MILLER'S
INTERNATIONAL
ANTIQUES
PRICE GUIDE

1992 AMERICAN EDITION

MILLER'S
INTERNATIONAL
ANTIQUES
PRICE GUIDE

1992 AMERICAN EDITION

COMPILED AND EDITED BY

JUDITH AND MARTIN MILLER

VIKING
STUDIO
BOOKS

HOW TO USE THE BOOK

Miller's uniquely practical *International Antiques Price Guide* has been compiled to make detailed information immediately available to the consumer.

The book is organized by category of antique: e.g. Pottery, Porcelain, Furniture, etc. (see Contents List on page 6); within each major category there are sub-categories of items in alphabetical order: e.g. basket, bowl, candlestick, etc., and these in turn are ordered by date. There are around 10,000 photographs of antiques and collectibles, each with a detailed description and price range. There is also a fully cross-referenced index at the back of the book.

This 1992 Edition contains 144 pages in full color — illustrating over 1,500 exceptional or attractive pieces.

In addition to individual entries there are special features throughout the book, giving pointers for the collector — likely condition, definitions of specialist terms, history, etc. — together with general articles, chapter introductions, glossaries, bibliographies where further reading is important, tables of marks, etc. As all the pictures and captions are new every year the selection of items included quickly builds into an enormously impressive and uniquely useful reference set.

PRICES

All the price ranges are based on actual prices of items bought and sold during the year prior to going to press. Thus the guide is fully up-to-date.

Prices are *not* estimates: because the value of an antique is what a willing buyer will pay to a willing seller, we have given not just one price per item but a range of prices to take into account regional differences and freak results.

This is the best way to give an idea of what an antique will *cost*, but should you wish to *sell* remember that the price you receive could be 25-30% less — antique dealers have to live too!!

Condition

All items were in good merchantable condition when last sold unless damage is noted.

ACKNOWLEDGEMENTS

Judith and Martin Miller wish to thank a large number of International auctioneers, dealers and museums who have helped in the production of this edition. The auctioneers can be found in our specialist directory towards the back of this edition.

Copyright © Millers Publications 1991

Viking Penguin, a division of Penguin Books U.S.A. Inc. 375 Hudson Street, New York New York 10014, U.S.A.

Penguin Books Canada Ltd. 10 Alcorn Avenue, Suite 300 Toronto, Ontario, Canada M4V 3B2

Designed and created by Millers Publications Sissinghurst Court Sissinghurst Cranbrook Kent TN17 2JA, England

All rights reserved.
First published in 1991 by Viking Penguin, a division of Penguin Books U.S.A. Inc.
Published simultaneously in Canada
ISBN: 0-670-84086-6

Typeset in England by Ardek Photosetters, St. Leonards-on-Sea, England.
Color originated by Scantrans, Singapore
Printed in Singapore

Editor's Introduction

by

Judith Miller

Martin and I started *Miller's Antiques Price Guide* in 1979. We produced a book which we believed was greatly needed by virtually everyone who had some interest in antiques, whether professional or as a collector.

We firmly believed that what was needed was a guide to the antiques market which was photographically illustrated, with detailed, concise descriptions and price ranges. The last 13 years have convinced me that this is what the buying public want. Initially, of course, we produced the kind of book that Martin and I wanted — and since we now sell well in excess of 100,000 copies of the British edition, it would seem we were not alone. The book in its various editions is now used all over the world as a major reference work to antiques and since we use in the region of 10,000 new photographs every year, the issues of the British Guide provide an unrivalled source to 100,000 different antiques.

Seven years ago we decided, in conjunction with Viking Penguin, to produce a U.S. edition of the Guide. We were convinced that the U.S. market needed the clear, high quality photographs, detailed descriptions, and the price ranges which give a "ball park" figure for the thousands of items featured in *Miller's International Antiques Price Guide*. These price ranges are researched from sold items and give readers an essential tool for buying and selling antiques and collectibles. We are constantly trying to improve our product and give the U.S. consumer information relevant to the antiques market in the States.

One interesting development I have noticed over the years is that the antiques market is becoming more international. Of course, each country has a special interest in items made by native craftsmen and it is the general trend that such pieces will sell better at a major saleroom in their country of origin. However, to balance this, when general prices achieved at auction in New York, London, Geneva and Hong Kong are compared, they show a striking similarity.

We try to include as many color photographs as is possible, and this year we have well over 1,500 items illustrated in color, all of which have been on the market in the year prior to compilation. All the pieces included, either in color or black and white, are antiques which have been available through dealers or auction houses; they are not museum pieces. The result is a strongly visual and encyclopedic reference guide to recognizing and buying antiques, to detecting trends and to planning one's future collecting. On my monthly trips to the U.S. I am in constant touch with dealers, antiques centers and auction houses to check and verify prices.

Finally our thanks are due to all those experts whose invaluable help and guidance has contributed so much toward this new edition.

CONTENTS

A pair of Royal Worcester porcelain New Large Grecian Water Carriers, one decorated in shades of russet and pale green, the other in green, raised upon gilt decorated waisted bases, printed mark in puce and numbered 2 over 125, date cipher 1915 and 1916, 20in (51cm) high.
$2,700-3,600

POTTERY

There have been no great surprises in the pottery market this year. Sales at the lower end of the market have been very slow with a definite drop in price on previous years. Some dealers and auction houses have been slow to recognise this with the result that many of them are still looking at last year's stock or having difficulty obtaining high reserve prices. The middle ground of good quality, but not too rare, 18thC pottery has more or less maintained its price level but more as a result of shortage of supply rather than a maintenance of demand level. It would appear that potential sellers are holding back their goods until a more vibrant market comes again. At the top end of the market, good and rare pieces still attract very high prices but are not reaching the dizzy heights of three years ago. There are some relative bargains to be picked up by those who are prepared to invest in these pieces, such as the Whieldon creamware arbour group sold at Bearne's, Torquay, for $56,000 + premium. It would have fetched much more three years ago.

The same market trends apply to the 19th and early 20thC collectors pottery fields of Wedgwood, Wemyss, Mason's, Moorcroft et al. Up to 50% of the more mundane pieces are being bought in at auction whereas the rare and unusual pieces are still fetching very high prices and are maintaining their value. A fine early Moorcroft vase sold at Neales, Nottingham, for $11,000 against an estimate of $3,600-5,500, and a Wedgwood Fairyland lustre vase of the Ghostly Wood pattern reached $15,500 at Bearne's.

Bottles

A Staffordshire saltglazed bottle, c1755, 9½in (24cm).
$1,000-1,100

Four South Staffordshire opaque white cruet bottles, named within branches of green foliage, the rims with puce 'feuilles-de-choux', with pierced and turned wood domed covers with knob finials, some damage, c1760, 7 and 6in (18 and 15cm).
$1,400-1,800

A Persian polychrome bottle, c1850, 6½in (16cm).
$160-200

Bowls

An English delft 'birdcage' bowl, painted in blue with birds and foliage behind vertical bars, probably Liverpool, damaged and repaired, c1770, 10in (25.5cm).
$270-370

A Bristol tin glazed bowl, c1765, 9in (23cm) diam.
$1,800-2,000

An English delftware butter dish and cover, the cover with blue sponged tree decoration, the glazed interior with a conical spur, probably Bristol, c1740, 5in (12.5cm).
$7,200-8,000

A Staffordshire slipware three-handled tyg, by Robart Pool, the rim inscribed in dark brown with cream dots on a cream ground with the inscription ROBART:POOL:MADE:THIS:CVP:WITH: A:CVP:POSET:FIL, the lower part in dark brown with cream stylised tulips and with 3 small loop handles flanked by rudimentary handles, extensively damaged and repaired, early 18thC, 7½in (18.5cm).
$8,000-10,000

A London delft dated blue and white bleeding bowl, the centre inscribed A.H.1673, extensively damaged and repaired, 7½in (19cm) wide.
$5,500-6,500

A creamware char dish, probably Yorkshire, the exterior painted in green, ochre and brown enamels, minor chip to foot, 8½in (22cm).
$450-550

A slipware bowl, with small loop handle and central conical spike, the dark brown ground decorated in cream slip with the initials IC and the date 1702, the overturned top rim with cream slip dots, rim chip and minor flaking, restoration to rim and handle, 1702, 8½in (21cm) wide.
$2,000-3,000

A slipware flared bucket shaped bleeding bowl, with pierced foliate handle, the interior striated with dark brown, light brown and cream slip marbling, the exterior covered in cream slip, cracked and repaired, early 18thC, 6in (15cm) wide.
$3,000-3,600

A salt glazed punch bowl, mid-18thC, 9in (23cm).
$1,000-1,200

A slipware two-handled porringer, decorated in brown slip with cream slip stylised foliage and wavy lines, minor cracks and chips to rim, slight chip and chip to handle, early 18thC, 6½in (17cm) wide.
$2,500-2,800

Boxes

A large Italian majolica bowl, probably Savona, late 17thC, 13in (33cm).
$900-1,000

An extremely rare Wedgwood & Bentley paint box, damaged, paint pots missing, 18thC, 6in (15cm) wide.
$1,500-1,600

A slipware money box, c1760, 5in (12cm).
$900-1,000

Commemorative

A creamware box and cover, the upper surface of the screw top cover moulded in relief with a titled portrait of John Wilkes, within a framework of flowers and scrolls, beadwork rims, c1770, 3½in (8cm).
$4,200-5,500

A pearlware and copper lustre small 'Green Bag' jug, printed in puce with a bust portrait of Queen Caroline, captioned 'God Save Queen Caroline', the reverse printed with the 'Green Bag Crew' rhyme in a puce cartouche with the names of her supporters, some damage, early 19thC, 5in (13cm) high.
$270-360

Cottages & Pastille Burners

A Mexborough rock pottery cottage money box, moulded upon 'The Wesleyan Chapel, Bank Street, Mexborough', inscribed 'Sarah Ducker Fendall, Bourne 20 August 1846', mid-19thC.
$1,500-1,625

A Staffordshire pottery money box, modelled as a house and decorated in Pratt colours, c1820, 4in (10cm).
$500-540

A Staffordshire pottery money box, modelled as a cottage, c1860, 4in (10cm).
$180-200

Cow Creamers

A Staffordshire cow creamer, c1775, 4½in (12cm).
$1,800-2,350

A Staffordshire pottery model of a house, c1860, 6in (16cm).
$160-180

A Pratt-Yorkshire church, c1820, 10in (24cm).
$1,000-1,200

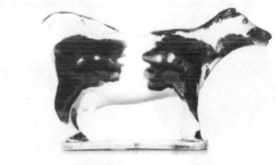

An English creamware cow creamer, its coat splashed with large brown patches, on a green base, c1810, 7in (18cm) long.
$360-540

A Staffordshire pink lustre cow creamer, c1830.
$540-650

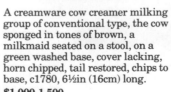

A Staffordshire pearlware cow creamer milking group, the cow sponged in grey, the milkmaid in blue blouse and pleated skirt, cover lacking, horns, ear and base with repairs and restorations, c1780, 7in (18cm) long.
$720-900

A creamware cow creamer milking group of conventional type, the cow sponged in tones of brown, a milkmaid seated on a stool, on a green washed base, cover lacking, horn chipped, tail restored, chips to base, c1780, 6½in (16cm) long.
$1,000-1,500

Cups

A London delft dated fuddling cup, formed as 3 globular bottles with entwined handles, one with the initials 'I S' above a flourish, another with the date '1633', the initialled vase with rim repair and repair to glaze patches, all with chips to feet and rims, and with glaze flaking to handles, 1633, 3½in (8.5cm).
$12,000-13,000

A fuddling cup is an earthenware vessel of several cups linked in such a way that anyone challenged to empty one of the cups was in fact forced to drain them all!

A London delft dated armorial caudle cup of squat baluster form with loop handle, painted with the Arms of the Watermen's and Lightermen's Company and with the initials 'D/I A' and the date '1682', extensively damaged and repaired, 1682, 3½in (9cm).
$18,000-20,000

Caudle: Spiced gruel laced with wine.

A Liverpool delft inscribed and dated blue and white cup with loop handle, inscribed 'A. Wigglesworth 1767' within a scroll and foliage cartouche surmounted by a winged cherub's head and flanked by grapes, beneath an ochre line rim, slight rim chips and 2 cracks, 1767, 2½in (6.5cm).
$3,600-4,000

A Staffordshire salt glazed cup and saucer, c1745, cup 2½in (6cm), saucer 4½in (11cm) diam.
$1,500-1,800

Ewers

A Minton majolica ewer, impressed marks and date code for 1867, 14½in (37cm).
$1,200-1,230

Figures – Animals

A Hall pearlware group of a ewe and lamb, their coats splashed in iron red, on green glazed base, repair to branch of bocage, impressed mark at back, c1820, 6½in (15.5cm).
$720-900

A Newport pottery model of an owl wearing a suit, signed M. Epworth, 7½in (18.5cm).
$180-235

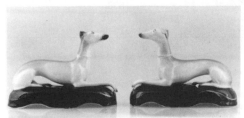

A pair of Staffordshire pen holders modelled as recumbent whippets, c1860, 5in (12cm).
$320-360

A Staffordshire pearlware model of a swan, with manganese beak and incised wing and tail feathers, on green mound base, c1790, 4in (10cm).
$1,800-2,350

A rare Staffordshire group, early 19thC, 8in (21cm).
$4,500-5,500

A pair of Prattware type figures of birds, 3½in (9cm).
$1,200-1,400

A Prattware figure of a lion, probably Staffordshire, c1800, 5½in (14cm).
$2,700-3,300

A Staffordshire pearlware figure of a lion, his paw raised upon a yellow ball, his coat predominantly salmon pink with a brown glazed mane and facial details picked out in black, restored hair crack to base, c1800, 8in (20cm).
$2,700-3,600

A Staffordshire figure of a cockerel, the cream coloured bird lightly sponged in brown and yellow, on a green glazed base, minor restoration, c1800, 8½in (21.5cm).
$1,800-2,700

A pair of Staffordshire models of a milkboy and milkmaid with cows, c1860, 6½in (16cm).
$685-720

A pair of Staffordshire creamware spaniels, with incised brown coats and light brown collars, on oval green-glazed foliage moulded bases, c1800, 4in (9.5cm).
$1,800-2,700

A rare Staffordshire rabbit, c1865.
$1,600-2,000

A Staffordshire spill vase, modelled as an eagle over a sleeping child, c1860, 8½in (21cm).
$180-200

A pearlware model of a recumbent ram, with yellow horns, his fleece sponged in yellow, blue and brown, on green mound base, c1790, 5½in (14cm) long.
$1,200-1,500

A Staffordshire pen holder modelled as spaniels and pup, c1860, 6½in (16cm).
$280-320

A pair of Staffordshire figures of spaniels, with both front legs separate, restored, c1850, 8in (20cm).
$450-500

A Staffordshire spill vase, modelled as a hound, c1870.
$500-540

A Staffordshire figure of an elephant, c1870.
$650-800

A pair of Staffordshire spill holders, modelled as a ram and ewe, c1860, 6in (15cm).
$500-540

A Staffordshire spill vase with coloured glaze, by the Wood family c1780.
$3,300-4,000

A Staffordshire standing hound spill vase, c1870.
$360-430

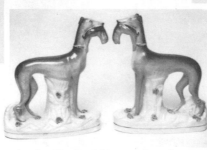

A pair of Staffordshire greyhounds, c1870.
$450-650

A Staffordshire group of 2 seated spaniels, one chained to a barrel, with iron red fur markings, on a shaped oval base, 9½in (24cm).
$360-450

A creamware model of a fox of Ralph Wood type, naturally modelled with brown coat, a bird beneath his right forepaw, on a shaped mound base streaked in grey, green and yellow, slight cracks, chip to base, crack to right forepaw, c1780, 4in (10cm).
$2,800-3,600

A pair of Staffordshire models of greyhounds, one with a hare in its mouth, the other with a hare at its feet, each on a green mound base, one with firing crack, 10½in (26.5cm).
$720-800

Figures – People

A Poole pottery figure of Buster Boy, modelled by Phoebe Stabler, naturalistically painted, impressed CSA mark, 7in (18cm).
$300-370

A matched pair of Staffordshire figures of cricketers, c1870.
$2,520-2,800

A Staffordshire pottery group in the Walton manner, slight damage, 5in (12.5cm).
$650-720

A pair of Staffordshire pearlware figures of Apollo and Diana, of Ralph Wood type, the god draped in a green lined pale mauve robe, the goddess wearing a green and grey dress, her neck and right arm repaired, part of quiver and head-dress lacking, his lyre chipped, both with chips to the bases, c1775, 9in (22cm).
$3,300-4,000

A Staffordshire pearlware figure of a gardener of Ralph Wood type, wearing black hat, white open-neck shirt, green jacket, blue sash and light brown breeches, left arm and spade restored and restored through legs, pedestal and base, flower pot lacking, c1785, 8in (19.5cm).
$650-900

A Staffordshire pottery group of 2 drunken men, The Night Watchmen, set on an oval mound and octagonal base, 10in (25cm).
$540-900

A Staffordshire pearlware figure of a bagpiper of Ralph Wood type, wearing black hat, green jacket and brown breeches, his manganese pipes under his arm, very slight chipping to base, c1785, 7½in (19cm).
$1,600-2,000

A pair of Robinson and Leadbeater coloured parian figures of a gypsy and his companion, he wearing a red and gold braid tunic with a broad cummerbund holding a violin, she with a red headscarf, pale blue bodice holding a lute, both on coloured rockwork bases, impressed marks, restoration to the violin, lute and her hand, 16½in (42cm).
$300-400

13

A Staffordshire group depicting
Charity, decorated in Pratt colours,
c1820, 8½in (21cm).
$450-485

A Staffordshire group of Persuasion,
she wearing a yellow hat, puce
blouse and long floral skirt, her
suitor sporting a black hat, green
coat and cream breeches, offering
her a ring, minor chips and
restoration, c1820, 7in (17.5cm).
$3,600-4,500

A Staffordshire figure depicting
Hope, c1820, 9in (23cm).
$280-320

A pair of Staffordshire figures of
Molyneux and Cribb, c1820.
$4,500-5,500

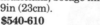

A Staffordshire rural group of
musicians, bocage missing, c1820,
9in (23cm).
$540-610

A pair of Staffordshire groups of
Flight and Return, on green
rockwork bases applied with moss
and flowers, Infant Jesus's head, one
tail and tip of one ear lacking,
damages and repairs to extremities
and foliage, slight glaze flaking,
perhaps Walton, c1820, 9in (23cm).
$5,100-5,850

A pair of Staffordshire pearlware
groups of The Flight to Egypt and
Return from Egypt, on rockwork
bases applied with flowers and
foliage, perhaps Walton, some
damage and repairs, c1820, 11 and
10in (28 and 25cm).
$3,000-4,000

A Staffordshire model of a cavalier
and his female companion, on gilt
lined base, c1850, 16in (41cm).
$270-360

A Staffordshire group of The New
Marriage Act, typically modelled
with a priest, the couple and a young
boy all within an arched interior,
picked out in bright enamels, the
stepped base in blue and iron red,
inscribed label restored, c1835,
6½in (16cm).
$1,800-2,520

A Staffordshire group of the
Proposal, c1830, 7½in (19cm).
$5,500-7,000

A pair of Staffordshire pottery figures of a young man and woman, he with a monkey, she with a tambourine, 7in (18cm).
$180-270

A Staffordshire figure, St. George and the dragon, the dragon painted green, slightly damaged, 19thC, 10in (25cm).
$145-180

A pair of Staffordshire square based pottery figures of children, each carrying a bird, painted in Pratt enamels, 5in (12.5cm).
$360-415

An early Staffordshire pottery group of a shepherd playing a flute, his companion standing at his side, a dog, lamb and goat at their feet, some damage, 10in (25cm).
$650-900

A pair of Staffordshire pottery groups, each in the form of a cow by a stream with a farmer or a milkmaid, 8½in (21cm).
$450-540

A pair of creamware figures of Ralph Wood type, each modelled as a youth in translucent blue, yellow and manganese clothes, both bases with some restoration, c1780, 5in (12.5cm).
$720-1,000

A German pottery figure of a barefoot boy, draped in a shawl, playing a mandolin, minor damage, late 19thC, 23½in (61cm).
$450-540

A figure of Apollo covered in coloured glazes, by the Wood family, 9in (22.5cm).
$1,800-2,000

Three creamware figures emblematic of Faith, Hope and Charity, of Pratt type, wearing ochre, dark blue and brown robes, on bases moulded with ochre and green stiff leaves, Faith's right arm restored, perhaps Yorkshire, c1790, 8½ and 9½in (21.5 and 23.5cm).
$1,200-1,800

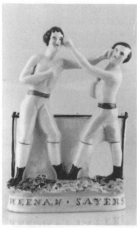

A Staffordshire figure of Malakoff, an outwork of Sebastopol, in salmon colour, c1854, 7in (17cm), (C,69/180). **$865-900**

A Staffordshire group portraying the prize fight between John Heenan and Tom Sayers, c1860, 10in (24cm), (F,7/15). **$900-1,000**

A Staffordshire figure portraying Ellen Bright, 'Death of the Lion Queen', c1850, 15in (38cm), (E,80/154). **$1,200-1,500**

A Staffordshire figure of Stanfield Hall, c1849, 8in (20cm), (G,20/46). **$500-575**

A pair of titled Staffordshire figures modelled as Moody and Sankey, each wearing a black frock coat, waistcoat and trousers, resting a hand on a book surmounted pedestal, both titled in black raised script, on oval gilt lined bases, c1873, 11in (28cm), (D,4/8/9). **$900-1,200**

A Staffordshire figure of John Liston as Swam Swipes, in a green jacket, white apron and brown breeches, standing before a marbled square column, printed 'Lo am I a Gentleman? Upon Your Soul Tho Mother', enamels flaked, restoration to feet, 6½in (16.5cm), (E, 48/85). **$360-450**

A Staffordshire figure of the Russian fortress of Sebastopol, in salmon colour, c1854, 10in (25cm), (C,69/181). **$755-865**

Flatware

A Staffordshire flatback figure entitled Miss Nightingale on base, Miss Nightingale standing beside a seated wounded soldier, in polychrome colours to the front and rear, c1860, (C,55/143). **$800-900**

Two similar Bristol delft plates, 9in (22cm) diam.   **$1,000-1,200**

A London delft blue and white Act of Union plate, painted with a thistle and rose beneath the Royal crown, flanked by the initials A R, within a concentric blue line and band rim, c1707, 9in (22.5cm) diam.
$2,340-3,300

A Llanelly pottery cockerel plate, with a border of continuous blue sponged flowerheads within red lines, the centre with typical cockerel and foliage in blue, red, green, brown enamel, unmarked, 9½in (24cm) diam.
$450-550

A large Irish delftware tureen stand by the Delamain factory, with underglaze blue floral decoration on white ground, mid-18thC, 22in (56cm) wide.
$1,200-1,300

A rare English delft stand dish, c1740, 10in (25cm) diam.
$2,000-3,000

A pair of English delft lobed plates, 6½in (16cm).
$1,000-1,200

A Bristol delft tulip charger, painted with a blue and yellow striped tulip flanked by iron red-centred flowers and green and yellow foliage, within a concentric blue line cartouche, the border with green and yellow leaves alternating with striped yellow fruits and blue fronds within a powdered blue rim, glaze flaking to rim, c1740, 13in (33cm) diam.
$3,500-4,500

An English delft powdered manganese ground plate, with the initial A/HT and the date 1740 in an hexagonal cartouche at the top, chip to well, minor rim chips, Bristol or Wincanton, c1740, 8½in (22cm) diam.
$3,000-3,700

A Lambeth delft Merryman plate, c1734, 7½in (18cm).
$550-650

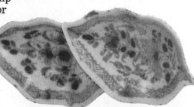

A pair of English delftware leaf dishes, 4in (10cm) wide.
$1,200-1,500

A pair of English delft dated plates, with a cartouche reserved on a ground of plants and stylised flowerheads and dot pattern, one with slight rim chip, the other cracked across and repaired, Bristol or London, 1709, 8½in (21.5cm) diam.
$900-1,000

A Dillwyn & Co. pottery plate, the shaped rim moulded with roses and other garden flowers, painted in bright enamel colours, the centre printed in black with the seated figure of the young Queen Victoria, 8in (20cm).
$550-650

A pair of Mason's leaf dessert dishes, decorated with the Pagoda Tree pattern, c1835.
$800-900

A Dutch Delft lobed dish, painted in yellow, blue and green, foot pierced, minute rim chips, c1700, 13½in (34.5cm).
$750-1,000

A Mason's Ironstone shell dessert dish, decorated with the Japan pattern, c1820, 11in (28cm) long.
$350-450

A Liverpool tin glazed blue and white plate, c1760, 8½in (22cm) diam.
$250-280

A Mason's Ironstone drainer, decoration with the Japan pattern, c1820, 6in (15cm) diam.
$270-320

A Lambeth tin glazed plate, c1780, 9in (23cm) diam.
$320-380

A set of 4 Ironstone plates, Royal Mail, 9½in (24cm) diam.
$50-90

An English polychrome plate, 9in (23cm) diam.
$700-800

A pair of Staffordshire leaf dishes, c1765, 10 by 9in (25 by 23.5cm).
$2,700-3,200

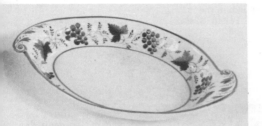

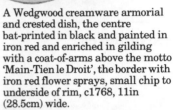

A pair of early English pottery dishes, with scroll side handles, painted with red and green fruiting vine borders, gilt highlights, 11in (28cm) wide.
$120-180

A majolica bread dish, 'Where Reason Rules, the Appetite Obeys', 13in (33cm) wide.
$120-150

A Wedgwood creamware armorial and crested dish, the centre bat-printed in black and painted in iron red and enriched in gilding with a coat-of-arms above the motto 'Main-Tien le Droit', the border with iron red flower sprays, small chip to underside of rim, c1768, 11in (28.5cm) wide.
$800-1,200

The arms are those of James Brydges, Marquis of Caernarvon (1731-89), who in 1753 married Margaret Nicol (d.1768) whose arms are shown on an escutcheon of pretence. Caernarvon succeeded his father as third Duke of Chandos in 1771.

A pair of Dutch Delft dated blue and white plates, cartouche outlined in black, enclosing the initials WWM and the date 1705, one cracked, rims chipped, c1705, 8½in (21cm) diam.
$900-1,000

A pair of Dutch Delft lobed dishes, 18thC, 13½in (34cm).
$450-550

An Hispano Moresque saucer dish, early 18thC, 7½in (19cm) diam.
$450-550

A Spode meat dish and pierced drainer, printed with the Tiber pattern, printed mark, 19in (48cm) wide.
$1,000-1,200

A small Hispano Moresque saucer dish, 16thC, 8in (20cm).
$550-750

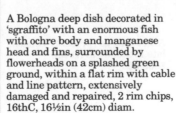

A Bologna deep dish decorated in 'sgraffito' with an enormous fish with ochre body and manganese head and fins, surrounded by flowerheads on a splashed green ground, within a flat rim with cable and line pattern, extensively damaged and repaired, 2 rim chips, 16thC, 16½in (42cm) diam.
$2,300-2,800

A Frankfurt faience dish, decorated in the Wanli style, c1700, 15in (39cm).
$900-1,000

An Italian majolica dish in the Castelli style, 18thC, 12½in (32cm) diam.
$1,200-1,500

A Staffordshire meat dish printed with the Rural Scenery pattern, within a border of flowers and scrolling foliage, the reverse with a named panel, 19in (49cm)
$540-740

Jardinières

A pair of Wedgwood jardinières, c1872, 9½in (24cm).
$2,000-2,700

A pair of Minton turquoise jardinières, with ram's head handles, the blue ground reserved with cherubs on 3 scrolling legs and ribbed base, impressed marks, 12½in (32cm).
$900-1,000

A pair of George Jones majolica jardinières, moulded in relief and picked out in strong colours over the navy blue ground, all beneath a yellow rim, pale blue interior, minor restoration, impressed G.J. monogram, black painted pattern No. 3326/D(2), c1865, 15in (38cm).
$3,700-4,700

Jars

Two London delft blue and white wet drug jars for S:DE:SPIN:CER and S:E:RUB:IDAEIS with cartouches, surmounted by 2 songbirds among foliage flanking a basket of fruit and with a winged cherub's head suspending swags of fruit and tassels below, one with crack to body, chips to rim and footrim, the other with chip and repair to rim and crack to footrim, both with glaze flaking, c1700, 8in (20cm).
$1,000-1,500

A London delft blue and white drug jar, c1690, 9½in (24cm).
$2,000-2,700

A pair of Dutch Delft blue and white jardinières, blue painted mark for the Greek 'A' pottery, mid-18thC, 8in (20cm).
$4,500-5,500

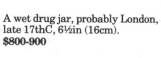

A wet drug jar, probably London, late 17thC, 6½in (16cm).
$800-900

An English delft cylindrical drug jar, probably London, c1760.
$350-450

A London delft blue and white wet drug jar named for O.EXCESTREN:, crack to foot, rims chipped, c1720, 7in (17.5cm).
$650-800

A Bristol delft blue and white wet drug jar, named in manganese for MEL:ROSACEUM, chips to footrim and glaze flaking to rim and spout, manganese 'eye' mark to base, c1740, 8in (20cm).
$650-1,000

An English delftware dry drug jar, inscribed in blue E.LENITIV within a central cartouche between a scallop shell and a winged cherub's mask, flanked by 2 cherubs holding floral sprays and a pair of floral swags, minor rim chips, early 18thC, 10½in (26cm).
$1,200-1,500

A pair of Lambeth delft blue and white baluster drug jars for P:THEBAICAE and P:PACIFICAE, rim chips and cracks, c1770, 3½in (9cm).
$1,800-2,800

A Dutch Delft ovoid tobacco jar, with brass cover, 18thC, 13in (33cm).
$1,400-1,500

A Savona blue and white wet drug jar, named for OI:ANETHI on a ribbon cartouche, pharmacy mark F.R at the base of the handle, rim and spout chipped, blue watchtower mark, late 17thC, 8½in (21cm).
$2,700-3,700

A Dutch Delft ovoid tobacco jar, with brass cover, 18thC, 11in (28cm).
$1,000-1,200

An Hispano Moresque ovoid jar, 16thC, 12in (31cm).
$5,500-6,500

21

An English delft drug jar, named in manganese for OPII:PURIFICAT: on a strapwork cartouche with a shell and winged cherubs above and flowers and tassels below, rim chips, Bristol or London, c1760, 3½in (9cm).
$1,000-1,200

A London delft blue and white drug jar named for U.NEAPOLIT, minor crack to rim, rim chips, c1720, 7in (17.5cm).
$650-800

Three Dutch Delft blue and white oviform tobacco jars, each painted with a Red Indian smoking a pipe, seated beneath a tree beside a jar named with the type of tobacco, St. Omer with slight rim chips, contemporary brass covers, 2 with blue 3 bells mark and one with B?P in blue, c1740, 9 and 10½in (23 and 27.5cm).
$5,500-6,500

An English delft drug jar, named in manganese for EX:GENISTAE: on a blue strapwork cartouche, with a shell flanked by winged cherubs above and a winged cherub's head and flowerheads below, Bristol or London, c1760, 3½in (9cm).
$800-1,000

A French faience wet drug jar, with short straight spout and loop handle, named in manganese for S.BERBERIS within a blue berried foliage cartouche, on a circular foot, late 18thC, 8½in (20.5cm).
$350-450

Jugs

A Hicks & Meigh jug and bowl set, decorated in polychrome colours, c1825, jug 8in (20cm), bowl 9in (23cm) diam.
$450-550

A Dutch Delft oviform jar, painted in tones of blue and outlined in manganese with Orientals in an extensive rocky wooded river landscape, between bands of radiating stiff leaves and scrolling foliage, slight rim chips and glaze flaking, c1700, 9½in (24cm).
$1,600-2,000

A London delft blue and white drug jar named on a ribbon, with a winged angel's head above and fluttering pennants below, minute crack to rim, c1680, 3½in (9cm).
$1,600-2,000

A Copeland parianware jug, with relief cherub figures picking grapes, late 19thC, 9in (23cm).
$160-200

A Leeds creamware jug with reeded body, mask-head spout and pierced rim, painted with underglaze green streaks, late 18thC, 3in (7.5cm).
$1,200-1,500

A Leeds creamware baluster jug, boldly painted with a portrait of the Princess of Orange, reserve within a foliate cartouche, slight restoration, late 18thC, 5½in (14cm).
$220-320

An early Mason's Ironstone jug, with strap handles, painted in polychrome enamels, unmarked, c1815, 11in (29cm).
$1,000-1,200

A Liverpool delft blue and white puzzle jug of conventional type, with hollow rim and handle with 3 spouts, the neck pierced with hearts and ovals, the body inscribed with a four-line verse 'Here Gentle-men Come Try Your Skill . . .', glaze flaking to handle, rim and spouts, c1760, 6½in (17cm).
$1,500-2,000

An early Mason's jug and bowl set, impressed mark, c1815, 7½in (19cm).
$1,800-2,000

A Mason's Ironstone jug, decorated with the Heron pattern, No. 311 on base, c1830, 8in (20cm).
$450-650

A Mason's Ironstone jug with strap handle, c1820, 6½in (16cm).
$450-550

An English delft blue and white puzzle jug, c1760, 7in (17.5cm).
$1,800-2,000

A Mason's Ironstone blue ground octagonal jug, with a snake moulded handle enriched in gilding, painted with butterflies and dragonflies in gilding, gilding rubbed, 8½in (21cm).
$180-380

A Minton majolica jug, lip and base repaired, impressed mark, date code for 1864, 12in (31cm).
$700-900

A pearlware pink lustre jug printed and coloured with a view of the Sunderland Bridge, stained, 4½in (11cm).
$270-370

A Staffordshire transfer decorated jug with good colours, c1830.
$120-160

A Mason's Ironstone jug with dragon handle, c1840, 7in (17.5cm).
$550-650

Again, this interesting handle is reflected in the price.

A Minton majolica jester jug, with impressed marks for 1870, 13in (33cm).
$650-750

A Minton grey stone Drunken Silenus jug, base cracked, impressed No. 16 on a scroll, 9in (23cm).
$180-240

A Staffordshire buff stoneware Tam O'Shanter and Souter Johnnie jug, neck and lip cracked, 9½in (24cm).
$120-220

A Wedgwood pearlware jug, with an orange ground border reserved with flowering prunus within bands of gilding, cracked and enamels slightly worn, 6½in (16cm).
$180-240

A Sunderland Bridge pink lustre ground pearlware jug, printed and coloured with a view of Sunderland Bridge flanked by 2 mottos within flower and floral cartouches, crack to the rim and base of handle, 9in (23cm).
$350-550

A Staffordshire saltglazed white pecten shell-moulded baluster cream jug, with reeded scroll handl and on 3 paw feet, moulded with shell ornament and with snails to each side of the lip, small crack to rim, c1755, 3½in (8.5cm).
$1,500-1,800

A W. Ridgway & Co. green stoneware Tam O'Shanter and Souter Johnnie jug, impressed mark, 8in (20cm).
$120-180

A fine quality creamware jug, c1775, 7in (18cm).
$3,700-4,700

A Sunderland pink lustre jug with a loop handle, printed in black with a view of the cast iron bridge over the River Weir, flanked by a verse and by a three-masted sailing ship, Northumberland 7, 8in (20cm).
$350-550

A Staffordshire saltglazed white pecten shell moulded baluster cream jug, with reeded loop handle, on 3 mask and paw feet, moulded with shell ornament and with trailing foliage, crack to base of handle, c1755, 3½in (9cm).
$900-1,000

A Minton dark green stoneware Drunken Silenus jug, damage and restoration to rim, impressed No. 19 on a scroll, 8½in (21cm).
$200-300

A Staffordshire jug with coloured, raised hunting scene and leaf decoration, cracked, 19thC, 5in (13cm).
$180-220

A creamware jug printed in black, on one side a couple in a blacksmith's shop, entitled 'Gretna Green' or the 'Red Hot Marriage', and on the other an inn interior with a verse, 8½in (21cm).
$450-650

A German blue and white faience jug, painted with stylised flowers, the handle with blue scrolls, perhaps Hanau, 5½in (14cm).
$550-700

A Sunderland Bridge pink lustre pearlware jug, printed and coloured with a view of Sunderland Bridge, the reverse with a Seaman's Verse within a flower and floral cartouche, the rims enriched in pink lustre, the top of the handle and base cracked, 8½in (21cm).
$250-320

A Don pottery jug with loop handle and a grip, printed with the 'Italian Residence of Solinenes, near Vesuvius', below a border of putti amongst flowers and foliage, slight chips, printed marks, 11½in (30cm).
$2,700-3,700

Toby Jugs

A Ralph Wood long-faced Toby jug, with creamware body, unglazed bottom of base, decorated in green and manganese translucent glazes, c1770, 10in (25cm).
$7,000-9,000

A rare and particularly well modelled example.

A Whieldon type creamware Toby jug with step base, decorated with translucent green glazed coat and manganese to face, hose and shoes, c1760, 9½in (24cm).
$4,500-5,500

A Staffordshire pearlware oviform jug, printed and coloured with farmer's emblems and trophies and inscribed 'A N' in gilding, enamels and gilding slightly worn, 6in (15.5cm).
$350-450

A small Staffordshire Coachman Toby jug, c1830, 6in (14cm).
$1,500-2,000

A Walton impressed Toby jug, c1820, 11½in (29cm).
$1,600-2,000

A pearlware Toby jug and cover, probably Yorkshire, painted in blue, green, ochre and brown enamels, minor damage, 10½in (26.5cm).
$1,200-1,700

Three miniature Toby jugs, c1820-40. **$180-240**

A Prattware Martha Gunn Toby jug, c1800, 10½in (26cm).
$3,600-5,600

A creamware Toby jug on Georgian base, decorated in translucent glazes, with green waistcoat and blue taupe patterned coat, c1790, 10in (25cm).
$1,200-1,500

A French version of the Toby jug from the Porquier factory, 19thC, 11½in (29cm).
$1,600-1,800

A Victorian Toby jug in overglaze enamels, with brown coat, lime waistcoat and yellow breeches, small sparrow beak jug, decorated with rust flower, c1870, 10in (25cm).
$270-370

A squat Toby jug with painted face and unusual pink swirled coat, green vest and chair, c1800, 8½in (21.5cm).
$350-450

A Yorkshire thin man Toby jug, c1780, 8½in (21cm).
$6,500-7,500

A Ralph Wood traditional model Toby jug, c1780.
$1,500-2,500

A Staffordshire stepped base Toby jug, c1780, 10in (25cm).
$1,800-3,200

A large impressed Hollins Toby jug, c1805, 9½in (24cm).
$2,700-4,500

A Staffordshire Toby jug of Mr. Punch seated on 3 volumes in a red hat and red striped suit, enriched in gilding, gilding slightly rubbed, 10in (25cm).
$270-370

A Martha Gunn Toby jug by Ralph Wood, c1780, 11in (28cm).
$4,500-6,500

A Ralph Wood type Toby jug, with measure, c1780, 9in (23cm).
$2,000-3,000

A Ralph Wood longface Toby jug, c1780, 10in (25cm).
$2,700-4,700

A Staffordshire Collier Toby jug, c1780.
$2,700-4,000

A Prattware Toby jug, c1800, 10in (25cm).
$650-950

A Ralph Wood Toby jug, c1780.
$2,000-3,000

A Wilkinson Toby jug, modelled as George V by Francis Carruthers Gould in a limited edition of 1,000, sparsely coloured, mainly in underglaze blue, c1919, 12in (30cm).
$700-900

A Hearty Good Fellow Toby jug, in underglaze colours, with overglaze turquoise coat, restoration to hat, c1815, 11in (28cm).
$1,000-1,500

Wilkinson Limited First World War Toby Jugs, designed by Sir F. Carruthers Gould, all with printer's marks and facsimile signature, from left:
President Wilson dressed as Uncle Sam with a bi-plane between his legs, 10½in (26cm).
$350-550

Admiral Beatty dressed in naval uniform, supporting a shell entitled 'Dreadnought' between his legs, slight damage to the right hand, 10½in (26.5cm).
$350-550
King George V dressed as an Admiral, 12in (30cm).
$900-1,000

Lloyd George dressed as Admiral of the Fleet, supporting a shell between his legs, 10in (25cm).
$350-550
Marshall Foch dressed as an Infantry Officer toasting to The Devil, The Kaiser, 12in (30cm).
$450-550

Mugs

A Nottingham salt glazed stoneware bulbous mug, the neck applied with a silver metal mount and flanked by a grooved strap handle, the silver mount engraved N.R.E, hair crack to neck, late 17thC, 3½in (9cm).
$3,600-4,600

A Mason's Ironstone cider mug with flared base, c1820, 4in (10cm).
$550-650

A Staffordshire slipware mug, c1700, 3in (7cm).
$3,600-4,000

A creamware cylindrical veilleuse of Whieldon type, with moulded female masks with pendant plaits of hair, the front with an ogee arch to take a burner, slight crack and chip to top rim, c1760, 7in (17.5cm).
$1,000-1,800

A Staffordshire redware baluster mug with grooved loop handle, the brown ground with a cream slip band with a 'sgraffito' bird flanked by trailing flowers and the initials 'g B' beneath a cream slip rim, crack to one side, chip to rim, handle repaired, perhaps Newcastle-Under-Lyme, c1745, 6in (15cm).
$3,600-4,600

A Staffordshire creamware mug, c1775.
$1,000-1,200

An English creamware mug printed in black, chipped, c1790, 4½in (11cm).
$320-420

A child's beaker, c1840.
$100-140

A Staffordshire tapering cylindrical
agate-glazed mug, the interior with
an applied frog, chipped and
cracked, 6in (15.5cm).
$350-450

A blue and white mug, probably
Liverpool, c1740, 4in (9cm).
$700-900

Plaques

A glazed and polychrome
earthenware domed panel of the
Virgin and Child in a niche, within a
fruiting border, in the manner of
Della Robbia, 27in (68cm).
$900-1,000

A Prattware plaque, Liverpool
Volunteers, 5in (13cm) square.
$1,200-1,500

A Cistercian black glazed mug,
restored lip, c1600, 4½in (11cm).
$550-650
*The mug was excavated from a
pavement in Finsbury*

A pottery plaque, moulded and
painted with the bust of Queen
Caroline wearing a plumed hat, a
crown and the initials 'Q.C.' above,
framed in a copper and purple lustre
border, 5½in (13.5cm).
$900-1,000

A Wedgwood & Bentley blue and
white jasper portrait medallion of
Voltaire, the solid blue ground
applied with his portrait, impressed
lower case mark, contemporary gilt
metal frame with beaded border,
c1775, 3½in (8.5cm) high.
$2,700-3,700

A Toby Phillpot plaque, c1830, 9in
(23cm) diam.
$700-1,400

A pair of creamware plaques,
moulded and coloured in blue and
brown with The Dipping of Achilles,
within brown reeded and leaf
moulded rectangular frames,
pierced for hanging, both with slight
crack to rim, c1800, 3½ by 3in (8.5
by 7.5cm).
$650-1,000

Pots

An English delft polychrome
baluster posset pot and cover, with
blue dash ornament, painted in iron
red, blue and green, hair crack to pot
and chips and glaze flaking to rim
and rim of cover, London or Bristol,
c1710, 8in (19cm).
$8,000-10,000

A Staffordshire redware flower pot, c1765, 5in (13cm).
$2,000-2,700

A Wedgwood caneware bough pot, painted on a blue ground, within an oval gilt line cartouche and painted in a bright blue palette, crack to one angle at back, c1790, 8in (20cm).
$1,000-1,200

Pot Lids

Yardley's Tooth Paste, London and Paris, B.162, coloured square lid, together with 13 other assorted monochrome pot lids, including: Army & Navy Almond Shaving Cream, D.I. green, Army & Navy Cold Cream of Roses, Army & Navy Areca Nut Tooth Paste, 2 square Tooth Paste lids and various Cold Cream, Tooth Paste and other lids.
$350-450

A Staffordshire redware cylindrical mustard pot and cover, with loop handle, applied in cream relief with 2 cockerels, a flowerhead and foliage, the cover extensively restored, some chipping to relief, c1745, 3½in (9cm).
$700-1,000

Sauceboats

A Staffordshire salt glazed sauceboat, c1765, 3in (8cm).
$2,000-2,700

A Pratt pottery sauceboat moulded in the form of a dolphin, painted in green, brown and ochre enamels, 6½in (16cm) long.
$550-750

A Staffordshire creamware shell shaped sauceboat, with double entwined reeded handle, the rim moulded with feathered scrolls on a spreading foot, chipped and stained, 6½in (16cm).
$180-280

Services

A Leeds pottery white glazed part dessert service, moulded in the form of leaves with twig handles, comprising: a comport and 19 dishes in 5 sizes, minor chips, impressed mark Leeds Pottery, 19thC, largest dishes 13in (33cm) wide.
$1,400-1,500

Did you know

MILLER'S Antiques Price Guide builds up year by year to form the most comprehensive photo-reference system available

A Mason's Ironstone part dessert service, transfer printed and coloured with flowers within an elaborate diaper and whorl pattern border, reserved with pink flowerheads and blue foliage, comprising: 2 oval two-handled sauce tureens, covers and stands, 12 dishes and 22 plates, printed mark, c1820.
$4,500-5,500

Tiles

A London delft tin glazed tile, c1740, 5½in (13.5cm).   **$140-160**

A Bristol tile depicting Jonah and the Whale, c1750, 5in (13cm) square. **$120-180**

A Liverpool black transfer ware tile, c1765, 5in (13cm) square. **$200-260**

A London delft blue and white tile, c1770, 5in (13cm) square. **$90-120**

Tureens

An early Mason's Ironstone china covered sauce tureen, painted in Imari style, early impressed mark, c1820. **$450-550**

A Staffordshire sauce tureen and stand, with rosebud finial lid, early 19thC, 6in (15cm) high. **$350-450**

A London delft tile, c1740, 5in (12cm). **$220-280**

A George Jones majolica sardine box and cover, covered in a brown glaze with turquoise interior, small chip inside cover, impressed registration diamond, black painted numerals 3541/111, c1865, 9in (23cm). **$900-1,000**

A Liverpool black transfer ware tile, restored, c1765, 5in (13cm) square. **$90-110**

A Liverpool black transfer printed tile, c1770. **$200-260**

A Mason's Ironstone dessert tureen, richly gilded, c1820, 7½in (18.5cm). **$700-900**

A Mason's Ironstone vegetable tureen, decorated with the Burning Bush pattern, c1835, 13½in (33cm) wide. **$650-750**

31

A Staffordshire hen on nest, c1880.
$300-400

A Hicks, Meigh & Johnson vegetable tureen, c1830, 15in (38cm) wide.
$650-800

Use the Index!
Because certain items might fit easily into any of a number of categories, the quickest and surest method of locating any entry is by reference to the index at the back of the book.
This has been fully cross-referenced for absolute simplicity

A John Rogers & Son tureen and cover, decorated with blue floral transfers, lid surmounted by a lion head and with 2 lion masks handles, impressed factory mark to base, early 19thC, 8in (20cm).
$450-550

A Staffordshire soup tureen and cover, with a rose finial, printed with the Bridge of Lucano, the base with a named ribbon, one handle damaged and restuck, 12½in (32cm).
$540-740

A rare salt glazed butter tub and cover, moulded with a seeded diaper ground beneath a single band of small ovolos, the domed cover divided into 4 segments, each pierced with 3 square holes, and surmounted by a recumbent bull, c1760, 4½in (11cm).
$2,000-3,000

Vases

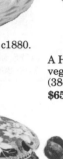

A Minton majolica two-handled game pie tureen, cover and liner, covered in a brown glaze encrusted and entwined with green oak leaves and acorns, the cover surmounted by a dead hare, duck and jackdaw lying on ferns and leaves, restoration, impressed marks and date cypher, 1878, 13½in (34cm) wide.
$1,200-1,500

A pair of Mason's Ironstone hall vases, with applied rich floral decoration, elaborate dragon handles and matching covers with dragon finials, slight damage to covers, c1820, 26in (66cm).
$8,000-9,000

A Liverpool vase, painted with buildings beside a willow tree issuing from rockwork, a figure crossing a bridge and 2 figures in a landscape, with birds above, crack to body and 2 cracks to rim, incised 6 mark, Pennington's factory, c1770, 9in (22.5cm).
$1,500-1,800

A Mason's Ironstone vase with centurion handles, with lustre decoration, c1820, 6in (15cm).
$320-420

A Bristol delft boldly painted baluster vase, extensive glaze flaking to body, foot chipped, c1730, 12in (31cm).
$2,000-2,700

A pearlware bear-baiting group, Staffordshire or Yorkshire, crack to bear's left flank, c1790, 12½in (31.5cm) wide. **$18,000-21,000**

A Staffordshire creamware equestrian group of Hudibras of Ralph Wood type, some damage and restoration, c1785, 12in (30cm). **$27,000-32,000**

A London delft armorial wine bottle, chipped and restored, c1650, 8in (20cm). **$32,000-38,000**

An opaque white candlestick with enamel drip pan, and a similar pair, South Staffordshire, damage, c1760, 10in (25cm) and 7in (18cm). l.&r. **$12,000-14,500** c. **$5,500-9,000**

A London delft candlestick with wide drip pan, cracks and glaze flaking, 1653, 10in (25.5cm). **$300,000-320,000**

A saltglaze moulded candlestick, c1760, 8in (20cm). **$11,000-18,000**

A small London delft royal portrait wine bottle with loop handle, inscribed ChARLS THE 2D, chipped and cracked, c1660, 6½in (16cm). **$300,000-320,000**

A rare Whieldon-type glazed slipware figure of a hawk, chips to base, late 18thC, 7in (17.5cm). **$9,000-12,000**

A Mason's Ironstone punch bowl, decorated with the table and flower pot pattern, c1820, 13in (33cm) diam. **$2,000-2,200**

An English delft inscribed and dated punch bowl, the underside with the initials K/WA and the date 1740, perhaps Bristol, some damage, 12½in (32cm). **$56,000-68,000**

A Staffordshire saltglaze two-handled cup, incised with the initials H:N above the date 1756, with three cracks to the rim, 12in (30.5cm) wide. **$23,000-27,000**

A pair of very rare Staffordshire figures of the royal children, Edward and Victoria, by Thomas Parr, 1850, 10in (25.5cm) high. **$2,500-3,300**

A creamware model of a falcon of Whieldon type, with moulded and incised plumage, c1770, 12in (30cm) high. **$18,000-21,000**

A previously unrecorded Staffordshire group of Jesus and the Woman of Samaria, decorated in enamel colours, c1820, 8in (20cm). **$4,500-5,500**

A Staffordshire watch holder modelled as whippets chasing a hare, watch missing, c1860, 8½in (21.5cm) high. **$450-500**

A saltglaze model of an owl, with deeply moulded and incised plumage, eyes and short beak, on triangular mound base, some minute glaze fritting, c1750, 8in (20cm) high. **$127,000-135,000**

A creamware model of a parrot of Whieldon type, with incised wing feathers and eyes, streaked in green and brown glazes, perched astride a conical tree stump, c1760, 7in (17cm) high. **$27,000-32,000**

A Mason's Ironstone cider mug, decorated with chinoiserie panels, c1820, 5in (13cm) high. **$800-900**

A pair of Staffordshire pottery poodles with flower baskets in their mouths, c1860, 3½in (18cm) high. **$270-320**

A creamware model of a squirrel of Whieldon type, ears restored, c1765, 7½in (19cm) high. **$16,500-21,000**

A Staffordshire figure, probably of Lablache as Falstaff, c1845, 6in (15cm). **$270-300**

A pair of Staffordshire figures portraying the Turkish general, Omar Pasha, on horseback, c1854, 4½in (11.5cm) high. $800-900

A rare Staffordshire figure of Daniel O'Connell, c1845, 15½in (39cm). $1,500-1,600

A Staffordshire figure of the Duke of Wellington, c1850, 12in (30cm) high. $900-1,000

A rare Staffordshire figure of Admiral Sir Charles Napier, c1854, 12½in (32cm). $1,400-1,500

A rare Staffordshire penholder depicting Lambton, c1845, 4in (10cm). $160-180

An unrecorded English delftware blue-dash charger, decorated with a shepherd playing the bagpipes, probably London, c1700, 12½in (32.5cm). $36,000-45,000

A Staffordshire group portraying standing Miss Florence Nightingale and a seated wounded officer, c1854, 10in (25.5cm). high. $1,000-1,200

A Southwark delft polychrome La Fécondité dish of conventional type, marked with initials R over N.A and with the date 1659, 18½in (46.5cm) wide. $45,000-54,000

A Savona figure of Winter, with minor chips and slight restoration, the underside incised with date 1779, 13½in (33.5cm) high. $4,500-7,000

A creamware arbour group of Whieldon type, with two women in crinolines in a garden shelter with a dove roosting on the roof, cracked, 6in (14.5cm). $56,000-63,000

A creamware figure of a mounted officer of Astbury/Whieldon type, saddle cloth with the initials GR, on fluted base, restoration to his left arm and tail of horse, c1760, 10½in (25.5cm) high. $36,000-45,000

A Lodi tray with Moses striking the rock, slight chipping, c1720, 19in (48cm) wide. **$11,000-13,000**

A German faience armorial dish, damaged and restored, early 18thC, 20in (50cm). **$7,000-10,000**

A Folch and Sons polychrome plate, c1820, 10in (26cm) diam. **$270-360**

A Faenza blue and white crespina, the underside moulded with shells and painted with San Bernardino rays, slight cracks, c1650, 12in (30.5cm). **$2,700-3,600**

A pair of marked dishes by Folch, c1820, 9½in (24cm) wide. **$800-1,000**

An Urbino Piatto di Pompa from the Guidobaldo II service, chipped, c1566, 16½in (42cm). **$54,000-58,000**

A Castelli Tondino paint by Niccoló Tommaso Gru with 6 figures beside a class ruin in a sunset woode landscape, c1755, 6½in (16.5cm) diam **$3,600-5,500**

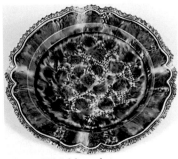

A large Whieldon plate, mid-18thC. **$2,700-4,500**

An Hispano Moresque armorial dish, damaged and repairs, late 15thC, 19in (48cm). **$16,500-20,000**

A pair of Mason's Ironstone dess plates, c1820, 9in (23cm) diam. **$650-720**

A very rare dated and inscribed delftware puzzle jug, probably Bristol, 1771, 8½in (21.5cm) high. **$7,000-8,000**

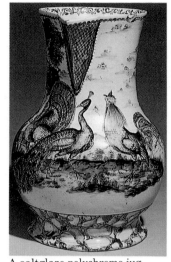

A saltglaze polychrome jug, cracked, restorations, cross mark, c1760, 13½in (34.5cm). high. **$40,000-45,000**

Two Faenza waisted albarelli, decorated in the workshop of Virgiliotto Calamelli, some damage, c1525, 10½in (27cm) high. **$42,000-43,000**

A Staffordshire slipware dated and inscribed bragget-pot, some damage and restored, 1709, 10½in (27cm) high. **$18,000-21,000**

A creamware jug with unusual handle, probably Greatbatch, Staffordshire, 9in (23cm). **$5,500-6,000**

A Davenport Toby jug of Drunken Sal, c1840, 13in (33cm). **$1,800-2,700**

A matched pair of majolica jardinières, probably Minton, each moulded and painted with ferns, foxgloves and convolvulus, with matching stands, some damage, c1865. **$2,700-3,600**

A Dutch Delft 'bleu persan' pewter mounted jug, makers marks, c1720, 9½in (24cm) high. **$10,000-12,000**

A pair of faience jardinières, probably Nevers, bases drilled, some damage, c1680, 5½in (13.5cm). **$7,000-9,000**

A Castel Durante albarello, rim chipped, c1555, 12in (30.5cm) high. **$9,500-11,000**

A creamware coffee pot of Whieldon type, c1765, 9½in (24.5cm). **$9,000-14,500**

A Wedgwood blue and white jasper 'Ruined Column' vase, impressed mark, c1795, 8½in (21cm) wide. **$10,000-18,000**

A Mintons pâte-sur-pâte vase by M. L.Solon, marked, c1894, 22in (56cm) high. **$16,500-20,000**

A creamware dovecote of Whieldon type, stem, foot and top with extensive restoration, some other restoration, c1760, 10½in (26.5cm). **$75,000-82,000**

A pottery barrel decorated in prattware colours, c1810. **$450-540**

An Isle of Man majolica three-legged teapot, late 19thC, 9in (23cm) high. **$650-1,000**

A Prattware figure of seated Toby jug wearing striped breeches, c1800. **$1,200-1,600**

A saltglaze teapot, slight damage, c1760, 6½in (16.5cm). **$40,000-45,000**

A pair of Staffordshire garden seats in the Mason's Ironstone mould, early 19thC. **$6,000-7,000**

A Yorkshire figure of a Toby jug holding a goblet and a jug, impressed crown mark, c1810, **$2,000-2,800**

Two Worcester bottles and a Worcester jug, c1753, bottles 4½in (11.5cm), jug 3½in (8cm). l.**$7,000-9,000**, c.**$14,500-16,500** r.**$6,000-11,000**

A London delft pill tile, pierced for hanging, with wood stand, cracked and repaired, chips, c1750, 13½in (34.5cm) high. **$27,000-30,000**

A pair of part glazed architectural reliefs, slight damage, 19thC. **$11,000-12,000**

A Worcester fable-decorated bowl, painted in the atelier of James Giles, chip to inside of footrim, c1765, 9½in (23.5cm) diam. **$28,000-32,000**

A pair of Bow globular bottles, painted in the Kakiemon palette with flowering shrubs, c1755, 8in (20.5cm) and 8½in (21cm) high. **$21,000-27,000**

A Meissen silver-gilt mounted squat bottle and cover, c1725, 6in (15cm). **$27,000-32,000**

A Chelsea cabbage leaf moulded bowl, red anchor mark, c1755, 5½in (16cm) high. **$9,000-10,000**

A London delft dated salt modelled as a youth, brightly painted, the underside with a blue dragonfly, repairs, chipping, c1676, 7½in (19.5cm). **$300,000-330,000**

A pair of Longton Hall leaf-moulded bowls and stands, chips and some restorations, c1755, the bowls 5in (12.5cm). **$11,000-13,000**

Six Meissen coffee cups and saucers and a coffee pot and cover, damaged, marked, c1750. **$9,500-12,000**

A Worcester coffee cup, teacup and saucer and bowl, c1768, cups and saucer. **$9,000-10,000** bowl.**$9,000-10,000**

An English porcelain bust of George II on later socle, damage, c1755, 13½in (34cm). **$67,000-72,000**

A gilt-metal mounted box of 'Girl in a Swing' type, modelled as a recumbent pug dog and pups, cover chipped and cracked, c1750, 2in (5cm) wide. **$6,000-9,000**

An early Derby figure of a Florentine boar, on oval mound base, damaged **$4,500-6,000**

A pair of Böttger beakers and saucers, slight damage, gilders numerals 17, c1725. **$14,500-18,000**

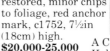

A Chelsea model of a little hawk owl astride a tree stump, restored, minor chips to foliage, red anchor mark, c1752, 7½in (18cm) high. **$20,000-25,000**

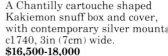

A Chantilly cartouche shaped Kakiemon snuff box and cover, with contemporary silver mounts c1740, 3in (7cm) wide. **$16,500-18,000**

A Meissen gilt metal mounted snuff box, slight rubbing, c1750, 3in (7.5cm). **$10,000-12,000**

A Meissen gold-mounted snuff box, with contemporary vari-coloured gold mounts, c1755, 3½in (8cm) high. **$27,000-32,000**

A pair of English porcelain models of dogs, perhaps Coalport, c1810. **$13,000-15,000**

A Staffordshire porcelain pastille burne modelled as a church, c1835, 5½in (14cm) high. **$1,200-1,400**

A Chelsea white figure of a sphinx, her lioness's body with shaped tasselled cloth, tip of tail missing, chip to base, c1750, 5½in (14.5cm). **$9,000-10,000**

A Kloster Veilsdorf figure of Pierrot by Wenzel Neu, restored, marked, c1765, 5½in (16cm) high. **$18,000-21,000**

A Liverpool group of La Nourrice, Richard Chaffer's factory, cracks, glaze flaking, c1760, 6in (15.5cm). **$5,500-7,000**

A pair of Fulda figures of a Turk and companion, restored, marked, c1770, 6in & 6¼in (15 & 15.5cm). **$58,000-63,000**

A Bow figure of The Doctor, his left hand raised and his right hand on his hip, colourfully clothed, on shaped painted base, restoration to brim of hat and left arm at shoulder, slight chip to jacket, c1755, 6½in (16cm) high. **$5,700-7,000**

A Chelsea group of La Nourrice modelled by Joseph Willems, cracked, c1756, 7½in (19cm). **$16,500-18,000**

A pair of Frankenthal figures of a gallant and companion in winter clothes, by J F Lück, both slightly chipped, makers marks, c1760. **$14,500-16,500**

A Capodimonte group of a youth riding a mastiff by Guiseppi Gricci, some damage, c1755, 6½in (17cm). **$8,000-9,500**

A pair of Bow sphinxes by the Muses modeller, on rococo scroll-moulded bases, both chipped, c1750, 4½in (12cm) long. **$6,000-8,000**

A pair of Bow white figures of Kitty Clive and Henry Woodward, both restored c1750, 10in (25cm).
$63,000-70,000

A Bow pierced basket, painted within a waved brown line rim, crack to base and footrim, c1760, 11½in (30cm) diam. **$27,000-32,000**

A Kloster Veilsdorf figure of Harlequin, c1765, 5½in (14.5cm). **$18,000-21,000**

A Nymphenburg figure of a mushroom-seller by Bustelli, hat restored, impressed marks, c1755, 8in (20cm).
$68,000-72,000

A Ludwigsburg group of Bacchus and a Bacchante, chips, marked, c1765, 9½in (24cm). **$5,500-7,000**

A pair of colourful Strasbourg figures of gardeners, heads and one arm re-stuck, one hand and spade missing, c1750, 7½in (19cm) high.
$6,000-8,000

A Meissen group of The Hand Kiss, by JJ Kändler, restored, chipped, marked, c1740, 7in (18cm).
$8,000-9,500

A rare Vincennes figure of a water nymph, probably by Fournier, c1750, 8in (20.5cm).
$20,000-24,000

A Kloster Veilsdorf figure of Gobiel, modelled by Wenzel Neu, in green striped snood, cloak, tunic and trousers, standing on tip-toe before a tree trunk on a mound base, left hand restored replacement, blue CV mark, incised EZ over a script B, c1765, 6½in (16cm).
$32,000-36,000

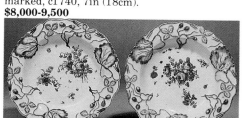

A pair of Longton Hall strawberry leaf moulded soup plates, each with one minute rim chip, c1755, 9½in (23.5cm). **$12,000-14,000**

A Meissen group of satyrs supporting a shell, c1734, 11in (28cm). **$4,500-6,000**

A pair of Meissen blue and white plates, blue crossed swords marks, Pressnummern 20, c1735, 10in (25.5cm).
$16,500-18,000

A Worcester Flight, Barr and Barr platter, small rim chips, slight wear to paint and gilding, marked, c1820, 22½in (57cm).
$12,000-14,500

Three Worcester fable-decorated plates, painted in the manner of Jefferyes Hammett O'Neale, c1768, 7½in (19cm). **$14,500-16,500**

A 'Girl in a Swing' cream jug, some chipping, c1750, 3½in (8.5cm) high.
$27,000-30,000

A Worcester cabbage leaf moulded jug with double scroll handle, c1768, 10½in (27cm) high. **$9,000-10,000**

A Chelsea fluted cream jug, two small rim chips, firing crack to handle, marked, c1745, 5in (12cm). **$16,500-18,000**

Three Worcester fable-plates, c1768, 7½in (19cm).
l. **$18,000-21,000** c.&r. **$9,000-10,000 each**

A framed English plaque, painted, signed and dated by Bessie Gilson, 1882, 20½in (51.5cm) high. **$3,600-5,500**

A Chelsea beaker, spirally moulded with coloured teaplants, minor chipping to rim and some staining to foot, c1745, 3in (7.5cm) high. **$5,500-7,000**

A Meissen cream jug and cover, supported on three paw feet, painted in 'famille verte' style with an exotic bird perched on a branch, the cover with brown-edged rim, crossed swords in underglaze blue, c1730, 4½in (11.5cm). **$8,000-9,500**

A framed Berlin plaque, painted with a young girl in satin dress, some surface pitting, c1880, 9in (23cm) high. **$5,500-9,000**

A Meissen 'famille verte' dish, painted in underglaze blue within an overglaze enamel band of zig-zag panels, blue crossed swords mark, blue K to rim for Kretschmar, and Dreher's 4 to foot, c1730, 15in (38cm) diam. **$30,000-36,000**

A Berlin plaque, painted with a gypsy girl, in velvet mount and giltwood frame, signed C.S., impressed marks, c1880, 9½in (23.5cm) high. **$5,500-7,000**

A Nymphenburg plate, probably painted by J Zächenberger, with a bouquet and insects beneath the gilt rococo scroll and blue line border, the rim further enriched with gilding, chip to one scroll, minor rubbing on rim, impressed shield mark and 4PM, c1760, 10in (25.5cm). **$22,000-25,000**

A Chelsea white teapot on 6 pad feet, the tip of spout with silver attachment disguising damage, marked, c1745, 4in (9.5cm). **$16,500-20,000**

A Chelsea asparagus tureen, one asparagus curled to form the finial, repaired, marked, c1755, 7½in (18.5cm) wide. **$6,000-8,000**

Three Worcester teapots and covers, c1765, l. **$7,000-9,000**, c. **$9,000-10,000**, r. **$1,800-3,600**

A Meissen chinoiserie teapot, chipped and repaired, blue K.P.M. and crossed swords mark, gilder's numeral, c1723, 6in (15.5cm). **$16,500-18,000**

A Paris gold ground coffee pot and cover, finial repaired, incised 8, c1800, 7½in (18.5cm) high. **$3,600-5,500**

A framed Meissen plaque, crossed swords in underglaze blue, slight bevelling of edges, late 19thC, 7½in (19cm) high. **$5,500-7,000**

A Bristol armorial baluster coffee pot and cover from the Ludlow of Campden Service, Richard Champion's factory, with entwined branch handle, painted with loose bouquets and scattered flower sprays, the domed cover with bud finial and with gilt dentil rim, c1775, 9½in (24cm) high. **$5,500-7,000**

A part armorial dinner service, perhaps H&R Daniel, with gilt line and leaf motifs, c1835. **$1,600-1,800**

A Venice (Vezzi) teapot and contemporary cover with fruit finial, short crack to rim, cover chipped, incised Z mark, c1725, 6½in (16.5cm) wide. **$21,000-25,000**

45

Part of the Sèvres Louis Philippe hunting service, with LP monograms, comprising 85 pieces, some damage, various marks, date codes for 1838-48. **$21,000-27,000**

A Meissen (Marcolini) tête-a-tête, painted in colours, comprising 13 pieces, slight wear to gilding, blue crossed swords and other marks, c1775, **$7,500-9,500**

A Meissen (Marcolini) composite dessert service comprising 89 pieces, some damage, various marks, c1790. **$40,000-45,000**

A Sèvres later decorated 'bleu celeste' part dessert service, comprising 59 pieces, slight chips, marks, 18thC. **$11,000-13,000**

A Meissen dinner service, comprising 169 pieces, some Berlin replacements, minor damage, makers marks, c1755. **$65,000-70,000**

A Meissen JAGD part coffee service, 11 pieces, some damage, various Pressnummern and marks, c1745. **$9,000-10,000**

A Meissen composite pierced part dessert service comprising 12 pieces, some damage, various marks, c1880. **$7,000-9,000**

A Meissen (Marcolini) part dinner service comprising 181 pieces, some damage, minor rubbing to gilt rims, blue crossed swords and other marks, c1790. **$60,000-68,000**

A Meissen tea service, comprising 36 pieces, with gilt edged rims, restored, minor rubbing, makers marks, c1750. **$14,500-16,500**

Six Naples coffee cans and saucers, damaged and repaired, incised marks, c1800. **$72,000-80,000**

A Worcester blue and white tureen and cover, with moulded dolphin finial, chips to finial, c1756, 16in (40.5cm) wide. **$52,000-58,000**

A Worcester beaker vase, slight damage, c1754, 6in (15cm) high. **$21,000-25,000**

A Worcester hexagonal vase and domed cover, c1770, 11½in (29cm). **$27,000-32,000**

A Meissen écuelle, cover and stand from the St Andrew The First Called Service, restored, blue crossed swords mark and pressnummer 6, c1745, 7in (18cm). **$10,000-12,000**

A Worcester garniture of vases, painted in the atelier of James Giles, restorations and replacements, c1770, tallest 12in (30cm). **$32,000-36,000**

A Meissen Augustus Rex beaker vase, chipped, blue AR mark, c1730, 15½in (39cm). **$52,000-56,000**

A Chelsea lobed baluster vase, slight damage, c1750, 5in (13cm) high. **$9,500-11,000**

A pair of Meissen Imari tureens, damage, marks, c1735, 13½in (34cm). **$65,000-70,000**

A Worcester baluster vase and a pair of Worcester oviform vases, the pair slightly damaged, c1756, 5in (12.5cm) and 6½in (16cm). **$15,400-12,500** **$16,500-18,000 the pair**

A Chelsea baluster vase and a pair of Chelsea oviform vases, baluster vase slightly damaged, all with red anchor marks, c1756, **$4,500-6,000** and **$15,500-16,500** the pair.

A pair of Berlin armorial tureens, damaged, marks, c1820. **$40,000-45,000**

A Derby elongated campana vase, decorated on both sides, 10½in (26cm) high. **$4,140-4,500**

A pair of Worcester sauce tureens, c1765, 8in (21cm) wide. **$13,000-14,500**

COLOUR REVIEW

An ormolu-mounted English porcelain and kingwood encrier, lacking inkwells, pen tray inlaid à quatre faces.
$7,000-9,000

A Wucai fish bowl, extensively restored, Wanli marks, 19in (48.5cm) diam.
$18,000-21,000

An Imari deep bowl, slight chip to rim restored, late 17thC, 10in (25cm) diam.
$9,000-10,000

A pair of 'famille rose' vases, iron red Qianlong seal marks, 19thC, 23in (59cm). **$20,000-25,000**

A rare Chinese Imari armorial ribbed basin, one handle restored, c1720, 11½in (29cm) wide. **$11,000-13,000**

A Ko-Imari globular ewer, pierced hole for silver mount, slight damage, late 17thC, 9in (22cm).
$30,000-34,000

A blue and white bottle vase, the slender handle modelled as a dragon head, Kangxi period, 11in (27cm).
$5,500-7,000

A Meissen clock case, damaged and repaired, marked, c1745, 16in (41cm) high. **$8,000-11,000**

A Kakiemon bowl, decorated in enamels and gilt, slight crack, c1680, 9½in (23.5cm) high.
$110,000-118,000

A Derby crayfish sauceboat, Andrew Planché's period, minor chips to applied shells and rim, crayfish lacking front pincers, c1750.
$12,000-14,500

A Chelsea crayfish salt, some damage, c1745, 5in (12cm) wide.
$20,000-23,000

A Sèvres porcelain vase, designed by Decoeur, decorated by Gaucher, printed marks, 20in (50cm).
$11,000-13,000

A pair of 'famille verte' Buddhistic lions and detachable stands, two paws and ball restored, 18th/19thC, 21 in (53cm). **$16,500-20,000**

A pair of exportware dishes, of European silver form, depicting a lady adorning her hair before a mirror on a table in the garden, with 7 ladies in waiting, Qianlong, 17in (43cm). **$5,500-7,000**

A pair of 'famille verte' helmet-shaped ewers, one foot restored, rim frits, chips, Kangxi period, 11 in (28.5cm) high. **$21,000-27,000**

A pair of turquoise and yellow glazed temple figures, each on a base decorated on each side with stylised clouds on a green ground, some damage to one dragon mouth, Ming Dynasty, 29in (74cm). **$18,000-21,000**

A pair of 'famille rose' models of pheasants, crests chipped, enamels flaked, base cracks, Qianlong, 12in (30.5cm) high. **$40,000-45,000**

An erotic 'famille rose' plate, decorated within eight foliate cartouches, early Qianlong, 8½in (21.5cm). **$5,500-7,000**

A late Ming blue and white 'Kraak porselein' dish, the well with eight lappets alternately painted with auspicious emblems and fruiting foliage, some rim frits, Wanli period, 20in (50.5cm). **$9,500-11,000**

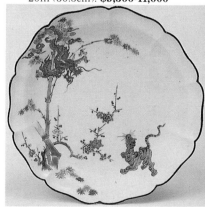

A pair of export figures of cranes, modelled in mirror image, with 'lingzhi' extremities chipped and slightly restored, early 19thC. 18½in (47cm) high. **$32,000-36,000**

A 'famille verte' biscuit wine ewer, Kangxi, 17½in (44.5cm) high. **$13,000-15,000**

A Kakiemon moulded foliate rimmed dish, decorated with a tiger prowling beneath a dragon coiled in branches of bamboo amongst plum blossom, slight firing crack, c1680, 7in (18cm) diam. **$45,000-50,000**

A 'famille verte' tureen and cover, surmounted by a cockerel finial, minor frits, Kangxi, 10½in (25cm). **$16,500-18,000**

An Imari dish, decorated in iron red enamel and gilt on underglaze blue, late 17th/18thC, 12½in (31.5cm). **$18,000-21,000**

An Imari jar and cover, cover cracked and 'karashishi' tail damaged, c1700, 23½in (60cm) high. **$12,000-14,500**

An Arita blue and white jar, slight chip to neck, cover missing, late 17thC, 24½in (62cm) high. **$12,000-14,500**

A large Imari dish, the reverse painted with 'ho-ho' birds signed Dai Nihon Hichozan Shinpo zo, 19thC. **$21,000-25,000**

A Kakiemon style blue and white tureen and cover, decorated with a continuous band of pavilions beneath pine trees, the domed cover similarly decorated and surmounted by a gilt metal finial, finial later replacement, c1680, 10½in (27cm) high. **$12,000-14,500**

An Arita blue and white ship's tureen with large finial, decorated with peony and plum blossom, late 17thC, 11½in (29cm). **$7,000-9,000**

A set of 5 graduated sepia Fitzhugh pattern armorial dishes, each painted with a crest below the motto 'Essayez', one cracked, c1800. **$9,000-10,000**

An Arita blue and white jar, decorated in the Kakiemon manner, c1680, 16in (40cm) high. **$72,000-78,000**

A 'famille rose' Masonic armorial dish, the initials MJD on two sides, Qianlong, 15½in (39.5cm). **$7,000-9,000**

A 'famille rose' eggshell dish, the reverse painted with 3 simple flower sprays, chips, early Qianlong, 8½in (21cm), fitted box. **$7,000-9,000**

51

A Transitional brush pot, 'bidong', painted with two bearded scholars playing 'weigi', two travellers and a 'qui'-bearing attendant, hallmarked, c1645, 8in (19.5cm) **$10,000-12,000**

A pair of 'famille verte' baluster vases, both cracked and chipped, Kangxi period, 23in (58cm). **$10,000-16,500**

A pair of 'famille rose' garden seats, one with foot chips, small areas of enamel flaking, 19thC, 19in (48cm) high. **$10,000-12,000**

A rare early Ming blue and white bottle vase, 'yuhuch-unping', Yongle period, 10½in (26cm) high. **$750,000-820,000**

A large porcelain garden lanter in seven sections, restored, sign Nihon Seto Kato Keisa sei, late 19thC, 69in (175cm). **$29,000-32,000**

A pair of 'famille rose' vases and covers, minute restorations, Qianlong period, 18½in (46.5cm) high. **$22,000-27,000**

An Imari tureen, decorated in enamels and gilt on underglaze blue, a peony spray on the interior of the tureen and cover, c1700, 10in (25cm). **$54,000-60,000**

A large Imari vase, decorated in various coloured enamels, 19thC, 34½in (88cm) high. **$16,500-18,000**

A pair of 'famille rose' tureens and covers, one finial restored, Qianlong, 14in (36cm) wide. **$14,500-18,000**

An Imari tureen and cover, the cover with large knop finial, cover restored, c1700, 15½in (39cm) high. **$10,000-12,000**

A Korean Punc'hong ware va decorated in 'hakeme-e' style restored, 15th/16thC, 11in (28cm). **$160,000-170,000**

A set of 6 green wine glasses, with conical bowls, bladed knop stems and plain conical feet, c1830, 5in (13cm) high. **$650-800**

An amethyst cream jug with loop handle, c1820, 4in (9.5cm) high, and a smaller pale amethyst cream jug with folded rim, c1820, 4in (9.5cm) high. **$270-450 each**

Two 'onion' shaped carafes, c1840, 8in (20cm). **$270-450 each**

A set of 6 green wine glasses with round funnel bowls and plain stems, c1840, 5in (12cm) high. **$380-500**

A pair of wrythen spirit bottles, c1830. **$800-1,000** An amber spirit bottle, c1845. **$180-270**

A pair of blue spirit bottles, c1830. **$1,200-1,500** and an amber spirit bottle with cork/metal stopper, c1850. **$270-360**

A pair of green spirit decanters of ovoid shape, with bevelled lozenge stoppers, c1790, 6½in (16cm) high. **$1,000-1,200**

A pair of magnum wine bottles, with raised seals, inscribed J Mason, 13in (33cm). **$360-720**

A very rare beer jug, with strap handle and ribbed rim, c1780, 7½in (19.5cm) **$1,400-1,500**

A cream jug and sugar basin with cold enamelled floral decoration, c1800, 4½in (12cm). **$900-1,000**

An export type wine glass, the double ogee bowl on plain stem with domed foot, c1760, 6in (15cm). **$1,500-1,800**

COLOUR REVIEW

A wine glass on wrythen knopped stem, with plain conical foot, c1760, 5½in (13.5cm). **$1,400-1,500**

A 'Façon de Venise' flute, on folded foot, 17thC, 10½in (26.5cm). **$14,500-16,500**

A peacock green wine glass, the cup bowl on a wrythen knopped stem and plain conical foot, c1760, 5½in (14cm). **$1,400-1,500**

A Hall-in-Tyrol 'Façon de Venise' goblet, perhaps from the workshop of Sebastian Höchstelter, 16thC, 10½in (26cm). **$30,000-34,000**

A German green tinted puzzle goblet, with a central column supporting a detachable stag, slight damage, 17thC, 14in (35.5cm). **$11,000-13,000**

A Netherlandish roemer, on a high trailed conical foot and with a kick-in base, mid-17thC, 10½in (26cm). **$10,000-12,000**

A Venetian latticinio tazza, decorated with vertical bands of lattimo thread and gauze, with shallow bowl above a knopped baluster section, on conical foot, 17thC, 6½in (16.5cm) diam. **$23,000-27,000**

A polychrome enamelled armorial opaque twist wine glass, attributed to William Beilby, the bowl enamelled in yellow heightened in iron-red, black, white and gilt, the reverse with a branch of fruiting vine, on double series stem and conical foot, c1765, 6in (15.5cm). **$18,000-21,000**

A rare blue wrythen ale glass, with everted rim, knopped stem on plain foot, c1810, 4½in (11cm). **$700-800**

A wine glass with incurved ogee bowl on stem with a multiple spiral air twist, c1760, 6½in (16cm). **$7,000-9,000**

A set of 10 amber wine glasses, with flute cut trumpet bowls, the stems with collars and cushion knops, on plain conical feet, c1845, 5in (13cm) high. **$1,200-1,400**

54

A French scent with silver mount, c1780, **$540-650** an amethyst scent with gilt decoration, **$540-650** and a blue scent with embossed silver mount, **$300-450**

A St Louis cruciform millefiori carpet-ground weight, very small chip, mid-19thC, 3in (7cm). **$9,000-10,000**

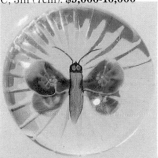

A Baccarat butterfly weight, the insect with translucent mauve body, multi-coloured wings, on a star cut base, mid-19thC, 3in (7cm). **$3,600-5,500**

A blue scent with later mount, c1800, **$500-550** an 'Oxford Lavender' type scent, c1850, **$180-270** and a blue scent with gilt decoration & silver mount, c1780, **$800-900**

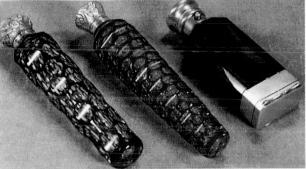

A blue overlay scent with embossed silver mount, and a similar red one, c1860, 5in (12.5cm) **$300-400 each** and a red scent with silver gilt mount and vinaigrette compartment at base, c1878, 4in (9.5cm). **$1,000-1,100**

A St Louis concentric millefiori mushroom weight, mid-19thC, 3in (7cm). **$5,500-7,000**

Four scent bottles, all with embossed silver mounts, c1870. **$180-450 each**

A German enamelled Humpen or Pasglas, dated 1723, 8in (20.5cm) high. **$5,000-6,000**

A German amethyst flask and screw stopper, the foot with silver stiff leaf mount, slight damage, 17thC, 11in (28cm). **$3,600-5,500**

A St Louis faceted panelled carpet-ground weight, with closely packed brightly coloured canes, slight chips, mid-19thC, 3in (7cm). **$11,000-13,000**

A red satin scent with darker stripes and silver mount, c1896. **$360-540** and a blue scent with silver mount, c1900. **$90-180**

l. A red vinaigrette/scent, with cut decoration, 1in (3cm) c. A double ended scent with chased gilt mounts, 5in (12cm) r. A clear scent with opaque overlay, 3in (7.5cm) c1870. **$360-900 each**

A rare Zwischen goldglas scent, c1850, 3½in (9cm). **$2,000-2,500,** an overlay scent with gilt decoration, c1860, 4½in (11cm). **$1,400-1,500,** and a rectangular overlay scent with embossed silver mount, c1860. **$450-540**

Three cut glass scent bottles, with silver moun c1860, 3in (7cm). **$300-450 each**

l. A prism cut scent with silver mount, c. A horn scent with silver gilt mounts and r. A cut scent with siver mount c1870. **$180-650 each**

An oval clear scent bottle, with enamelled decoration, c1880, 4in (10.5cm). **$300-360**

Three red glass scent bottles with silver gilt mounts, l & r hallmarked Samson & Mordan London 1878, 3½in (9cm) high. **$540-1,000 each**

Four glass scent bottles, all with silver gilt mounts, 1850-1892, 4in to 6in (10.5cm to 15cm) long. **$270-800 each**

A Mason's Ironstone large vase and cover, with mythical beast lug handles, the cover with entwined dolphin knop, decorated in shades of blue and orange, with printed and impressed marks, some damage and repair, c1840, 25in (63cm) high.
$1,000-1,200

A large Mason's Ironstone two-handled vase on hexagonal foot, with cover, painted with a frieze of classical figures, above and below a band of Greek key, on iron red body, with dragon moulded handles and fish entwined knop, 19thC, 25.5in (65cm).
$1,200-1,400

A Mason's Ironstone alcove vase, with lion handle, c1835, 17½in (44cm).
$700-900

A pair of Mason's Ironstone vases and covers.
$1,000-1,200

A Mason's Ironstone lidded vase, with Dog of Fo finial and Chinese seal mark, lid restored, c1830, 10½in (26cm).
$550-650

A salt glazed baluster vase, covered in a Littler's blue glaze, glaze fault to shoulder, slight crack to rim, c1760, 7in (17.5cm).
$3,500-4,500

A Minton vase by Christopher Dresser, shape No. 2693, c1885.
$450-550

A pottery treacle-glazed stoneware vase with gilt-metal mounts, painted all over in gilding with scrolling foliage and flowers, on a spreading foot with engine-turned metal rims and base, the base with an incised mark, gilding slightly rubbed, 10½in (26cm).
$550-900

William Littler and Aaron Wedgwood shared a pot bank at Brownhills 1745-63. Littler moved to Longton Hall to concentrate on porcelain production leaving Wedgwood on his own. In the sales account book of Thomas and John Wedgwood they refer to their cousin's wares as 'Aaron's Blue'.

Three Dutch Delft blue and white vases and covers, painted with a river landscape within a scroll cartouche flanked by trailing flowers, between shaped fluted and panelled borders with flowers, the covers with hound and shield finials, minor rim restorations to vases and covers, slight flaking, 2 finials restored, c1740, 18in (46cm).
$4,500-6,000

A Dutch Delft fluted globular vase, with tapering garlic neck, painted in manganese and blue, slight chips to rim, manganese 8 mark, c1700, 12in (31cm).
$1,800-2,800

Wemyss

l. A large Wemyss pottery model of a pig, with black patch markings, the ears, snout and mouth coloured in pink wash, one ear restuck, impressed Wemyss Ware, 17½in (45cm) long.
$2,700-3,600
r. A small Wemyss pottery model of a pig, with black patch markings, the face and trotters detailed in pink, inscribed Wemyss, printed Made in England, 6½in (16cm).
$700-950

A Scottish Wemyss ware pottery pig, painted with pink roses and foliage, early 20thC, 16½in (42cm).
$6,500-7,000

A Wemyss jug and basin, painted with fruiting cherries within a blue/green rim, impressed and painted marks, T. Goode & Co. retailer's marks, jug 6in (15cm) high, bowl 11½in (29cm) diam.
$650-900

A Wemyss chocolate pot, painted with brown cockerels, 5½in (14cm) high.
$350-550

A Dresden oviform vase and domed cover, with moulded female mask handles, painted within richly gilt scroll, foliage, 'gitterwerk' and strapwork cartouches, cracks to shoulder and body, one handle repaired, imitation blue AR mark, c1890, 17½in (44cm).
$800-1,200

A Wemyss pommade pot, painted with roses, 3½in (8cm) diam.
$350-550

In the Ceramics section if there is only one measurement it usually refers to the height of the piece

A Wemyss dog bowl, with impressed mark, 7in (17cm) diam.
$650-800

A Wemyss 'violet' plaque, with hair cracks, 5½ by 3½in   **$350-550**

A Wemyss square honey pot, stand and cover, with thistle finial, painted in colours within a dark green dentil border, inscribed marks, 7in (18cm) wide.
$900-1,200

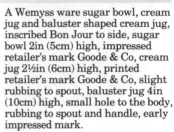

A Wemyss ware sugar bowl, cream jug and baluster shaped cream jug, inscribed Bon Jour to side, sugar bowl 2in (5cm) high, impressed retailer's mark Goode & Co, cream jug 2½in (6cm) high, printed retailer's mark Goode & Co, slight rubbing to spout, baluster jug 4in (10cm) high, small hole to the body, rubbing to spout and handle, early impressed mark.
$300-400

A Wemyss pig painted with clover, 6½in (16cm) long.
$900-1,200

A pair of Wemyss candlesticks with rose design, 12in (30.5cm).
$1,200-1,600

A Wemyss jug and basin set, including a sponge bowl and soap dish, jug 10in (25cm) high.
$2,700-4,500

A Wemyss bowl painted with buttercups, 6½in (16cm) diam.
$700-900

A Wemyss plate with wisteria, 5in (13cm) diam.
$350-700

A Wemyss black and white pig, 6in (15cm) long.
$550-900

A Wemyss thistle vase, 5½in (14cm) high.
$270-360

A pair of Wemyss cats with pink bows, 12½in (32cm) high.
$5,500-7,000 each

A Wemyss biscuit pot, painted with apples, 4in (10cm).
$550-900

A Wemyss goose, 8in (20cm) high.
$1,000-1,600

A Wemyss porridge bowl, stained,
6in (15cm) diam.
$540-740

A Wemyss Japan vase, painted with
herons, 8in (20cm) high.
$1,000-1,200

A Wemyss beaker vase, painted
with sand martins, 11½in (29cm)
high.
$2,700-3,700

A Wemyss teapot, painted with
brown cockerels, 4½in (11cm) high.
$450-550

A Wemyss pin tray, painted with
violets, 5½ by 3in (14 by 7cm).
$160-360

A Wemyss
quaiche with
handles, painted
with plums, 7½in
(19cm) diam.
$550-750

Miscellaneous

A Wemyss brush vase, painted with
mallard ducks, 4½in (11cm).
$540-740

An English
creamware basket
and stand, c1820.
$380-500

A rare salt glazed model of a shoe,
finely tooled over the upper surface
and around the welt and sole,
washed in a chocolate brown
ferruginous dip, probably
Nottingham, c1700, 4½in (12cm).
$1,600-2,000

A pair of blue and white flower
bricks, possibly Liverpool, 4½in
(11cm) wide.
$1,500-1,700

A treacle glazed egg stand, formed s 7 receptacles for eggs, covered in treaked brown glazes divided by opetwist, on a spreading partially lazed foot, minor rim chips, erhaps Sussex, late 18thC, 4½in 11.5cm).
1,000-1,200

A large Continental painted table centre figure group, some minor chips and restoration, mid-19thC, 18in (46cm) high.
$450-650

An English earthenware blue and white footbath, printed with a river landscape and trailing rose border, old restoration to one handle, early 19thC, 18½in (47cm) wide.
$1,400-1,500

A creamware flask, painted in the manner of David Rhodes in iron red nd black, the reverse with a utterfly and loose bouquets, within ircular moulded bead cartouches, ith short cylindrical neck, perhaps Vedgwood, c1775, 4½in (11.5cm).
1,000-1,200

A Staffordshire inkstand, possibly made by John Forster, c1820, 5½in (14cm). **$650-800**

A Davenport two-handled foot bath, printed with the Mosque and Fisherman pattern, within a border of roses and diaper panels, slight glaze cracks, impressed mark.
$3,200-4,500

A Staffordshire polychrome drainer, 9thC, 12in (31cm) wide.
270-370

A pepper pot and a vinegar bottle, by Samson and Smith, with gold anchor mark, 5in (12cm).
$70-140

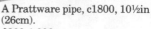

A Prattware pipe, c1800, 10½in (26cm).
$900-1,000

A pair of Mason's Ironstone letter acks in the Japan pattern, mpressed mark, c1815, 3½in 8.5cm) high.
1,500-1,600

A blue and white supper set, each piece printed with a Chinese landscape, with 4 crescent dishes and 2 covers, each with a lion's head knop, probably by Ralph Wedgwood, some damage, complete with mahogany tray, 23½in (60cm) wide.
$800-1,200

A rare Wedgwood stoneware pestle and mortar, the exterior decorated in white over a chocolate brown ground above a speckled green glazed ground, the plain white glazed pestle mounted on a turned wooden handle, small chip to spout, impressed Wedgwood 3 on the mortar and Wedgwood 4 on the bowl, c1800, bowl 5½in (14cm) diam.
$2,000-2,700

It is probable that this pestle and mortar formed part of a set produced by Wedgwood for someone of some note, probably as a luxury item for domestic use, although there would appear to be no record of who may have ordered the set in the Wedgwood archives.

QUIMPER

Pottery had been made at Quimper in Brittany since Roman times, but the characteristic style of the 'Petit Breton' peasant figure surrounded by floral garlands in the 'a la touche' techniques (single brush stroke) and concentric blue and yellow borders emerged only about 1870 when interest focused on Brittany with the building of the railways.

Trading on the Quimper success, similar wares were produced at Malicoine in the Sarthe region from about 1870 in a softer, more fluid style in a matt pink glaze on a reddish body. At the same time from Desvres in the Pas de Calais came a large variety of decorative forms in the Rouen manner, boldly painted in primary colours upon rococo shapes. Proximity to England resulted in a considerable quantity reaching these shores.

The two main faience factories were the Grande Maison de la Hubaudiere and the former Dumaine Stoneware pottery acquired by Jean-Baptiste Tanquerey whose grandson Jules Henriot gave the establishment its main impetus when he took over in 1884. Their marks were HB and HR respectively until 1922 when a legal suit obliged Henriot to use his full name.

A pair of Quimper plates, c1893, 9in (23cm).
$320-380

If they were c1920 they would be half the price.

A pair of Malicoine potter bells, c188(
$160-220 eac

A pair of Quimper plates, c1890, 9½in (24cm).
$550-650

A Quimper vase, c1880, 4in (10cm). **$300-360**

A Quimper match striker, c1890, 3in (8cm) high. **$180-220**

A Quimper menu, c1890, 6½in (16cm) high. $480-550

A French spill vase, c1900, possibly Malicoine, 7in (18cm) high. $180-240

An early Quimper bénitier, c1890, 9½in (24cm) long. $350-450

A Desvres Pas de Calais plate, 1892, 10in (25cm). $340-380

'Justice is on the side of the strongest' was the title of the original watercolour from which this subject derives, hence the see-saw and in this plate the tables are turned and the citizen/peasant is winning.

A Quimper inkstand, 7in (18cm) wide. **$650-800**

A Quimper bowl, some rim chips, c1890, 3½in (9cm) diam. **$25-40**

A Quimper bonbonnière, c1895,
4½in (11cm) diam.
$230-270

An early Quimper shoe, signed,
c1880, 6½in (16cm) long.
$100-150

A Desvres figure
Fourmaintraux Frères, c1890, 7½in
(19cm).   **$120-180**

A Desvres Pas de Calais plate,
centenary of the revolution, c1893,
10in (25cm).
$350-400

A Desvres egg cup Fourmaintraux
Frères, c1900, 3in (8cm) high.
$30-70

A Desvres Pas de Calais plate,
commemorating the centenary of
the revolution, with inscription,
c1891, 9in (23cm).
$300-400

A Malicoine pin tray, c1880, 4½in
(11cm) long.
$50-70

A Quimper vase, c1890, 5in (13cm
$200-270

A Devres snuff flask,
Fourmaintraux Frères pottery,
c1880, 3½in (8cm).
$180-220

A Quimper cornucopia, possible
Adolphe Porquier, c1880, 4½in
(11cm) high.
$270-320

An early Quimper plate, c1875, 9in (23cm).
$180-220

A Quimper jug, restored crack, c1890, 9in (23cm) high.
$400-450

An early Quimper dish, c1880, 10½in (26cm).
$300-370

A Desvres plate, centenary of the revolution, c1893, 9in (23cm) diam.
$340-380

A Quimper mug, 6in (15cm) high.
$250-280

A Quimper mug with damaged handle, c1925, 5½in (14cm) high.
$120-180

A Quimper bowl, some damage and restoration, c1880, 10in (25cm) diam.
$350-550

A Malicoine flask with stopper, c1875, 7½in (19cm) high.
$350-400

Make the Most of Miller's

In Miller's we do NOT just reprint saleroom estimates. We work from realised prices either from an auction room or a dealer. Our consultants then work out a realistic price range for a similar piece. This is to try to avoid repeating freak results – either low or high

A Malicoine plate, c1890, 7½in (19cm).
$120-180

A Quimper pot with lid, c1920, 6in (15cm) diam.
$250-280

A Quimper bud vase, c1890, 5in (13cm) high.
$230-270

PORCELAIN

As with the pottery market, last year's trends have continued with no real surprises. Quality and rarity still count! It was noticeable at the summer specialist ceramic fairs that the rarities had their red sold dots attached within a few minutes of opening but that the good but not too rare pieces were still available at the end of the show. The traditionally much sought after factories are still bid to high prices as was evident at Lawrence's sale in December when Lund's Bristol coffee cans were sold up to $3,150 each. Figure studies have maintained a stable price and unless of high quality and condition have not readily found a buyer. Good 19thC porcelain has been much in demand, particularly if painted and signed by the top ceramic artists. There has been a considerable upsurge in the demand for porcelain plaques with prices beginning to push $18,000 for the better pieces. These plaques have long been undervalued for the fine works of art that they undoubtedly are. Good, preferably complete, well painted services are still in demand. An Albert Gregory painted Royal Crown Derby dessert service realised $13,000 at Bearne's, Torquay. Porcelain from the Royal Worcester factory is still much in demand for the best signed pieces even though the year has seen a diminishing interest from Japanese buyers.

EUROPEAN PORCELAIN

Good early Meissen continues to be the international currency of the ceramics world and you do not have to sell it in Geneva to realise its potential. A 12-piece part Meissen breakfast service painted in the Herold style and dating from the 1730s fetched $43,200 at Riddetts auction rooms, Bournemouth. Although collectors are still chasing the rarest 18thC figurines the 19thC Meissen figures still represent very good value at $360-540, particularly if compared to some of the bizarre prices being paid for 20thC Staffordshire pieces of questionable quality. Large, attractive Continental figures still find a ready market in the decorative field with good pieces being attained for Sevres biscuit wares if in good condition. The market for Berlin plaques has stabilised with subject matter becoming more important; pretty ladies being the most desirable!

Baskets

A Caughley pierced two-handled basket in the Worcester style, transfer printed with The Pine Cone and Foliage pattern, blue C and raised T mark, c1785, 9in (22.5cm) wide. **$900-1,000**

An English porcelain basket, probably Coalbrookdale, applied and painted with flowers, some damage, 10½in (27.5cm) wide. **$450-650**

A Rockingham flower encrusted basket, the flowers and foliage picked out in gilding, all beneath an entwined twig handle, also picked out in gilding, minor chips to foliage, puce printed griffin mark, red painted title, c1835, 9in (23cm). **$1,600-2,000**

A Derby chestnut basket and pierced cover, the interior painted with an Oriental building on an island, finial damaged and restuck, inscribed inside the cover August 1762, Wm. Duesbury & Co. 1762, 7in (18cm) diam. **$2,700-3,700**

A Worcester pierced basket, painted over a white ground, the exterior with yellow and green flowerheads at the angles, and painted on the interior with smaller scattered sprays of flowers, applied hand written paper label to base and remains of a collection label, c1760, 6½in (17cm) diam.
$1,000-1,200

A Worcester blue and white basket, transfer printed with The Pine Cone and Foliage pattern, the exterior with flowerheads at the intersections, blue crescent mark, c1770, 6in (15cm) diam.
$1,800-2,800

Bottles

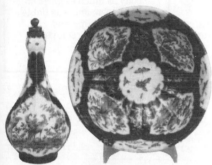

A Worcester powdered blue ground faceted bottle and a basin, painted within shaped gilt scroll cartouches reserved on powdered blue grounds gilt with flowersprays, the bottle with later giltmetal mount and giltmetal-mounted cork stopper with chain attachment, with repair to rim of neck, c1765, the bottle 10½in (27cm) high, the basin 11in (28cm) diam.
$12,000-14,500

A Worcester blue and white pear shaped bottle, transfer printed with The Pine Cone and Foliage pattern, blue crescent mark, c1775, 11½in (29cm).
$1,000-1,500

Bowls

A Chelsea white sugar bowl, the exterior moulded in relief in the Fujian style with branches of flowering prunus, slight damage to rim, c1750, 4in (9.5cm) diam.
$1,500-1,600

A Bow baluster finger bowl with shaped rim, painted in an Imari palette with pierced blue rockwork, the interior rim with loop pattern and pendant foliage, incised R mark, c1750, 3in (7.5cm).
$1,500-1,600

A Bow baluster finger bowl, the interior rim with iron red and gilt flowerheads suspended from blue foliage, cracks to base, slight rim chips and staining, incised line mark, c1750, 2½in (7cm).
$650-800

A pair of Worcester blue and white patty pans, with flared sides and flat rims, transfer printed with trailing loose bouquets, blue crescent marks, c1770, 4½in (12cm) diam.
$650-800

A Royal Worcester bowl, decorated by Chivers, signed, printed marks for 1902.
$1,700-2,000

A pair of Sèvres pattern ormolu mounted bowls, painted in a bright palette, the interiors similarly painted within the 'bleu nouveau' borders, on ormolu four-footed bases, both with restoration to sides and bases, imitation blue interlaced L marks, both with incised number 25, mid-19thC, 10½in (27.5cm) diam.
$6,000-7,000

A Meissen, Marcolini, bowl and a cover with flower finial, painted on a ground of gilt diaper enclosing flowerheads, the bowl with blue crossed swords and star mark, and impressed numbers, worn and small chips to extremities, late 18thC, 7½in (19cm) wide.
$1,700-1,800

Boxes

A Royal Worcester lobed and fluted bowl in blush ivory, with gilt scroll handles, initialled B.T. and marked in green on base, 8in (21cm) diam. **$650-800**

A Meissen gilt metal mounted snuff box and cover, painted in colours within a gilt floral scroll border, the base finely decorated with a 'Kauffahrtei' scene in purple 'camaieu', gilt interior, cover cracked, c1740, 3in (7.5cm), the chased metal mounts 19thC.
$6,000-7,000

The initials M.S. could possibly refer to Marc Solon who, after retiring from Mintons in 1904, worked independently decorating blanks.

A pair of Berlin boxes and covers, each cover decorated in 'pâte-sur-pâte' over a pale green ground, signed M.S., within a gilt rim, the sides in pale pastel shades picked out in gilding with panels and foliate scrollwork, sceptre mark in underglaze blue, feint K.P.M. and orb mark and impressed marks, late 19thC, 3½in (8.5cm) diam.
$1,200-1,500

Please refer to index for other sections on boxes.

A Furstenberg snuff box, moulded with scales and gilt scrolls, painted in colours, the inside cover with flowers tumbling from an upturned gilt basket on a marble plinth, with gilt metal mount, c1770, 4in (10cm) long. **$1,200-1,500**

A Meissen box and cover, painted in puce, enriched in gilding within gilt lined rims, blue crossed swords mark, 3in (7cm) diam, and a Meissen rectangular box, similarly decorated in yellow monochrome within gilt lined firms, blue crossed swords mark, 3in (7cm) wide. **$90-180**

A Mennecy white snuff box, moulded with radiating flutes and sprigs of flowers, crack to back and base, contemporary silver mounts with décharge mark for Julien Berthe, c1740, 3in (8cm) wide. **$1,000-1,500**

A Mennecy snuff box as a seated man wearing a blue night-cap and yellow flowered robe, the interior painted with a flowerspray, cracked, yellow enamel rubbed, contemporary silver mounts with décharge mark for Julien Berthe, c1750, 2½in (5.5cm). **$1,000-1,500**

Caskets

A Paris, Jacob Petit, gilt metal mounted casket, the cover with a porcelain panel painted on a shaded ground within an oval gilt dot cartouche and reserved on a richly gilt green ground, the gilt metal mounts elaborately chased and moulded with foliage scrolls and with a standing putto playing the pipes at each angle, c1830, 9½in (24cm) wide. **$3,800-4,200**

A French porcelain and ormolu mounted casket, heightened in gilt, on caryatid putti supports, 19thC, 8in (20cm) wide. **$1,600-2,000**

Centrepieces

A pair of Sèvres pattern turquoise ground and ormolu mounted centre dishes, the flared bowls painted on turquoise grounds gilt with swags and floral foliage, the ormolu mounts to the rims applied with Bacchus masks with elaborate pineapple, foliage scroll and snake terminals, the ormolu supports modelled as 4 paws above fluted cylindrical and laurel wreath stems, the bases with a canted section inset with porcelain plaques painted with flowers, one bowl broken in two, the other cracked, c1865, 16in (41cm). **$8,000-9,000**

A Royal Dux centre bowl, modelled as 2 nymphs scantily clad and seated on the side of a conch shell, shell cracked, slight wear, pink triangle mark and impressed number 1066. **$450-540**

A Bevington centrepiece, set on a rococo foliate moulded base, some damage, 18in (45cm). **$1,200-1,400**

A pair of English porcelain two-handled pierced tazzas, enriched in gilding and supported by 2 children in loosely draped robes, on rockwork bases, gilding rubbed and damage to extremities of the tazzas, 11in (29cm).
$360-540

A Sèvres pattern and gilt metal mounted centre bowl, the blue ground reserved with 18thC lovers in a garden with a raised gilt scroll and flower cartouche, on a socle stem with square metal mount cast with a laurel wreath and with Vitruvian scrolls, mid-19thC, 13in (33cm).
$3,600-5,500

A Carl Thieme Potschapel pierced centrepiece, applied with flowers, painted in colours and enriched in gilding, some damage, blue mark, 12½in (31cm).
$720-800

A Meissen centrepiece, with 2 cherubs on a scroll and flower encrusted base, the flared column supporting a pierced scroll basket, minor chips, crossed swords in underglaze blue and incised M141, c1880, 11in (28cm).
$3,000-4,500

A Sèvres porcelain comport, signed F. Roper in gilt borders, with deep blue background and floral interior, on raised foot with moulded ormolu base, 15in (38cm) wide.
$1,000-1,200

Clocks

A French clock set, comprising a clock case and 2 nine-light candelabra, on gilt marbled bases, edged with blue beading, the clock case fitted with an 8-day striking movement with an enamel dial, each candelabra with one branch damaged, the top-most nozzle a replacement, minor chipping to all pieces, imitation blue crossed swords and x marks, c1880, candelabra 27in (69cm) high, clock case 18½in (47cm) wide.
$6,000-9,000

A Meissen mantel clock, the rectangular plinth base with a broken front, painted with gilt panels of birds perched amongst branches, minor chips and restoration, crossed swords mark in underglaze blue and incised numerals, c1880, 16in (40cm).
$3,000-3,600

A Rudolstadt-Volkstedt porcelain cased mantel timepiece.
$1,400-1,500

A French three
-piece clock garniture in the manner of Jacob Petit, the clock with white enamel dial and 8-day bell striking movement by Henri Marc, small faults, 19thC, 16 and 17½in (41 and 44cm). **$1,500-1,800**

A Sèvres pattern garniture-du- cheminée, the dial set into a gilt metal surround above a porcelain plaque, with turquoise ground pillars at the angles, flanked by 2 gilt metal figures of Cupid, the upper part surmounted by a gilt metal and porcelain vase held by 2 putti, the 2 flanking vases with turquoise ground porcelain bodies, c1900, clock with gilt wood and plush shaped stand, vases 15in (39cm), clock 20½in (52cm). **$1,800-2,700**

Cottages & Pastille Burners

A Staffordshire porcelain pastille burner, modelled as an octagonal cottage with bun feet and detachable roof, c1835, 5in (12cm) high. **$450-540**

A Staffordshire porcelain pastille burner, modelled as a house, c1835, 5in (12cm) high. **$450-540**

l. A pastille burner in the form of a yellow gazebo with an integral base and a fluted roof, 5in (13cm).
c. A pastille burner in the form of a cottage, applied with green clay chips and flowerheads, 4in (10cm). All with damages.
r. A Staffordshire porcelain pastille burner in the form of a church with a tower and arched windows, applied with coloured clay chips, 5in (13cm). **$800-1,000**

An English cottage pastille burner, applied with foliage and enriched with colours and gilt, 5in (13cm). **$450-540**

A Staffordshire porcelain pastille burner with applied foliage, enriched in yellow and gilding, 6in (15cm), together with 2 others, similarly decorated, one with chimney restored. **$360-450**

A pastille burner in the form of a pale yellow octagonal cottage with 'parasol' roof, applied with flowers and mosses, slight damage, 8in (20cm). **$450-550**

Cups

A Bow white libation cup after a Fujian original, moulded with prunus and resting on a pierced oval foot, minor staining to rim, c1755, 4in (9.5cm) wide.
$2,000-2,700

A Worcester fluted teabowl and saucer, painted with green diaper panels edged with gilt scrolls alternating with puce floral swags, c1765.
$900-1,200

An early Worcester coffee cup, painted in a 'famille verte' palette with flowering Oriental shrubs alternating with insects, applied paper label for D.M. & P. Manheim, c1753, 2½in (6cm).
$1,800-2,700

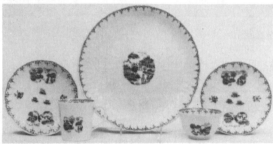

l. A Worcester coffee can and saucer, painted in the 'famille rose' palette, minute rim chips to underside of saucer, c1758.
$5,000-6,000
c. A Worcester moulded saucer dish, the centre painted in a 'famille rose' palette, the border with moulded scrolling foliage within a puce scroll rim, c1758, 8in (20cm) diam.
$5,500-7,000
r. A Worcester pleated teabowl and saucer, painted in a 'famille rose' palette, within moulded foliage scroll cartouches, the borders with puce C-scrolls and stylised pendant foliage, minute glaze flake to rim of teabowl, c1758.
$4,000-4,500

A Worcester teacup and saucer, painted in puce with sprigs and sprays of flowers within a gold line rim, hair crack to handle, crossed swords and numeral mark in underglaze blue, c1760.
$450-650

A Bow cup, applied with prunus pattern decoration, 2½in (6cm).
$210-270

A Chelsea teabowl and trembleuse saucer, with chocolate brown rims, red anchor marks, c1755.
$4,500-5,500

A pair of Doccia teabowls and saucers, painted 'alla Sassonia' in landscapes within gilt 'Laub-und-Bandelwerk' cartouches with iron red scrolls and purple panels within gilt line rims, one saucer with very slight rubbing, c1770.
$3,000-4,000

A Worcester teacup and saucer, c1770, saucer 5in (13cm) diam.
$300-340

Did you know
MILLER'S Antiques Price Guide builds up year by year to form the most comprehensive photo-reference system available

A Chamberlain's Worcester documentary blue ground cylindrical cup and saucer, painted by Humphrey Chamberlain with 'Penelopel (sic) weeping over the Bow of Ulyfses', within a gilt band cartouche, reserved on a dark blue ground gilt with stylised ornament above a black band, with gilt interior, the saucer with a central gilt medallion, with gilt dentil rims, small star crack to base, signed H. Chamberlain pinxt. on a shell cartouche beneath The Prince of Wales feathers in iron red and with script marks, c1815.
$3,600-4,500

A Royal Worcester coffee cup, the exterior painted by Harry Davis with a misty view of Venice, the interior painted in gold, printed mark and date code for 1926.
$400-450

A Royal Worcester cup and saucer, pierced in the manner of George Owen, with honeycomb decoration heightened in turquoise and with equally spaced iron red and gilt medallions, the borders of rose pink with white and turquoise jewelled ribbon decoration, compressed year mark for 1877.
$1,400-1,500

A Worcester faceted coffee cup and saucer, painted in the atelier of James Giles with alternate blue panels and bands of gilt trailing foliage on a white ground, the centre of the saucer with a gilt bouquet, the cup with a bouquet in green 'camaieu', blue square seal mark.
$800-1,000

A Worcester teabowl and saucer, with The Three Flowers pattern, 4½in (11cm).
$300-360

A Berlin K.P.M. cabinet cup and saucer, with central panel painted with a portrait of Frederick the Great in military uniform, enriched in gilt, the interior with a wide band of gilt, c1847, 4in (11cm) high.
$300-360

A Böttger two-handled chinoiserie slender beaker and saucer, painted in the manner of J. G. Höroldt with figures at various pursuits, within gilt 'Laub-und-Bandelwerk' cartouches with panels of 'Böttgerluster' and iron red scrolls, the underside of the saucer moulded with 3 gilt chrysanthemum branches, beaker with restored crack, 2 rim chips and a footrim chip to saucer, c1725.
$2,700-3,600

A Chamberlain's Worcester cup and saucer.
$320-400

A Worcester, Barr, Flight & Barr, cup, cover and stand, painted with brightly coloured feathers within a rectangular gilt line cartouche, with richly gilt angular handles and loop finial, finial restored, chip to rim of cover, puce script marks to cup, incised B marks to cup and stand, c1810.
$1,800-2,700

A Meissen turquoise ground teabowl and saucer, painted within elaborate gilt and brown borders, very slight rubbing, crossed swords in underglaze blue, gilder's numeral 80, impressed Drehermarke xx, c1740.
$3,000-4,500

A Meissen, Marcolini, blue ground coffee can and saucer, painted within a gilt tooled band reserve, the rims enriched with gilt egg-and-dart ornament, the base inscribed 'd'apres l'original de Raphael dans la Gallerie de Sa Majesté le Roi de Saxe', blue crossed swords and star marks, Pressnummer 23 and B9 to can, c1800.
$900-1,500

A Fürstenberg teacup and saucer, decorated with monkeys smoking, marks in blue.
$2,000-2,800

A Staffordshire porcelain hound's head stirrup cup, the white body with black patches and muzzle details, black whiskers and yellow and black eyes, wearing a gilt bordered collar with central gilt oval tag, hair crack to rim, early 19thC, 4in (10.5cm).
$800-1,200

A Derby trout's head stirrup cup, painted in shades of green puce and pale pink, the rim inscribed in gilt 'The Angler's Delight', between gilt lines, Robt. Bloor & Co., c1825, 5½in (13.5cm).
$2,700-3,600

A Worcester blue and white teabowl and saucer, in Rock Warbler pattern, c1760, 4½in (11cm).
$1,200-1,500

Ewers

An English miniature blue ground ewer and basin, perhaps Coalport, 4½in (11cm).
$500-600

A Paris powder blue ground ewer and basin, painted in colours with richly gilt rims, c1830, ewer 10½in (26cm) high, basin 16½in (42cm) wide.
$900-1,000

A German gold ground ewer in the form of a rhyton, the short foot with a band of false gadroons, some damage and restoration, mid-19thC, 9in (23cm).
$1,000-1,800

A Royal Worcester ewer with leaf and flower decorated scrolled handle, painted by Harry Stinton with highlight landscape and cattle, 11½in (29cm).
$2,700-3,600

Figures – Animals

An English white model of a finch, naturally modelled with incised and moulded plumage, on an oval base, chipping to leaves, probably Chelsea, c1750, 8in (19cm).
$10,500-21,000

Two Meissen models of hoopoe birds, naturalistically modelled with feathered crests and with shaded black, cream and brown plumage, damage to extremities, blue crossed swords marks, incised and painted numbers, c1860, 12in (31cm).
$1,000-1,200

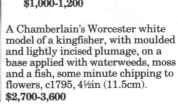

A pair of 'Sèvres' gilt-bronze ewers, the bodies painted between white beaded borders, the reverse with a landscape scene, reserved on a turquoise, gilt and 'jewelled' ground, some glaze flaking, c1870.
$1,500-1,800

A Chamberlain's Worcester white model of a kingfisher, with moulded and lightly incised plumage, on a base applied with waterweeds, moss and a fish, some minute chipping to flowers, c1795, 4½in (11.5cm).
$2,700-3,600

A Meissen group of 3 dogs, modelled as a pug wearing a blue and gilt collar, a brown and white spaniel and a black and white spaniel scratching its face, slight chip to one ear, blue crossed swords and incised numeral marks, c1880, 8in (20cm) wide.
$3,000-4,000

A large Meissen elephant and rider group, the rider wearing a richly embroidered and colourful robe holding a sceptre and a censer, on grey elephant with a tasselled saddle cloth, minor chips and repairs, c1870, 16½in (42cm).
$6,000-8,000

Two Meissen models of parrots with long tail feathers and brightly coloured plumage, on rockwork bases enriched in gilding, one with tail feathers broken, one beak and leaves chipped, blue crossed swords marks and impressed and incised numbers, c1880, 8in (20cm).
$1,500-1,800

A Samson 'famille rose' model of a horse, with tasselled saddle cloth, enamels worn, 13½in (34cm).
$720-800

A Meissen group of a pug bitch suckling its puppy, its brown coat with dark extremities, slight chips to claws, blue crossed swords and incised numeral marks, c1880, 9in (22.5cm).
$2,500-3,000

A Meissen model of a turkey, beak repaired, blue crossed swords mark and incised and impressed numbers, c1890, 4in (10cm).
$270-360

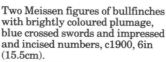

Two Meissen figures of bullfinches with brightly coloured plumage, blue crossed swords and impressed and incised numbers, c1900, 6in (15.5cm).
$1,500-1,700

A large Meissen model of a monkey snuff taker, seated on a tree stump, realistically enamelled, damage to one foot, 20thC, 19in (48cm).
$3,600-5,500

A group of 8 Meissen and one Berlin
mute swans, mostly with wings
outstretched in various poses, the
Berlin example with wings folded,
all with white feathers and faces
with red and black markings, minor
chips, crossed swords in underglaze
blue, incised and impressed marks,
printed K.P.M. orb and sceptre
marks, late 19thC, tallest figure
11in (28cm).
$7,000-9,000

A Meissen figure of a cockerel,
naturally modelled with brightly
coloured plumage in shades of
yellow, brown, iron red, mauve,
green and black, damage to comb
and damage and restoration to tail
feathers, blue crossed swords and
impressed marks, late 19thC, 12in
(31cm) wide.
$1,600-2,000

Figures – People

A Bow white glazed figure of a
seated nun wearing a voluminous
habit and reading her breviary,
minor chips, c1755, 6in (15cm).
$800-1,000

A pair of Bow figures, a gallant and
his companion, on rococo turquoise
and gilt scroll bases, minor damage,
red enamelled sword and anchor
marks, 18thC, 8in (20cm).
$2,000-2,700

A Bow white glazed figure of a
seated nun wearing a voluminous
habit and reading the Divine Office,
minor chips and damage to base,
c1755, 6in (15cm).
$720-1,000

A Bow figure of Harlequin, wearing
yellow hat, chequered jacket and
trousers and yellow shoes, enriched
in turquoise and puce, damage to
hat, slap-stick and his right hand,
chips to flowers, c1765, 7in (18cm).
$2,000-3,200

A Chelsea Derby group of Venus by
a rocky outcrop, Cupid at her feet
with his bow and quiver of arrows,
minor damage, late 18thC, 8in
(20cm).
$900-1,000

A Bow figure of a nun, reading from
an iron red bound book, wearing a
mauve veil, the sleeves to her white
robe edged in mauve and with
mauve shoes, with an iron red and
gilt rosary, book and left hand
repaired and chipped, chips to edge
of veil, sleeves and base, c1765,
6½in (16.5cm).
$1,200-1,400

77

Two Derby figures of Sight and Smell, from a set of the Senses, restored, incised No. 59, late 18thC, 6½in (17cm).
$1,200-1,400

A Derby figure of David Garrick as Richard III, c1790, 11½in (29cm).
$900-1,000

A Derby porcelain figure of The Farmer, wearing a jacket and black hat, russet yellow breeches, standing on a flower encrusted pad base, minor restoration, c1765, 7in (17.5cm). **$720-800**

A Derby figure of Shakespeare, c1770-75, 11½in (29cm).
$1,500-1,600

A Derby figure of John Wilkes, c1770-75, 13in (33cm).
$900-1,000

A Royal Worcester figure of a Cairo water carrier, in a gold decorated dress, slight damage, shape No. 1250, printed mark and date code for 1899, 10in (25cm).
$450-650

A Derby figure of a gardener, restored, late 18thC, 7½in (18cm).
$360-650

A Derby figure of a Lady Musician, her hair tied back with a pale blue ribbon, minor chips, incised model No. 311, c1775, 8½in (21cm).
$1,400-1,500

According to Haslem's list of Derby figures, model No. 311 is for a pair of musicians, the male figure playing an end flute and the female figure playing a tambourine.

A pair of Derby figures of a youth and companion, he wearing a white nightshirt and yellow-lined turquoise jacket, his companion wearing pink-lined pale yellow dress, her underskirt painted in purple and gilt with flowers, he on a washed green base, his chair back restored, minor chipping, incised No. 71, Wm. Duesbury & Co, c1775, 6in (15cm).
$1,700-2,000

A Derby figure of Britannia, wearing yellow-lined pink drapery, gilt scale cuirass and her dress painted with purple and gilt flowers, the base enriched in turquoise and with gilding, chip to hat, tip of flag-pole lacking, chips to foliage, incised 3 mark, Wm. Duesbury & Co, c1770, 10½in (27cm).
$800-1,000

A Royal Dux bisque porcelain figure group.
$900-1,000

A Derby figure of a young boy, late 18thC, 6in (15.5cm).
$360-540

A Derby figure of Fame, her dress painted and gilt with pink flowing drapery, base enriched in turquoise and with gilding, trumpet lacking and minor chipping to foliage, Wm. Duesbury & Co, c1770, 10in (25.5cm).
$900-1,500

A pair of Royal Worcester figures modelled by James Hadley in the Kate Greenaway style, painted in muted enamel colours, printed mark, c1895, 10in (25.5cm).
$1,600-2,000

A Royal Worcester figure of a female water carrier, with a floral dress, shape No. 637, printed mark and date code for 1912, 6in (14cm).
$540-720

A Royal Worcester figure, The Parakeet, modelled by F. G. Doughty, printed mark in black, 7in (17cm).
$360-450

A rare and previously unrecorded Plymouth figure of The French Shepherd, in white jacket lined in pale puce with similar striped waistcoat and breeches decorated with iron red flower sprigs, his feet with red buckled shoes, a small puppy with forepaws on his chest, some damage, c1770, 5½in (14cm).
$2,700-3,600

A pair of Worcester figures modelled as the Cairo Water Carriers by James Hadley, in tones of blush ivory, marked in puce, date code for 1919, 20in (51cm).
$1,800-2,700

Three Frankenthal figures of Chinamen, modelled by K. G. Lück, one wearing yellow, white, puce and iron red, another wearing pink, green and iron red, and the other wearing white, puce, blue and yellow, all standing on scroll-edged gilt and green moulded bases, chips and restoration, part of musician's triangle missing, all with crowned CT mark, one with 77, in underglaze blue, c1777, 5in (12.5cm). **$3,000-4,000**

A pair of Royal Worcester figures of cherub musicians, impressed marks, c1880, 6in (15.5cm). **$800-1,000**

A Royal Worcester bronzed new large Grecian Water Carrier, class 2/125, c1916, 15in (38cm). **$1,000-1,200**

A pair of Royal Worcester 'Kate Greenaway' figures by James Hadley, shape No. 893, printed mark and date code for 1886, 9in (22.5cm). **$1,500-1,600**

A Longton Hall figure of Harlequin wearing a black mask, yellow jacket and chequered trousers, repaired through tree stump, c1753, 5in (12.5cm). **$3,600-4,500**

A Royal Worcester 'Ivory' group of 2 children after the model by James Hadley, the boy holding a gilt jug to the lips of his companion, their features and hair naturalistically painted and enriched in gilding, his right cuff with minute chip, impressed Hadley on the back, the base with green printed marks and No. 813, date code for 1898, 7in (17.5cm). **$720-1,000**

A pair of Meissen figures emblematic of Summer and Autumn, from a set of the Seasons, Summer as a scantily draped woman, Autumn with grapes in his hair, painted in colours and enriched in gilding, on high mound bases moulded with white and gilt scrolls, Summer with one hand restored, slight chipping, blue crossed swords and incised marks, c1900, 9in (22.5cm). **$800-1,000**

A pair of Meissen figures of a fisherman and fishwife, the man wearing a black hat, a lilac smock and purple, green and yellow striped breeches, his companion wearing a lilac dress edged in yellow and a white apron with yellow, iron red and purple stripes, each standing on rococo scroll bases applied with flowers, the girl's fishing net restored and her hat repaired, the man's fishing net restored and rim of hat restored, feint crossed swords mark and impressed numerals 3 and 1, c1760, 6in (15.5cm).
$3,600-4,500

A pair of Royal Dux figures of a shepherd boy playing pipes, wearing green classical dress and sheepskin robe, and his companion similarly attired, pink triangle mark and impressed Nos. 579 and 580, 17in (43cm).
$1,500-1,700

Two Limbach figures of the Continents, Europe as a king in armour, wearing an ermine-lined purple cloak, Asia as an Oriental wearing a turban, on scroll moulded bases, outlined in purple, 2 hands restored and minor chipping and restoration, crossed swords in purple, c1775, 7½in (19cm).
$4,500-5,500

A large Meissen pastoral group, after a model by Acier and Schönheit, picked out in bright enamel colours and gilding, minor chips and repairs, crossed swords in underglaze blue, incised D.46 and with impressed and script numerals, c1880, 18½in (47cm).
$6,000-8,000

A Meissen figure of Schindler modelled by J. J. Kändler, wearing a buff hat with a fur brim, buff jacket and trousers with gilt frogging, purple belt and red boots, holding a goat formed as bagpipes, a black and white dog at his feet, on gild edged base, damaged, c1740, 6½in (17cm).
$5,500-9,000

A Meissen group of Neptune, seated in a chariot and dressed in a red flowing robe, coloured in bright enamels and enriched in gilding, crossed swords in underglaze blue and incised 2189, c1880, 6½in (16cm).
$1,600-2,000

A pair of Meissen figures of a Turk and his companion, 7in (17.5cm).
$2,700-3,600

A Meissen group of a gallant and companion, he in frock coat, blue sash, striped waistcoat, black breeches and shoes, holding a snuff box, she in a flowered crinoline dress and lilac underskirt, holding a fan, on a brown base, minute chip to back of dress, nosegay and ribbon, blue crossed swords mark and incised 556, c1880, 8½in (21.5cm).
$1,000-1,800

A Meissen group of School for Love after a model by Acier, picked out in bright enamel colours on a green and brown rockwork base, area of the base restored, crossed swords in underglaze blue, c1880, 11½in (29cm).
$2,700-4,500

A Meissen figure of Sight, from a set of the Five Senses, modelled as a young woman seated at a dressing table admiring herself in a mirror, very minor chips, crossed swords in underglaze blue, incised E.3 and impressed 127, late 19thC, 5½in (14cm).
$1,600-2,000

A pair of Meissen figures of a youth and a girl, their clothes painted in colours and enriched in gilding, on rockwork bases enriched with gilt lines, minor chipping to flowers, blue crossed swords and incised numeral marks, c1880, 6½in (16.5cm).
$2,000-2,500

A Berlin figure of a classical maiden, allegorical of Spring from a set of the Seasons, the low drum shaped base raised on a separate waisted socle, moulded in relief with gilt scrollwork panels painted with colourful flowers, minor chips to extremities, cancelled sceptre mark in underglaze blue and impressed numerals, c1880, 19in (49cm).
$1,800-2,700

A Sèvres white porcelain group of Diana the Huntress and 2 other figures, on a rocky outcrop, some damage, 13in (33cm).
$900-1,000

A Meissen group of the Seasons, each putto with flowers or a sheaf of corn or seated on a barrel holding a wine goblet, base of goblet restored and minor chips, crossed swords in underglaze blue and incised 1068, c1880, 6in (15cm).
$2,700-3,600

A Meissen figure of a boy as a gardener carrying a hoe and a basket of flowers, wearing a pink hat and turquoise and yellow clothes, chips to flowers and leaves, blue crossed swords mark and incised 14, c1750, 5½in (13.5cm).
$1,200-1,600

A pair of Meissen groups of Bacchic putti, representing the Four Seasons, on rocky bases with scroll moulded rims picked out in gilding, minor chips, crossed swords in underglaze blue, incised numerals 230 and 1236, c1860, 8½in (22cm).
$3,600-4,500

A Meissen group of a Domestic Incident, the whole group in bright colours and gilding, some minor restoration, crossed swords in underglaze blue and incised D.64, c1875, 8in (20cm).
$1,600-2,000

A Meissen group depicting Venus and Cupid riding in a large clam shell, minor restoration, crossed swords in underglaze blue and incised 127, c1880, 13½in (34cm).
$4,500-5,500

A pair of Meissen 'Bouquetier' figures after models by J. J. Kändler, the woman in black, white and gilt, and an apron decorated with 'indianische Blumen', her companion in green and white, with yellow shoes, some damage, crossed swords mark in underglaze blue, mid-18thC, 7½in (19cm).
$4,500-6,000

A Meissen group of 2 semi-naked children, chip to base, impressed H.88, cancelled crossed swords mark, 6in (15cm).
$720-800

A Royal Worcester figure from The Countries of the World series by James Hadley, in the form of a Scotsman, minor damage under base, shape No. 913, printed mark and date code for 1899, 6in (15cm).
$450-540

A Meissen group of the Druken Silenus, painted in colours, on an oval rockwork base moulded with white and gilt scrolls, tip of donkey's ear and tail lacking, slight damage to basket and foliage, chip to footrim, blue crossed swords and incised numeral mark, c1880, 8½in (21cm).
$900-1,200

A Meissen figure, after a model by Jüchtzer and based on the marble by Bernini, depicting a naked Daphne changing into a tree and pursued by Apollo who wears a green robe, gilt lined base, crossed swords in underglaze blue and incised J.9, c1875, 14in (36cm).
$2,000-2,700

A Meissen group after a model by Acier and Schönheit, with grinning marble muse of Music overlooking the proceedings, all in bright polychrome enamels, crossed swords in underglaze blue and incised G.32, c1880, 10½in (27cm).
$3,600-5,500

A Meissen apple-picking group, decorated in bright enamel colours on a scroll moulded gilt lined base, minor restorations, crossed swords in underglaze blue and incised 2229, c1870, 10½in (26cm).
$2,000-2,700

A pair of Meissen musician figures, on scroll moulded gilt lined bases, minor repairs, crossed swords in underglaze blue and incised 1351, c1875, 13in (33cm).
$2,500-3,000

A Meissen group of 'Das Verlobnis' or 'The Betrothal', after an 18thC original by J. J. Kändler, the man wearing a red jacket picked out in gilding, the lady wearing a mauve-lined dress painted with colourful sprays of flowers on a white ground edged in gilding, and a white cap with a pale blue ribbon on her head, minor chips to foliage, c1880, 7½in (19cm).
$2,000-2,700

A Meissen figure group of a lady with a spinning wheel, 'Leserin am Spinnrocken', modelled in the 18thC taste, she holds a gilt bound book, all on a rococo base with relief moulded gilt scroll rim, minor chips and restoration, crossed swords in underglaze blue, incised numerals 2685 and impressed numerals 127, c1880, 6½in (16cm). **$3,000-3,600**

A Nymphenburg figure of an egg-seller, 'Eiergretel', modelled by Franz Anton Bustelli, wearing a black neckerchief, green bodice, a yellow skirt and holding her white puce-spotted apron, on a flat base washed in grey, base restored, incised 43, c1755, 5½in (14.5cm).
$1,800-2,700

A Samson figure of a young woma seated in a sleigh with a swan support, painted with flowers and moulded and pierced with gilt scrolls, the lady wearing a tricorn hat, grey flowered skirt and a feather muff, blue marks, 6½in (16cm).
$720-800

A pair of Samson figures of musicians in the Chelsea style, on rococo scroll moulded bases enriched in puce and gilding, chips to extremities, 9½in (24cm).
$720-900

A pair of Royal Dux figures of classical maidens, wearing long pink robes picked out in gilding, pink triangles, impressed numerals 2018/2019, early 20thC, 18½in (47cm).
$2,700-3,600

A pair of Continental coloured bisque figures, probably French, about to lose his tricorn hat, she with her parasol blown inside out and about to lose her bonnet, min restoration, incised A.M. in scroll frame, mid-19thC, 15in (38cm).
$720-800

Flatware

A Bow patty pan, the exterior to the flared sides with stylised flowers, small hair crack, painter's numeral 8, c1758, 4in (10.5cm) diam.
$650-800

A Bow dish, the white body painted with a colourful spray of flowers, fruit and foliage, within a border moulded in relief with fruiting vines picked out in puce, green and yellow, all within a shaped wavy rim with gilt edge, restored chips, red painted anchor and dagger mark, c1765, 10½in (26cm).
$1,200-3,000

A Bow dish, 10½in (26cm) wide.
$650-750

A Caughley plate decorated with the full Nanking pattern, 8in (20cm).
$280-320

A Caughley powdered blue ground dish, painted with flowering plants within a circular cartouche, the powdered blue border reserved with shaped panels enclosing stylised flowers, utensils and zig-zag ornament, blue C mark, c1775, 10in (24.5cm) wide.
$720-800

A Caughley dish, 7½in (19cm).
$450-500

A Chelsea leaf-moulded dish, the centre painted in the manner of Jeffereys Hammett O'Neale with 2 cows with black and pale brown markings, standing and recumbent in a landscape vignette, wear to decoration, small rim crack, red anchor mark, c1758, 8½in (21cm).
$3,000-4,000

A Caughley spoon tray, 6in (15cm) wide.
$300-360

A pair of Coalport shell shaped dishes, early 19thC, 9½in (24cm).
$540-720

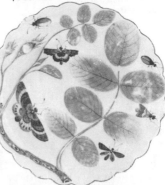

Two Worcester Blind Earl pattern plates, painted in the atelier of James Giles, in brown, green and puce over the white ground, all within a gilt fluted rim, one restored, c1765, 7½in (19cm).
$2,000-2,800

A Coalport plate, painted and signed by Fred Sutton, c1850, 9in (23cm).
$235-270

Two Sèvres pattern yellow ground plates, painted in the Japanese taste in a bright palette, with lobed gilt rims, imitation interlaced L marks, c1880, 9½in (24cm).
$1,000-1,200

85

A Caughley lozenge dish, decorated with the Fisherman pattern, c1770, 10½in (26cm) wide.
$360-540

A Chelsea red anchor miniature dish, with twig handles, the centre painted with exotic birds, the pierced rim applied with flowerheads, slight discolouration, mid-18thC, 4½in (11cm).
$1,000-1,200

A pair of Chelsea plates, crazed, brown anchor marks, c1758, 9in (22.5cm) diam.
$900-1,500

top. A Chelsea dish boldly painted within a brown and green feather-moulded rim, minute rim chip, slight rubbing, crazed, brown anchor mark, c1758, 11in (28cm) wide.
$650-800
below. A Chelsea dish, painted in a light palette, brown anchor mark, c1758, 10in (24.5cm) wide.
$900-1,000

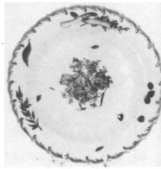

A Chelsea plate, painted with a tight bouquet of flowers and fruit within a border of asparagus, flowers, nuts and insects, within a gilt and turquoise scroll and feather-moulded rim, paint worn, gold anchor mark, 8in (20cm) diam.
$360-540

A Caughley patty pan, decorated with the Fisherman pattern, 10in (25cm) wide.
$450-540

A Worcester dish painted in the 'famille verte' palette with Chinese figures in a garden, the rim painted with a flowerhead and diaper design, mid-18thC, 10½in (26cm).
$1,200-1,500

A pair of Copeland & Garrett plates, with named views, c1840, 9½in (24cm).
$400-450

A Chamberlain's Worcester 'Aesop's Fables' dessert plate, the centre painted in dark brown enamel with a scene from the hare and the tortoise story, the lightly fluted rim decorated in gold on a blue band, late 18thC, 8½in (21.5cm).
$720-900

A Worcester pickle dish, transfer printed after Robert Hancock with Winter, the pencilled diaper pattern border reserved with foliage, slight rim chip, c1755, 4in (10cm) wide.
$2,000-2,700

A Chelsea dish, painted with flowers over the white ground, within a shaped brown rim, minor chip to rim, red anchor mark, c1765, 15in (38cm).
$2,500-3,000

A Paris blue ground plate, painted within a circular cartouche with oval cartouches of flowers and flowerheads, the border with sprigs of flowers within diamond cartouches on a gold ground, the base inscribed in gilt, gilding slightly rubbed, printed retailer's mark, 8½in (21cm).
$800-1,000

A Vienna dish, the centre painted with Venus, Cupid and Minerva, the border with maroon coloured panels painted in white and gilt, signed F. Koller, 9½in (23.5cm).
450-540

A Worcester pickle dish, the centre transfer printed after Robert Hancock with Spring, depicting a gardener and companion standing beside a flower pot with flowers and a watering can, the pencilled diaper pattern border reserved with foliage, rim chips, c1755, 4in (10cm) wide.
$1,800-2,700

A Worcester blue scale plate, painted within gilt vase and mirror shaped cartouches, reserved on a well defined blue scale ground, minute rim chip, blue square seal mark, c1770, 8in (20cm).
$270-360

A pair of Vienna plates, inscribed to rear 'Marie Mancini' and 'Montesson', 19thC, 10in (25cm).
$3,000-4,000

A Worcester fable-decorated deep plate, painted within a gilt band and turquoise husk cartouche reserved with foliate ornament and edged in gilding, the well painted with 3 sprays of fruit and 3 exotic birds, the fluted border with a bright blue band edged with gilt scrolls and 'feuilles-de-choux', within a waved gilt dentil rim, slight wear to gilding, blue crescent mark, c1775, 8½in (22cm).
$5,500-6,500

A pair of Derby plates, some restoration, c1800, 10in (25cm).
$800-900

A set of 4 Berlin porcelain plates, c1760, 10in (25cm).
$1,600-2,000

A set of 12 Royal Worcester dessert plates, after originals by Dorothy Doughty, each moulded and painted on a cream ground within a gold painted wavy rim, 9½in (23.5cm).
$650-1,000

A Royal Worcester plate with pierced rim, painted by Charles Henry Clifford Baldwyn, with white swans flying amongst reeds, the moulded border painted in gold, printed mark and date code for 1905, 8½in (21.5cm).
$2,700-3,600

A Worcester dish, the border with bright blue band edged with gilt scrolls, within a gilt dentil rim, gilding to rim slightly worn, blue crescent mark, c1775, 10in (25cm)
$720-900

A Worcester pink scale fluted soup plate, painted in the atelier of James Giles, with a central loose bouquet and with trailing flowers pendant from a cornucopia-shaped puce scale border edged with gilt scrolls, within a waved gilt rim, c1770, 10in (25cm).
$5,500-6,000

A Böttger chinoiserie saucer, painted within a gilt quatrefoil cartouche with Böttger lustre panels, iron red and puce scrolls within a band of gilt interlocking scrolls, gilt line rim, slight rubbing, gilder's numeral 34, c1725.   **$1,000-1,200**

A set of 6 Sèvres soup plates, each painted in colours with sprays of flowers, gilt dashed blue line borders, gilt and shaped rims, interlaced L marks and date letter in blue and black, painter's marks in blue and black, various incised marks, c1773.
$900-1,500

A large Sèvres portrait charger, the centre painted with a titled portrait of Louis XVI, surrounded by 8 titled medallion portraits, each within a gilt ribbon border flanked by gilt scrolls, pendants and 'fleur-de-lys' motifs reserved on a pale pink ground, minor wear to gilding, interlaced L's in blue and incised numerals, black painted titles for portraits, c1880, 19in (48.5cm).
$1,000-1,500

A Worcester shell dish, decorated with the 2 peony, rock and bird pattern, 5in (13cm) diam.
$700-750

A Derby deep plate, painted in a 'famille verte' palette after a Chinese original, with false gadroon bands and a waved gilt rim, crown crossed baton and D mark in carmine, Duesbury & Kean, c1800 10in (25cm).
$1,500-1,600

A Meissen 'pâte-sur-pâte' plate, decorated with a classical female wearing a diaphanous white robe, all reserved on a pink ground, the pierced border gilt with interlinking ovals centred by tiny florets in relie crossed swords in underglaze blue c1880, 9½in (24cm).
$3,000-3,600

A Worcester spoon tray of scroll outline, painted in a 'famille rose' palette with Putai and 2 attendants on a lightly moulded pleated ground edged with scrolls, within a gilt rim, rubbing to enamels and slight rim chip, c1760, 5½in (14cm) wide.
$3,000-4,000

A gilt metal mounted Paris porcelain tray, with scroll ends, Egyptian masks and winged lion masks on the gilt underside, finely painted in the centre, within a tooled gilt border, fitted into a later gilt metal frame of fruiting vines and raised on 4 short lappet feet, c1830, 18in (46cm).
$4,000-5,000

A Sèvres armorial two-handled tray, later decorated, the centre painted within a gilt dentil quatrefoil cartouche reserved on a 'bleu celeste' ground enriched with gilding, the border reserved with a coat-of-arms and a mirror monogram within oval cartouches, the rim gilt, gilding slightly rubbed, imitation interlaced L marks, c1875, 12in (31cm) wide.
$1,000-1,500

A Liverpool blue scale saucer dish, slight rim chip, Philip Christian's factory, c1770, 6½in (16cm) diam.
$360-510

A set of 6 Vienna plates painted in Imari style on alternating underglaze blue and white grounds, shield marks and 8 in underglaze blue, painter's numerals in iron red, impressed and incised numerals, c1750, 8½in (21.5cm).
$3,600-4,500

A Worcester, Flight, Barr & Barr dish, the centre painted with a pink rose within a gilt band cartouche, the border with a band of pink roses beneath a gilt shaped gadrooned rim, impressed mark, c1815, 9½in (23.5cm).
$800-1,000

A Worcester, Flight, Barr & Barr plate, painted by Simon Astles with a gilt band well, the border with gilt stylised anthemion beneath a shaped gilt gadrooned rim, script marks, c1820, 10in (25cm).
$4,500-5,500

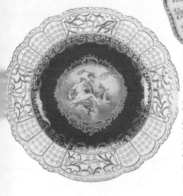

A Meissen cabinet plate, painted with a titled scene of 'Der Frühling', after Watteau', between a gilt scroll border on a blue ground, the rim pierced with floral designs, rim chip, crossed swords in underglaze blue and script title, c1870, 10in (25cm).
$1,200-1,500

A Vienna plate by Hav.(?) Sartory, signed, painted after Ch. du Jardin with a rural scene, one flake, shield mark in underglaze blue, impressed date code and numeral, inscribed in black enamel 'L' original 'peint par Charles du Jardin, se trouve dans la galerie de Mr = le Comte Ant:de Lamberg à Vienne, cop:par Hav:Satory 1815', dated 1815, 9½in (24.5cm).
$3,000-4,000

Inkwells

An English inkwell, with lion mask terminals and 4 paw feet, painted in colours, the lid with finial, painted with flowers, 3in (7cm).
$210-360

A Staffordshire porcelain inkwell modelled as a gazebo, c1835, 4in (10cm).
$400-450

A Marseilles inkstand, wing restored, c1790, 7½in (18cm) wide.
$650-720

Factory closed in 1793.

A late Meissen blue ground inkstand, reserved with cherubs amongst clouds and with flowers within gilt scroll cartouches, the tray fitted with 2 inkwells and covers, blue crossed swords mark, 8½in (21cm) wide.
$360-540

A Fürstenberg square section inkwell and matching sander, 4in (9cm).
$470-600

A Worcester, Barr, Flight & Barr pale blue ground inkwell and cover, painted with a white and tan spaniel within a gilt line cartouche, enriched with gilt 'vermicule', the gilt scroll handle with male mask terminal flanked by 2 containers for sand, slight rim chip and gilding rubbed, printed marks, c1810, 5½in (13.5cm).
$1,500-1,600

Jardinières

A Worcester blue and white jardinière, chip to footrim and warped in firing, blue crescent mark, c1770, 10in (24cm).
$6,000-7,000

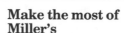

A Royal Worcester 'Gloire de Dijon' moulded jardinière in Hadley style, painted by Harry Martin, the body with 3 panels of red, pink and yellow roses on a shaded ivory ground and with gilded base, signed H. Martin, shape No. 1295, subject No. 1275, date mark 1911, 9½in (23.5cm).
$2,500-2,800

A Royal Worcester jardinière, painted by Harry Stinton.
$6,000-7,000

Make the most of Miller's

Unless otherwise stated, any description which refers to 'a set' or 'a pair' includes a valuation for the entire set or the pair, even though the illustration may show only a single item

A pair of Sèvres-pattern turquoise ground ormolu mounted jardinières, each on 4 cast foliage feet, one extensively damaged, imitation blue interlaced L marks, c1880, 12in (30cm).
$3,000-4,000

A Royal Worcester biscuit ground blush ivory jardinière, with weave body with leaf decoration including 3 folding leaves extending to outer rim forming side handles, shape No. 1947, puce mark 1918, 14in (36cm) diam.
$1,000-1,200

Jugs

A Caughley cream jug, with the
Temple pattern, 3in (7.5cm).
$400-450

A Derby blue and white creamer,
3in (7.5cm).
$1,400-1,500

A Caughley cabbage leaf moulded
mask jug, painted in the Chantilly
style with scattered flowersprays,
the spout moulded with a bearded
mask and with double scroll handle,
blue S mark, c1790, 9in (23cm).
$800-1,000

A Worcester blue and white cabbage
leaf moulded jug, the rim moulded
with a band of stiff leaves, painter's
mark, c1758, 8½in (21cm).
$1,200-1,500

A Caughley claret ground
pear-shaped milk jug and cover, the
shaped claret borders gilt with
flowersprays and edged in gilding,
the domed cover with gilt knob
finial, c1785, decoration later, 5in
(12.5cm).
$2,800-3,600

A Caughley inscribed and dated
cabbage leaf moulded mask jug,
inscribed 'Griffin Beaufoy White'
and with the date 1791, the spout
with a bearded mask and with
double scroll handle, cracked, blue
S mark, 1791, 9in (23cm).
$1,000-1,200

A Worcester herringbone moulded
baluster cream jug, painted with
blue flowers and with traces of
gilding, with scroll handle, small
chip and haircrack to rim, painter's
mark, c1758, 3½in (9cm).
$650-800

A Pinxton creamer, c1800, 4½in
(11cm) wide.
$400-500

A Caughley cabbage leaf moulded
mask jug, transfer printed with the
Fisherman pattern, with a bearded
male mask beneath the spout, blue
Sx mark, c1785, 8½in (22cm).
$720-800

A Liverpool baluster jug, with scroll handle and cornucopia moulded spout, decorated in light relief with fruiting vine, painted with a European landscape vignette, some damage, c1762, Richard Chaffer's factory, 8½in (22cm) high.
$2,800-3,600

A Liverpool baluster mask jug with elaborate scroll handle, transfer printed, the spout moulded with a female mask, Penningtons factory, c1775, 7in (18cm) high.
$1,000-1,200

A Worcester yellow ground cabbage leaf moulded mask jug, the body transfer printed and coloured after Robert Hancock with Milk Maids, within puce scroll cartouches, the handle enriched in puce and with a bearded mask beneath the spout, with brown line rim, chips to spout and small chip to rim, c1765, 7in (17.5cm).
$6,000-7,000

A Worcester blue and white cabbage leaf moulded mask jug, transfer printed with flowers, small chip to spout, blue script W mark, c1775, 8½in (22cm).
$500-550

A Worcester blue and white herringbone moulded cream jug, painted with trailing flowersprays and an insect on a crisply moulded ground, with scroll handle, painter's mark, c1758, 3½in (9cm).
$1,200-1,500

A Worcester blue and white baluster mask jug, transfer printed with loose bouquets and scattered butterflies, with a bearded mask beneath the spout, minute chip to spout, crescent mark, c1770, 7½in (18.5cm).
$800-1,000

A Worcester sparrow beak jug, c1775.
$320-360

A Liverpool cabbage leaf moulded mask jug, with scroll handle, painted with loose bouquets beneath a border moulded with dot and stiff leaf ornament, the spout moulded with a female mask, some damage and restoration, Philip Christian's factory, c1770, 9½in (24cm) high.
$900-1,500

A Liverpool baluster jug with scroll handle, painted with peony and a willow tree beside a fence, some damage, Richard Chaffer's factory, c1765, 7½in (19cm) high.
$1,800-2,000

A Worcester clobbered baluster cream jug with grooved loop handle, painted in underglaze blue, decorated in overglaze enamels, the top rim inscribed in iron red 'Desire the sincere milk of the world.i Peter', the lip restored, blue crescent mark, c1770, the overglaze decoration slightly later, 3½in (9.5cm).
$450-650

A Worcester baluster cream jug, painted within an iron red and gilt line cartouche, the reverse painted in puce monochrome with an Oriental in a sampan, reserved on a gilt foliate scroll ground, tiny chip to spout, c1770, 3½in (9cm).
$1,000-1,200

A Liverpool cream jug, 4in (10cm) wide.
$300-360

A Worcester Imari pattern baluster jug, cover and deep basin, painted with The Kempthorne pattern, the radiating flowering shrubs within an elaborate flowerhead and diaper pattern border, c1770, jug 10in (25cm), basin 11in (28.5cm) diam.
$8,000-9,000

Mugs

A Derby baluster mug, transfer printed with The Boy on a Buffalo pattern, with ribbed loop handle, minute rim chip, Wm. Duesbury & Co, c1770, 5in (12.5cm).
$800-900

A Liverpool mug with scroll handle, painted beneath a diaper border, on a grooved circular foot, some damage, c1765, 6in (15cm) high.
$1,200-1,500

A Liverpool mug with scroll handle, painted with bamboo beside a fence flanked by rockwork, Richard Chaffer's factory, c1765, 5in (12cm) high.
$2,700-3,600

A Derby mug, painted in a bright palette in the Oriental style, with scroll handle, cracked, Wm. Duesbury & Co, c1765, 4in (10cm).
$650-720

A Derby mug, painted in a soft palette in the manner of the Cotton Stem painter, with a large spray of flowers on either side, flanked by smaller sprigs all beneath the brown line rim, applied paper label for the Cottam Collection, c1760, 3½in (9cm).
$1,800-2,700

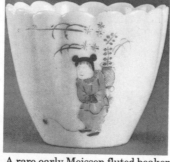

A rare early Meissen fluted beaker, painted in Kakiemon style and gilding, crossed swords mark in blue enamel, incised Johanneum mark N = 362/W and //, c1725.
$3,600-4,500

A Liverpool baluster mug with scroll handle, some damage, Philip Christian's factory, c1768, 7in (17cm) high.
$800-900

A Worcester blue and white mug, with ribbed loop handle, haircrack round top of handle, c1765, 3½in (9cm).
$720-1,000

A Chamberlain's Worcester mug, painted with a portrait of the Duke of Wellington within an oval gilt line and foliate wreath cartouche, the ground with scattered gilt leaves and with the monogram IP, named in black script on the base, slight wear to gilding, c1828, 3in (8cm).
$900-1,000

A Worcester blue and white baluster mug, transfer printed with loose bouquets and scattered flowers, blue crescent mark, c1770, 6in (15cm).
$720-800

A Plymouth mug with grooved loop handle, painted in an inky blue, tiny rim chip, base cracked, blue 24 mark, Wm. Cookworthy's factory, c1770, 5½in (13.5cm).
$1,800-2,700

A Worcester mug in 'La Peche' pattern, c1770, 3½in (9cm) diam.
$650-720

A Chamberlain's Worcester beaker, finely painted with a colourful arrangement within a broad gilt border, the reverse with a plain pale yellow panel framed by a narrower gilt line border, all between gilt line rims, script Chamberlains Worcester in orange, c1800, 3½in (9cm).
$1,500-1,600

A Worcester blue and white baluster mug, crescent mark, c1768, 6in (15cm).
$950-1,000

Plaques

An English plaque, by F. N. Sutton, signed, c1880, 11 by 7½in (28 by 18.5cm).
$1,800-2,700

F. N. Sutton worked at the Royal Worcester factory during the 1880s.

A Berlin plaque, painted with a Vestal Virgin after Angelica Kaufmann, wearing filmy white robes with a blue sash, signed with the initials F St, impressed K.P.M. and sceptre marks, c1880, claret plush mount and carved giltwood frame, 10½ by 9in (26.5 by 22cm).
$4,000-4,500

A Berlin plaque, painted with a portrait of a saint wearing dark red drapery, seated in a rocky landscape reading from a book, impressed K.P.M. and sceptre marks, c1880, 12½ by 10in (32 by 25.5cm).
$1,500-2,000

A Berlin dated plaque, painted by E. Böhm with Jupiter and Antiope after Corregio, chips to edge on reverse, impressed K.P.M. and sceptre marks, signed and dated Paris 1863, carved giltwood frame, 13½ by 9½in (34 by 23.5cm).
$7,000-9,000

A Meissen plaque after Corregio, depicting The Repentant Magdalene, lying in a forest landscape and reading from the Scriptures, crossed swords in underglaze blue, c1870, 8 by 11½in (21 by 29cm).
$2,800-4,500

A Berlin plaque, painted with a portrait of the bearded old man, his eyes raised heavenwards and his hands resting on the hilt of a sword, impressed K.P.M. and sceptre marks, c1880, 12½ by 10in (32 by 25.5cm).
$1,500-2,000

A Berlin plaque, painted after Boucher with a pastoral scene, impressed K.P.M. and sceptre marks, c1880, 14in (35.5cm).
$1,500-1,800

A Berlin plaque of rococo inspiration, painted all within an elaborate border of scrolling cartouches picked out in gilding and painted with scattered sprays of flowers and insects, minor chips and restoration, sceptre mark in underglaze blue, printed K.P.M. Orb mark in red and impressed numerals, late 19thC, 22in (55cm).
$2,000-3,000

A Berlin plaque, impressed K.P.M. sceptre and H marks, c1880, giltwood frame, 9½ by 6½in (23.5 by 16cm).
$7,000-8,000

A Limoges plaque, later painted with a south view of Christchurch from the meadows by Turner, signed in the bottom left hand corner 'Leighton', the view named on the reverse, 20thC, 13½in (34cm), in ornate gilded frame.
$1,200-1,600

A Meissen plaque after Raphael, painted with the Virgin Mary wearing a blue robe and red and gold skirt, with the infant Christ by her knee and St. John kneeling at her side, the front inscribed in gilding C. Raphalo, crossed swords in underglaze blue, c1865, 11 by 8in (28 by 20cm), framed.
$8,000-9,000

The original painting of La Belle Jardinière after Raphael hangs in the Louvre.

A Berlin K.P.M. plaque, in original frame, signed and dated 1884, 11in (29cm) high.
$2,000-2,500

A Continental porcelain plaque painted with 'Murillo's Children', the 2 children with a basket of grapes, 19thC, 6 by 4½in (15 by 11cm), framed.
$900-1,000

A pair of 'Vienna' plaques, painted with three-quarter length portraits of a girl wearing a puce, yellow and white dress and with long hair, and with a girl wearing a blue dress seated beside a ledge leaning on her elbow, signed with 'CR' monogram, late 19thC, 9in (22cm), plush and giltwood frame.
$3,600-4,500

Pots

A Worcester mustard pot and cover, cracked cover.
$800-900

A Berlin plaque, painted with a mother and child, impressed K.P.M., Sceptre, 111, Z, 19thC, 7 by 5in (17 by 13cm), framed.
$1,500-1,800

A Worcester baluster dry mustard pot, outline-printed and coloured with The Red Ox pattern, the interior with a brown line to the rim, c1758, 3in (7.5cm).
$2,000-3,000

A Worcester inverted baluster wet mustard pot and a cover, printed and coloured with Oriental figures and a youth at various pursuits, the cover with insects and green and iron red knob finial, small restoration to rim of pot and crack near top of handle, c1760, 3in (7.5cm).
$3,600-4,500

A Worcester blue and white sauceboat, minute glaze blemish to rim, minute crack to handle, painter's mark to base of handle, c1756, 6in (15cm) wide.
$1,600-2,000

A small Derby sauceboat, painted with a landscape vignette and lightly moulded with C-scrolls, Wm. Duesbury & Co, c1765, 6in (14.5cm) wide.
$1,000-1,200

Sauceboats

A Liverpool sauceboat in the Worcester style, painted with an Oriental lady and a boy with a bird on a pole, Richard Chaffer's factory, c1765, 8½in (20cm) long.
$3,000-3,600

A small Derby sauceboat, moulded with fruit and painted with stylised flowersprays, Wm. Duesbury & Co, c1765, 6in (15cm) wide.
$800-900

A Bow sauceboat with diaper and foliate border, on 3 lion's mask and paw feet, c1752, 8½in (21cm) long.
$1,000-1,200

A sauceboat with scroll handle in the manner of Worcester, in underglaze blue, damaged handle.
$450-650

A Worcester blue and white sauceboat of compressed form, painted with The Plantation pattern, crack to rim and round foot, c1756, 8in (20cm) long.
$450-650

A Longton Hall sauceboat, painted with foliage within relief moulded cartouches of flowersprays tied with ribbon, with waved rim, chip to rim and firecrack, c1755, 7in (18cm) wide.
$720-800

A First Period Worcester sauceboat of cos lettuce form, branch loop handle, painted with insects, flowerheads and leaves, on stem foot, c1756, 9½in (24cm) wide.
$1,500-1,800

A Longton Hall sauceboat, painted in the Oriental style, crack to base of handle, c1755, 8in (20cm) wide.
$540-900

A Lowestoft creamer, 6½in (16cm) wide.
$450-540

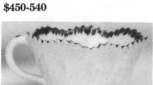

A Derby leaf moulded butter boat, the interior painted with flowers beneath a shaped blue dentil rim, Wm. Duesbury & Co, c1765, 3½in (9cm) wide.
$800-900

A Derby blue and white sauceboat, 8in (20cm) long.
$600-650

Services

A Coalport dinner service, each piece decorated with an emerald green band dispersed with pale yellow panels and leaves, all highlighted in gilt and on a white ground, comprising 96 items, pattern No. S.1931, c1820.
$3,600-4,500

A Copeland topographical part dessert service, each piece painted with a named view within a cerise band and gilt reticulated border, comprising: 16 plates, 2 damaged, 3 dishes, 4 circular tazza on three-footed bases, one with damage, c1850.
$1,500-1,700

An English dessert service, possibly John Ridgway, painted within cobalt blue borders reserved with a scrolling foliate or lobed orange and gilt designs, comprising: 18 plates and 8 dishes, 2 plates cracked, pattern number in red 6/2767, c1835, plates 9½in (23.5cm).
$9,000-9,500

A Royal Crown Derby dessert service, each piece enamelled by W. E. J. Dean, with fishing scenes within cobalt blue borders with raised gilt scroll and foliage decoration, comprising: 12 plates and 5 dishes, c1900.
$4,500-6,000

A Minton dessert service, with central monogram E.M.B, impressed date code for 1858.
$650-720

A Royal Crown Derby part tea service, printed in iron red, enriched in underglaze blue with scrolls and foliage in gilding, comprising: a tray, a teapot and cover, a milk jug, a two-handled sugar bowl, a slop bowl, 10 side plates, 13 cups and 14 saucers, some damage and gilding slightly rubbed.
$1,500-1,600

An English dessert service, probably Minton, painted over a white ground within a 'malachite' border and shaped gilt rim, comprising: one tall pierced two-handled comport, 3 dishes and 12 dessert plates, minor hair cracks, red painted pattern No. 2311/1, c1830.
$1,800-2,700

A Minton dessert set, decorated with fine picture panels, comprising 8 pieces, dated 1888.
$1,200-1,500

A composite Royal Derby tea service.
$1,000-1,200

A Coalport part dessert service, painted in the studio of Thomas Baxter, the centres with loose bouquets within gilt line cartouches reserved on iron red grounds gilt with dots and stars, the borders with flowersprays alternating with yellow ground lozenge shaped and diamond shaped panels of pink roses edged in gilding, the rims gilt, comprising: a two-handled centre dish, an oval tureen stand, 10 dishes, 14 plates, gilding rubbed and some rubbing and flaking to enamels, some damage, c1805.
$5,000-6,000

A Davenport part dessert service, painted within a gilt foliate hexafoil cartouche suspending salmon pink medallions, beneath border of pink roses and gilt C-scrolls, comprising: 2 sauce tureens and covers with gilt bud finials, slight damage to one finial, 7 dishes, c1820.
$4,500-5,500

A Derby part tea service, printed in iron red and underglaze blue, enriched in gilding, comprising: a bread plate, 12 side plates, a slop bowl, 9 cups and 10 saucers, some damage, gilding rubbed.
$650-720

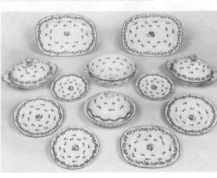

An English dinner service, painted in green, blue, pink and gilt, comprising 123 pieces, probably Coalport, early 19thC.
$3,000-3,600

A Meissen coffee service, each piece painted with trailing green ivy between gilded borders, comprising: 14 cups, 14 saucers, 14 dessert dishes, a coffee pot and cover, a teapot and cover, 2 cream jugs, a sucrier and cover, some minor chips and rubbing, crossed swords in underglaze blue and script numerals, c1885, coffee pot 10½in (27cm).
$5,500-7,000

An English part dessert service, each piece painted in the centre with a floral bouquet, enclosed by an elaborate gilt and pea green border, comprising: 12 plates, 4 dishes and one medium tazza, c1820.
$1,500-1,800

An English part dessert service, comprising: 2 comports, 4 low stands and 12 plates, each painted with a spray of flowers within a lobed rim, in green enamel and gold, some damage.
$800-900

A Coalport tea and coffee service, painted in a bright palette and gilt beneath gilt dentil rims, comprising: a teapot, cover and stand, a sugar bowl and cover, a milk jug, a slop bowl, small star crack to base, 2 bread and butter plates, 24 cups and 12 saucers, one with star crack, one cracked, gilding slightly rubbed, pattern No. 830, c1825.
$3,000-4,000

A Staffordshire porcelain part dessert service, painted in colours on an apple green ground within beaded rims, comprising: 2 tall comports with dolphin supports, 4 similar shallow comports and 12 plates, some damage and repairs, pattern No. 1797, 19thC.
$1,800-2,700

A Royal Worcester dessert service, with impressed marks and registration No. 198236, printed marks for 1898.
$5,500-6,000

A Worcester, Flight & Barr and Flight, Barr & Barr composite part dessert service, painted in dark brown monochrome and gilt with a band of foliage beneath gilt rims, comprising: 8 dishes, a two-handled sauce tureen and cover, and 7 plates, some damage, script and impressed marks, c1805 and c1815.
$1,800-2,700

A Rockingham part tea service, with leaf and scroll moulded rim, painted in grey with grapes and foliage, all enriched in gilding, comprising: a teapot and cover, a two-handled sugar bowl and cover, a milk jug, a slop bowl, 3 bread plates, 11 teacups and 12 saucers, pattern No. 12/61, and another teacup, some damages and gilding rubbed.
$1,600-1,800

A Berlin cabaret set, painted with bouquets and sprays of flowers within gilt cartouches, including an oval tray with scroll moulded handles, blue sceptre and iron red K.P.M. and globe marks, various impressed and painted numerals, c1880, the tray 16½in (42cm) wide.
$7,000-9,000

A Nantgarw part dessert service, possibly decorated by Thomas Pardoe, painted over a white ground within a 'bleu celeste' border, framed by gilt foliage, all within a shaped gilt dentil rim, comprising: 2 dishes and 3 dessert plates, one dish restored, impressed marks, c1820, dessert plates 8½in (22cm).
$2,800-3,600

Tankards

An early Worcester tankard, painted in blue with a palm and a fir tree before a pagoda, the reverse painted with a fishing boat beside a shrine, all under a diaper border, 2 chips to foot rim, 4½in (11cm).
$450-650

A Worcester tankard, printed in blue with The Plantation pattern, c1765, 5½in (14cm).
$540-650

Tureens & Butter Tubs

A Worcester blue and white butter tub and cover, on 4 scroll feet, with bud finial, stalk to finial lacking, blue crescent mark, c1760, 5½in (14cm) wide.
$2,700-3,600

A Berlin tureen and cover, painted with panels of 18thC gentlemen engaged in scenes of revelry and festivity, the domed cover surmounted by a Bacchic cherub knop, minor chip to cherub, sceptre mark in blue, late 19thC, 14in (36cm).
$1,500-2,000

A Worcester white partridge tureen and cover with incised plumage, the edge of the cover with stylised entwined straw and feathers, the basket weave moulded base with feathers and corn, c1765, 6½in (16cm) long.
$3,200-4,000

A Meissen hen and chick tureen and cover, the hen picked out in black and brown, the base with 6 chicks and the cover surmounted with a single chick, cover restored, crossed swords in underglaze blue and incised D,9, c1870, 7½in (19cm).
$1,000-1,500

A pair of Worcester quatrefoil tureens, covers and stands, painted in underglaze blue and gilt within blue borders, gilt with foliage and entwined ribbon and edged with C-scrolls, with gilt dentil rims, blue crescent marks to the stands, c1780, stands 10½in (26cm) wide.
$7,000-9,000

A Barr, Flight & Barr two-handled sauce tureen, cover and stand, raised on a pedestal base with radiating gilt lines, finely painted with a chinoiserie pattern of flowers and 'mon' in iron red, green, pink and gilding, brown printed and impressed marks, c1810, 7in (18cm).
$1,200-1,400

A pair of Chamberlain's Worcester pedestal sauce tureens and covers, painted with the Dejeuney pattern on a gold decorated rich blue band, bearing the crest and motto of Sir James Yeo, one cover with some restoration, 8in (20cm).
$2,700-3,600

A pearlware shaped dish and cover, printed and coloured with scrolling foliage and flowers enriched in gilding, slight rubbing and flaking, damage to one corner, 9½in (24cm) diam.
$180-270

A Derby blue and white tureen and cover, 5in (13cm).
$1,500-1,600

Vases

A pair of Bow baluster frill vases of conventional type, with female mask and flower handles, the shoulders pierced and with blue and yellow flowerheads at the intersections, both with chips to flowers and handles, one with cracked neck, c1765, 8in (19.5cm).
$1,800-2,700

A Chelsea pot pourri vase and cover, enriched in pale puce and with gilding, the pierced domed cover with flower finial, restoration to vase, her right arm and drapery and to hound, cover restored, gold anchor mark, c1765, 16½in (42.5cm).
$1,600-2,700

A Derby type porcelain tulip vase, with yellow petals enriched in orange and puce, on sinuous green stems and surrounded by green foliage, all on a naturalistic base applied with smaller coloured flowers, minor chips, restoration to bud, c1800, 6in (15.5cm).
$1,800-2,700

An early Derby pedestal vase, c1810.
$1,500-2,000

A pair of Derby flower encrusted vases, moulded with scrollwork picked out in shades of green and puce, minor chips, c1765, 9in (23.5cm).
$3,600-4,500

A pair of Derby bottle vases and stoppers, early 19thC.
$1,000-1,200

A pair of Coalport baluster two-handled vases and covers in the Chelsea style, enamelled in colours within gilt reserves and on a blue scale ground, florid ribbon and leaf scroll handles and finials, one finial and one scroll on handle repaired, unmarked, 14½in (37cm).
$2,000-2,800

A pair of Derby spill vases, 4in (10cm).
$1,600-1,700

A Meissen vase, finely painted with various birds perched on a dead tree covered in ivy, gilt scroll border, rim restored, crossed swords in underglaze blue, c1755, 6in (15cm).
$3,600-4,500

A pair of Staffordshire porcelain urn shaped vases, the blue scale ground reserved with bouquets of flowers within gilt scroll cartouches, with flared necks and on socle stems and square bases, 11in (29cm).
$540-650

A small Spode blue ground two-handled vase of Warwick shape, reserved on a dark blue ground gilt with scale pattern, the looped snake handles and rims gilt, marked in red and pattern No. 1166, c1820, 4in (10cm) wide.
$1,500-1,700

A pair of Mintons turquoise ground tapering vases and covers, painted in colours, signed 'Dean', printed globe mark, 8in (19cm).
$210-360

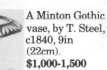

A Minton Gothic vase, by T. Steel, c1840, 9in (22cm).
$1,000-1,500

A pair of Derby vases and covers, with polychrome floral on gilt decorated white reserves with blue ground, 9in (24cm).
$2,700-3,200

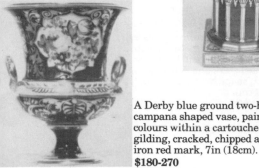

A Derby blue ground two-handled campana shaped vase, painted in colours within a cartouche and gilding, cracked, chipped and worn, iron red mark, 7in (18cm).
$180-270

In the Ceramics section if there is only one measurement it usually refers to the height of the piece

A pair of Worcester vases, signed and painted by Harry Stinton, shape No. 2471, marked in puce and retailer's mark Townsend and Company, Newcastle on Tyne, date code for 1914, 6in (14.5cm).
$2,700-3,600

A Worcester oviform pot pourri vase and pierced hexagonal cover, transfer printed in black after Robert Hancock, within a gadrooned rim, part of cover lacking, c1765, 11in (29cm).
$4,500-5,500

l. & r. A pair of Worcester vases and covers, signed and painted by Harry Stinton, in shades of green and coral with highland cattle watering and grazing by a stream, slight damage to covers, marked in green, date code for 1909, shape No. H 247, 10in (25.5cm).
$4,500-5,500

c. A Worcester vase, signed and painted by Harry Davis, in tones of blush ivory, with a recumbent ram lying amongst heather and grass, marked in green, date mark for 1907, shape No. G 1040, 5½in (13.5cm).
$1,800-2,700

A Grainger's Worcester reticulated bottle vase.
$720-900

A Royal Worcester vase and cover, the ivory and gilt body painted with cattle by John Stinton, signed, printed mark and date code for 1907, shape No. 1572, 11in (28cm).
$3,600-4,500

A Royal Worcester vase and cover, painted and signed by John Stinton, shape No. 151, printed marks, rd. No. 168915, 8in (21cm).
$3,600-4,500

A Worcester vase by Harry Stinton, in green and gilt, slight crack on reverse, marked in green, date code for 1901 and shape No. G.32, 8½in (22cm).
$1,500-2,000

A small Royal Worcester vase, painted by Harry Stinton with cattle in a highland landscape, printed mark and date code for 1911, shape No. G.923, 4½in (11.5cm).
$800-900

A late Victorian Royal Worcester vase and cover, painted by C. H. C. Baldwyn.
$8,000-9,000

A Royal Worcester two-handled vase and lid, painted and signed by Harry Davis, pattern No. 2453, damage to lid, dated 1913, 12in (31cm).
$2,700-3,600

A Royal Worcester vase, with scroll feet and pierced rim, decorated by Raymond Rushton with a thatched cottage in a country landscape entitled 'Ripple', shape No. G.42, printed mark and date code for 1929, 8½in (22cm). **$900-1,000**

A large Dresden flower encrusted vase and a cover of rococo inspiration, with a pair of nymph head handles picked out in pale green and gilt, minor chips to flowers, cancelled mark, late 19thC, 26in (67cm).
$5,500-6,000

A pair of English blue ground faceted vases, painted in bright colours, enriched with gilt flower, leaf and scale patterns, one repaired at foot, both with wear to gilding, 8in (21cm).
$1,000-1,200

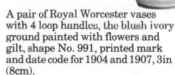

A pair of Royal Worcester vases with 4 loop handles, the blush ivory ground painted with flowers and gilt, shape No. 991, printed mark and date code for 1904 and 1907, 3in (8cm).
$450-540
A Royal Worcester blush ivory bottle shape vase, painted with flowers, shape No. 2491, printed mark and date code for 1912, 5½in (14cm).
$130-180

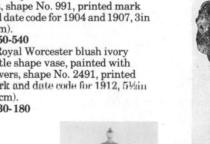

A pair of Worcester vases and covers, signed and painted by Harry Stinton in shades of green and gold, marked in puce, date mark for 1911, 4½in (11.5cm).
$6,000-7,000

A pair of Worcester bottle vases, decorated on pale blue ground with gilt banding, 15in (39cm).
$1,500-1,800

A pair of Berlin pot pourri urns and cover, raised on square gilt plinths with a central band painted on either side, flanked by 2 ram mask handles above vine leaves and branches tied by pale blue ribbons, all over a puce scale ground gilt with stars, each pierced cover similarly decorated and surmounted by a gilt artichoke knop, minor chips, one knop restored, sceptre mark in underglaze blue, c1880, 14in (35cm).
$2,700-3,600

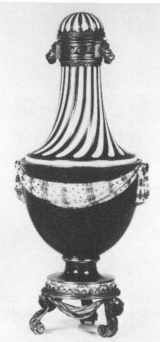

A garniture of 3 English vases, with foliate and goat head handles, each painted with a basket of flowers on a puce ground, early 19thC, 6½ and 7½in (16.5 and 18.5cm).
$450-650

A Sèvres covered vase, the base with swagged tied drapery, the ground colour in 'bleu de roi', decorated 'oeil de perdrix' mounted with chased and chiselled classical ormolu, lacks chains, interlaced 'A' mark, the ormolu with Fondeurs mark, 18thC, 13in (33cm).
$450-540

A pair of Royal Worcester peach ground two-handled vases, each with hand painted picture panels of long horned highland cattle, signed H. Stinton, shape No. 2425, date code 1911, 8in (20cm).
$2,700-3,600

A pair of Sèvres pattern gilt metal mounted blue ground oviform vases and covers, with cast rope-twist, scroll and mask handles, painted by L. Bertion, the waisted necks and spreading feet enriched with gilding, gilt metal mounts to feet and rims, imitation blue interlaced L and F marks, c1900, 20½in (51.5cm).
$3,000-3,600

A Vienna vase, the handles, foot and plinth gilt, chipped, shield mark in underglaze blue, c1830, 25in (64cm).
$9,500-10,000

A German porcelain blue ground urn shaped vase and cover, moulded with mythological dancing figures between moulded gilt swags, leaves and gadroons, the fretwork handles, berried finial and rims enriched with gilding, perhaps Fürstenberg, chips to stem, chip to base and underside of cover, c1790, 16in (41cm).
$7,000-8,000

A 'Vienna' vase, painted by Kray, signed, reserved on a pale green ground with complex gilded and coloured panels, painted shield mark and script title 'Wasser trägerin', c1890, 12½in (32cm).
$1,800-2,000

A pair of Helena Wolfsohn vases and covers, painted in colours with alternate panels of 18thC lovers in landscapes and sprays of summer flowers on a black ground within gilt scroll borders, 12in (30cm).
$1,200-1,400

Miscellaneous

A Worcester blue and white spittoon, transfer printed with loose bouquets, scattered flowers and insects, blue W mark, c1775, 4½in (11.5cm).
$900-1,000

Four Worcester blue and white asparagus servers, painted beneath a cell pattern border, the pierced upright sides edged with a foliate border, one with a small extended firing crack, c1765, 3in (7.5cm).
$2,500-3,000

A 'Vienna' vase, indistinctly signed, painted with a forest setting, reserved on a lustrous purple and blue ground brightly painted and enriched with gilding, shield mark and script title, c1885, and a 'Vienna' stand, en suite, in burnished gilt with a scroll border, 10in (25cm).
$7,000-8,000

A pair of Bow white pistol-shaped knife and fork handles, mounted with a steel blade and a two-pronged fork, c1753, 3½ and 4in (9 and 10cm).
$180-270

> In the Ceramics section if there is only one measurement it usually refers to the height of the piece

A Bristol salt spoon, the fluted bowl painted with bouquets within a gilt line rim, the handle moulded with gilt foliage and painted with a pink Martagon Lily, the reverse with an iron red flower, Richard Champion's factory, c1775, 4½in (11cm).
$3,200-4,000

A large 'Sèvres' gilt metal mounted vase, painted with a continuous scene of Venus, Cupid, maidens and cherubs at play in a woodland setting, reserved on a light blue and gilt ground, some gilding rubbed, interlaced L's in blue, c1860, 36in (91cm), giltwood foot.
$5,500-9,000

A Worcester ladle, the bowl painted in an Imari palette with The Old Mosaik pattern, slight rim chips, c1768, 6½in (17cm) long.
$900-1,000

A Worcester ladle, the bowl gilt with a loose bouquet within a scroll cartouche reserved on a blue ground, the top of the curved handle with gilt ornament on a similar ground, c1780, 6½in (16.5cm) long.
$540-650

Six Royal Crown Derby Imari pattern cake knife handles, painted in underglaze blue and iron red and enriched in gilding, with steel blades, in a plush lined box, 6 cake forks in a plush lined box en suite and 6 fruit knives in a plush lined box en suite, gilding very slightly rubbed.
$720-900

A Worcester mustard spoon, the shell moulded bowl painted with a flowerspray within a gilt rim, the handle enriched with puce, c1768, 3½in (9cm) long.
$5,500-6,000

A Worcester white salt spoon, the handle moulded with scrolling foliage, tiny chip to rim of bowl, c1765, 4in (10cm).
$450-650

An English porcelain pod of peas, probably Coalport, the naturalistic green painted pod with one seam split to reveal the pale cream coloured peas inside, minor chips at either end, c1830, 3½in (9cm).
$650-900

A rare Chelsea shell salt, painted in the London workshop of William Duesbury, in orange and green, with a winkle shell centred by fronds of coral and seaweed, raised on a colourful base of sea shells, coral and seaweed, minor rim chips, feint incised triangle mark, c1745, 3in (7.5cm).
$6,000-7,000

Twelve St. Cloud blue and white knife handles, painted with bands of lambrequin and scrolls, the rounded ends with false gadroons, 9 cracked, contemporary silver ferrules, finials and steel blades with cutler's mark of a crowned I, c1715, handles 3½in (8cm) long.
$1,400-1,500

Jars

Five Royal Worcester candle snuffers:
l. to r.
A Royal Worcester candle snuffer modelled as Granny Snow, wearing a pink dress and yellow bonnet, marked in puce, date code for 1930, 3in (7.5cm).
$180-360
A Royal Worcester candle snuffer modelled as a French nun, wearing a black and white habit and carrying a bible under her arm, no mark, 4in (10cm).
$180-360
A Royal Worcester candle snuffer modelled as the head and shoulders of Mr. Caulder from Punch, wearing a nightcap and a blanket wrapped around him, marked in puce, date code for 1920, 3in (7.5cm).
$180-360
A Royal Worcester candle snuffer modelled as a monk wearing a brown habit and reading from the bible, marked in puce, date code for 1922, 5in (12.5cm).
$180-360
A Royal Worcester candle snuffer modelled as a French cook, marked in puce, date code indistinct, 2½in (7cm).
$180-360

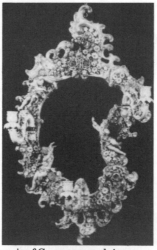

A pair of German porcelain kidney-shaped girandoles with elaborate moulded rococo scrolls enriched in pink, pale blue and gilding, applied all over with flowers and putti, the branches with leaf moulded sconces, some damage, 30in (76cm) high.
$2,700-3,600

A Royal Worcester lobed jar and cover, with long horned cattle in highland setting, signed John Stinton, marked in green on the base, date code for 1912, 7½in (18.5cm).
$3,600-4,500

ORIENTAL POTTERY & PORCELAIN

The year has seen great variance in demand and prices with the best fetching the expected high prices and the run of the mill hard to sell. The Oriental porcelain market is one of the most fickle, depending to a large extent on the buying fashions of a few very wealthy Far East buyers. The recent upsurge in demand for Qing mark and period pieces would appear to have levelled as supply has met demand and many Oriental dealers are well stocked. There has been renewed interest in Korean ceramics, particularly from Korea itself, which has pushed up the prices of the better pieces. At Christie's a small Yi Dynasty blue and white tortoise shaped

kendi with underglaze blue and copper red decoration fetched $93,500 and a superb early 15/16thC brown on white Korean bottle vase sold for $145,000.

Exceptional pieces of Ming and Yuan blue and white are still contested to high prices but Dingyao and other Song ceramics are in the main ignored. There will never be a better time to buy early Chinese pieces with many desirable objects being available for a few hundred pounds.
Isnik pottery continues to be in

great demand. Prices have continued to soar for high quality, perfect pieces. The end of the year saw $90,000 being paid in Phillips for a 16thC blue Isnik dish painted in imitation of the 15thC Ming original.

Japanese ceramics still maintain a buoyant market for the better pieces of any period. Good 17thC Imari is still in demand although collectors are being more selective with condition and pattern playing a more important role. A well decorated, signed Meiji period Makuzu vase sold at Sotheby's Sussex for $21,000.

Bottles

A Japanese celadon glazed bottle, carved with sprays of leaves below a band of key pattern at the shoulder, glaze cracks and staining, 17thC, 13in (33cm).
$2,700-3,600

An Imari bottle, painted in underglaze blue, slight colours, enamels and gilt with a sparse river landscape, with iron red and gilt scrolling foliage, c1700, 9in (23cm).
$650-1,000

A pair of blue and white decanters, each painted in deep blue tones, one with rim chips, Kangxi, 9in (23cm).
$3,600-4,500

Bowls

An Imari deep bowl, painted in iron red, yellow and aubergine enamels, underglaze blue and gilt, base crack, c1700, 6in (15cm) diam.
$650-1,000

A Japanese Cha-Wan bowl, Ko-Imari Edo, repaired, 17thC, 3½in (8.5cm) diam.
$210-250

A pair of Hirado blue and white oviform bottles, painted with wooded landscapes, each with 3 indentations, modelled in relief with a chrysanthemum head and leaves, 6½in (16cm).
$3,000-4,000

A Sancai moulded pottery bowl, the exterior decorated overall in relief with four-petalled blooms on a granular ground, coloured in spotted green, cream and chestnut glazes, restored break, Tang Dynasty, 4in (10cm).
$1,500-1,700

A small Arita bowl with foliate rim, painted in the interior in iron red, green and aubergine enamels, underglaze blue and gilt, the exterior with iron red and underglaze blue emblems, early 18thC, 5½in (14cm) diam.
$720-900

An Arita polychrome wucai style deep dish, with everted rim painted with the Eight Immortals around a central dragon and wave medallion, the rim with flowersprays, flaking to enamels, early 18thC, 8½in (21cm) diam.
$350-550

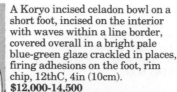

A Koryo incised celadon bowl on a short foot, incised on the interior with waves within a line border, covered overall in a bright pale blue-green glaze crackled in places, firing adhesions on the foot, rim chip, 12thC, 4in (10cm).
$12,000-14,500

A Japanese Cha-Wan bowl, E-Karatsu, 18thC, 4in (10cm) diam.
$720-900

A pair of Transitional dated blue and white bowls, freely painted with an abstract band around the interior rim, inscribed with a regnal date Tianqi qinian, Tianqi 7th year, corresponding to AD 1628, and of the period, 4½in (11cm) diam.
$1,800-2,700

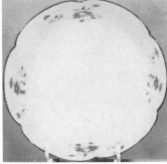

A Kakiemon shallow bowl, with chocolate brown hexafoil rim, painted in the interior with 4 groups of flowering shrubs, rubbed, c1700, 10½in (26cm) diam.
$2,500-3,200

A Cantonese bowl made for the export market, 18thC, 2½in (6cm) high.
$270-360

A Chinese tea bowl and saucer, with eggshell finish, Yongzheng, c1730, saucer 4½in (11cm) diam.
$320-360

A Japanese Arita bowl, early 18thC, 4½in (11cm) diam. **$720-900**

Chinese dynasties and marks

Earlier Dynasties

Shang Yin, c.1532-1027 B.C.
Western Zhou (Chou) 1027-770 B.C.
Spring and Autumn Annals 770-480 B.C.
Warring States 484-221 B.C.
Qin (Ch'in) 221-206 B.C.
Western Han 206 BC-24 AD
Eastern Han 25-220
Three Kingdoms 221-265
Six Dynasties 265-589
Wei 386-557
Sui 589-617
Tang (T'ang) 618-906
Five Dynasties 907-960
Liao 907-1125
Sung 960-1280
Chin 1115-1260
Yüan 1280-1368

Ming Dynasty

洪武年製

Hongwu (Hung Wu)
1368-1398

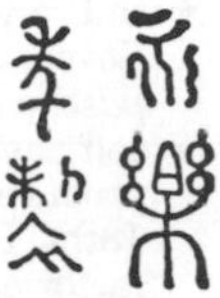

永樂年製

Yongle (Yung Lo)
1403-1424

大明宣德年製

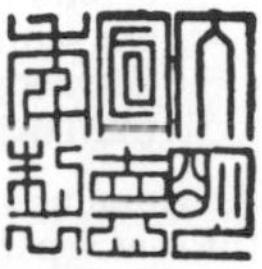

Xuande (Hsüan Té)
1426-1435

大明成化年製

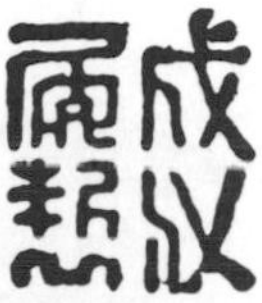

Chenghua (Ch'éng Hua)
1465-1487

大明弘治年製

Hongzhi
(Hung Chih)
1488-1505)

大明正德年製

Zhengde
(Chéng Té)
1506-1521

大明嘉靖年製

Jiajing
(Chia Ching)
1522-1566

大明隆慶年製

Longqing
(Lung Ching)
1567-1572

大明萬曆年製

Wanli (Wan Li)
1573-1620

大明天啟年製

Tianqi
(Tien Chi)
1621-1627

崇禎年製

Chongzhen
(Ch'ung Chêng)
1628-1644

Qing (Ch'ing) Dynasty

大清順治年製

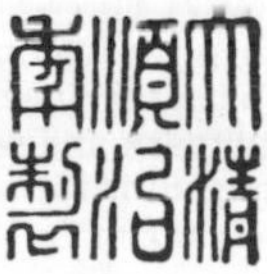

Shunzhi
(Shun Chih)
1644-1661

大清康熙年製

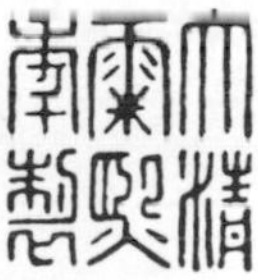

Kangxi (K'ang Hsi)
1662-1722

大清雍正年製

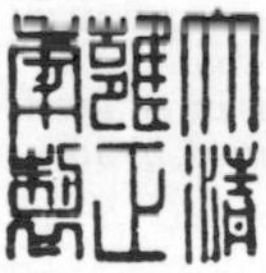

Yongzheng (Yung Chêng)
1723-1735

大清乾隆年製

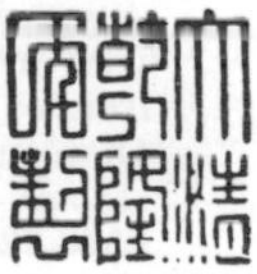

Qianlong (Ch'ien Lung)
1736-1795'

嘉慶年製

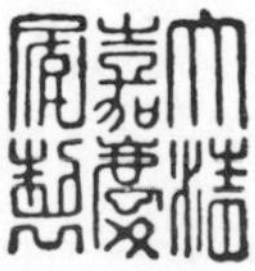

Jiaqing (Chia Ch'ing)
1796-1820

大清道光年製

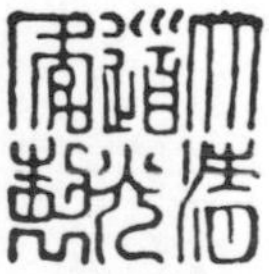

Daoguang (Tao Kuang)
1821-1850

大清咸豐年製

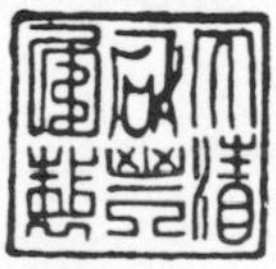

Xianfeng (Hsien Féng)
1851-1861

大清同治年製

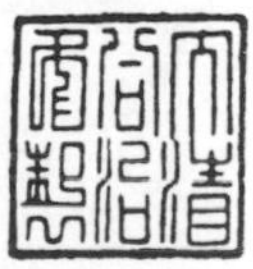

Tongzhi (T'ung Chih)
1862-1874

大清光緒年製

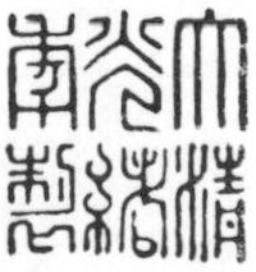

Guangxu (Kuang Hsu)
1875-1908

大清宣統年製

Xuantong
(Hsuan T'ung)
1909-1911

洪憲年製

Hongxian
(Hung Hsien)
1916

A large Cantonese punch bowl, painted within gold key pattern surrounds divided by butterflies, birds, flowers and emblems, restored, Daoguang, 23in (59cm) diam. **$5,500-7,000**

A large 'famille rose' punch bowl, painted on the exterior with bands of pink lotus petals and iron red and gilt scrolling foliage, restored, Qianlong, 16in (40cm). **$2,700-3,600**

An Annamese blue and white bowl, the centre painted with a fish, the exterior with 2 dragons between lappet and diaper borders, late 16th/early 17thC, 6in (15cm) diam. **$650-800**

A wucai bowl, the exterior painted with dragons in green enamel and iron red, hair crack and rim chipped, Qianlong mark and period, 5½in (13cm). **$540-720**

A blue and white Immortals bowl, painted in underglaze blue with the Eight Immortals, the interior with a medallion of Three Immortals seated in a garden under a pine tree within a double line repeated at the rim, seal mark and period of Daoguang, 6in (15cm). **$2,000-3,000**

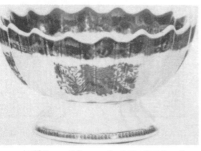

A 'famille rose' export punch bowl, painted with green and gilt roundels of iron red baskets of flowers below pink, green and gilt bands at the borders, late Qianlong, 14in (36cm) diam. **$1,800-2,700**

A Chinese blue and white Fitzhugh pattern fluted bowl, with serrated rim and spreading foot, after a silver rose bowl original, painted with groups of flowers and emblems around a central medallion below trellis pattern, flowers and key pattern, minor restoration to rim, c1800, 11½in (30cm). **$1,500-1,600**

A set of 4 Chinese porcelain dishes with shaped sides, 19thC, 8in (21cm) wide. **$650-750**

A blue and white 'poem' tea bowl, inscribed around the exterior with a poem running in a band around the bowl, with the seals of the Emperor Jiaqing and dated to the spring of the year 'dingsi' (1797), between a 'ruyi' border reserved in white on blue above and below, seal mark and period of Jiaqing, 4in (10.5cm). $7,000-9,000

A Junyao deep bowl under a streaked pale lavender glaze, turning to pale brown at the rim, the interior with one purple splash, the glaze finishing irregularly above the foot, Song Dynasty, 8in (20cm) diam. $1,800-2,700

A pair of copper red decorated phoenix medallion bowls, decorated around the exterior with 5 roundels of phoenix, with wings displayed and long tails curled underneath, small chip to one, seal marks and period of Daoguang, 6in (14.5cm). $2,800-3,600

A Tao-Kung Chinese porcelain bowl, with 'famille verte' dragon decoration, c1850, 13in (33cm). $550-900

An unusual blue and white bowl, painted in underglaze blue of slightly pale tone with a design of the 'sanyou', 'Three Friends', of pine, prunus and bamboo on either side, above a continuous square scroll band around the foot, the interior white, seal mark and period of Daoguang, 10in (26cm). $6,000-8,000

It is rare to find a bowl of this type of oval section, with flared sides, although the design is well known on smaller rounded bowls.

A large Cantonese bowl, 19thC, 20in (51cm) diam. $1,700-2,000

A pair of Chinese blue and white dishes, painted with pagodas in wooded rocky river landscapes within borders of scrolls, stylised flowers and butterflies, one with rim chip and associated hairline, the other with body crack, Qianlong, 21½in (54cm) wide. $1,800-2,000

In the Ceramics section if there is only one measurement it usually refers to the height of the piece

A 'famille rose' bowl, the exterior painted with 3 poppy blooms, one striated pink, one shaded white and one in iron red, all borne upon slender hairy stems with leaves in shaded tones of bluish-green and yellowish-green, the interior with 3 fallen blossoms in pink and white, restored, mark and period of Yongzheng, 3½in (9cm). $9,500-13,000

A pair of 'famille rose' ruby ground bowls, painted to the exterior with chrysanthemum issuing from leafy stems, the interiors plain, ruby enamelled Kangxi 'yuzhi' marks, 19thC, 4½in (11.5cm), wood stands, box.
$2,000-3,000

Two 'famille rose' bowls, with rounded sides rising to flaring rims with plain interiors, painted to the exterior with flowersprays, both with iron red Guangxu six-character marks and of the period, 6½in (17cm) diam.
$4,500-6,000

A 'famille rose' yellow ground bowl, painted with a bird below blossoms among flowers and bearing the mark of the Empress Dowager, 5in (12.5cm) diam.
$800-1,000

A rare Korean blue and white bowl, with stoutly potted steep rounded sides standing on a straight foot, the exterior with 2 sprays of fruiting finger-citron and a stylised flowerhead within a double line medallion in the centre, Yi Dynasty, 19thC, 10in (26cm).
$72,000-80,000

A fragment with a similar cobalt blue design, excavated from the Punwonli kiln site at Namchong-myon, Kwangju-gun Kyonggi-do is now in the National Museum of Korea, Seoul.

A large Cantonese punch bowl, painted with panels of figures on terraces and birds and butterflies among flowers on a green scroll gold ground, base cracked, 16in (41cm) diam.
$1,800-2,700

An Imari monteith, decorated in typical coloured enamels and gilt on underglaze blue, late 19thC, 12½in (31.5cm) diam.
$4,500-5,500

A Cha-Wan bowl with documentary inscription, c1906, 5in (13cm) diam.
$540-720
Awarded as 1st school prize.

A large Kaga ware deep bowl, decorated in iron red and green enamels and gilt, late Kutani, late 19thC, 12in (30.5cm).
$4,500-5,500

A pottery deep dish, the coarse pale grey body burnt to a brick red and glazed in Ki-Seto style, with patches left unglazed and pooling in the well, gold lacquer 'naoshi' in the rim, signed 'to', 12in (31cm) diam.
$3,000-4,000

A Cantonese bowl, painted inside and out with panels containing figures in conversation, the rim painted with a wide band of birds, insects and flowers, 16in (41cm) diam, with damaged wood stand.
$3,600-4,500

A Bencharong bowl, 7in (17.5cm) diam.
$180-210

A Chinese 'famille rose' bowl, Tongzha mark and of period, 7in (17.5cm).
$1,800-2,000

Cups

A 'famille rose' wine cup, painted around the exterior in enamels with a peony plant bearing one pink bloom, growing beside a chrysanthemum bush bearing 3 yellow blooms, the reverse with a purple butterfly, the interior white, Yongzheng mark and of period, 2½in (6cm).
$5,500-6,300

An Imari tankard decorated in iron red, green, yellow, aubergine and black enamels and gilt on underglaze blue, the loop handle with scrolling foliage and flowerheads, body crack and chip to rim, late 17thC, 8in (20cm).
$2,600-3,000

A 'famille rose' European Subject teacup and saucer, enamelled with 'The Ascension', Christ in Majesty above a group of 9 adoring, standing and kneeling Apostles, all on a plain grassy terrace, Yongzheng.
$3,000-4,500

A matching pair of 'blanc de chine' libation cups of rhinoceros horn form, moulded in relief, 18thC, 3in (8cm).
$900-1,000

A Chinese yellow ground trio, Guangxu mark and period, plate 6in (15cm) diam.
$720-900

A pair of Imari beakers and saucers, decorated in iron red enamel and gilt on underglaze blue, and 6 Imari beakers and 3 saucers of similar design, one beaker and one saucer with a hairline crack, c1700, beakers 3½in (9cm) high, saucers 6in (15.5cm) diam.
$3,000-4,000

Ewers

Figures – Animal

A painted pottery figure of a camel, with traces of pigment overall, Wei Dynasty, 9in (23cm).
$30,000-$36,000

An Imari ewer, decorated in iron red enamel and gilt on underglaze blue with sprays of chrysanthemum and wild pinks surrounding a roundel containing the letter 'O' (olieum), loop handle, slight chips to neck, c1700, 7in (17.5cm).
$1,200-1,500

A turquoise glazed figure of a water buffalo, c1800, 14in (35.5cm) wide. **$1,000-1,600**

An Arita polychrome group of a cockerel flanked by half grown chicks, the plumage painted in iron red and black with green and aubergine enamels heightened in gilt, the rockwork base predominantly black, green and white, heightened in iron red, comb restored, late 17thC, 6in (15cm).
$6,400-8,000

An Imari model of 2 'Oshidori' decorated in iron red, green, brown and black enamels and gilt, one beak restored, 19thC, 9½in (23.5cm).
$2,000-3,000

A large Japanese porcelain figure of a sleeping cat with gilt fur markings, an iron red and green decorated bow around its neck, 12in (30cm) long.
$1,500-1,550

Figures – People

A pair of turquoise glazed parrots, their wing feathers naturalistically moulded, chipped, c1850, 14½in (36.5cm).
$3,600-4,500

A turquoise and mustard glazed roof tile, modelled as a standing scholar, with a wise expression and wearing long loose robes, chip to finger, slightly degraded, Ming Dynasty or later, 17in (43cm).
$2,000-2,700

A pair of painted pottery figures of ladies, with features picked out in black, with detailing in red pigment on an ivory ground, Han Dynasty, 12in (30cm).
$6,000-8,000

A 'blanc de chine' seated figure of Guanyin, her flowing robes forming the base, 17th/18thC, 8½in (21cm). **$1,700-2,000**

An Imari model of a bijin decorated in iron red, green and black enamels and gilt on underglaze blue, old damage to her hair, some old cracks, c1700, 15in (39cm). **$1,200-1,400**

A black, green and mustard glazed equestrian roof tile, modelled as an official on a horse with an elaborate saddle cloth, Ming Dynasty or later, 13in (33cm). **$2,600-3,000**

A large Imari model of a bijin decorated in iron red, green, aubergine and black enamels and gilt on underglaze blue, late 17thC, 20in (50cm). **$6,000-8,000**

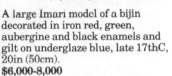

A pair of Satsuma figures, each in colourful floral dress, holding a fan and a cone, slight damage, 6½in (16cm). **$270-450**

A pair of Arita models of Kintaro astride a carp decorated in iron red, green and black enamels and gilt, c1700, 10in (25cm) long. **$4,500-6,300**

An Imari figure of a woman, her kimono painted with small birds in flight among hanging wisteria and fences, chips, 11in (27cm). **$540-720**

A pair of Imari bijin, decorated in iron red, green and aubergine enamels and gilt on underglaze blue, the kimono with peony sprays and cloud scrolls, minor damage and cracks, c1700, 10½in (26.5cm). **$3,000-4,000**

A Dehua 'blanc de chine' figure of Guanyin wearing long flowing robes and a high cowl on her knotted hair, late Qing Dynasty, 15in (37.5cm). **$1,800-2,700**

An export figure of a lady, holding an underglaze blue and white jar and wearing a gown over a long yellow ground robe, painted in underglaze blue, turquoise, yellow, blue, iron red, green and gilt, base possibly not original, head cracked, hands and base of robe restored, base chipped, Qianlong, 12in (31cm). **$3,600-4,500**

Flasks

A pair of Satsuma flasks, painted in colours and gilt, the short cylindrical necks with key pattern, one foot repaired, 5in (12cm).
$2,700-3,600

A large blue and white saucer dish, painted in underglaze blue, extensively restored, early Ming Dynasty, 16in (41cm).
$4,500-5,500

A Chinese blue and white 'Rotterdam Riot' plate, painted with a scene representing the demolished house of Jacob van Zuylen, 2 small rim chips, Chenghua six-character mark, Kangxi, 8in (20cm).
$2,000-2,800

Flatware

A late Ming blue and white blue ground lobed dish, painted with a central roundel of waves with cranes among lotus, rim frits, Chenghua six-character mark, Tianqi/Chongzheng, 8½in (21cm).
$720-900

A Chinese blue and white plate, painted with 2 ladies, within a trellis pattern border reserved with 4 panels of fruit, Kangxi six-character mark within a double circle and of the period, 8in (20cm).
$1,200-1,600

A Chinese yellow ground underglaze blue decorated saucer dish, painted with 3 phoenix amongst clouds, the reverse with 2 further phoenix and flowers, small rim cracks, Chenghua six-character mark, Kangxi, 6in (15cm).
$720-900

A late Ming blue and white saucer dish, Tianqi four-character mark within a double circle and of the period, 6½in (16cm).
$900-1,000

A pair of 'famille verte' plates, painted to the centre of the interior with auspicious emblems and scholars' objects, the exterior with 6 loose ribboned emblems, the base painted in underglaze blue with a 'lingzhi' spray, rim chip restored, rim chips, Kangxi, 8½in (22cm).
$1,600-2,000

A Ming blue and white deep saucer dish painted within a double circle, the border with stylised trailing flowers and the reverse with 6 cranes in flight divided by stylised clouds, 16thC, 17in (43cm).
$3,600-4,500

A dish in the form of a peach with short lipped upright sides, painted in underglaze blue heightened in copper red, the base unglazed, cracked from firing fault in rim, Kangxi, 10in (25cm). $2,700-3,600

Fifteen Chinese blue and white plates, each painted with a central flowerspray medallion within a dense panel of flowers and foliage, the rims with sprays of chrysanthemum and daisies, 5 cracked, most with small chips or frits, Kangxi, 10in (24cm). $1,500-1,900

A large 'famille verte' dish, painted with a central roundel of a small bird among flowers and rockwork within 2 phoenix, the border with 4 panels of sea creatures and with moulded iron red and gilt rim, restored, Kangxi, 15in (37cm). $720-1,000

A pair of 'famille verte' plates, each painted at the centre with a boy on a terrace, within a band of floral roundels and scholars' utensils beneath cash emblems at the rim, Kangxi, 9in (22.5cm). $4,000-4,800

A 'famille verte' dish painted within a seeded green border reserved with panels of vessels, rim frit, Kangxi, 14in (36cm). $1,800-2,700

A 'famille verte' dish painted at the centre, the piecrust rim decorated in iron red and gilt, fritted, rim chip and associated short crack, Kangxi, 14in (35.5cm). $2,700-3,600

An Imari deep dish, painted to the centre with a roundel of a jardinière of pine and plum on a wooden terrace, the border with 3 panels of flowering chrysanthemum and gilt quail below grasses, divided by dark blue ground panels of flowers and leaves, crack, late 17thC, 19in (48cm). $4,500-5,500

A Chinese blue and white dish, with scroll border, early 17thC, 8in (20cm). $720-800

A set of 4 Arita blue and white kraak style deep dishes, painted to the centre with a deer below pine and overhanging rockwork within panels of flowersprays, the everted rims with masks, c1700, 7in (17.5cm). $2,000-2,700

A pair of 'famille verte' plates, each painted at the centre with a bird perched above dense prunus and tree chrysanthemum, the seeded border reserved with butterfly cartouches, one cracked, Kangxi, 8½in (24cm). $1,800-2,000

TRANSITIONAL WARES

★ these wares are readily identifiable both by their form and by their style of decoration

★ forms: sleeve vases, oviform jars with domed lids, cylindrical brushpots and bottle vases are particularly common

★ the cobalt used is a brilliant purplish blue, rarely misfired

★ the ground colour is of a definite bluish tone, probably because the glaze is slightly thicker than that of the wares produced in the subsequent reigns of Kangxi and Yongzheng

★ the decoration is executed in a rather formal academic style, often with scholars and sages with attendants in idyllic cloud-lapped mountain landscapes

★ other characteristics include the horizontal 'contoured' clouds, banana plantain used to interrupt scenes, and the method of drawing grass by means of short 'V' shaped brush strokes

★ in addition, borders are decorated with narrow bands of scrolling foliage, so lightly incised as to be almost invisible or secret (anhua)

★ these pieces were rarely marked although they sometimes copied earlier Ming marks

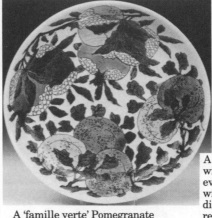

A 'famille verte' Pomegranate saucer dish, painted in aubergine, yellow and shades of green with fruiting peach and pomegranate, outlined in black over a lightly incised design of five-clawed dragons, the exterior similarly decorated, riveted, cracked, encircled Kangxi six-character mark and of the period, 10in (25cm), wood stand. **$2,000-3,000**

A 'famille rose' deep dish, painted with 4 figures in conversation, the everted cell pattern rim reserved with 4 river landscape panels divided by flowers, one area of rim restored, early Qianlong, 15½in (39cm) diam. **$1,200-1,500**

A Kakiemon blue and white foliate rimmed dish, decorated with a lakeside landscape, the reverse with scrolling 'karakusa', small silver lacquer repair, late 17thC, 7½in (18cm) **$1,200-1,500**

A Japanese Arita blue and white plate, late 17thC, 8½in (21cm). **$550-720**

A large Chinese blue and white shallow dish, the centre painted with deer in a landscape, the rim with a band of insects, flowers and foliage, 2 hair cracks, minor glaze chipping to rim, Transitional, 17½in (44cm). **$450-650**

A Hausmaler decorated Chinese porcelain dish, painted in 'Schwarzlot' and gilding by Ignaz Preissler, in iron red, turquoise, blue and gilt, small chips, c1715, 8½in (21cm). **$5,000-6,400**

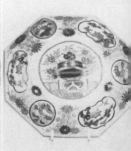

A Chinese Imari foliate muffin dish and domed cover, rim repairs, early 18thC, 11in (29cm). **$2,500-3,000**

A set of 3 'famille rose' plates, the rims with iron red and gilt bands, one with hairline crack and chip, Qianlong, 9in (23cm).
$1,000-1,200

A 'famille rose' armorial plate, painted with the large iron red and gilt arms of Lauder, with the motto 'Turris Prudentia Custos ut Migaturus Habita' within a border of flowersprays and gilt spearhead bands, rim chip, Qianlong, c1760, 9in (23cm).
$1,000-1,200

A 'famille rose' pseudo tobacco leaf meat dish, painted with large overlapping serrated leaves and flowerheads, 2 rim chips, Qianlong, 18½in (47cm) wide.
$5,000-5,800

A Chinese blue and white thickly potted saucer dish, densely painted with Ming-style scrolling flowers and leaves divided by bands of whorl pattern, the exterior similar, small rim crack, rim chip restored, Qianlong, 14½in (37cm).
$1,600-2,700

A blue and white dragon dish, painted in the centre in deep underglaze blue with a large leaping dragon enclosing a 'shou' character, chip on rim, seal mark and period of Qianlong, 17½in (45cm).
$9,000-10,000

A pair of 'famille rose' plates, painted with sprays of peony, chrysanthemum and daisy, within borders of flower and fruit sprays within iron red and gilt whorl pattern surrounds, divided by blue enamel clouds and iron red half flowerheads, one cracked, Qianlong, 11in (28cm).
$1,800-2,700

A pair of Chinese export 'famille rose' meat dishes, Qianlong, 15in (38cm) wide.
$3,000-3,600

A pair of Chinese blue and white warming dishes, each painted with a pagoda in a riverside garden, Qianlong, 11in (29cm).
$540-720

A pair of Japanese Kakiemon fluted saucer dishes, late 18thC, 6in (15cm) diam.
$1,800-2,000

A Chinese porcelain blue and white saucer, Qianlong.
$160-210

A popular item of salvage from the Nanking Cargo.

A large blue and white deep dish, painted at the centre below a band of trellis pattern at the border, the exterior with 3 flowersprays, Qianlong, 17in (43.5cm).
$2,000-3,000

A pair of Chinese export 'famille rose' plates, Qianlong, 8½in (22cm).
$720-900

A pair of 'famille rose' plates, painted within a band of iron red and gilt spearheads, the border with 3 branches of peony and fruit, chipped, one with hairline crack, Qianlong, 12in (30.5cm).
$1,800-2,700

A set of 10 Chinese deep dishes, brightly painted in 'famille rose' enamels with crabs, lilies and a spray of peonies, 4 cracked, the rest with minor glaze damage, Qianlong, 9in (23cm).
$1,400-1,500

A pair of Chinese Imari armorial plates, fritted, one repaired, c1720, 12in (30.5cm).
$3,600-5,500

A 'famille rose' plate, painted with a traveller and attendant, Qianlong, 9in (23cm).
$360-540

A 'famille rose' dish, painted within an iron red and gilt spearhead well and rim, the border with trailing flowers, fritted, Qianlong, 14in (36cm).
$1,800-2,700

A 'famille rose' dish, painted in a pierced iron red and gilt border, Qianlong, 14in (36cm).
$2,500-3,000

A set of 3 Chinese export 'famille rose' plates, Qianlong, 9in (23cm).
$1,000-1,200

A Chinese 'famille rose' quatrefoil dish, with Mandarin pattern, c1770, 8in (20cm) wide.
$650-720

A Chinese blue and white charger, painted within a border of stylised pomegranates and floral designs, Qianlong, 21½in (54cm).   **$1,800-2,500**

A dragon dish, later enamelled in green and iron red, the centre painted in underglaze blue, seal mark and period of Qianlong, 17½in (45cm).
$12,000-14,500

A pair of Chinese 'famille rose' dishes, late 18thC, 10in (25cm) wide.
$1,500-1,800

A pair of 'famille rose' armorial plates, each painted to the centre with an elaborate coat-of-arms, small rim chips, Qianlong, 9in (23cm).
$1,500-1,600

The Arms are those of Carr, c1765-70.

A set of 10 Chinese blue and white plates with foliate rims, minor damages and rubbing, Qianlong, 9½in (24cm).
$3,600-4,500

A blue and white dragon saucer dish, painted in the centre with a leaping scaly dragon chasing a flaming pearl, the reverse similarly painted with a frieze of 2 dragons, all between line borders, seal mark and period of Daoguang, 6½in (16cm). **$1,500-1,600**

A large iron red and gilt dragon dish, the centre of the interior enamelled with 2 five-clawed dragons pursuing a flaming pearl, with similar exterior, rim crack, iron red Guangxu six-character mark and of the period, 20½in (51.5cm).
$3,600-4,500

A late Ming blue and white kraak dish, painted within alternate panels of flowers and emblems, repaired, Wanli, 20in (51cm).
$1,000-1,500

A blue and white saucer dish, the interior decorated within a double line border repeated around the rim, the underside with similar phoenix and clouds, mark and period of Xianfeng, 6½in (16.5cm).
$3,000-3,600

A 'famille rose' export deep dish for the Danish market, painted with a central pink ground portrait medallion, with white brickwork and green enamel and gilt rim, late Qianlong, 6½in (15.5cm) wide.
$650-800

A Chinese blue and white plate, decorated in underglaze blue, the central panel depicting a fisherman and a young child walking alongside a river bank with trees in the background, mid-19thC, 13in (33cm).
$300-400

Fourteen Arita style blue and white dishes, painted with a butterfly hovering above flowers issuing from pierced rockwork, four-character mark, early 19thC, 8in (20cm).
038   **$540-720**

An Imari deep dish, painted with 2 bijin among pine in a landscape beside dense flowering shrubs reserved with panels of 'ho-o' and foliage, the everted rim with gilt cranes among blue clouds and dragons behind blue lattice-work, 20½in (52cm).
$4,200-4,700

A Cantonese plaque, the centre painted with a basket of flowers reserved on a ground of insects, fruit and foliage, 14½in (37cm).
$670-750

A pair of 'famille verte' dishes, each painted with a pair of peacocks among flowering shrubs issuing from pierced iron red rockwork, 16in (41cm).
$540-720

A pair of Chinese blue and white meat dishes, painted with peacocks before flowers, 10½in (26cm) wide.
$540-720

A Satsuma sauce, the cavetto dish painted with warriors on the bank of a river, within a rim painted with a band of stylised flowerheads, 10in (25cm).
$720-800

A pair of Imari dishes, decorated in ochre, underglaze blue and gilt, c1800, 14in (36cm).
$2,000-3,000

A set of 7 Satsuma plates, decorated with scenes progressing through the seasons, 8½in (21cm).
$3,200-4,000

A Satsuma shallow dish, 12in (30.5cm).
$1,400-1,500

A Satsuma fluted dish, painted with panels containing figures in conversation, reserved on a brocade ground, 10in (25cm).
$800-900

A Japanese earthenware galleried tray, painted in enamels, on a deep blue ground gilded with stylised blooms, painted and impressed seal mark of Kinkozan, 5½in (14.5cm) wide.
$1,000-1,200

Jardinières

A Satsuma thickly potted fluted saucer dish, painted in coloured enamels and richly gilt, 13in (33cm).
$1,200-1,800

A wucai jardinière, painted on the exterior with 3 yellow Buddhistic lions among dense scrolling iron red peony and green leaves, fritted, Transitional, 9½in (24cm) wide.
$2,700-3,200

A 'famille rose' jardinière, painted on the exterior with 4 panels of baskets of flowers, on a yellow ground reserved with dense scrolling flowers and leaves, below a trellis pattern band at the rim, 18in (46cm) diam.
$2,700-3,600

A large Ming blue and white jardinière, firing crack, hipped and scratched, Jiajing six-character mark and f the period, 16½in (42.5cm) diam.
8,000-9,500

An Imari porcelain jardinière, with fluted body, 12in (30cm).
$900-1,000

Jars

Chinese jar and cover, Han ynasty, 8in (20cm) high.
800-1,000

A late Ming blue and white jar and domed cover, painted with 2 Buddhistic lions among scrolling flowers and leaves below a band of lappets at the shoulder, the cover with 4 flowersprays, Wanli, 6in (16cm).
$540-720

A green glazed pottery jar with lipped mouth, applied with a minutely crackled olive green glaze falling in an uneven line revealing the buff ware below, Tang Dynasty, 6½in (16.5cm).
$2,700-3,600

A wucai baluster jar and a domed cover, fritted, c1650, 15in (38.5cm).
$5,500-7,000

Two Chinese blue and white broad oviform jars, each painted with 3 shaped panels of 'qilin' on a cracked ice pattern ground, reserved with sprays of prunus, Kangxi, 8in (21cm), with pierced wood covers.
$1,800-2,700

A wucai broad baluster jar, painted below iron red scale pattern and floral lappets at the shoulder, rim restoration, Transitional, 10½in (26cm).
$800-1,000

A wucai baluster jar, painted with dragons and phoenix amongst cloud scrolls and above foaming waves crashing on the rocks, the neck with stiff leaves, damaged, Transitional, 12½in (31cm).
$1,600-2,000

A Transitional blue and white jar and cover, decorated beneath a band of descending leaves on the cylindrical neck, the cover decorated with 3 figures on a terrace, cover restored, vase cracked, c1650, 12in (30.5cm).
$3,600-4,500

A Korean blue and white jar, painted in underglaze blue, crack and chips, Yi Dynasty, 19thC, 5in (12.5cm).
$2,000-2,700

A pair of blue and white jars and shallow domed covers, decorated on the exterior with 4 foliate panels of scholars' utensils divided by lotus and peony sprays, the covers similarly decorated, one foot rim chipped, 19thC, 13in (33cm).
$3,200-4,000

A blue and white oviform jar, painted with 4 panels alternately depicting figures in mountainous riverscapes and archaistic vessels amongst precious emblems, all reserved on a trellis pattern ground between 'ruyi' lappets at the foot and on the shoulder, Kangxi, 12½in (32cm), wood cover.
$5,500-6,000

A Satsuma moulded jar and cover, decorated in various coloured enamels and gilt on a brocade ground, signed 'Nihon Bijitsuto Satsuma yaki Shuko', late 19thC, 8in (20cm), wood stand.
$7,000-8,000

A Korean blue and white faceted jar, with a band of 8 facets around the middle, decorated in underglaze blue with a line around the low foot, 4 scroll motifs around the middle and on the angled shoulders with 3 'shou' characters interspersed with foliate sprays centred with a bloom, chip to inside of foot, Yi Dynasty, 19thC, 5in (12cm).
$3,000-4,000

A pair of Imari jars and covers, each painted with a figure standing outside a house by a river, reserved on a foliate decorated orange and blue ground, one cover chipped, 13in (33cm).
$2,500-3,200

A pair of late Kutani squat pear-shaped jars and domed covers, painted in green, yellow, blue enamels and iron red, one cover repaired, 11½in (29.5cm).
$800-1,000

A pair of Imari jars, each with inner and outer covers, each facet painted with a jardinière of chrysanthemum or peonies within a gold decorated deep blue border, 10in (24.5cm).
$1,800-2,700

Tureens

A pair of Imari oviform jars and high domed covers, with 'shi-shi' finials, densely painted in gold ground panels, some repairs, 21in (53cm).
$7,000-8,000

A Chinese blue and white tureen and domed cover, with fruit finial and lion mask handles, painted with sprays of flowering shrubs, finial chipped, 10½in (26cm) wide. **$1,500-1,800**

A Chinese export tureen and cover, with animal head handles, each piece boldly painted with scrolls, flowers and insects in the tobacco-leaf palette, Qianlong, 13½in (34.5cm).
$10,000-11,000

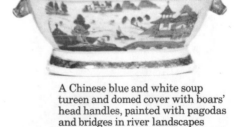

A Chinese clobbered blue and white tureen stand, later ormolu mounted on 4 rams head feet and with flowerspray handles, the porcelain 18thC, 20in (50cm) wide.
1,500-1,800

A Chinese blue and white soup tureen and domed cover with boars' head handles, painted with pagodas and bridges in river landscapes within trellis pattern bands, c1800, 12½in (32cm) wide.
$1,600-2,000

A Chinese blue and white soup tureen, cover and shaped stand, with lion mask handles and Buddhistic lion finial, painted with scattered flowersprays within borders of further flowers, trellis pattern and cell pattern, Qianlong, stand 15in (38cm) wide.
$2,700-3,600

A pair of Cantonese 'famille rose' oval vegetable tureens and covers with gilt berry finials, and a matching rectangular tureen and cover with bamboo handle, one rim chip, gilt slightly rubbed, 19thC, oval tureens 10½in (26.5cm) wide, rectangular tureen 9½in (24cm) wide.
$1,800-2,700

A Chinese porcelain covered bowl with tab handles, painted in 'famille rose' colours with peonies, 19thC, 9in (23cm). **$900-1,000**

Vases

A Cantonese vegetable tureen and domed cover, painted on a green scroll gold ground, 9½in (24cm) wide.
$720-900

A Sancai glazed vase, the body liberally splashed overall in chestnut and green on a straw-coloured ground, the glaze falling in an uneven line around the base, showing the pale buff ware of the low flat-bottomed foot, 2 restored rim chips, Tang Dynasty, 4½in (11cm).
$1,800-2,000

A pair of late Ming blue and white 'kraak porselein' double gourd vases, moulded and decorated on the exterior one neck cracked and chipped Wanli, 12in (30.5cm)
$6,000-7,000

A Transitional polychrome baluster vase, of characteristic tall shouldered form with a flared neck, painted in different shades of underglaze blue and bright polychrome enamels, damage to rim, 20in (50cm).
$2,700-3,600

A Dehua 'blanc de chine' slender pear shaped vase, with flared neck modelled in relief with a coiled dragon, chips to extremities, 17thC, 14in (36cm).
$540-650

A Transitional blue and white sleeve vase, decorated in underglaze blue, the base unglazed, slight wear, 19in (48cm).
$5,500-6,300

Two Transitional blue and white bottle vases, the tall flaring neck painted with flowersprays, one with 2 insects in flight, c1640, 13½in (34cm).
$4,500-5,500

An unusual pear shaped vase, decorated with a pair of undulating green dragons pursuing flaming pearls amid cloud scrolls, all reserved on a white ground with details in 'an hua', the base with a Hongzhi six-character mark, Kangxi, 16in (41cm).
$3,000-3,600

A pair of Imari vases, the exteriors with an allover deep cobalt underglaze blue and decorated in gilt, the inside of the rims decorated in iron red enamel and gilt on underglaze blue with sprays of peony, one with some restoration to the rim, c1700, 12½in (32cm).
$2,000-2,700

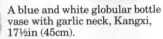

A blue and white globular bottle vase with garlic neck, Kangxi, 17½in (45cm).
$4,000-5,000

A 'famille verte' rouleau vase, the neck with bamboo sprays, encircled Xuande six-character mark, Kangxi, 7in (18cm).
$1,800-2,700

A large 'famille verte' vase with rounded shoulder and short flared neck, painted with 2 panels of equestrian figures before buildings and among clouds divided by panels of scrolling leaves, restored, Kangxi, 20in (51cm).
$1,800-2,000

A blue and white gu-shaped beaker vase, foot chip restored, rim with one small chip, encircled Chenghua six-character mark, Kangxi, 18½in (47cm).
$2,700-3,600

A 'famille verte' rouleau vase, base repaired, Kangxi, 17½in (44.5cm).
$3,600-4,500

An Arita 'Tokkuri', decorated in iron red, green, aubergine and black enamels and gilt on underglaze blue, chip to neck, c1700, 7½in (18.5cm).
$1,800-2,700

Two blue and white square vases, painted on each side with an audience scene below birds amongst lotus scroll on the sloping shoulder and precious emblems on the slightly waisted shoulders, one chip restored, fritted, impressed Xuande four-character marks, Kangxi, 11½in (29cm), wood stands.
$5,000-6,000

A 'famille rose' Mandarin pattern three-piece garniture, all reserved on a white raised-dot ground embellished with flowersprays and iron red and gilt bats, one foot rim chipped, one small rim chip re-stuck, Qianlong, 10in (25cm).
$4,000-5,000

An Imari polychrome bottle vase, painted in typical enamel colours and gold, minor glaze chip to rim, late 17thC, 12in (30.5cm).
$2,700-3,600

A pair of 'famille rose' vases and covers, each painted beneath a band of turquoise lappets embellished with flowers at the shoulder, the covers similarly decorated and surmounted by knop finials, necks with hairline cracks, covers chipped, one repaired, Qianlong, 14in (36cm).
$2,700-3,600

A 'famille verte' vase, painted with flowers issuing from rockwork between ascending and descending lappets, the shoulder with a band of half flowerheads on a green ground, Kangxi, 9in (22.5cm), wood cover.
$1,800-2,500

Two blue and white baluster vases and covers, the domed covers surmounted by lion finials, one with neck restored, one with small rim chip and cover chipped, Qianlong, 15in (38cm).
$2,000-2,800

A blue and white bottle vase, reserved on a dark blue ground, late Qianlong/Jiaqing, 17in (43.5cm).
$1,600-2,000

A Chinese 'famille rose' vase, Qianlong mark, Jiaqing, 10in (25cm).
$1,000-1,500

A rare copper red and blue and white dragon bottle vase, on a slightly splayed foot, boldly painted in copper red and underglaze cobalt blue, restored neck, cracked, seal mark and period of Qianlong, 20½in (52cm).
$8,000-9,500

A moulded Satsuma vase, decorated in various coloured enamels and gilt, neck restored, signed 'Dai Nihon Satsuma yaki Meigyokudo', late 19thC, 10in (25cm).
$3,000-4,000

A large Satsuma vase, decorated in various coloured underglaze enamels and gilt, base restored, unsigned, late 19thC, 19½in (49cm).
$5,500-6,300

An Arita polychrome vase decorated in the late Ming style, horizontal Wanli six-character mark at the rim, 19thC, 24in (61cm).
$7,000-8,000

A pair of Cantonese vases, with handles in the form of standing figures, applied at the shoulders with dragons, reserved within a diaper border on a ground painted with flowers and insects, each with an interior hair crack, 25in (63cm).
$1,500-2,000

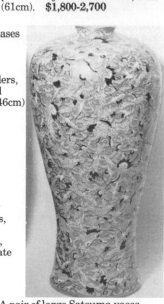

A Cantonese vase with flared neck and scalloped collared shoulder, with gilt elephant head handles, painted with Immortals divided by precious objects and flowers, 24in (61cm).   **$1,800-2,700**

A pair of Satsuma vases, decorated in various coloured enamels and gilt, signed 'Gyokushu' with impressed seal 'Taizan', late 19thC, 5in (12.5cm).
$5,500-7,000

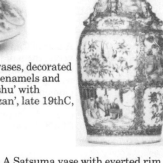

A pair of Cantonese vases with wavy rims, gilt Buddhistic lion cub handles and 'guei' dragons to the shoulders, painted on green gold scroll grounds, 18in (46cm)
$1,000-1,200

A Satsuma vase with everted rim, the blue ground finely gilded, chip to underneath rim, late 19thC, 8in (21cm).
$550-650

A pair of Satsuma oviform vases, decorated in various coloured enamels and gilt, with gilt rims, signed 'Dai Nihon Taizan sei', late 19thC, 12in (30cm).
$2,800-3,600

A pair of large Satsuma vases, decorated in enamels and gilt with a multitude of Manchurian cranes in flight, 20thC, 31½in (80cm).
$2,700-3,600

An Imari bottle vase, painted on a ground of flowering shrubs and 'ho-o', the neck with 2 dragon roundels on a ground of dense flowers, Fukugawa mark, 16in (40cm).
$1,800-2,500

A pair of Cantonese vases, with slender rounded cylindrical bodies and slightly flared necks, painted within gold key pattern surrounds divided by smaller similar panels and roundels, on grounds of butterflies, flowers and emblems, 15½in (39cm).
$2,700-3,600

A pair of Imari flattened flask-shaped oviform vases with flared rims, 9½in (24cm).
$1,200-1,500

A Satsuma vase of slender ovoid form and short neck, 9in (23cm) high.
$2,000-3,000

A Satsuma porcelain vase, with flared rim, gilt dragon handles and allover polychrome figure decoration on patterned gilt ground, 10in (25cm).
$1,200-1,400

A pair of Cantonese 'famille verte' vases, the handles modelled as standing Immortals, painted allover with groups of vessels, furniture and emblems among flowers, below green key pattern bands at the rims, one neck repaired, 24in (61cm).
$1,500-1,800

A pair of Satsuma vases, each painted on one side with warriors in a mountain landscape and on the other with a panel of flowers and birds, 6in (15cm).
$300-450

A pair of Japanese Satsuma heart-shaped vases, decorated within shaped cartouches with floral strewn borders, having square necks and pedestal bases, late 19thC, 3½in (8.5cm).
$3,000-3,600

A pair of Imari hexagonal waisted beaker vases with bulbous feet, 14in (36cm).
$2,700-3,600

A pair of Satsuma vases, painted
with panels of geese, fish beneath
wisteria, river landscapes and ladies
before flowers, all on a dark blue gilt
ground, signed, 7in (18cm).
$1,600-2,000

A Satsuma slender oviform vase,
painted in colours and gilt on one
side, the shoulder within iron red
ground band of emblems, 6½in
(17cm).
$6,500-8,000

A Satsuma vase with rounded
shoulder and foot, painted in colours
and richly gilt with 2 rectangular
panels of 'bijin', signed Seizan, 10in
(25cm).
$3,000-3,600

A large Imari vase, decorated in
typical palette, foot damaged, piece
missing, Meiji period, 42½in
(108cm).
$3,000-3,600

A pair of Satsuma vases, painted
and heavily gilt with panels of
Immortals in river landscapes, and
ladies and attendants in gardens on
a ground of stylised flowerheads,
signed, 15in (38cm).
$2,700-3,600

A Satsuma square vase with floral
decoration, 5in (13cm).
$125-180

A pair of Japanese
Satsuma vases,
highlighted in gilt,
7in (18cm).
$650-720

A pair of small Japanese Satsuma
ovoid two-handled vases, signed,
2½in (6cm).
$200-280

An Arita blue and white vase,
painted with floral medallions on a
cracked ice and prunus ground,
applied with 2 confronting dragons
in high relief, Meiji period, 17in
(44cm).
$1,200-1,500

A pair of Satsuma vases, painted in
colours and richly gilt, 7½in
(18.5cm).
$1,500-1,700

133

A pair of Imari vases of ovoid form, decorated in typical palette with birds amongst pine trees and flowering peony between formal borders, both with rim restoration, Meiji period, 18in (46cm). **$1,200-1,600**

A Japanese Kutani vase, decorated with extensive crowd scenes amidst orange and gilt highlighted clouds, Daini Pon Kutani mark on a yellow enamel rectangular panel, Meiji, 12in (30cm). **$1,800-2,700**

A Japanese Satsuma vase of tapering square section, the shoulders and foot allover decorated with gilt diaper patterns, each face with numerous figures, Meiji, 8½in (21cm). **$720-80**

A Satsuma vase and stand, with long cylindrical neck, decorated in enamels and gilt, raised on a stand with 5 mask-head feet, stand chipped and tassel chipped, Meiji period, 34½in (87cm). **$900-1,500**

A Kinkozan pottery vase of globular form, painted with an encircling band of women in conversation under sprays of wisteria, the foot and neck painted with flowers, 5in (12.5cm). **$1,700-2,000**

A Japanese porcelain vase decorated on an iron red ground, Meiji period, 11½in (29cm). **$720-90**

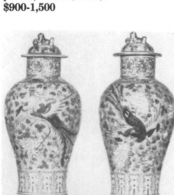

A pair of 'famille rose' turquoise ground vases and domed covers, the yellow ground necks with scrolling foliage, the covers with pink everted rims, 14in (36cm). **$900-1,000**

A pair of Kyo-Satsuma vases with waisted rims and feet, each painted in colours and gilt with a band of 'karako' among furniture on a ground of 4 birds among bamboo, 7in (18cm). **$1,400-1,800**

A pair of Chinese yellow ground Cong-shaped vases, painted in blue, green and aubergine and modelled in relief on each side with 8 trigrams, 9½in (24cm), wood stand. **$350-45**

A Chinese underglaze blue and copper red decorated vase, with angled shoulder and flared neck with pierced handles, Qianlong, 19in (48cm).
$2,700-3,600

A 'famille rose' garniture, restoration to 2 cover rims, the necks of the vases and the rim of one beaker, early Qianlong, 6½ and 7in (16 and 18cm).
$4,000-5,000

A pair of Kutani vases, each decorated with a continuous landscape with figures and buildings, Meiji period, 18in (46cm).
$7,000-8,000

A Chinese monochrome vase, with incised decoration, mid-19thC, 9in (23cm).
$320-400

A pair of important documentary Yixing vases, with superb calligraphy, signed and dated 1926, 12in (31cm).
$1,000-1,500

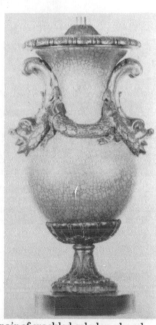

A pair of crackled celadon glazed pear-shaped vases, ormolu mounted as lamps, 24in (61cm) overall.
$3,600-4,500

A Fukagawa vase, decorated in various coloured enamels and gilt on underglaze blue and brown, signed in underglaze blue 'Dai Nihon Arita-cho Fukagawa sei', late 19thC, 15in (38cm).
$5,500-6,300

A Chinese blue and white garniture, comprising: 3 slender baluster vases and domed covers and a pair of gu-shaped beaker vases, small restorations to cover rims and one beaker rim, small hairline to one rim, Kangxi, 9½ and 11½in (24 and 29cm).
$9,000-10,000

Miscellaneous

A 'famille rose' shell-shaped cup stand, painted with sprays of flowers on the moulded dish, below a pierced holder, rim chips, Qianlong, 9in (23cm) wide.
$900-1,000

A pair of 'famille rose' Sèvres-style ice pails, each decorated with flowersprays below a floral garland, divided by gilt shell-shaped handles, chipped, one restored, Qianlong, 10in (25cm) wide.
$4,500-5,500

A Chinese green glazed brush rest, modelled as a five-peak group of craggy rocks, one peak repaired, 18thC, 6in (16cm) wide, wood stand.
$650-800

Two 'blanc de chine' joss stick holders, modelled as seated Buddhistic lions with brocade balls, one holder restored, 18thC, 10½in (26cm).
$1,000-1,200

A Chinese underglaze blue and iron red decorated compressed brush washer, painted with scrolling lotus below a band of trailing foliage and above stylised linked leaves near the foot, Qianlong, 4in (9cm).
$2,700-3,600

An Imari spitoon, painted in iron red, underglaze blue and gilt with pine branches and flowering shrubs, the globular body with a flowerspray on each side, c1700, 7in (17.5cm) diam.
$1,500-1,800

A 'famille rose' brush pot, painted around the exterior in bright enamels, the base and interior glazed turquoise and the rim gilded, seal mark and period of Jiaqing, 5½in (12.5cm).
$3,600-4,500

A Canton 'famille rose' bough pot and a cover, with 2 gilt rope-twist handles, all reserved on a relief-decorated squirrel and vine ground, 19thC, 8½in (21.5cm).
$3,000-3,600

GLASS – PRICE TRENDS 1990-91

Unlike most areas of the antiques field where a general depression exists, and where some salerooms are either shedding staff or closing down, glass has held its own and has advanced in varying degrees in many specialisations. The reason for this bucking of the trend is probably because of the general shortage on the market, an increasing interest and the often expressed statement that glass has for a long time been under-valued.

There is little point in quoting increased prices for particular glasses because in the following pages readers can compare for themselves the broad spread of prices obtained. Having said that, I give some examples of English and Continental glass that is either of interest, not in the limelight, or is not easy to obtain because of rarity and/or high price.

For instance, at a well publicised Hampshire house sale there was a broad spread of good glass and high prices were obtained from the large number of dealers and collectors present. Some good cut glass,

always difficult to find, remains in my mind; $3,960 for a pair of 'Irish' oval turnover bowls (5¾in), c1800, and $2,370 each for two larger similar bowls, $800 for a good Irish cut cream jug and $3,150 for a pair of cut 'honey jars' (comports with covers), c1800.

Of lesser value, but not of lesser interest, a large collection of 19thC coloured hyacinth bulb glasses which made about $45-65 each, and a large collection of 19/20thC witches' balls, sold in lots of five or six, which made over $180 each (a very good price).

Back to 18thC drinking glasses, Beilbys go 'marching on' and a Beilby in pristine condition with the usual enamelled fruiting vine can now easily fetch over $1,800, whereas damaged (chipped) or restored examples can still be had for $1,000 upwards. The moral is obvious and any 18thC decanter with good engraving, particularly those with the beverage engraved within a cartouche of scroll, will easily fetch over $900.

A large and varied collection, including about 60 glasses, tumblers, beakers and decanters

came onto the market late last year, instead of going into a museum as had been hoped. However, looking back at what I paid for rummers and decanters in 1981, the prices realised for similar examples in this sale showed no, or very small, increases in what I paid then. For example, two dram firing glasses with opaque twist stems with white enamelled symbols (often mistakenly attributed to the Beilby workshop) made $2,800 and $1,980 compared with $1,800 I paid for a plain stem example in a London saleroom in 1981.

In conclusion, although glass is in a rising market, which I think will continue while so little is available, prices can be unpredictable. I have always counselled that it is better to save one's money and buy one good example instead of two or three mediocre items, and if one sees a very good specimen that is needed to fill a particular gap in one's collection, then forget about price trends, guides and saleroom estimates and buy it, as in later years invariably one will not be disappointed with the purchase.

R. G. Thomas (January 1991)

Beakers

An engraved beaker, monogrammed CW, c1810, 3½in (9.4cm) high.
$150-200

A Venetian latticinio beaker in vetro a reticello, supported on 3 bun feet, early 18thC, 4in (10cm) high.
$6,500-8,000

Bottles

A 'Façon de Venise' beaker, the lower part applied with 2 rows of small curled bosses enriched with gilding beneath a milled band similarly enriched, the conical foot with applied trailed ornament, perhaps Italian or Spanish, early 17thC, 6½in (15.5cm) high.
$3,500-4,500

A South Netherlands beaker, the lower part of the cylindrical body moulded with 'nipt diamond waies' and with kick-in base, on 3 flattened bun feet, crack to base, 17thC, 5½in (14.5cm) high.
$1,500-2,000

A set of 3 blue cruet bottles, with gilt labels 'Soy', 'Ketchup' and 'Kyan', in a leather covered iron stand, c1800.
$1,200-1,600

A pair of barrel shaped spirit bottles with flute cutting and bands of diamonds, and cut ball stoppers, c1820, 6½in (17cm) high.
$300-350

A novelty duck amber glass sauce
bottle, with silver head spout, with
hinged cover, set glass eyes, by
Akers & Co., Birmingham, c1919,
6½in (16cm).
$700-800

Three square spirit bottles with
vertically fluted bodies and cut ball
shaped stoppers, in a silver plated
trefoil frame, c1820, 7in (18cm) high.
$800-1,000

An enamelled bottle and stopper,
inscribed in white 'Betty Hodgon
AP 1767' within a C-scroll and
'feuilles-de-choux' cartouche, with
teared flattened knob stopper,
slightly damaged, perhaps Scottish,
7½in (18.5cm) high.
$1,000-1,500

An 'onion' olive green tint serving
bottle with kick-in base, the applied
scroll handle with pincered
thumbpiece, c1725, 6½in (16.5cm)
high.
$1,500-1,800

A set of 3 blue club shape cruet
bottles, with gilt labels and gilt
lozenge stoppers, c1800, 4in (10cm)
high.
$1,000-1,200

Bowls

A fruit bowl with turned over rim,
diamond, serrated and geometric
cut body, on a knopped stem and
lemon squeezer foot, c1800, 8in
(20cm) high, 10½in (27cm) diam.
$2,600-3,600

A Venetian diamond engraved
armorial tazza, with a coat-of-arms
and a circle of turquoise chain
ornament between milled bands,
the waisted spreading foot applied
with a trailed collar and folded rim,
c1600, 13in (33.5cm) diam.
$15,500-16,500

*The arms are those of the Vangelisti
family of Verona.*

A Venetian enamelled deep bowl
with everted folded rim, gilt with a
wide band of scale ornament
embellished with enamelled dots in
white, iron red, green and blue, with
upturned folded blue rim, slight
damage to rim, c1500, 9½in (24cm)
diam.
$5,500-7,500

A Venetian footed bowl, the body
with gadrooned underside and with
2 applied blue filigree threads to the
folded rim, the spreading vertically
ribbed foot with an upturned folded
blue rim, 16thC, 10½in (27cm) diam.
$3,000-4,000

A Venetian enamelled bowl, with
everted folded rim and gadrooned
lower part, decorated with a gilt
band embellished with blue dots
and edged with pink and white dots
above an applied trailed blue
thread, the kick-in base with an
applied footring, mid-16thC, 6in
(14.5cm) diam.
$3,500-4,500

A tazza, the flat platform on a stem
with moulded Silesian decoration on
domed folded foot, c1750, 10in
(25cm) diam.   **$450-650**

Decanters

A Venetian tazza, the tray with upturned rim decoration on the underside with applied turquoise chain ornament between clear milled bands, supported on a waisted spreading stem with a trailed collar and folded foot, early 17thC, 11in (27.5cm) diam.
$2,500-3,500

A pair of Webb rock crystal shallow dishes, engraved by W. Fritsche in an intaglio technique with swags of fruit including pineapples and pears encircling oval bosses enclosed within berried foliage, one signed, c1890, 6½in (15.5cm) diam. **$1,800-2,800**

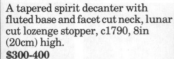

A tapered spirit decanter with fluted base and facet cut neck, lunar cut lozenge stopper, c1790, 8in (20cm) high.
$300-400

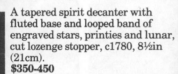

A tapered spirit decanter with fluted base and looped band of engraved stars, printies and lunar, cut lozenge stopper, c1780, 8½in (21cm).
$350-450

An engraved ale decanter, the reverse inscribed Mathew Tankey Harble Down Kent, c1775, the inscription perhaps later, 10½in (26.5cm) high.
$700-900

A pair of clear spirit decanters with a gilt band of fruiting vine and labelled 'Brandy' and 'Rum', with gilt lozenge stoppers, c1790, 8in (20cm) high.
$700-800

A pair of glass decanters and stoppers, each painted in gold with an encircling band of scrolling foliage above a flute cut base, the shoulder cut with a diamond and fan design below a faceted triple ring neck, slight damage to one stopper, 19thC, 9½in (24.5cm).
$350-450

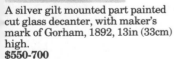

A silver gilt mounted part painted cut glass decanter, with maker's mark of Gorham, 1892, 13in (33cm) high.
$550-700

Four blue decanters with gilt cartouches and gilt lozenge stoppers, c1800, 7 to 7½in (18 to 19.5cm) high. **$350-450 each**

l. A spirit decanter, engraved with fleur de lys and looped decoration, c1790, 8in (20.5cm) high.
$350-450

r. A decanter with cut star and looped decoration, lunar cut stopper, c1780, 9½in (24cm) high.
$700-800

l. An ovoid decanter with flute cut base and shoulder, three plain neck rings and with target stopper, c1810, 8in (20cm) high.
$300-380
c. A cylindrical spirit decanter with flute, prism and diamond cutting and prism cut neck, with mushroom stopper, c1825, 7½in (19cm) high.
$150-200
r. An ovoid decanter with cut neck rings and mushroom stopper, c1820, 9in (22.5cm) high.
$300-350

l. & r. A pair of blue spirit decanters with three neck rings and plain lozenge stoppers, c1800, 8in (19.5cm) high.
$900-1,000
c. A blue spirit bottle with everted rim, c1820, 9½in (24cm) high.
$250-350

Two 'Bristol' blue decanters with gilt labels for 'Hollands', and gilt stoppers, c1790, 7in (18cm) high.
$350-450 each

l. & r. A pair of plain ovoid spirit decanters with three bladed neck rings and target stoppers, c1810, 7in (18cm) high.
$350-450
c. An ovoid spirit decanter with flute cut tapered body, spiral neck ring and diamond cut, with lozenge stopper, c1800, 7½in (19cm) high.
$320-420

l. An ovoid spirit decanter with three cut neck rings and mushroom stopper, c1810, 7in (18cm) high.
$200-300
r. An ovoid decanter with three plain neck rings and target stopper, c1810, 8½in (21.5cm) high.
$350-450

l. A flute cut ovoid decanter with annulated neck rings, and target stopper, c1810, 9in (23cm) high. **$270-450**
r. A straight sided decanter with plain neck rings and cut mushroom stopper, c1810, 8½in (21cm) high.
$270-370

l. & r. A pair of ovoid decanters with wide base fluting and flute cut necks, with target stoppers, c1810, 8½in (21cm) high.
$1,000-1,200
c. A tapered decanter engraved with looped ribbon, bows and Prince of Wales' feathers, flute cut base and neck, lozenge stopper, c1780, 8in (20cm) high.
$270-370

l. An ovoid decanter with flute cut base and neck, and cut mushroom stopper, c1810, 8in (20cm) high.
$200-300
c. A spirit decanter with a band of small cut diamonds, c1810, 7½in (19cm) high.
$200-300
r. An ovoid spirit decanter with flute cut neck and base, cut mushroom stopper, c1810, 7in (18cm) high.
$150-200

l. & r. A pair of round spirit decanters, with base flute cutting and a band of diamonds, prism cut necks and cut mushroom stoppers, c1815, 6½in (16.5cm) high.
$450-650
c. A barrel shaped spirit decanter with moulded prism bands, pouring neck and cut ball stopper, c1825, 6in (15.5cm) high.
$150-350

l. A pair of flute and diamond cut decanters, with cut neck rings and flat topped mushroom stoppers, c1830, 9in (22cm) high.
$800-1,000
r. A pair of decanters with ovoid bodies, flute, diamond and prism cutting, cut mushroom stoppers, c1830, 7½in (19cm) high.
$1,000-1,200

l. & r. A pair of square spirit decanters, with prism and strawberry diamond cutting, cut ball stoppers, c1825, 7in (17cm) high.
$350-550
c. A pair of round spirit decanters, with flute and diamond cutting, annulated neck rings, cut mushroom stoppers, c1820, 7in (17cm) high.
$450-550

A pair of cut glass ship's decanters, with cut triple neck rings and mushroom stoppers, c1880, 9½in (24cm) high.
$800-900

l. A cylindrical shaped decanter with flute and diamond cutting, diamond cut neck rings and cut mushroom stopper, c1825, 9in (23cm) high.
$300-400
c. A plain ovoid decanter with flute cut base and shoulder, plain neck rings, engraved with the initials 'MG', target stopper, c1810, 9in (22.5cm) high.
$350-450
r. A decanter with plain neck rings, c1825, 9in (23cm) high.
$300-400

A set of 3 spirit decanters with prism, small diamond and printy cutting, 2 neck rings and cut mushroom stoppers, c1825, 8in (19.5cm) high.
$800-900

A set of 4 cut glass cordial decanters without stoppers, with knopped and faceted necks above sloping faceted shoulders, the sides with a central engraved medallion bearing the titles 'Shrub', 'Mint', 'Raspberry' and 'Lovage' respectively, within an engraved grapevine garland, on star cut bases, 19thC, 11in (28cm) high.
$700-900

Drinking Glasses

A set of 10 dwarf ale glasses, with conical bowls wrythen moulded at their bases, on plain conical feet, c1810, 5in (13cm).
$800-1,000
A tazza with hollow Silesian stem, domed folded foot, c1760, 8½in (21cm) diam.
$450-550

An ale glass, with engraved deep funnel bowl, on a stem with a double series opaque twist stem, plain conical foot, c1760, 8in (19.5cm).
$900-1,000

A slender ale glass, the trumpet bowl engraved with a Jacobite rose and bud, the reverse with hops and barley, on a drawn stem with air twist cable on folded conical foot, c1750, 8in (19.5cm).
$3,000-3,500

GLASS

l. A dwarf ale glass, with engraved conical bowl on an unusual stem and plain conical foot, c1790, 6in (15cm).
$70-110
c. A fluted wine glass, on a drawn stem with centre knop and plain conical foot, c1830, 5in (13cm).
$35-90
r. A pair of Wellington flutes, the conical bowls flute cut at the bases, collared and bladed knop stems and plain feet, c1825, 7in (17cm).
$110-180

An unusual ale glass, the trumpet bowl engraved with fruiting vine, on a plain drawn stem with air tear, folded conical foot, c1750, 7½in (18.5cm).
$650-800

An ale flute, with flared waisted bowl on air twist stem enclosing central spiral column, 18thC, 8½in (21cm).
$900-1,000

l. A dwarf ale glass, engraved with hops and barley on plain drawn stem and folded conical foot, c1790, 6in (15cm) high.
$70-100
r. A dwarf ale glass, the plain conical bowl on a short knopped stem and folded conical foot, c1790, 5in (13cm) high.
$55-90

An ale glass, with round funnel bowl set on a double series opaque twist stem and plain conical foot, 7in (17cm).
$235-320

A set of 4 dwarf ale glasses, with engraved conical bowls on plain conical feet below plain drawn stems, 6in (15cm).
$90-145 each

Two dwarf ale glasses, with engraved conical bowls on plain drawn stems with folded conical feet, 5½ and 6in (14 and 15cm).
$90-145 each

A 'Façon de Venise' flute, the slender funnel bowl supported on a flattened ribbed knop set between 2 mereses, on a conical foot with thinly folded rim, The Netherlands, mid-17thC, 11in (28cm).
$3,500-4,500

A composite stemmed wine flute of drawn form with a slender bell bowl, the stem filled with air-twist spirals and set into a beaded inverted baluster knop, on a domed foot, c1750, 8½in (21cm).
$1,500-1,700

A dwarf ale glass, the conical bowl on a stem with a collar and bladed knop, plain conical foot, c1825, 6in (14.5cm).
$55-110

A champagne flute, with honeycomb moulded lower part supported on a shoulder knopped stem above a conical foot, mid-18thC, 8in (20cm). **$350-450**

A cordial glass, with engraved funnel bowl on a double series air-twist stem and plain conical foot, c1745, 7in (17cm). **$900-1,000**

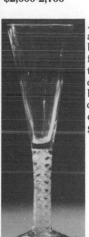

A Williamite opaque twist cordial glass, the funnel bowl inscribed 'Our Glorious & Immortal King William III', the stem with two entwined corkscrew spirals, on a conical foot, c1770, 7in (17cm). **$2,000-2,700**

A baluster goblet, the stem with an angular knop above a true baluster section, on a conical foot, c1730, 8½in (21.5cm). **$1,200-1,600**

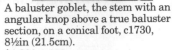

A Williamite cordial glass, the funnel bowl inscribed below the rim 'The glorious memory of King Will III', above a band of foliate ornament, supported on a plain stem above a domed foot, small chip to footrim, c1750, 7in (17cm). **$2,600-3,600**

A set of 9 opaque twist ale flutes, the bowls with hammered flutes to the lower parts, the stems with gauze corkscrew cores within ten-ply spirals, on conical feet, 4 with chips, c1765, 7in (17cm). **$2,600-3,000**

A set of 10 opaque twist ale flutes, the funnel bowls with hammered flutes to the lower parts, the stems with gauze corkscrew cores entwined by ten-ply spirals, on conical feet, 4 with chips, c1765, 7in (18cm). **$3,000-3,500**

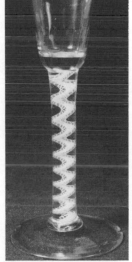

A cordial glass, the round funnel bowl on a double series opaque twist stem and plain conical foot, c1760, 6½in (16.5cm). **$800-900**

A baluster cordial glass, the waisted bucket bowl supported on a flattened knop, the stem with swelling waist knop enclosing a large and a small tear, on a conical foot, c1725, 6in (15cm). **$900-1,000**

A baluster goblet, supported on a ball knop terminating in a basal knop and enclosing 2 small tears, on a folded conical foot, c1700, 6½in (16cm). **$1,800-2,200**

A goblet with trumpet bowl, on a drawn plain stem with small air tear, plain conical foot, c1745, 9in (22cm).
$350-550

A pair of goblets, with trumpet bowls and drawn plain stems with air tears, folded conical feet, c1730.
$1,000-1,200

A cordial glass with engraved ogee bowl, on a stem with a double series opaque twist stem, and plain conical foot, c1760, 5½in (14cm).
$800-1,000

GLASS APPENDIX

Drinking glasses

STEM FORMATIONS

 ball knop

  collar

 annular knop

annulated knop

 true baluster

swelling knop

 flattened knop

 cushioned knop

 inverted baluster

the knop proper

cone knop

 angular knop

 acorn knop

 drop knop

 cylinder knop

 wide angular knop

shoulder knop

mushroom knop

 true baluster ridged

BOWL FORMS

 lipped bucket

 incurved bucket

 bucket

 conical

 bell, with solid base

 waisted, with solid base

 waisted, with solid base

 round funnel

 cup

 waisted ogee

 waisted bucket

 hexagonal

 thistle

 trumpet

 waisted

 bell

 lipped

 pan-topped

 bucket-topped

 pointed

 ogee

 trumpet

 waisted

 saucer-topped

FOOT FORMS

 folded

firing

solid conical

plain conical

pedestal

stepped square foot

domed square foot

flanged

terrace-domed solid square foot

domed and folded

A champagne or ale glass, the very deep bowl fluted at base on double series opaque twist stem and plain conical foot, c1760, 10in (25cm). **$650-800**

A pair of Richardson's 'Waterlily' goblets, painted with a continuous frieze of flowering waterlilies, marked Richardson's Vitrified and with registry mark for 1848, 6½in (16.5cm). **$2,000-2,800**

A baluster goblet, the funnel bowl supported on an inverted baluster stem above a folded conical foot, c1705, 7in (17cm). **$1,000-1,200**

An engraved air-twist goblet of Jacobite significance, with double knopped stem filled with spiral threads, on a domed foot, c1750, 8in (20cm). **$1,200-1,500**

A light baluster armorial goblet, in the manner of Jacob Sang, the funnel bowl engraved with the crowned arms of Willem V of Orange and Nassau within the Garter, above the motto 'Je Maintiendrai', on an angular knop, above a beaded inverted baluster stem and base knop, on a domed conical foot, c1760, 8in (19.5cm). **$1,000-1,500**

A Nuremburg engraved goblet, attributed to Herman Schwinger, supported on hollow cushion and inverted baluster knops divided by plain sections and sets of mereses, base of stem and foot damaged, c1680, 13in (33cm). **$6,500-7,000**

A cordial glass, with drawn trumpet bowl and multiple series air-twist stem, small chip to foot rim, 18thC, 7in (17cm) high. **$650-800**

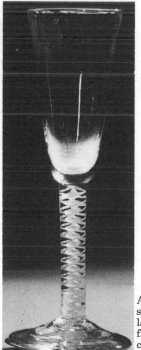

A goblet, with engraved bowl, the air-twist stem with swelling waist knop and filled with spiral threads, on a conical foot, c1750, 9in (22cm). **$900-1,000**

A set of 6 opaque twist flutes with slender funnel bowls, the stems with laminated corkscrew cores within five-ply spirals, on conical feet, c1765, 7in (18cm). **$2,600-3,600**

A Venetian goblet, the funnel bowl moulded with vertical ribs and supported on a merese over a barley sugar twist stem and conical foot, early 17thC, 8in (20cm).
$4,500-5,500

A Sunderland Bridge rummer with engraved bucket bowl, on bladed knopped stem and plain conical foot, c1820, 5½in (14cm).
$650-800

A Sunderland rummer, with engraved bowl, inscribed 'Sunderland Bridge' in diamond point with cut tasselled drapery below, the reverse inscribed 'C.F. Barber Golden Inn Boston' and with a rampant lion, flanked by sprays of rose, thistle and shamrock, on a short knopped stem and circular foot, c1825, 9in (22cm).
$1,400-1,500

l. A round funnel bowl wine glass, engraved with fruiting vine, and plain conical foot, c1750, 6in (15cm).
$350-450
c. A trumpet bowl wine glass, on drawn stem and folded conical foot, c1745, 7½in (19cm).
$270-370
r. A trumpet bowl wine glass, with solid section double knop stem and plain domed foot, c1745.
$450-650

A baluster wine glass, the bell bowl supported on a slender inverted baluster stem enclosing a large tear and terminating in a basal knop, on a folded conical foot, c1715, 7in (17cm).
$800-900

l. & r. A pair of bucket bowl rummers, with flute cutting on bladed knop stems and plain feet, c1825, 5½in (14cm).
$180-280
c. A bucket bowl rummer, c1825, 5in (13cm).
$90-140

A pair of wine glasses, with waisted trumpet bowls on stems with multiple spiral air-twists, with central vermicular collars and plain conical feet, c1745, 7in (17cm).
$650-800 each

Three ovoid rummers, with collars, square domed lemon squeezer feet, c1800, 5 and 5½in (13 and 13.5cm).
$110-140 each

A heavy baluster wine glass, the thistle bowl with solid base and air tear, on a stem with annulated and base knops with air tear, domed folded foot, c1710, 6½in (15.5cm).
$1,800-2,800

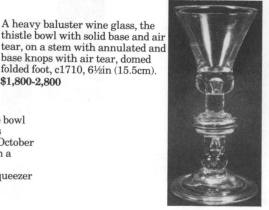

A Nelson ovoid rummer, the bowl engraved 'Trafalgar may his memory never be forgotten October 21st 1805', with an anchor in a shield, reverse shield with monogram, square lemon squeezer foot, c1805, 5½in (14cm).
$1,200-1,400

A Bohemian blue overlay cut goblet and cover with oviform hexagonal finial, gilding rubbed and foot chipped, 13in (33cm).
$1,600-2,000

A small rummer, the flared bucket bowl inscribed 'Wellington for Ever' above a naked sword, the reverse with a bird in flight with a twig in its beak, early 19thC, 4½in (11cm).
$270-370

A wine glass, with trumpet bowl on a drawn stem with multiple spiral air-twist and plain conical foot, c1745, 6½in (16.5cm).
$280-450

A baluster wine glass, the bell bowl with a tear to the solid lower part, supported on an annulated knop above a plain section enclosing an elongated tear and basal knop, on a folded conical foot, c1725, 6in (15cm).
$650-800

Two similar ovoid rummers with capstan stems and plain feet, c1825, 4½ and 5in (12 and 13cm).
$90-120 each

A heavy baluster wine glass, the conical bowl with deep solid section and air tear, on a stem with an inverted baluster and base knop, folded conical foot, c1710, 7in (17cm).
$2,000-2,700

A balustroid wine glass of 'Kit Kat' type and drawn trumpet shape, the stem with a slender tear, set on an inverted baluster section above a folded conical foot, c1740, 7in (17cm).
$650-800

A large Victorian rummer, the upper part wheel engraved with a boxing scene, the lower part diamond cut, 7in (17cm).
$300-360

A Jacobite wine glass, the trumpet bowl engraved with the Jacobite rose, 2 buds, oak leaf and star, a drawn multiple spiral air-twist stem and folded conical foot, c1745, 6in (15cm).
$2,600-3,600

A wine glass with bell bowl, on a stem with an inverted baluster and base knop, folded conical foot, c1715, 6in (15cm).
$650-800

A trumpet bowl wine glass, on a stem with multiple spiral air-twist, and plain conical foot, c1745, 7½in (19cm).
$550-700

l. A double ogee bowl rummer, with capstan stem and plain foot, c1830, 5in (12.5cm).
$110-130
c. A rummer with round bowl and capstan stem, on domed plain foot, c1810, 5½in (13.5cm).
$110-140
r. A rummer with ovoid bowl, capstan stem and plain conical foot, c1810, 5in (13cm).
$110-140

A wine glass with the trumpet bowl, on a drawn stem with multiple spiral air-twist, folded conical foot, c1750, 6in (15cm).
$270-470

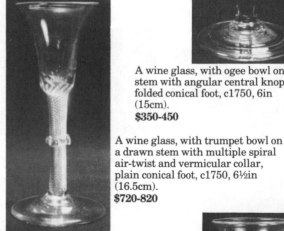

Four small wine glasses, one with engraved rim, two with engraved bowls and one plain, 1750-1810.
$55-75 each

A bobbin knopped wine glass with an ogee bowl, the stem formed as 8 cushion knops above a domed and folded foot, mid-18thC, 6½in (16.5cm).
$1,200-1,500

A wine glass, with ogee bowl on a stem with angular central knop, on folded conical foot, c1750, 6in (15cm).
$350-450

A wine glass, with trumpet bowl on a drawn stem with multiple spiral air-twist and vermicular collar, plain conical foot, c1750, 6½in (16.5cm).
$720-820

l. A plain stem wine glass, with trumpet bowl on folded conical foot, c1750, 5in (13cm).
$270-370
c. A plain stem wine glass on folded conical foot, c1750, 7½in (18cm).
$270-370
r. A wine glass with round funnel bowl, rim engraved with a band of hatched curtain decoration, plain stem, on plain conical foot, c1750, 5in (13cm).
$270-370

A glass with bell bowl, on a stem with a collar and centre swelling knop, domed base knop and folded foot, c1750, 5in (13cm).
$350-550

A Jacobite air-twist wine glass, with engraved funnel bowl, the stem filled with spiral threads above a domed foot, c1750, 7in (17cm).
$1,600-2,000

Three air-twist wine glasses:
l. With trumpet bowl on drawn multiple spiral air-twist stem and folded conical foot, c1745, 6½in (16cm).
$350-450
c. With round funnel bowl with single series air-twist cable stem, on plain conical foot, c1745, 6in (15.5cm).
$550-650
r. With bell bowl and multiple spiral air-twist stem with shoulder knop, on plain conical foot, c1750, 6in (15.5cm).
$260-360

A 'Newcastle' wine glass, the round funnel bowl engraved with a band of cross hatching and stars with a floral meander below, angular and air-beaded inverted baluster and base knops, on plain conical foot, c1750, 7½in (18cm).
$1,800-2,800

A wine glass, the round funnel bowl on a stem with double series air-twist, plain conical foot, c1750, 6in (15cm).
$450-550

A Williamite plain stemmed wine glass of drawn shape, the bell bowl inscribed 'The Glorious Memory of King William III', on a conical foot, mid-18thC, 6½in (16cm).
$1,500-2,000

A pair of wine glasses, with round funnel bowls on stems with shoulder cushion knop and multiple spiral air-twist stems, and plain conical feet, c1750, 7in (18cm).
$900-1,200

A wine glass, the round funnel bowl on a stem with multiple spiral air-twist, on plain conical foot, c1750, 7in (18cm).
$450-650

A wine glass, the bowl on a stem with multiple spiral air-twist with swelling knop, plain conical foot, c1750, 6in (15.5cm).
$900-1,000

A wine glass, the trumpet bowl on a drawn plain stem, plain conical foot, c1750, 6in (15.5cm).
$280-380

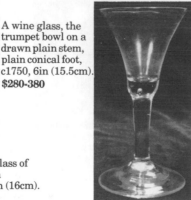

A Jacobite air-twist wine glass of drawn trumpet shape, with engraved bowl, c1750, 6½in (16cm).
$1,800-2,800

l. A wine glass, the moulded round funnel bowl on a stem with a double series opaque twist, plain conical foot, c1750, 6in (15cm).
$350-450
r. A cordial glass, the small round funnel bowl on a stem with a double series opaque twist, plain conical foot, c1760, 6in (15cm).
$800-900

l. A plain stem wine glass, the trumpet bowl with air tear at base, on folded conical foot, c1750, 6in (14.5cm).
$210-280
c. A wine glass, with engraved ogee bowl, plain stem, on folded conical foot, c1750, 5½in (14cm).
$260-360
r. A wine glass, the round funnel bowl on plain stem with folded conical foot, c1750, 5½in (14cm).
$180-250

Three wine glasses with multiple spiral air-twist stems, on plain conical feet:
l. With bell bowl and shoulder knop, c1750, 6½in (16cm).
$300-380
c. With trumpet bowl and plain stem, c1750, 5½in (14cm).
$320-350
r. With round funnel bowl and shoulder knop, c1750, 6½in (16cm).
$450-550

A balustroid wine glass, the bell bowl on a stem with angular knop above a true baluster knop, and plain conical foot, c1745, 7in (18cm).
$900-1,000

JACOBITE GLASSES

Jacobite glasses, which began to be engraved c1730, have commanded much attention and popularity among collectors. The dating and the significance of the various motifs on these glasses is still the subject of debate and disagreement, but considered opinion is that few of them can be dated to before Culloden in 1746. Jacobite engraved glasses continued to be produced through the various stem formations (plain, air-twist, opaque and faceted) until the death of Prince Charles Edward Stuart in 1788. Countless numbers of old glasses have been later engraved. There were also the counter Jacobite glasses supporting the Loyalists but these are considerably fewer in number.

A pair of Dorflinger engraved colourless glass goblets, minor chip on lip of one, each with paper label on the base, Brooklyn, New York, c1900, 10½in (26cm) high.
$800-1,200

A light green balustroid wine glass of export type, with cup bowl and knopped stem on plain domed foot, c1760, 6½in (16cm).
$900-1,000

A wine glass, the ovoid body engraved with a band of hatched decoration and rosebud spray, single series opaque twist, on plain conical foot, c1760, 5½in (13cm).
$250-450

Three opaque twist wine glasses with double series twists and plain conical feet, c1760, 5½ to 6in (14.5 to 15.5cm).
$280-380

A wine glass, the trumpet bowl with honeycomb moulded, incised twist stem, on plain conical foot, c1750, 6½in (16cm).
$650-800

l. A 'Newcastle' wine glass, the trumpet bowl with air beaded, knopped stem, on folded conical foot, c1750, 7½in (18cm).
$1,500-1,600
c. A cordial glass, the moulded round funnel bowl on a double series opaque twist stem, on plain conical foot, c1760, 6½in (17cm).
$1,000-1,600
r. A wine glass, the trumpet bowl on a drawn plain stem, with air tear, on plain conical foot, c1750, 6½in (16cm).
$200-300

A Jacobite light baluster wine glass, with engraved bowl, on conical foot, c1750, 6½in (16cm).
$2,600-3,600

A Jacobite air-twist wine glass, with engraved bowl, the stem with a swelling waist knop and filled with spiral threads, on a conical foot, c1750, 6in (15cm).
$900-1,000

An engraved quadruple knopped opaque twist wine glass, the bell bowl with a border of beehives and bees, the stem with a gauze core entwined by 2 spiral threads, on a conical foot, c1765, 7in (17cm).
$1,500-1,600

A Lynn wine glass, the round funnel bowl with horizontally ribbed bands, with a double series opaque twist stem, on plain conical foot, c1760, 6in (15cm).
$1,400-1,600

A Williamite wine glass of drawn shape, the bell bowl engraved and inscribed 'The Glorious Memory of King William III', the rim with hatched ornament, the plain stem enclosing an elongated tear and on a conical foot, mid-18thC, 7in (17cm).
$1,700-2,700

A Jacobite wine glass, the round funnel bowl engraved with rose and a bud, on a multiple spiral air-twist stem, on plain conical foot, c1750, 6½in (16cm).
$1,400-1,500

A wine glass, the ovoid bowl engraved with stars and printies on a drawn stem, diamond facet cut with centre knop and plain conical foot, c1770, 5in (13cm).
$300-380

l. A wine glass, with pan top bowl on a stem with a multiple spiral air-twist, on folded conical foot, c1750, 7in (17cm).
$700-800
r. A wine glass, the bell bowl on a drawn stem with multiple spiral air-twist, on plain conical foot, c1750, 7½in (18cm).
$500-700

l. A set of 3 green wine glasses, with cup shaped, honeycomb moulded bowls, on facet cut baluster stems, with plain conical feet, c1850, 5½in (13cm).
$120-160 each
r. A set of 4 amber, rib moulded bowl wine glasses, with plain stems, and plain feet, c1840, 5in (12cm).
$90-120 each

l. A green wine glass with cup shaped bowl, ball knopped stem and plain conical foot, c1770, 5in (12cm).
$250-450
r. A green wine glass, with conical bowl, ball knopped stem and plain conical foot, c1820, 5½in (13cm).
$90-120

A set of 4 unusual emerald green wine glasses, with cup shaped bowls and everted rims, bladed knop stems and plain conical feet, c1830, 4in (10cm).
$650-800

A composite stemmed wine glass, the funnel bowl supported on an annulated knop above an opaque twist shoulder knopped stem with a gauze core enclosed within 2 spiral threads, on a conical foot, c1765, 6½in (16cm).
$900-1,000

A set of 10 green wine glasses, with bladed knop stems, on plain conical feet, c1830, 5in (13cm).
$1,000-1,200

A round funnel bowl wine glass, on single series opaque twist stem, on conical foot, 6in (15cm).
$120-180

A set of 4 small wines, from a part service consisting of wine glass cooler, spirit decanter, 2 tumblers, c1820, wines 4½in (11cm).
$650-800 the set

l. A pair of wines, with bucket bowls, band of engraving, knopped stems and plain feet, c1870, 4½in (11cm).
$40-90
r. A pair of wines, with conical bowls, star and printy engraving, drawn stems and folded conical feet, c1820, 5in (12cm).
$40-90

A wine glass, the ogee bowl engraved with an entwined Jacobite rose and a thistle, set on a double series opaque twist stem and conical foot, 6in (15cm).
$650-800

Four wine glasses, 2 with drawn stems, c1825, 3½ and 4in (9 and 10cm).
$50-90 each

A set of 6 green wine glasses, with conical bowls and bladed knop stems, on plain conical feet, c1825, 5½in (13cm).
$380-480

An ogee bowl wine glass with multi-spiral opaque twist stem, on conical foot, chips to foot, 5in (12.5cm).
$210-280

A pair of wine glasses with bell bowls, on multi-spiral opaque twist stems, chips to foot, 5in (12.5cm).
$300-380

l. A pair of wine glasses with engraved bowls, on plain drawn stems, with plain conical feet, c1820, 4in (10cm).
$110-180
r. A pair of wine glasses cut with stars, c1820, 4in (10cm).
$110-180

A wine glass with bell bowl, on multi-spiral opaque twist stem and conical foot, 6½in (16cm).
$110-150

A round funnel bowl wine glass, on multi-spiral opaque twist stem, and conical foot, 7½in (19cm).
$150-200

A trumpet drawn wine glass, the stem with tear inclusion on domed and folded foot, 6½in (16cm).
$180-220

Three plain stem wine glasses, the trumpet bowls on drawn stems with air tears, c1750.
l. 5½in (14cm). **$200-280**
c. 6½in (16cm). **$200-280**
r. 7in (17cm). **$250-350**

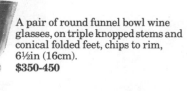

An armorial opaque twist wine glass, the bowl engraved with a coat-of-arms surmounted by a crest within scroll mantling, on a double series stem and conical foot, chip to footrim, c1765, 6in (15cm).
$350-450

An engraved wine glass with bell bowl, with fruiting vine on a multi-spiral opaque twist stem and conical foot, chips to foot, 6½in (16cm).
$180-240

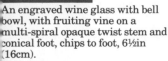

A pair of round funnel bowl wine glasses, on triple knopped stems and conical folded feet, chips to rim, 6½in (16cm).
$350-450

A wine glass, the ogee bowl set on a double series opaque twist stem and plain conical foot, 5½in (14cm).
$180-280

153

A pan topped bowl wine glass, with double series opaque twist stem and conical foot, chips to foot, 6in (15cm).
$100-160

A pair of ogee bowl wine glasses, on double series opaque twist stems and spreading feet, chips to foot, 5in (12cm).
$450-550

A panel moulded ogee bowl wine glass, on multi-spiral opaque twist stem and conical foot, 6½in (16cm).
$250-300

An engraved water glass, with engraved bell bowl, on a spreading conical foot with folded rim, c1740, 4½in (11cm).
$450-550

A dated, engraved barrel shaped tumbler, one side with a view of Yarmouth Church, named above, the reverse with the initials 'JRP' above the date '1798', and inscribed above and below 'Plenty to a Generous Mind/Success to Farming', the lower part cut with flutes, 5in (12cm).
$1,600-2,000

A dated engraved tumbler inscribed 'Mary Moody 1766', within a shaped scrolling foliage cartouche, 4½in (11cm).
$650-700

An engraved water glass of Jacobite significance, the bell bowl engraved with a sunflower and a moth, c1870, 3in (7cm).
$900-1,000

Four trumpet drawn wine glasses, on multi air-twist stems and conical feet.
$550-650

A Jacobite wine glass, with bucket bowl engraved with flower and moth, on air-twist stem, with double knop, 6in (15cm).
$730-800

A firing glass, the ovoid bowl fluted at base, on a drawn stem with a conical undersewn foot, c1780, 3½in (9cm).
$230-300

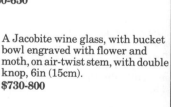

Three dram glasses with ogee bowls and plain drawn stems, c1780.
l. 3½in (9cm). **$50-90**
c. With rare undersewn foot, and moulded bowl, 4in (10cm).
$250-300
r. 4in (10cm). **$50-90**

A crested shipping tumbler, inscribed 'Suc^s to the Bee' beneath a sailing ship, flanked by ears of barley, the reverse with the initials 'RG' beneath a crest with a bird to the left, late 18thC, 5in (13cm).
$650-700

l. A barrel shaped tumbler with band of hatched decoration, c1800, 4½in (11cm).
$140-180
r. A tapered beaker engraved with band of hatched roses and inscription 'George and Mary Owen 1835', 4in (10cm).
$150-200

An engraved cylindrical tumbler decorated with a continuous scene, with facet cut footrim and the base with 'LLH' monogram, c1800, 4½in (11cm).
$700-800

l. A dwarf ale glass, the conical bowl engraved with hops and barley, plain drawn stem, on conical foot, c1790, 6in (15cm).
$200-270
c. A port glass, with engraved band, plain stem, c1830, 5½in (14cm).
$40-80
r. A wine glass, the ovoid bowl with band of looped star and printy cutting and engraving, on plain conical foot, c1790, 5in (12cm).
$90-140

A firing/dram glass, the ogee bowl on a short plain stem and terraced conical foot, c1760, 3½in (9cm).
$230-300

A panel moulded ogee bowl wine glass, on double series opaque twist stem and conical foot, chips to foot, 6in (15cm).
$200-300

Jugs

A two-handled baluster mug, with lightly ribbed everted rim and on a circular foot, mid-18thC, 5in (12cm).
$650-720

A green glass claret jug and stopper, of faceted form with ribbed neck, early 19thC, 11in (28cm).
$650-750

Four Nailsea jugs, with olive green bodies and opaque white marvered splashes, c1810, 4½ to 7½in (11 to 19cm).
$450-900 each

A pair of Continental cut glass claret jugs, with bracket handles and domed hinged covers with artichoke finials, the mounts die stamped with rococo flowers and foliage incorporating vacant cartouches, 11½in (29cm).
$1,600-2,600

A claret jug, the globular body with broad cut fluting, 2 neck rings, and cut spout, applied strap handle similarly cut and mushroom stopper, c1840, 10½in (26.5cm).
$650-750

A Georgian ale jug, with engraved hops, barley and monogram, with pinched loop handle, 7in (18cm).
$650-750

An oviform cut jug, with an applied opaque panel painted in colours within a cartouche of scrolls and foliage in gilding, on an octagonal knopped stem and foot, handle damaged and repaired, gilding rubbed, 13½in (34cm) and a pair of goblets.
$900-1,000

Paperweights

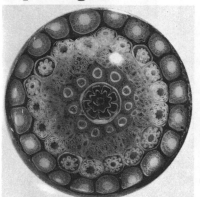

A Bacchus close concentric millefiori weight, in shades of pink, blue, white and yellow about a central red and white lobed cane and with a circle of green lined hollow crimped tubes at the periphery, mid-19thC, 3½in (8.5cm) diam.
$1,200-1,400

An Islington Glass Co., close concentric millefiori mantel ornament, in shades of pink, white and dark blue, supported on a facet cut knop and fluted inverted baluster stem, above an hexagonal foot, late 19thC, 5½in (14cm) high.
$1,700-2,000

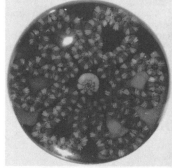

A Clichy blue ground patterned millefiori weight, the central pale blue and white cane enclosed by a hexafoil looped garland of green centred pink and white canes, set on a translucent dark blue ground, mid-19thC, 3in (7.5cm) diam.
$1,200-1,500

A Paul Stankard spray weight, with pink flowers and buds with green leaves and brown stalk, the underside of the spray with a cane inscribed 'S', 1970s, 2½in (7cm) diam.
$800-1,000

A Baccarat flower paperweight, with millefiori flowers on a bed of 5 leaves within a border of star and pastry mould canes on an amber ground, cut with 6 side printies, chipped, mid-19thC, 3in (8cm) diam.
$540-740

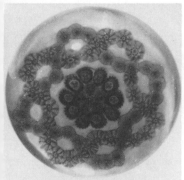

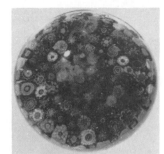

A Clichy 'Sodden Snow' patterned millefiori weight, in pale green, red, blue and pink, on an opaque white ground, mid-19thC, 3in (8cm) diam.
$800-900

A small clear glass paperweight, enclosing a single pink clematis flower flanked by 2 buds and 5 leaves, with star cut base, probably Baccarat, 2in (4.5cm) diam.
$750-850

A Clichy close millefiori weight, with pink, green and white staves, slight bruising, mid-19thC, 2½in (6.5cm) diam.
$2,700-3,700

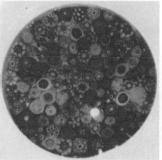

A Clichy close millefiori weight, with pink, dark blue, pale blue, white and green staves, mid-19thC, 3in (7cm) diam.
$1,000-1,200

A Bacchus close concentric millefiori weight, in shades of red, blue, pink, white and pale mauve, mid-19thC, 3½in (8.5cm) diam.
$1,000-1,200

A Clichy swirl weight, the alternate turquoise and white staves radiating from a large red, white and blue cane with a yellow stamen centre, mid-19thC, 3in (8cm) diam.
$1,200-1,500

Vases

A Venetian mould blown vase, the body with flared neck moulded with a frieze of cherub's heads alternating with escutcheon and with stylised foliage between, the lower part with radial gadroons, supported on a lightly ribbed compressed knop above a spreading foot with folded rim, 16thC, 8½in (22cm) high.
$21,000-25,000

A Bohemian glass vase, the body painted with cows wading in a stream before a house, enclosed by gilt medallion, the reverse painted with a floral bouquet also enclosed by gilt medallion, interspaced by a white fluted lozenge shaped panel above acanthus leaf lappet, on scrolling gilt ivy leaf and tendril on clear glass, 19thC, 16½in (42cm) high.
$1,200-1,800

A small opaque white vase, with enamelled floral and bird decoration, London or South Staffordshire, c1765, 5in (12cm) high.
$1,600-2,000

A decalomania vase and cover, transfer printed with religious subjects, and including the Sacred Monogram, the domed cover with birds, butterflies and loose bouquets within a floral band and with knob finial, minor damage, mid-19thC, 21½in (55cm) high.
$1,200-1,800

A Federzcichnung style cased air-trap glass vase, with cylinder neck, being clear glass over brown with air-trap decoration, external gilded body decoration, pattern No. on base 9159, c1890, 11in (28cm) high.
$3,000-3,600

A Stourbridge three overlay cameo bulbous vase, with tapering cylinder neck, with latticed satin opal over ruby over citrine, c1880, 15½in (39cm) high.
$350-450

A pair of blue overlay tulip shaped vases with castellated rims, the Persian style blue panels decorated with scrolls in gilding, on knopped stems and hollow bases, 11in (28cm) high.
$520-720

A pair of Bohemian white overlay green glass lustre vases, decorated with alternate panels of foliage and diamond designs on a ground painted in gold with scrolling foliage, hung with clear glass prism drops, minor chip to foot rim, mid-19thC, 11in (28cm) high.
$1,500-2,000

Miscellaneous

A Stourbridge glass inkwell and stopper, the base and domed cover decorated with concentric bands of coloured canes, c1850, 6in (15cm) high.
$270-470

A 'Façon de Venise' latticinio two-handled vase, in vetro a retorti, decorated with bands of white gauze cable, the clear scroll handles with lion's mask terminals, Low Countries or Venice, early 17thC, 6in (14.5cm) wide.
$2,000-3,000

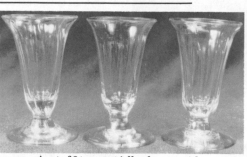

A set of 6 trumpet jelly glasses, with flute moulded bodies and plain conical feet, c1810, 4in (10cm).
$400-450

Two trumpet bowl jelly glasses, with vertical ribbing on plain feet, c1780.
$60-90 each

A sweetmeat, the double ogee bowl with flute cutting over cut with ladder cutting, the knopped stem similarly cut, with domed scallop cut foot and crenellated rim, c1770 6½in (17cm).
$650-750

A leaded glass roundel, unmarked, early 20thC, 10in (25cm) diam.
$900-1,200

A pair of bonnet glasses, with diamond cut double ogee bowls, with square domed lemon squeezer feet, c1820, 3½in (9cm).
$150-250

A 'coin' tankard, with trailed rim, central trailed band and base gadrooning on hollow conical foot, with applied strap handle, the base containing a silver George II coin, c1757, 6½in (17cm) high.
$1,000-1,200

A baluster 'coin' tankard and cover, the base set with a George III silver threepence dated 1762, the domed cover with acorn knop finial, some damage, c1765, 7½in (19cm) high.
$800-950

Scent Bottles

Three oval blue scent bottles with cut decoration.
l. Blue with gilt decoration, c1780, 4½in (11cm).
$800-1,000
c. Blue with embossed silver mount, c1780, 4½in (11cm).
$450-550
r. Blue with copper gilt mount, c1780, 4½in (11cm).
$350-450

A Fürstenberg scent bottle and gilt metal stopper, after a Chelsea model, in a simulated wicker basket, a gilt chain moulded about the shoulders, with a label inscribed 'Eau de Senteur', the neck with sprigs of flowers, blue script F mark, gilt metal mount and stopper with broken chain, c1770, 3½in (9cm).
$2,700-3,700

Three double ended scent bottles, with gilt brass mounts.
top. Blue opera glass type, c1870, 5½in (14cm).
$280-380
c. Red, c1880, 4in (10cm).
$100-180
bottom. Red, with embossed mounts, c1880, 5½in (14cm).
$230-270

A clear glass double travelling perfume flask, with lozenge and diamond decoration, each end with silver gilt mounts and covers, stamped London hallmarks for 1874, 6½in (16cm).
$250-450

A Venetian scent bottle, attributed to Franchini, the multi-coloured scrambled glass with aventurine inclusions set with 5 portrait canes and panel 'Venise', with silver screw top, 3½in (9cm).
$650-800

A Venetian scent bottle, attributed to Franchini, the multi-coloured scrambled glass with aventurine inclusions set with 2 portrait canes and silhouette of a gondola, with hinged gilt metal cover and chain, repaired, 2½in (6cm).
$50-100

159

A Venetian scent bottle, attributed to Franchini, the multi-coloured scrambled glass with aventurine inclusions set with 4 portrait canes, with hinged gilt metal cover and chain, 3in (8cm).
$450-550

A deep blue stained scent bottle for Worth, the spherical body moulded with stars, the disc stopper with 'dans la nuit', moulded R. Lalique, 4in (10cm).
$800-1,000

A frosted grey stained perfume pendant, moulded on 2 sides with curved spear shaped leaves, pierced at the shoulders for suspension cord and with matching mushroom stopper, moulded Lalique, 2in (4.5cm).
$5,500-6,500

A clear glass double travelling perfume flask, cut with a zigzag design, with gilt metal mounts and chased screw tops, 5in (12cm).
$180-220

A clear and blue stained scent bottle for Forvil, chipped stopper, moulded R. Lalique Paris France, 4½in (11cm).
$650-800

A Venetian scent bottle attributed to Franchini, of flattened and tapering ovoid shape, the multi-coloured scrambled glass with aventurine inclusions set with 5 portrait canes, the hinged gilt metal cover with inset green cut 'jewel' finial, 3in (8cm).
$550-650

A clear and frosted scent bottle, enclosing a plaque moulded in intaglio with 2 nude female figures amongst flowering branches, the stopper moulded as 2 nude female figures holding up a garland of flowers, small chip, engraved R. Lalique France, 5½in (14cm) high.
$12,000-14,500

'Vers le Jour', an amber frosted and clear scent bottle for Worth, moulded with a repeating triangular design and Worth in the bottle, with matching stopper, moulded R. Lalique, France, 5½in (14cm).
$3,500-4,500

'Ramses', a crystal bottle for Ramses Inc., with chamfered shoulders, the ribbed lotus flower stopper suspending a nude female figure dipper, 8in (20cm).
$450-550

A pear shaped atomizer, enclosed in a white metal cage of pierced scrolling foliage and stamped sterling, 5in (13cm) high.
$180-280

A Baccarat bottle, intaglio moulded with a figure teasing a woodpecker, the stopper moulded as a large woodpecker, 6½in (16cm).
$550-650

A clear green scent bottle for Worth, flattened circular, with Worth moulded in the bottle, and stepped disc stopper, moulded R. Lalique France, 3in (8cm).
$800-1,000

A frosted and clear glass bottle, flanked by 2 female nude figures seated at the base, with shallow conical moulded foliate stopper, heightened with green and amethyst staining, 5in (13cm).
$270-320

'L' Amour dans le Coeur', a clear scent bottle for Arys, one side moulded with Cupid within a heart, with moulded flower stopper, heightened with sienna staining, minute chip, moulded R. Lalique, 4in (10cm).
$550-750

A clear green scent bottle for Worth, cylindrical with stepped disc stopper, on original square metal/wood base, some chips, impressed Worth, moulded R. Lalique, stopper and bottle with engraved No. 102, 4½in (11cm).
$900-1,200

An amber opalescent scent bottle for Morabito, moulded with 4 turtles, the spherical stopper with turtle shell markings, base moulded in intaglio Morabito No. 7 Paris, etched Lalique France, 5½in (14cm).
$8,000-10,000

A cut glass scent bottle of inverted fan shape, the frosted stopper pierced and moulded with a courting couple within a garland of roses, 8in (20cm).
$270-370

An ornate fan shaped bottle, moulded at the base with frosted flowers, beneath vertical ribbing, the stopper moulded as a large orchid, 9in (22cm).
$270-370

A set of 3 clear and blue shaded bottles, with white metal collars and diamond cut glass stoppers, encased in a pierced cylindrical white metal mount, 5in (12cm).
$350-450

An ornate pierced and cut glass bottle, modelled as a crown with orb stopper, 6½in (16cm).
$270-450

A Cartier amber lozenge shaped scent bottle, with ornate pierced gilt mount at the base, inset with simulated lapis lazuli cabochons and other coloured stones, the angular stopper intaglio moulded with a kneeling female figure, small chip, inscribed Cartier Paris, 5in (13cm).
$270-370

A cobalt blue and white overlay perfume flask, of slender tapering form, with chased gilt metal cover, 4½in (11cm) high.
$200-270

'Jolanda', a large amphora shaped clear bottle on gilt pedestal, with gilt metal mount at the shoulders, cast with roses, square stopper and label, 10in (25cm).
$120-220

An opalescent glass 'pedestal' bottle, the stepped base rimmed with malachite glass segments, the 'pedestal' stopper moulded in green glass as a bust of Pan, 9in (23cm) high.
$550-650

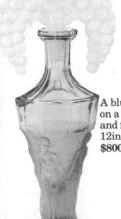

A blue tinted scent bottle, decorated on a frosted ground, with polished and frosted berried tiara stopper, 12in (31cm).
$800-1,000

A clear and sepia stained bottle, with graduated base, on hexagonal foot, moulded with stylised flowers, with matching spire stopper, 7in (18cm).
$550-650

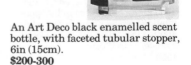

An Art Deco black enamelled scent bottle, with faceted tubular stopper, 6in (15cm).
$200-300

A frosted and clear perfume counter tester for D'Orsay, each of the 5 testers with flowerhead dipper, the body moulded with brambles and the word 'D'Orsay', 9in (22cm) long.
$2,700-3,700

A ruby glass and gilt double scent and vinaigrette flask, with foliate chased mounts and covers, 4in (10cm).
$450-550

A Meissen scent bottle and 2 stoppers, modelled as the Provender of the Monastery, wearing a brown habit, carrying a dead pigeon, a young lady hidden in a wheatsheaf with cornflowers on his back, the pink ground base with indianische Blumen, restored, blue crossed swords mark under base decoration, c1770, 3in (8cm) high.
$1,800-2,200

'Iris', a clear scent bottle for Houbigant, the front moulded with interlaced strapwork, with matching stopper, heightened with blue staining, moulded Lalique, 3in (8cm).
$350-450

A clear scent bottle for Worth, moulded with an allover design of flowerheads with gilt label at the centre, with matching flowerhead stopper, moulded R. Lalique, in original case, 3½in (8cm).
$540-740

A clear glass perfume pendant, enclosed in an ornate scrolling white metal and gilt mount and with filigree metal 'crown' stopper, on suspension chain, 3in (7cm).
$270-370

A Baccarat bottle for Christian Dior, with gilt decoration, in red velvet coffret lined with red satin, chipped stopper, 9in (23cm).
$1,500-1,800

'Tentacion', a novelty bottle for Parera, the stopper moulded as the half length figure of a woman, the bottle as her long skirt, with paper label, 7½in (19cm).
$180-280

A clear scent bottle for Worth, with scalloped edging stained in blue, the flat topped tapering stopper moulded with the letter W, moulded Lalique France, 3in (7cm).
$550-800

A gilt enamelled ruby glass perfume flask, of faceted conical form enamelled with scrolls and foliage, gilt metal scroll mount and hinged cover, the whole resembling a dagger, on gilt suspension chain, 5in (13cm).
$350-450

A clear glass double travelling perfume flask, cut with a lozenge design, with chased gilt metal mounts and covers, 5in (13cm).
$200-270

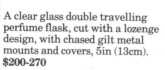

A clear and frosted glass cologne flask, etched on one side with a wild rose spray, and with matching gilt metal top, 5½in (14cm) long.
$350-450

'L'Origan', a clear display bottle for Coty, the cushion shaped frosted and sienna stained round stopper moulded with entwined branches, applied gilt label, moulded Coty France, 11in (28cm).
$550-900

'Tulipes', a clear and green stained scent bottle for Jay-Thorpe, the compressed globular body moulded with tulip blooms, and with flowerbud stopper, one bud moulded Jaytho, with crack, moulded R. Lalique France, 3in (8cm).
$270-470

OAK & COUNTRY FURNITURE

Beds

An oak bed, with arched plank ends, one with faceted ball finials, joined by plain rails, the rails lengthened, lacking bolts and slats, 17thC, 82½in (209cm) long.
$3,200-4,200

MONARCH CHRONOLOGY		
Dates	**Monarchs**	**Period**
1558-1603	Elizabeth I	Elizabethan
1603-1625	James I	Jacobean
1625-1649	Charles I	Carolean
1649-1660	Commonwealth	Cromwellian
1660-1685	Charles II	Restoration
1685-1689	James II	Restoration
1689-1694	William & Mary	William & Mary
1694-1702	William III	William III
1702-1714	Anne	Queen Anne
1714-1727	George I	Early Georgian
1727-1760	George II	Georgian
1760-1812	George III	Late Georgian
1812-1820	George III	Regency
1820-1830	George IV	Late Regency
1830-1837	William IV	William IV
1837-1860	Victoria	Early Victorian
1860-1901	Victoria	Late Victorian
1901-1910	Edward VII	Edwardian

An oak tester bed, the panelled canopy with a flute carved frieze, the back with deep moulded panels with baluster turned front posts, plain panelled footboard, 17thC and later, 84in (213cm) long.
$6,500-7,500

This bed has been made up using old parts.

A heavily carved oak tester bedstead, part 17thC, 83in (210cm) long.
$17,000-20,000

Bureaux

A small early oak bureau, with interior drawers, c1780, 32in (81cm).
$3,000-3,500

An oak bureau, with reading ledge and fitted interior, on bracket feet, lock missing and replacement handles, 18thC, 35½in (90cm).
$3,500-4,500

A George I oak bureau bookcase with stepped interior, well and secret drawers, original brasses, c1725. **$15,000-20,000**

Use the Index!

Because certain items might fit easily into any of a number of categories, the quickest and surest method of locating any entry is by reference to the index at the back of the book.
This has been fully cross-referenced for absolute simplicity

A mahogany and oak sided bureau, with stepped fitted interior, on bracket feet, 18thC, 32in (81cm).
$1,800-2,800

A mid George III oak bureau, with a later sloping fall enclosing a fitted interior, on bracket feet, minor restoration, 36in (92cm). **$1,500-1,800**

The later fall will have affected the price.

A George III provincial oak bureau, the fall enclosing a fitted interior of a small door flanked by drawers and pigeonholes. **$1,800-2,000**

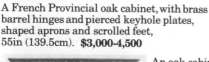

A George III oak bureau, the fall revealing stationery compartments, on bracket feet, restored, c1770, 35½in (90cm). **$2,700-3,700**

Cabinets

OAK

★ oak was the principal material for all furniture up to c1670 and well into the 19thC for country furniture

★ early oak has character and although originally a golden honey colour, it will have aged to a warm chestnut to black colour with a rich patination from centuries of polishing and handling

★ stripping and refurbishing destroys colour and sheen and substantially devalues a piece

★ best prices are paid for exceptional condition, even if the piece is of relatively common type

A French Provincial oak cabinet, with brass barrel hinges and pierced keyhole plates, shaped aprons and scrolled feet, 55in (139.5cm). **$3,000-4,500**

An oak cabinet on stand in the Gothic style, with moulded cornice, burr veneered, fitted pair of arch panelled doors enclosing 12 small drawers around a recess, 19thC, 50in (127cm). **$1,800-2,800**

An oak cabinet with geometrically panelled doors enclosing 14 drawers, the sides with carrying handles, on later bun feet, adapted, mid-17thC, 30½in (77.5cm). **$3,500-5,500**

Chairs

A Windsor settee, feet slightly reduced, c1810, 77in (196cm) long. **$5,500-6,500**

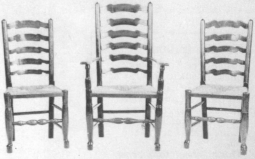

A set of 8 Yorkshire elm dining chairs, with wavy ladder backs, rush seats, turned supports terminating in pad and block feet, late 18thC. **$5,000-5,500**

A Charles I carved oak armchair, the solid seat above a chevron inlaid apron and bobbin turned legs joined by stretchers, c1640.
$2,000-3,000

An oak and walnut panel back open armchair with scroll cresting, the solid seat and rail with a scrolling apron, on baluster legs joined by stretchers, late 17thC.
$12,000-14,500

A Charles I oak panel back armchair, the arms with plain turned cap and cover supports, on similarly turned legs, Salisbury, lacking finials.
$1,500-1,800

A North Cheshire oak panel back open armchair with a blind parapet toprail, the panel carved with stylised foliage with solid seat, on ring turned baluster legs joined by stretchers, late 17thC.
$11,000-12,000

A well proportioned chair in original condition and good contemporary carving.

An oak open armchair with carved panelled back, the arms carved with conforming decoration, with panelled seat on spirally twisted and rectangular legs joined by conforming stretchers, 17thC and later. **$1,500-2,000**

An oak panel back open armchair, the solid seat on ring turned baluster legs joined by stretchers, late 17thC. **$8,000-9,500**

A late George III yew and elm Windsor armchair, the bowed railed back above a saddle seat, on turned tapering splayed legs joined by a crinoline stretcher. **$1,000-1,200**

A pair of William and Mary oak side chairs with carved rails and panelled backs, English, c1695.
$2,700-3,700

A set of 8 Charles II style carved walnut and beech chairs, including a pair of armchairs, with oval cane splats and cane seats with cushions, c1870.
$5,500-6,500

An oak open armchair, the panelled back with pyramid finials, with slightly spreading arms on turned supports with plank seat, on turned legs with block feet joined by square stretchers, South Lancashire/North Cheshire, seat possibly replaced, second half 17thC.
$1,800-2,800

Pyramid finials are a characteristic feature of chairs made in South Lancashire and North Cheshire from the mid-17thC.

A Derbyshire ash and fruitwood lambing chair, 18thC.
$1,500-2,000

The fact that this piece has been heavily restored is reflected in the price.

An early Georgian lambing chair in elm with original paint.
$12,000-13,000

An oak chair, 18in (46cm) wide.
$650-750

A yew and elm wheelback Windsor chair, with a pierced solid splat above a solid seat tied by spindle turned stretchers, 19thC.
$450-550

A set of 6 Windsor bow back side chairs, each stamped on the underside of the seat E. Tebbets, c1820. **$2,500-4,000**

A Windsor writing armchair, with dark green/brown stained surface, drawer restored, probably Pennsylvania, c1800. **$3,000-3,500**

A George III ash comb back Windsor chair, c1800.
$2,700-4,500

A yew and elm broad arm Windsor chair, 19thC.
$2,700-3,700

Being yew will boost the price.

A pair of richly carved oak wainscot chairs, with pierced scalloped cresting rail, with solid seats, raised upon bobbin turned and block carved front supports and plain stretchers, dated 1629.
$1,000-1,500

A Charles II oak nursing chair, English, c1680.
$900-1,800

A North Cheshire oak chair, the panelled back with a pierced parapet cresting initialled S.E., the solid seat on baluster legs joined on stretchers, some restoration to toprail, late 17thC.
$4,500-5,500

A yew and elm wheelback Windsor armchair, some restorations, 19thC.
$300-450

A set of 8 oak and ash spindle back chairs, including a pair of armchairs with rush seats, on turned tapering legs with pad and ball feet, late 18th/early 19thC. **$6,500-7,000**

A matched set of 6 ash ladder back chairs, with rush seats, on turned legs with pad and ball feet, Lancashire/Cheshire, requiring re-seating and joints tightening, late 18th/early 19thC.
$3,000-3,500

A set of 3 William and Mary oak and beech chairs, with scroll cresting rail, with conforming stretchers, on scroll legs, some variations.
$1,000-1,200

A William and Mary oak side chair, with carved rail, English, c1695.
$900-1,800

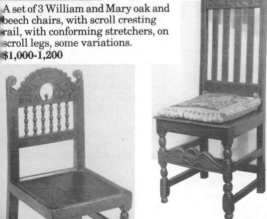

A Derbyshire oak chair with spindle filled back beneath an eared arch cresting with pierced finialled roundel, the solid seat on baluster turned legs joined by a bobbin turned front stretcher, late 17thC.
$2,700-3,700

A pair of North Cheshire oak chairs, decorated with stylised foliage and initials G.B., on ring turned baluster legs joined by stretchers, late 17thC. **$10,000-12,000**

A single chair would probably only command a quarter of this price – pairs are at a premium.

A later carved North German ash turner's chair with chip carved toprail and triangular solid seat, on turned legs joined by turned stretchers, basically 18thC. **$700-1,000**

An oak corner chair, the elevated canopied panelled back above a solid seat and base drawer, basically 17thC. **$5,000-6,000**

A set of 6 Lancashire dining chairs, with slightly dipped cresting rails, 2 sets of spindle splats, rush seats and on turned and tapering front supports terminating in pad and block feet, with baluster turned seat rails and turned stretchers, 18thC. **$2,700-3,700**

A Bavarian stained oak seat in the form of a bear with outstretched arms, late 19thC, 51in (129cm) high. **$2,700-3,700**

Three turned Windsor fan back side chairs, c1790. **$3,000-3,500**

A child's painted chair, 11in (28cm) wide. **$270-370**

A Windsor turned lowback armchair, Pennsylvania, c1765. **$6,500-7,500**

A Charles II oak settle, the panelled strapwork and lunette carved back with later stylised floral inlay, the solid seat above turned and square legs joined by stretchers, restored, c1680, 70in (178cm) wide. **$1,600-2,000**

A fruitwood and mahogany child's high chair, the finialled back with a marquetry panel, the panelled arms and tasselled seat on square chamfered legs joined by a foot-rest and turned stretchers, early 19thC. **$1,400-1,600**

An oak panelled and carved settle, English, excellent colour and patina, late 17thC. **$3,600-5,600**

A carved oak settle, the scrolled cresting above a grape vine frieze with the date 1651, the hinged box seat with a panelled front, 48in (122cm) wide. **$1,500-1,800**

An oak settle, the box seat half hinged, with steel H hinges, and with panelled fascia, on fluted extended stile supports, some later additions, hence price, 18thC, 67in (171cm). **$1,200-1,500**

The later additions are reflected in the price.

A William and Mary oak chest in two parts, with mitred and bobbin turned mouldings, the drawers with walnut veneered panels, inlaid with mother of pearl and bone floral scrolls, including the date and initials Anno 1568, E.B.:J.B., on stile feet, 40½in (102cm). **$3,500-4,500**

A Charles II oak chest of 4 drawers, decorated with geometric moulding and split balusters, on original bun feet, English, c1670. **$10,000-14,500**

Rare to find original feet these days.

Chests

An oak geometrically moulded chest of drawers with lifting lid top section, English late 17thC. **$3,500-5,500**

A George II oak chest of drawers with walnut veneer, excellent colour and patina with original brasses, English, c1730. **$3,600-5,600**

An early George III oak small chest with mahogany crossbanded drawers, 34in (86cm). **$2,000-3,000**

A George III oak chest, the top above a brushing slide and 4 drawers, on bracket feet. **$750-1,000**

An oak 6 drawer chest, c1870, 42in (106.5cm). **$800-1,000**

An oak chest with panelled drawers, on stile feet, late 17thC, 38½in (98cm). **$3,000-3,500**

A James I oak coffer, with null carved front, on trestle supports, 35in (89cm). **$4,800-5,800**

An oak coffer with hinged top above a front carved with guilloche and inlaid with stars, on stile feet, early 17thC, 42in (106.5cm). **$2,700-3,700**

An oak chest with moulded top and 3 geometrically panelled drawers, on stile feet, late 17thC, 31½in (80cm). **$3,500-4,500**

169

A Charles I carved oak boarded coffer, the hinged cover with hasp, the front with incised twin lozenge carving and palmettes, together with an iron escutcheon, c1620, 48in (122cm).
$1,600-2,000

A Charles I oak boarded coffer, the front with twin stylised quatrefoils and punchwork, c1630, 42½in (107cm).
$1,000-1,600

A Charles I oak coffer, with moulded three panel top and front, on stile feet, some damage, c1640, 50½in (128cm).
$1,200-1,600

A Commonwealth oak coffer, the moulded hinged top above a twin panel front, on stile feet, c1650, 37½in (95cm).
$1,600-2,000

A Charles II oak boarded coffer, the front with iron escutcheon and nailed border, c1680, 53½in (136cm).
$750-1,000

A Charles II oak boarded coffer, the cover with iron hasps, the front with iron escutcheon and gouge borders, c1680, 65in (165cm).
$1,500-1,600

A Charles II oak coffer, c1680, 43in (109cm).
$1,200-1,800
A panelled top would be more valuable.

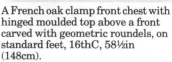

A French oak clamp front chest with hinged moulded top above a front carved with geometric roundels, on standard feet, 16thC, 58½in (148cm).
$8,000-10,000

Fine example of the carver's art.

Cupboards

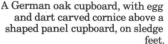

A German oak cupboard, with egg and dart carved cornice above a shaped panel cupboard, on sledge feet.
$1,200-1,800

A Louis XV Provincial oak buffet, with cartouche shaped mouldings and roundels, the 3 frieze drawers above a pair of fielded panel doors, on later bun feet, raised back now missing, c1750, 63in (160cm). **$3,500-4,500**
Less valuable than an English dresser base.

An oak corner cupboard, with fitted interior. **$700-900**

A George III hanging press, with brass knob handles throughout, bracket feet missing, 53in (134.5cm). **$2,700-3,700**

An oak press cupboard, the ogee moulded cornice above a pair of arched fielded panel cupboard doors, the lower section with an arrangement of 5 short drawers, on square section feet, mid-18thC, 53in (134.5cm). **$3,000-3,500**

An oak barrel back corner cupboard, with restorations, late 18thC. **$1,200-1,600**

An oak double corner cupboard, 18thC. **$3,000-4,500**

A Charles II panelled and carved fitted cupboard, English, c1680. **$1,800-2,800**

A George II oak press cupboard, the base with 3 dummy drawers and 2 real drawers, on ogee bracket feet, c1750, 65in (165cm). **$1,800-2,800**

A Louis XV carved oak armoire, the cornice above a pair of arched later glazed panelled doors, enclosing 3 drawers and a shelf, on stile feet, c1770, 67in (170cm). **$3,600-4,600**

An oak court cupboard, the canopied superstructure with moulded frieze, the lower part with a pair of moulded doors, with iron butterfly hinges throughout, the feet being continuations of the stiles, and with shaped brackets, late 17thC, 57in (144.5cm). **$7,000-9,000**

A carved oak court cupboard, with 2 recessed doors, 2 panelled doors below and a further pair of drawers, on block feet, dated 1685 and initialled H.I.K., 64½in (163cm). **$3,500-4,500**

A Louis XV Provincial oak armoire, with brass hinges and escutcheons, the interior with hanging space, on stile feet, c1740, 64in (162.5cm). **$2,400-3,400**

A French Provincial brass mounted chestnut armoire, with arched moulded cresting above 2 doors enclosing shelves, with waved apron on scrolled feet, minor restorations, late 18thC, 61in (155cm).
$2,700-3,000

A Charles I oak cupboard, with square and turned supports with platform undertier, restored, c1640, 36in (92cm).
$3,300-4,500

An oak credence cupboard, on ring turned baluster legs joined by square moulded stretcher, the top and door later, 39in (99cm).
$6,500-8,000

An original would be worth considerably more.

Dressers

An oak dresser, with brass knobs and escutcheons and 3 tier fitted back, 18thC, 63in (160cm).
$5,500-6,500

An oak Welsh dresser, with delft rack, the projecting base crossbanded in fruitwood, over a deep scalloped apron, raised upon cabriole front supports with pointed pad feet, and square back supports on block feet, 18thC, 80in (203cm).
$8,000-10,000

A Charles II carved oak livery cupboard, the plank top above a pair of perforated panel doors enclosing a shelf, on tall stile supports, c1680, 43½in (110cm).
$1,800-2,800

An oak cupboard with rectangular moulded top above 2 doors, each with a carved panel between fluted uprights headed by lions' masks (formerly a linen press), 30in (76cm).
$1,500-2,000

A George III oak dresser and rack, English, c1795.
$10,000-14,500

An oak dresser, 18thC, 65in (165cm).
$4,500-5,500

A mid-Georgian oak dresser, with 3 mahogany banded frieze drawers and an arcaded apron, on cabriole legs and pad feet, the 2 parts associated, restorations, 80½in (204.5cm).
$3,500-4,500

A Dutch oak low dresser, profusely carved with urns, roundels, strapwork and guilloche, the planked top above 3 frieze drawers and a pair of fielded panelled doors on bracket feet, 19thC, 62in (157cm). **$1,500-2,000**

An earlier piece that has been modified later in the 19thC.

Stools

An oak box stool with hinged, moulded top above a cabled frieze, on baluster turned legs joined by stretchers, mid-17thC, 20½in (52cm). **$7,000-9,000**

An oak joint stool with moulded top and frieze, on ring turned slightly splayed baluster legs joined by stretchers, late 17thC, one stretcher replaced, 19in (48cm). **$1,200-1,500**

Replaced stretcher will reduce the price.

A Charles II oak joint stool, the plain frieze with a scroll apron, the scroll and baluster turned legs joined by peripheral stretchers, c1680, 16in (41cm). **$1,500-2,000**

An oak joint stool, the moulded top and rail with a separate profile-shaped apron, on complex baluster turned legs joined by stretchers, late 16thC, 19in (48cm). **$8,000-9,000**

Early joint stools in original condition are rare today.

Tables

A William and Mary oak gateleg table, with a drawer, on baluster turned legs joined by stretchers, c1690, 42in (107cm) extended. **$1,800-2,800**

Did you know
MILLER'S Antiques Price Guide builds up year by year to form the most comprehensive photo-reference system available

Oak & Country Furniture
TURNED TABLE LEGS

A Charles II style oak centre table, made-up, the carved frieze with 2 end drawers, the spiral twist legs above square feet joined by square stretchers, 51½in (130cm).

$700-900

'Made-up' is a trade term used to describe a piece which has been constructed from old materials but which is not genuine.

An oak gateleg dining table, on moulded frieze with single drawer, on baluster turned legs joined by stretchers, minor restorations, late 17thC, 55in (139cm).

$6,500-8,000

An oak counter table, the sliding top above a triple parchment panelled front, on moulded stile feet joined by a stretcher, the sliding mechanism replaced, the apron later, the toes replaced, mid -16thC, 47in (119cm).

$4,500-6,500

An oak 8-seater bobbin turned gateleg table, English, excellent condition, colour and patina, c1695.

$10,000-14,500

Large gateleg dining tables now fetch a premium price.

A William and Mary chestnut and beechwood gateleg table, on baluster turned and square legs, joined by stretchers, c1700, 54½in (138cm).

$1,500-2,000

A walnut gateleg table, including later timber, the moulded top above spiral twist and square legs, joined by stretchers, late 17thC, formerly with a frieze drawer, 59in (150cm).

$2,700-3,700

The missing drawer will lower the price.

A small Queen Anne oak gateleg table, good colour and patina, English, c1710.

$2,500-4,500

A Jacobean style drawer leaf table, the planked top above a moulded frieze on bulbous baluster legs, joined by cross stretcher, 116in (294cm), extended.   **$6,500-8,000**

174

PATINA
Surface colour of genuinely old wood resulting from the layers of grease, dirt and polish built up over the years, and the handling the piece of furniture has received in that time. It differs from wood to wood, and is difficult to fake.

A red walnut gateleg table, the moulded single flap top and frieze drawer on ring turned baluster legs joined by a square stretcher, on Spanish scroll feet, mid-18thC, 34in (86cm).
$1,800-2,800

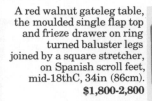

An oak gateleg table, the demi-lune foldover top on baluster column supports joined by stretchers, 37½in (95cm).
$2,500-3,500

An oak gateleg dining table, on turned baluster supports with plain stretchers, with inset quadrant outer corners, 51in (129cm).
$1,600-2,000

An oak side table with crossbanded full width drawer with cockbeading and brass swan neck handle, supported on tapering circular legs with pad feet, mid-18thC, 32in (81cm).
$1,200-1,600

The oak refectory table was the only type until gateleg tables and side tables appeared in the early 17thC. From the turn of the 18thC tables were increasingly designed to serve a specific purpose.

An oak refectory table with a planked top above a lunette carved frieze on baluster turned legs joined by stretchers, parts late 17thC, top and frieze later, 121in (307cm).
$7,000-9,000

Charles I oak refectory table, the guilloche and paterae carved frieze above bulbous turned supports joined by peripheral stretchers, one support bears the initials R.D. and the date 1637, top bears indistinct branded initials, including restorations, surfaces distressed, 114in (290cm).
8,000-10,000

A William and Mary oak X-stretchered side table, on original bun feet, excellent colour and patina, English, c1695.
$2,700-4,500

A Charles II oak side table, the frieze drawer above square and bobbin turned legs joined by peripheral stretchers, c1680, 29in (74cm).
$1,800-2,800

A Spanish chestnut side table, the projecting top above a frieze carved with stylised flowerheads, including a pair of drawers, on square legs, joined by stretchers, 76½in (194cm). **$1,800-2,800**

A Dutch oak side table with planked top above a long frieze drawer on bobbin baluster legs, joined by stretchers, late 17thC, 36in (92cm). **$1,800-2,200**

A George III oak candlestand, with one-piece top, excellent colour and patina, English, c1790. **$2,000-3,000**

A George III oak 2-tier cricket table, the triple splayed supports with an undertier, c1800, 23½in (60cm) diam. **$1,200-1,800**

A small George III applewood tripod table, English, c1795. **$1,500-2,000**

A rare tiny William and Mary oak tripod table, English, c1695 **$10,000-14,500**

An oak lowboy with brass swan neck drop handles with backplates, shaped apron beneath, supported on circular tapering legs with pad feet, mid-18thC, 33in (84cm). **$2,700-3,700**

A George III elm tripod table with tilt top, one piece, well figured top, English, c1820. **$1,200-2,000**

A Georgian burr yew tripod table, excellent colour and patina, English, c1820. **$3,500-6,500** *Yew is always highly collectable.*

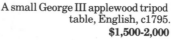

A cherry wood dining table, 63in (160cm) **$1,800-2,200**

Miscellaneous

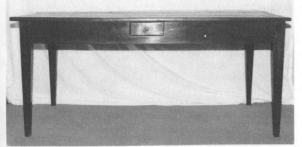

A French fruitwood table, 71in
(180cm).
$1,800-2,400

A fruitwood table, 68in (172cm).
$1,500-1,800

An oak box, the hinged lid above a
carved panelled front, the end
boards extending to form feet, 20in
(51cm).
$700-900

An oak desk box, the hinged
rectangular slope with a
gouge-carved edge above front and
sides carved with scrolling dragons,
late 17thC, 27½in (70cm).
$700-900

A small 16thC oak plank coffer,
English.
$5,500-7,000
Pieces of this early date are now rare.

A rare oak box on cabriole legs,
English, c1760.
$3,500-4,500

An oak desk box, the moulded slope
with a book ledge, on an associated
stand fitted with a frieze drawer, on
baluster turned legs joined by
square stretchers, some restoration,
17thC, 27in (69cm).
$2,600-3,600

Miller's is a price Guide not a price List

*The price ranges given
reflect the average price a
purchaser should pay for
similar items. Condition,
rarity of design or pattern,
size, colour, provenance,
restoration and many
other factors must be
taken into account when
assessing values.
When buying or selling, it
must always be
remembered that prices
can be greatly affected by
the condition of any piece.
Unless otherwise stated,
all goods shown in Miller's
are of good merchantable
quality, and the valuations
given reflect this fact.
Pieces offered for sale in
exceptionally fine
condition or in poor
condition may reasonably
be expected to be priced
considerably higher or
lower respectively than
the estimates given herein*

FURNITURE

Beds

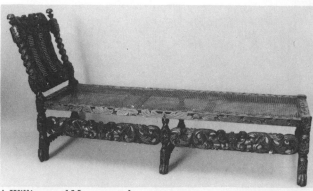

An early Victorian mahogany full tester bed, with moulded cornice, carved acanthus capitals and bases, 54in (137cm) wide, 102in (259cm) high, 84in (213cm) long.
$7,000-9,000

This bed was formerly the property of the Watt family of Abney Hall, Cheadle, Nr. Stockport, Cheshire. Agatha Christie was a frequent house guest at Abney Hall as her sister married James Watt and during her visits would always sleep in this bed. Such visits influenced the 'Adventures of the Christmas Pudding' which was dedicated to the memory of Abney Hall and in which there is mention of a 'big four poster bed'.

A William and Mary carved walnut and cane day bed, made up, the hinged end panel with spiral twist supports and coronet cresting rail, with square and spiral twist legs, 72in (183cm) long.
$1,800-2,800

DAY BEDS
Early versions reflect contemporary chair styles. Later, under French Empire influence, they became increasingly elaborate with rich upholstery, gilding, paint and exotic motifs.

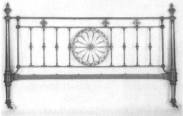

A mid-Victorian brass half tester bedstead, with railed headrest and footboard, centred by a pierced roundel with paterae between finialled uprights, 76in (193cm).
$11,000-13,000

A Victorian brass and black painted iron bedstead, with brass label R.W. Winfield & Son Pattentees and Manufacturers, London & Birmingham, with registry mark for 1856, lacking slats and mattress, 54½in (138cm) wide, 78½in (99cm) long.
$3,000-4,000

The firm of R. W. Winfield were manufacturers of metal furniture and appear in Pigot's Directory in 1839. Among the large variety of goods which they made in iron and brass were metallic military bedsteads for which they claimed to be 'Proprietor of the English Patent'. They exhibited beds of various styles at the 1851 Great Exhibition and were patronised by Queen Victoria.

A Victorian mahogany bed, the headboard with moulded frame inset with a pleated cream panel, the footboard with a moulded panel complete with base, c1860, 63in (160cm).
$1,800-2,800

A Victorian brass and iron bedstead, the foot and headboard with scrolling toprail cast with simulated bamboo on column supports cast with foliate mouldings, on porcelain casters, no slats or mattress, 81½in (207cm) long.
$5,500-6,500

A red painted ebonised and parcel-gilt boat shaped day bed, of antique Egyptian style, the dished seat covered in black horsehair, the seat rail painted with a border of anthemia, the prow in the form of a gazelle's head on oar feet and H-shaped base, 76in (193cm) wide.   **$2,600-3,600**

A French Empire mahogany and parcel gilt bed, the panelled ends with sphinx and lantern finials above columnar pilasters with foliate capitals, including side rails and box spring mattress, c1815, 84in (213cm).   **$3,500-5,500**

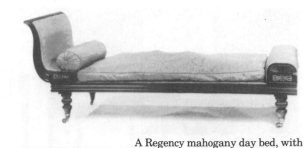

A Regency mahogany campaign bed, with hinged top enclosing hinged side panels and hinged slatted base, on turned tapering legs, labelled Patent, John Durham, London, 42in (106cm) wide. **$5,500-6,500**

John Durham, foreman of Morgan and Sanders, 16 Catherine Street, Strand, took over their patent furniture business in 1820 and specialised in cabinet, camp and field-beds.

A Regency mahogany day bed, with a scrolled guilloche carved end, on baluster turned legs with lobed collars, headed by gilt metal opposing anthemia, 80in (203cm) wide. **$1,500-1,800**

A mahogany child's rocking cradle, with domed hood, 18thC, 36in (92cm) long. **$270-370**

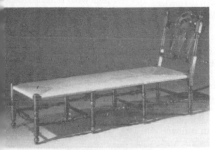

A William and Mary maple daybed, replaced rush, Philadelphia, c1730, 75in (191cm) long. **$900-1,500**

A Federal birchwood and pine pencil post bedstead, with later tester, New England, c1800, 77in (196cm) long. **$4,000-6,000**

An Italian giltwood cradle, with ribbed hull and scrolling ends, hung with a blue velvet curtain, the sides with gilt metal railings, the padded interior lined with blue velvet with padded cushion, with scrolling end supports joined by a waved stretcher on scrolling feet carved with acanthus, repaired, mid-19thC, 57in (145cm) long. **$6,000-8,000**

A Federal maple four-poster bedstead, 80in (203cm) long. **$3,000-4,000**

A Charles X inlaid bird's-eye maple bed, with solid headboard and solid footrest and one concave side, the other plain side of oak, no box spring or mattress, 76½in (194cm). **$3,500-4,500**

A Federal crossbanded birchwood and pine four-poster bedstead, Eastern New England, c1810, 76in (193cm) long. **$3,000-4,000**

Bonheur du Jour

A Regency rosewood bonheur du jour, the superstructure with brass pierced key pattern three quarter gallery, the slightly projecting base with a drawer, opening to reveal a hinged and ratcheted blue morocco writing surface, flanked by wells for pens and ink, over a long drawer with brass knob handles. **$9,500-11,500**

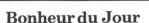

A Louis XV style tulipwood and gilt metal mounted bonheur du jour, with Sèvres style plaques, stationery compartments above a frieze drawer, on cabriole legs, c1870, 24½in (62cm). **$4,500-5,500**

A late Victorian painted satinwood and mahogany bonheur du jour, with overall neo-Classical trailing floral decoration, a pierced three quarter brass gallery above open shelves flanked by doors, with grisaille painted classical figures, on square tapering legs joined by an undershelf, 25in (64cm). **$3,500-4,500**

A mahogany and painted bonheur du jour, the galleried superstructure decorated, above a hinged writing slope and fitted drawer, on square tapered legs, part late 18thC, adapted, 24in (61cm). **$2,600-3,600**

A Napoleon III ebonised, gilt metal mounted and tortoiseshell and brass inlaid bonheur du jour, with a frieze drawer with writing slide on cabriole legs with female mask headings and gilt sabots, restored, 32in (81cm). **$2,600-3,600**

An inlaid rosewood bonheur du jour, with folding baize-lined top and frieze drawer with turned wood knob handles, the superstructure with brass galleried shelf and gilt tubular and spindle supports, cupboards each with an interior 2 side drawer, one with 2 glass ink and sand receivers, on tapered squared supports with fitted casters, early 19thC, 27in (69cm). **$8,000-9,000**

An ormolu and porcelain-mounted amaranth bonheur du jour, banded in tulipwood, the fold-out top inlaid with strapwork and lined in green leather, the shaped frieze drawer mounted with tassels on cabriole legs with scroll and rockwork clasps reaching to sabots, late 19thC, 32½in (82cm). **$7,000-9,000**

An Edwardian mahogany lady's bonheur du jour, with inlaid stringing and rosewood banding, the top with tooled leather inset and brass gallery, with 2 front frieze drawers with brass handles, the square tapering legs on casters, 36in (92cm). **$1,800-2,400**

Breakfront Bookcases

A George III style mahogany breakfront bookcase, the dentil moulded cornice with a blind fretwork frieze, above 3 astragal glazed doors, the lower section with a blind fret frieze above panel cupboard 3 cut corner doors, on bracket feet, late 19thC, 80in (203cm). **$4,500-6,500**

A Regency pale mahogany breakfront library bookcase, 140in (355cm). **$26,000-36,000**

A Regency breakfront secretaire library bookcase, inlaid with radial boxwood lines, on later bracket feet, some restoration, 82in (208cm).
$18,000-21,000

A Regency rosewood small breakfront bookcase, the upper part with 4 grille and glazed doors, enclosing shelves, the base enclosing 9 graduated drawers, the side cupboards with shelves, on plinth base, the lower doors with later panels, 66½in (168cm).
$3,500-5,500

A mahogany breakfront bookcase, of George III design, the moulded cornice above 8 astragal glazed doors centred by 4 frieze drawers, on plinth base, 92in (234cm).
$6,500-7,000

A William IV rosewood breakfront bookcase, with an arrangement of open adjustable shelves, divided by moulded pilasters, on a plinth base, c1835, 63½in (161cm).
$3,400-4,500

A mahogany bookcase of mid-Georgian design, the breakfront lower section with central panelled door flanked by 4 astragal glazed doors on plinth base, 19thC, 124in (315cm). $4,500-5,500

A Victorian burr walnut veneered breakfront library bookcase, the base with mahogany lined frieze drawers above cupboards, fitted shelves, enclosed by domed top panelled doors, the flanking pilasters with scroll scale carved brackets above floral drapes, on a plinth base, 100in (254cm).
$20,000-23,000

A Victorian walnut breakfront open bookcase, with leather trimmed open shelves flanked by gilt metal mounted pilasters, on a plinth base.
$2,400-3,000

A Continental satinwood breakfront secrétaire bookcase, the moulded cornice above 4 astragal glazed doors, the lower section with a secrétaire drawer above 2 further drawers, flanked by cupboard doors inlaid with oval fan paterae, on turned tapered legs, probably Scandinavian.
$2,700-4,500

A Victorian mahogany breakfront bookcase, the ogee moulded cornice above 4 arched glazed doors with horizontal astragals, the flanking pilasters with lotus caps, above 4 arched panel cupboard doors, on a plinth base.
$8,000-9,000

Did you know

MILLER'S Antiques Price Guide builds up year by year to form the most comprehensive photo-reference system available

Bureau Bookcases

A Federal inlaid mahogany cylinder front desk and bookcase, Boston area of Massachusetts, c1815, 35in (89cm). **$6,000-7,000**

A banded walnut bureau bookcase of George II design, 'made up', 37in (94cm). **$3,600-5,600**

A George III mahogany bureau bookcase, with inlaid sloping fall front, the drawers below with brass loop handles, and shaped back plates, on ogee bracket feet, the whole with chequered and boxwood stringing, 44in (112cm). **$5,500-6,500**

A mid George III inlaid mahogany bureau bookcase, with a pierced broken scroll well shaped pediment and dentil moulded cornice above a pair of astragal glazed doors, on moulded bracket feet, associated, 41in (104cm) **$8,000-9,000**

A George III mahogany bureau bookcase, hinged sloping flap with a fitted interior, on later bracket feet, 52in (132cm). **$4,300-5,000**

A George III mahogany bureau bookcase, the later top with a pair of geometrically glazed astragal doors above sloping flap and 4 graduated long drawers, on bracket feet, 42in (106.5cm). **$2,000-3,000**

A Chippendale carved walnut bureau bookcase, with restorations to cornice and feet, Philadelphia area, c1770, 94in (238cm) high. **$15,000-20,000**

A mahogany bureau bookcase, with a dentilled cavetto cornice and enclosed by a pair of glazed astragal doors above a hinged sloping flap with a fitted interior and 4 graduated long drawers, on bracket feet, late 18thC and later, 41in (104cm). **$6,800-7,400**

An unusual Edwardian mahogany inlaid bureau bookcase, the breakfront cornice with chequer inlaid frieze, the lower section with central writing slope opening to reveal an interior of pigeonholes and small drawers, flanked by 3 further drawers on each side, over cupboard base, raised on tapering supports with spade feet, 49½in (126cm). **$3,600-4,600**

An Edwardian mahogany bureau bookcase, the moulded cornice above a pair of astragal glazed doors, the fall enclosing drawers and pigeonholes, on cabriole legs **$1,000-1,500**

A George III mahogany bureau bookcase, with fall front enclosing drawers and pigeonholes over 4 graduated long drawers with brass drop handles, on bracket supports, 45in (114cm).
$4,800-5,800

A late George III inlaid mahogany bureau bookcase, with a satinwood fitted interior, on bracket feet, adapted, 43in (109cm).
$5,500-6,500

A late Victorian mahogany bureau bookcase, the upper section with a moulded cornice above a pair of astragal glazed doors, the base with a fall enclosing a fitted interior above 4 long graduated drawers, on bracket feet.
$1,500-2,000

A Victorian walnut cylinder bureau bookcase, the shutter fall enclosing a sliding leather lined writing panel and fitted interior above a pair of panelled doors, on plinth base, 49½in (126cm).
$3,600-4,500

Dwarf Bookcases

An Edwardian satinwood revolving bookcase, the top inlaid with tulipwood bandings and stringing, the open sides with pierced fret panels, on cabriole legs joined by an undertier, 18in (46cm). **$2,800-3,600**

A late Victorian mahogany satinwood crossbanded square shaped revolving bookcase raised on dwarf cabriole legs with pad feet, 24½in (62cm).
$1,600-2,000

Library Bookcases

A pair of Victorian walnut library bookcases, the lower section of inverted breakfront form with 2 frieze drawers over 2 mirrored doors flanked by carved brackets raised on moulded plinth bases, 49in (124cm).
$18,000-21,000

A George III mahogany library bookcase, inlaid with satinwood, the base with a slide above a pair of doors enclosing an adjustable shelf with oval segmented veneers and flanked by 8 short drawers, on a plinth base, c1800, 70in (178cm).
$10,000-11,000

Basically a fine piece requiring sympathetic restoration.

A Georgian mahogany book cabinet.
$8,000-9,000

A George IV mahogany and marquetry inlaid bookcase, with moulded cornice and a pair of geometrically glazed doors above 2 drawers and a pair of panelled cupboard doors, on bracket feet, 62in (157cm).
$4,800-6,400

A Regency mahogany bookcase, with an associated moulded cornice above 2 glazed doors, 2 drawers below and doors, on plinth base, possibly a section from a larger bookcase, 40in (101cm).
$2,340-3,000

A late George III mahogany open bookcase on chest, on turned tapered feet, 29in (74cm).
$2,520-3,300

A Colonial padouk cabinet bookcase, the moulded cornice above a pair of arched glazed doors enclosing adjustable shelves, on shaped bracket feet, c1830, 30in (76cm).
$3,600-5,500

A William IV rosewood bookcase, with moulded cornice above 2 sets of adjustable shelves, the lower part with similar adjustable shelves, on a plinth base, c1835, 70½in (179cm).
$2,700-3,600

An Edwardian mahogany and satinwood crossbanded cabinet bookcase, on tapered square legs, 42in (106cm).
$1,200-1,800

A late Victorian oak bookcase, the fielded panelled doors enclosing drawers and shelves, 90in (228cm).
$1,200-1,400

An Edwardian mahogany bookcase, the arched pediment inlaid with scrolls and swags in satinwood and stinkwood, the base with drawers above 2 panelled doors inlaid with ribbons, on bracket feet, 49in (124cm).
$6,700-7,360

A Victorian mahogany library bookcase, 102in (259cm).
$7,000-9,000

A Victorian mahogany bookcase with a pair of glazed doors enclosing adjustable shelves above a pair of panel doors enclosing a shelf and a drawer, 35½in (90cm).
$1,500-1,800

Secrétaire Bookcases

A Victorian carved oak bookcase in the Gothic style, the raised back with turned finials, below are 3 adjustable shelves and a pair of panel doors, 47½in (120cm).
$1,200-1,400

A Regency mahogany and ebony-strung breakfront secretaire bookcase, with a fitted interior with 2 panels below, flanked by glazed doors with drawers and cupboards below, on plinth base, with later bun feet, 90in (228cm).
$14,000-18,000

A Victorian mahogany secrétaire bookcase, the drawer falling to reveal 6 small drawers with maple fascias, centred by pigeonholes, 50in (127cm).
$2,700-3,600

A Victorian mahogany secrétaire bookcase, the lower section with a secrétaire door and fitted interior above a pair of arched panelled doors, on a plinth base.
$2,700-3,600

A late Regency mahogany secrétaire bookcase, with a cavetto moulded cornice and enclosed by a pair of arched lancet astragal doors above a deep drawer with a fitted writing interior and 3 graduated long drawers, on splayed bracket feet, 45in (114cm).
$3,600-5,500

A mahogany secrétaire bookcase, the serpentine scrolling pediment carved with flowerheaded paterae and enclosed by a pair of glazed panelled doors above a writing drawer and 3 graduated drawers, on splayed bracket feet, early 19thC and later, 45in (114cm).
$3,000-4,000

A George IV mahogany secrétaire bookcase, the secrétaire drawer enclosing a satinwood interior of drawers and pigeonholes around a cupboard door concealing secret compartments, and with one of the drawers inscribed on the base, Mr. Baldy, Surgeon, Cornwall Street, Plymouth, on bracket feet, 43in (109cm).
$2,700-3,600

Buckets

A mahogany brass-bound plate bucket, with pierced sides and brass loop handle, late 18thC, 12in (28cm) high.
$1,400-1,800

A George III mahogany and brass-bound pail, with a hinged brass handle, 16½in (42cm) high. **$2,700-3,600**

A George III brass-bound mahogany peat bucket, the tapering sides with carrying handles, lacking liner, 16in (41cm) high. **$2,000-2,800**

An Irish Regency brass-bound mahogany peat bucket with brass carrying handle, scrolling hinge, tapering ribbed sides and tin liner, 17in (43cm) high. **$5,000-5,860**

A brass-bound mahogany bucket of navette shape, with brass liner and carrying handle, 19thC, 13in (33cm) high. **$900-1,500**

Bureaux

A walnut bureau, the fall front enclosing an interior of drawers and pigeonholes above a well, with 2 short and 2 long drawers divided by half round mouldings, on bracket feet. **$3,000-4,000**

A walnut and feather banded bureau, with hinged slope and fitted interior with well above 3 graduated drawers, on bun feet, 38in (96cm). **$3,600-4,500**

A Queen Anne walnut bureau, the crossbanded top above a hinged slope enclosing a fitted interior and well above 4 drawers, on turned bun feet, adapted, 33in (84cm). **$3,600-5,500**

A Queen Anne bureau, on later shaped apron and bracket feet, c1710, possibly Colonial, 35in (89cm). **$2,700-3,600**

A William III figured walnut veneered bureau in 2 sections, the feather banded base with brass handles and raised on later bracket feet, 36½in (93cm). **$8,000-11,000**

Early bureaux were made in two parts.

An early Georgian figured walnut bureau with feather banding, the flap enclosing a stepped and shaped fitted interior, on later plinth base, 37in (94cm). **$6,500-7,000**

A walnut bureau, with flap enclosing a fitted interior above 4 long graduated drawers, on bracket feet, parts 18thC, 36in (92cm). **$2,000-3,300**

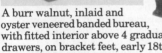

A George II mahogany bureau, the fall above 4 long graduated drawers, on shaped bracket feet, c1750, 35½in (90cm). **$1,800-2,700**

A burr walnut, inlaid and oyster veneered banded bureau, with fitted interior above 4 graduated long drawers, on bracket feet, early 18thC and later, 31in (79cm). **$4,500-7,000**

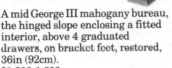

A mid George III mahogany bureau, the hinged slope enclosing a fitted interior, above 4 graduated drawers, on bracket feet, restored, 36in (92cm). **$1,200-1,800**

A George II crossbanded figured walnut bureau, with fitted interior, the drawers all with brass swan neck handles, on bracket feet, 37in (94cm). **$3,600-4,800**

A George II mahogany bureau, the fall revealing stationery compartments, the 4 long graduated drawers above bracket feet, handles replaced, c1750, 39in (99cm). **$1,500-2,160**

A George III mahogany bureau, the fall enclosing a fitted interior, on bracket feet, basically 18thC with restorations. **$2,000-3,000**

A George III mahogany bureau, the fall front enclosing an interior of drawers and pigeonholes around a cupboard door, on later bracket feet, 35½in (91cm). **$2,000-3,000**

A George III mahogany bureau, the hinged sloping flap enclosing a fitted interior, above 4 graduated long drawers, on bracket feet, adapted, 36in (92cm). **$3,600-4,500**

A George III mahogany bureau, the hinged sloping flap enclosing a fitted interior, above 2 short and 2 graduated long drawers, on bracket feet, 36in (92cm). **$1,800-2,700**

A mid George III mahogany bureau, the hinged slope enclosing a fitted interior above 4 graduated drawers, on bracket feet, slight restoration, 39in (99cm). **$2,700-3,600**

187

A Dutch mahogany bureau, the fall revealing a well and shaped stationery compartments centred by a door and brass mounted secret drawers, on ogee-shaped base, above a carved and shaped apron, on claw and ball feet, c1750, 38in (98cm).
$3,600-4,500

A Victorian Sheraton revival inlaid satinwood cylinder bureau de dame, enclosed by a tambour shutter with a fitted interior and sliding writing panel, on square tapering legs with spade feet, 17in (43cm).
$2,700-3,600

A George III inlaid mahogany cylinder bureau, the crossbanded top with a tambour shutter enclosing a fitted interior above a leather-lined writing slide and long frieze drawer, on square tapering legs, 34in (86cm).
$3,000-4,500

A Dutch walnut bureau, inlaid overall with chequer lines, the top and hinged fall with shell motifs enclosing a fitted interior, on later bracket feet, late 18thC, 41in (104cm).
$4,500-6,500

A walnut and feather banded miniature bureau on stand, of early 18thC design, with a hinged slope enclosing a fitted interior with a concave frieze drawer below and shell headed cabriole legs with pad feet, 18in (46cm).
$1,600-2,000

An Anglo Indian padouk bureau, the hinged sloping flap enclosing a fitted interior, on bracket feet, with later handles and loper stiles, 44½in (113cm).
$1,800-2,700

A George III Irish mahogany bureau, inlaid overall with barber pole stringing, the fall front enclosing fitted interior, with door inlaid with Prince of Wales feathers, above 2 short and 3 long drawers, on bracket feet, bearing a retail label from Millar & Beatty, Grafton Street, 41in (104cm).
$3,000-4,000

A George III mahogany cylinder bureau, the tambour fall revealing stationery compartments and a pull-out ratchet adjusted writing surface, on panelled tapered square legs with spade feet, c1790, 32½in (82cm).
$4,500-6,500

A Portuguese hardwood bureau, inlaid overall with ivory and ebonised panels of classical design, the sloping front revealing a fitted interior, on ebonised cabriole legs, the knees carved with foliage ending in French-knot feet, 19thC, 28in (71cm).
$3,000-4,500

Antiques - Antiques - FOR SALE WHOLESALE

20-foot and 40-foot Containerized Hand Picked to Suit Your Requirements

DIRECT TO YOU FROM SWAINBANK ANTIQUES

THE GATEWAY TO A NEW WORLD OF ANTIQUES

OLD ENGLAND BROUGHT TO YOU IN FAMILY TRADITION
DELIVERED TO ANYWHERE IN THE WORLD. ESTABLISHED SINCE 1890

TO PURCHASE IMMEDIATELY CALL: 0114 494 872534

We offer a unique concept in buying antiques. You may select your merchandise from our special 100-page color brochure. Sent to you **free of charge**.

Why not invest your money wisely and turn over your capital into big profits from sales of antiques (off the floor sales) or (auction), whatever you prefer!

We guarantee excellent merchandise (30 days delivery). Just look at the prices of shipments for sale.

References available from many satisfied customers.

ANTIQUES SHIPMENT PRICE LIST
CONTAINER GRADES AVAILABLE

The price of container required depends upon the Quality of Antiques you require for your clientele.

U.S. $s

Price	Quality/Grade
$9,000	☐ ECONOMY (20ft. containers only)
$12,000	☐ BETTER ECONOMY
$15,000	☐ AUCTIONEERS WHOLESALE PACK
$20,000	☐ QUALITY WHOLESALE PACK
$25,000	☐ FINE ECONOMY (Extra)
$30,000	☐ SUPER QUALITY
$45,000	☐ DEPARTMENT STORE SPECIAL 18th & 19th Centry (bric-a-brac)
$50,000	☐ VIENNA HIGH GRADE ANTIQUES
$60,000	☐ MUSEUM QUALITY PACK (VIENNA)
$75,000	☐ CONTINENTAL ASSORTED PACK (EUROPE)
$100,000	☐ HISTORICAL/MUSEUM PACK (INC. ORIENTAL) Please check box required

Prices shown are for supply of 40 ft. Containers.
20 ft. Containers available to suit your requirements.

NOTE: PACKING BY EXPERTS *FREE OF CHARGE*

**Calling Auctioneers
Antique Shop Owners
Antique Mall Owners
Collectors, Museums**

*We can supply
you immediately*

Please write today
or telephone
011-4494-872-534
Head Office (U.K.)

we provide
24 hours response
by facsimile

"We're Ready"
TO DEAL!!
Call us, Today!

"PERSONAL CALLERS TO ENGLAND ALWAYS WELCOME"

A late Regency mahogany and ebony strung cylinder bureau, the top and sliding fall enclosing a fitted interior, above a long frieze drawer and 2 drawers to either side of the kneehole, on turned legs, 44in (111cm).
$5,500-7,000

A Viennese mahogany cylinder bureau, the tambour fall revealing stationery compartments, restored, c1820, 26½in (67cm).
$4,500-5,500

A William and Mary style walnut bureau, on inverted baluster turned legs.
$650-900

A North Italian figured inlaid walnut bureau of serpentine and bombe shaped outlines, the hinged sloping flap enclosing a fitted interior above 2 long drawers, on cabriole legs with knob feet and foliate carved headings, 43in (109cm).
$3,600-4,500

A German mahogany cylinder bureau, with fitted interior and 3 graduated long drawers, early 19thC, 39½in (100cm).
$2,700-3,600

A George III satinwood tambour cylinder bureau, inlaid throughout with stringing, the fall revealing stationery compartments and a pull-out writing surface, the frieze drawer above tapered square legs with brass casters, 36in (92cm).
$5,500-7,000

A small Edwardian satinwood cylinder bureau, the cylinder painted with figure and scrolls, 24in (61cm).
$3,600-4,500

A Dutch walnut bureau, with writing slope and fitted interior, profusely inlaid with marquetry flowers and scrolls, on bracket feet, early 18thC, 36in (92cm).
$10,000-12,000

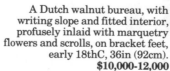

A Victorian satinwood small collectors cabinet, the drawers lined in green printed paper and with a locking pilaster, on a plinth base with ivory ball feet, c1880, 16in (41cm).
$1,600-2,000

Display Cabinets

A Victorian mahogany collectors cabinet, with a pair of arched panelled doors, 40 glazed graduated drawers enclosing a collection of Lepidoptera, on plinth base, labelled J. Thorne, 1 Gernon Road, Esmond Road, Victorian Park, also part of the collection of Egar Greenwood Esq. S.E.S., F.Z.S. presented by Jennifer Greenwood, 1933.
$4,800-5,800

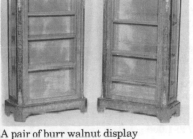

A pair of burr walnut display cabinets, 19thC, 29in (74cm) each.
$6,500-7,800

A Dutch walnut display cabinet, the arched moulded cornice with broken pediment centred by a finial, the glazed door with conforming glazing bars, enclosing 4 shelves, formerly the top section of a bureau bookcase, early 18thC, 40in (102cm).
$2,700-4,000

A giltwood display cabinet, in the William and Mary taste, with a central glazed door flanked by glazed panels, enclosing shelves, the whole decorated with floral carving.
$1,800-2,800

A Dutch walnut hanging display cabinet, with moulded serpentine top and central carved cartouche above glazed doors flanked by canted glazed side panels, late 18thC, 46in (116.5cm).
$1,800-2,800

A Queen Anne style mahogany inlaid dome shaped bookcase/display cabinet, the base with fitted cupboards and double opening doors, supported on shaped cabriole legs with shell carved knees, 1920s.
$2,000-2,800

A mahogany display cabinet, in the 18thC style, with an elaborately inlaid central door in the manner of Chippendale, flanked by a pair of bevelled glass doors, with shaped and pierced apron and satinwood inlay throughout, early 20thC.
$4,000-5,500

An Edwardian inlaid mahogany display cabinet, with a moulded pediment and cavetto cornice above a pair of astragal glazed doors on square tapering legs, 35in (90cm).
$1,500-2,000

A brass banded display cabinet, enclosed by 2 side panelled doors with a mirror lined interior and adjustable rectangular shelves mounted on a gilt wood 18thC style stand, 55in (140cm).
$3,600-5,600

A French mahogany and gilt metal mounted vitrine of Louis XV design, on cabriole legs with gilt paw sabots, signed Albertini, 40in (101.5cm).
$4,500-5,500

A late Victorian mahogany and marquetry standing display cabinet, with satinwood banded outline, on square tapering legs, 26in (67cm).
$1,500-1,800

An Edwardian mahogany display cabinet, with cavetto cornice above the satinwood ribbon tied bellflower swag and astragal glazed door and side panels above, on square section legs tied by a shelf stretcher.
$900-1,200

A Georgian style mahogany display cabinet, with carved decoration, on square tapering supports, 34in (86cm).
$720-1,000

A mahogany display cabinet, of George II design, on a stand with chamfered square legs with Marlborough block feet and pierced wings, 50½in (128cm).
$3,000-4,500

An Edwardian inlaid mahogany glazed fronted display cabinet, with 3 internal adjustable shelves lined with silver floral patterned damask, the base with inlaid and crossbanded drawer with brass knobs, on turned tapering legs.
$4,500-5,500

A rosewood mirror backed display cabinet, with pierced galleried surmount, moulded and beaded cornice and base with protruding corners and wrythen supports to the front, on squat bun front feet, 19thC, 48in (122cm).
$6,500-7,500

An early Victorian rosewood display cabinet, 1866, 30in (76cm).
$1,600-2,000

An Edwardian mahogany and boxwood strung display cabinet, the frieze inlaid with floral swags above an arched glazed apron, inlaid with an urn and floral scrolls, on square tapered legs with spade feet tied by a shelf stretcher.
$1,500-1,800

An early Victorian satinwood and gilt metal mounted display cabinet, with glazed door on bracket feet, 26in (66cm).
$2,000-3,000

A French ormolu-mounted inlaid kingwood vitrine, with serpentine glazed door and sides with bombe lower parts, painted with Vernis Martin allegorical groups, velvet-lined interior, marble top, 32in (81cm).
$5,000-6,500

A giltwood vitrine of Louis XVI design, with beaded and foliate carved outlines, enclosed by a bevelled glazed door and side panels, on cabriole legs with scroll feet, 33½in (85cm).
$1,600-2,500

A French beech salon cabinet in the Louis XV-style, with rococo scroll arched cresting over crimson velvet backed glass shelves, raised upon fluted scroll supports terminating in knurl and peg feet, 19thC, 27in (69cm).
$1,800-2,700

A Louis XVI-style rosewood and tulipwood vitrine, with gilt metal mounts, the brèche d'alep marble top above a glazed door enclosing a lined interior with glass shelves, the sides with inlaid fluting, on toupie feet, c1900, 27½in (70cm).
$2,700-3,600

Cabinets on Stands

A North Italian walnut and marquetry cabinet-on-stand, with ripple moulded banded outlines, the coffered top above drawers flanking a central panelled door enclosing small drawers, 19thC, 30in (76cm), the later stand with a simulated frieze drawer and spiral tapering baluster legs joined by stretchers.
$3,600-4,500

A walnut and feather-banded cabinet on associated stand, of Queen Anne design, with broken pediment above a pair of arched bevelled mirrored doors, fitted with 3 drawers below, above a shaped apron on cabriole legs with pointed pad feet, 39in (99cm).
$3,000-4,000

A Dutch burr walnut side cabinet, the ogee base fitted with 2 short and 2 long drawers and ogee chamfered ends, cross grain mouldings, raised on lion paw feet, restored, early 18thC, 48in (122cm). **$8,000-10,000**

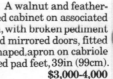

A Victorian mahogany and marquetry cabinet-on-stand, the top with a pierced three-quarter brass gallery fitted with 3 drawers above a rectangular plateau and long frieze drawer, on square tapering legs, 20in (51cm).
$1,600-2,500

Side Cabinets

A George IV breakfront cabinet, 48in (122cm).
$4,500-5,500

A late George III mahogany side cabinet, the sides with an arrangement of 5 opposing drawers, on turned feet, c1805, 50in (127cm).
$4,500-5,500

A pair of mahogany tulipwood banded and marquetry bowfront corner cabinets, inlaid with floral scroll motifs on fluted tapering legs joined by a shaped undertier, possibly reconstructed from a Regency sideboard, each 51½in (131cm).
$4,700-5,500

A pair of mid-Victorian gilt metal, walnut and marquetry dwarf side cabinets, with glazed panelled doors between mask mounted pilasters, on plinth bases, 31in (79cm).
$4,000-4,800

A Regency style mahogany breakfront side cabinet, the crossbanded top above a central brass grille door, flanked by fluted pilasters and bowed cupboard doors, on lobed tapered legs.
$1,000-1,500

A French kingwood and parquetry side cabinet, the mirror with gilt metal cresting centred by a ribbon tied Sèvres style plaque, the lower section with similar plaques on quatrefoil parquetry reserves, on a plinth base, 72in (183cm).
$7,000-9,000

A Victorian burr walnut and inlaid credenza, with serpentine fronted glazed doors on each side, a central panelled door, gilt metal mounts, 59in (149.5cm).
$3,300-4,000

A mid-Victorian walnut and marquetry dwarf side cabinet, applied with gilt metal mounts, the ebonised banded top above 2 glazed panelled doors between pilasters, on turned tapering bun feet, 42in (107cm).
$1,500-1,800

A Victorian walnut and gilt metal mounted side cabinet, inlaid throughout with amboyna bandings and stringing, the serpentine top with a geometric inlaid frieze, the columnar pilasters terminating in a plinth base with turned feet, c1870, 72in (182cm).
$5,500-6,500

A Victorian burr walnut bowfront dwarf side cabinet, inset with painted decorated oval plaques and applied with gilt metal mounts in tulipwood banded borders, on a shaped plinth with block feet, 47in (119cm).
$4,500-6,500

A Victorian burr walnut serpentine dwarf side cabinet, the eared Carrara marble top above a pair of arched mirror panelled doors, between canted angles applied with foliate carved mouldings, on plinth base, 60½in (154cm).
$2,500-3,600

An ebonised, boulle and gilt metal mounted side cabinet, the eared Carrara marble top above an oval panelled door, between canted angles headed by putti, on plinth base, 36in (92cm).
$1,600-2,700

A Louis Philippe ebony, thujawood banded, marquetry and gilt metal mounted side cabinet, with Carrara eared marble top and gilt foliate border, on plinth base, 33in (84cm).
$3,000-4,000

A Dutch satinwood and marquetry corner cabinet, the crossbanded bowfront above 2 frieze drawers and 2 doors, on square tapering legs with ball feet, damaged, 37in (94cm).
$1,700-2,000

A Victorian burr walnut and gilt metal mounted side cabinet, inlaid throughout with laburnum bandings and stringing, the panel doors with Sèvres style plaques, the sides enclosed by a pair of bowed glazed doors, on a plinth base with bun feet, c1870, 72½in (184cm).
$5,500-6,500

A rosewood and brass strung pedestal cabinet, stamped 'Maigret', 19thC.
$2,000-2,800

A mid-Victorian burr walnut and marquetry dwarf side cabinet, with amaranth bands and applied with gilt metal mounts, on bracketed plinth base, 33in (84cm).
$3,600-4,500

A German mahogany side cabinet, with a long frieze drawer above a pair of cupboard doors, on a plinth base with block feet, mid-19thC.
$720-1,000

A boulle and gilt metal side cabinet, with velvet lined shelves and applied mounts in the form of child-like figures and scroll mounts, all on a blind plinth, early 19thC, 64in (162.5cm).
$2,700-3,600

A mid-Victorian inlaid walnut and gilt metal mounted credenza of broken D-shaped outline with inlaid panelled door between column uprights and bowed glazed doors, on plinth base, 70½in (179cm).
$6,000-6,500

A pair of Louis XVI style marble topped and ormolu mounted side cabinets, on turned tapered legs.
$2,700-3,600

Canterburies

An early Victorian rosewood canterbury, the 4 divisioned rectangular top carved with foliage above a base drawer, on turned tapering baluster legs, 21in (53cm).
$1,200-1,600

FURNITURE

CANTERBURIES

CANTERBURIES

- ★ the first canterburies were made c1700, originally as plateholders to stand by the supper table
- ★ Sheraton attributed the name to the first piece having supposedly been commissioned by an Archbishop of Canterbury
- ★ the earliest canterburies are of mahogany but satinwood examples are known
- ★ the number of divisions varies, though four is common. Tops are square or slightly convex, with a drawer below
- ★ early pieces are pleasingly simple with decoration generally limited to the legs and corner supports, sometimes with stringing. Rare 'colonnaded' examples in which all the supports are carved to resemble pillars are highly desirable
- ★ square legs are an indication of an early date, round tapered and turned legs appeared c1810
- ★ in the 19thC canterburies were used to hold sheet music, and the Victorians' passion for the piano accounts for the large number of such pieces surviving
- ★ 19thC canterburies became increasingly elaborate with barley-twist supports, fretwork side panels and ingeniously shaped racking
- ★ later still it was common to add a superstructure to the racks, so combining the functions of canterbury and étagère, sometimes with a music stand in the top tier
- ★ elegance is the quality most sought after by collectors, and elaborate pieces often do not command such good prices as a simple, well proportioned piece
- ★ high prices are paid for rare shapes, crisp deep carving and canterburies decorated with musical motifs, e.g. lyre sides. Rosewood pieces often achieve better prices than walnut

A Victorian burr walnut canterbury and whatnot, the top with three-quarter gallery over reeded and carved supports, the lower section with spindle divisions and frieze drawer, raised on ribbed bun feet with casters, 24in (61cm).
$2,700-3,600

A Victorian burr walnut music canterbury, with 4 divisions above a single drawer, resting on turned legs with brass casters, 19½in (50cm).
$2,000-3,000

Open Armchairs

A Victorian gentleman's walnut open armchair, the spoon back, arm pads and serpentine seat upholstered in floral machine woven tapestry, the legs terminating in knurl and peg feet and ceramic casters.
$1,500-2,000

A pair of beechwood armchairs, each with cartouche shaped padded back, armrests and seat upholstered in blue patterned cotton, in a moulded frame, the cresting and seat rail carved with a cabochon and scrolling foliage, on cabriole legs, stamped C. Mellier & Co 50 Margaret Street W, late 19thC.
$4,600-5,500

A walnut open armchair, with padded back and seat upholstered in floral material with slightly scrolled arms, on bobbin turned and square legs joined by scrolling stretchers.
$1,500-2,000

A pair of Victorian rosewood armchairs, in the French taste, the carved shell and flowerheaded cresting above upholstered panelled backs, serpentine seats and armpads upholstered in Aubusson tapestry, on cabriole legs with knob feet.
$3,600-4,500

196

A Georgian style mahogany open arm children's chair, with drop-in seat upholstered in gold Regency stripe, 20in (51cm) high.
$540-720

A George III mahogany open armchair, with waved eared toprail carved with C-scrolls centred by acanthus with confronting C-scrolls with pierced vase-shaped splat, the arms with channelled down scrolling supports, with bowed drop-in seat upholstered in beige floral silk, on square chamfered legs joined by an H-shaped stretcher.
$1,800-2,700

A mahogany open armchair, the arched toprail carved with paterae, the scrolling arms with channelled downward scrolling supports, with serpentine drop-in seat covered in beige floral damask, on square chamfered legs with H-shaped stretchers.
$2,000-2,700

An Edwardian satinwood armchair, with caned seat, on turned tapered legs, the whole with floral painted decoration, stamped WBL.
$800-1,200

A pair of George III style mahogany upholstered armchairs, on ogee bracket feet.
$1,500-2,000

A William and Mary painted maple bannister back armchair, one finial restored, Connecticut River Valley, c1710.
$2,000-4,000

A George III mahogany open armchair, with shield shaped back and pierced splat carved with wheat ears above demi-star, the bowed seat covered in cut floral velvet, on square stop-fluted legs and block feet, later blocks, some restoration.
$2,000-3,000

A pair of 17thC style beech armchairs, with close nailed serpentine tapestry panelled backs and seats, pierced aprons carved with foliage, on baluster legs with paw feet joined by stretchers.
$2,700-3,600

A pair of Swiss walnut open armchairs, each with caned cartouche shaped back and bowed seat, with moulded arms and seat rails, on stop fluted turned tapering legs, headed by gadrooning and paterae, late 18thC.
$3,000-4,000

A Hepplewhite style mahogany open elbow desk chair, the arms with reeded supports on turned reeded tapered legs.
$2,000-3,000

A pair of late Regency simulated rosewood open armchairs, with padded drop-in seats covered in white cotton, on sabre legs, restored.
$2,000-3,000

A pair of painted satinwood open armchairs, the bowed cane filled seats with patterned squab cushions, on turned tapering sabre legs.
$6,700-7,360

These chairs are Sheraton revival and date from the late 19thC, if they were period (late 18thC) the price would be doubled.

A George IV rosewood tub shaped library chair.
$1,200-1,600

A late Regency painted and decorated armchair, the tablet railed radial moulded back above a cane filled seat, on square tapering legs.
$540-1,000

A pair of Regency open armchairs, each with curved toprail, and channelled X-shaped splat centred by a patera the channelled arms on baluster supports, the seats covered in yellow striped cotton, on turned tapering legs, some restorations.
$5,500-6,500

Two George III black painted and parcel gilt open armchairs, one with scrolled cane filled back, the other with back pierced with ovals, each with cane filled seat and squab cushion covered in blue floral damask, on turned tapering legs, re-caned, one partially re-decorated.
$2,700-3,600

A maple rush seat bannister back armchair, painted black, Connecticut River Valley, c1765.
$1,500-2,000

A pair of Regency mahogany open armchairs, each with curved toprail inlaid in ebony with geometric stringing, with drop-in seat covered in striped silk, on moulded sabre legs, some restorations.
$3,600-5,500

A Federal mahogany lolling chair, restorations, New England, c1810.
$3,000-5,000

A Louis XIV silvered and cream painted open armchair, lacking upholstery, the scrolling arms carved with foliage and flowerheads, the S-scroll legs with paw feet joined by a foliate carved front stretcher and H-shaped stretchers bearing printed label Fundacao Ricardo Do Espirito Santo Silva Exposicao D Arte Decorativa Inglesa Peca Que Figurou No Catalogo Com O N.36, re-decorated, some restorations.
$2,700-3,600

The closest parallel to this chair is the giltwood armchair from the collection of the Duke of Buccleuch and Queensbury, Boughton House, now in the Victoria and Albert Museum. It is possible that the Buccleuch armchair, previously thought to be English, formed part of the furnishings of Montagu House and was acquired by Ralph, Duke of Montagu, who was twice ambassador to the French court (1669-72 and 1676-78). Peter Thornton has argued that this chair together with the Dolphin Chairs at Ham House, represents the stage of development of the Parisian fauteuil by about 1675.

A Louis Philippe mahogany open armchair, the moulded solid toprail carved with flowerheads, scrolled horizontal splat and leather padded seat, on baluster tapering legs.
$1,500-2,000

A suite of American rococo revival laminated rosewood seat furniture, comprising a settee and an open armchair, by J. and J. W. Meeks, in the Stanton Hall pattern, mid-19thC.
$8,500-9,000

A pair of walnut open armchairs, of Louis XV style, covered in olive velvet, the arms with scrolled terminals on downward scrolling channelled supports, with channelled waved seat rail on channelled cabriole legs, later blocks, Italian, one with repairs.
$2,700-3,600

A pair of Spanish walnut Gothic revival open armchairs, the padded seats covered in white cotton, on turned legs and block feet, later blocks, mid-19thC.
$3,300-3,600

A pair of late Victorian mahogany open armchairs, the casters stamped Hamptons & Sons, Pall Mall.
$3,600-4,800

A mid-George III mahogany and blue upholstered Gainsborough armchair, restored.
4,500-5,500

A pair of Italian throne chairs, with acanthus finials, above flat arms with baluster turned supports and deep box seat, on short turned legs and sled feet with paws, late 17thC.
$1,600-2,000

Upholstered Armchairs

A William IV library armchair, with brown upholstery, the waisted back, padded seat, reeded scroll arms and seat rail on reeded tapering legs. **$1,600-2,000**

A mid-Georgian mahogany wing armchair, covered in bargello patterned material, on square chamfered legs joined by an H-shaped stretcher, and cushion. **$2,700-3,600**

A mahogany wing armchair, of Queen Anne design, upholstered in figured pink damask, on cabriole legs with shell headings joined by stretchers. **$1,800-2,000**

A Victorian walnut gentleman's armchair, with buttoned spooned back, serpentine seat and side panels upholstered in green velvet, on cabriole legs with scroll knob feet. **$1,200-1,400**

A Regency mahogany bergère armchair, with reeded surround above padded arms with spiral turned uprights and a loose red leather cushion, on turned legs and splayed back legs. **$3,600-4,500**

A mahogany armchair, of George III design, the eared back, seat and scrolling arms upholstered in tapestry, on cabriole legs with ball and claw feet, with acanthus carved headings, and a similar armchair. **$1,800-2,520**

A 6 piece walnut drawing room suite, of Louis XV design, comprising a pair of canapés en cabriolet carved with flowerheads and acanthus C-scrolls, 2 armchairs and 2 side chairs, upholstered in printed linen, on cabriole legs with knob feet.
$2,700-3,600

A George IV library chair, on fluted mahogany front legs, back legs restored.
$5,500-6,500

A Regency simulated rosewood and cane bergère, the seat with a buttoned velvet cushion, the turned and reeded legs ending in brass cappings and casters, bearing the label of Gill & Ryegate Ltd., Oxford Street, London, seat rail stamped G.R. 35P107, cane brittle.
$2,000-2,800

A walnut wing armchair, with a bowed seat and scrolling side panels, upholstered in tapestry, on pad feet, early 18thC and later.
$2,700-4,500

A Victorian walnut armchair, the shell cresting above a buttoned ballooned back, seat and scrolling arms upholstered in orange velvet, on cabriole legs with ribbon carved headings and knob feet.
$1,000-1,500

Corner Chairs

A mahogany corner chair, with curved toprail and twin vase shaped splat, with drop-in seat covered in red velvet, on square chamfered legs joined by an X-shaped stretcher.
$1,600-2,000

An inlaid rosewood splat back corner chair, on turned legs and stretcher frame with stuff over tapestry upholstered seat, late 19thC.
$450-550

These chairs fetch more if they have cabriole legs.

A George IV mahogany tub shaped library chair, upholstered in pale brown leather, on reeded tapering legs.
$3,600-4,500

A pair of George II style walnut corner chairs, with drop-in seats, on carved front cabriole legs with claw and ball feet, c1900.
$2,000-2,800

Did you know

MILLER'S Antiques Price Guide builds up year by year to form the most comprehensive photo-reference system available

201

Dining Chairs

A set of 12 Carolean style walnut dining chairs, the cane filled seats above a scrolling arcaded carved apron on inverted baluster column supports with Spanish scroll feet joined by stretchers, early 20thC.
$2,520-3,300

A set of Chippendale period mahogany dining chairs, comprising 6 side chairs and 2 armchairs.
$16,000-21,000

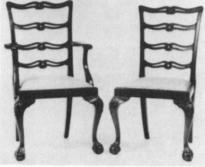

A set of 8 mahogany dining chairs, including 2 carvers, each with an eared shaped toprail and pierced ladder back carved with stiff leaves, above a padded drop-in seat, on cabriole legs with cabochon headings and claw and ball feet.
$3,000-3,600

A set of 6 late Victorian mahogany dining chairs, of George III design, including an armchair, each with a serpentine and foliate carved toprail above a pierced scrolling splat, with leatherette drop-in seats below, on cabriole legs with claw and ball feet and scroll headings.
$2,000-3,000

A George I walnut dining chair, the cresting rail with compressed centre panel, over a solid vase splat, drop-in seat raised upon cabriole front supports terminating in pad feet and turned and block carved back supports tied by baluster turned and block carved stretchers.
$665-900

A pair of early George III mahogany dining chairs, the drop-in seat covered in bargello patterned material, on cabriole legs headed by scallop shells on claw and ball feet, both with later blocks, some damage and restoration.
$1,600-2,000

A pair of mahogany George III Chippendale style chairs, with raised scrolling bead moulded front legs, loose seats, c1780.
$900-1,200

A set of 4 single and 2 arm mahogany dining chairs, in George II style, with drop-in seats above the gadrooned apron raised on heavy cabriole legs with claw and ball feet.
$1,800-2,700

THERE ARE MANY ANTIQUE
SHIPPERS IN BRITAIN BUT...

... few, if any, who are as quality conscious as Norman Lefton, Chairman and Managing Director of British Antique Exporters Ltd. of Burgess Hill, Nr. Brighton, Sussex.

Nearly thirty years' experience of shipping goods to all parts of the globe have confirmed his original belief that the way to build clients' confidence in his services is to supply them only with goods which are in first class saleable condition. To this end, he employs a cottage industry staff of over 50, from highly skilled antique restorers, polishers and packers to representative buyers and executives.

Through their knowledgeable hands passes each piece of furniture before it leaves the B.A.E. warehouses, ensuring that the overseas buyer will only receive the best and most saleable merchandise for their particular market. This attention to detail is obvious on a visit to the Burgess Hill showrooms where potential customers can view what must be the most varied assortment of Georgian, Victorian, Edwardian and 1930s furniture in the UK. One cannot fail to be impressed by, not only the varied range of merchandise, but also the fact that each piece is in showroom condition awaiting shipment.

As one would expect, packing is considered somewhat of an art at B.A.E. and the manager in charge of the works ensures that each piece will reach its final destination in the condition a customer would wish. B.A.E. set a very high standard and, as a further means of improving each container load, their customer/container liaison dept, invites each customer to return detailed information on the saleability of each piece in the container, thereby ensuring successful future shipments.

This feedback of information is the all important factor which guarantees the profitability of future containers. "By this method" Mr. Lefton explains, "we have established that an average £15,000 container will immediately it is unpacked at its final destination realise in the region of £25,000 to £30,000 for our clients selling

the goods on a quick wholesale turnover basis."

In an average 20-foot container B.A.E. put approximately 75 to 100 pieces carefully selected to suit the particular destination. There are always at least 10 outstanding or unusual items in each shipment, but every piece included looks as though it has something special about it.

Burgess Hill is 15 minutes away from Gatwick Airport, 7 miles from Brighton and 39 miles from London on a direct rail link, (only 40 minutes journey), the Company is ideally situated to ship containers to all parts of the world. The showrooms, restoration and packing departments are open to overseas buyers and no visit to purchase antiques for re-sale in other countries is complete without a visit to their Burgess Hill premises where a welcome is always found.

BRITISH ANTIQUE EXPORTERS LTD,
SCHOOL CLOSE, QUEEN ELIZABETH AVENUE,
BURGESS HILL, WEST SUSSEX RH15 9RX, ENGLAND.
Telephone BURGESS HILL (04 44) 245577.
Fax (04 44) 232014.
Tel from USA 011 44 444 245577

MEMBER
LAPADA
MEMBER

203

A set of 6 late George III mahogany dining chairs, including an armchair, the turned and panelled crestings above pierced rail backs, the pale blue moiré fabric drop-in seats on turned legs, c1805.
$5,500-7,000

A set of 6 George III mahogany dining chairs, the backs with pierced stick splats each inlaid with an oval floral harewood medallion, the bowed nailed hide upholstered seats above tapered square legs, c1790.
$4,500-6,500

A set of 6 William IV mahogany dining chairs, including 2 armchairs, the rail backs with carved clasps above loose seats, on turned legs.
$3,600-4,800

A set of 6 George IV mahogany dining chairs.
$2,000-2,800

A set of 6 Regency mahogany dining chairs, the scroll bar draped cresting and railed backs above upholstered drop-in seats, on sabre legs.
$4,500-6,500

A set of 4 Regency padouk dining chairs, the rope twist toprails above splats incorporating circular tablets carved with paterae, supported by S scrolls, above caned seats, on sabre legs.
$2,700-3,600

A set of 6 Victorian mahogany dining chairs, the arched toprail with a double C-scroll pierced splat above button down spring seats, on turned baluster legs.
$2,000-3,000

A set of 6 Regency rosewood grained and parcel gilt dining chairs, the bowed upholstered backs with moulded stiles and scroll supports, above caned seats, on moulded sabre legs.
$4,500-6,500

A set of 10 mahogany dining chairs, the brocade upholstered seats on square tapering legs joined by stretchers, parts late 18thC.
$4,600-5,500

A set of 8 Edwardian mahogany dining chairs, including 2 armchairs, outlined in boxwood stringing, the open oval backs with pierced splats, on square tapered legs.
$3,600-4,500

A pair of George III mahogany dining chairs, the spindle splat hung with drapery, the bowed seat covered in pink floral silk, on square tapering legs joined by an H-shaped stretcher, on spade feet, one block replaced.
$1,500-1,800

A set of 6 William IV mahogany dining chairs.
$2,700-3,600

James Buckingham

COLLECTION OF ENGLISH PERIOD COPIES

At factory prices

TWIN PEDESTAL DESKS

*Also available,
L-shape Computer Desks
with side returns.*

REVOLVING BOOKCASE

BRASS MARQUETRY TOP CHAIRS

BREAKFAST TABLE

ALL ITEMS AVAILABLE IN MAHOGANY WALNUT AND YEW

LOWBOY

DINING TABLE

FILING CABINET

CHIPPENDALE RIBBON BACK CHAIRS

BACHELOR CHEST

NEST OF 4 TABLES

205

A set of 10 William IV mahogany dining chairs, upholstered in brown leatherette, raised on formal foliate, sheathed, melon fluted, turned and tapering front supports, terminating in peg feet.
$8,000-10,000

A set of 6 William IV rosewood dining chairs, the foliate carved scrolling semi-balloon backs above serpentine brocade upholstered seats, on turned tapering legs.
$2,700-3,300

A set of 6 early Victorian rosewood dining chairs, with flower carved crest rail
$3,600-4,500

A set of 10 mahogany dining chairs, of Hepplewhite design, including 2 elbow chairs.
$5,500-6,500

A set of 6 Victorian walnut dining chairs, the serpentine cresting and S scrolling balloon backs above upholstered tapestry seats, on turned legs.
$2,000-2,800

A set of 5 Victorian walnut balloon back dining chairs, shaped overstuffed seats and scrolled cabriole front legs with peg feet.
$1,500-2,000

A set of 6 Victorian mahogany dining chairs, on turned baluster legs.
$1,800-2,520

A set of 6 mid-Victorian walnut dining chairs, on cabriole legs with foliate carved feet, one stamped 849.   **$4,500-5,500**

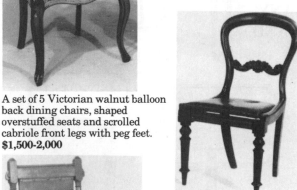

A set of 9 late Victorian oak dining chairs, with padded seats, on turned supports tied by block stretchers, including one armchair.
$1,400-1,800

A set of 5 late Victorian oak and leather upholstered dining chairs, of Gothic revival design, and another almost matching, each stamped Gillow & Co., Lancaster, some with maker's stamp W. Bromfitt, NoLL5178, also with various names inscribed in pencil. **$1,600-2,520**

A set of 4 Italian parcel gilt and cream painted chairs, upholstered in striped gold velvet, with moulded frames and square fluted legs, late 18thC, with painted inventory number 1163, 1164, 1166 and 116?, later blocks, slight damage.
$2,800-3,600

Hall Chairs

A pair of George III mahogany hall chairs.
$1,500-2,000

A pair of George IV carved mahogany hall chairs, with shell shaped backs and solid seats, on ring turned splayed legs, c1820.
$1,200-1,800

A pair of Tuscan walnut high panelled back side chairs, with moulded narrow tapering backs, one roundel cresting carved with the Arms of the Medicis with octagonal seats and spreading square legs carved with rope twist decoration.
$4,000-5,500

A set of 8 George III mahogany hall chairs, each with vase shaped back, dished bowed seat and vase shaped support to front and back, on splayed feet joined by a waved stretcher, one with repair to seat.
$5,500-7,000

A Regency mahogany and ebonised hall chair, the back on lotus leaf support, the bowed solid seat on ring turned and tapering fluted legs, with splayed feet, stamped T. Luke, later blocks, minor restorations.
$1,000-1,600

A pair of Victorian mahogany hall seats, with turned toprails above partially pierced fret backs and solid seats, on pierced fret trestle supports joined by turned stretchers, c1850.
$2,000-2,700

A set of 3 George III mahogany hall chairs, each with solid shield shaped back centred by a painted oval with crests and the motto Constantia et Vigilantia, with dished solid seat, on square tapering legs and spade feet, some restoration.
$3,600-4,500

Side Chairs

A pair of Chippendale carved mahogany side chairs, Boston-Salem area, Massachusetts, c1780.
$5,500-7,000

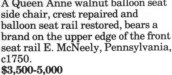

A Queen Anne walnut balloon seat side chair, crest repaired and balloon seat rail restored, bears a brand on the upper edge of the front seat rail E. McNeely, Pennsylvania, c1750.
$3,500-5,000

A pair of Federal carved mahogany side chairs, possibly New York, c1790. $1,700-2,700

A pair of Chippendale carved mahogany side chairs, possibly Southern, c1770, together with a Chippendale carved cherrywood side chair, New England.
$3,000-4,000

Chests of Drawers

A Federal mahogany bowfront chest of drawers, New England, c1810, 40½in (103cm).
$3,500-5,000

A rare George II mahogany small chest, with caddy top, 24in (61cm).
$5,500-6,500

The small size is a major factor here.

A William and Mary walnut and crossbanded chest, inlaid throughout with stringing, minor restorations, on later bracket feet, c1700, 37½in (95cm).
$4,500-5,500

An inlaid walnut and elm chest, with crossbanded top, on bracket feet, basically early 18thC, 37in (94cm).
$4,000-4,800

An inlaid walnut chest, with crossbanded top above 3 frieze drawers and 3 long drawers, on bracket feet, basically 18thC, 37½in (95cm).
$1,800-2,700

An early Georgian walnut, crossbanded and herringbone inlaid chest, of 4 graduated oak lined long drawers, with brass handles and escutcheons, fitted with a brushing slide, on bracket feet, small pieces of veneer missing, 31in (79cm).
$45,000-54,000

These early 18thC walnut small chests with figured veneers and in original condition now fetch large sums.

A William and Mary walnut and featherbanded chest, with quarter veneered and crossbanded top, handles replaced, on later bun feet, c1700, 38in (97cm).
$4,500-5,500

A burr walnut and feather banded bachelor's chest, of George I design, the fold-over top above 2 short and 3 graduated long drawers, on bracket feet, with side carrying handles, 32in (81cm).
$2,520-3,000

A George I style burr walnut bachelor's chest, the top with feather banding, on bracket feet.
$1,800-2,520

A mahogany chest with moulded top edge, brass handles with pierced plates and keyhole plates, on bracket feet, 18thC, 32½in (83cm).
$1,800-2,520

A Georgian mahogany chest of drawers, with brass handles, on bracket feet, 27in (69cm).
$7,000-8,000

A Chippendale carved mahogany block front chest of drawers, formerly the bottom section of a chest-on-chest, the top added later, Massachusetts, c1770, 43in (109cm).
$10,500-12,000

An early George III mahogany chest of drawers, the moulded top with canted angles above 2 short and 3 graduated long drawers, on ogee bracket feet, 33½in (85cm).
$3,000-3,600

A Chippendale carved mahogany block front chest of drawers, restoration to feet, Boston area, Massachusetts, c1760.
$10,000-20,000

A George III mahogany chest of drawers, 41in (104cm).
$1,400-1,600

A late Georgian mahogany chest, the drawers with cockbead borders and brass loop handles, the top with ogee edge, on shaped bracket feet, 40½in (103cm).
$1,400-1,800

A George III style mahogany crossbanded chest of drawers, with brushing slide, brass drop handles and escutcheons, supported on bracket feet.
$4,000-4,500

A George III mahogany chest of drawers, on bracket feet, 37in (94cm).
$1,200-1,500

A mahogany bow fronted chest of drawers, early 19thC, 42in (107cm).   **$1,200-1,500**

A George III mahogany chest, with later ogee bracket feet, restorations, 36in (92cm).
$2,520-3,600

A Chippendale carved mahogany block front chest of drawers, restoration to lower part of feet, Boston area, Massachusetts, c1765, 36in (92cm).   **$20,000-22,000**

A mahogany serpentine fronted chest of drawers, 19thC, 34in (86cm).
2170   **$2,000-2,700**

A Regency inlaid mahogany bowfront chest of drawers, the crossbanded top above 2 short and 3 graduated long drawers and serpentine apron, on splayed bracket feet,
$1,200-1,400

A Federal inlaid mahogany bowfront chest of drawers, some repairs to veneers, Middle Atlantic States, probably Maryland, c1810, 39½in (100cm).
$4,500-5,500

A Regency inlaid mahogany bowfront chest of drawers, with rosewood crossbanded top, on splayed bracket feet, 41in (104cm).
$800-1,200

The large proportions of this chest restrict the price.

A Federal inlaid cherrywood bowfront chest of drawers, New England, c1810, 41½in (106cm).
$4,500-5,500

A late George III mahogany, satinwood and tulipwood banded chest of drawers, the later inlaid top above a brushing slide, 2 small and 3 long graduated drawers, on later bracket feet, 30½in (78cm).
$2,000-2,800

A Chippendale mahogany oxbow front chest of drawers, restoration to 2 rear feet, Massachusetts, c1775, 36in (92cm).
$5,500-7,000

A Chippendale birchwood oxbow front chest of drawers, some damage and repair, New England, probably Massachusetts, c1785, 38in (97cm).
$10,000-12,000

A George IV mahogany bowfront chest of drawers, with gadrooned mouldings, flanked by turned pilasters, on turned feet, c1820, 42in (107cm).   **$1,600-2,000**

A George III mahogany chest, with 4 long drawers, 34in (86cm).
$1,800-2,700

A Dutch mahogany and brass inlaid chest of drawers, on square tapering legs, late 18thC, 46in (117cm).
$1,600-2,000

A Federal inlaid mahogany butler's desk, New York, c1805, 42in (106cm).
$4,000-6,000

A George III mahogany chest, on later ogee bracket feet, c1770, 38in (97cm).
$2,000-3,000

A serpentine fronted black japanned chest of drawers, 18thC, 27in (69cm).
$3,600-4,500

A George III mahogany chest of drawers, with moulded top, on ogee bracket feet, 43½in (110cm).
$1,800-2,520

A Dutch burr walnut and inlaid elm chest of drawers, of bombe outline, on an inverted plinth, on turned bun feet, 18thC, 28½in (73cm). **$8,000-10,000**

A mahogany bowfront chest of drawers, 19thC, 42in (107cm).
$1,200-1,600

A George III mahogany chest-on-chest, the upper section with moulded cornice above 5 drawers flanked by fluted canted corners, the lower section with a brushing slide above 3 further drawers, 42in (107cm). **$2,700-3,600**

Chests-on-Chests

A Chippendale curly maple tall chest of drawers, New England, probably Rhode Island, c1780, 38in (96cm).
$9,000-12,000

A walnut and feather tallboy of William and Mary design, on a finialled arcaded base, with 6 frieze drawers, on bracket feet, part 18thC, 40in (102cm).   **$2,000-2,800**

A mahogany secretaire tallboy, with rococo gilt metal handles and keyhole plates, bracket feet, 18thC, 42½in (108cm).
$7,000-9,000

The secretaire drawer is an interesting feature that enhances the value of this piece.

A Chippendale inlaid walnut tall chest of drawers, some restoration, Middle Atlantic States, probably Pennsylvania, c1790, 48in (122cm).
$4,000-6,000

A Chippendale figured maple tall chest of drawers, restored feet, New England, c1780, 42½in (108cm).
$4,500-6,000

A late George III mahogany chest-on-chest, the frieze inlaid with 3 oval shell paterae over drawers, flanked by satinwood banded canted stiles, on slightly projecting base, with brass swan neck loop handles, on bracket feet, 44in (112cm). **$1,800-2,700**

A George III mahogany chest-on-chest, the lower section with a brushing slide above 3 long graduated drawers, on bracket feet, 44in (112cm). **$2,000-3,000**

A mid-Georgian tallboy, with moulded cornice between fluted canted angles, the base with a slide and 3 long drawers, on bracket feet, 43in (109cm). **$4,500-6,500**

A George III mahogany and blind fret carved chest-on-chest, with dentilled cornice, on bracket feet, c1760, 44in (112cm). **$2,000-2,800**

A Chippendale walnut tall chest of drawers, Pennsylvania, c1770, 44½in (113cm). **$6,500-8,000**

A late George III mahogany tallboy, with a cavetto moulded cornice above 3 short and 6 graduated long drawers between fluted angles, on bracket feet, 43in (109cm). **$2,700-3,600**

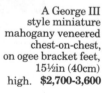

A late George III mahogany chest-on-chest, with a brushing slide and 3 drawers below, on bracket feet, 44in (112cm). **$4,000-4,800**

A George III style miniature mahogany veneered chest-on-chest, on ogee bracket feet, 15½in (40cm) high. **$2,700-3,600**

A Georgian mahogany tallboy with a dentil cornice, with fitted moulded brass handles and lock escutcheons, the upper section flanked by blind fret carved corners, 43in (109cm). **$1,800-2,700**

A Regency mahogany bowfront chest-on-chest, the scrolled pediment above an ebony strung frieze, on splayed bracket feet. **$1,500-2,000**

Chests-on-Stands

A Queen Anne inlaid walnut high chest-on-stand, probably Massachusetts, 40in (101cm).
$5,500-7,000

A Queen Anne style walnut tallboy, the moulded broken arched cornice above a small drawer with 2 short and 3 long further drawers below, the lower section with a brushing slide, 2 long drawers, on cabriole legs and claw and ball feet.
$4,000-4,600

A Queen Anne style walnut chest-on-stand, fitted with a cushion moulded frieze drawer above 9 drawers, on plain cabriole legs.
$1,200-1,500

An American cherrywood chest-on-stand, the stand with waved apron, on club legs and pad feet, Salem, Massachusetts, 40½in (102cm).
$6,500-8,000

A walnut chest on later stand, with a moulded cornice, the stand with a shaped apron, on turned legs and feet joined by flattened stretchers, 38in (97cm).
$2,000-2,800
This piece would be worth at least three times the price if the stand was original.

A Queen Anne curly maple flat top tallboy, top and bottom associated, New England, c1760, 39½in (100cm).
$8,000-9,000

A Queen Anne carved cherrywood tallboy, some repairs, Coastal Connecticut, c1765, 44in (112cm).
$7,000-10,000

A Queen Anne cherrywood high chest-on-stand, some restorations, probably Connecticut, c1745, 40in (101cm).
$4,500-6,000

A William and Mary walnut and marquetry chest-on-stand, the stand with one long drawer, on later baluster turned oak supports joined by waved stretchers and with bun feet, some moulding missing, c1690, 40in (102cm).
$3,300-4,000

213

A William and Mary walnut and crossbanded chest-on-stand, the quarter veneered top above 2 short and 3 long graduated drawers, the stand with one long drawer, on later turned feet, restored, c1700, 38in (97cm).
$4,500-6,500

A Queen Anne walnut and crossbanded tallboy, with moulded cornice, the upper stage with 5 drawers, with pierced brass drop handles, the lower stage with 3 drawers, shaped frieze and cabriole legs with pad feet, 39½in (101cm).
$4,500-6,500

A walnut chest-on-stand, the upper section with shallow ogee moulded cornice, the projecting base with chamfered edge, with brass baluster pendant handles, circular back plates and pierced shaped lock escutcheons, and crossbanded, raised upon 6 ring turned inverted trumpet shaped supports tied by a wavy flat stretcher, on onion feet, some later additions, early 18thC, 41in (104cm).
$3,600-5,500

Wellington Chests

A Victorian burr walnut Wellington chest, the top above 6 graduated drawers flanked by hinged locking stiles, with carved acanthus scroll headings, on a plinth base, damaged, 20in (51cm).
$1,000-1,200

A small mahogany Wellington Chest of 7 graduated drawers, handles not original.
$1,000-1,500

A Victorian walnut Wellington chest with 8 drawers and locking pilaster, 23½in (60cm).
$2,700-3,700

A William IV rosewood Wellington secretaire chest with moulded top, leaf carved brackets, one upper drawer, secretaire and fully fitted interior over 4 lower drawers, turned knobs and plinth, 26in (66cm).
$2,900-3,600

Commodes

A George III mahogany tray bedside commode, with satinwood strung front, ceramic liner and cover, c1790, 20in (51cm).
$1,600-2,000

A George III mahogany tray top bedside commode, the frieze drawer above a pair of doors and a converted apron drawer, on square legs, c1790, 22in (56cm).
$2,000-2,800

A George II mahogany commode, with tray top, the waved pierced sides with carrying handles above a hinged flap and sliding front, the sides with brass carrying handles, on club legs and pad feet with later base, 23in (59cm).
$4,600-5,500

A George III mahogany commode, the top above a tambour shutter and a simulated drawer, on square chamfered legs, 19in (48cm).
$2,000-2,800

A George III mahogany tray top night commode.
$1,500-1,800

Commode Chests

A late George III mahogany night commode.
$800-1,000

A George III mahogany tray top tambour fronted commode, the apron drawer with ceramic liner, c1790, 21in (54cm).
$2,700-3,600

A Louis XV style marquetry petite commode, with galleried top, understage and 3 drawers inlaid with flowers, birds, trophies and writing motifs, 19½in (50cm).
$3,600-4,500

A George III Hepplewhite concave commode.
$15,500-18,000

A rosewood, marquetry and gilt metal mounted serpentine commode, with a rouge marble top above 3 drawers between foliate scroll clasps, on splayed legs with gilt sabots, 39in (99cm).
$3,300-4,000

An Italian walnut serpentine commode, with crossbanded top, 2 drawers with original brass drop handles, on carved rococo and floral parcel gilt base and cabriole legs, early 18thC, 34in (86cm).
$10,000-12,000

A Queen Anne style walnut and lacquer commode, the top with radiating veneer with herringbone and above 2 lacquer drawers flanked by 2 doors, on cabriole legs, decorated with chinoiserie scenes.
$1,200-1,600

An Italian walnut commode, with armorial mask handles and original locks, flanked by caryatids, the moulded base raised on lion's paw supports, 17thC, 58in (147cm).
$22,000-29,000

A Dutch walnut and floral marquetry commode, of serpentine outline, on angled scroll feet, 34½in (88cm).
$6,500-7,000

A South German marquetry serpentine petite commode with bombé sides, the top and drawers with satinwood and ivory inlaid hunting scenes, the legs and sides with scrolling foliage, 19thC, 30in (76cm).
$3,600-4,500

A South German walnut serpentine fronted commode, the top decorated with a panel of cubed marquetry, 18thC, 47in (119cm).
$5,500-6,500

A Continental crossbanded walnut commode of small proportions and serpentine form, fitted with 4 long drawers and resting on short cabriole legs, 19thC, 23½in (60cm).
$5,500-6,500

A rosewood, kingwood floral marquetry and gilt metal mounted bombé commode, with serpentine rouge marble top above 3 drawers between foliate scroll rocaille clasps, on splayed legs with gilt sabots, labelled C. Sale, Antique Furniture Store, Church Street, Kensington, possibly Spanish, late 19thC, 36in (92cm).
$4,500-5,500

A Swedish marquetry and gilt metal mounted bombé commode, of serpentine outline with a moulded verde antico marble top above 3 drawers between foliate scroll clasps, on splayed legs, 35½in (91cm).
$1,800-2,700

A Dutch bowfront commode, with 2, and 2 false, frieze drawers above a pair of tambour doors, on square tapered feet, the whole inlaid with chequered stringing, restorations, 18thC.
$1,600-2,350

A French kingwood and tulipwood marquetry commode, the serpentine red marble top above gilt metal mounted sides and 3 gilt metal mounted drawers, on splayed legs, inside loose lock stamped Paris, c1900, 27½in (70cm).
$1,800-2,700

A Louis XVI walnut commode, with an eared top of brocatelle marble above 3 graduated drawers between fluted uprights, on turned feet, restorations, 53in (135cm).
$5,500-6,500

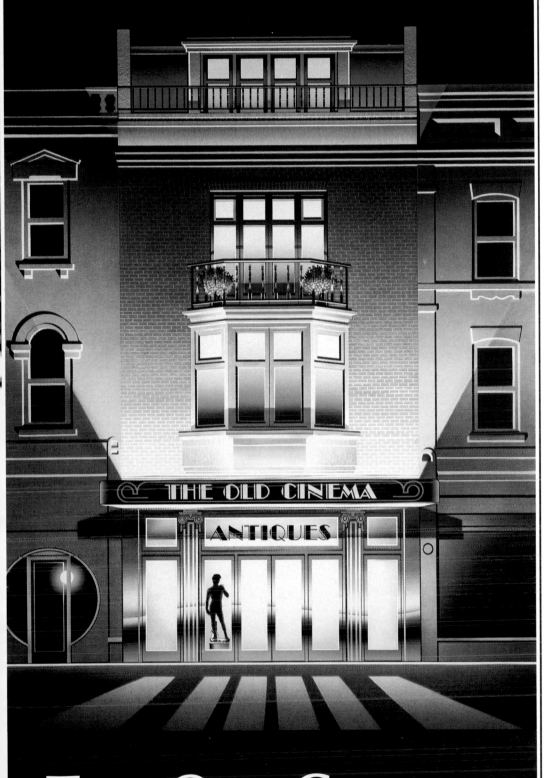

COLOUR REVIEW

A matched set of 6 Charles II carved oak Yorkshire chairs, now with figured seat cushions and loose covers, c1680. **$10,000- 12,000**

A Charles I oak coffer with moulded top above a fluted frieze, the three-panelled front carved with stylised flowerheads and the initials AW flanked by foliate strapwork and stile supports, Somerset, c1640, 42in (106cm) wide. **$2,700-4,500**

A mahogany Windsor chair, one arm repaired, mid-19thC. **$4,500-6,000**

An oak bench with padded seat covered in close-nailed brown leather, on turned legs and square channelled stretchers, basically 17thC, 60in (152.5cm) wide. **$5,000-7,000**

An ebonised oak and fruit wood chest, inlaid with ivory and mother-of-pearl in two sections, the panelled drawer inlaid with the date 1652, 19thC **$5,500-9,000**

A Charles II oak bench with solid seat, the plain frieze with channels, on four baluster legs joined by stretchers, one stretcher replaced, 67in (170cm) wide. **$4,500-6,500**

A William and Mary burr yew chest inlaid with geometric lines, on later bun feet with later veneer. **$10,000-12,000**

A primitive Welsh chair, dry scraped down to it's original paint finish. **$1,800-2,700**

A Queen Anne oak bureau bookcase, with associated top, the featherbanded fall revealing stepped interior, on later bun feet, c1710, 79in (199cm) high. **$4,500-6,500**

An oak bureau, the fall front revealing a fitted interior, with two short and three long drawers, on bracket feet, early 19th C, 36in (92cm) wide. **$2,700-4,500**

A William and Mary burr yew wood and yew wood side table, the legs joined by wavy double Y stretchers, on later inverted cup feet. **$14,500-18,000**

A George I oak lowboy, with crossbanded top, on pad feet, c1715. **$18,000-21,000**

A George II mahogany side table, with moulded top above waved apron, on cabriole legs headed by acanthus on claw-and-ball feet, small repair. **$10,000-14,500**

A Charles II oak side table, the plank top enclosing a well, the front with two simulated drawers, on bun feet, back feet replaced, restorations. **$8,500-10,000**

A pot board dresser, with plate racks over three drawers, with original fretwork, South Wales, c1785. **$9,000-10,000**

A George III oak cupboard dresser with a rare three cupboard formation, North Wales, c1780. **$16,500-21,000**

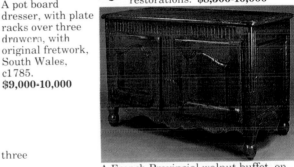

A French Provincial walnut buffet, on later beechwood ball feet, mid-18th C. **$4,500-6,000**

A George III oak dresser, the raised back with moulded cornice, the base flanked by reeded quarter turned pilasters, on stile feet, c1790. **$5,500-9,000**

A George III oak and pine dresser, with associated back, on stile feet, base c1780, top early 19thC. **$4,500-7,000**

A pair of Regency oak and ebonised daybeds, covered in blue striped repp, on hairy monopodia with paw feet, inscribed in ink underneath 5244, repair to seat rail. **$27,000-35,000**

A George III mahogany and painted four-poster bed, the arched tester painted with flowers on a cream ground, the reeded end posts carved with wheat ears and with reeded lower parts, with box-spring and mattress, 1790. **$21,000-27,000**

A black and gilt japanned four-poster bed, on turned feet, late 19thC. **$6,000-8,000**

A walnut and parcel-gilt lit en bateau, the curtain edged with original bobbin tassels, probably German, early 19thC. **$32,000-40,000**

An Empire mahogany bed, each end faced by a free-standing column, c1810, 60in (152.5cm) wide, 83in (210.5cm) long. **$18,000-21,000**

A blue and grey painted lit à la polonaise, with domed hanging canopy, on scroll feet joined by a waved rail carved and decorated on one side only, one rail later. **$14,500-18,000**

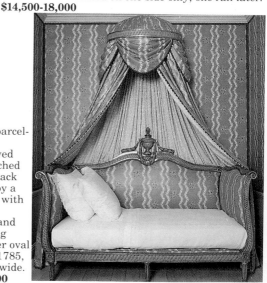

A Louis XVI painted and parcel-gilt bed, with guilloche-carved frame, the arched upholstered back surmounted by a swagged urn, with over-scrolled padded ends and fluted tapering legs, with later oval corona, circa 1785, 76in (193cm) wide. **$21,000-27,000**

A mahogany tester bed, with two George III front posts, made up and requires restoration. **$3,600-5,500**

A George III mahogany breakfront bookcase with some alterations. **$18,000-21,000**

A Regency mahogany and ebony bookcase, on bun feet, restorations to one back foot. **$16,500-20,000**

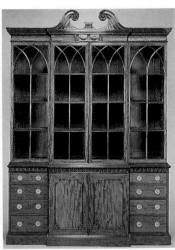

A George III mahogany breakfront bookcase cabinet in two parts, 3rd quarter 18thC. **$54,000-72,000**

A George III mahogany bookcase in three sections, 88in (224cm) wide. **$14,000-16,500**

An Edwardian satinwood and painted display cabinet, feet, 78in (198cm) high. **$9,000-12,000**

A Louis XV ormolu mounted tulipwood, kingwood and marquetry secrétaire à abattant, with 'arc-en-arbalette' breccia marble top, stencil marks. **$50,000-70,000**

A George II mahogany breakfront bookcase, the broken architectural pediment above 4 glazed doors, on plinth base, originally fitted in an alcove. **$11,000-13,000**

pair of Regency mahogany, arcel-gilt bookcases, adapted. 33,000-40,000

A George II mahogany breakfront bookcase in the manner of Thomas Chippendale, on shaped bracket feet. **$145,000-160,000**

A George I small walnut bureau cabinet, with moulded swan neck cornice, c1720. **$66,000-80,000**

A George III satinwood secrétaire cabinet crossbanded in amarillo, the cornice surmounted by four later urn-shaped finials, the base with fall flap and mahogany lined drawers. **$48,000-55,000**

A George I figured walnut bureau cabinet, the broken scroll pediment with 3 later urn finials above a pair of later bracket feet, restorations. **$45,000-54,000**

A George I figured walnut bureau cabinet, the base in two parts, inlaid with featherband the flap enclosing a fitted interior, on later bun feet. **$18,000-27,000**

A Biedermeier birch secrétaire à abattant, on block feet, some restorations. **$5,500-9,000**

A George II mahogany bureau bookcase, 77in (196cm) high. **$9,000-12,000**

A Louis XVI kingwood and marquetry secrétaire à abattant, with grey fossil marble top, the interior of the fall lined with leather, 56½in (143.5cm) high. **$23,000-28,000**

A George II walnut bureau bookcase, with 4 long cockbeaded drawers, on later bracket feet, c1750. **$25,000-32,000**

A Queen Anne walnut escritoire, formerly on bun feet. **$20,000-25,000**

A Queen Anne burr walnut bureau cabinet in three sections, on later bun feet, the sides with carrying handles, some restorations, 76½in (194cm) high. **$29,000-36,000**

A George I figured walnut bureau cabinet, with fitted interior and well, on later bun feet. **$38,000-45,000**

A Venetian yellow painted lacquer povera bureau cabinet, with fitted interior, on cabriole legs and paw feet. **$13,000-16,500**

A George I walnut bureau, inlaid overall with featherbanding, on bracket feet, 43in (110cm) high. **$18,000-21,000**

A pair of ormolu mounted open bookcases with inset Basque Jaspe marble tops. **$10,000-14,500**

A George III mahogany corner cabinet, the triangular pediment with dentilled border, on moulded plinth, 91¹/₂in (233cm) high. **$8,000-10,000**

A Victorian ormolu mounted amboyna display cabinet, one putto mount lacking, 26¹/₂in (67cm). **$3,600-5,500**

A Queen Anne walnut bureau with featherbanding, the flap lined with green baize, 30in (76cm). **$7,000-9,000**

A Victorian walnut display cabinet, with ormolu mounts, 30in (76cm). **$1,000-1,500**

A Queen Anne walnut bureau, inlaid overall with boxwood stringing above a flap enclosing fitted interior, restorations, 31in (79cm). **$10,000-14,500**

A George I inlaid walnut bureau, with herringbone crossbanding, on bracket feet, restorations, 36in (92cm). **$20,000-22,000**

A boulle, ebony and brass side cabinet, the doors inlaid with foliate strapwork, 40¹/₂in (103cm) wide. **$3,600-5,500**

A Portuguese carved rosewood bureau, the sloping front enclosing a fitted interior with small drawers, pigeonholes and a central cupboard, the serpentine lower part with four graduated long drawers flanked by carved canted corners, mid-18thC 43in (110cm) high. **$40,000-54,000**

A Louis XV marquetry bureau, with pull-out leather lined writing slide, on cabriole legs, all inlaid with naive marquetry 39¹/₂in (100cm). **$72,000-90,000**

A George III mahogany bonheur du jour, banded in satinwood and inlaid overall with boxwood stringing, on brass paw feet, 36in (92cm). **$16,500-20,000**

A Regency kingwood and tulipwood cylinder bureau, inlaid with boxwood and ebony lines. 30in (76cm). **$10,000-14,500**

A Regency amaranth, satinwood and ebony cabinet-on-stand, on beaded turned tapering legs with lotus leaf capitals with concave-fronted undertier, feet damaged, 50in (127cm) wide. **$9,000-14,500**

A Portuguese brass mounted rosewood, ebonised and tortoiseshell cabinet-on-stand, with trade label, with brass finials, on bun feet, 19thC, 48in (122cm). **$21,000-27,000**

A figured walnut cabinet-on-stand, inlaid overall with featherbands, the stand with a frieze drawer, on multi-baluster legs and bun feet, 22in (56cm). **$9,000-12,000**

A Louis XIV marquetry bureau mazarin, with two drawers in the frieze, a recessed cupboard with four further drawers, the whole inlaid with floral marquetry on an ebony ground, late 17thC, 44¹/₂in (113cm). **$30,000-36,000**

A Charles II japanned cabinet on a silvered wood stand, the stand with rich foliate scrollwork, the decoration re-painted, c1680, 42¹/₂in (108cm). **$16,500-20,000**

A Flemish silver-mounted parcel gilt, tortoiseshell, ebony, rosewood and marquetry cabinet-on-stand, the sides inlaid with vases of flowers, 76¹/₂in (193cm). **$130,000-180,000**

A pair of mid-Victorian ormolu mounted, amboyna and walnut side cabinets, 51in (129.5cm). **$30,000-36,000**

A pair of ormolu mounted kingwood and parquetry side cabinets c1875. **$12,000-16,500**

A William IV amboyna and parcel gilt side cabinet, the doors enclosing purple velvet-lined shelves, on plinth base, 72in (182.5cm). **$9,000-10,000**

A lacquer and kingwood parquetry side cabinet with portor marble top, stamped P. Garnier, part c1780, altered, 88in (224cm). **$45,000-63,000**

An early Victorian ormolu mounted and brass inlaid calamander side cabinet with marble top, 80½in (204cm). **$9,000-12,000**

A George IV mahogany folio cabinet with twin reading stand, each end with door enclosing two vertical dividers, 39in (99cm). **$5,500-9,000**

An Edwardian satinwood and painted side cabinet, 48in (122cm). **$7,000-9,000**

A pair of late Victorian amboyna cabinets by Gillow & Co. **$10,000-14,500**

A George III mahogany collector's cabinet-on-stand, with 20 small drawers, and contents list in French, stamped. **$27,000-36,000**

A German walnut and marquetry cabinet, with cast iron handles, 17th/18thC. **$12,000-16,500**

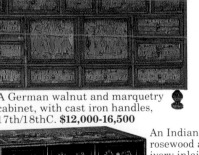

An Italian ebony and white metal inlaid cabinet, early 18thC with later back, 34in (86cm). **$16,500-21,000**

An Indian rosewood and ivory inlaid cabinet, with chequered band to the base, restorations, 21in (53cm). **$9,000-10,000**

An Italian bone and ebony cabinet with later stand, restorations, the cabinet 17thC. **$36,000-45,000**

A Louis XV painted desk armchair, mid-18thC. **$11,000-14,500**

A matched pair of Louis XV giltwood bergères, re-gilded, stamped. **$27,000-36,000**

An early George III mahogany wing armchair. **$21,000-27,000**

A Louis XV walnut large bergère, cabriole legs, mid-18thC. **$32,000-36,000**

A George III mahogany library armchair. **$5,500-7,000**

A Queen Anne walnut armchair on later blocks. **$12,000-16,500**

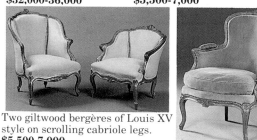

Two giltwood bergères of Louis XV style on scrolling cabriole legs. **$5,500-7,000**

A pair of Louis XV walnut bergères, arched stuffed backs, padded arms, loose cushioned seats and cabriole legs, mid-18thC. **$14,500-18,000**

A George II walnut wing armc. on cabriole legs and pad feet, l blocks, minor restorations. **$14,500-16,500**

A William and Mary elmwood wing armchair, on pointed pad feet, c1700. **$10,000-14,500**

A George III mahogany armchair, with waved padded back, arms and seat upholstered with floral needlework, on cabriole legs carved with acanthus and flowerheads, claw-and-ball feet, seat rail reconstructed, restored. **$16,500-20,000**

A George II walnut wing armchair, on cabriole legs, minor restorations. **$16,500-20,000**

A Queen Anne beechwood wing armchair, restorations to front legs, later blocks, some replacements. **$14,500-18,000**

A pair of walnut bergères, arched padded backs, sides and cushions covered in moiré silk, on short cabriole legs with scroll toes, restorations. **$12,000-14,500**

A George III mahogar armchair, restoration **$7,000-10,000**

A William and Mary beechwood and fruitwood one later armchair, stretcher. **$14,500-18,000**

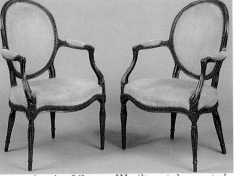

A pair of George III gilt metal mounted ebonised open armchairs, on turned tapering fluted legs headed by anthemia, redecorated, the gilt metal added in 19thC. **$9,000-10,000**

A George II mahogany open armchair, with later upholstery and blocks. **$45,000-54,000**

A George II red japanned caned armchair, attributed to G. Grendy. **$9,000-12,000**

A Russian ormolu mounted mahogany bergère, on sabre legs, early 19thC. **$70,000-95,000**

A pair of George III mahogany library armchairs, on square fluted tapering legs, c1775. **$36,000-45,000**

A Chippendale walnut armchair **$29,000-36,000**

A George I burr walnut armchair, restorations. **$72,000-90,000**

A George I walnut open armchairs, formerly with stretchers, restorations. **$24,000-28,000**

A set of 6 Dutch walnut open armchairs, on scrolled pad feet. **$7,000-9,000**

A pair of George II japanned chairs. **$14,500-21,000**

A pair of George III mahogany chairs, restorations. **$18,000-27,000**

A George III mahogany desk chair, with pierced splat, on chamfered legs joined by stretchers, later blocks. **$7,000-9,000**

An ormolu mounted mahogany revolving desk chair, restorations. **$3,500-5,500**

A Regency mahogany library bergère, with cane filled back, arms and seat, lacking part of one arm support. **$3,600-5,500**

A Regency mahogany tub chair, with cane filled arched back and seat and squab cushion, stamped S. **$3,500-4,500**

A giltwood open armchair, with arched padded panel back, early 19thC. **$9,000-10,000**

A pair of modern ebonised and parcel gilt open armchairs. **$5,500-9,000**

A George III mahogany bergère, numbered in ink no.397, indistinct inscription. **$2,700-4,500**

A George III mahogany tub armchair, upholstered in close nailed leather. **$9,000-10,000**

A pair of George III mahogany open armchairs. **$17,000-18,500**

A Regency mahogany bergère, partially re-railed, and another matching chair. **$5,500-7,000**

Two French open armchairs, one walnut, one elm, late 17thC. **$6,000-7,500**

A pair of George III beechwood open armchairs, restorations. **$3,500-5,500**

A pair of George III mahogany open armchairs. **$11,000-14,500**

Two Flemish open armchairs, late 17thC tapestry. **$9,000-10,000**

A Pair of George III giltwood open chairs. **$36,000-40,000**

A pair of George III giltwood open armchairs, re-gilded, minor variations in size. **$7,000-9,000**

A George III giltwood open armchair. **$3,500-5,500**

A Napoleon III rosewood prayer seat, with hinged back, covered in needlework. **$1,200-1,600**

A Regency rosewood library open armchair, lacking reading stand. **$3,800-4,500**

A pair of Louis XVI carved giltwood armchairs, c1780. **$20,000-22,000**

A pair of Italian walnut and parcel gilt open armchairs, basically 17thC. **$4,000-4,500**

A Victorian parcel gilt and polychrome painted Gothic suite, comprising a sofa and 2 open armchairs. **$6,000-7,500**

A North Italian simulated rosewood and parcel gilt Klismos armchair, c1820. **$12,000-14,500**

A pair of Empire white painted and parcel gilt fauteuils, stamped Cressent. **$28,000-36,000**

A rare Empire mahogany Campaign chair, stamped J D c1805. **$10,000-12,000**

A pair of Empire mahogany fauteuils, plain frame and armrests. **$7,000-10,000**

A pair mahogany armchairs, the arm rests with ball finials and baluster supports c1800. **$18,000-21,000**

A pair of Louis XVI painted armchairs, stamped Jacob, c1785. **$9,500-11,000**

A Restauration rosewood armchair, c1830. **$14,500-18,000**

A set of 4 North Italian parcel gilt and grained open armchairs. **$16,500-18,000**

A harlequin pair of Venetian silvered grotto chairs, with scallop backs and seats, dolphin arm supports and shaped legs carved with rockwork and scrolls. **$14,500-18,000**

A pair of Louis XVI fauteuils, stamped G. Jacob, restored. **$9,500-11,000**

229

A pair of Empire chairs, later blocks. **$2,000-2,700**

A set of 6 Regency mahogany dining chairs, and 2 others of later date, one with Norman Adams label. **$9,200-10,000**

A set of 4 George IV mahogany hall chairs, by Gillows, slight variations in carving. **$6,000-7,500**

A set of 10 Regency dining chairs, stamped Ford, damage. **$21,000-25,000**

An Empire mahogany chair, perhaps Jacob Desmalter, c1810. **$4,500-6,000**

A set of 12 Regency mahogany dining chairs, minor restorations. **$72,000-80,000**

A set of 4 Piedmontese painted chairs, 2 repaired, redecorated, traces of old gilding, late 18thC. **$9,000-12,000**

A set of 12 Regency mahogany dining chairs, restored. **$36,000-40,000**

A set of 12 William IV rosewood dining chairs, with variously upholstered seats above cane filled seats, one lacking splat, one re-railed. **$14,500-16,500**

A set of 4 satinwood dining chairs, each with pierced shield shaped back painted with an oval. **$4,500-6,000**

A set of 12 Regency parcel gilt simulated rosewood dining chairs, by Gee. **$46,000-54,000**

A set of 4 Regency gilt metal mounted ebonised chairs, on X-frame supports, stamped IW, minor restorations, decorations retouched. **$7,500-9,500**

A George I walnut tallboy, inlaid with featherbands, on later bracket feet, 41in (104cm). **$10,000-14,500**

A George III walnut tallboy, with fluted quadrant columns and brass mounts, c1765, 44in (112cm). **$10,000-14,500**

A Queen Anne walnut tallboy, Pennsylvania, c1750, 41½ in (105cm). **$16,500-20,000**

A mid-Georgian mahogany bachelor's chest, with hinged top, 33in (84cm). **$23,000-28,000**

A mid-Georgian mahogany tallboy, 41in (104cm). **$14,500-18,000**

A walnut oyster veneered chest, inlaid and crossbanded with fruitwood, part early 18thC. **$3,500-5,500**

A Chippendale carved mahogany chest of drawers, c1780, 41in (104cm). **$8,000-10,000**

A George II mahogany tallboy, with dentil cornice and broken dentil triangular pediment, c1755, 48in (122cm). **$9,500-10,500**

A Chippendale carved mahogany chest of drawers, original brasses, Massachusetts, 37½in (95cm). **$22,000-25,000**

A George III mahogany secrétaire tallboy, with moulded broken swan neck pediment centred by scrolling acanthus above a band of blind fretwork, the secrétaire drawer with fitted interior, 46½in (116.5cm). **$18,000-21,000**

A Queen Anne figured maple tallboy, in 2 sections, New England, c1750, 40½in (102cm). **$14,500-18,000**

A George III mahogany chest, inlaid with chevron bands, 42½in (107cm). **$18,000-21,000**

A North Italian walnut bombé commode, 38in (96.5cm). **$14,500-18,000**

A Regency mahogany chest, inlaid with fruitwood, with waved apron and sabre legs, 42in (106cm). **$5,500-7,00**

A George III mahogany dressing chest, the top drawer with a slide, previously fitted, 43½in (110cm). **$14,500-18,000**

A George III mahogany dressing commode. **$12,000-16,500**

A late Victorian satinwood and marquetry commode, by Edwards & Roberts, banded and inlaid with kingwood and harewood, 60in (152cm). **$18,000-21,000**

A George III mahogany chest, inlaid with ebonised lines, with slide above 2 short and 4 graduated mahogany lined drawers, on angled bracket feet and later blocks, 40in (102cm). **$9,500-11,000**

A George III mahogany and marquetry chest, inlaid with fruitwood lines, the top with an oval medallion with an urn, 41½in (105cm). **$7,000-9,000**

A George III parquetry commode, the do with central medallions fram by parquetry, enclosing slides, 66in (168cm). **$100,000-130,00**

A George III satinwood commode, crossbanded with amaranth and inlaid with boxwood and ebonised lines, restorations, 39½in (100cm). **$34,000-36,000**

A German walnut parquetry commode, inlaid with simple parquetry, c1740, 46in (117cm). **$14,500-18,000**

A bird's-eye maple chest, slide, early 19thC, with restorations, 30in (76cm). **$3,500-5,500**

A Louis XIV boulle commode, inlaid partly in coloured shell on a brass and tortoiseshell ground, 37in (119cm). **$215,000-230,000**

A Louis XVI style kingwood and ormolu commode, by Henry Dasson, dated 1889, the doors inlaid with a trellis pattern, 54½in (138cm). **$16,500-20,000**

A Dutch black and gilt commode, redecorated, 36½in (93cm). **$7,500-9,500**

A Louis XV Provincial walnut commode, 50in (127cm). **$10,000-14,500**

A Danish walnut and parcel gilt commode, the pierced frieze carved with acanthus, C-scrolls, rockwork and flowerheads, on cabriole legs headed by acanthus with scroll feet, mid-18C, 37in (94cm). **$36,000-40,000**

A Venetian walnut, olivewood and marquetry commode, heightened with mother-of-pearl and bone, inlaid with Apollo within a scrolling cartouche, the drawers inlaid with a putto and scrolling foliage, the sides inlaid with vases of foliage, early 18thC, 30½in (77cm). **$27,000-32,000**

An Italian walnut commode, with 3 drawers, on later short cabriole legs, restorations, 47in (119cm). **$10,000-14,500**

A South Italian walnut commode, banded overall with tulipwood with moulded quarter veneered top, minor restorations, 3rd quarter 18thC, 50in (127cm). **$32,000-36,000**

A Louis XV ormolu mounted kingwood commode, 58in (147cm). **$30,000-32,000**

A North Italian walnut, barr beech, ebonised and marquetry commode, 18thC, 56in (143cm). **$16,500-21,000**

A Louis XIV olivewood veneered commode, c1710, 52in (130cm). **$14,500-16,500**

A Regency mahogany pedestal desk, outlined with ebony stringing, with leather-lined top, c1805, 61½in (155cm). **$50,000-54,000**

A Louis XV style kingwood, parquetry and ormolu bureau, late 19thC, 50in (127cm). **$12,000-16,500**

A George III mahogany tambour desk in Chippendale style, c1780, 50½in (128cm). **$14,500-18,000**

A mahogany kneehole desk, with 4 banks of drawers below slides, handles replaced, c1800, 47in (119cm). **$22,000-25,000**

A satinwood double-sided library desk, now stamped Gillows, part early 19thC, 79in (200cm). **$14,500-18,000**

A George III pedestal partners desk, leather-lined top, by S&H Jewell, 71½in (180cm). **$16,500-18,000**

A George III mahogany double-sided library desk, with leather-lined top, c1769 (175cm) **$45,000-55,0**

A George III mahogany pedestal partners desk, with leather-lined top, locks stamped Lingham, 61in (155cm). **$20,000-22,000**

A William IV mahogany Gothic revival pedestal desk with leather-lined top, c1830, 58in (147cm). **$7,000-9,000**

An early Georgian walnut kneehole desk, 31in (78.5cm). **$12,000-16,500**

A George I walnut dressing chest of drawers, crossbanded throughout, 33in (84cm). **$12,000-16,500**

A mid-Victorian walnut and marquetry davenport, 23in (59cm). **$4,500-6,000**

A George III giltwood mirror, with pierced carved frame, re-silvered, 38in (96.5cm). **$12,000-16,500**

A Pair of George III giltwood, églomisé two-light girandoles, 37in (94cm). **$13,500-14,500**

A George II giltwood mirror, c1740. **$14,500- 16,500**

A George II walnut and parcel gilt mirror, 50in (127cm). **$9,000-10,000**

A Queen Anne giltwood overmantel mirror, with triple engraved plates, and moulded frame, 55in (140cm) wide. **$6,000-7,500**

A George III giltwood mirror, c1760, 54in (137cm). **$20,000-22,000**

A George II mirror, c1730. **$6,000-7,500**

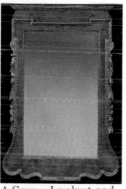

A George II giltwood mirror, re-gilt. **$9,000-10,000**

A George I walnut and parcel gilt mirror, lacking cresting. **$3,600-5,500**

A George II giltwood mirror, embellished, 76in (193cm). **$13,500-14,500**

A George II giltwood mirror, possibly Irish, c1755. **$9,000-10,500**

A pair of George I gilt gesso mirrors, each two-part bevelled and arched plate within mirror borders 1725, 60in (152cm). **$85,000-95,000**

A George II giltwood mirror, c1755, 52½in (133cm). **$9,000-10,000**

A George III giltwood mirror, 69in (175cm). **$20,000-22,000**

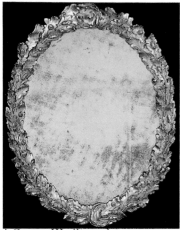

A George III giltwood mirror, the frame with acorns and oak leaves, re-gilt, 34¹/₂in (87cm).
$12,000-16,500

An Irish George II giltwood grotto mirror, restored, 60in (152cm).
$18,000-21,000

A George III giltwood mirror, the frame pierced and carved, damage and restored, 48in (122cm). **$21,000-25,000**

A George III giltwood overmantel mirror, restored, 29in (74cm). **$12.000-16,500**

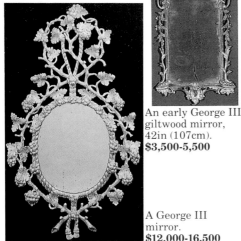

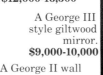

An early George III giltwood mirror, 42in (107cm). **$3,500-5,500**

A George III mirror. **$12,000-16,500**

A George III style giltwood mirror. **$9,000-10,000**

A George II wall mirror, some damage, c1750. **$12,000-18,000**

A George III giltwood mirror, with later plates, 49in (124.5cm). **$7,000-10,000**

A pair of George III carton-pierre mirrors, later plate and restored, 92in (234cm). **$27,000-28,500**

A George III mirror, in John Linnell style, re-gilded, 53in (134.5cm). **$23,000-28,000**

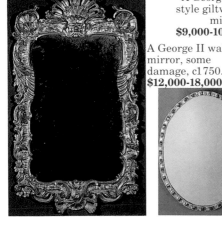

A pair of Regency cobalt and mirrored glass mounted mirrors, slight losses, c1800, 24in (61cm). **$11,000-12,000**

A Regency gilt and composition wall mirror, 52¹/₂in (132cm). **$3,500-5,500**

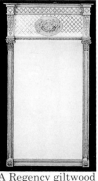

A Regency giltwood and verre églomisé mirror, restored,49in (125cm). **$3,500-4,500**

A giltwood mirror, 19thC, 62¹/₂in (158cm). **$2,000-2,700**

A Florentine giltwood mirror, with pierced carved frame, some losses, 64in (163cm). **$7,500-9,500**

A Danish parcel gilt and walnut mirror, mid-18thC, 53in (135cm). **$14,500-16,500**

A Scandinavian giltwood mirror. **$3,500-5,500**

A giltwood mirror, 59in (150cm). **$4,500-5,500**

A giltwood and ebonised mirror, re-gilt. **$3,500-5,500**

A Regency giltwood mirror, with convex plate and ebonised slip, 30in (76cm) diam. **$4,500-6,000**

A giltwood mirror,some damage, c1850, 52in (132cm). **$7,000-9,000**

A German verre églomisé mirror, 18thC. **$9,000-10,000**

A Regency giltwood mirror, 41¹/₂in (105cm). **$3,500-5,500**

An early Victorian giltwood and composition 4-light Gothic girandole, 75in (190.5cm). **$5,500-7,000**

A pair of mahogany and parcel gilt mirrors, 19thC, 53in (135cm). **$5,500-7,000**

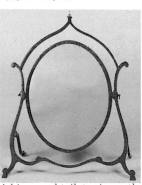

A kingwood toilet mirror, the frame edged with boxwood, bone finial, restored, 24in (61cm) high. **$6,000-7,500**

A Regency giltwood mirror, restored, 42in (107cm). **$3,500-4,500**

 A Dutch six-leaf painted leather screen, with imitation coromandel lacquer, the panelled back painted later, distressed, 18thC, 90in (229cm). **$6,000-7,500**

A painted leather six-leaf screen, late 17thC, borders refreshed, 77½ (197cm). **$18,000-21,000**

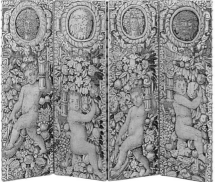

A four-leaf screen with 17thC wool and silk Brussels tapestry, minor restoration, mark of Jean Rals, 61in (155cm). **$9,000-10,000**

An Empire ormolu mounted burr maple firescreen, with later gros point floral needlework panel, possibly German, 41in (104cm) high. **$5,500-7,000**

A carved giltwood firescreen, stamped G. Jacob, with trestle feet, 40in (101.5cm). **$6,000-8,000**

A George III mahogany two-leaf screen, with later painted canvas panels, 45in (114cm) high. **$3,500-5,500**

Two Louis XVI giltwood firescreens, by Jean Baptiste-Claude Sené, with Beauvais tapestry panels. **$27,000-29,000**

A Dutch six-leaf painted leather screen, the reverse painted later, restored, 18thC, 96½in (245cm) high. **$6,000-7,500**

A Regency bronze mounted mahogany firescreen, with pleated silk panel, 55in (140cm) high. **$7,500-9,500**

A Dutch six-leaf leather screen, painted with chinoiserie scenes, the leather 18thC, frame later, 98in (249cm) high. **$18,500-21,000**

A George III mahogany sideboard, the bowfronted top crossbanded in satinwood and tulipwood, above a central drawer and tambour shutter flanked by a cellaret drawer, on square tapering legs and spade feet, 36in (92cm). **$20,000-22,000**

A Regency mahogany breakfront sideboard, banded with fruitwood and ebonised lines, repair to leg, 75in (191cm). **$3,500-5,500**

A George III mahogany pedestal sideboard, with cellaret drawers, 91in (231cm). **$7,000-9,000**

A George III mahogany bowfront sideboard, leg repaired, 72in (182cm). **$5,500-7,000**

A Regency mahogany sideboard, restorations, one drawer lacking back, 82in (208cm). **$7,500-9,500**

A George III mahogany sideboard, with bowfront top, central drawer and 2 cellaret drawers, inlaid with boxwood and ebonised lines and satinwood fan-shaped paterae, restoration to one front foot, 43in (109cm). **$5,500-7,500**

A Federal maple sideboard, with line inlays, probably Massachusetts, legs warped, 77½in (197cm). **$22,000-25,000**

A George III mahogany sideboard, with serpentine front, c1780, 60in (152cm). **$7,000-9,000**

A Federal mahogany and mahogany veneer sideboard, New York, labelled Thomas Burling, c1785, 68in (172.5cm). **$30,000-35,000**

A George III mahogany sideboard, banded with tulipwood and inlaid with chequered lines, probably Scottish, 72in (182.5cm). **$16,500-18,000**

A mid-Victorian conversation settee, each end with rotating seat, on turned tapering legs, 68½in (173cm). **$9,000-10,000**

A George III mahogany sofa, upholstered in close nailed wool, restoration, 94in (238cm). **$5,500-7,000**

A George III needlework upholstered mahogany settee, alterations, 68in (173cm). **$6,000-7,500**

A George IV beechwood two-part sofa, later brackets partially re-supported, 93in (236cm). **$9,500-10,500**

A Louis XV giltwood marquise, stamped Delanois, c1765, 43in (109cm). **$28,000-32,000**

A George III giltwood sofa, restorations and re-gilt, 96in (244cm). **$18,000-21,000**

A Regency brass inlaid rosewood sofa, the waved padded back with inlaid tablet, 75in (191cm). **$6,000-7,000**

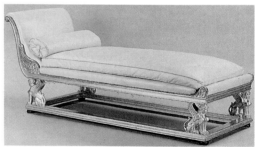

A gilt mahogany chaise longue, covered in close nailed leather, gilding later, 77in (196cm). **$5,500-7,000**

An Italian giltwood canape, upholstered in silk velvet, seat frame partially reinforced, mid-18thC, 77in (196cm). **$12,000-14,500**

A Regency giltwood chaise longue, the moulded frame carved with eagle's head terminals, on eagle's claw-and-ball feet, with interchangeable side , 89in (226cm). **$10,000-12,000**

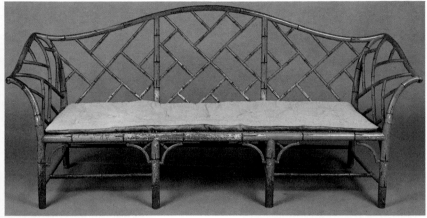

A George III simulated bamboo settee, with hump back and outscrolled arms filled with paling, the drop-in rush seat with squab covered in buttoned linen, on turned legs with pierced angle brackets joined by stretchers, seat distressed, 82½in (209cm). **$40,000-45,000**

A double spoon ended giltwood settee, early 19thC. **$1,500-2,000**

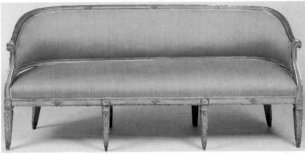

An Italian neo-classical grey painted and parcel gilt canape, redecorated, c1800. **$5,500-7,000**

A Russian Nicholas I parcel gilt mahogany sofa, the padded back and drop-in seat upholstered in printed cloth, with solid scrolling arm supports and shaped legs 74in (188cm). **$6,000-9,000**

A Louis XV beechwood sofa with flower carved moulded frame, arched stuffed back, padded arms, double serpentine fronted seat and cabriole legs, 51½in (131cm). **$14,500-18,000**

An Italian giltwood sofa, upholstered in leather, the channelled seat rail on turned fluted tapering legs, late 18thC, 104in (264cm). **$21,000-27,000**

A Louis XV beechwood sofa, with carved moulded frame, arched stuffed back, padded arms, loose cushioned seat and cabriole legs, mid-18thC, 77in (196cm). **$18,000-21,000**

241

A George III mahogany dumb waiter, 59¹/₂in (150cm) high.
$4,500-6,000

An early George III mahogany urn stand, with pierced fret gallery, c1765, 12in (305cm) wide.
$5,500-7,000

A George II mahogany bowl stand, 29¹/₂in (75cm).
$4,500-6,000

An early George III mahogany torchère, 49in (122cm) high.
$3,500-5,500

A pair of George II giltwood torchères, re-gilded, 43in (108cm).
$27,000-30,000

A George III satinwood whatnot, with cedar lined drawer, 52in (132cm) high.
$21,000-27,000

A pair of parcel gilt and ebonised pedestals, re-decorated, basically early 19thC, 47¹/₂in (120cm) high.
$27,000-32,000

A pair of George III mahogany washstands, inlaid with ebony stringing, formerly with mirrors, 19in (48cm) wide.
$3,500-5,500

A pair of ormolu mounted ebony boulle pedestals, 51in (130cm).
$18,000-21,000

A pair of mahogany dining room pedestals, each with a cellaret drawer, on later blocks, 36¹/₂in (93cm) high.
$10,000-14,500

A pair of Italian walnut and parcel gilt stands, each with later verde antico marble top, lacking one mask, previously washstands, 30¹/₂in (77cm) high.
$9,000-10,000

A Victorian mahogany reeded column, with acanthus leaf decoration, 39in (99cm).
$540-720

An early Victorian mahogany folio stand, by Kendell & Co., 36in (92cm).
$28,000-32,000

A walnut and parcel gilt stool, the cabriole legs carved with foliage, claw-and-ball feet, 19thC, 27in (69cm). **$4,500-6,000**

A William and Mary walnut dressing stool, the over-upholstered seat raised on gadrooned trumpet legs, c1690, 23in (58cm). **$15,000-18,000**

A pair of George III mahogany stools, the legs carved with blind fretwork, later cross struts, 19in (48cm). **$14,500-18,000**

A Regency mahogany stool, in the manner of C. H. Tatham, the seat with scroll ends, 20½in (52cm). **$9,000-10,000**

A George III Gothic cream painted stool, lacking upholstery, 16in (40.5cm). **$2,500-3,500**

A mahogany stool, the padded seat covered in close nailed needlework, on carved cabriole legs headed by lion masks, on paw feet, 19thC, 26½in (67cm). **$6,000-7,500**

A pair of George II mahogany stools, each with rounded rectangular drop-in seat covered in bargello pattern, the waved frieze on cabriole legs and pad feet, 17in (43cm). **$18,000-21,000**

A William and Mary beech and walnut stool, the padded seat covered in 17thC tapestry, formerly decorated. **$5,500-7,000**

A Regency white painted and parcel gilt stool, the padded seat covered in calico, on X-framed legs carved with flowerheads and cleft feet joined by a baluster stretcher, 20in (51cm). **$4,500-6,000**

A matched pair of Regency mahogany X-frame stools, by Gillows, restored, 20½in (52cm). **$18,000-21,000**

A Regency painted and parcel gilt stool, after a design by Thomas Hope, c1810, 34½in (87cm). **$40,000-45,000**

A second Empire ormolu footstool, the bowed upholstered top in floral velvet, with foliate 'pied-de-biche', 12½in (32cm). **$2,000-2,500**

A giltwood stool, covered in tapestry, labelled S. Dawes & Sons, early 19thC, 19½in (49cm) **$5,500-7,000**

A William IV mahogany bench, the waved frieze carved with acanthus and S-scrolls, 91in (231cm). **$5,500-7,000**

A Louis XIV style giltwood stool, the X-shaped stretchers carved with conforming acanthus scrolls, 43in (109cm) **$3,500-5,500**

A mahogany stool, with adjustable support and turned baluster legs, c1820, 17in (43cm). **$5,500-7,000**

Two Victorian giltwood simulated bamboo stools, covered in green cotton, on turned sabre legs joined by X-shaped stretchers, 19in (48cm). **$6,000-7,500**

A pair of Regency mahogany footstools, after a design by George Smith, minor restorations, 16in (41cm). **$3,500-5,500**

A Regency beechwood tabouret, the waved seat rail centred with scallop shells and carved with acanthus, 21in (53cm). **$10,000-12,000**

A French giltwood stool, after a design by A. C. M. Fournier, the seat rail, legs and X-shaped stretcher carved in the form of knotted rope, 19in (48cm) diam. **$5,500-7,000**

A pair of white painted benches, after a design by C. H. Tatham, slight differences, re-decorated, 57in (144.5cm). **$25,000-28,000**

An ebonised scroll and cane footstool, early 19thC, 16in (41cm). **$250-350**

A George III satinwood card table, banded in amaranth and inlaid with boxwood and ebonised lines, the top crossbanded in rosewood, restored, 36in (91cm). **$3,500-4,500**

A George I laburnum concertina action card table, inlaid with featherbanding, 35in (88cm). **$14,500-18,000**

A Russian mahogany architect's table, with double ratchet support, c1795, 40½in (102cm). **$23,000-27,000**

A pair of George III painted and satinwood card tables, crossbanded with rosewood and decorated overall with swags of flowers, foliage and husks, decoration later, gateleg action replaced, 36in (92cm). **$21,000-25,000**

A pair of George III satinwood bedside tables, inlaid with mahogany lines, with hinged tops, restored. **$25,000-27,000**

A mid-Georgian triple leaf tea and card table, the baize lined flap with counter wells above a deep frieze with hinged top, 29½in (75cm). **$10,000-12,000**

A George III satinwood card table, crossbanded and inlaid with rosewood, decorated with flowers, 36in (91cm). **$16,500-18,000**

A George III mahogany architect's table with pull-out section enclosing a fitted interior, 40in (101.5cm). **$10,000-14,500**

A pair of mahogany card tables, with hinged tops, one later drawer, 36in (92cm). **$12,000-14,000**

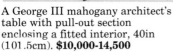

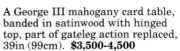

A George II mahogany concertina action card table, in the manner of Benjamin Goodison, restored 36in (91cm). **$21,000-27,000**

A George III mahogany card table, banded in satinwood with hinged top, part of gateleg action replaced, 39in (99cm). **$3,500-4,500**

A pair of Federal inlaid mahogany card tables, attributed to Jacob Forster, Massachusetts, c1800, 35in (89cm) diam. **$45,000-50,000**

A Dutch walnut and marquetry card table, inlaid with flowers, birds and foliage, the baize lined interior with wells and inlaid with cards, 33½in (85cm). **$7,000-9,000**

A pair of French ormolu mounted amaranth, burr walnut and marquetry card tables, inlaid with boxwood, 34in (86cm). **$18,000-21,000**

A Regency mahogany, ebony and ebonised card table, inlaid with yew wood, 36in (92cm). **$10,000-12,000**

A George III satinwood card table, inlaid with ebonised and boxwood lines and banded with thuya, with folding top above panelled frieze, 36in (92cm). **$9,000-10,000**

A Regency brass inlaid rosewood card table, inlaid with boxwood and ebonised stringing, the D-shaped top with panelled frieze, on sabre legs headed by anthemia, the back support and part of gateleg replaced, 36in (92cm). **$4,500-6,000**

A George III satinwood and marquetry card table, crossbanded with mahogany, gateleg action later, 44in (112cm). **$18,000-21,000**

A Regency ormolu-mounted brass inlaid rosewood card table, crossbanded in ebony, restorations, 36in (92cm). **$12,000-14,500**

A William IV mahogany centre table, crossbanded with maple, parts later and re-supported, 60in (152cm). **$9,000-12,000**

A mahogany centre table, with pierced fretwork gallery top, 28in (71cm). **$7,000-9,000**

A mid-Victorian walnut and marquetry centre table, top formerly with tilt, 51½in (131cm). **$12,000-14,500**

A rosewood and parcel gilt centre table, modern, 29½in (75cm). **$6,000-7,500**

A pair of George I Irish giltwood and lacquer centre tables, the Japanese export tops late 17thC with some English decoration, traces of original 'Nashig' border, 34in (86cm). **$90,000-100,000**

A Dutch marquetry, simulated tortoiseshell, ebonised and parcel gilt centre table, distressed, 42in (107cm). **$13,000-16,500**

A William IV fruitwood centre table, the segmented tilt top banded in rosewood, on turned shaft and concave sided base on bun foot, 48in (122cm). **$3,500-5,500**

A Regency rosewood and parcel gilt centre table, with tilt top, 54in (137cm). **$12,000-14,500**

A William IV giltwood centre table, with Florentine pietra dura top inlaid in marbles and semi-precious stones 29½in (75cm). **$80,000-90,000**

A mahogany centre table, the apron centred by a bearded mask flanked by acanthus scrolls, on cabriole legs headed by lion ring masks, with claw-and-ball feet, 19thC, 55in (140cm). **$10,000-14,500**

247

A Swedish neo-classical bronzed and gilt centre table, with later marble top, c1800, 42in (106cm). **$5,500-7,000**

A Louis XV giltwood console table, with marble top, and another matching table, restored and re-gilded, marble 18thC, 52in (132cm). **$20,000-23,000**

A pair of Italian giltwood centre tables, with marble tops, re-gilded, early 19thC, 30¹/₂in (77cm) high. **$27,000-30,000**

A Spanish ormolu mounted mahogany centre table, the top inset with black fossil marble, restored mid-19thC, 47¹/₂in (120cm). **$16,500-21,000**

A George III pine pier table, with bardiglio marble top, the fluted frieze centred by a tablet carved with a patera and husks, 55¹/₂in (141cm). **$14,500-18,000**

An ormolu centre table, the pietra dura top banded with porphyry and malachite, 19thC, 41in (104cm). **$80,000-85,000**

A Flemish ebony and marquetry centre table, inlaid with bone and mother-of-pearl, 19thC, 58¹/₂in (148cm). **$7,000-9,000**

A George III giltwood console table, with Sicilian jasper marble top, inlaid with various marbles, re-gilded, 38in (97cm). **$20,000-23,000**

A Regènce giltwood console table, with veined marble top, restorations, 46in (117cm). **$5,500-7,000**

A pair of Italian silvered wood tables, with simulated marble tops, mid-18thC, 52in (132cm). **$63,000-72,000**

A Pair of Genoese giltwood corner consoles, with mottled marble tops, the pierced friezes carved with foliage and acanthus, one inscribed 'an Boffi', mid-18thC, 30in (76cm). **$12,000-14,500**

A pair of giltwood console tables, with marble top, carved with rockwork, 54in (137cm). **$20,000-25,000**

A pair of Spanish painted and parcel gilt corner tables, mid-18thC, 34¹/₂in (87cm). **$6,000-7,500**

A pair of Louis XVI painted console tables, with later marble tops, restored and reduced, 21in (54cm). **$9,000-10,000**

A Restauration rosewood console table, stamped Jacob, with later marble top, c1830, 53in (135cm). **$35,000-45,000**

A pair of Italian giltwood console brackets, 27in (68cm). **$5,500-7,000**

A pair of Italian giltwood corner console tables, c1750, 32in (81cm). **$48,000-54,000**

A Louis XV console table, the frieze with ribbon tied flowers, 48in (122cm). **$32,000-36,000**

A pair of Italian silvered and painted console tables, 41¹/₂in (105cm). **$16,500-18,000**

A North Italian painted and parcel gilt console table, with later simulated scapliola top, late 18thC, 50in (127cm). **$4,500-6,000**

COLOUR REVIEW

A George III mahogany gateleg table, the twin flap top on square chamfered legs, 67in (170cm). **$6,000-7,500**

A George III mahogany dining table, crossbanded in satinwood, lacking extra leaf, later section to edge, 70in (178cm). **$18,000-21,000**

A pair of North Italian rosewood and marquetry console tables, Milan, mid-19thC, 65in (165cm). **$9,000-10,000**

A mid-Georgian mahogany concertina-action dining table, restorations, the back legs possibly associated, 66in (168cm). **$7,000-9,000**

A Regency mahogany dining table, the base associated, 4 leaves in a baize lined box, 84in (213cm) extended. **$63,000-72,000**

A Regency mahogany breakfast table, with tilt top, the quadripartite base with downswept legs and brass cap 63in (106cm). **$9,500-12,500**

An early Victorian oak dining table, with 3 extra leaves, 117in (297cm) extended. **$9,000-12,000**

A Regency mahogany revolving library table, labelled Waring & Gillow, 69^{1}/2in (176cm). **$9,500-10,500**

A late Regency mahogany pedestal dining table, adapted, 223^{1}/2in (568cm) long. **$32,000-36,000**

A George III mahogany drum table, crossbanded with rosewood, the drawers crossbanded with tulipwood, 24in (61cm). **$16,500-18,000**

A Regency brass mounted rosewood games table, restored and adapted, 28in (71cm). **$6,000-7,500**

A French ormolu mounted kingwood gueridon, with brocatelle marble top, 19thC, 21in (53cm). **$3,500-5,500**

A late Louis XV marquetry gueridon table, with later marble top, 29½in (75cm). **$6,000-8,000**

An ormolu mounted mahogany and marquetry gueridon, by H. Dasson, with spring operated drawer, c1888, 15in (38cm). **$6,000-8,000**

A Regency rosewood and parcel gilt games table, formerly with work basket, 31½in (80cm). **$10,000-12,000**

An Austrian walnut games table, with parquetry lifting top, 41in (104cm). **$4,500-6,000**

A Regency ormolu mounted mahogany and parcel gilt occasional table, with later leather lined top, restorations, 24in (61cm). **$3,500-4,500**

A Regency kingwood games table, with frieze drawer and silk work box, 31½in (80cm). **$3,500-4,500**

A William IV figured walnut drum table, one leg spliced, 28in (71cm). **$4,500-5,500**

A Victorian figured mahogany library table, with scrolled carved frieze, fluted and carved dual ends to cross stretchers, 48in (122cm). **$1,600-2,000**

A satinwood occasional table, the panelled frieze fitted with a drawer, 26in (66cm). **$1,600-2,000**

A black and gold
japanned pedestal
table, the tilt-top
with a Chinese
lacquer panel, early
19thC, 30in (76cm).
$21,000-24,000

A George III mahogany supper table, 3 sides filled
with gilt chicken wire, 42in (106cm). **$9,000-10,000**

A George III satinwood
Pembroke table, crossbanded
with rosewood, oval twin flap
top with central oval, 33in
(84cm). **$8,000-9,500**

A Restauration mahogany
reading table, adjustable in
height, 30in (76cm).
$5,500-7,000

A Louis XV kingwood
table, the serpentine top
inlaid with a diamond
shaped panel, 14in (36cm).
$5,500-7,000

A George III mahogany and marquetry Pembroke
table, 42in (107cm). **$11,000-13,000**

A pair of brass gueridon
tables, marble tops, 29in
(74cm). **$12,000-14,500**

A George III harewood, satinwood and marquetry
Pembroke table, 36½in (93cm). **$48,000-54,000**

An ormolu
mounted kingwood
and tulipwood
table, 12½in
(32cm).
$3,500-5,500

A George III mahogany
Pembroke table, with twin flap
banded in rosewood, single
frieze drawer, square tapering
legs with brass caps, 39in
(99cm). **$4,500-6,000**

A George III mahogany serving table,
the edge applied with blind fretwork
moulding with C-scroll brackets, legs
reduced in height, 74in (188cm).
$6,000-8,000

A mahogany side table, with the inlaid specimen marble top, 37½in (95cm). **$12,000-14,500**

A George III harewood marquetry and parcel gilt side table, 64½in (163cm). **$215,000-230,000**

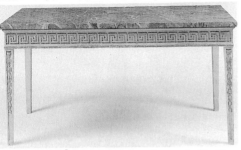

A pair of Irish Regency brass mounted rosewood and parcel gilt side tables, the marble tops supported by winged eagle monopodiae, restorations, 46in (117cm). **$18,500-20,000**

A George III white painted and parcel gilt side table, with later simulated marble top, restorations, redecorated, legs spliced, 67½in (171cm). **$9,500-11,000**

A satinwood side table, with a thuya oval and chequered lines, restorations, 44in (112cm). **$10,000-12,000**

A pair of early Victorian oak side tables, by J. D. Crace, tops cracked and repaired, 66in (168cm). **$63,000-72,000**

A German walnut, burr walnut, ebony and parquetry side table, mid-19thC, 43½in (110cm). **$3,500-5,500**

A pair of George III satinwood side tables, the tops crossbanded with harewood and rosewood and inlaid with ebonised and boxwood lines, branded BO, 33in (84cm). **$24,000-28,000**

A Regency parcel gilt and brass mounted side table, banded with satinwood, mahogany lined frieze drawers, parts lacking, 36in (92cm). **$6,000-7,500**

A Federal inlaid cherrywood tray top table, attributed to John Dunlap II, Antrim, New Hampshire, c1800, 35in (89cm). **$10,000-12,000**

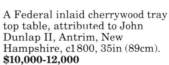

A mahogany side table, with Italian specimen marble top, 69¹/₂in (176cm). **$72,000-80,000**

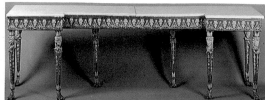

An Italian parcel gilt painted breakfront side ta 113in (287cm). **$36,000-45,000**

A Portuguese palisander side table, with eared serpentine moulded top and a frieze drawer, the apron carved with rockwork, on foliate cabriole legs and claw-and-ball feet, partly re-lined, mid-18thC, 42in (107cm). **$18,000-21,000**

A pair of Italian giltwood side tables, one supported by Bacchus and Flora, 59¹/₂in (151cm). **$21,000-27.000**

A Regency rosewood sofa table, inlaid with fruitwood stringing, banded in burr yew, stretcher possibly replaced, restored, 59in (149cm). **$10,000-12,000**

An ormolu, mahogany and ebony side table, stamped H. Fourdinois, 32¹/₂in (82cm). **$27,000-29,000**

A Regency gilt metal mounted rosewood sofa table, the twin flaps banded with maple and ebonised lines, one foot with wooden replacement, restorations, 62in (157cm). **$21,000-27,000**

A Regency mahogany sofa table, banded in satinwood and ebony, restored, 72in (182cm). **$14,500-16,500**

A Regency mahogany sofa table, inlaid with boxwood and ebonised lines, crossbanded in fruitwood and rosewood, 61¹/₂in (156cm). **$10,000-14,500**

A Regency brass mounted rosewood sofa table, inlaid with boxwood, restored, 62in (152cm). **$12,000-14,500**

A pair of George III mahogany tea tables, crossbanded with satinwood and tulipwood and inlaid with boxwood lines, restorations, 34in (86cm). **$18,000-21,000**

A mahogany tripod table, the top with spindle gallery, 10in (25.5cm). **$16,500-18,000**

A mahogany tea table, the tilting top on a ball turned pedestal, c1770, 36in (92cm) diam. **$14,500-18,000**

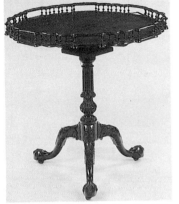

A mahogany tripod table, the tilt top with spindle gallery inlaid with brass, restoration to one leg, 30in (75cm) **$30,000-36,000**

An Empire bronze and ormolu gueridon, the marble base on brass casters, 19in (49cm). **$45,000-54,000**

A George II mahogany tripod table, with fret pierced gallery, 26½in (67cm) diam. **$30,000-35,000**

A George III mahogany tea table, the twin flap top enclosing a well, with plain frieze and waved apron, 30in (76cm). **$7,000-9,000**

A Regency mahogany sofa table, inlaid with ebony, with cedar lined drawer, 30½in (77cm). **$7,000-9,000**

A mahogany tripod table, the top with raised waved rim, 17in (43cm). **$4,500-6,000**

A Regency ormolu mounted rosewood and parcel gilt work table, the top with a contemporary English School watercolour, 18in (46cm). **$40,000-45,000**

An Austrian mahogany work table, with hinged top enclosing an architectural fitted interior, 37in (94cm) high. **$16,500-21,000**

A Regency brass inlaid rosewood sofa table, with crossbanded twin flap top, restored, 60in (152cm). **$9,000-10,000**

COLOUR REVIEW

A Regency rosewood wrting table, with easel reading slope, 29in (75cm). **$28,000-23,000**

A George IV rosewood writing table, with rounded top, 2 panelled frieze drawers, on solid panelled end supports and tapering bun feet, 60in (152cm). **$7,000-9,000**

A Regency rosewood writing table, th scalloped frieze with milled ormolu drops, 40in (102cm). **$36,000-40,000**

A Regency mahogany writing table, with leather lined top and 2 frieze drawers, 45¹/₂in (115cm). **$10,000-12,000**

A mahogany writing table, with 2 drawers back and front, adapted, part early 19thC, 59in (150cm). **$9,000-12,000**

An ormolu mounted rosewood amboyna and marquetry writing table, labelled G. Trollope & Sons, 43in (109cm). **$5,500-7,000**

A Louis XV tulipwood parquetry bureau plat, in the manner of Jacques Dubois, mid-18thC, 51in (129cm) **$160,000-180,000**

A Regency rosewood writing table, the frieze with 2 drawers and 2 false drawers, restored, 44in (111cm). **$7,000-9,000**

A mahogany writing table, with leather lined top, restored, 62in (157cm). **$7,000-9,000**

A Louis XV ormolu mounted rosewood and tulipwood bureau plat, 19thC locks, 57¹/₂in (146cm). **$54,000-63,000**

A Regency rosewood writing table, with leather lined top, the frieze with 2 mahogany lined drawers, with ormolu paw feet, 45in (115cm). **$14,500-16,500**

A Louis XV style ormolu mounted kingwood and fruitwood bureau plat, English, mid-19thC, 67in (170cm). **$12,000-16,500**

A Regency brass inlaid mahogany writing table, inlaid with ebonised lines, some damage and restorations, 54¹/₂in (138cm). **$11,000-12,500**

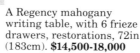

A Regency mahogany writing table, with 6 frieze drawers, restorations, 72in (183cm). **$14,500-18,000**

A French ormolu mounted rosewood, mahogany and burr walnut writing table, mid-19thC, 55in (140cm). **$9,000-10,000**

A Louis XV marquetry writing table, perhaps Strasbourg, c1765, 19¹/₂in (49cm). **$56,000-63,000**

A George IV mahogany wine cooler, with later fitted interior, 33in (84cm). **$6,000-7,500**

A Spanish mahogany centre table, c1835, 27in (69cm). **$3,500-6,000**

A lacquer, gilt bronze and mahogany writing table, stamped P. A. Foullet, 31¹/₂in (80cm). **$63,000-72,000**

A matched pair of George III mahogany hanging shelves, with later mirror and back, 24in (61cm). **$10,000-12,000**

A Transitional kingwood table à écrire, 17¹/₂in (45cm). **$16,500-18,000**

A Louis Philippe boulle centre table, with 3 drawers and 3 dummy drawers, c1830, 47in (120cm). **$9,500-11,000**

A Louis XV/XVI Transitional tulipwood parquetry writing table, stamped RVLC, c1775, 19¹/₂in (50cm). **$90,000-108,000**

An ormolu mounted tulipwood, kingwood and marquetry table à écrire, restored. **$50,000-54,000**

A Transitional tulipwood and marquetry table à écrire. **$75,000-80,000**

A Louis XV style ormolu mounted painted bureau plat, 75in (190cm). **$20,000-21,500**

A George III mahogany breakfront wardrobe, the cupboard doors enclosing 5 shelves to the centre, 104¹/₂in (265cm). **$8,000-9,500**

A Louis XIV boulle and ebony cabinet en armoire, 57in (154cm). **$190,000-215,000**

An oak and inlaid sideboard, c1890, 80¹/₂in (204cm). **$5,500-8,500**

A pair of malachite and Belge-noir table tops, with a sunburst within a Greek border, 24in (61cm) diam. **$16,500-18,000**

A German black and gilt japanned armoire, 18thC, 63in (160cm). **$14,500-16,500**

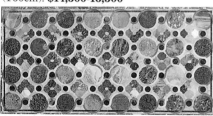

An Italian specimen marble table top, on a modern painted iron stand, 52in (132cm). **$21,000-25,000**

An Italian specimen marble table top, late 18thC, **$63,000-72,000**

A French Provincial mahogany armoire, mid-18thC, 66in (168cm). **$6,000-7,500**

A mahogany tambour pedestal desk, inlaid with box and ebony, c1850, 70in (178cm). **$14,500-26,000**

A Regency mahogany cellaret, with domed hinged lid with gadrooned edge, 34in (86cm). **$16,500-18,000**

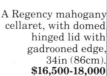

A pair of Regency mahogany bed steps, by Gillows, with leather lined steps, 21in (53cm). **$9,500-10,000**

A George III mahogany cellaret, banded in satinwood, one leg repaired, lacking interior, 20in (51cm). **$3,600-4,500**

A George III mahogany inlaid wine cooler, 21in (53cm). **$4,500-5,500**

A George III mahogany cellaret-on-stand, banded and inlaid, 16in (40cm). **$3,600-4,500**

An early George III mahogany wine cooler, with brass and loop handles, restored, 24in (61cm). **$5,500-7,000**

An oak hall letterbox, by A. Rodrigues, 42 Piccadilly, dated 7th May 1872, 17in (43cm) high. **$3,600-6,000**

A Biedermeier mahogany teapoy, with hinged lid, inlaid with boxwood and ebonised lines, with fitted interior, restored, 20¹/₂in (52cm). **$3,600-4,500**

A George III mahogany cellaret, 16in (41cm). **$4,000-4,500**

A pair of George III giltwood wall brackets, 21in (30.5cm). **$18,000-21,000**

A George III mahogany bottle holder, brass carrying handles, 25in (63cm). **$7,000-9,000**

George III mahogany wine cooler, with brass bands and op handles, 27in (69cm). **,500-7,000**

A George III brass bound mahogany cellaret-on-stand, with lead lined interior with compartments, 18¹/₂in (47cm). **$9,500-12,000**

A mid-Georgian mahogany butler's tray, containing 6 glass decanters, one broken, 21in (53cm). **$3,500-5,500**

COLOUR REVIEW

A pine sideboard, c1850, 96in (244cm). **$1,000-1,500**

A pitch pine wardrobe, c1870, 48in (122cm). **$800-900**

A pine cupboard base, c1800, with later breakfront display plate rack, 60in (152cm). **$1,000-1,500**

A pine delft rack, c1840, 60 by 42in (152 by 106.5cm). **$540-650**

A pine dresser base with gallery back, c1860, 66in (168cm). **$1,200-1,500**

A hazel pine wardrobe, c1890, 39in (99cm). **$720-800**

A pine and elm dresser base, c1850, with later plate rack, 72in (182cm). **$2,000-2,700**

A pine serpentine front Yorkshire dresser base, c1860, with later plate rack, spice drawers original, 54in (137cm). **$1,800-2,000**

A pitch pine dresser base, c1900, with later plate rack, 42in (107cm). **$1,000-1,500**

COLOUR REVIEW

A four door pine cupboard, County Limerick, with shaped interior and panelled sides, c1780, 72in (182.5cm). **$4,500-6,000**

A pine chest of drawers, with waved gallery, c1820, 39in (99cm). **$650-800**

A hazel pine dressing chest, c1890, 36in (92cm). **$720-900**

A pine farmhouse larder cupboard, with 4 drawers, c1850, 66in (167.5cm). **$1,800-2,000**

A pine glazed display cabinet, c1880, 39in (99cm). **$450-650**

A pine veterinary medicine chest, marked 'Restorine Remedies', c1890, 24in (61cm). **$270-450**

A pitch pine and pine glazed bookcase, c1870, 48in (122cm). **$800-1,000**

A pine mule chest, with 2 short drawers, c1800, 44in (112cm). **$450-650**

A pine mule chest, with long drawer and brass handles, c1800, 42 in (107cm). **$450-650**

An Empire ormolu and steel fender, the lions on stepped plinths linked by a chain, 40in (101.5cm) closed. **$2,700-3,600**

A mid-Victorian steel and brass fender, stamped No. 178 and with registry mark for 15 March 1858, 61in (155cm). **$2,200-3,200**

A Restauration gilt bronze fender, adjustable in width, c1830. **$4,000-4,500**

An early Victorian steel and ormolu fender, with Registry mark for 1845, the frieze with restoration, 67in (170cm). **$2,300-3,200**

A Restauration adjustable bronze and gilt bronze fender, c1830. **$6,000-6,800**

A bronze and gilt bronze fender, adjustable in width, mid-19thC, 56in (142cm). **$9,000-10,000**

A Restauration adjustable gilt bronze fender, c1820. **$2,200-2,900**

A pair of cast iron lion chenets, the confronting roaring beasts with brass rings supporting cartouches on pierced scrolling bases, late 19thC, 19in (49cm) high. **$4,500-6,000**

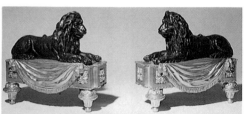

A pair of Louis XVI ormolu and bronze chenets, modelled as recumbent lions on draped plinths, 14in (35.5cm) wide. **$8,000-9,000**

A Regency brass mounted polished steel and cast iron fire grate, in George Bullock style, repaired, 40in (102cm). **$7,000-9,000**

A set of gilt bronze and steel fire irons and stand, each piece with a finely cast dog's head handle, mid-19thC, 29¹/₂in (75cm). **$20,000-21,000**

A Regency ormolu mounted steel fire grate, attributed to George Bullock, the railed front with pyramid finals, the U-shaped side and back on scrolling pilasters with acanthus headings and paw feet with plinth bases, 34in (86cm) **$16,500-18,000**

A statuary marble chimneypiece, the siena marble frieze embellished with scrolling Roman acanthus foliage, 63 by 86in (160 by 219cm). **$36,000-54,000**

A Georgian statuary marble chimneypiece, with engraved steel slip, 60 by 73in (152 by 185cm). **$38,000-45,000**

A Louis XV style rosewood and gilt metal mounted bombé commode, the serpentine white marble top above 2 short and 2 long drawers inlaid with stringing, the splayed bracket feet on later blocks, 53½in (136cm).
$4,000-4,800

A North German brass mounted mahogany commode, with eared top, one panelled drawer and 2 further drawers between canted angles, on later square tapering legs, c1800, 50½in (128cm).
$9,000-10,000

This commode is possibly Russian.

A French Provincial walnut commode, with moulded top and 3 long drawers with rounded angles, waved apron and panelled sides, on cabriole feet, mid-18thC, 49in (125cm).
$4,600-5,500

A Louis XV walnut petite commode, with waved breccia marble top above a slide with reading ledge and 2 drawers, the right hand side with a small drawer, on square tapering cabriole legs with brass caps, stamped MO and ON, formerly with ormolu mounts, reconstructed, 24½in (62cm).
$6,500-7,000

The stamp does not appear to match that of Francois Mondon, 1694-1770.

A pair of Dutch colonial hardwood serpentine commodes, the moulded tops each above 2 short and one long drawer, the shell flanked by cabriole legs on claw and ball feet, carved aprons late 19thC, 40in (102cm). **$2,700-3,600**

A Scandinavian yew veneered commode, the single frieze drawer and sides inlaid with sphinxes and scrolling designs above 2 deep drawers, on tapering block feet, early 19thC, probably Swedish, 50in (127cm).
$3,300-4,000

A North Italian ormolu mounted kingwood and mahogany bombé commode, with moulded serpentine top inlaid à quatre faces above 3 conforming graduated drawers between keeled angles, 41½in (106cm).
$2,700-3,600

A Dutch mahogany breakfront commode, with a later top, with drawers between fluted uprights, on tapering fluted legs, late 18thC, 41½in (106cm).
$4,000-4,800

An Empire mahogany commode, with later white marble top and overhanging frieze drawer flanked by turned columns with panelled sides, on turned tapering front feet, possibly Italian, 50in (127cm).
$6,500-8,000

Cupboards – Armoires

An Austrian grained armoire with arched scrolling cornice and a pair of panelled cupboard doors painted with vases of flowers, with moulded square base, re-decorated, mid 18thC, 59½in (151cm).
$5,500-7,000

A South German painted and grained marriage armoire, with moulded cornice, the frieze inscribed Andre Anna Kech 1850, above 2 doors painted with religious scenes, with central spirally turned pilaster upright, the canted sides with flower festoons on block feet, mid 19thC, 53in (135cm).
$4,500-5,500

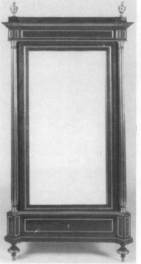

A brass-mounted mahogany armoire, the top with finials above a panelled frieze and long mirrored door with bevelled plate enclosing shelves and a drawer between fluted spreading pilasters, above one long drawer with a slide on toupie feet, possibly Russian, 19thC, 44in (111cm).
$3,600-5,500

Corner Cupboards

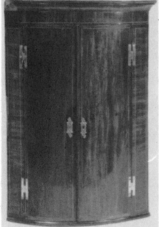

A George IV mahogany bowfronted hanging corner cupboard, the cavetto cornice above a pair of boxwood strung doors, c1780, 31in (79cm).
$1,200-1,500

A Victorian mahogany bowfronted corner cupboard on stand, with cornice, brass escutcheon and door plate, central fitted drawer, supported on stand with shaped legs, 36in (92cm).
$700-900

A Georgian mahogany corner cupboard.
$900-1,000

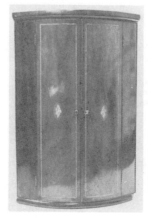

An Edwardian mahogany and satinwood inlaid double corner cupboard, the moulded overhanging cornice with sunburst frieze, over a pair of 13 pane astragal glazed doors opening to reveal shelving, the lower section with a pair of 5 pane astragal glazed doors, raised on shaped bracket feet, 35in (89cm).
$4,000-5,000

A George III mahogany bowfront hanging corner cupboard, inlaid with oval shell paterae, crossbanded in satinwood and strung with ebony and box, 26in (66cm).
$1,600-2,000

A Regency mahogany linen press, the finialled classical apex pediment above a pair of radial panelled doors and drawers, on splayed bracket feet, 46½in (118cm).
$1,600-2,000

A George III mahogany hanging corner cupboard, the cavetto cornice above a frieze inlaid with urns, drapes and a vase of flowers, above a pair of doors, 29in (74cm).
$1,800-2,800

A Dutch mahogany standing bowfront corner cupboard, inlaid with boxwood geometric lines and rosewood bands, 3 short and 4 graduated long drawers, on bracket feet, late 18thC, 31½in (80cm).
$4,600-5,500

Linen Presses

A George III mahogany clothes press, the moulded cornice with key pattern dentils above a frieze inlaid with paterae, and a pair of panelled doors with re-entrant corners and similar paterae, the base with 2 short and one long drawer, on bracket feet, resupported, 51in (130cm).
$7,000-9,000

This press is in fine condition and of good colour all over; the panels, unlike those of many presses, have not suffered from splitting.

A George III mahogany linen press, the upper section with dentil carved cornice over slides enclosed by a pair of beaded panelled doors, the slightly projecting base set with 2 short and 2 long drawers, with brass swan neck loop handles, on bracket feet, 51in (129cm).
$3,500-4,500

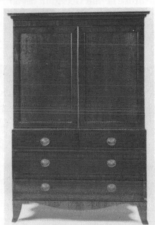

A George III plum pudding mahogany wardrobe inlaid overall with ebonised lines, the top section with moulded rectangular cornice, above 2 panelled doors enclosing 2 later shelves and hanging space, the lower section with 2 short drawers and 2 graduated long drawers, on splayed bracket feet, 51in (129cm).
$2,800-3,600

A Victorian inlaid satin birch linen press, by Morant & Co., 91 New Bond Street.
$1,600-2,000

A mahogany linen press, with shelved upper section enclosed by a pair of panelled doors, with lower section with 2 long and 2 short drawers with circular brass handles, on bracket feet, 19thC, 48in (122cm).
$1,500-1,800

A mahogany linen press with
4 shelves to the upper section
enclosed by a pair of panel doors,
3 long drawers below with wooden
knob handles, turned side columns,
on plinth base, 19thC, 56in (142cm).
$1,000-1,500

A late Victorian mahogany
wardrobe of mid Georgian design,
on scroll carved bracket feet, 53in
(134cm).
$2,700-3,600

A late George III inlaid mahogany
gentleman's press, with a broken
scroll pediment inlaid with urns
above a simulated fluted frieze with
a pair of oval panelled doors and
2 short and 2 long drawers, on
bracket feet, 48½in (123cm).
$5,500-7,000

A George II mahogany linen press,
the moulded top above a pair of
fielded panel doors, now enclosing
hanging space, on shaped bracket
feet, c1750, 47½in (120cm).
$2,700-4,500

A George IV mahogany
dwarf breakfront clothes
press, the 4 sliding trays
enclosed by a pair of
crossbanded beaded
panel doors, between
4 short drawers on
either side, on reeded
bun feet, 74in (188cm).
$4,500-5,500

Wardrobes

A George III mahogany clothes
press, the dentil moulded cornice
above a pair of curvilinear fielded
panels with 2 short and one long
graduated drawers, on bracket feet,
54½in (138cm).
$3,500-4,500

A late George III mahogany linen
press, with moulded dentil cornice
above a pair of fielded panelled
doors, with similar doors below,
enclosing 4 drawers, on ogee
bracket feet, 53in (134cm).
$3,500-4,500

A Dutch mahogany wardrobe with a
dentil cornice, above a pair of fielded
panel doors decorated with applied
swags and paterae, flanked by a pair
of Corinthian pilasters, 2 dummy
and one long drawers below with
moulded handles, raised on square
tapering legs, early 19thC, 61in
(155cm).
$2,700-3,600

A reproduction Georgian style mahogany breakfront wardrobe, 97in (246cm).
$1,000-1,200

An early Victorian mahogany breakfront wardrobe, the moulded cornice above 4 fielded panelled doors flanking 4 central drawers, on plinth base, 109in (276cm).
$2,700-3,600

A William IV mahogany breakfront wardrobe, with cavetto moulded cornice above 3 fielded panelled doors, enclosing central sliding shelves and 4 graduated drawers, on plinth base, 81in (205cm).
$3,000-3,600

A burr walnut and banded hanging cupboard of William and Mary design, with 2 simulated drawers, with 2 drawers to the apron on faceted turned tapering baluster columns and turned bun feet, joined by scrolling flat stretchers, 38½in (98cm).
$3,000-3,600

A Victorian mahogany and satinwood banded wardrobe, inlaid with geometric boxwood lines, the cavetto banded pediment above 2 fielded panelled doors and 2 base drawers, on bracket feet, 49in (124cm).
$1,200-1,600

Davenports

A George IV rosewood davenport, the sliding box top with a spindled baluster three-quarter gallery with a leather lined folding flap enclosing fitted interior, above 4 graduated side drawers, on plinth base, 18½in (47cm).
$3,000-3,600

A William IV mahogany davenport, the sliding top with fretwork gallery and hinged slope inset with original tooled leather, opening to reveal a polished, fitted interior, the lower section fitted with slide to each side and 4 drawers to one face, opposed by 4 dummy drawers, all with rosewood handles, on moulded base and ribbed bun feet, with casters, stamped GILLOW, 20in (51cm).
$8,000-10,000

A late Victorian burr walnut and oak davenport, carved overall with fruiting vine leaves, with a hinged pencil compartment superstructure above a leather lined slope, 18in (46cm).
$2,700-3,600

Did you know
MILLER'S Antiques Price Guide builds up year by year to form the most comprehensive photo-reference system available

269

A William IV rosewood davenport, with spindle filled three-quarter gallery, tooled leather inset to the flap, hinged pen and ink drawer, above a door enclosing sliding trays, and on lotus headed columnar supports, with bun feet and casters, 23½in (60cm).
$1,400-1,700

A William IV rosewood davenport.
$3,600-4,600

A late Victorian rosewood veneered davenport, 23in (59cm).
$1,600-2,000

An early Victorian rosewood davenport, the inset leather lined sloping flap enclosing a maple lined interior, on an inverted plinth base, 19in (49cm).
$1,500-2,000

A Victorian ebonised and amboyna davenport, inlaid with geometric boxwood lines, with leather lined hinged sloping flap below a brass galleried lidded stationery compartment, above 4 side drawers, on bar and scroll block feet, 22in (56cm).
$1,600-2,000

A Regency rosewood davenport with a three-quarter pierced gallery above a lined slope enclosing a fitted interior, on bun feet, 20in (51cm).
$5,000-6,000

A late Victorian walnut and marquetry davenport, with three-quarter galleried top and hinged fall, decorated with figures before a church in a foliate landscape, the marquetry panels probably German, late 18thC, 26in (66cm).
$1,500-2,000

A late Victorian ebonised davenport, banded in burr walnut, 22in (56cm).
$1,600-2,000

★ davenports are small desks derived from a design ordered by Captain Davenport in 1790
★ qualities adding substantially to the value are fine veneering in figured walnut, bird's-eye amboyna, tulipwood, kingwood, rosewood or speckled veneer; crisp deep carving to the brackets, brass stringing to the writing surface and ingenious fittings such as a rising top and concealed drawers
★ mass produced versions in bleached oak, elm, Virginia walnut or light mahogany are considerably less valuable
★ beware: marriages are commonplace. Check veneer match and colour between desk top and base, back, sides and front
★ look for evidence of replaced desk supports, rising top and drawer knobs. In particular, a plain writing top may have been replaced with a piano top to increase value

Desks

A mahogany partners' desk, the inset top with bevelled edge above 6 frieze drawers on pedestals of 3 drawers opposing panelled cupboard doors, with plinth bases, stamped W. Priest 17 & 24 Water St., Blackfriars, early 19thC.
$5,500-6,500

An Edwardian mahogany partners' desk, with divided red leather lined top, each end with 3 frieze drawers flanked by 6 pedestal drawers, on a moulded bases, minor restorations, 60½in (154cm).
$6,500-7,000

A Regency mahogany kneehole desk, with red leather lined top and bead and reel moulded frieze, the sides applied with split mouldings, the back with false drawers, on stiff leaf scroll feet, 45in (114cm).
$22,000-24,500

A mahogany kneehole desk, the rounded top centred by a conch shell motif, with 7 drawers about the kneehole, fitted with a door and secret drawer, on bracket feet, late 18thC, the inlay later, 28½in (72cm).
$3,600-4,600

A partners' mahogany pedestal desk, late 19thC, 60in (152cm).
$1,800-2,950

A George III mahogany partners' desk, with green leather lined top, on pedestals each fitted with 3 graduated short drawers opposing another 3 drawers, on plinth bases, fitted with side carrying handles, restored, 64in (162cm).
$11,000-13,000

A Victorian mahogany partners' pedestal desk, the inset leather lined top above 6 drawers and a panelled door, the same to the reverse, on plinth bases, 59½in (151cm).
$4,500-5,500

> **Did you know**
> *MILLER'S Antiques Price Guide builds up year by year to form the most comprehensive photo-reference system available*

A Victorian mahogany partners' desk, with maroon leather lined top, on plinth bases, 72in (183cm).
$5,500-6,500

A William IV mahogany kneehole double pedestal desk, with 4 graduating drawers on either side and a central drawer with turned wooden handles and inset green leather top.
$1,600-2,520

A Victorian mahogany partners' desk, with green leather lined top, on pedestals each with a door opposed by 3 drawers, on bracket feet, 60in (152cm).
$1,800-2,700

A Victorian mahogany partners' desk, with green leather lined top, on pedestals each with a door opposed by 3 drawers, on plinth bases, 60in (152cm).
$5,500-6,500

A partners' mahogany kneehole desk, the inset leather lined rectangular top above 6 drawers and a panelled door, the same to the reverse, on plinth bases, 72in (183cm).
$1,500-2,160

A mahogany pedestal desk, the top inset with gilt key pattern tooled red leather top, with gadroon carved edge, the 3 drawers to the frieze with foliate carved fascias and brass knob handles, each pedestal set with drawers opposing a cupboard enclosed by panelled door carved with a musical trophy, and flanked by fluted column stiles with acanthus carved capitols, with 2 fielded side panels and on a plinth and casters, late 19thC, 59in (150cm).
$3,600-4,800

A Victorian burr walnut kneehole desk, with coffered and inset leather lined top, on plinth bases, 54in (137cm).
$9,000-10,000

A late Victorian walnut and rosewood banded pedestal desk, the inset leather lined rectangular top above 9 drawers between canted angles, on bracket feet, 51in (130cm).
$2,700-3,600

A mid-Victorian mahogany clerk's desk, with lined top and shelved superstructure incorporating a hinged slope and 8 small drawers, with 9 drawers about the kneehole, on plinth bases, 60in (152cm).
$2,700-3,600

A Victorian mahogany pedestal desk, on plinth bases and casters, c1850, 47½in (121cm).
$2,000-2,800

A Second Empire plum pudding mahogany pedestal desk, with inset leather lined top above 9 drawers and reverse panelled door between quadrant angles, on plinth and turned bun feet, 60in (152cm).
$2,700-3,700

A Victorian stained oak twin pedestal desk, stamped Edwards & Roberts, 48in (122cm).
$1,500-2,160

A mahogany kneehole writing desk, the inset leather lined inverted rectangular top above 7 drawers, on fluted turned tapering legs, 42in (107cm).
$1,800-2,700

A Federal inlaid mahogany tambour desk, 42in (107cm).
$2,500-4,000

A Victorian carved oak pedestal partners' desk, the leather inset top with carved edge, the drawers with mask handles, on pedestals of 3 similarly covered drawers opposing panelled cupboard doors covered with lions' masks.
$1,800-2,700

A late Victorian mahogany roll top desk, with a tambour fall enclosing drawers and pigeonholes and an adjustable writing slope, on pedestals of 3 drawers, with plinth bases.
$1,600-2,000

A Victorian mahogany cylinder top desk with original interior, c1870, 48in (122cm).
$3,000-4,000

A Queen Anne walnut desk-on-frame, later top and lid, skirt reshaped, Pennsylvania, c1735, 29in (74cm).
$4,000-5,000

A partners' kneehole desk with foliate lunette and gadrooned carved banded borders, with inset leather lined top, basically early 19thC, 60in (152cm).
$4,700-5,800

A Victorian mahogany partners' kneehole desk, with inset leather lined top above 6 drawers and enclosed by a panelled door, the same to the reverse, on plinth bases, 60in (152cm).
$7,000-9,000

A late Victorian mahogany partners' desk, inlaid throughout with stringing and narrow satinwood bandings, with leather inset top, on shaped bracket feet, one pedestal now with 2 drawers converted to a deep drawer, c1900, 54in (137cm).
$7,000-8,000

A walnut S-shape roll top desk, with panel sides and finished reverse, c1910, 60in (152cm).
$3,200-4,200

Dumb Waiters

A South German/North Italian walnut, rosewood and foliate scroll marquetry kneehole desk, of broken serpentine outline, the geometrically inlaid top with central motif of deer, with 3 drawers and hinged doors to either side of the arched kneehole, on turned feet, reconstructed, the marquetry possibly 18thC, 47in (119cm).
$8,000-10,000

An early Victorian metamorphic occasional table/dumb waiter, the rising circular top with moulded rim containing 2 further shelves, usable in any combination, on octagonal stem and concave platform base.
$1,500-2,000

A William IV mahogany dumb waiter, the 3 graduated tiers with three quarter galleries, the tapering square supports surmounted by anthemion finials, on foliate moulded platform bases with bun feet, c1835, 48in (122cm).
$1,800-2,700

A pair of early Victorian mahogany dumb waiters, each with 2 galleried moulded tiers and a baluster shaft with turned boss, on tripod base with splayed feet, one leg broken and repaired, 27in (69cm).
$3,000-4,000

A George III mahogany dumb waiter, the 3 dished circular tiers on gun-barrel turned columns and cabriole tripod support, slight restoration.
$1,200-1,800

An early Victorian 3-tier adjustable dumb waiter, with rounded rectangular divisions, on dual scroll carved supports with turned feet, 48in (122cm).
$1,200-1,500

A George IV mahogany dumb waiter, with brass column supports and embossed mouldings.
$4,500-5,500

Mirrors & Frames

A George I carved and gilt gesso wall mirror, the broken arch cresting with a central cartouche above foliate scrolls, the later plate with a shaped shell carved apron mounted with gilt metal candle sconce brackets, c1720, 40 by 24in (102 by 61cm).
$2,000-3,000

A pair of George II style gilt gesso mirrors, the scrolled pediments centred by eagles with outspread wings, the friezes decorated with foliage and cherub masks, the shaped aprons centred by scallop shells.
$800-1,000

A mahogany and parcel gilt mirror, of early Georgian design, the frame with scrolled cresting headed by a basket of flowers flanked by C-scrolls and acanthus leaves, the sides carved with fruit, flowerheads and leaves, 43 by 22in (109 by 56cm).
$4,800-5,500

An Adam style gilt gesso wall mirror, with an oval plate surrounded by subsidiary plates, with a jasperware patera crest.
$650-800

A Regency giltwood mirror, with original plate and moulded frame, 58 by 33in (147 by 84cm).
$6,500-7,400

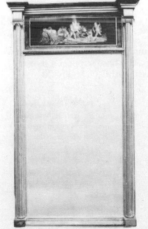

A Regency giltwood and gesso wall mirror.
$1,500-1,800

A George II wall mirror, the walnut veneered frame with giltwood and gesso borders and pendants, 56 by 28in (142 by 71cm).
$8,000-9,000

A William and Mary white painted overmantel mirror, with bevelled plate and cushion frame, 31 by 41½in (79 by 104cm).
$4,600-5,800

An early George III mahogany and parcel gilt mirror, 43 by 25in (109 by 64cm).
$7,000-8,000

A giltwood mirror, the bevelled plate in a foliate gesso re-entry banded frame below a pierced leafy C-scrolling cabochon cresting and base, 18thC, 36 by 22in (92 by 56cm). **$1,500-2,000**

A Regency mahogany cheval mirror, with swing plate on ring turned column supports and reeded downswept legs, with 2 brass adjustable candle holders, 32½in (83cm) wide. **$5,500-6,500**

A Dutch mahogany and marquetry inlaid toilet mirror, the base inlaid with foliate marquetry and fitted with a single drawer, 19thC, 17in (44cm) wide. **$650-800**

A Regency style mahogany and boxwood strung cheval mirror, the plate within a square section frame on outsplayed legs terminating in brass lion's paw feet. **$1,000-1,200**

A gilt pier mirror, the pronounced leaf and foliate crest above foliate swags, the base support a pair of sconces, 19thC. **$680-830**

A Chippendale style mahogany and parcel gilt triple plate overmantel, the plates with gilt inner slips and surmounted by a shaped crest with gilt ho-ho bird finial, 55 by 50½in (140 by 128cm). **$1,200-1,500**

A Regency green painted and parcel gilt overmantel, the sphere applied cornice above a frieze centred by a scallop shell flanked by floral scrolls above a bevelled mirror plate, flanked by moulded pilasters with leaf carved capitals. **$1,000-1,500**

A mahogany and parcel gilt mirror, the moulded frame with scrolling cresting centred by a roundel mounted with a ho-ho bird, with scrolling apron, 34½ by 19½in (88 by 50cm). **$1,500-1,800**

A George III mahogany and parcel gilt toilet mirror, on square spreading supports with brass finials, the base with concave front and 3 drawers, on bracket feet, 25in (64cm) high. **$2,000-2,700**

A George III mahogany toilet mirror, the crossbanded and strung plinth with 3 drawers, restored, c1790, 16½in (42cm) wide.
$720-1,000

A late Regency giltwood and gesso convex girandole, with foliate cresting piece surmounted by an outstretched eagle, the glass with an ebonised slip and 2 scroll candle branches below, 21in (53cm) diam.
$1,000-1,200

The reverse bears the trade label J. F. Barber, Newark. This being composition rather than carved wood is reflected in the low price.

A George III style mahogany overmantel with 3 bevelled mirror glass panels with carved gilded surround, pierced and carved shaped finial with bird and floral gilded decoration, 34in (86cm) high.
$540-720

A giltwood and gesso mirror frame, boldly carved with flowerheads, foliage and scrolls, late 18thC, the glass later, 32 by 28in (81 by 71cm).
$1,000-1,200

A Regency ornate gilt plasterwork overmantel, with original mirror glass, 60in (152cm) high.
$1,800-2,700

A Venetian painted mirror, the plate surmounted by a cartouche and within a carved and moulded frame, painted with flowers and leafy tendrils, 29½ by 18½in (75 by 47cm). **$3,600-4,500**

Regency giltwood mirror, the plate in an ebonised slip and moulded foliate frame, the cresting with an eagle on a tapering plinth between dolphins, with foliate apron, 38 by 22in (97 by 56cm).
1,800-2,800

A late Victorian giltwood and red and black painted overmantel mirror, of Gothic revival design, with a cornice of rope mouldings above a bevelled plate between Gothic arched columns with foliate capitals and oak leaf mouldings, on a moulded plinth, 72 by 51½in (183 by 131cm).
$1,030-1,600

A French giltwood and grey painted overmantel mirror, above an 18thC style painted panel with figures in a pastoral setting, an arched plate below within a ribbon tied surround flanked by female busts above foliate leaf moulded uprights, 19thC with some later decoration, 95 by 62in (241 by 157cm).
$6,700-9,000

An Edwardian mahogany and satinwood banded cheval mirror, the swan neck pediment flanked by reeded finials, above a plate on outswept supports.
$900-1,000

A Venetian wall mirror, with pierced scroll surmount, bevelled plate with etched and chamfered margin plates, c1900, 39 by 37in (99 by 94cm).
$3,400-4,500

An Italian carved giltwood wall mirror, the later plate within a pierced foliate scroll surround interspersed with putti, early 18thC, 24 by 19½in (61 by 50cm).
$1,500-1,800

A Regency giltwood and composition mirror, with later plate below a verre eglomisé panel painted with a vase of flowers with inverted breakfront cornice cast with balls above an acorn frieze, the sides with cluster columns, re-gilt, the cornice later, restorations, 51 by 32in (130 by 81cm).
$3,000-3,600

A rococo revival giltwood mirror, the shaped plate framed by C-scrolls, rockwork and foliage, incorporating brackets, and surmounted by an open lattice C-scroll, Italian, mid-19thC, 48 by 32in (122 by 82cm).
$1,500-2,000

A walnut mirror, the sides carved with flowerheads and foliage, with broken pediment cresting centred by rockwork, the waved apron carved with acanthus, 55½ by 32in (141 by 81cm).
$4,500-5,500

A William IV giltwood overmantel, the plate in a moulded frame with arched cresting with broken pediment centred by acanthus scrolls and flowerheads, stencilled on reverse From W. Froom's Looking Glass Warehouse, 136 Strand, London, 74 by 59in (188 by 150cm).
$3,600-4,500

William Froom is recorded as a carver, gilder and looking glass manufacturer from 1825 to 1839.

A pair of Victorian gilt gesso girandoles, with pierced cartouch crests and pierced aprons issuing 3 scrolled branches.
$1,000-1,200

A giltwood mirror, with cartouche shaped plate, the eared frame carved with acanthus, the moulded cresting mounted with martial trophies, the apron centred with a scallop shell, 19thC, 29 by 21in (74 by 53cm).
$720-1,000

A mahogany and parcel gilt mirror, with bevelled plate, the moulded frame with scrolling cresting and roundel mounted with a ho-ho bird, with scrolling apron, 18thC and later, and an additional mirror plate, 49 by 24in (125 by 62cm).
$3,600-4,500

An Italian giltwood mirror, with later bevelled plate, the frame boldly carved with pierced foliate scrolls, the cresting with an oval plate and gadrooned surround surmounted by sunflowers, 17thC, 55 by 35in (140 by 89cm).
$3,600-4,800

A giltwood wall mirror, of rococo scrolling form, carved with overlapping leaves, and of 2 shaped mirrored panels, late 18thC, 36in (92cm) wide.
$3,000-3,600

A George III style mahogany wall mirror, the bevelled plate within a gilt slip, the pierced scroll crest centred by a ho-ho bird, the scrolled apron centred by an inlaid shell.
$450-540

A George III mahogany and satinwood inlaid swing frame toilet mirror, the serpentine plateau with 3 drawers, on bracket feet, 18in (46cm) wide.
$1,400-1,800

A Flemish tortoiseshell and ebonised mirror, with later stepped bevelled plate, the channelled frame with ripple moulded corners and scrolled cresting, 19thC, 33 by 29in (84 by 74cm).
$2,000-2,800

A late Victorian composition mirror, the bead and stiff leaf frame decorated with berried trailing foliage on a velvet ground, with pierced urn and scroll cresting and conforming apron, 70 by 42in (178 by 107cm).
$4,500-5,500

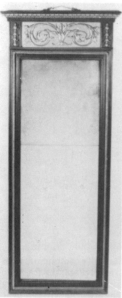

A pair of stained wood and gilt gesso pier mirrors, each with a moulded cornice above a foliate scroll frieze and divided rectangular plate within a rope twist surround, early 19thC, probably Scandinavian, 59 by 24in (150 by 61cm).
$2,700-3,600

Screens

A French four-leaf screen, each leaf painted with rural scenes on leather, 19thC.
$1,500-1,700

A four-leaf painted leather screen, depicting Chinese figures of various pursuits, hunting and entertaining, with panels of blossoming foliage and birds above, within a red leather surround, 19thC, each leaf 28in (71cm).
$2,700-3,600

The condition of the leather is an important factor in assessing the value.

A French giltwood cheval firescreen, inset with an Aubusson tapestry panel, on downward scrolling end supports carved with acanthus, the tapestry 18thC, the frame 19thC, 29in (74cm).
$2,000-3,600

A George II mahogany tripod polescreen, with a silk and woolworked adjustable panel, on a fluted column with shell carved downswept supports and club feet, converted from a tripod table, c1750.
$1,200-1,800

This polescreen bears the Nostell Priory inventory mark.

l. A Regency rosewood polescreen, with carved corners and inset with Victorian wool and silk canvaswork flowers, the brass pole on reeded column and concave triangular base.
$350-450
r. A Regency rosewood polescreen, the brass pole of concave triangular form, on reeded column and concave triangular base.
$450-540

A Victorian walnut fire screen, carved in 17thC style, with 18thC gros and petit point panel.
$720-800

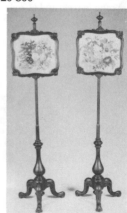

A pair of Victorian rosewood polescreens, with needlework banners.
$900-1,000

An early Victorian rosewood and gilt brass polescreen, the adjustable guard with needlepoint panel, on trefoil base with scroll feet, 55in (140cm) high.
$450-650

A William IV giltwood cheval fire screen, with a needlework panel woven with a basket of flowers and a parrot, the cresting centred by an anthemion, on turned end supports and downswept legs, on bun feet, 29½in (75cm).
$1,500-2,000

A mahogany cheval fire screen, with arched needlework panel depicting a parrot and peacock, the moulded frame joined by a turned stretcher, on downswept legs and pad feet, the needlework 18thC.
$720-1,000

Settees

A mahogany sofa, upholstered in yellow floral damask, the curved toprail and waved seat rail carved with gadrooned edge, on cabriole legs headed by foliate scrolls and scrolling feet, 19thC, 80in (203cm).
$7,000-8,000

A William and Mary style walnut framed two-seater settee, the shaped back and scroll arms raised on scrolling front supports united by stretchers.
$1,000-1,200

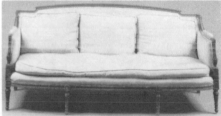

A George III beechwood sofa, upholstered in yellow silk, the arms with spirally fluted turned supports, on turned tapering fluted legs, lacking finials, minor restorations, 80in (203cm).
$3,500-5,500

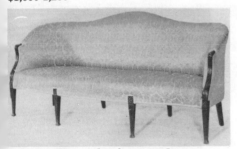

A George III carved mahogany sofa, upholstered in green brocade, the moulded arm facings above fluted and stop fluted tapered square legs headed by paterae, c1780, 76½in (194cm).
$4,000-5,500

A George III sofa, of Chippendale design, 86in (219cm).
$8,000-10,000

A pair of George I style mahogany framed two-seater sofas, on shell capped cabriole legs, with brown floral embroidered upholstery.
$2,700-3,600

A Victorian chaise longue, on carved walnut cabriole legs.
$500-575

The price reflects the state of the upholstery.

A Regency mahogany sofa, with blue floral upholstery, on reeded splayed legs and 2 similar legs to the centre, legs strengthened, upholstery distressed, 92in (234cm).
$2,700-3,600

A Regency giltwood framed settee, upholstered in eggshell damask, on lotus carved tapering legs with reeded brass casters, 90in (229cm).
$3,600-4,500

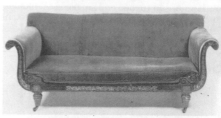

A Regency mahogany sofa, with pale green floral upholstery, on turned tapering legs, restored, back legs replaced, 77½in (197cm).
$1,800-2,700

A Regency brass inlaid simulated rosewood sofa, upholstered in green corduroy, inlaid with anthemia and foliate scrolls, on short gadrooned cylindrical tapering legs, 84in (213cm).
$2,700-3,600

A Federal mahogany sofa, New England, c1810, 78in (198cm) long.
$3,500-5,000

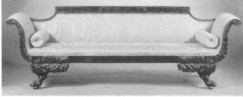

A Federal carved mahogany settee, New York, c1815, 103in (262cm) long.   **$3,500-5,000**

An Italian walnut three-seater sofa, in Louis XVI style, on fluted turned tapering legs, with loose seat squab, 19thC, 61½in (156cm).
$1,600-2,000

A Victorian walnut, three-seater settee, on cabriole legs with original casters, upholstered in ivory ground floral patterned linen, 78in (198cm).
$4,500-5,500

A suite of Renaissance revival walnut furniture, comprising a pair of canapes, a pair of armchairs, and a pair of side chairs, attributed to John Jelliff, c1875.   **$7,500-8,000**

A Louis Philippe rosewood and gilt metal mounted canapé, lacking upholstery, the seat rail applied with gilt foliate mounts, on cabriole legs, 65in (165cm).
$1,800-2,700

A Victorian walnut framed nine-piece suite, comprising a sofa, a pair of lady's and gentleman's armchairs and 6 side chairs, the backs with imbricated moulding surmounted by acanthus carved crests, the arms with husk carved supports continuing to turned and fluted legs, the sofa 68½in (174cm).
$5,500-9,000

A William and Mary style sofa, 56in (142cm).
$1,000-1,200

A Victorian sofa, with shaped curved back in buttoned red velvet.
$1,200-1,400

A mid Victorian walnut chaise longue, buttoned and upholstered in bottle green, on cabriole legs with scroll feet.
$2,000-3,000

A Knole sofa, upholstered in Gothic style gros point tapestry.
$1,500-1,800

A Regency mahogany sofa, upholstered in cream and crimson striped fabric, on turned reeded legs, replacements, 76in (193cm).
$2,700-3,600

A William IV mahogany chaise longue, with green upholstery and dual foliate carved scroll ends and scroll back, with a moulded seat rail and reeded baluster turned legs, 81in (206cm).
$3,600-4,500

A Victorian mahogany open arm sofa, of George III design, with figured brocade drop-in seat, on cabriole legs with claw and ball feet, 41in (104cm).
$900-1,500

A North German mahogany sofa, upholstered in yellow moiré silk, on splayed legs and paw feet, 76in (193cm).
$900-1,200

A pair of giltwood sofas, of Louis XVI design, upholstered in scarlet damask, the channelled frame elaborately carved, the arms terminating in rams' heads, the seat rail with guilloche pattern, on turned stop fluted legs carved with lotus leaves and headed by fleurs de lys, one stamped 2 on seat rail, one stencilled 17, the other 18, 56in (142cm).
$3,600-4,500

A Victorian walnut chaise longue and a lady's salon chair, the cushion moulded cresting rails richly carved, the frames pierced and richly carved, raised upon cabriole supports carved at the knees, terminating in knurl and peg feet and ceramic casters, the whole upholstered in floral machine woven tapestry.
$1,600-2,000

A late Victorian mahogany and crimson upholstered chaise longue, with a scroll and berry carved back rail and similarly carved single scroll end, on reeded bun feet, 75in (191cm). **$2,700-3,600**

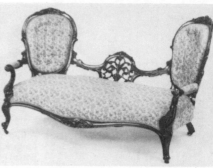

A George III painted chair back settee, black and gilt with pierced lattice splats with oval cresting panels of gilt chinoiserie scenes, the scrolling arms to lion's paw and ball supports, the front turned splay legs to brass casters, c1805, 72in (183cm). **$14,500-16,500**

A Knole style upholstered modern settee, covered in pale green damask, with twin seat cushions, 67in (170cm). **$1,600-1,800**

A mid Victorian walnut double chair back settee, with beige floral upholstery, on cabriole legs, 67½in (171cm). **$4,500-5,500**

A rosewood sofa, carved with cabochon and acanthus scrolls, upholstered in figured brocade, on cabriole legs, with knob feet, late 19thC, 66in (168cm). **$1,500-2,000**

A Victorian mahogany sofa, of early Georgian design, upholstered in pink velvet, with cabriole legs and hairy paw feet, 78in (198cm). **$2,000-3,000**

A Federal carved mahogany settee, casters missing and minor repairs, labelled and stamped Sypher & Co., New York City, late 19thC, 44in (112cm). **$2,000-3,000**

A Classical mahogany recamier, patches to veneers, c1820, 87in (221cm) long. **$2,000-4,000**

A Victorian four-seater Chesterfield sofa, upholstered in lining, on foliate carved rosewood bun feet, with loose floral cover, 94in (238cm). **$1,000-1,600**

A walnut three-piece drawing room suite, comprising a two-seater sofa, with a serpentine crested back, on cabriole legs with knob feet, 67in (170cm), and 2 open armchairs upholstered in velvet and leather. **$2,700-3,600**

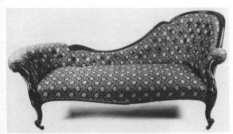

A Victorian rosewood scroll end settee, with scroll arm terminals extending down to cabriole front supports terminating in knurl and peg feet, all carved with scrolling acanthuus leaves, the buttoned back, arms and overstuffed seat upholstered in blue floral brocade.
$2,200-3,000

A walnut three-piece bergère suite, comprising a three-seater sofa with double caned back and side panels, above a tapestry upholstered seat with pierced scrolling apron on stump feet, 72in (183cm), and 2 armchairs with loose cushions.
$3,600-4,500

Shelves

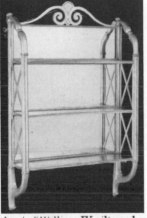

A set of William IV giltwood and simulated rosewood hanging shelves, with later pierced scrolling cresting and 3 shelves with mirrored back, the concave fronted top with pierced X-shaped sides, 34in (86cm) high.
$3,500-3,750

A pair of French Provincial cream painted and polychrome corner hanging shelves, with bowed stepped shelves and pierced backs, above tambour shutters painted with floral sprays, 41in (104cm) high.
$3,600-4,500

A Biedermeier mahogany scroll end sofa, the serpentine back and seat upholstered in green fabric, the splayed supports headed by paterae, c1840, 79in (201cm).
$3,500-4,500

A George III inlaid mahogany bowfront sideboard, the top above a frieze drawer flanked by swivelling cellarette drawers, on square tapering legs and spade feet, adapted, 61in (155cm).
$6,700-7,400

Sideboards

A George III mahogany sideboard, with a single frieze drawer flanked by 2 further drawers, on square tapering supports with spade feet, c1800, 90in (229cm).
$3,600-5,500

A George III mahogany breakfront sideboard, decorated with rosewood crossbanding and boxwood stringing, with octagonal handles, raised on square tapering legs and spade feet, 84in (213cm).
$7,000-8,000

A late Regency mahogany sideboard, with eared concave top, on turned tapering reeded legs, top restored, 84½in (215cm).
$3,000-4,000

A Victorian inlaid mahogany sideboard, the rosewood banded top above an arcaded frieze, fitted with 3 drawers and a simulated cellaret drawer, on square tapering legs with spade feet, 58½in (148cm).
$2,000-2,700

An early Victorian mahogany sideboard, on plinth base, 70½in (179cm).
$1,600-2,000

An early Victorian mahogany sideboard, 66in (168cm).
$3,600-4,500

A Federal inlaid mahogany sideboard, left front leg repaired, Middle Atlantic States, c1805, 44in (112cm).
$4,500-6,000

An inlaid mahogany bowfront sideboard, with cellaret drawer, on ring turned tapering legs, basically early 19thC, 35½in (91cm).
$2,700-4,500

A Federal painted and inlaid mahogany sideboard, some damage and repair, New York, c1800, 68in (172cm).
$4,500-6,000

A mahogany and marquetry bowfront sideboard, the satinwood and rosewood banded top with low ledge back above 2 central drawers flanked by a panelled door and cellaret drawer, on square tapering legs, basically early 19thC, 46½in (118cm).
$2,700-3,600

The inlay is a later addition.

A late George III mahogany and ebony strung bowfront sideboard, with an eared top above a central frieze drawer with arched apron drawer flanked by cupboards, on turned legs, 63½in (161cm).
$4,000-5,000

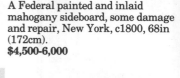

A late George III mahogany sideboad, with brass baluster pillar uprights with urn finials, the doors with brass loop handles and elliptical back plates, raised upon square tapering supports with collar divides, the whole crossbanded with circular and oval double stringing in box, 76in (193cm).
$4,500-5,500

A George IV mahogany pedestal sideboard, with brass rail and urn finials, 76in (193cm).
$1,600-2,000

For many years this type of sideboard has been undervalued but they are now quickly rising in price.

An inlaid mahogany serpentine sideboard, the rosewood banded top above 3 frieze drawers and a cellaret drawer, on square tapering legs with spade feet, basically early 19thC, 46in (117cm).
$3,000-4,000

A profusely carved Anglo-Indian rosewood sideboard, the doors flanked by a pair of cellarets with ribbed lids, brass lined interior and bottle holders, on turned pedestals, on canted rectangular base and winged scrolled feet, c1830, 94in (238cm).
$2,000-3,000

A Regency mahogany and ebony string inlaid bowfronted sideboard, the raised back containing shallow cupboard with sliding drawer fronts, on 6 turned and reeded supports, 84½in (215cm).
$3,000-4,000

A Regency mahogany pedestal sideboard, inlaid with ebonised stringing, the superstructure with canted, moulded top, above a panelled tablet flanked by sliding doors above a bowfronted centre section, each pedestal with a drawer and a door flanked by monopodia, on a plinth base, each enclosing a single drawer with compartments, later bases, restorations, 84½in (215cm).
$2,700-3,600

Stands

A George IV mahogany folio stand, 45½in (115cm) wide.
$5,500-6,500

An Eastern carved hardwood plant stand, with inset marble top and carved floral decoration. $350-450

A Victorian walnut duet stand, with 2 pierced scroll carved panels, each rising on a ratchet, on a turned column, with moulded downswept supports, c1870, 63in (160cm) extended.
$1,200-1,600

A parcel gilt and satin birch easel, with foliate finial and scrolling shoulders with splayed supports and 2 adjustable shelves, 73in (185cm) high.
$3,500-4,500

A George III mahogany urn stand, 12in (31cm).
$3,000-3,600

A carved maple hall tree, New England, c1830, 79in (200cm) high.
$1,500-3,000

A walnut, marquetry and gilt metal mounted candle stand, inlaid with flowering foliage on a pierced spiral twist support, with dished circular base with trailing fruiting vines, 19thC, 12in (30cm) diam.
$900-1,200

A satinwood duet stand, the back-to-back adjustable ratcheted music stands on turned and knopped stem, united to the single drawer box pattern base by 4 scroll shaped members, decorated throughout with painted scrolls, flowers and oval reserves, 19thC, 48in (122cm) high.
$7,000-8,000

A Regency mahogany metamorphic library chair, with scroll arms and rope twist back, on sabre supports folding over to form 4 steps.
$7,000-9,000

Steps

A matched pair of Regency mahogany bedsteps, inlaid with ebony stringing, inset with panels of patterned Brussels carpet, the hinged top step enclosing a well, on turned tapering legs, each with label inscribed in ink 'Trader', one with damage to back and top step loose, 22in (56cm) high.
$3,000-3,600

Pairs are very rare today, and highly sought after as bedside tables.

A set of early Victorian mahogany bed steps, inset with panels of patterned Brussels carpet, the second step enclosing a pull-out commode drawer with porcelain pan, on turned legs, 25½in (65cm) high.
$1,200-1,400

A late Victorian mahogany chair/library steps.
$540-720

Stools

A late Regency rosewood stool, the floral woolworked padded top on X-form supports, joined by a turned pole stretcher, c1820.
$1,800-2,800

A pair of William IV mahogany stools, with needlework tops, on baluster turned legs, 11in (28cm).
$700-900

A pair of George IV walnut X frame stools, 23in (59cm).
$3,500-4,500

A Victorian rosewood and button upholstered stool, covered in pink chintz, the carved apron with cabriole legs, on scroll feet, c1850, 39in (99cm).
$2,400-3,000

An early Victorian walnut stool with padded seat and waved channelled seat rail centred by flowerheads, the channelled cabriole legs headed by flowerheads, on foliate feet, 20in (51cm).
$1,600-2,000

A William IV rectangular stool, in the manner of Bulloch, 15in (38cm).
$650-800

A George III cream painted and parcel gilt stool, the padded seat covered in close nailed yellow cotton, on cabriole legs headed by flowerheads, redecorated, previously gilt, 19½in (49cm).
$2,700-3,700

A George IV round adjustable music stool.
$650-750

A pair of Victorian walnut footstools, with upholstered tops, on cabriole legs with scroll feet, 13in (33cm).
$540-720

A rococo rosewood piano stool, attributed to John Henry Belter, New York, c1855.
$5,500-6,500

A George II walnut stool, the padded drop-in seat on cabriole legs with pad feet, restorations, 17½in (44cm).
$1,200-1,500

A pair of Regency beech framed footstools, 9½in (24cm) square.
$2,000-3,000

A Federal brass inlaid mahogany window bench, alterations, 45in (114cm) long.
$5,000-6,000

A mid Victorian walnut stool, covered in modern floral needlework, on cabriole legs and scrolling feet, woven with OS 1961, 48½in (123cm).
$6,500-7,000

A George IV rosewood and cut brass inlaid music seat, with a pierced lyre shaped splat, the hide upholstered revolving seat on a brass mounted turned pillar and gadrooned triform base with scroll feet, c1825.
$2,700-3,700

A pair of giltwood stools of Louis XV style, each with padded seat upholstered in floral embroidered silk, the waved channelled seat rail carved with S-scrolls, acanthus, C-scrolls and rockwork on channelled cabriole legs headed by rockwork within confronting C-scrolls.
$3,000-4,000

A George II style mahogany stool, the stuffed seat covered in needlework, the scroll cabriole legs with elongated cabochon motifs and cabochon scroll feet, c1910, 23in (58cm).
$1,500-1,800

A Dutch walnut and marquetry window seat, 30in (76cm).
$900-1,200

A George I style walnut stool, with slip-in needlework seat, the hipped cabriole legs with fan and leaf scroll motifs to the knees, on claw and ball feet, 21in (53cm), together with a similar walnut stool, 22in (56cm), both c1920.   **$3,000-3,600**

A carved walnut stool with floral carved front panel, supported on shaped matching carved cabriole legs, upholstered in sage green floral patterned cut velvet, 19thC, 42in (106cm) long.
$650-800

Make the Most of Miller's

Every care has been taken to ensure the accuracy of descriptions and estimated valuations. Price ranges in this book reflect what one should expect to pay for a similar example. When selling one can obviously expect a figure below. This will fluctuate according to a dealer's stock, saleability at a particular time, etc. It is always advisable to approach a reputable specialist dealer or an auction house which has specialist sales

A James II brown painted stool with padded seat, covered in tapestry style material, on cabriole legs headed by foliage and punched trellis work, joined by a waved and H shaped baluster stretcher, 20½in (52cm) wide.
$1,500-2,000

A Regency mahogany footstool, after a design by George Smith, of lotus carved S-scroll form, with reeded rails and on bun feet, some restoration.
$550-900

TABLES
Breakfast Tables

A Victorian mahogany breakfast table, the top on a baluster turned column and 3 carved outswept legs, terminating in scroll feet.
$1,800-2,400

A Regency rosewood circular breakfast table, on triform base, 51in (129cm).
$3,500-4,500

A Regency mahogany breakfast table, with gadrooned tip-up top, on a reeded turned shaft and quadripartite platform, with 4 reeded splayed legs, 44in (111cm).
$3,500-4,500

A Victorian giltwood stool, the green velvet upholstered seat on cabriole legs with scroll feet and cabochon headings, 25in (64cm).
$550-900

A late George III mahogany breakfast table, with a reeded top above a turned shaft and splayed legs, 48½in (123cm).
2532a   **$2,400-3,000**

Larger sizes will be considerably more expensive.

A William IV mahogany breakfast table, the tip-up top above a carved and lappeted central shaft on a triform platform base, with paw feet, 52in (132cm).
1983   **$3,000-3,600**

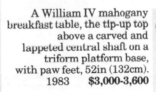

A mid Victorian rosewood breakfast table, the snap-top on octagonal baluster pillar issuing from concave square platform, on compressed bun feet and casters, 51in (129cm).
$1,800-2,800

A Victorian inlaid walnut breakfast table, the amboyna banded oval tip-up top on quadruple baluster columns, with splayed legs and foliate carved terminals, 48in (122cm) wide.
$1,600-2,000

A Victorian walnut breakfast table, the moulded top raised on a bulbous stem, with downswept supports, carved with leafage, stamped 216, 48in (122cm).
$3,000-4,000

A green painted breakfast table, including 4 extra leaves to add to the outer rim, in a fitted black painted box, modern, 76½in (194cm) extended.
$7,000-9,000

A Victorian rosewood breakfast table.
$2,600-3,600

An early Victorian burr walnut breakfast table, with a quarter veneered circular moulded top on a baluster and gadrooned shaft and 3 splayed scroll carved legs, 50in (127cm).
$2,800-3,200

A Victorian rosewood breakfast table, the tilt-top with a moulded border, on a bulbous leaf cast baluster support, on triple downswept legs profusely carved with flowers, c1845, 54in (137cm).
$3,500-4,500

A Regency mahogany breakfast table, with rosewood crossbanding, the ring turned pillar on quadruple splayed legs ending in brass cappings and casters, c1810, 54in (137cm).
$3,400-4,000

An early Victorian mahogany breakfast table, on turned column and tripod base, top and bottom associated, base stamped A Blain, Liverpool.
$2,400-3,200

A mid-Victorian burr walnut breakfast table, the tilt-top on a tripod base, with bulbous fluted shaft, with splayed legs and scroll feet, 52in (132cm).
$4,200-5,000

A George III mahogany pedestal breakfast table, the tip-up top on a tapering shaft and quadruple splayed legs, with brass box terminals, 57in (144cm).
$2,000-3,000

A William IV mahogany tip-up breakfast table, on 4 acanthus carved hipped splayed legs with brass caps and casters, 54½in (138cm).
$2,600-3,600

A Regency rosewood, marquetry and brass inlaid breakfast table, the tip-up top with a trailing floral border, on a faceted tapering shaft and beaded concave platform with foliate carved paw feet, 50in (127cm).
$7,000-8,000

The price of this piece reflects the quality and inlaid decoration.

A William IV mahogany breakfast table, of good colour, on bulbous turned column with moulded outswept legs and lappet carved feet, 56in (142cm).
$1,600-2,000

A mid-Victorian walnut breakfast table, with a burr veneered tip-up top on a fluted and beaded turned column and 4 splayed foliate and flowerhead carved legs, with scroll feet, the base stamped Lamb, Manchester, 19189, 51in (129cm) wide.
$3,000-4,000

Card Tables

A George III mahogany and boxwood strung semi-circular card table. **$2,000-3,000**

A George III mahogany concertina action card table, with a hinged top, above a blind fret frieze, on square chamfered legs, 36in (92cm). **$3,200-4,000**

This piece is decorated in typical Chinese Chippendale style.

A George II style mahogany tea/card table, the twin shaped panelled folding top enclosing a baize lined interior, above 2 frieze drawers on blind fret square moulded legs, with pierced wings, 35in (89cm). **$2,600-4,600**

A Classical carved mahogany swivel-top card table, Philadelphia, c1815. **$4,500-6,500**

An Edwardian mahogany and satinwood banded card table, the envelope folding top above a frieze drawer, on square tapering legs, 22in (56cm). **$1,600-2,000**

A Victorian rosewood envelope card table, 21in (53cm). **$720-800**

A George III mahogany card table, the top crossbanded in satinwood and rosewood, on square tapered legs inlaid with boxwood stringing, 35½in (91cm). **$2,600-3,600**

A Georgian inlaid rosewood folding card table. **$3,000-3,600**

A George II mahogany card table, the fold-over top with counter wells, above a concertina action base with cabriole legs, on pad feet, 34in (86cm) wide. **$2,000-3,000**

A mahogany and satinwood crossbanded folding card table, with boxwood and ebony stringing, the frieze similarly inlaid, on square tapering supports, 19thC, 37in (94cm). **$1,600-2,000**

A late George III inlaid mahogany demi-lune card table, the tulipwood banded baize lined top with central fan inlay on square tapering legs, 36in (92cm). **$1,600-2,000**

A Regency satinwood ebonised and brass inlaid card table, with a canted hinged baize lined top, above a reeded frieze on turned uprights, the platform on 4 reeded splayed legs, restored, 36in (92cm). **$3,500-4,500**

A Georgian mahogany and ebony strung demi-lune card table, on square tapered legs with spade feet.
$1,500-1,800

An inlaid satinwood card table, the hinged baize lined top inlaid with fan motifs on square tapering legs, with spade feet, 34in (86cm).
$1,500-1,800

An Adam style satinwood and mahogany banded serpentine card table, the fan inlaid top above a deep frieze, on square tapered legs inlaid with bellflower chains, late 19thC.
$2,700-3,700

An Edwardian mahogany card table, 34in (86cm).
$2,700-3,700

An early Victorian rosewood crossbanded fold-over card table, on shaped and fluted columns with 4 carved legs.
$2,700-3,200

A William IV rosewood pedestal card table, the swivelling fold-over top enclosing a baize lined interior, on a collared tapering shaft and concave sided platform base, 36in (92cm).
$1,200-1,500

A Regency mahogany card table, the rosewood crossbanded hinged top on a turned column with moulded downswept supports and brass casters, c1810, 36in (92cm).
$1,000-1,600

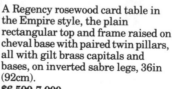

A Regency rosewood card table in the Empire style, the plain rectangular top and frame raised on cheval base with paired twin pillars, all with gilt brass capitals and bases, on inverted sabre legs, 36in (92cm).
$6,500-7,000

The value of this piece is greatly enhanced by the fact that the legs close up when the top is rotated.

A George IV rosewood and brass inlaid pedestal card table, with a baize lined interior, on a bulbous tapering column and concave sided platform base and splayed legs, with brass paw feet, 36in (92cm).
$1,200-1,600

A Regency rosewood card table, inlaid throughout with cut brass floral motifs, the top above a vase shaped pillar and quadruple splayed legs ending in brass paw feet and casters, c1815, 36in (92cm).
$4,500-5,500

A Federal inlaid mahogany card table, with repairs to feet, probably Baltimore, c1800, 38½in (98cm).
$3,500-5,000

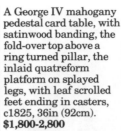

A George IV mahogany pedestal card table, with satinwood banding, the fold-over top above a ring turned pillar, the inlaid quatreform platform on splayed legs, with leaf scrolled feet ending in casters, c1825, 36in (92cm).
$1,800-2,800

A Victorian rosewood and inlaid envelope card table, fitted with a drawer, on tapered square legs joined by an undertier, 31in (79cm) open.
$1,400-1,600

A Louis Philippe style ormolu mounted burr walnut and marquetry card table inlaid with scrolling foliage and a central urn of flowers on dark ground, protruding corners, baize lined inlaid folding and swivelling top, on ebonised fluted tapered legs, 34in (86cm).
$4,000-5,000

A Dutch marquetry card table, the top inlaid with bands of cattle in landscape, and a chess board inside, the square tapering legs folding flat, allowing the top to be displayed vertically, 19thC, 36in (92cm).
$1,200-1,800

A boulle and gilt metal mounted card table, the serpentine top centred by putti, the frieze centred by a mask medallion, on cabriole legs with caryatids and sabots, c1860, 36in (92cm).
$2,700-3,700

A Napoleon III walnut and gilt metal mounted card table, inlaid throughout with tulipwood bandings and stringing, on cabriole legs ending in sabots, c1870, 33in (84cm).
$2,700-3,700

An ormolu mounted tulipwood and marquetry card table, the folding swivelling baize lined top inlaid with a central bowl of fruit in stained woods and scrolling foliage and banding, on fluted ebonised supports with cross stretchers, 24½in (62cm).
$2,700-3,700

A Louis XV style walnut and gilt metal mounted card table, the serpentine top with narrow tulipwood banding, the cabriole legs ending in sabots, probably English, c1870, 36in (92cm).
$2,200-3,200

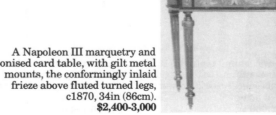

A Napoleon III marquetry and ebonised card table, with gilt metal mounts, the conformingly inlaid frieze above fluted turned legs, c1870, 34in (86cm).
$2,400-3,000

Centre Tables

A mid Victorian walnut and gilt metal mounted centre table, inlaid with geometric scrolling motifs, the moulded top on 4 turned supports with finialed platform on splayed legs, 47½in (121cm).
$2,000-2,700

A Victorian rosewood and marquetry centre table, the top segmentally veneered, on baluster column and 3 hipped downscrolled legs, 48½in (123cm).
$4,500-5,500

A Regency rosewood centre table, banded with ebony and satinwood, on column end supports joined by a turned stretcher, on downswept legs with brass caps, 49in (125cm).
$5,500-6,500

A Regency rosewood centre table, with 2 true and 2 false frieze drawers, on end standards with scroll mouldings, joined by a stretcher, on turned feet, 60in (152cm).
$4,000-4,600

A Regency mahogany centre table, crossbanded with rosewood, on end supports and scrolling capitals, inlaid with ebonised lines joined by a high plain stretcher, on downswept legs with brass paw feet, 36in (92cm).
$3,300-4,000

A French tortoiseshell brass inlaid and gilt metal mounted centre table, in the manner of A C Boulle, of broken recessed outline, the top with egg and bellflower border above 2 frieze drawers centred by a female mask, on cabriole legs headed by bearded masks trailing to leaf and paw sabots, distressed, early 19thC, 41in (104cm).
$3,000-3,600

A walnut and red walnut centre table, with claw-and-ball feet with acanthus carved headings, early 18thC and later, 40½in (103cm).
$1,500-2,000

A Victorian giltwood and composition centre table, with an inset glazed tapestry panelled top, 51in (130cm).
$2,000-2,800

A Victorian walnut centre table, of serpentine outline, the top inlaid with arabesques above a drawer, on gilt metal mounted cabriole legs.
$1,600-2,000

A late Victorian rosewood and marquetry centre table, with 4 swivelling drawers, on square tapering legs joined by stretchers, 21½in (54cm).
$1,200-1,600

An early Victorian rosewood centre table, 40in (102cm).
$1,600-2,000

A Victorian burr walnut and carved centre table, the top with stipple ground border, on conjoined quadruple scroll supports and ceramic casters, c1855, 60in (152cm).
$3,600-4,500

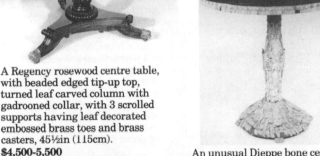

A gilt gesso table, carved in low relief, divided by strapwork within a flowerhead border with plain frieze and shaped apron with shells and foliage, on club legs and pad feet with acanthus trailing husks, 37½in (95cm).
$3,600-4,500

A Regency rosewood centre table, with beaded edged tip-up top, turned leaf carved column with gadrooned collar, with 3 scrolled supports having leaf decorated embossed brass toes and brass casters, 45½in (115cm).
$4,500-5,500

An unusual Dieppe bone centre table, with later mirrored top, the whole applied with overlapping leaves incorporating dolphins and mythological figures, c1860, 36in (92cm).
$1,600-2,000

A Victorian marquetry and gilt metal mounted centre table, in the Louis XV style, inlaid throughout with deities and cherubs within floriated leafy scrolls, the serpentine kingwood banded top above a concealed frieze drawer, the cabriole legs ending in sabots, c1870, 36in (92cm).
$4,000-5,500

A Biedermeier walnut centre table, with spreading hexagonal and ribbed pedestal on concave sided tripod base, with downward scrolling legs, restorations to top, 42in (107cm).
$4,500-5,500

A Victorian rosewood centre table, the top above 2 frieze drawers, on end column supports, with platform supports and paw feet.
$1,500-2,000

A giltwood centre table, of late 17thC design, with mottled marble top and stiff leaf carved border, on carved bun feet joined by flattened stretchers centred by an acorn finial, 39½in (100cm).
$2,700-3,600

A Victorian walnut centre table, the serpentine quarter veneered top with leaf carved baluster supports joined by a pole stretcher, c1850, 48in (122cm).
$2,000-2,700

Console Tables

A green veined, cream painted console table, of Louis XV design, with moulded eared serpentine grey marble top, cabriole legs joined by a scrolling stretcher on scroll feet, 46½in (118cm). **$2,000-2,800**

A pair of gilt decorated and later blue painted console tables, of Louis XVI design, each with a white marble top, on turned fluted legs joined by a concave stretcher centred by an urn, on turned feet, 51in (130cm). mid-19thC, **$4,500-6,500**

A pair of early 20thC console tables and a round table en suite, with marble tops. **$2,000-2,700**

An Anglo-Indian rosewood console table, with scagliola top above a plain frieze, on S-scroll end supports carved with acanthus leaves and paterae, on concave fronted moulded rectangular plinth base, restorations, 19thC, 48in (122cm). **$3,600-4,500**

A Napoleon III ebonised gilt metal mounted and boxwood strung console table, on paw sabots, 55in (140cm). **$2,000-3,000**

Dining Tables

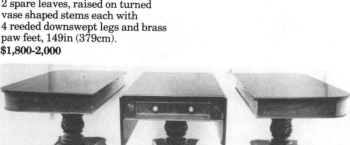

A Georgian style mahogany three-pillar dining table, with 2 spare leaves, raised on turned vase shaped stems each with 4 reeded downswept legs and brass paw feet, 149in (379cm). **$1,800-2,000**

A William IV mahogany D-end extending dining table, the drop-leaf top with telescopic action, on reeded turned legs with brass casters, including 3 leaf insertions, lacking clips, c1830, 88½in (225cm) long extended. **$5,000-5,500**

A William IV mahogany three-pedestal extending dining table, the centre piece in the form of a Pembroke table, 96in (244cm) long. **$9,000-10,000**

A mahogany triple pedestal D-end dining table, on later tripod supports, with 2 extra leaves, basically early 19thC. **$4,500-5,500**

A mahogany concertina action extending dining table, with moulded edge and 2 drop flaps, raised on melon fluted turned and tapering supports terminating in casters, each end drawing out to incorporate the 3 additional leaves, with a central melon fluted turned support, early 19thC, 104in (264cm) long extended. **$5,500-7,000**

A Regency mahogany draw leaf table, with D-shaped end sections and central section with reeded edge and 2 frieze drawers, on turned shaft with downswept reeded legs and brass caps, minor restorations, 60in (152cm).
$5,500-6,500

An early Victorian mahogany secrétaire dining table, the extending coffered top revealing a frieze writing drawer with a leather lined writing plateau, including an extra leaf, 75in (191cm) long.
$7,000-9,000

A Victorian mahogany extending dining table, the top with telescopic action, the lobed baluster turned legs on brass casters, including 4 leaf insertions, c1850, 148in (376cm) long extended.
$5,500-7,000

A mahogany extending D-end dining table, in 3 sections with a central drop leaf, on square tapering legs, adapted, late 18thC.
$4,500-5,500

A Victorian mahogany dining table, on turned tapering legs with link cabochon headings, including 3 extra leaves in a grained pine housing unit, 119in (302cm) long extended.
$5,000-5,500

A Regency mahogany dining table, on splayed legs with brass block terminals, including an extra leaf, extending to 67½in (171cm).
$3,300-4,500

A George IV mahogany extending dining table, with veneered friezes, ribbed panels above turned ribbed tapering legs to onion feet, on brass casters, 106in (269cm) extended.
$9,500-10,000

An early Victorian mahogany extending dining table, 98in (249cm).
$5,000-5,500

A George III mahogany dining table, inlaid with ebonised banding, with 2 extra leaves, on square tapering legs, with gateleg action, restorations, 99in (252cm) long, including leaves.
$3,000-4,000

A George III mahogany twin pedestal dining table, with spare leaf, supported on twin fluted columns with 4 shaped legs, ornate brass feet and casters, 78in (198cm) long.   **$9,000-10,000**

A George III mahogany drop-leaf dining table, on square tapered legs.
$1,000-1,500

A late Georgian mahogany D-end dining table, on square tapering legs with spade feet, including an extra leaf, 68½in (174cm) long.
$3,600-4,500

A Victorian mahogany dining table, on reeded turned tapering legs, including 2 extra leaves, 81in (206cm) long extended.
$2,200-2,800

A mahogany framed dining/snooker table by E. J. Riley.
$2,000-2,800

A Federal mahogany three-part dining table, restored, c1820, 48in (122cm). **$4,000-5,000**

An Edwardian Chippendale revival carved mahogany dining table, on cabriole legs with acanthus knees and claw-and-ball feet, including 2 spare leaves and winding key, c1910, 96in (244cm) long extended.
$2,5000-3,000

A Biedermeier bird's-eye maple expanding dining table, with later top, opening to enclose 3 later leaves, on pierced shaped trestle ends joined by a ring turned stretcher and bun feet, including 3 leaves, adapted, 94in (238cm) extended. **$6,500-7,000**

A Regency mahogany three-pillar dining table, 130in (330cm) long. **$72,000-81,000**

A Restoration walnut extending dining table, with metal label inscribed T.P. Sherborne/Patent Right Secured 1849 No. 127 Walnut St/Philadelphia, c1849, 104½in (265cm) extended.
$5,500-7,000

A Regency mahogany dining table, on reeded turned legs, including a later spare leaf, c1810, 82in (208cm) long extended. **$3,600-4,500**

A William and Mary walnut gateleg dining table, some restoration, Pennsylvania, c1740, 56in (142cm) extended. **$4,500-6,000**

Display Tables

An Edwardian satinwood and marquetry vitrine table, inlaid overall with scrolling foliage with glazed hinged top and sides enclosing an interior with green velvet lined base, on square tapering legs joined by an X-shaped stretcher, on spade feet, damage to stretcher, 24in (61cm).
$2,700-3,600

Dressing Tables

A Chippendale carved walnut dressing table, Philadelphia area, c1770, with later carving, 33½in (85cm). **$46,500-48,000**

An Empire mahogany and gilt metal mounted dressing table, the arched swing-plate above a single frieze drawer, on turned column supports with concave platform base, adapted, 32in (81cm).
$3,600-4,350

A French Second Empire kingwood and gilt metal mounted vitrine table, the glazed top with three-quarter pierced gallery above a shaped apron, on cabriole legs with gilt foliate clasps, 25½in (65cm).
$1,500-1,800

A Venetian giltwood and blue and floral painted vitrine table, with a hinged lid, on cabriole legs headed by foliate mouldings and armorial devices with turned feet, 36in (92cm).
$3,000-3,600

A William and Mary inlaid walnut veneer dressing table, some restorations, New England, early 18thC, 34in (86cm).
$10,000-11,000

A French kingwood and ormolu mounted bijouterie table, with shaped bevelled glass top enclosing velvet lined interior, the bombé sides with torch, mask and floral motifs, on cabriole legs, 19thC, 30in (76cm).
$7,350-8,000

A rosewood and marquetry display table, late 19thC, 24in (61cm).
$1,600-1,800

A Victorian burr walnut dressing table and matching washstand, 48in (122cm).
$1,200-1,500

A black and gilt japanned dressing table, the top with three-quarter gallery with 4 short drawers around a kneehole drawer, on turned tapering legs with brass caps, stamped 1033, early 19thC, 42in (107cm).
$5,500-6,500

A George III mahogany dressing table, with hinged top, the interior banded in tulipwood with easel mirror flanked by lidded compartments with chased ormolu handles, on square tapering legs joined by a concave side undertier, 28in (71cm).
$2,800-3,600

A Biedermeier rosewood dressing table, banded overall with fruitwood lines, the base with grey veined white marble top with single ash lined frieze drawer with compartments, on S-scroll supports joined by double U-shaped stretcher, on downswept legs, 32in (81cm).
$3,600-4,500

A mahogany tray top dressing table, early 19thC, 38½in (98cm).
$900-1,000

A mahogany dressing table, inlaid with boxwood stringing, on square tapering legs, one front leg broken and repaired, 37½in (95cm).
$3,000-3,600

Drop-leaf Tables

A mahogany drop-leaf table, with double gateleg action, on turned tapering supports with pad feet, 63½in (161cm).   **$1,200-1,400**

> ### Did you know
> *MILLER'S Antiques Price Guide builds up year by year to form the most comprehensive photo-reference system available*

A Regency mahogany drop-leaf dining table, with twin flap top, on turned tapering legs and brass caps, previously the centre section of a larger table, some repairs, 64in (163cm).
$3,600-4,600

A George II mahogany drop-leaf table, the top on round tapering legs, with plain husk outline mouldings to the knees, on pad feet, some damage, 56in (142cm).
$1,200-1,400

A Queen Anne cherrywood small dropleaf dining table, New England, c1760, 41in (104cm) extended.
$2,500-3,500

A George II mahogany oval drop-leaf table, with single extension to either side, small fitted drawer, plain cabriole legs having scroll carved knees with pointed pad feet, 45in (114cm).
$1,800-2,700

A Queen Anne curly maple dropleaf dining table, New England, c1760, 52in (132cm) extended.
$2,500-3,500

Games Tables

A Dutch mahogany and marquetry games table, the fold-over top enclosing a recess above a frieze drawer, on cabriole legs with claw-and-ball feet, 19thC, 27in (69cm). **$3,500-4,000**

A mahogany games table with an eared hinged top, the baize lined surface with gaming dishes above a dummy frieze drawer, on cabriole legs with pad feet, adapted, mid-18thC, 32in (81cm).
$1,500-2,000

This table is adapted and this is reflected in the price.

A New Zealand thuyawood parquetry games and work table, the hinged top revealing a chessboard and compartments, the hexagonal pillar support on a shaped platform base with bun feet, with original trade label of James Annear, Sydney Street, Wellington, New Zealand, c1840, 27½in (70cm).
$4,500-5,500

An inlaid maple and walnut pool table, with metal label of Sandford, Bell & Lahm, New York, 61 Fourth Ave.
$14,500-16,000

A mahogany games table with eared folding top, inset with counter wells and a gaming board, on cabriole legs headed by acanthus and hoof feet, with folding backgammon board, drawer distressed, adapted, 31½in (80cm). **$3,600-4,500**

A Regency rosewood games table, the top with pierced brass gallery flanking a panel, sliding to reveal a chessboard and a backgammon board, on ring turned legs with splayed feet joined by twin turned stretchers, gallery loose, c1815, 31in (79cm).
$2,000-2,800

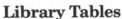

A French kingwood and harewood inlaid tic-tac games table, the rimmed detachable top with a central chessboard and enclosing a backgammon board above 2 side drawers, on cabriole legs, 19thC, 33½in (85cm).
$5,500-6,500

Library Tables

A George III mahogany library table, the top with replacement green hide, 42in (107cm).
$4,600-5,500

A George III mahogany partners' library table, with inset leather writing surface, with reeded edge, each side fitted with 3 drawers, on turned and finely fluted tapering supports, brass toe caps and casters, 60in (152cm).
$6,000-6,500

A mahogany library table, with a leather lined top above 3 frieze drawers, on square tapering legs, late 18thC and later, 48in (122cm). **$4,500-5,500**

A mid Victorian mahogany library table, with a reeded top above 3 frieze drawers to either side, on turned tapering legs, 54in (137cm).
$3,300-4,000

A William IV rosewood library table, the top with a gadrooned border and a pair of frieze drawers, the reeded and fluted supports on platform bases with gadrooned bun feet, c1830, 45½in (115cm).
$3,600-4,500

A late Regency rosewood library table, the leather lined top with hinged reading slope, above 3 frieze drawers, on pierced end standards with bun feet, 34in (86cm).
$2,700-3,600

A George IV mahogany library table.
$5,500-6,500

A George IV mahogany library table, with 2 frieze drawers to either side, on panelled end supports with scroll brackets, and bun feet, 57in (145cm).
$3,000-3,600

A Georgian style quartetto of mahogany coffee tables, inlaid with fruitwood.
$1,600-2,000

A William IV library table, the top on twin reeded turned end supports, with shaped platform bases and scroll feet, c1835, 50in (127cm).
$1,500-2,000

Nests of Tables

A set of George III style mahogany quartetto tables, outlined in boxwood stringing, the rosewood banded tops on twin ring turned column supports, on downswept feet, late 19thC.
$1,500-1,600

A set of Regency mahogany quartetto tables, with beaded tops on slender turned legs joined by later stretchers, on splayed feet, smallest table stamped Wilkinson, Ludgate Hill, 11781, c1815, 19in (48cm).
$3,500-5,000

The firm of William Wilkinson operated from 14 Ludgate Hill from c1808 and continued to stamp products Wilkinson, Ludgate Hill until c1820 when the business traded as William Wilkinson & Sons. After this date furniture was stamped Wilkinson & Sons, 14 Ludgate Hill. The company remained in business at these premises until c1840.

A nest of Victorian mahogany and marquetry quartetto tables, the tops painted within satinwood banded borders, on twin column end standards and splayed feet joined by stretchers, labelled F.W. Greenwood & Sons Ltd., 24 Stonegate, York, 22in (56cm) and smaller.
$2,800-3,500

Occasional Tables

A French ormolu mounted occasional table, fitted with 2 small drawers, 18½in (47cm).
$900-1,000

A Regency mahogany three-tier occasional table, on plinth base.
$800-1,000

A Louis XV style occasional table, 16in (41cm) diam.
$1,600-2,000

Pedestal Tables

An early Victorian burr elm and amboyna pedestal table, in the manner of Edward Baldock, the marquetry tip-up top with yew banded borders, on a triform stem and scroll block feet, 26in (66cm).
$6,500-7,000

A Regency rosewood library table, in the manner of Thomas Hope, 48in (122cm).
$20,000-23,500

A French marquetry occasional table, in the Louis XVI style, the top with paterae at each corner within ormolu border, the top frieze and platform with dotted marquetry trellis on satinwood ground, with frieze drawer, on square tapered mahogany legs encased in ormolu foliage with slender twist turned acanthus sabots, 19thC, 16in (41cm).
$2,700-3,600

A Victorian walnut and floral marquetry pedestal table, inlaid on ebonised grounds within crossbanding, the lobed baluster support on a scrolled tripod base, c1860, 57½in (146cm).
$9,500-10,000

A mid Victorian gilt metal pedestal table, with octagonal Derbyshire spire and black slate top, on tripod stand with scrolling feet, 20in (51cm).
$2,000-3,000

A Victorian rosewood pedestal table, the tilt-top above a baluster turned pillar, on quadruple scroll carved supports, c1845, 63in (160cm).
$2,700-3,600

An early Victorian Derbyshire slate pedestal table, the top inset with a band of trailing white flowers in pietra dura on baluster shaft with concave sided canted triangular base, on bun feet, 20in (51cm).
$1,800-2,700

A Victorian walnut pedestal table, the quarter veneered tilt-top inlaid with arabesques and stringing, c1870, 51½in (131cm).
$1,200-1,800

A Victorian walnut pedestal table, the tilt-top inlaid with various segmented veneered woods, on a spiral turned shaft with splayed legs and scroll feet with bell flower headings, 16in (41cm).
$1,200-1,800

An early Victorian walnut and parquetry pedestal table, on tapering faceted shaft on tripartite platform base, with carved claw feet, 32in (81cm).
$1,500-1,600

Pembroke Tables

A George III mahogany Pembroke table, the folding top with serpentine outlines, with 2 frieze drawers, on square chamfered moulded legs joined by a pierced flat stretcher, 34in (86cm).
$3,000-3,600

A George III mahogany Pembroke table, outlined in boxwood stringing, the crossbanded top above an end drawer, on square tapering legs headed by oval fan paterae, 29in (74cm).
$3,600-4,500

A Federal inlaid mahogany Pembroke table, New York, c1805, 41in (104cm) extended.
$5,000-6,000

A Chippendale mahogany Pembroke table, some damage, Philadelphia, c1775, 44in (112cm) extended.
$4,000-6,000

A George III mahogany Pembroke table, with moulded twin flap top above 2 cedar lined drawers and 2 simulated drawers inlaid with ebonised stringing, on a turned shaft with quadripartite base with reeded legs and brass caps, the top possibly associated, 35½in (91cm) open.
$2,000-2,700

A George III mahogany and rosewood banded Pembroke table, the top with 2 hinged flaps above a bowfront frieze drawer, on square tapering legs, 38in (97cm).
$2,700-3,600

A George III style satinwood Pembroke table, the kingwood crossbanded top outlined in barber pole stringing, above an end drawer, on similarly inlaid square tapering legs, late 19thC, 36in (92cm).
$2,000-2,800

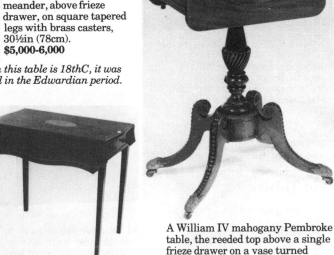

A George III satinwood Pembroke table, with painted top, the double crossbanding painted with ribbon and a bay leaf meander, above frieze drawer, on square tapered legs with brass casters, 30½in (78cm).
$5,000-6,000

Although this table is 18thC, it was decorated in the Edwardian period.

A George III inlaid mahogany Pembroke table, the rosewood banded folding top above a frieze drawer, on square tapering legs, 41½in (105cm) extended.
$5,000-5,500

A Sheraton style small mahogany and satinwood inlaid Pembroke table, with small marquetry panel and serpentine top and flaps.
$800-1,000

A William IV mahogany Pembroke table, the reeded top above a single frieze drawer on a vase turned column with beaded downswept supports, with leaf cast brass casters, Scottish, c1835, 29in (74cm).
$3,200-4,200

Serving Tables

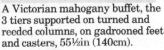

A Victorian mahogany buffet, the 3 tiers supported on turned and reeded columns, on gadrooned feet and casters, 55½in (140cm).
$1,800-2,000

A George III mahogany Pembroke table, 38in (97cm).
$1,800-2,000

A William IV mahogany Pembroke table, the top with opposing frieze drawers, the turned pedestal support on quadruple moulded splayed legs ending in brass paw casters, c1825, 44in (112cm) open.
$1,200-1,400

A George IV mahogany Pembroke table, the top with opposing frieze drawers, the turned pedestal support on quadruple moulded splayed legs ending in brass paw casters, c1825, 44in (112cm) open.
$1,200-1,400

A late George III mahogany serpentine serving table, on square tapering legs headed by paterae and ribbon tied trailing bellflowers terminating in spade feet, some carving of a later date, 63in (160cm).
$5,500-6,500

A mahogany and marquetry serpentine serving table, the top crossbanded in rosewood, on square tapering legs with block feet, adapted, some repair, late 18thC, 60in (152cm).
$3,500-4,500

A William IV mahogany serving side table, with tongue and dart and beaded carved outlines, on cabriole front column supports with a concave platform base, 66½in (169cm).
$7,000-9,000

The bold designs of this period are now much in vogue.

A sycamore sideboard, 19thC, 83in (210cm).
$2,900-3,600

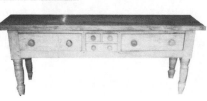

A mahogany serving side table of George III design, the top with gadrooned carved borders above a ribbon banded frieze fitted with 3 drawers, on cabriole legs with claw-and-ball feet with acanthus and bellflower carved headings, 72in (182cm).
$2,000-3,000

Side Tables

A George III mahogany side table, the veined Carrara marble top above a frieze, on square tapering legs carved with blind fret bands and paterae, raised on later pine column supports, 41in (104cm).
$10,000-11,000

A Victorian walnut side table, on fluted column supports tied by a shelf stretcher, on turned feet carved with floral swags.
$650-750

A South German parcel gilt and cream painted side table, with simulated marble top, on claw-and-ball feet, joined by a later scrolling X-shaped stretcher, centred with a later vase of flowers, 41in (104cm).
$3,000-4,000

A mid Victorian satinwood and kingwood banded bowfront side table, the quarter veneered top above 2 frieze drawers, on square tapering legs with spade feet, 44in (111cm).
$2,600-3,600

A kingwood, tulipwood and parquetry table a ecrire, inlaid overall with a sycamore leaf pattern, with eared waved sliding top above a drawer, with 2 lidded compartments with waved frieze, on cabriole legs with foliage scroll sabots, 32in (81cm).
$3,000-4,000

A William IV mahogany breakfront serving table with beaded frieze carved with lotus leaves, on turned tapering ribbed legs, each headed by a patera and with a stiff leaf collar, 120in (305cm).
$18,000-21,000

It is possible that this serving table was provided for the Stone Banqueting Hall. An important piece of its period.

A walnut veneered side table, the top with boxwood outline and crossbanded, the feet restored, early 18thC, 53in (134cm).
$6,500-7,000

A George III mahogany serpentine side table, the moulded top above 3 frieze drawers, on square tapering supports, reconstructed, 35in (89cm).
$2,000-3,000

A George III mahogany and boxwood strung side table, the top above a frieze drawer, on square tapered legs. **$900-1,000**

A William IV mahogany side table, with marble top and cushion frieze, on foliate and scroll headed monopodia supports, with hairy paw feet, 40in (101cm).
$2,900-3,900

A Venetian 18thC style green painted side table, the moulded top painted with a floral bouquet, above a similarly decorated wavy frieze containing a drawer, on floral carved moulded cabriole legs. **$1,600-2,000**

An early George III walnut side table, the quarter veneered and crossbanded top above 2 frieze drawers, on square chamfered legs, 32in (81cm). **$2,000-3,000**

A George III mahogany side table, the top inlaid with an oval in ebony, the waved frieze, on cabriole legs, 33in (84cm). **$3,000-4,000**

An Irish mahogany side table, surmounted by a moulded verde antico marble top, on foliate and feather carved tapering legs, with paw feet, 71in (180cm). **$5,800-9,000**

A walnut side table, on baluster turned legs, joined by a waved X stretcher, centred by a vase, on bun feet, with paper label Messrs. Stair & Andrew Ltd., restorations, part late 17thC, 38in (96cm). **$6,500-7,000**

A William IV rosewood side table, raised on standard carved supports, c1835, 24in (61cm). **$800-1,000**

A reproduction mahogany serpentine fronted side table, crossbanded in rosewood with shell inlay, with brass drop handles, on spade feet, bearing the Redman and Hales Limited trade label, 58in (147cm). **$900-1,000**

A Georgian style mahogany serpentine front side table, with later raised back, decorated with crossbanding and stringing, the drawers stamped M. Butler, 61in (155cm). **$1,600-2,000**

A William and Mary style walnut side table, the top inlaid with 2 panels of arabesque marquetry, the borders similarly inlaid, on slender inverted baluster turned legs joined by wavy stretchers, stamped Gillows, 32in (81cm). **$1,200-1,800**

A George III mahogany kneehole side table, the serpentine top above 5 drawers, on tapered square legs, with spade feet, c1785, 42in (106cm). **$3,500-4,500**

A Portuguese rosewood side table, with the frieze with convex panel and rippled borders, fitted with 3 drawers, on bulbous turned legs joined by spirally twisted stretchers, with bun feet, 19thC, 54in (137cm).
$7,000-8,000

Sofa Tables

A Regency mahogany sofa table, with 2 frieze drawers, on end standards joined by a turned stretcher, on splayed legs, 54in (137cm).
$3,000-3,600

A Venetian polychrome blackamoor side table, the top draped with an imitation rug supported by a kneeling girl, on stepped base carved with lotus leaves and paw feet, 19thC, 21in (53cm).
$4,500-5,500

A calamander sofa table, with twin flap top above 2 frieze drawers, on end standard supports, with dual legs joined by a stretcher, early 19thC and later, 58in (147cm).
$6,500-7,500

A mahogany and satinwood banded sofa table, possibly Dutch, lacks casters, early 19thC, 61in (155cm).
$3,600-4,900

A mahogany sofa table, on solid end standards, with fluted splayed legs and brass paw terminals, early 19thC and later, 66in (167cm) extended.
$3,000-3,600

A pair of late Regency mahogany sofa tables, with rosewood banded tops, fitted with 2 drawers with ebony banding and brass lion mask ring handles, on trestle end supports, the swept legs with ebony line brass sabots and casters, 61½in (156cm) extended.
$30,000-36,000

A Regency rosewood and banded sofa table, with 2 hinged flaps above 2 frieze drawers, on square tapering end standards with splayed legs and brass terminals, 58in (147cm).
$7,500-8,500

A mahogany sofa table, with 2 frieze drawers, on solid end supports and outsplayed legs, part early 19thC.
$1,200-2,000

A mahogany and ebony strung sofa table of Regency design, on brass paw terminals, 59in (149cm).
$1,800-2,200

A Regency mahogany sofa table, crossbanded with boxwood stringing, with turned central stretcher and shaped feet with ebony stringing and brass lion paw feet with brass casters, 51in (129cm).
$4,500-5,500

A George III mahogany sofa table, inlaid overall with ebony and boxwood stringing, each side with a drawer and a dummy drawer, on downswept legs and brass caps, platform carved with W, 61in (155cm).
$7,000-9,000

A Regency rosewood sofa table, outlined with brass stringing, with 4 hipped splayed legs, brass caps and casters, top and frieze varnished, 55½in (141cm).
$3,000-4,000

A George IV brass inlaid rosewood sofa table, with inlaid border, the frieze decorated with foliage and scrolls, with single mahogany lined drawer, on square spreading shaft and concave sided rectangular base, on scrolling feet, 59in (150cm).
$9,000-10,000

A Regency mahogany and satinwood banded sofa table, on end standards joined by a later stretcher, on dual splayed legs with spiral inlay, 63in (160cm).
$7,000-9,000

An inlaid rosewood sofa table, the crossbanded top with 2 frieze drawers, on twin S-scroll end standards and octagonal platform with quadruple splayed legs with brass paw feet, basically early 19thC, 60in (152cm).
$4,800-5,500

A George III style mahogany and painted sofa table of Sheraton design, the frieze with a pair of real and opposing dummy drawers, on rectangular end supports with splayed legs ending in brass paw feet and casters, 61in (155cm), extended.
$3,600-4,600

A Regency mahogany sofa table, inlaid overall with ebony stringing, the frieze with 2 drawers and 2 false drawers, on vase shaped end supports inlaid with scrolls, on downswept legs with brass caps, restorations, 57½in (146cm).
$4,800-5,500

A William IV rosewood sofa table, decorated with crossbanding, raised on solid end supports with splay legs and paw feet, 41in (104cm).
$2,800-3,600

Sutherland Tables

An early Victorian rosewood Sutherland table, 52in (132cm). **$1,800-2,700**

A Victorian burr walnut Sutherland table, with pierced shaped end supports and slender turned tapered legs. **$1,200-1,500**

A Victorian walnut Sutherland table, on pierced end supports and outswept legs. **$800-1,000**

A Victorian walnut Sutherland table, with baluster turned end supports joined by a conforming stretcher, on flower carved splayed feet with casters, some restoration, 41in (104cm). **$1,500-1,800**

A mid Victorian walnut Sutherland table, with twin flap top, on turned supports and dual scroll feet joined by a stretcher, 36in (92cm). **$650-1,000**

Tea Tables

A Georgian mahogany tea table, with semi-circular fold-over top, on turned tapering supports with pad feet, 27in (69cm). **$1,000-1,200**

Tavern Tables

A George III mahogany and fretwork tea table, in the Gothic manner, with pierced gallery above a drawer, supports loose, c1760, 21½in (54cm). **$5,200-6,500**

A William and Mary maple and pine tavern table, New England, c1725, 27in (69cm). **$5,500-7,000**

A George III mahogany tea table, with hinged top with plain frieze, on square chamfered legs with pierced brackets, 28in (71cm). **$2,700-3,600**

A Queen Anne maple and birchwood oval top tavern table, New England, c1760, 34in (86cm). **$5,500-6,500**

A pair of late 18thC mahogany D-shaped tea tables, folding to double gate supports, on later legs, 29in (74cm). **$11,000-13,000**

A Regency mahogany fold-over swivel top tea table, with mahogany crossbanding and 2 rosewood bandings, shaped panel and string inlay, raised on square tapered pillar rectangular platform with coved sides and paterae, 4 sabre legs with scroll tops terminating in pot casters, 35in (89cm). **$2,000-3,000**

A late Victorian satinwood and marquetry tea table, inlaid with classical urns and acanthus scrolls, on square tapering legs. **$1,200-1,600**

A mahogany satinwood inlaid fold-over tea table, with centre drawer, on square tapered legs, mid-19thC, 38in (97cm). **$1,500-1,600**

A George IV mahogany tea table, the hinged moulded top swivelling to reveal a recess, on a double column stem and platform base, with reeded downswept supports, c1825, 35in (89cm). **$2,000-3,300**

A pair of mahogany tea tables, each with rectangular fold-over top above a frieze drawer, on square tapering reeded legs with spade feet, early 19thC, 33½in (85cm). **$1,200-1,500**

A Regency mahogany tea table, the yew wood crossbanded top inlaid with ebonised stringing, the gilt metal mounted ring turned pillar above quadruple splayed legs ending in chased brass cappings and casters, c1815, 42in (107cm). **$2,700-3,000**

A late Regency rosewood tea table, on a U-shaped scroll support and lobed column, on 4 acanthus carved hipped outswept legs, 36in (92cm). **$1,400-1,600**

Toilet Tables

A Georgian mahogany toilet table, on squared sectioned supports with undertier, the top opening to reveal a mirror, 36in (92cm) high. **$2,000-2,700**

A George III mahogany pedestal toilet stand, the folding top enclosing bowl apertures above a simulated drawer front enclosed by a pair of panelled doors and base drawer, on square tapering legs, flanking a side bidet with creamware liner, 23in (59cm). **$1,000-1,200**

Tripod Tables

An early 19thC mahogany round tip-up table, 22in (56cm).
$1,200-1,600

A George II walnut tripod table, with associated top, formerly with spindle gallery now with hobnail edge, on plain turned shaft with spirally reeded urn, on arched cabriole tripod base and pad feet, 11½in (29cm).
$1,600-2,000

A George III mahogany round tip-up table, 33in (84cm).
$1,000-1,200

A mid Georgian mahogany tripod table, with tilt-top, now fixed, on a turned pedestal and arched cabriole legs with pointed pad feet, 24in (61cm).
$1,500-1,600

A mahogany table, the top made from a single piece of timber, c1780, 32in (81cm).
$650-720

A George III mahogany round tip-up table, on turned and spiral fluted column, 30½in (77cm).
$1,000-1,200

With contemporary carving and a dished top this table would fetch a higher price.

A mahogany tripod table, the hinged top with pierced gallery and birdcage support, on a stop fluted spirally twisted spreading shaft, on downswept legs headed by acanthus and rockwork, on claw-and-ball feet, branded TMW, 24½in (62cm).
$1,600-2,000

This table is out of period otherwise the price would be considerably higher.

Wine/Lamp Tables

A pair of rosewood and satinwood banded lamp tables, each with an octagonal top and faceted shaft, on 3 splayed legs with gilt metal ball feet, modern, 14in (36cm).
$2,700-3,600

A Victorian walnut wine table, with floral marquetry inlay, raised on a spiral turned column, with cabriole tripod, with retailer's stamp beneath, 22in (56cm).
$1,000-1,200

A small lamp/chess table, 28in (71cm) high. **$720-800**

Work Tables

A George IV mahogany Pembroke work table, with 2 real and 2 opposing dummy frieze drawers the pierced lyre shaped supports joined by a turned stretcher, on splayed legs ending in brass cappings and casters, c1820, 29½in (75cm).
$2,600-3,600

A Federal curly maple inlaid mahogany two-drawer work table, some restoration, Philadelphia, c1810, 21in (53cm).
$18,000-19,000

A Federal curly maple single drawer work table, Massachusetts, c1815, 19in (48cm).
$7,500-9,000

A Federal carved mahogany work table, Hains-Connelly School, Philadelphia, c1810, 20in (51cm).
$2,500-3,500

A kingwood, tulipwood and end cut marquetry work table, the lifting top inlaid with scrolls, enclosing a divided interior of satinwood and bird's-eye maple, on square cabriole legs mounted with chased ormolu plaques and Joseph pattern angles, bearing trade label of Edwards & Roberts, 20 & 21 Wardour St. and 7 Chapel St. Oxford St., London, mid-19thC, 23in (59cm).
$1,800-2,800

A George III rosewood and painted work table, banded overall with boxwood and ebonised lines, the top banded with satinwood enclosing a green pleated repp well on square tapering legs headed by anthemia and husks and joined by a later X-shaped stretcher, 16in (41cm) wide. **$2,000-2,700**

A Federal carved mahogany two-drawer work table, Philadelphia, c1825, 20in (51cm).
$5,000-6,000

A satinwood and painted work table, the sides each with one drawer, one lacking compartments, with red pleated silk work basket, on square tapering legs headed by husks and joined by an X-shaped stretcher, on spade feet, 18in (46cm).
$3,000-3,600

A Regency mahogany work table, with sliding semi-circular box with support, on rectangular platform with coved sides, 4 sabre legs terminating in claw box casters, 24in (61cm). **$2,000-3,000**

A late Federal carved mahogany sewing table, lacking sewing bag, attributed to Samuel Field McIntire, Salem, Massachusetts, c1820, 18in (46cm). **$3,000-5,000**

Writing Tables

A Regency mahogany writing table, by Gillows, Lancaster, 31in (79cm).
$7,000-8,000

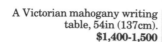

A Victorian mahogany writing table, 54in (137cm).
$1,400-1,500

A mid-18thC style mahogany and ebony banded writing table, by Maple & Co., on plain cabriole legs.
$900-1,200

A lady's French kingwood and parquetry writing table, the sliding tray top with parquetry centre enclosed within wide bandings above fitted writing drawer, fitted with leather lined slide, on square tapered legs, with gilt metal sabots,19thC, 16in (41cm).
$2,400-3,200

A Louis Philippe ebony, floral marquetry and gilt metal mounted bureau plat, of Louis XV design, on cabriole legs with gilt sabots, 51in (129cm).
$2,600-3,600

A Victorian boulle bureau plat in Louis XV style, the serpentine top inlaid in première partie, fitted with 2 drawers on gilt metal mounted cabriole legs.
$1,400-1,500

A French kingwood and gilt metal mounted bureau plat of Louis XV design, with a leather lined top above 3 frieze drawers with shell and foliate scroll mounts, on cabriole legs, 59in (150cm).
$2,600-3,600

A mid Victorian oak writing table, with green leatherette lined top, the panelled apron carved with Gothic tracery, on C-scroll end supports carved with trefoils joined by a square stretcher on foliate scroll feet, 46in (116cm).
$3,200-4,000

A black lacquer and chinoiserie decorated kneehole writing table, the coffered top above 3 frieze drawers, on square tapering legs, early 19thC and later, 31in (79cm).
$2,000-3,000

An early Victorian rosewood writing table, with leather lined top and three quarter pierced brass gallery above end standards, with scroll mouldings joined by a turned stretcher, on dual reeded bun feet, 43in (109cm).
$4,000-5,000

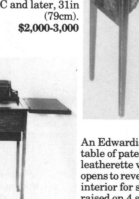

An Edwardian mahogany writing table of patent design, with purple leatherette writing slope which opens to reveal crimson taffeta lined interior for sewing accessories, raised on 4 square section supports, 20in (51cm).
$350-550

Washstands

A black lacquered washstand with gold design, 34in (86cm).
$1,000-1,200

Whatnots

A Victorian burr walnut canterbury whatnot, with a finialled three-quarter fret gallery, the top on spiral supports above a three divisioned box base fitted with a drawer, on turned tapering legs, 24in (61cm).
$1,800-2,700

A Regency mahogany two-teir corner washstand, the top lacking bowls and 2 false frieze drawers, on splayed square section legs tied by a platform stretcher.
$450-650

A Regency mahogany whatnot, with drawer below the third tier, 13½in (35cm).
$1,200-1,600

A Victorian rosewood four-tier corner whatnot, 23in (59cm).
$1,000-1,200

A Second Empire mahogany washstand, the Carrara marble top below a C-scrolling elevated shelved back above 2 frieze drawers and a panelled door, between quadrant angles, on bracket feet, 27½in (70cm).
$1,500-1,800

A rosewood tricoteuse, with veneered shelves, early 19thC, 30in (76cm).
$2,800-3,600

A George IV mahogany three-tier whatnot, on plain end standards, with scrolling supports, 36in (92cm).
$2,700-3,600

A Regency mahogany five-tier whatnot, the 3 lower shelves with drawer beneath, on turned supports, 22in (56cm).
$2,700-3,600

An early Victorian rosewood serpentine three-tier whatnot, with pointed finials, on brass caps and casters, 18in (46cm).
$1,500-1,800

317

A mahogany whatnot, early 19thC.
$1,400-1,500

A Regency mahogany four-tier whatnot, each tier with baluster turned column supports, with a frieze drawer to the base, on turned tapered legs.
$1,800-2,000

A Victorian rosewood whatnot, with 3 serpentine tiers between barleytwist columns, with a centre single drawer, on turned supports with brass casters, c1860, 23in (59cm).
$1,200-1,700

A George IV mahogany standing whatnot, with a three-quarter gallery above triple undertiers, on finialled ring turned baluster column supports and casters, shelves adapted, 54in (137cm) high.
$2,000-2,700

Miscellaneous

A mahogany pedestal artist's necessaire, the detachable boxed top with a fitted zinc lined interior and inset brass side carrying handles, above 3 graduated drawers and a concave undertier, on turned tapering legs with casters, basically early 19thC, 18in (46cm).
$1,200-1,800

A walnut lap desk, by Halstaff and Hannaford, London, with pierced brass mounts, parquetry inlaid fall front, domed lid enclosing fitted interior, with embossed red leather covered light and ink well, stamped Berry's Patent, on moulded base, 14½in (37cm).
$800-1,000

A German iron bound casket with studded hinged lid enclosing a formerly fitted interior, 17thC, 14in (36cm).
$700-900

A Spanish carved walnut marriage chest, the hinged top revealing a carved giltwood picture frame and a void interior, the front with 3 formal buildings flanked by a pair of scrolls, on a punched ground interspersed with flowerheads, on projecting fluted bases, mid-17thC, 42in (106cm).
$2,000-3,000

A Dutch child's sleigh, the front runner ending in eagle masks, with bobbin turned back handles, the sides with painted panels, c1870, 44in (112cm) long.
$6,500-7,000

ARCHITECTURAL ANTIQUES

Fireplaces

A late Georgian stripped pine fire surround, with leaf carved inner fillet, cut down, 60in (152cm), together with a green marble mantelpiece, 46in (117cm).
$540-720

An early Victorian white statuary marble fire surround with finely carved brackets, 61in (155cm).
$5,500-6,500

A cream painted pine and composition fire surround flanked by fluted split Corinthian column stiles, with grey veined white marble fillet with moulded edge, early 19thC, 82in (208cm).
$1,000-1,500

A late Georgian pine and carved walnut mounted chimney piece, carved with central tablet supporting a medallion carved with 'blind Justice', flanked by flaming torchères, 68½in (174cm).
$11,000-12,000

A pine and gesso fire surround, 19thC, 73in (185cm).
$540-720

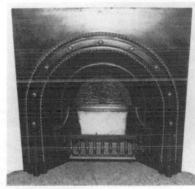

A cast iron fire insert, with brass buttons and double row of ogg and dart trim, c1840, 39in (99cm).
$2,000-3,000

A George II style pine fire surround, with carved border and plain central tablet, the scrolled jambs carved with flowerheads and bell husks, 60in (152cm).
$900-1,000

A Louis XV white marble bedroom fire surround, 38in (97cm).
$5,500-7,000

Use the Index!

Because certain items might fit easily into any of a number of categories, the quickest and surest method of locating any entry is by reference to the index at the back of the book.
This has been fully cross-referenced for absolute simplicity

A pine and gesso chimney piece, the breakfront shelf above a central tablet decorated with a figure of Plenty being driven in a chariot, 19thC, 90½in (230cm).
$1,500-2,000

A French statuary marble chimney piece, Louis XIII style, 55in (140cm).
$11,000-13,000
and fire basket with brass fretwork apron.
$1,500-1,600

A French/Grecian style white marble fire surround, the moulded shelf above a panelled frieze centred by a medallion of the Goddess Juno, the projecting end tablets embellished with rosettes supported on scroll brackets with guilloche bands and a large acanthus leaf at the base, 19thC, 76½in (194cm).
$7,000-9,000

A George III style steel and brass basket grate, of serpentine form with pierced foliate apron and cluster column front supports surmounted by urn finials.
$2,600-3,600

A Regency pine and gesso chimney piece, with a tablet depicting Cupid and Psyche, with rosette roundels at the angles above quiver jambs, 70½in (179cm).
$5,500-7,000

A Victorian white marble fire surround, with half columns, 66in (168cm).
$1,000-1,500

A Victorian white statuary marble fire surround of architectural design, 77in (196cm).
$12,000-16,000
and cast iron fire basket with applied brass rococo decoration.
$2,000-2,700

A George III style carved pine fire surround, the shelf above a central tablet carved with ribbon tied floral swags flanked by floral scrolls, the jambs carved with floral trains.
$5,500-6,500

A Victorian cast iron kitchen range, by James Work, Liverpool, restored, c1890.
$2,700-3,200

A white Sicilian marble fire surround, c1840, 71in (180cm).
$3,500-4,500
with Carron Co. cast iron insert.
$1,200-1,500

An Edwardian fire basket.
$1,500-1,800

A circular iron fire basket, with dragons heads and sunburst decoration, c1920.
$650-800

An iron fire basket with cut fretwork front.
$1,200-1,400

An early cast iron fire grate, made by A. Oakley, Hurst Green, E. Sussex, c1820, 40in (102cm).
$1,000-1,200

A fire basket, 35in (89cm).
$540-720

A Victorian slate fire surround, with pink fantasy marble decorated panels with Victorian cast iron arched interior, restored, c1870.
$2,700-3,200

An Adams style brass and cast iron serpentine fronted fire grate, 20thC.
$1,000-1,200

A French ormolu and steel fender, of serpentine outline, the scrollwork frieze with pierced and chased meandering foliage, mid-19thC, 60in (152cm).
$1,500-1,800

A pair of brass and wrought iron andirons, signed Wittingham, New York, c1790, and a pair of brass and wrought iron andirons.
$3,300-3,800

A cast iron fender, 45in (114cm).
$450-650

A pair of brass and wrought iron andirons, Philadelphia, c1790, 26in (66cm) high.
$1,700-2,000

A Regency brass fender, 36in (92cm).
$450-650

Fire Irons

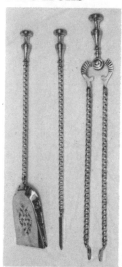

A set of 3 Victorian brass fire irons.
$450-650

A set of 3 Victorian brass fire irons.
$350-550

A set of 3 early Victorian brass and steel fire irons, each with foliate knop and spirally twisted shaft, comprising a pair of tongs, a pierced shovel and a poker, the tongs 30in (76cm) long.
$1,000-1,200

A set of 3 Victorian brass fire irons.
$450-650

A brass coal box, early 20thC, 13 by 15in (33 by 38cm).
$350-550

Did you know

MILLER'S Antiques Price Guide builds up year by year to form the most comprehensive photo-reference system available

An Edwardian oval brass coal box, with decorative fretwork, 16 by 16in (41 by 41cm).
$350-550

A set of brass rests and fire irons, c1870.
$720-900

Furniture

A pair of green painted Coalbrookdale type armchairs, of fern leaf design, the pierced backs cast with foliate motif, on wood slatted seats.
$3,500-4,500

A helmet shaped copper coal scuttle, 19 by 20in (48 by 51cm).
$350-550

A set of 3 Victorian brass fire irons, c1890.
$350-550

A white painted wrought iron 2 seater garden bench, on straight legs with pad feet, early 19thC, 43in (109cm).
$2,600-3,600

A set of 4 wrought ironwork chairs, the waisted backs above pierced seats, square feet with X shaped cross stretchers, 20thC.
$450-650

A Victorian white painted cast iron garden seat, the pierced drop-in seat with stiff leaf back and grape vine feet.
$700-1,000

A white painted wrought iron 2 seater seat, on cabriole legs with pad feet, early 19thC, 36in (92cm).
$2,000-3,000

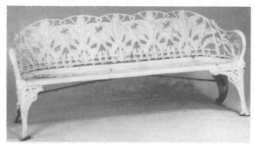

A Coalbrookdale cast iron lily of the valley pattern garden seat, the pierced cast back and arm rests with wood slat seat, 71in (180cm).
$2,700-4,500

A cast iron garden seat, the scrolled over back with mask surmount and pierced trailing nasturtium decoration, and slatted roll edged wooden seat, 19thC, 53½in (136cm).
$1,200-1,800

This seat was very nearly forgotten in the nettle bed of an estate.

A reeded wrought iron garden seat, with paw feet, early 19thC, 95½in (242cm).
$4,500-5,500

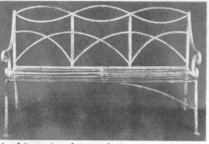

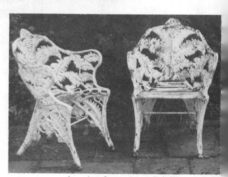

A Regency white painted garden bench, on splayed legs joined by stretchers, 62in (157cm).
$800-1,200

A white painted wrought iron garden seat, early 19thC, 67in (170cm).
$3,500-4,500

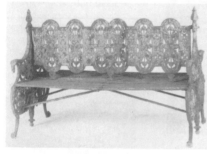

A cast iron double sided garden bench, the panelled back pierced with foliate motifs, the end pieces similarly decorated with eagle mask hand terminals, on paw feet, with pierced iron slatted seat, 57in (145cm).
$4,500-5,500

A pair of cast iron Coalbrookdale fern leaf pattern armchairs, the pierced cast backs above slatted seats, some slats lacking.
$1,500-2,000

A Coalbrookdale cast iron garden seat of unusual small size, of Gothic design, the pierced cast back centred by a crest, with scroll arm rests and iron slatted seat, 37in (94cm).
$2,600-3,600

A cast iron Coalbrookdale nasturtium pattern seat, the pierced cast back and ends with wood slatted seat, stamped Coalbrookdale, 71in (180cm).
$4,800-6,500

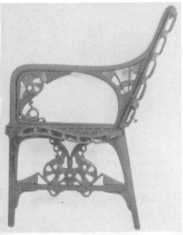

A Coalbrookdale cast iron and polychrome painted nasturtium pattern seat, the pierced cast back above wood slatted seat and scrolled uprights, stamped C.B. Dale and Co., 71in (180cm).
$2,600-3,600

A set of Coalbrookdale cast iron bench ends, designed by Dr. Christopher Dresser, with elaborate pierced scrolling decorations, each stamped Coalbrookdale and 206162.
$1,200-1,600

A set of 6 white painted cast iron chairs, the waisted backs above pierced seats and cabriole legs.
$1,500-2,000

A pair of white painted Coalbrookdale cast iron fern leaf pattern seats with pierced backs and uprights above wood slatted seats, 59in (150cm).
$2,000-3,000

A green painted cast iron bench, the pierced back, sides and seat cast with leafy branches, 50½in (128cm).
$2,000-3,000

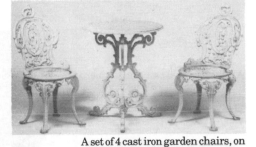

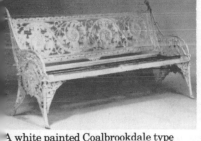

A set of 4 cast iron garden chairs, on cabriole legs with paw feet, and a cast iron table, on triple scroll support, 23in (59cm) diam.
$1,700-2,700

A white painted Coalbrookdale type cast iron bench, the pierced and cast back and sides cast with foliate arabesques, on slatted seat, 73in (185cm).
$3,500-5,500

A white painted reeded wrought iron garden seat, with down curved arm rests, the legs with paw feet and curved cross stretcher, early 19thC, 71in (180cm).
$1,500-2,000

A green painted cast iron garden bench, the pierced scrolled back on S-scrolled end supports pierced with foliate scrolls and wood slatted seat, 28½in (73cm).
$750-1,200

A white painted cast iron garden seat, with down curved arm rests and wood slatted seat, 47½in (120cm).
$2,000-3,000

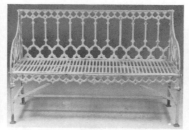

A white painted cast iron chair, the pierced floral back above a drop-in pierced seat and scrolled cabriole legs.
$1,500-1,800

A pair of white painted cast iron garden benches, of Gothic design, the pierced backs with down curved arm rests and iron slat seats, with later feet and cross stretchers, 57in (145cm).
$1,700-2,700

A white painted cast iron garden bench of Gothic design, with down curved arm rests and honeycomb pierced seat, 56½in (143cm).
$2,600-3,600

A pair of green painted cast iron rustic garden armchairs, the backs and seats pierced and cast with foliate branches.
$1,700-2,700

A white painted cast iron Gothic armchair, the pierced back and down curved arm rests on iron slat seat.
$800-1,200

A pair of Verona marble seats, the curved backs with lion mask terminals with paw feet, centred by an anthemion motif, and a table of rectangular oval form with egg and dart rim and winged lion supports, the seat 30in (76cm) high and the table 57in (145cm) long.
$14,500-18,000

A set of 4 French folding iron garden chairs, on wicker work simulated seat and X frame feet.
$3,500-4,500

Four white painted galvanised wire framed garden chairs and a matching circular table.
$1,500-1,800

A Coalbrookdale cast iron garden seat of Louis XV design, the arched pierced back cast with a central flower motif, with pierced trellis work and angled arm rests, on wood slatted seat, 75in (191cm).
$4,500-5,500

A white painted cast and wrought iron bench, the swept back and seat on splayed legs, with paw feet, 58in (147cm).
$800-1,000

A rare George V pub table.
$350-450

A pub table, with a cast iron base and wooden top, 24in (61cm) diam.
$180-280

Garden Statuary

A white marble bust of the Apollo Belvedere, after the antique, the head turned to sinister, with draped shoulders, on socle, 30in (76cm) high.
$5,500-7,000

A stone figure of a dog, ears pricked, on rectangular shaped base with cut corners, 23½in (60cm) high.
$800-1,200

A white marble figure of Diana the Huntress, with hound, on square base, 19thC, 52in (132cm) high.
$7,350-9,000

A white marble figure of Ariadne, the classical figure leaning against a rock signed Calvi, Milano, 19thC, 37in (94cm) high, on cylindrical granite plinth, 20in (51cm) high.
$4,500-6,500

A large white marble bust depicting The Lord of the Isles, the bearded figure with long flowing hair and draped shoulders, signed on back J. Hutchison Sc, Edinr, 32in (81cm) high.
$2,600-3,600

John Hutchison was born in Lauriston, Edinburgh, in 1833, and died there on 23 May 1910. He was apprenticed to a wood carver but also studied at the Antique and Life School of the Trustees' Academy, Edinburgh, and went to Rome in 1863. He exhibited at the Royal Scottish Academy from 1856, being elected A.R.S.A. in 1862 and R.S.A. 5 years later. He also exhibited at the Royal Academy from 1861 onwards.

A white marble group of Venus and Cupid, on cylindrical marble plinth, fingers and arrow missing, weathered, 19thC, 77in (196cm) high overall.
$3,500-5,500

A variegated white marble bust, lacking head, the torso dressed as a Roman Emperor, on a later metallic plinth, 15½in (40cm) high.
$2,600-3,600

A pair of white marble figures of seated lions, 19in (48cm) high.
$5,500-7,000

A white marble figure depicting an allegory of Wealth, clasping a wreath of berries with a bird at her feet, a pile of coins below, on circular base, 43in (109cm) high.
$9,000-10,000

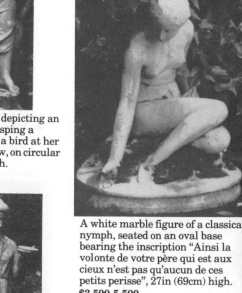

A white marble figure of Athena, right arm lacking, 19thC, 48in (122cm) high.
$3,500-5,500

A Coade stone type figure of a recumbent lion, on rectangular shaped base, some chipping, 22in (55cm) wide.
$1,200-1,500

A white marble figure of a classical nymph, seated on an oval base bearing the inscription "Ainsi la volonte de votre père qui est aux cieux n'est pas qu'aucun de ces petits perisse", 27in (69cm) high.
$3,500-5,500

A pair of modern white marble figures of lions with heavily carved manes, on rectangular bases, 40in (101cm) wide.
$4,500-6,500

A white marble figure of Hebe holding a tazza and a ewer, left arm loose, 19thC, 62in (157cm) high.
$6,500-8,000

A pair of lead figures of eagles with wings outstretched, on square bases with cut corners, 24in (61cm) high.
$1,700-2,700

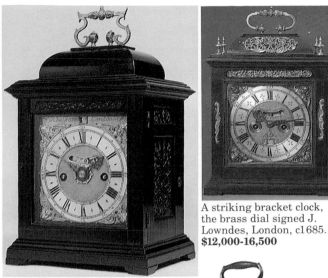

A striking bracket clock, the brass dial signed J. Lowndes, London, c1685. **$12,000-16,500**

A Charles II striking bracket clock, signed Cha. Gretton, London, 12in (30.5cm) **$32,000-40,000**

A Charles II ebonised striking bracket clock, dial signed J. Gerrard, London, strike/silent lever above XII, some restoration, 15in (38cm). **$16,500-21,000**

A William III kingwood quarter repeating bracket clock, the 6 pillar movement signed James Tudman, Londini Fecit, 15in (38cm). **$11,000-15,000**

A George II mahogany striking bracket clock, by Delander, 16in (40.5cm). **$18,000-21,000**

A Charles II ebony veneered bracket clock, signed Joseph Knibb, Londini Fecit, c1670, 14in (35cm). **$72,000-90,000**

An ebony veneered bracket clock, by John Barnett, London, 17thC, 15in (38cm). **$11,000-13,000**

A George I ebony grande sonnerie bracket clock, by Dan Delander, altered. **$150,000-175,000**

A Queen Anne striking bracket clock, signed Jos. Windmills. **$25,000-28,000**

329

A French brass carriage clock, with striking movement, 5½in (12.5cm). **$1,000-1,500**

A Louis XV boulle bracket clock, dial now signed Glaesner à Lyon, 37in (94cm). **$7,000-10,000**

A William IV gilt metal carriage timepiece, made by Howell & James, c1835, 4in (10cm). **$11,000-12,500**

A German walnut bracket clock, with quarter strike on 2 gongs, by Lenkirsh, c1880, 10in (25.5cm). **$1,800-2,000**

A gilt brass striking carriage clock, Japy Frères. **$9,000-10,000**

A miniature 8-day carriage timep[...] restorations, 3in (7cm). **$5,500-7,[...]**

A French repeating and alarm carriage clock, the gong striking movement stamped Pons. Medaille D'or 1827, with lever escapement, c1865, 6in (15cm). **$1,600-2,000**

A repeating carriage clock, the enamel dial signed for Dent, the bell striking movement No.301 with a lever platform escapement, in gorge case, c1870, 5in (12cm). **$3,200-3,600**

A Louis XV boulle bracket clock, the dial and movement signed Bertrand à Paris, surmounted by a trumpeting angel, c1730, 35in (89cm). **$2,000-3,200**

A French enamel mounted repeating carriage clock, stamped E. M. & Co, later lever escapement, c1900. **$2,700-3,600**

A brass alarm carriage clock, by Henri Jacot. **$1,600-2,000**

A porcelain mounted repeating carriage clock, c1870 6in (15cm). **$3,500-4,500**

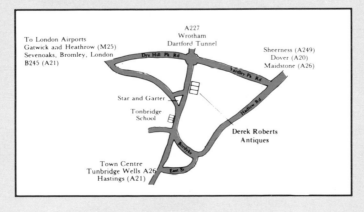

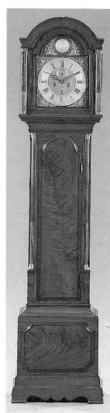

A mahogany longcase clock, by Blackwood, N. Shields, c1820. **$6,000-7,500**

A country oak longcase clock by Friend, Lyme Regis, 8-day movement striking on a bell, c1830. **$3,500-4,500**

A George III mahogany longcase clock. **$12,000-14,500**

A mahogany longcase clock, signed Samuel Guy, London, c1750. **$7,000-9,000**

A Charles II ebonised longcase clock, Henry Jones, c1685. **$50,000-54,000**

A mahogany longcase clock, c1830. **$14,500-16,500**

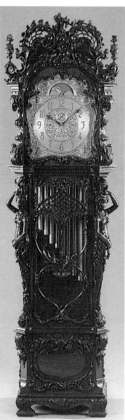

A burr elm longcase clock, the brass dial signed Jno Clowes, Russell St., Covent Garden, the 6-ringed pillar movement with bolt and shutter maintaining power, late 17thC. **$32,000-36,000**

A George II walnut longcase clock, John Ellicott, c1740. **$65,000-72,000**

An Edwardian mahogany chiming longcase clock, c1905. **$40,000-45,000**

A William & Mary marquetry longcase clock. **$9,000-10,000**

A burr walnut longcase clock, signed Chas. Blanchard, London,104in (264cm) **$1,800-2,000**

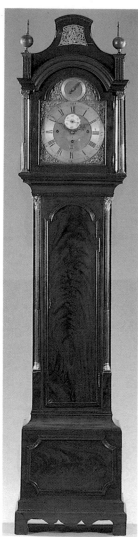

A George III longcase clock, Thos. Wilkinson, c1770. **$12,000-14,500**

A Charles II burr walnut longcase clock, 78in (198cm). **$54,000-63,000**

A mahogany longcase clock, by William Scott, London, c1770. **$15,000-17,000**

A William and Mary walnut marquetry longcase clock, J. Wise. **$21,000-24,000**

An oak and mahogany longcase clock, c1820. **$5,000-5,700**

A William and Mary walnut longcase clock, late 17thC. **$16,000-18,000**

A miniature oak and mahogany month-going longcase clock, signed J. Windmills, London, early 18thC, 66in (168cm). **$12,000-14,500**

A mahogany longcase clock, James Robertson, c1800. **$8,000-9,500**

An ormolu mantel
clock, for J. Carter,
c1840, **$1,800-2,700**

A French boulle mantel
clock, by Japy & Fils.
$650-1,000

A Louis Philippe ormolu
mantel clock, signed
Dd Fe Dubois à Paris,
17in (43cm).
$3,500-5,500

An Empire ormolu mantel
clock, by Lesieur, 18½in
(47cm) wide. **$8,000-9,500**

A Viennese mantel
clock, 19thC.
$10,000-14,500

An Empire ormolu and
mahogany mantel
timepiece, the fusee
movement signed
Burwisc, London on the
backplate, 23in (59cm).
$12,000-16,500

An Empire ormolu clock, 15in
(38cm). **$5,500-7,000**

A Louis XVIII ormolu and bronze
mantel clock, signed, 30in (76cm).
$14,500-18,000

An Austrian ormolu and
bronze troubadour mantel
clock of Gothic form, the
pinnacle with a bell above
a pointed arch, the quarter
striking movement with 2
gongs, mid 19thC, 19½in
(49cm). **$1,600-2,000**

A Louis XV1 mantel clock, 19in (48cm)
wide. **$21,000-25,000**

A George III ormolu, jasperware and biscuit
mounted mantel clock, by Benjamin Vulliamy,
c1799, 13½in (34cm). **$18,000-21,000**

A French 'singing bird'
mantel clock, c1880, 16in
(41cm). **$9,000-10,000**

An ormolu mantel clock,
c1870, 16½in (42cm).
$3,200-4,500

A Charles X ormolu clock, signed Le Roy, 17½in (44cm). **$4,500-6,000**

A French ormolu mantel clock with calendar, c1850, 17½in (44cm). **$4,500-6,000**

A 'Sèvres' mounted ormolu clock, signed, 21½in (54cm). **$9,500-11,000**

A Vienna regulator, c1810. **$54,000-72,000**

A Vienna regulator, c1835. **$9,500-11,000**

A striking clock, by Vulliamy, London, 19thC, 23½in (60cm). **$2,000-2,700**

A wall clock, by T. Amoore, mid-19thC. **$720-800**

A German brass mounted mahogany mantel clock, late 18thC. **$15,000-17,000**

A Vienna regulator, c1825. **$21,000-27,000**

A Vienna regulator, c1830. **$45,000-63,000**

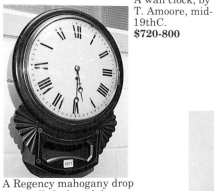

A Regency mahogany drop dial wall clock with brass inlay. **$800-950**

A Louis XVI ormolu mantel clock, signed Peignat A Paris. **$5,500-7,000**

A Louis XV ormolu and tôle mantel clock, signed Thibault A Paris, adapted, 8in (20cm). **$7,000-9,000**

A German brass mounted mahogany obelisk mantel clock, late 18thC, 29in (74cm). **$30,000-36,000**

A minute repeating chronograph, by JW Benson, with 18ct gold hunter case, glass missing. **$13,000-15,000**

An 18ct gold hunter cased keyless lever watch, E. F. Ashley, No.03747, 5cm. **$2,700-4,500**

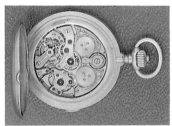

A Swiss 18ct gold hunter cased minute repeating grande and petite sonnerie watch, signed Invar. **$7,000-9,000**

A gold and enamel musical automaton verge watch, by Isaac Daniel Piguet, quarter repeating on 2 gongs, Numbered 98, 5.8cm. **$40,000-45,000**

A silver and tortoiseshell quarter repeating watch, for Turkish market, 1798. **$20,000-23,000**

A gold and enamel verge watch, by Gregson, c1790. **$5,500-7,000**

A gold and enamel hunter cased minute repeating keyless lever automaton watch, by LeCoultre, c1890. **$10,000-14,500**

A quarter repeating Jacqumart watch, signed Dubois & Comp. No.23114, in silver gilt plain case with push pendant, 5.8cm. **$6,000-7,500**

A gold pocket watch, by Vacheron & Constantin, numbered 319021, 4.5cm. **$1,800-3,000**

A gentleman's Patek Philippe keyless lever open face pocket watch, No.198950, in 18ct gold case, London 1936. **$2,000-2,700**

A silver keyless lever Karussell, signed F. A. Chandler. **$5,500-6,500**

A gold repoussé pair case verge pocket watch, by James Cowan, Edinburgh, hallmarked London 1772, 4.7cm, with chain and gold pencil. **$3,200-4,000**

A gilt metal striking watch, signed Timy Williamson, c1780. **$13,000-15,000**

A Cartier 18ct gold lady's wristwatch, No.780950832, c1977. **$2,000-2,700**

An 18ct gold moonphase calendar chronograph, by Baume & Mercier. **$5,500-6,500**

An 18ct gold five minute repeating keyless lever watch, c1890, stamped J. E. Caldwell & Co. **$4,500-6,500**

A steel cased Cosmonaut Navitimer chronograph, by Breitling, c1950. **$2,000-3,600**

A stainless steel reverso wristwatch, by Jaeger LeCoultre, with later engraved coat-of-arms, c1940. **$2,000-2,700**

An 18ct pink gold single button chronograph, signed Election, subsidiary dials for seconds and minutes, outer telemetric and tachometric scales. **$900-1,500**

An 18ct gold and diamond skeleton wristwatch, by Audemars Piguet, with 17 jewels and adjusted to 5 positions, the dial with diamond rope-twist surround, No.B41172, c1975. **$10,000-14,500**

An 18ct gold and steel centre seconds reverso wristwatch, by Jaeger LeCoultre, c1940. **$5,500-6,500**

A 9ct gold reverso wristwatch, signed LeCoultre Co, London import mark for 1936. **$2,700-3,600**

An 18ct gold wristwatch, by Audemars Piguet, c1950. **$2,000-2,700**

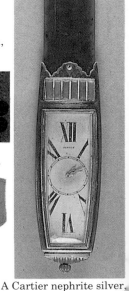

A Cartier nephrite silver, gold, coral and enamel watch set paperknife, blade repaired. **$15,000-17,000**

A Cartier platinum, gold and diamond lady's wristwatch, signed European Watch & Clock Co Inc., No.429765, c1930. **$7,000-9,000**

A Heuer gentleman's chronograph wristwatch, in 18ct gold case. **$1,800-2,700**

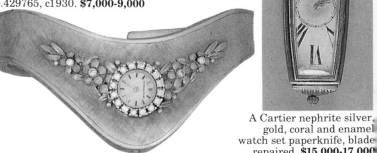

An 18ct gold wristwatch, by Audemars Piguet, London import mark for 1959. **$4,000-4,500**

A steel automatic water resistant calendar chronograph, by Girard Perregaux, 1989 and unworn. **$1,500-1,700**

An 18ct gold day/date Rolex Oyster Perpetual wristwatch, 1974. **$7,000-8,500**

A 9ct gold Rolex bubble back Oyster Perpetual wristwatch, c1940. **$2,000-2,700**

A stainless steel wristwatch, by Patek Philippe, c1934. **$3,000-3,600**

A Vacheron & Constantin 18ct pink gold wristwatch, c1945. **$2,000-2,700**

A Rolex 18ct two-colour gold wristwatch, import mark for 1927 **$3,600-4,500**

A Universal 18ct pink gold Tri-Compax chronograph wristwatch, c1940. **$4,500-5,500**

A steel and gold Rolex Datejust Oyster Perpetual wristwatch. **$1,600-2,000**

A 14ct gold chronograph, Tourneau watch Co, c1945. **$3,000-3,600**

A 9ct pink gold Rolex wristwatch, the circular movement with 15 jewels, 1953. **$1,800-2,700**

A Vacheron & Constantin 18ct gold automatic wristwatch, c1900. **$1,000-0,600**

A Rolex 9ct gold wristwatch. **$1,200-1,600**

A stainless steel and gold Rolex Oyster Perpetual wristwatch, c1940. **$2,000-2,700**

A lady's Rolex gold and stone set wristwatch, set with rubies and diamonds, numbered 23844 2697. **$1,500-1,800**

An 18ct gold automatic nautilus wristwatch, by Patek Philippe, with intergral bracelet, modern. **$10,000-14,500**

A silver Rolex Prince wristwatch, case worn, 1930. **$2,000-2,700**

A rosewood wheel barometer, with mother-of-pearl inlay, by Bramwell-Alston, c1860.
$1,500-2,000

A lacquered brass 2¼in reflecting telescope, signed J. Bird, London, the 10in body tube with screw rod focusing , 18thC, 17in (43cm).
$12,000-14,500

A Smith's 18in (45.5cm) diam celestial globe, by G Phillip & Son Ltd, on turned wood stand, 22in (56cm).
$3,000-4,500

A rare demonstration orbital globe, by W&S Jones, with painted wood dial, 24in (61cm).
$20,000-21,000

A Spanish gilt brass and silver universal equinoctial dial, signed Juanin Cocart fecit, early 17thC, 5.4cm long. **$75,000-80,000**

A 5in reflecting telescope, signed Naire & Blunt, London, replacement mirror, late 18thC, 42in (106.5cm) long.
$9,000-10,000

A 'Solnhofer' stone horizontal dial, signed Isaak Kiening fecit, late 16thC, 10in (26cm) wide.
$15,000-16,500

A celestial globe, the axis through the celestial poles and mounted on a painted wood stand, early 18thC, 16in (39cm) diam. **$16,500-18,000**

A brass transit telescope, signed Troughton & Simms, London, with 2 mahogany carrying cases, early 19thC, 20in (50.5cm).
$12,000-16,500

A New Universal double microscope, mid-18thC, 9in (23cm) wide.
$40,000-45,000

A gilt brass universal ring dial, possibly Flemish, late 17thC, 8in (20cm). **$12,000-14,500**

An Italian 1¹/₂in telescope body tube cum-case, of leather and pasteboard, decorated in gilt with gilt brass and amber cap and fish scale covered outer tube of mother-of-pearl. **$1,600-2,000**

A mahogany wheel barometer, by Borelli, Farnham, c1840, 8in (20cm) diam. **$1,000-1,500**

A pair of 12in (31.5cm) terrestrial and celestial globes, by W & A. K. Johnston Ltd, Edinburgh. **$6,000-7,000**

A rosewood wheel barometer, with tulip top, c1860. **$650-800**

A Newton's New & Improved Terrestrial pocket globe, dated 1817. **$3,200-4,500**

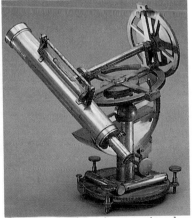

A 4¹/₄in reflecting telescope, signed on the back plate James Innes 1796, with mahogany carrying case, 26¹/₂in (67cm). **$650-800**

A simple orrery, the 2in terrestrial globe with maker's label inscribed S. Fortin Rue de la Harpe, 1773. **$6,000-8,000**

A Louis XVI style ormolu barometer and a matching thermometer, 15¹/₂in (39cm). **$4,500-5,500**

A pair of George II candlesticks, later three-light branches, William Gough, London 1750, branches 19thC, 118oz. **$6,000-7,500**

A pair of William and Mary cast tablesticks, maker's mark overstruck for Edward Gibson, 6in (15cm), 26oz. **$28,000-32,000**

A pair of five-light candelabras, c1840. **$32,000-36,000**

A pair of French silver gilt candlesticks, by P. Paraud, Paris, 1797, 8$^1/_2$in (21cm), 23oz. **$10,000-11,000**

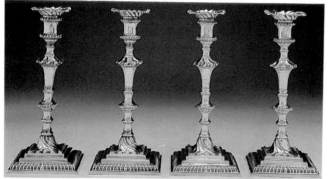

Four George III candlesticks, by William Cafe, London, marked on bases and nozzles, c1766, 10$^1/_2$in (26cm). **$15,000-18,000**

A George III silver gilt basket, by Thomas Arden, 1805, 13in (33cm), 54oz. **$12,000-14,500**

A set of 4 George II table candlesticks, by Edward Wakelin, 1747, 8$^1/_2$in (21.5cm), 79oz. **$21,000-27,000**

A centrepiece bowl, the sides decorated with elephants in relief, gilt interior etched with stylised foliage, by Tiffany & Co. New York, marked, c1885, 11in (28cm) diam, 52oz. **$18,000-21,000**

A pair of Charles II candlesticks, maker's mark TD in script monogram, London 1683, 6$^1/_2$in (16cm), 534gr. **$22,000-27,000**

A George II shaving bowl, by John Edwards II, London 1729, marked on base, 13in (33cm), 28oz. **$6,000-7,500**

A George II punch bowl, Gabriel Sleath, London 1727, 9$^1/_2$in (24cm) diam, 1415gr. **$32,000-36,000**

A pair of George III vegetable dishes and covers, by Paul Storr, London 1805, 11in (28cm) diam, 121oz. **$26,000-30,000**

A Victorian centrepiece and cover, by John S Hunt, 1861, 20in (51cm) high, 266oz. **$14,500-18,000**

A George III centrepiece, on triangular plinth with 3 bracket feet, the base on 3 horned and bearded mask feet, engraved with coat-of-arms, 1815, 18½in (47cm), 233oz. **$50,000-55,000**

A French parcel gilt centrepiece, signed H. Wadere, 1897, 34½in (87cm), 25,860 gr. gross. **$28,000-32,000**

A George III epergne, by Emick Romer, fully marked, London 1771, 21in (53cm), 97oz. **$20,000-23,000**

An early Victorian five-light candelabrum centrepiece and mirror plateau, engraved with a coat-of-arms and presentation inscription dated 1843, by Richard Sawyer, Dublin 1843, 25in (64cm), 254oz. **$10,000-14,000**

A pair of George IV entrée dishes and covers, by Paul Storr, London, marked, 12½in (32cm), 155oz. **$14,500-18,000**

Four George III meat dishes, engraved with a baron's armorials, marked by Robert and Thomas Makepeace, 1794, largest 23in (59cm) wide, 278oz. **$16,500-18,000**

A George III epergne, with removable cut glass dishes, by William Grundy, London 1767, fully marked, 21in (53cm) wide, 86oz. **$20,000-22,000**

A George III epergne, maker's mark IP Pellet between oval punch, London 1799, 15in (38cm). **$15,000-18,000**

A teapot, by William Ball, Baltimore, with script initials 'M.G.' marked twice on base, c1800, 11½in (29cm) high, 28oz gross. **$10,000-14,500**

A George I coffee pot, by Humphrey Payne, 1716, 9in (23cm) high, 19oz gross. **$20,000-23,000**

A George II coffee pot, by Paul de Lamerie, 1742, 8½in (21cm) high, 23oz gross. **$80,000-90,000**

A George I chamber pot, Isaac Liger, engraved with contemporary armorials, London 1714, 7in (17.5cm) diam, 861gr. **$36,000-40,000**

A Belgian coffee pot, by Jan Baptist Verberckt I, marked and 19thC control marks, 1781, 14in (35cm), 50oz. **$27,000-32,000**

Two George III honey pots, formed as bee skeps, by Paul Storr, c1797, one with clear glass liner, 4½in (11cm) high, 13oz each. **$27,000-36,000 each**

A Belgian chocolate pot, maker's mark and Rome town mark, Mons 1773, 13in (33cm), 1206gr. **$40,000-45,000**

A George III inkstand, with inscription, by John Parker and Edward Wakelin, 1771, 12in (30cm) long, 56oz. **$32,000-36,000**

A George I inkstand, by Lewis Mettayer, London 1716, with later bell, 12½in (32cm) long, 58oz. **$16,500-20,000**

A French silver gilt inkstand, by E. D. Tetard, Paris, marked on base, c1870. **$13,000-16,500**

A George III inkstand, by Paul Storr, London 1803, 15in (38cm) wide, 3351 gr. **$80,000-90,000**

A George III tankard, by Benjamin Smith, 1812, 6½in (16cm) high, 45oz. **$13,000-15,000**

A tankard, by Philip Syng, probably Jr, Philadelphia, c1730, later monograms, 7in (17.5cm), 31oz. **$32,000-36,000**

A German parcel gilt coin set tankard, by David Splitgerber, Kolberg, c1670, 20in (51cm) high, 233oz. **$210,000-215,000**

A William IV silver gilt presentation tankard, inscribed, 13in (33cm) high, 91oz. **$54,000-63,000**

A pair of Charles I silver gilt flagons, maker's mark RS, with mallet above and below, London 1638, 13in (33cm) high, 4381 gr. **$108,000-125,000**

A George II sugar box and matching tea caddy, by Elizabeth Godfrey, London 1749, with 6 teaspoons by Jessie McFarlan, c1754, 40oz. **$30,000-36,000**

A French silver gilt part dinner service, by Tetard Frères, late 19thC, meat dish 17½in (45cm) wide, 286oz. **$18,000-21,000**

A pair of George II tea caddies and a matching sugar box, by Paul de Lamerie, London, 1736, 34oz, with ebony case. **$38,000-40,000**

A composite George III/IV tea and coffee service, by Paul Storr and others, c1820, stand modern, stand 12in (30.5cm), 136oz. **$16,500-18,000**

A set of George III tea caddies, by Frederick Vonham, 1763, with 12 teaspoons, 18thC, and sugar tongs, 49oz. **$18,000-21,000**

A George III tray, by Robert Garrard, 1809, 30in (76cm) wide, 303oz. **$58,000-63,000**

A George III two-handled soup tureen and cover, by Thomas Robins, 1809, 15in (38cm) wide, 111oz. **$12,000-14,500**

A pair of Brazilian processional lanterns, struck with marks for Oporto, maker's mark A'S, late 18thC, 76in (193cm) high, 300oz weighable silver. **$55,000-63,000**

A Mexican hanging lamp, with spurious marks for Miguel Maria Martel, Mexico City, c1800, with 8 later branches, 63in (160cm) high. **$12,000-13,500**

A George II cheese stand, by Edward Wakelin, London 1754, 14in (35.5cm) wide, 69.5oz. **$145,000-180,000**

An Austrian dressing table set, c1850, 72.75oz silver. **$9,000-10,000**

A pair of George III tea caddies, by Hester Bateman, marked, London 1779, 4½in (11cm) wide, 24.5oz. **$10,000-14,500**

A Victorian model of The Master of a hunt and his mount, by Hunt & Roskell, 1869, 12in (30.5cm) high, 2873gr, on wooden plinth. **$9,000-10,000**

A pair of George III sauce tureens and covers from the Hamilton service, by Paul Storr, London 1806, 10in (25.5cm) wide, 85oz. **$40,000-45,000**

A pair of Regency soup tureens and covers, by Kirkby, Waterhouse & Hodgson, Sheffield, 1810, 15in (38cm), 168oz. **$30,000-36,000**

A pair of George III wine coolers, by Paul Storr, London 1800, 7½in (18.5cm) high, 96oz. **$33,000-36,000**

A pair of Louis XIV ormolu mounted boulle plinths, one stamped E. Levasseur and JME, 9in (23cm) high, **$30,000-36,000**

A pair of George III ormolu candlesticks, possibly Italian, 13in (33cm) high. **$15,000-17,000**

An 18ct gold presentation casket, by Goldsmiths and Silversmiths Company, 1927. **$18,000-21,000**

A Roman ormolu vase, by Benedetto Boschetti, on marble pedestal, mid-19thC, 26in (66cm) high. **$54,000-63,000**

A George III ormolu figure of Minerva, on marble plinth and blue john plinth, 13in (33cm). **$6,000-7,500**

An Empire ormolu vase, cast with Cupid and Psyche, with reeded female mask handles, 21¼in (54cm) high. **$14,500-18,000**

A Charles X ormolu centrepiece, 20in (51cm) high. **$21,000-25,000**

Five ormolu plaques, emblematic of Astronomy and Music, 11in (28cm). **$4,500-6,000**

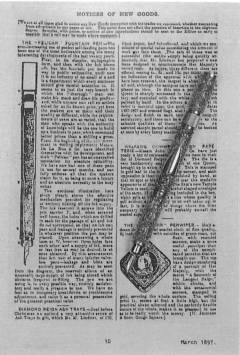

An ornate 9ct gold Pelican self-feeding pen, with iridium 14ct gold overfed nib, De la Rue, hallmarked 1897. **$9,000-10,000**

347

COLOUR REVIEW

A gilt bronze bust, 'Salammbo', by L. Moreau, 29½in (74.5cm). **$8,000-9,500**

A pair of Regency bronze, ormolu and marble lions, by Thomas Hope. **$5,500-6,500**

A Venetian bronze centrepiece, some damage, c1674, 6½in (16cm). **$9,500-11,500**

A Franco-Flemish bronze group of Venus and Cupid, late 16thC, 16½in (42cm) high. **$55,000-65,000**

A pair of patinated bronze and ormolu models of deer, possibly Italian, 19thC, 13in (33cm). **$32,000-36,000**

A Florentine bronze group of Diana, mid-17thC, 16in (40cm) high. **$400,000-420,000**

A French silvered bronze figure of Pandora with her open box, silvering rubbed, 19thC. **$7,000-9,000**

An Italian bronze figure of a kneeling satyr, late 16thC, 7in (17cm) high. **$12,000-14,500**

A bronze group, 'Valkyrie', by Stephan Sinding, 22in (56cm). **$5,500-6,500**

A French bronze figure of 'L' Effroi', by Gustave Doré, late 19thC, 23in (59cm). **$9,500-10,500**

An Italian bronze portrait head of Beethoven, by Alfredo Pina, early 20thC. **$13,000-15,000**

A Louis XV gilt bronze and lacquer inkstand, mid-18thC, 13in (33cm) wide. **$10,000-12,000**

348

A pair of Italian marble busts of a Roman official and his wife, on rouge marble socles and scagliola columns, late 17thC, 25in (64cm) high. **$36,000-40,000**

A marble statue of Cleopatra, early 17thC. **$58,000-63,000**

A pair of Italian marble figures, early 19thC, 53in (135cm). **$48,000-54,000**

An English white marble group of a mother and child, by Edward Gustavus Physick, c1827, 22in (56cm) high. **$22,000-28,000**

A French marble sculpture of Peace, by Albert Carrier-Belleuse, 19thC, 23½in (60.5cm) high. **$16,500-21,000**

An Italian marble figure of a young street musician, signed J. Bottiglioni. **$21,000-25,000**

A German ivory relief of The Dream of Constantine, attributed to Antonio Leoni, 18thC, 4in (10cm) high. **$18,000-21,000**

An Eastern French Gothic ivory group, early 14thC, 8in (21cm) high. **$22,000-27,000**

An Italian white marble bust of Caesar Augustus, some damage and repair, 30in (76cm) high. **$18,000-21,000**

An Irish marble bust of Pope Clement XIV, by Christopher Heweston, c1772, 25in (63cm) high. **$27,000-30,000**

349

A carved and polychrome painted wood panel, with the Royal arms of King William III, 19thC, 28in (71cm) high. **$8,000-9,500**

A French terracotta bust of Rouget de L'Isle, c1835, on wooden socle, 17½in (45.5cm). **$16,500-18,000**

A pair of Empire carved giltwood columns, early 19thC, **$12,000-14,500**

A Florentine glazed terracotta statue, attributed to Benedetto Buglioni, damage and repairs, c1510. **$80,000-95,000**

An Hispano-Flemish polychrome and giltwood reliquary bust, early 16thC, 22in (56cm) high. **$32,000-36,000**

An Italian variegated white marble urn, distressed, early 19thC, 16in (40.5cm). **$5,500-7,000**

An Italian marble figure of a Greek slave girl, by Scipione Tadolini, some damage, late 19thC, 97in (246cm). **$160,000-180,000**

A Tinos marble urn, with gadrooned body and fluted foot, with a beaten copper liner, early 19thC, 11in (28cm) high. **$7,000-9,000**

An Italian white mottled marble mortar, with circular lobed rim, 18thC, 21in (53.5cm) diam. **$3,200-4,000**

A Swabian painted wood group of St.Christopher, some damage, c1500, 31in (79cm). **$22,000-27,000**

A giltwood figure of a poodle, with brown glass eyes, 19thC, 30½in (77cm), on modern wooden base. **$28,000-32,000**

A gold mounted enamel box, with mythological scenes, emblematic of Love, possibly German, c1770, 3½in (8.5cm) wide. **$3,600-5,500**

A Swiss gold and enamel snuff box, Neuchâtel, c1840, 3½in (9cm) wide. **$3,600-4,500**

A Meissen gold mounted snuff box, with gilt interior, c1755, 9cm wide. **$160,000-180,000**

A Doccia snuff box, painted by J. K. Anreiter, c1750, silver gilt mounts London 1855. **$7,000-9,000**

A gold snuff box set with a Roman micro-mosaic, by S. Chaligny, Geneva, c1820. **$38,000-40,000**

A George II gold snuff box, with portrait of Mary, Countess of Bute, by Christian Friedrich Zincke, c1750, 7cm wide. **$72,000-75,000**

A Meissen gold mounted snuff box, with gilt interior, enamels rubbed, gilder's numeral 18, c1740, 9cm wide. **$190,000-215,000**

A Swiss vari-coloured gold, enamel and diamond set presentation snuff box, c1830, 3½in (9cm). **$10,000-12,000**

A Swiss gold and enamel bonbonnière, probably Geneva, c1800, 3in (8cm) wide. **$7,000-9,000**

A German gold mounted hardstone portrait snuff box, set with diamonds, unmarked, c1780, 7.5cm wide. **$10,000-12,000**

A gold, enamel and gem set presentation snuff box, mid-19thC, with later French import marks, 3½in (8.5cm) wide. **$7,000-9,000**

A Meissen gold mounted snuff box, c1770, in contemporary leather box with gilt tooling, 8.5cm wide. **$24,000-28,000**

A Swiss gold presentation snuff box, probably Neuchâtel, maker's mark CCS in a lozenge, c1840. **$9,000-10,000**

A Victorian Diamond Jubilee heavily embossed casket, with leather covered case, **$210-270**

A pair of cutlery urns, with enclosed fitted interior, 29in (74cm) high. **$6,000-7,500**

A George III scrolled paper tea caddy, c1790, 8¹/₂in (21cm) wide. **$2,000-2,700**

An Upper Rhine wooden Minnekästchen, lock replaced, stamped AC, 15thC, 9in (23cm) wide. **$9,500-11,000**

A Zurich wooden box, 15thC, 11¹/₂in (29cm) wide. **$8,000-9,500**

An Upper Rhine Minnekästchen, late 14thC. **$27,000-30,000**

A French oak casket, with bronze mounts, c1850, 8in (20cm) wide. **$900-1,000**

A pair of japanned cutlery urns, 23in (59cm) high **$18,000-21,000**

A French gilt casket, with silver plated plaques, c1860, 6¹/₂in (16cm) wide. **$1,400-1,500**

An Upper Rhine Minnekästchen, heavily carved, early 15thC, 9¹/₂in (24cm) wide. **$7,500-10,000**

A Killarney ware writing slope, c1840, 10in (25.5cm) wide. **$1,000-1,200**

A papier mâché, mother-of-pearl and gilt decorated box, 19thC, 11in (28cm) wide. **$270-360**

An Italian boulle casket, with steel and semi-precious stones inlaid to lid, late 17thC, 14in (35cm) wide. **$4,500-5,500**

A collection of 10 stone garden gnomes, some playing bowls, the others as attendants, 25in (64cm) high.
$3,300-4,000

A bronze figure of Venus Disrobing, standing on a circular base, signed Ferd. Lepke Fec, also inscribed Aktien-gessellschaft: Gladenpeck, Berlin-Friedrichshagen, early 20thC, 72in (183cm) high.
$25,000-36,000

Ferdinand Lepke was born in Coburg on March 23rd, 1866, he died in Berlin on March 13th, 1909. He studied at the Berlin Academy and worked in the studio of the Begas Brothers.

A white marble figure of Modesty, the draped female figure holding flowers, standing on a circular base and inscribed Modestia, 62in (157cm) high.
$6,500-8,000

An Italian white marble figure of a pensive classical lady, standing on a square base, 19thC, 49in (125cm) high.
$1,600-2,500

A Continental carved wood and polychrome saint, 18thC, 45in (114cm) high.
$1,200-1,600

A pair of lead fountain masks, depicting 'Winter' and 'Spring', of Baroque influence, spouts issuing from their mouths, raised on cloud motifs, 21in (53cm) high.
$4,500-6,500

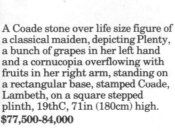

A Coade stone over life size figure of a classical maiden, depicting Plenty, a bunch of grapes in her left hand and a cornucopia overflowing with fruits in her right arm, standing on a rectangular base, stamped Coade, Lambeth, on a square stepped plinth, 19thC, 71in (180cm) high.
$77,500-84,000

A white marble fountain, carved as a young fisher boy with fish slung over his back, water spouting from its mouth, 19thC, 48½in (123cm) high.
$7,000-9,000

A pair of stone groups of putti, depicting Day and Night, one group with an owl, the other with a boar, on square bases, restored, 18thC, 29in (74cm) high.
$3,600-4,500

A bronze figure fountain, depicting a bearded man in mediaeval costume with peaked cap, holding a goose under each arm, incorporating spouts in their beaks, signed Ch. Lenz, Nuremberg, 19thC, 27in (69cm) high.
$1,200-1,800

An Italian white marble figure of Ariadne dressing her hair, leaning against a tree stump, on oval shaped base, some breaks, 19thC, 69in (175cm) high.
$12,000-14,500

A pair of white painted cast iron garden urns, of campana form, the beaded rims with gadrooned lower halves, with looped and mask handles, on circular fluted socles and square bases, 19thC, 31½in (80cm) high.
$2,700-3,600

A Neapolitan bronze figure of the Dancing Faun of Pompeii, 19thC, 31in (79cm) high.
$1,800-2,700

A pair of white painted cast iron garden urns, raised on stepped square plinths, the sides cast with wreaths, 19thC, 45in (114cm).
$2,700-3,600

A pair of lead urns, cast with roseheads with looped crestings, on circular socles and square bases applied with scroll mounts, one damaged, 19thC, 15in (38cm) high.
$4,000-4,600

A Coalbrookdale cast iron fountain, formed as 2 putti entwined, supporting a cornucopia, standing on naturalistic rocky base, 35½in (91cm) high.
$1,400-1,700

A set of 3 white painted cast iron urns, each semi-lobed body moulded with floral scrolls, and with mask hoop handles, on rising circular feet mounted on square tapered pedestals, 19thC.
$1,600-2,000

A pair of white painted cast iron garden urns, on fluted socles, some damage, 25in (64cm) high.
$450-720

A decorative pair of floral moulded lead planters.
$550-650

An Italian white marble wall fountain, the back inset with pink variegated marble panels, the mouths incorporating spouts, above rectangular basin with pedimented top, 18thC, 43in (109cm).
$12,000-16,500

A Victorian white painted cast iron garden urn, with looped carrying handles, the lower half capped with acanthus leaf scrolls, on fluted socle and square base, 46½in (118cm) high.
$3,500-4,500

A terracotta jardinière, the bowl with acanthus leaf scroll decoration, on twist turn support, with 3 figures of swans, on circular rocky naturalistic base, 35½in (91cm) high.
$3,000-3,600

A set of 4 white painted cast iron garden urns, 35in (89cm) high.
$1,800-2,700

A Doulton terracotta urn, on square plinth, stamped Doulton Lambeth, 40in (102cm) high.
$900-1,200

A white marble part urn, the bowl with fluted mask and loop handles, carved with anthemion and stiff leaf decoration, raised on square stepped base, the rim with stiff leaf decoration above a frieze centred by a harp flanked by floral wreaths, 18thC, the base 22in (56cm), the part urn 11in (28cm) high.
$4,000-5,000

A pair of white painted cast iron urns, of campana form, with mask and loop handles, fluted socles and square bases, 29½in (75cm) high.
$1,600-2,700

A lead urn, with flambeau finial, the sides applied with lion masks and cartouches with cherubs, on square base with cut corners, mid-19thC, 68½in (174cm) high.
$20,000-27,000

A cast iron urn, the ovoid fluted body with stiff leaf cast lower halves, with S-scrolled handles, beaded borders and circular base, 30½in (78cm) high.
$1,200-1,800

A pair of black painted cast iron urns, each raised on a square plinth, the sides cast with floral panels, on foliate decorated square stepped bases, stamped No. 1, Corneau Alfred, A. Charleville, French, 41½in (105cm) high.
$2,000-3,000

A pair of stoneware terracotta urns, of campana form, the wide plain rims above gadrooned lower half bodies, with scrolled handles, circular socles with foliate rims, mid-19thC, 18½in (47cm) diam.
$2,700-3,600

A set of 3 black painted cast iron urns, of Adam design, on circular spreading socles, 2 with gadrooned and foliate capped lids, 37in (94cm) high.
$2,700-4,600

A pair of lead troughs, in the 18thC style, the sides applied with lion masks within geometrical borders, 18½in (47cm) diam.
$1,200-1,600

A pair of Italian Verona marble tazzas, on central baluster and knopped support with square bases, 29in (74cm) diam.
$10,000-12,000

A set of 3 Regency cast iron urns, of campana form, with ring and mask handles, and another similar, with gadrooned lower half and the frieze depicting a classical scene, 23½in (60cm) high.
$3,000-4,500

A Doulton stoneware terracotta urn, the circular bowl cast with anthemion motifs, the frieze with trailing grapevine and gadrooned lower half, the foliate capped socle on square base, 22½in (57cm).
$1,200-1,500

A pair of cast iron urns, of campana form, with egg and dart rims, bodies cast with foliate arabesques and gadrooned lower halves, with mask and loop handles, on fluted socles and square bases, 30in (76cm) high.
$2,000-3,000

A white painted cast iron Medici urn, with classical frieze, mask and loop handles, on fluted circular socle and square base, raised on a square stepped plinth, 27in (69cm) high.
$900-1,200

A set of 4 grey painted cast iron garden urns, the beaded borders with waisted bodies, decorated with foliate arabesques, the gadrooned lower halves with loop and mask handles, above fluted socles and square bases, 24in (61cm) high.
$2,700-3,600

A pair of lead jardinières, the sides cast with lion masks, 10½in (27cm) high.
$650-900

A collection of 12 Georgian wrought iron railing panels, each panel centred by flower motif with friezes above and below, 27 by 35in (69 by 89cm).
$1,800-2,800

Four cast iron baskets, 18 to 26in (46 to 66cm) long.
$235-300 each

An urn shaped two-tier bronze fountain, the bulbous gadrooned dish with foliate capped border with central gadrooned urn, on fluted socle and square base, with central and rim spouts, 26in (66cm) high.
$3,500-5,500

A pair of white painted cast iron urns, 21in (53cm) high.
$1,400-2,000

A section of iron railing, comprising a number of panels centred by cartouches and framed by repoussé foliate scrolls, and a number of sections of frieze and alternating half columns with Corinthian capitals, early 20thC, each panel 73 by 47½in (185 by 121cm) approx.
$10,000-12,000

These panels were made by Mr Starkie Gardner in 1904.

A Coade stone urn, with lion mask ring handles, rosette frieze and stiff leaf decoration, on rectangular base stamped Coade, Lambeth.
$16,000-18,000

A wrought iron conservatory stand, 47 by 37in (119 by 94cm).
$180-270

A white marble trough, the front and sides carved with cherubs riding chariots, raised on winged sphinx supports, cracked, 45½in (115cm) wide.
$16,500-21,000

A pair of iron gates, each panel centred by scrolling iron work applied with repoussé foliate rosettes, with lower half as dog rail, surmounted by foliate motifs, 68 by 32½in (173 by 83cm).
$720-1,000

An Italian rosso antico Grand Tour souvenir modelled as a trough, on solid trestles with fluted sides, on claw feet and rectangular plinth base, base possibly associated, early 19thC, 7½in (19cm).
$7,000-8,000

A pair of cast and wrought iron gates, the scrolling iron work top with centred breakarched panel decorated with floral scrolling motif, 19thC, each panel 89½ by 42½in (227 by 108cm).
$2,700-3,600

Did you know
MILLER'S Antiques Price Guide builds up year by year to form the most comprehensive photo-reference system available

Miscellaneous

A pair of carved oak doors, each panel with a moulded surround and carved decorative scrolled crestings centred by a foliate motif within a circle and foliate surround, French, each panel 76 by 27½in (193 by 70cm).
$1,600-2,000

An Adam D-shaped fanlight, in pine frame, the sectioned sunburst effect with leaded scrolling work, applied with anthemion motifs, 78 by 40½in (198 by 103cm).
$2,500-3,600

A pair of stained glass pub screens, with green, red and white frosted glass.
$1,500-1,800

A cut sheet copper rooster weathervane, late 19th/early 20thC, 31½in (80cm) high.
$1,400-1,600

A pair of double oak doors with bevelled glazed spidersweb oval panels, 90 by 63in (229 by 160cm).
$2,000-2,700

An unusual cut cast iron locomotive weathervane, 19thC, 70in (178cm) long.
$4,000-4,500

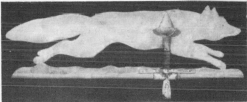

A zinc weather vane, formed as a figure of a running fox, 37 by 28½in (94 by 73cm).
$650-800

A door with glass panels painted with birds, 86½ by 28in (220 by 71cm). $540-720

A Coalbrookdale painted cast iron stick stand, with seated whippet between the 2 hoops and loose scallop bases, stamped C.B. Dale Co. No. 20 and Victoria Register Mark.
$6,500-7,000

A moulded copper sloop weathervane, late 19thC, 32in (81cm) high. $3,300-3,800

An unusual wrought iron 'bone-shaker' weathervane, 19thC, 21in (53cm) long.
$2,800-3,200

A painted sheet iron hunter and stag weathervane, c1930, 26½in (67cm) long.
$5,000-5,500

A terracotta plinth, the square top formed as a capital with acanthus leaf scrolls, on square base with cut corners and serpentine sides, indistinctly stamped on base, 41in (104cm) high.
$1,000-1,500

A lead cistern, the front panel cast with geometrical borders with griffin motifs, centred by the initials C.R.A. and dated 1740, 47½ by 36in (121 by 92cm).
$3,500-4,500

An unusual gilded sheet zinc rooster weathervane, late 19th/early 20thC, 25in (64cm) long.
$2,800-3,200

A pair of white painted cast iron radiator covers, the front and sides inset with pierced panels cast with foliate flowerheads, birds of paradise and foliate scrolls, each surmounted with a rouge marble top, 58½ by 38in (148 by 97cm).
$2,700-3,600

A pair of Gothic design terracotta chimney pots, the bases stamped Smith and Co., Old Kent Road, London, 43in (109cm).
$1,400-1,500

An early Victorian cast iron staircase balustrading, formed as panels pierced and cast with Gothic motifs, alternating with panels interlaced with initials and panels centred by a shield bearing the date of 1834, with newel post with castellated tops.
$1,500-1,800

A Victorian black painted cast iron umbrella stand, the backplate modelled with foliate and C-scrolls, the drip tray in the form of a shell, on shaped feet, 30in (76cm) high.
$550-720

A pair of brown glazed terracotta chimney pots, the 'crown' tops above octagonal shafts and square spreading bases, with another unglazed, 37½in (95cm) high.
$200-350

An unusual pair of cast iron gate weights, 19thC, 6in (15cm) high.
$1,400-1,800

A pair of pocket postal scales.
$200-250

A pair of white painted wirework plant stands, of D-shaped form, with 3 graduated tiers, with scrolled panels below and scrolled feet, 49½in (126cm) high.
$1,000-1,200

A carved stone royal coat-of-arms, flanked by lion and unicorn, supporting shields with George V monogram, the lion 60½in (154cm), the unicorn 58in (147cm), the crest 66½in (169cm) high.
$15,500-19,000

The crest formed part of the Old Royal Hotel in Lowestoft, Suffolk, which was demolished in 1974.

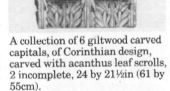

A collection of 6 giltwood carved capitals, of Corinthian design, carved with acanthus leaf scrolls, 2 incomplete, 24 by 21½in (61 by 55cm).
$1,400-1,800

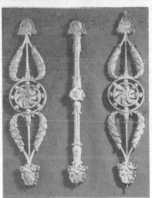

A quantity of cast iron balustrading, the cast and pierced balustrades centred by a rosette with foliate scroll motifs with anthemion cresting, early 19thC, 29½in (75cm) high.
$720-900

A cast iron boot scraper, on scroll uprights centred by lion mask motif, on rectangular base with egg and dart rim, 15½in (39cm), and another 14in (36cm).
$280-400

A gilt metal bed coronet with swag and rosebud decorations, French, c1880, 19 by 6in (48 by 15cm).
$450-650

An Edwardian cast iron spiral staircase, made by St Pancras Ironworks Company, London, with 14 treads 24in (61cm) wide, with handrail and balustrade, c1907, 114in (290cm) high.
$1,200-1,700

CLOCKS
Bracket Clocks

A Victorian brass inlaid rosewood chiming bracket clock, the 7in (18cm) dial signed Benson London, the massive 3-train fusee and chain movement with anchor escapement and chiming on 8 bells and a gong, the front inlaid with brass leaves and stringing, c1885, 29in (74cm). **$4,000-5,000**

A George III mahogany striking bracket clock, with carrying handle, the dial signed Wm Creake Royal Exchange London, with strike/silent ring to the arch, the 5-pillar twin fusee movement with verge escapement, pendulum holdfast to backplate, similarly signed, the case reconstructed, 14in (36cm). **$4,800-5,500**

A walnut bracket clock, the 6in (15cm) silvered dial signed Dent, 61 Strand and 4 Royal Exchange, the twin fusee movement gong striking, with stamped backplate. **$2,700-3,600**

A mahogany bracket clock, the 7in (18cm) brass dial with silvered chapter ring, strike/silent ring and signed at centre Fra. Dorrell, London, date aperture, the fusee movement with replaced verge escapement, pull repeat and leafy scroll engraved backplate, 16½in (42cm). **$3,500-4,500**

A Regency mahogany and brass inlaid bracket clock, on brass ball feet, the white painted dial, chipped, with Roman numerals, inscribed Duncan, London, the twin chain fusee movement striking on a bell, bell missing, 20in (51cm). **$1,500-1,800**

A Regency brass inlaid mahogany bracket clock, with 8in (20cm) convex painted dial signed Brugger London, the 5-pillar bell striking fusee movement with unusual pin wheel escapement, on ball feet, c1820, 18in (45cm). **$2,700-3,600**

An ebonised bracket clock, with a 6in (15cm) brass dial signed Chr. Gould, London, with silvered chapter ring, matte screwed putto spandrels, the movement with 7 latched pillars, verge escapement, foliate engraved backplate and scroll pierced cock, on bun feet, 11½in (30cm). **$12,000-14,500**

A mahogany striking bracket clock, with 8in (20cm) convex painted dial signed William Grace, Cheapside, London, 2-train fusee movement with anchor escapement, 15in (38cm). **$2,000-2,700**

A George III ebony veneered striking bracket clock, the 7in (18cm) brass dial with silvered chapter ring, mock pendulum aperture and date in the matted centre, signed on a plaque between the dials and on backplate Thomas Carrington, London, the movement now with striking train removed and replaced with one at the hour strike, verge escapement, the case with pineapple finials and carrying handle, 19in (48cm). **$2,700-3,600**

A George IV mahogany bracket clock, with an 8in (20cm) painted dial indistinctly signed Frodsham Gracechurch St London, the repeating 5-pillar twin fusee movement with anchor escapement and rack and bell striking, c1830, 17in (43cm). **$1,500-2,000**

A rare George III ebonised musical bracket clock, the enamelled and brass dial with chime/not chime and gavot/hornpipe/air/gavot/song/cotillion, the 8-day 3-train fusee movement with a 3in (8cm) cylinder and 13 bells, 2 repeat pulls, by Charles Howse, London, 19in (48cm).
$11,000-12,000

Charles Howse produced clocks at 5 Great Tower Street, between 1768 and 1794, and was Master of the Clockmakers Company 1787.

A Victorian chiming bracket clock, in 17thC style, the 7in (18cm) dial signed Thurlow Ryde, with subsidiary dials, the 3-train fusee and chain movement with anchor escapement and chiming on 8 bells and a gong, in a William III style ebonised case with gilt brass basket top, carrying handle and further embellished with gilt brass mounts, side frets and paw feet, c1865, 16½in (42cm).
$4,800-6,000

An ebonised bracket clock, with a 6in (15cm) brass dial signed at the centre Robt. Henderson, London, date aperture, strike/silent in the arch, the movement with verge escapement, bell striking with pull repeat, the backplate signed, 16in (41cm).
$6,500-7,000

CLOCKS
Factors influencing prices of clocks

★ **Size.** Small size is a premium factor with most clocks, especially longcase and bracket clocks. Conversely large size is a negative factor except perhaps with special or complicated clocks, where complexity of mechanics may dictate more functional space.

★ **Woods.** The woods used may have a considerable bearing on value with longcase or bracket clocks. Wood is only one of many value factors but if it could be seen in isolation then the order of values based on woods alone would be: ebonised (black stained); oak; pine; mahogany; walnut (with or without marquetry) – all in ascending order. Pine should strictly rate on the lowest level but the scarcity of pine clocks of serious age in good condition tends to lift this level. The woods used will naturally depend to some extent on the period. For example most walnut clocks would date before 1750 and so age is a considerable influencing factor on walnut values.

★ **Auction estimates.** Values given by auctioneers as estimates of anticipated price levels may prove very different from actual bid prices. Prices paid may be much higher than estimates, and often have an added premium of 10% plus VAT on the premium. However high the estimate, some items will fail to sell at all, often for reasons which are not obvious from the illustration alone.

★ **Originality.** Clocks have been subject to more change and alteration than many other antiques, and these changes are seldom apparent from an illustration. A clock not in its original case or with a non-original movement will bring a much lower price than a similar clock in original state. The same applies to a clock with important mechanical functions missing, or even one with such functions replaced later.

★ **Condition.** If a clock is complete it is not particularly important whether its mechanics are in clean condition, as long as the vital components are still present. On the other hand a clock in the lower value ranges may cost more to restore than its total value. Case condition is very important, and a clock in good state with its original patina and colour is much more valuable than a similar one which has had casework restoration, re-polishing, etc. These things can seldom be recognised by a novice.

A George II ebonised striking bracket clock, the dial signed Tho. Martin London, with silvered chapter ring, the matted centre with false pendulum and calendar apertures, pierced blued steel hands, female mask and foliate spandrels, the 5-ringed pillar twin gut fusee movement now with anchor escapement, the pull quarter repeat train removed, 17½in (44cm).
$2,800-3,600

A walnut bracket clock with an 8in (20cm) brass dial, silvered chapter ring and matted centre, signed on a plate Wm. Smith, London, the movement with replaced verge escapement, pull repeat and with an engraved backplate, the associated case with caddy top, brass handle and on bracket feet, 20in (51cm). **$2,700-3,600**

A mahogany bracket clock, with double fusee movement, silvered chapter ring, glass side panels, date aperture, strikes on bell, by Wm Morgan, London, c1760, 17in (43cm). **$3,600-4,000**

A George III ebonised bracket clock, the 8in (20cm) silvered dial signed Wm. Ray Sudbury with central calendar and strike/silent dial in the arch, the similarly signed 5-pillar bell striking repeating fusee movement with deadbeat escapement, c1800, 17½in (44cm). **$2,700-3,600**

A mahogany and brass inlaid bracket clock, the 7in (18cm) enamelled dial signed Marriott, London, the associated twin fusee movement quarter striking on 2 bells, 14½in (37cm). **$1,800-2,700**

A mahogany bracket clock, with an 8in (20cm) silvered dial signed Joseph Johnson, Liverpool, pierced gilt hands, the twin fusee movement with pull repeat and engraved backplate, the broken arch case with brass fish scale frets, brass mouldings and ball feet, 17in (43cm). **$3,300-4,000**

A mahogany striking bracket clock, the 8in (20cm) white painted dial with subsidiary date, strike/silent in the arch, anchor escapement, the backplate signed Green, Liverpool, 20½in (52cm). **$1,800-2,800**

A Regency mahogany bracket clock, with a 4in (10cm) enamel dial and brass hands, the 5-pillar fusee movement signed Perigal & Duterrau London, with shouldered stepped plates bordered by engraving, the front plate stamped Thwaites and numbered 4835, c1812, 11½in (29cm). **$1,600-2,000**

A George III ebonised bracket clock, the twin fusee and chain bell striking movement with anchor escapement, 11½in (29cm). **$2,700-3,600**

A French bracket clock veneered with arabesque green boulle supplied by Lee & Son, Belfast, mid-19thC, 12in (31cm). **$900-1,000**

A Victorian carved oak chiming bracket clock, with brass dial, silvered chapter ring and 3 subsidiary dials for chime/silent, regulation and chime select, the triple chain fusee movement chiming on 8 bells, 4 gongs and striking on one gong, 22½in (58cm). **$2,000-2,800**

An Austrian ebonised bracket clock, with 7in (18cm) dial signed Johan Schreibmayr, Wienn and 2 selection dials, dummy pendulum aperture and date, the triple train movement with grande sonnerie striking on 2 bells, the case with caddy top, c1770. **$2,700-3,600**

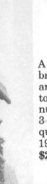

A South German automaton quarter striking bracket clock, with nun appearing at the quarters and monk appearing at the hours pulling ropes to the bells in the belfry, painted dial with Roman numerals and gilt decoration to the centre, the 3-train skeletonised movement striking the quarters on 2 bells, with pendulum and key, late 19thC, 30in (76cm). **$2,700-3,600**

A French boulle bracket clock, the Vincenti movement bell striking and with a 7in (18cm) cartouche dial, in a waisted case with putto mounts and scroll feet and a putto surmount, late 19thC, 24in (61cm), with a bracket en suite. **$2,700-3,600**

A late Victorian mahogany chiming bracket clock, with an 8in (20cm) brass dial, the triple fusee movement chiming on 8 bells and striking on a gong. **$2,800-3,600**

A George III mahogany striking bracket clock, the dial signed Willm. Fleetwood London, on a silvered arc to the arch with subsidiary strike/not strike ring below, silvered chapter ring, the matted centre with false pendulum and calendar apertures, pierced blued hands, foliate scroll spandrels, the 4-pillar twin gut fusee movement with verge escapement, the backplate with profuse inhabited floral engraving, securing brackets to case, 19in (48cm). **$9,000-10,000**

A George III mahogany striking bracket clock, the dial signed John Green London, with false pendulum and calendar apertures, pierced blued hands, foliate scroll spandrels, subsidiary strike/silent ring to the arch, the 5-pillar twin gut fusee movement with anchor escapement, restored and possibly associated, 23in (59cm). **$2,800-3,600**

Carriage Clocks

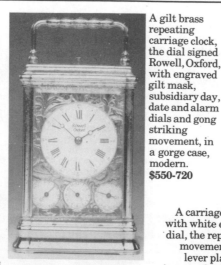

A gilt brass repeating carriage clock, the dial signed Rowell, Oxford, with engraved gilt mask, subsidiary day, date and alarm dials and gong striking movement, in a gorge case, modern.
$550-720

A carriage clock, with white enamel dial, the repeating movement with lever platform, in a moulded gorge case, 6in (15cm).
$1,400-1,500

A carriage clock with white enamel dial, the repeating movement stamped E.G.L. within an ellipse, lever platform, in Corinthian column case with fluted bands, 6in (15cm).
$1,000-1,200

A gilt brass repeating carriage clock, with 3in (8cm) white enamelled dial, gong striking movement and push button repeat, the case with spiral fluted columns and ripple moulded upper and lower friezes, 6½in (16cm).
$1,200-1,500

A brass carriage clock, with repeater movement, 8in (20cm).
$1,000-1,200

A rare Westminster chiming and repeating carriage clock, the enamel dial with a silent/chime dial below, the 3-train movement with lever escapement and chiming on 4 bells and a gong, with a travelling case, c1880, 7in (17cm). **$5,500-7,000**

A rare silver grande sonnerie carriage clock, the dial signed Dent, 1893, 4½in (11cm).
$7,000-8,000

An English gilt brass and bronze carriage clock, with silvered dial with moon hands, the movement with lever escapement visible through a panel in the top, slow/fast lever in the top, the base with spring clip and recess for the numbered key, both numbered 1069, with velvet lined glazed rosewood travelling case, c1840, 5½in (14cm).
$1,400-2,000

A miniature gilt brass carriage clock, the gilt dial with silvered scroll engraved mask, with cast scroll handle, in a leather travelling case with a key, 3½in (9cm).
$1,800-2,700

A carriage clock with cream enamel annular chapter ring against a pierced foliate mask, the movement with lever escapement, 5½in (14cm). **$900-1,000**

A gilt brass and enamel carriage clock, with a 2in (5cm) white enamelled dial, with gong striking movement, 6in (15cm). **$2,000-2,700**

A gorge cased carriage clock, Jacot No. 14694, with white enamel dial, the repeating movement bearing the parrot stamp of Henri Jacot, lever platform. **$1,400-2,000**

A brass repeating carriage clock, with painted pale blue dial with leafy scroll pierced mask and side panels, bevelled glasses, 5½in (14cm), in a leather case. **$1,600-2,000**

A French grande sonnerie calendar carriage clock, the enamel dial with subsidiary chapters for date and alarm, the movement No. 2414 striking on 2 bells and with a later lever escapement, in a gorge case with lever in the base for Gde. Sonnerie/Silence/Pte. Sonnerie, c1865, 6in (15cm). **$2,000-3,600**

A French decorative carriage clock, c1900, 5in (13cm). **$550-750**

A French brass grande sonnerie and alarm carriage clock, the dials with white chapter on a black and pink enamel ground, the movement, platform lever escapement striking on 2 gongs mounted on the backplate, late 19thC, 7½in (19cm). **$1,800-2,500**

A petite sonnerie alarm carriage clock, with cream enamel dial and subsidiary alarm dial beneath, the movement numbered 7851, quarter striking and repeating on 2 gongs, lever escapement, the sonnerie/silence lever in the base, 6in (15cm), with travelling case. **$1,400-1,600**

Garnitures

An ormolu and porcelain clock garniture, with later bell striking movement, No. 2853-92, contained in a 'bleu-royale' vase case with satyr mask handles, 20½in (52cm), together with a pair of conforming 5-branch candelabra, 23in (59cm). **$1,000-1,500**

A French white marble and gilt metal clock garniture, the clock striking on single bell, with white enamel dial, 15in (38cm), and a pair of 2-branch matching candelabra. **$2,000-3,000**

A French gilt and porcelain clock garniture, with a 4in (10cm) white enamelled dial and bell striking movement, 12½in (32cm), and a pair of matching 4-light candelabra, with plinths. **$2,000-3,000**

A French gilt mounted green marble garniture, the bell striking movement by Gustav Becker, the case applied with gilt caryatids, swags and trophies, 19in (49cm), and a pair of matching vases, 15in (38cm). **$2,700-3,500**

A black marble Egyptian style garniture clock set, comprising 8-day mantel clock striking with gong, designed as an Egyptian tomb with brass sphinx finial and 2 matching side winged sphinx, the dial marked Victor Emanuel & Co., Gantia De Chile, c1880, 18in (46cm), and a pair of matching stelae, 22in (56cm). **$2,000-2,800**

A French garniture, late 19thC. **$2,800-3,600**

A black marble clock garniture, the 5in (13cm) dial with exposed Brocot escapement and bell striking, 20½in (52cm) and a pair of matching tazzas, 12in (31cm). **$2,000-2,800**

A French green onyx and champlevé enamel clock garniture, with a 4in (10cm) enamelled dial and gong striking movement, the 4-glass case applied with enamelled mouldings and mercury pendulum, 13in (33cm), and a pair of matching vases, 10½in (26cm). **$1,200-1,600**

Longcase Clocks

An 8-day oak longcase clock, the 12in (31cm) brass dial signed around the arch John Bagnall, Dudley, subsidiary seconds and calendar sector in the scroll engraved centre, 4-pillar movement in a case with canted corners, break arch hood with pagoda pediment and giltwood finials, 94in (238cm). **$4,500-6,500**

An oak longcase clock, the 12in (31cm) arched brass dial signed Samuel Bryan, London, with 8-day bell striking movement, the associated case applied with a garland and spiral columns and with plain trunk and plinth, 82½in (209cm). **$2,000-3,500**

An oak longcase clock, with brass dial with pierced spandrels, silvered chapter ring, inscribed Thos. Carswell Hastings, 30-hour birdcage movement, with hour hand only, mid -18thC, 78in (198cm) **$900-1,000**

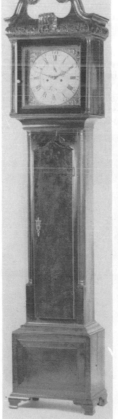

An Irish mahogany longcase clock, the 13in (33cm) brass dial signed Barny Delahoyde, Dublin, with date aperture and seconds dial, putto spandrels, 8-day bell striking movement, hood with lion mask carved mantling and swan neck pediment, 92½in (235cm). **$2,700-3,600**

An 8-day, brass dial longcase clock, with moonwork and tidal dial for high water, by John Baker of Hull, in original oak case crossbanded in mahogany and with shell motif inlays, fully restored, c1770, 92in (234cm). **$5,500-7,000**

An oak longcase clock, the 12in (31cm) brass dial signed on a disc John Barnet, London, with seconds dial and date aperture, 8-day bell striking movement, 89½in (227cm). **$1,800-2,800**

A Queen Anne painted and decorated walnut longcase clock, by Daniel Balch, Newbury, Massachusetts, some restoration, c1760, 93½in (237cm). **$5,500-6,500**

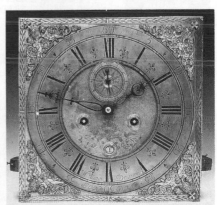

An oak and crossbanded longcase clock, the 12in (31cm) brass dial with engraved and signed chapter ring, Wlm. Davison, London, and with date ring and seconds dial, the 8-day bell striking movement with inside countwheel and cut out backplate, the associated oak case with crossbanded trunk door and plinth, 79½in (201cm). **$1,800-2,700**

An oak crossbanded longcase clock, the colourful dial with moon phase to the arch, signed Garrat Peterborough, mid-19thC, 81in (205cm). **$5,800-6,500**

A George III black japanned 8-day longcase clock, the 12in (31cm) brass dial signed Daniel Field, Hitchin, with date aperture and subsidiary seconds, the arch with strike/silent, foliate scroll spandrels, 5-pillar movement, the case decorated with gilt chinoiserie designs against a black ground, giltwood finials, 95in (241cm) **$4,500-5,500**

An 8-day longcase clock, with brass dial, with rocking Father Time, by Robert Henderson of Scarborough, in original dark blue lacquered case, fully restored, c1740, 94in (238cm). **$6,500-7,000**

A North Country carved oak 8-day longcase clock, with engraved brass dial with silvered chapter ring, date indicator and second hand, cherub head spandrels, moon indicator, trunk with door with key, clock No. 586, maker Kitchen & Lloyd Nantwich, Cheshire, late 18thC, 81in (206cm). **$3,000-4,500**

The carving on this clock is probably later.

A stencilled mahogany and églomisé banjo clock, by Aaron Willard, Jr., Boston, Massachusetts, c1825, 33in (84cm). **$5,500-6,500**

A Chippendale carved cherrywood longcase clock, by New London Co., some restoration, the movement possibly not original, 88½in (225cm). **$10,000-15,000**

A Federal inlaid mahogany dwarf longcase clock, by Joshua Wilder, Hingham, Massachusetts, 41½in (105cm). **$26,000-32,000**

A mahogany longcase clock, the 12in (31cm) dial signed McMaster, Dublin, with 8-day bell striking movement, 81in (206cm). **$2,600-3,600**

A mahogany longcase clock from the Liverpool region, the flame veneers with inlays and stringing, the trunk with reeded columns, the base with canted angles and an applied shaped panel, the dial with 4 seasons spandrels and a Rocking Father Time to the arch, the chapter ring with the maker's name, Lassel Paris. **$10,000-11,000**

371

An 8-day walnut longcase clock, the door with burr walnut veneer, the brass dial with raised silvered chapter ring, the moulded centre with raised silvered seconds ring and date aperture, gilt Indian head spandrels, signed in the arch on silvered plaque David Pain, London, No. 104, with strike/silent aperture below, mechanism lacking, the 5-ringed pillar movement striking on a bell, some restorations, 91in (231cm).
$7,000-8,000

A mahogany and brass inlaid longcase clock, with 12in (31cm) arched brass dial, silvered chapter ring and signed on a disc Thos. Milner, London, with date aperture and subsidiary seconds dial, 8-day bell striking movement, the hood with broken arch pediment, altered, the plinth inlaid with brass stringing, 92in (234cm).
$3,000-4,500

A mahogany longcase clock with crossbanding and boxwood stringing, the trunk with reeded columns, the hood with scroll pediment and blind frets, the painted dial with floral decorations, signed D. Norrie, Leith, c1795, 84in (213cm).
$7,000-8,000

An oak longcase clock, the 12in (31cm) brass dial signed Humphrey Mason, Gosport, with date aperture, seconds dial and applied spandrels symbolising the 4 seasons, with 8-day bell striking movement, the pagoda topped hood with brass ball and spire finials, 85in (216cm).
$2,000-3,000

A George III Lancashire mahogany longcase clock, by William Lawson, Newton-le-Willows, with brass dial with rolling moon, subsidiary seconds and date pointer, 8-day rack striking movement with anchor escapement, c1780.
$6,500-8,000

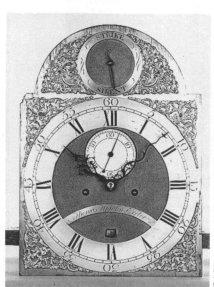

An 8-day oak longcase clock by Thomas Upjohn, Exeter, the movement with 12in (31cm) brass dial, strike/silent in the arch, recessed subsidiary seconds and date aperture, signed on a reserve to the dial centre, 5-pillar rack striking movement with anchor escapement, now contained in an early 19thC inlaid and crossbanded figured mahogany case with swan necked pediment, above free standing spirally fluted columns, 18thC, 81½in (206cm).
$2,600-3,600

An oak longcase clock, the 12in (31cm) brass dial signed Pattison, Halifax, with 30-hour bell striking movement, outside countwheel, hood with swan neck pediment, fluted columns, shaped trunk door and deep plinth, 86in (219cm).
$1,200-1,500

A walnut longcase clock, the 12in (31cm) brass dial with silvered chapter ring, subsidiary seconds dial, date aperture, urn and scroll spandrels and with matted and engraved centre, signed in the arch Will. Upjohn, Exon. with 8-day bell striking movement, 86½in (220cm). **$7,500-9,000**

An 8-day white dial longcase clock, by Alexander Sim of Aberdeen, in original mahogany case, fully restored, c1800, 87in (221cm). **$4,500-5,500**

An 8-day oak longcase clock, with 10in (25cm) brass dial with subsidiary seconds and date aperture, the arch signed James Smith, London, 4-pillar movement with anchor escapement, in a case with panelled plinth, the break arch hood with brass ball finials, 85in (216cm). **$2,600-3,600**

An unusual oak longcase clock, by John Seddon (Frodsham), the case profusely carved overall, with brass dial with pointer and penny moon in the arch, silvered chapter, signed, subsidiary seconds and date aperture, with spandrels and incised engraving to the dial centre, the 8-day movement with 4 finned pillars, 3-train movement quarter striking on a carillon of 8 bells, with anchor escapement, 100in (254cm). **$6,500-7,000**

An oak and mahogany longcase clock, the 13in (33cm) arched painted dial signed William Winder, Wreckington, with 8-day bell striking movement, broken arch hood, chamfered trunk and plain plinth, 81½in (206cm). **$1,800-2,800**

A mahogany longcase clock, the 12in (31cm) brass dial with silvered chapter ring and disc now signed Thomas Wagstaffe, with associated 8-day gong striking movement, 106in (269cm). **$5,500-7,000**

A George III oak and mahogany longcase clock, the cream enamelled dial with black Roman numerals and Arabic minutes, enclosing a subsidiary seconds dial, calendar aperture and maker's name Walker, Liverpool, the 8-day movement striking on a single bell, the case crossbanded in mahogany, together with 2 weights, a pendulum and a winding key, 90in (229cm). **$2,400-3,200**

An oak and crossbanded longcase clock, with 14in (36cm) painted dial, date aperture and seconds dial, the false plate stamped Walker, 82in (208cm).
$1,200-1,600

A George III 8-day mahogany longcase clock, the 12in (31cm) brass dial signed William Withers, London, subsidiary seconds and date aperture, the arch containing strike/silent, foliate spandrels, the 5-pillar movement in a case with brass inlaid corinthian pilasters to the trunk, 95in (241cm).
$4,500-6,500

A George III longcase clock with silvered chapter ring and Roman numerals, seconds dial, date aperture and gilt spandrels, a circular plaque to the arch engraved Jn. Walker, Newcastle, with 8-day striking movement, 89in (226cm).
$3,000-4,000

A Federal inlaid cherrywood longcase clock, New England, probably Connecticut, c1810, 91in (231cm).
$5,500-6,500

A late Stuart burr walnut longcase clock, the hood with giltwood capped columns, the dial signed Windmills London on the silvered chapter ring, with subsidiary seconds, ringed winding holes and calendar aperture, mask and foliate spandrels, the 5-ringed pillar rack striking movement with anchor escapement, associated, 84in (214cm).
$10,000-12,000

An oak and mahogany crossbanded longcase clock, the brass dial with raised silvered chapter ring and Indian head spandrels, Roman numerals and Arabic 5 minute divisions, the engraved centre with pie crust silvered seconds dial, silvered plaque in the arch inscribed Tempus Fugit, the 8-day movement striking on a gong, some restorations, finial missing, 87in (221cm).
$3,000-4,000

A pine longcase clock, c1840, 82in (208cm).
$2,000-3,000

An Edwardian inlaid mahogany longcase clock.
$2,000-3,000

A cut down oak cased crossbanded longcase clock, with silvered and brass chapter dial, Roman numerals, date and second hand, foliate spandrels, circular boss, marked William Yeadon, Stourbridge, with key, c1780, 78in (198cm).
$1,200-1,500

Mantel Clocks

A William IV rosewood mantel clock, with 5in (13cm) painted dial signed Huggins London, the fusee and chain movement with anchor escapement, c1835, 13in (33cm). $1,600-2,000

A mahogany and brass inlaid quarter repeating mantel clock, with an 8in (20cm) cream painted dial, with regulation dial and serpentine hands, the triple train fusee movement chiming on 8 bells and now on a gong, signed on the backplate W.L.M. Partington, Paddington Street, London, now on a rosewood base and brass claw-and-ball feet, 27½in (70cm). $3,000-3,600

A French ormolu and porcelain mantel clock, 2-train movement signed Martin & Co., with white enamel dial, 13½in (34cm). $800-1,000

An English burr walnut 4-glass clock, glazed to 4 sides and the top, white enamel dial signed F. Dent, 61 Strand, 1466, the single chain fusee movement with anchor escapement and pendulum cock, the pendulum with fine regulation, signed and numbered on the backplate, 10in (25cm). $5,500-6,500

A late Victorian ebonised quarter chiming mantel clock, with 3 subsidiary dials for chime/silent, slow/fast and Westminster/8 bells, the 3 train fusee movement chiming on 8 bells or 4 gongs, 27in (69cm). $3,000-4,500

A gilt brass Gothic mantel clock, with a 3½in (9cm) white enamelled dial signed E. White, 20 Cockspur Street, London, the substantial twin fusee movement gong striking and with a signed backplate, the case with onion dome and leafy scroll pierced frets and baluster finials, 17½in (44cm). $3,000-3,600

A 4-glass mantel clock with barometer and thermometer, the sunken 3½in (9cm) silvered dial with a gilt bezel set within an engine turned silvered mask, 2 dials mounted below for the thermometer and aneroid barometer, the MS gong striking movement with anchor escapement, c1880, 15in (38cm). $1,800-2,800

A William IV burr walnut mantel clock, with silvered brass dial signed Vulliamy, London, single fusee 4-pillar movement with anchor escapement and pendulum with adjustable brass bob, 10½in (26cm). $7,000-8,500

A gilt bronze and marble calendar mantel clock, with enamel dials, the bell striking silk suspension movement with a lever leading from the strike train to the calendar mechanism below indicating the date and the day of the week, the black marble case surmounted by an urn and profusely decorated with gilt and formerly patinated bronze mounts, c1840, 19½in (49cm).
$1,600-2,000

A satinwood and inlaid mantel clock, with a 7in (18cm) cartouche dial and bell striking movement, the waisted case with ebonised and mahogany stringing.
$900-1,000

A French ormolu and silvered mantel clock, the 2-train movement stamped Cleret, No. 4058, with silk suspension and floral bezel, 20in (51cm).   **$1,800-2,800**

A French porcelain mounted ormolu mantel clock, the 3½in (9cm) porcelain dial signed Bourdin à Paris, the similarly signed bell striking movement with Brocot escapement and outside countwheel, the sides and front inset with porcelain panels, c1850, 12in (31cm).
$4,000-4,800

A French ormolu mantel clock, the white enamelled dial signed Cachard successor to Ch. Le Roy and signed at the base Dubuisson, the movement with outside countwheel and bell striking, c1800, 22in (56cm).
$8,500-10,000

An unusual French bronze patinated brass mantel clock, with cast gilt brass dial with blue on white enamel Roman numeral panels, the bell striking 8-day movement inscribed P. Ltre, pendulum missing, 19thC, 23in (59cm).
$700-1,000

A French Empire mantel clock, in mahogany case, on gilt bun feet, the white enamel dial signed Devillaine, rue rive. des Pts. Champs No. 35, the large drum shaped movement with outside countwheel strike on a bell, 12in (31cm).
$1,600-2,000

A French porcelain and ormolu mantel clock, the 2-train movement stamped Deniere à Paris, lacking feet, 14in (36cm).
$2,000-2,800

A French ormolu and marble mantel clock, with a white enamel dial signed S. Devaulx, Palais Royal, the case with bands of green marble, with ormolu appliques, mask feet, 23in (59cm). **$2,800-3,600**

A French 4 glass mantel clock, the bell striking movement No. 2483 with enamel dial, visible Brocot escapement and Ellicott pendulum, c1875, 10in (25cm).   **$1,200-1,400**

A French ormolu and white mantel clock, with white marble dial, raised numerals, 8-day movement with outside countwheel strike on a bell, signed Rollin à Paris, 19thC, 14½in (37cm).   **$1,000-1,200**

A French gilt mounted marble mantel clock, the 4in (10cm) white enamelled dial signed Guydamour à Paris, with bell striking movement, c1800, 16in (40cm). **$2,000-3,000**

An unusual French Empire ormolu and simulated malachite mantel clock, the 2-train movement with silk suspension, 12in (31cm).   **$1,200-1,500**

A French faience mounted gilt brass mantel clock, with gong striking Achille Brocot movement and faience dial decorated against a cream ground, the gilt case flanked by faience columns, c1880, 15½in (39cm).   **$1,400-1,500**

A French gilt spelter and porcelain mounted mantel clock, on cast gilt feet, with porcelain dial, 8-day movement striking on a bell, bearing the maker's stamp Japy et ils, with pendulum, and giltwood base, 19thC, 14½in (37cm). **1,600-2,000**

A French 4 glass mantel clock, the 3½in (9cm) enamel dial signed Tiffany & Co., the Japy Frères gong striking movement with Brocot escapement and miniature set pendulum bob, the case with glazed cushion form cresting and a moulded base, c1900, 10½in (27cm). **$2,000-3,000**

A French brass mantel clock, the pendulum bob in the shape of a stewing pot with detachable cresset fender, on rouge marble base with bracket feet, with ivorine dial, the 8-day movement with outside countwheel strike on a gong, 17in (43cm). **$1,400-1,500**

An ormolu and bronze mantel clock, the countwheel striking movement now with Brocot suspended pendulum, 13in (33cm) wide. **$1,500-1,800**

A French ormolu and bronze automaton mantel clock, with a bell striking silk suspension movement and silvered engine turned dial with bronze plinth case, the automaton galleon driven by a separate key wound movement, c1840, 17in (43cm). **$2,600-3,600**

A sculptural bronze mantel clock, on Siena marble pedestal, the gilt dial with black on white enamel Roman numeral panels, 19thC, 21in (53cm). **$700-1,000**

A French brass mounted onyx mantel clock, with bell striking movement, 12½in (32cm). **$1,000-1,200**

A Danish coromandel and tortoiseshell veneered mantel clock, with plated and engraved dial, inscribed H.E. Holst, Kløbenhavn, and a Danish bell striking movement, 14in (36cm). **$3,000-4,500**

A champlevé enamel mounted 4 glass mantel clock, the 3½in (9cm) enamel dial painted with garlands of flowers and signed for Tiffany & Co., the Japy Frères gong striking movement with a mercury pendulum, c1900, 11in (28cm). **$1,500-2,000**

A French rouge and black marble perpetual calendar mantel clock, the 6in (15cm) white enamelled dial with exposed Brocot escapement, centre second hand, subsidiary calendar and barometer dials and with glazed pendulum aperture, the case mounted with Fahrenheit and Reamur thermometers, with mercury pendulum, 18in (46cm). **$3,500-4,500**

A French vari-coloured marble and gilt mantel clock, surmounted by a marble urn finial, the base with beading, on gilt turned feet, the white enamel dial with quarter hour divisions, with timepiece movement, 8in (20cm). **$650-1,000**

A bronze and ormolu French Empire mantel clock, 2-train movement with suspension, white enamel dial, in an arched case with ormolu trophies and cherub appliques, urn and butterfly finial, 12in (31cm), on ebonised base with bowfronted glazed dome, cracked. **$1,600-2,000**

A French boulle mantel clock, with a 5½in (14cm) cartouche dial and bell striking movement. **$1,200-1,400**

A French gilt mantel clock, with a 3½in (9cm) enamelled chapter ring, the drum movement with silk suspension and outside countwheel, the case in the form of a stylised chariot on a fanciful cloud base, 14½in (38cm). **$1,000-4,800**

A Dutch mahogany and marquetry mantel clock, with enamel dial, the movement stamped Dales Westbourne, the case inlaid with floral cornucopia with turned columns and plinth base, lacking cresting. **$1,600-2,600**

A French gilt brass and bronze mounted marble mantel clock, the bell striking movement with garland painted dial, the case flanked by a reclining putto, on white marble base, 10½in (26cm). **$1,000-1,200**

A Continental parcel gilt wood mantel clock, with enamel dial, asymmetrical winding holes, bell striking silk suspension movement with outside countwheel, bronze patinated wood figure of a near naked dancing woman to the side, c1770, 15in (38cm). **$1,500-1,800**

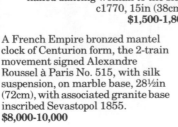

A French Empire bronzed mantel clock of Centurion form, the 2-train movement signed Alexandre Roussel à Paris No. 515, with silk suspension, on marble base, 28½in (72cm), with associated granite base inscribed Sevastopol 1855. **$8,000-10,000**

A French gilt brass and porcelain mantel clock, the 2-train movement with white enamel annular chapter ring, decorated in gilt against a dark blue ground, 16in (41cm). **$2,700-3,700**

Skeleton Clocks

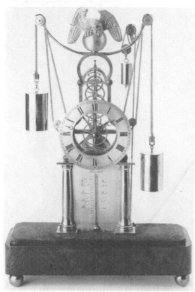

A French Empire weight driven skeleton clock, stamped on the rafter frame Augte. Moirau et Rolland Degrege, No. 33, the bullet shaped weight driving the maintaining power, the suspension chains of square section running over a series of pulleys, the movement supported on 2 brass columns inset with a silvered thermometer, on a walnut veneered base, 23in (59cm).
$5,500-7,000

A brass Cathedral skeleton clock, the pierced silvered chapter ring with black Roman numerals, the double fusee movement striking on a single bell and gong, surmounted on a grey veined white marble plinth under a glass dome, 19thC, 25in (64cm), together with an oak wall bracket.
$2,600-3,600

A Victorian skeleton clock, by Frodsham & Keen, with verge fusee and chain movement beneath a glass dome.
$3,500-4,500

Wall Clocks

A large wall clock in Act of Parliament style, single-train movement with anchor escapement, the moulded shield dial signed Robt. Peake, Dereham, brass spade hands with counter balance, the trunk decorated with florally painted panel against a green ground, 55in (139cm).   **$1,200-1,600**

A George III black lacquer wall clock, the convex glazed 11in (28cm) engraved silvered dial signed Jas Higgs Wallingford, with pierced blued hands, the 4-pillar single gut fusee movement with tapered plates, knife-edge verge escapement and bob pendulum, 16in (41cm).
$3,000-3,600

A Dutch oak alarm staartklok, the movement with turned baluster pillars with countwheel strike on 2 bells, 48in (122cm).   **$1,500-1,800**

An American late Federal mahogany wall clock of banjo type, the dial inscribed Panton on the reverse, the brass movement with 4 front-pinned pillars, anchor escapement, narrow diameter of barrel for the line the weight falling behind a tinplate divider from the pendulum with cranked rod clearing the cannon pinion, in a drum case with spreading shaft and plinth base, mid-19thC.
$1,800-2,800

Watches

A gentleman's 18ct gold key-wind open faced pocket watch, the gilt fusee movement with a lever escapement, mask engraved balance cock, the backplate signed Jas. Barclay, London, 2966, with a slow/fast regulator, with blued steel hands, and a key, mid-19thC.
$450-550

A silver pair case verge pocket watch, in plain outer case, with white enamel chapter ring, outer gilt rim with the motif 'keep me clean, use me well and I to you the truth will tell', the frosted gilt fusee movement signed Richd. Kevitt, London, 6cm.
$800-900

A gilt oignon verge pocket watch, in engraved case, with single steel hand, the frosted gilt fusee movement with silver chased, engraved and pierced bridge cock and pierced Egyptian pillars, signed on the backplate C.D.R. Angers, hinge to the movement broken, with gilt chatelaine, late 17thC, 5.6cm.
$2,700-3,300

An 18ct gold and enamel cylinder watch, with gilded bar movement, the back decorated with dark blue translucent enamel over a guilloche ground, centred with rose diamond set leaves and flowers, 3cm.
$700-800

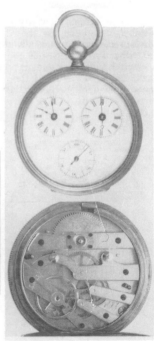

An English verge watch in silver pair cases, with silver regulator disc, plain steel balance, the outer with an engraved monogram and the date 1783, signed John Chapman Sheerness 213, hallmarked London 1781, 5cm.
$800-1,200

A gentleman's 18ct gold keyless wind full hunter cased minute repeating pocket watch, London, 1929, with an unsigned gilt jewelled Swiss lever movement, the cuvette presentation inscribed, with blued steel hands, the side with push-in minute repeat button, the case front monogram engraved, with a box.
$2,700-3,700

A Swiss cylinder Captain's watch, in a silvered open face case, with keywind gilt bar movement with suspended going barrel, plain 3-arm gold balance with blue steel spiral hairspring and gilt case interior, late 19thC, 5cm.
$650-800

An English verge in decorative silver pair cases, with engraved masked cock, silver regulator disc, fusee and chain with worm and wheel barrel setup between the plates, plain steel balance, later blue steel beetle, silver inner case with silver pendant and bow in a contemporary decorative silver outer case, signed Thos Reynolds London 435, hallmarked London 1742.
$1,000-1,200

A gold, enamel and diamond mounted fob watch, with gilded keyless lever bar movement jewelled to the centre, gilt dial, the back decorated with blue translucent enamel over a guilloche ground, and old cut diamonds set in a filigree band, with silver ribbon fob, 2.7cm.
$1,000-1,400

A silver and enamel Cartier purse watch, the translucent pale blue enamel on guilloche background, chipped, with brushed silvered dial, 4.6 x 3.1cm.
$1,600-2,000

A keyless open face Mickey Mouse novelty watch by Ingersoll, in plain white metal case, with unusual outer 13-24-hour ring, subsidiary seconds with 3 Mickeys, the time indicated by Mickey's hands, the signed engine turned back with monometallic balance and lever escapement, 4.9cm.
$800-1,000

Wristwatches

An early stainless steel wristwatch by Rolex, in tonneau case, the discoloured, engine turned silvered dial with subsidiary seconds, the case with hinged back and maker's mark numbered 578 02243, the signed movement jewelled to the third, 3.7 x 2.5cm.
$1,000-1,500

A gold steel Cartier automatic calendar wristwatch, the case with protected winder, signed to the reverse by the maker, with integral gold steel flexible bracelet and deployant clasp, 3cm.
$1,000-1,400

A stainless steel wristwatch, by International Watch Company, for military use, the black dial with luminous quarter hour marks, sweep centre seconds, the case with screwed back and ordinance number, 3.5cm.
$800-900

A stainless steel Rolex Oyster Perpetual chronometer bubble back wristwatch, the case with screw-down winder and screwed back numbered 2940, the signed movement numbered N18243, 3cm.
$1,200-1,600

A gentleman's 9ct gold cased automatic wristwatch by Jaeger le Coultre, London, 1955, with a gilt metal expanding bracelet.
$700-1,000

An 18ct gold calendar wristwatch by Record, the nickel movement jewelled to the centre, the dial with subsidiary seconds, apertures for day, month and moon, concentric date hand, with an associated 9ct gold flexible bracelet, 3.6cm.
$800-1,000

A duo plan Extra Prima movement wristwatch by Rolex, jewelled to the third and timed to 6 positions, the silvered dial, discoloured, with subsidiary seconds, square, signed Rolex Prince, now in gilt case, 3.2 x 1.7cm.
$2,600-3,600

A gentleman's stainless steel wristwatch by Vacheron & Constantin, Genève, in waterproof case, the discoloured silvered dial with luminous dots to the 5 minute divisions and luminous hands, subsidiary seconds ring, the case with screwed back, 2.8cm.
$1,600-2,000

A gold backwind wristwatch, the duo-plan nickel lever movement signed European Watch & Clock Co., 16 jewels, damascened dust cover, the white dial signed Cartier, the case mounted with crown at the back, the leather strap with gold Cartier deployant buckle, 3.1 x 2cm.
$7,000-9,000

An 18ct gold cased wristwatch.
$550-750

An 18ct gold wristwatch by Piaget, the 18 jewel movement with bark finish dial, the case with integral 18ct gold bracelet of herringbone design, 2.4cm.
$1,800-2,500

An 18ct gold lady's wristwatch, the nickel movement signed Cartier, the moulded ribbed case with sapphire set winding crown, with leather strap and tooled Cartier box, 3.1 x 2.4cm.
$4,000-4,800

A lady's diamond set wristwatch with diamond scroll and ring link articulated shoulders to a cordette bracelet, the movement signed Syntax, 17 jewels, 4 adjustments.
$1,000-1,200

A lady's platinum and diamond wristwatch, with a moiré strap.
$700-900

A lady's platinum, diamond and calibre emerald wristwatch, the dial signed Cito, with milanese bracelet.
$700-800

Chronometers

A 2-day marine chronometer, the
spotted movement with Earnshaw
spring detent escapement,
compensation balance, palladium
helical spring, free sprung,
numbered at the edge 13458,
silvered dial signed Kelvin White &
Hutton, 11 Billiter St. London, and
numbered 6038, in brass box
numbered 13458, in later brass
bound mahogany carrying case with
flush handles and named and
numbered roundel, 5in (13cm).
$1,600-2,000

An early 2-day marine chronometer,
signed on the movement John
Arnold London, Invt. et Fecit
No. 16, with Arnold's spring detent
escapement, early form of 2-armed
compensation balance with
bi-metallic rims with peripheral
adjustment and compensation, gold
helical spring with terminal curves
and adjustable stud with pointer
fitted to the clock, original dial,
cracked and chipped, steel hands, in
contemporary mahogany box with
brass bezel, c1791.
$48,500-54,000

A 2-day marine chronometer, the
silvered dial signed Ja. Edwards,
near the West India Docks, No. 282,
c1820.
$4,200-5,200

*This chronometer was sold with a
framed letter from E. J. Dent to Mr
Hawley dated July 11 1832, in
which it is stated that this is the
chronometer which proved to the
House of Commons Committee Mr
Arnold's priority of introduction of
the spring detent escapement.*

Stick Barometers

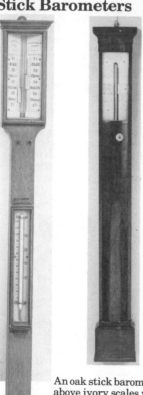

A mahogany
'upside down' stick
barometer, by
Naime & Blunt,
London, with

by the maker

enclosed mercury
tube with ball
reservoir at the top
and boxed cistern,
some restorations,
37½in (95cm).
$1,400-1,500

A rosewood barometer, the silvered
scales signed Adie & Son,
Edinburgh, the case with moulded
pediment, bowed front and plain
cistern, 41½in (106cm).
$3,500-4,500

Make the Most of Miller's

*CONDITION is absolutely
vital when assessing the
value of an antique.
Damaged pieces on the
whole appreciate much
less than perfect
examples. However a rare,
desirable piece may
command a high price
even when damaged*

An oak stick barometer with flat top
above ivory scales with vernier,
knobs lacking, signed J.H. Steward,
457 West Strand, London, cased
thermometer with turned cistern
cover, 36½in (93cm).
$800-1,000

A mahogany stick barometer,
signed on the silvered register
plates Berrenger, London, in a case
with crossbanding to the trunk, 38in
(96cm).
$1,600-2,000

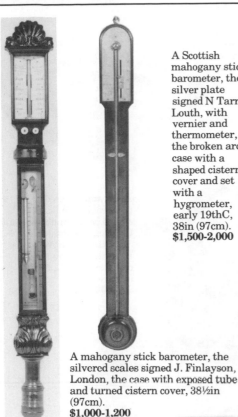

A Scottish mahogany stick barometer, the silver plate signed N Tarra Louth, with vernier and thermometer, the broken arch case with a shaped cistern cover and set with a hygrometer, early 19thC, 38in (97cm).
$1,500-2,000

A mahogany stick barometer, the silvered scales signed J. Finlayson, London, the case with exposed tube and turned cistern cover, 38½in (97cm).
$1,000-1,200

A mahogany stick barometer, the plates signed Polti-Exon, the case with hemispherical cistern cover, 39in (99cm).
$900-1,000

A rosewood marine barometer by Cameron, Glasgow, with ivory register, the trunk with sympiesometer, thermometer and hygrometer scales, with brass cistern cover and shell pediment, with provision for gimbal mount, 19thC, 40in (102cm).
$3,500-4,500

A mahogany stick barometer with boxwood and ebony herringbone inlay, the case with visible tube and plain turned cistern cover, the silvered dial with thermometer and vernier, signed F. Pellegrino Fecit, 39in (99cm).
$2,600-3,600

A George III mahogany stick barometer, the silvered plate signed B. Cole London, with vernier and thermometer, the case with kinked concealed tube, turned cistern cover and inset with a key adjustable hygrometer, c1770, 44½in (113cm).
$3,200-4,000

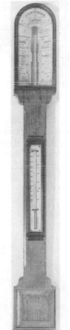

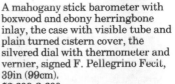

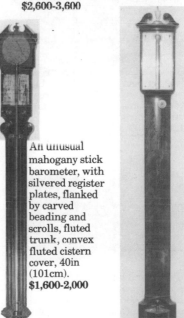

An unusual mahogany stick barometer, with silvered register plates, flanked by carved beading and scrolls, fluted trunk, convex fluted cistern cover, 40in (101cm).
$1,600-2,000

A Victorian rosewood marine barometer, the bone plates with vernier and signed B. Biggs Cardiff, the case with a brass cistern cover, later gimbals and set with a thermometer, with a later brass mount and wood shield, c1860, 34in (86cm).
$1,600-2,000

An oak stick barometer, the bone scales signed Steward, Strand & Cornhill, London, twin verniers, the case with thermometer on trunk, 39in (99cm).
$900-1,000

A stick barometer by Carey, London, late 18thC, 37in (94cm).
$6,500-7,000

SCIENTIFIC INSTRUMENTS

Dials

A brass compass dial, with folding gnomon and interior printed paper card, the brass circle pierced with Roman numerals, early 20thC, 5½in (14cm) wide.
$350-450

A gilt and silvered brass universal equinoctial dial, signed on the under side of the compass box Johan Schrettegger in Augsburg, in leather covered card case, late 18thC, 2½in (6cm) wide.
$2,600-3,600

A brass mining dial, signed on the silvered compass rose Cail, Newcastle-upon-Tyne No. 125, the corner engraved with scales for Diff of Hypo & Base, with staff mounting and T. B. Winter trade label, in mahogany case, 19thC, 13in (33cm) wide.
$550-750

Globes

A Smith's 12in (31cm) terrestrial globe, by George Philip & Son Ltd., the paper gores with ocean currents, the continents outlined in colours, with axis pins, 19thC.
$1,200-1,400

A 6in (15cm) terrestrial globe, by W & S Jones, London dated 1822, the printed and coloured paper gores with tracks of Admiral Anson, Capt. Cook and other explorers, 10in (26cm) high.
$4,500-5,500

A terrestrial globe, with maker's cartouche inscribed '18 inch Terrestrial Globe by W & A K Johnston Ltd., Geographers, Engravers and Printers, Edinburgh and London, Copyright 1910', the horizon dial 3in (8cm), on a mahogany stand terminating in lion paw feet and ball casters, 48in (122cm) high.
$7,000-9,000

A 1½in (4cm) terrestrial globe, inscribed 'Newton & Berrys New Terrestrial Globe 1831', with varnished and coloured paper gores, Australia as New Holland and with tracks of Capt. Cook and Clarke & Gore, in leather covered drum shaped case, early 19thC, 2in (5cm) high.
$3,000-3,600

A 3in (8cm) thread terrestrial globe, with coloured paper gores, the globe arranged to split and contain a reel of cotton, with interior trade label for Clark & Co., on ebonised stand, late 19thC, 4in (10cm) high.
$650-700

A Betts's patent portable globe, the waxed cotton collapsible sphere with folding umbrella frame, maker's trade label in case, 29in (74cm) long.
$650-900

A 10in (25cm) terrestrial globe by Ludw. Jul. Heymann, Berlin, the axis with part brass base, on turned beechwood stand, the base inset with a compass, 17½in (45cm) high.
$800-1,000

A 1in (3cm) terrestrial globe, unsigned, with varnished and coloured paper gores, in domed mahogany case, 19thC, 2in (5cm).
$2,000-2,700

A 2in (5cm) terrestrial globe, inscribed 'Woodward's Terrestrial Globe 18*6', the coloured and varnished paper gores printed with extensive geographical information, with brass meridian half-circle, on baluster turned support and base, globe cracked, 19thC, 6½in (17cm) high.
$1,600-2,000

A Betts's portable globe, the calico folding sphere on black japanned umbrella-type frame, in wood box, late 19thC, 29in (74cm) long.
$750-800

A 2in (5cm) terrestrial globe, inscribed 'New Terrestrial Globe' and with trade mark, the printed gores delicately coloured, delineated with the tracks of Capt. Cook, and Clarke and Gore, Australia as New Holland, late 18thC.
$1,000-1,200

An American 6in (15cm) Geographic Educator terrestrial globe, with printed and coloured paper gores, tracks of the transatlantic flights of Lindbergh and Chamberlin, arranged so as to divide into 7 sections containing jig-saw puzzles of the continents, on moulded tripod stand, 11in (28cm) high.
$1,000-1,400

A terrestrial globe, by Gilman Joslin, Boston, Massachusetts, some damage, early 19thC, 23in (59cm) high.
$1,800-2,200

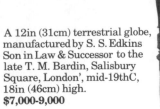

A 12in (31cm) terrestrial globe, manufactured by S. S. Edkins Son in Law & Successor to the late T. M. Bardin, Salisbury Square, London', mid-19thC, 18in (46cm) high.
$7,000-9,000

Surveying

A brass surveying level, unsigned, the telescope with a sliding draw-tube focusing, crosswires, bubble level, screw vertical adjustment, the limb with socket staff mounting, in case, 19thC, 13½in (34cm).
$260-360

An oxydised brass surveying compass, signed 'Designed & Made by Andrew Yeates 12 Brighton Place, New Kent Rd, London', with folding wire, prism and slit sights, bubble level, damaged, fixed telescope, finely engraved compass ring and steel bar needle on jewelled pivot, with trade label for Yeates 2 Grafton Street Dublin, in mahogany case, 19thC, 5½in (14cm) wide.
$900-1,000

A lacquered brass swinging arm protractor, with silvered scale and 2 verniers, signed 'Cail, Newcastle upon Tyne', with rack adjustment, in fitted mahogany case, 19thC, 7in (18cm).
$350-550

A Danish suspended deckhead compass, with dry card signed 'Rasmus Koch I Kiobenhavn 1772', 18thC, 8½in (21cm) diam.
$2,000-3,000

An oxidised and lacquered brass surveying level, signed W. & L.E. Gurley, Troy N.Y., the telescope with rack and pinion focusing, crosswires, eye-piece dust slide, with graduated level on limb with 2 clamps over the silvered horizontal circle with vernier and 4-screw tripod mounting, in carrying case, with maker's trade label, 14in (36cm) wide.
$700-800

An oxidised and lacquered brass theodolite, signed on the silvered compass dial Simms London, on 4-screw tripod mounting, 19thC, 9in (23cm) high.
$1,500-1,600

An oxidised brass double frame sextant, signed on the arc, with platina scale, 'Troughton & Simms, London', with rosewood handle, with accessories, in fitted mahogany case, 19thC, 12in (31cm) wide.
$1,000-1,500

An oxidised and lacquered brass sextant, signed 'Savill, Maker to the Royal Navy, Liverpool', with adjustable telescope socket, 7 shades, mirrors and index arm, late 19thC, 6½in (17cm), radius with vernier and magnifier, in mahogany case, 10in (25cm) wide.
$900-1,000

A geomancers compass, decorated with characters in black and red, the side and underside with other inscriptions, in carrying case, 19thC, 13in (33cm) diam.
$1,000-1,200

A black enamelled and lacquered brass theodolite, by T. Cooke & Sons Ltd, No. 7105, engraved Fergusson's patent surveying circle No. 6, on 3-screw tripod mounting, 13in (33cm) high.
$700-800

Telescopes

A 3in (7.5cm) refracting telescope, by Broadhurst Clarkson & Co., with rack and pinion focusing, lens cap and hood, the black crackle finished body tube with star finder, on trunnion and mahogany tripod, with accessories, in pine carrying case, 49in (125cm) long.
$1,500-1,600

An oxidised and lacquered brass sextant, signed on the arc with silvered scale Adams, London, with accessories in mahogany case, late 19thC, 11½in (29cm) wide.
$650-700

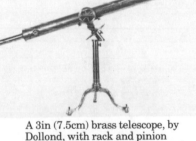

A 3in (7.5cm) brass telescope, by Dollond, with rack and pinion focusing, the tube on altitude and azimuth mount with slow motion adjustment, the ring with spirit level and vernier scale, the circular plate with scale, plain turned column support on a cabriole tripod with screw adjustment, 53in (134cm) tube inscribed Dollond, London, mahogany case, early 19thC.
$1,500-1,800

A 2¾in (7cm) brass reflecting telescope, signed on the backplate 'J. Bird London', the 16½in (42cm) long body tube with pin-hole and bead sights, screw-rod focusing, eyepiece and end cap, with speculum mirrors, on fine geared alt/azimuth mounting, unengraved and on tripod stand, the inswept cabriole legs terminating in scroll feet, late 18thC.
$2,600-3,600

An oxidised brass surveying level, signed on the telescope 'R.W. Street & Co., 39 Commercial Rd., Lambeth', with rack and pinion focusing graduated bubble, ray-shade and dust-cap, the limb on 4-screw tripod attachment, 19thC.
$260-360

A polished brass transit theodolite, by W. Ottway and Son Ltd, with micrometer eyepieces, silvered scales, bubble level and accessories, in mahogany case, 13in (33cm) wide.
$650-750

A lacquered brass 2⅛in (5cm) refracting telescope, signed on the backplate 'J.H. Dallmeyer, London', the 27in (69cm) long body tube with rack and pinion focusing, star finder, and mounted by 2 knurled nuts on a quadrant with clamp to an axis on the tapering pillar support, signed 'J.H. Dallmeyer London', on folding tripod stand, with 3 additional eye pieces, in fitted pine case, late 19thC, 38½in (98cm) long.
$1,400-1,500

Microscopes

An unusual miniature brass microscope, possibly French, unsigned, arranged so as to fold in mahogany case, late 19thC, 5in (13cm) long folded.
$550-750

A lacquered brass monocular microscope, unsigned, with rack and pinion coarse and micrometer fine focusing, the rack web with additional in/cm scale by The Lugkin Rule Co. Saginaw U.S.A., with accessories, in mahogany case, late 19thC, 14½in (37cm) wide.
$1,000-1,200

A black enamel and satin chrome binocular microscope, by Carl Zeiss Jena No. 207174, with rack and pinion coarse and micrometer fine focusing, quadruple nosepiece, micrometer circuit stage, sub-stage condenser and mirror.
$450-550

A lacquered and oxidised brass monocular microscope, signed 'J. Swift & Son, 81 Tottenham Court Rd., London', on horseshoe stand with accessories, in mahogany case, 16in (41cm) high.
$1,500-1,800

A lacquered brass polarising microscope, signed on the silvered horizontal scale to eyepiece 'W. Ladd & Co., Beak Street, W.' the polariser scale engraved in 2 quadrants with lens train swivel stage and plano concave mirror, in fitted mahogany case, 19thC, 15½in (39cm) wide.
$1,400-1,600

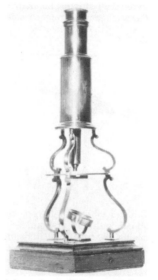

A large brass Culpepper tube microscope, unsigned, the body tube, stage and plinth base with accessory drawer united by scroll supports, in pyramid shaped mahogany case, 20in (51cm) high.
$900-1,000

A brass folding simple microscope, signed on the stage I. Cuff, Londini, Inv. & Fec. No. 18, with 4 objectives, forceps, talc box, rings and mirror, on oval base in plush lined fishskin case, 18thC, 7in (18cm) wide.
$4,000-4,800

A Nuremburg type tripod monocular microscope, of boxwood and pasteboard construction with 2 sliding body tubes, lens covers, slide clamp and mirror, the underside of the base with brand SIF, 19thC, 13in (33cm) high.
$1,700-2,700

A brass compound monocular microscope, signed 'B. Martin, Invt., London' on the body tube, focusing in the Cuff manner by sliding pillar and sleeve with long fine focus screw, in a red velvet lined fishskin covered case with a range of accessories and slides, late 18thC, 10in (25cm).
$3,500-4,500

Medical Instruments

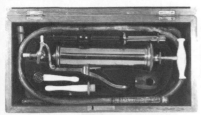

A lacquered brass enema stomach pump, unsigned, complete with ivory and vulcanite fittings, a set of catheters by Down, London, and a set of Clutton's pattern urethral sounds, all in cases, 19thC, 13in (33cm) wide.
$350-450

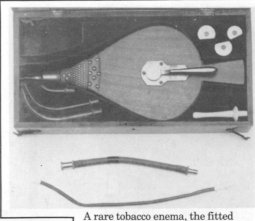

A rare tobacco enema, the fitted mahogany case containing bellows pump, tubing and assorted bone and pewter nozzles, a brass plaque on lid is engraved Bristol Humane Society 1833, 16in (41cm) wide.
$2,500-4,500

This apparatus for resuscitating the apparently drowned, was invented in the late 18thC and distributed by the Royal Humane Society to lock-keepers and docksides, and was used for pumping smoke up the victim's rectum, this practice was discontinued in 1865 after experimenting with pigs and sheep found that it only hastened their deaths!

A mahogany domestic medicine chest, with a steel balance with brass pans and weights, various jars and bottles, and 4-bottle poison compartment to rear, 19thC, 11in (28cm) high.
$1,000-1,200

A plaster phrenology bust, inscribed Pub. by J. DeVille, 367 Strand London 11 April 1821, the cranium incised with the numbered areas of the sentiments, 10in (25cm) high.
$450-650

A pair of iron spectacles of 'Martin's' margin pattern, one of the sides with loop ends stamped Froget, the lenses within horn rims, 18thC.
$800-900

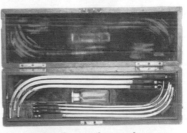

A set of 7 silver catheters, by Ferguson, with chequer grip ebony handles, a solution bottle and other items in plush lined, brass bound, rosewood case, 13½in (34cm) wide.
$350-450

A pair of brown/green tint globe shaped pharmacy carboys, with pontil marks and gilt labels for AQ:ANETH: and TR: RHETI:C, early 19thC, 11in (28cm) high.
$800-900

A minor operation set, by Cuzner Bristol, with chequer grip ivory handles with a bistoury knife by Coxeter, University College, in plush lined, gilt tooled leather case, 7½in (19cm) wide, the lid with silver plaque inscribed Bristol Infirmary surgical Prize Essay 1834 Hernia, presented to Mr. G. Cooper, mid-19thC.
$1,000-1,300

A large induction coil, by Harry W. Cox & Co. Ltd., 159 Great Portland St., London W., with vulcanite insulators, brass fittings, on oak base, late 19thC, 34½in (88cm) wide.
$1,400-1,600

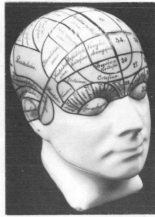

A phrenology head, the areas of the sentiments numbered and named, decorated in colours, late 19thC, 4½in (11cm) high.
$1,400-1,500

A part set of surgical instruments, by Arnold & Sons 35 & 36 West Smithfield, in brass bound mahogany case, 19thC, 17in (43cm).
$1,600-2,000

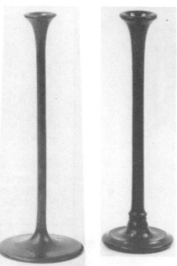

A fruitwood monaural stethoscope with wide plate, 7in (18cm) long, and a 3-part nickel plated brass and composition stethoscope, repaired, 19thC.
$475-575

A two-piece composition monaural stethoscope, with moulded plate, 19thC, 7in (18cm) long.
$350-450

A collection of surgical instruments, including a trephine, various knives, a tonsil guillotine and a chain lithotrite by S. Garie Gount, with a part mahogany case, 17½in (44cm) wide.
$450-550

A rare fruitwood Lannec monaural stethoscope, arranged in 3 parts, early 19thC, 1½in (4cm) diam, 12in (31cm) long.
$11,000-12,000

A rare Scottish paper cut out of a skeleton, with the inscription 'This representation of the human skeleton cutt with scizars by Thomas Hunter 1791 aged 82 years was presented by him to Doctor John Glendining during his residence at the University of Edinburgh', framed and glazed 10 by 5in (25 by 13cm), 18thC.
$1,600-2,000

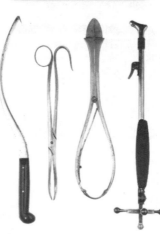

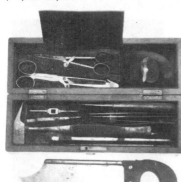

A post mortem set by Brady & Martin, Newcastle-on-Tyne, comprising saw, combination knife and chisels, hammer, skull rest and other items in brass bound mahogany case, late 19thC, 12in (31cm) wide.
$450-650

A burnished and blued steel lithotrite, stamped Charriere and with number 4, 11½in (29cm) long, the ebony handle with chequer grip, a pair of steel perforators, a stone forceps instrument and an ebony handled crochet, 19thC.
$450-550

A part set of surgical instruments, by Weiss No. 62 Strand London, one original Liston knife and 3 replacements, in plush lined brass bound mahogany case, 19thC, 17in (43cm) wide.
$1,000-1,200

A rare silver concealed tonsillectomy lancet, with sabre shaped steel blade and steel adjustment screws, maker CW, 18thC, 7½in (19cm) long.
$650-800

A burnished steel trepanning drill, unsigned, with tapering trephine perforator and lignum vitae stock, 18thC, 10½in (27cm) long.
$1,400-1,500

A rare set of acupuncture needles, the 6 steel needles with brass screw caps contained in a lignum vitae cylindrical case, the cap forming the needle handle, early 19thC, the case 3½in (9cm) long.
$450-650

Dental Instruments

A rare hand operated dental drill, unsigned with spring and ratchet operation, fitted with a single hardened steel 'bit' and ivory handle, 7in (18cm) long, and a collection of 6 burnished iron dental forceps by Pearce, Peyps, Weiss and others, mid-19thC.
$1,500-1,600

A dentist's drill, c1925.
$210-300

A set of dental scaling instruments, with ivory handles and mirror, in plush lined leather case, 18thC, 4in (10cm) wide, and a set of scalers in a case, 19thC, 5½in (14cm) wide.
$800-1,000

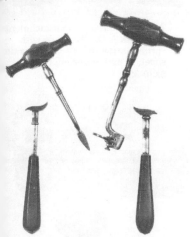

A black stained ivory handle tooth key, the moulded shank stamped CAEROM**, an elevator stamped BLANC, and 2 other elevators.
$575-650

A burnished steel tooth key, the cranked shank with claw and chequer grip ivory handle, and 2 shaped elevators with chequer grip bone handles, one stamped Everard, early 19thC.
$550-650

A plaster group of a dentist and patient, The extraction, on plinth, signed J. Pinas, 13in (33cm) high.
$700-1,000

Cameras

A whole plate brass and mahogany tailboard camera, with a brass bound lens with wheel stops and inset plaque W. Watson & Sons, 313 High Holborn, London.
$550-900

An early dry plate model.

A quarter-plate The Albemarle Postage Stamp camera, with 9 single meniscus lenses, mounted behind a 9 pinhole mask, single metal and wood darkslide, metal photograph holder and instruction card, in maker's original box.
$650-750

A quarter-plate Sibyl De Luxe camera No. D186, by Newman and Guardia, London, with a Carl Zeiss Jena Protarlinse VII 22cm lens No. 167955 and 2 single metal slides, in fitted leather case.
$450-550

A mahogany and brass fitted studio camera, with a J. H. Dallmeyer 4b f/3 patent portrait lens with variable soft focus adjustment, repeating back, leather bellows and rack and pinion focusing, mounted on a mahogany studio stand with elevation and adjustable camera geared table. **$675-800**

A 35mm twin lens Contaflex camera No. Y.84501, with a Carl Zeiss Jena Sucher-Objectiv f/2.8, 8cm viewing lens No. 1513358 and a Carl Zeiss Jena Sonnar f/1.5, 5cm taking lens No. 1753807, in maker's leather ever ready case.
$1,500-1,800

A Retina stereo prism attachment by Kodak A.G., Stuttgart, with sprung framefinder and instruction sheet, in maker's original box.
$230-330

A 35mm Olympus M1 camera No. 122910, with an Olympus M-System G. Zuiko Auto-S f/1.4 50mm lens No. 102161, in maker's leather ever ready case.
$700-800

The Olympus M1 camera was launched at Photokina in 1972 and was rapidly withdrawn and re-launched with the model name OM-1. Leitz had registered the M1 name in 1959. Very few of the M1 marked Olympus cameras found their way on to the open market. The lens engraving was also changed from M to OM-1.

A 35mm Widelux model FV camera No. 340815, by Panon Camera Shoko Co. Ltd., with a Lux f/2.8 26mm lens No. 46243.
$900-1,000

A 35mm Leica M2 camera No. 1004066 by E. Leitz, Wetzlar, with a Leitz Summilux f/1.4 50mm lens No. 1945430 and lens hood.
$1,000-1,250

A 35mm Canon IVSB camera No. 114746, with a Canon Camera Co. 50mm f/1.8 lens No. 95377, in maker's leather ever ready case.
$650-700

An 18 by 24mm film Ducati camera, No. 6909 with rangefinder and a Ducati Vitor f/3.5 35mm lens.
$350-550

A 35mm gilt and black karung leather Leica R3 Electronic camera, No. 1524066 by Leitz, Portugal, and commemorative serial No. 100-333, with a gilt and black Leitz Summilux-R f/1.4 50mm lens No. 2932005, camera top plate engraved O. Barnack, 1879-1979, in maker's fitted mahogany box, instuction booklets and guarantee cards, in maker's box.
$4,500-5,500

This camera was the first prize in the Barnack/Year of the Child Draw and was delivered by E. Leitz (Instruments) Limited Director A. H. Elder on Tuesday 4 March, 1980, to the winner in Wolverhampton. To commemorate the centenary of the birth of Oscar Barnack on 1 November 1879, 1,000 gold and skin covered Leica R3 and M4-2 cameras were produced. The Leitz packaging describes the camera as 24 carat gold plated, lizard skin.

A half plate mahogany wet plate sliding box camera, with removable focusing screen, lacking ground glass, single wet plate holder and a brass bound lens with rack and pinion focusing.
$1,500-1,800

Viewers

A mahogany body peep box, with 1¼in (3cm) peep hole, hinged legs, front and back mahogany panels, brass fittings and a 7 by 7in (18 by 18cm) linen backed coloured day and night engraving depicting the Thames tunnel.   **$1,600-2,000**

A mahogany body Designscope kaleidoscopic viewer, with lacquered brass and ebonised wood viewing column, meniscus viewing lens, 2 internal mirrors and rotating specimen tray.
$1,000-1,200

A mahogany body Kinora viewer, with inlaid wood decoration, ornamental embossed metal viewing hood and a picture reel No. 273 showing a white polar bear.   **$1,000-1,200**

Use the Index!

Because certain items might fit easily into any of a number of categories, the quickest and surest method of locating any entry is by reference to the index at the back of the book.

A wood body electrically operated wall mounted stereo viewer, with gilt coloured metal decoration, white fascia and text panels proclaiming 40 different pictures, 'You see ten for 3d and 3-D Beauty Parade' featuring stereoscopic pairs of posed nude and semi-nude women.
$2,600-3,600

SILVER
Baskets

l. A George III silver wirework sweetmeat basket, body with fruiting vine, London 1763, 6½in (16cm), 4½oz.
$700-800

r. A George III sweetmeat basket, embossed and pierced with flowers, London 1767, 6½in (16cm), 5½oz.
$900-1,000

A George III boat shaped cake basket, the spreading foot and body pierced and engraved with bright cut scrolls, urns, flowers and foliage, with reeded border and swing handle, engraved with a coat-of-arms within a foliage surround, by Charles Aldridge 1787, 15½in (39cm) wide, 32oz.   **$6,500-7,000**

The arms are those of Ridell impaling another.

A Kirk-style bridal basket, retailed by Loring Andrews Co., Cincinnati, c1900, 20in (51cm) high, 42oz.
$4,300-4,800

A George III sugar basket, with beaded edges, pierced and engraved roundels joined by foliate drapes, erect leafage and scrolls, maker's mark W P, probably William Plummer, London 1775, 5¾oz, with blue glass liner.
$1,200-1,400

A George III fruit basket, engraved with Royal crown and monogram, by John Wakelin and Robert Garrard 1797, 11in (29cm) diam, 41oz.
$11,000-13,000

The monogram is that of Queen Charlotte, wife of George III.

An Edwardian flower basket, with half pierced body and base, swing handle, London 1909, 17oz.
$900-1,000

A Victorian swing handled fruit basket, with chased vine pattern edging, on spreading base, by Robert Harper, London 1863, 9½in (24cm) diam, 15.1oz.
$450-550

A late Victorian pierced and fluted shaped cake basket, die stamped with rococo flowers and scrolling foliage and with shell terminals, B.B., Birmingham 1899, 10½in (26cm), 12.5oz.
$650-750

Beakers

A Swiss cylindrical beaker, punched with a broad band of matting and with moulded rim, engraved with a Latin presentation inscription and a name, Sion, maker's mark possibly that of Francois-Joseph Ryss, c1700, 3½in (9cm) high, 111gr.
$6,500-7,000

A French beaker, on a chased foot, the bowl engraved with a monogram and coronet within a rococo cartouche, with a moulded rim, maker's initials possibly B.C., Paris 1744, 4in (10cm).
$1,600-2,000

A Charles I beaker, the upper part of the body engraved with strapwork and foliage, pricked and engraved with initials, maker's mark I.S. a rosette below, 1640, 3½in (9cm) high, 4oz.
$3,500-4,500

Bowls

A beaker by Isaac Hutton, Albany, repairs to base, marked on base, c1800, 3½in (9cm) high, 4½oz.
$700-900

A gilt lined olive bowl and pair of olive tongs, by Gorham & Co., No. 515, 1892, the bowl 6in (15cm) wide.
$1,800-2,200

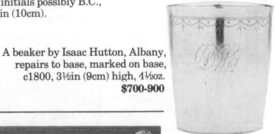

A silver two-handled punch bowl by Gorham Mfg. Co., Providence, RI, c1900, 19in (48cm) wide, 129½oz.
$4,500-5,000

A George III silver gilt bowl, with beaded border, London 1777, 4½in (11cm) diam, 6oz.
$550-650

A circular footed bowl, by Joseph Richardson, Sr., Philadelphia, marked 4 times on base, c1780, 6½in (16cm) diam, 15½oz.
$6,600-7,000

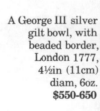

A silver bowl, with cast figure handles, gilt interior, standing on an oval base, London, 1899, 11oz.
$550-650

A two-handled footed centrepiece bowl by Gorham, No. A4984, 15in (38cm) wide, 37½oz.
$1,700-1,900

A trophy punch bowl by Ferd, Fuchs & Bros., 11in (28cm) diam, 54½oz.
$2,000-2,500

Boxes

BOXES
Please refer to the
index to locate
boxes elsewhere in
this guide

A George I tobacco box and cover, with moulded borders, the cover engraved with a coat-of-arms within shell and scroll cartouche, by Edward Cornock, 1716, 4in (10cm) long, 3oz.
$2,600-3,600

A Queen Anne tobacco box, with moulded borders, the detachable cover engraved with a coat-of-arms the base engraved 'Ste. Wright, Daventry', by Nathaniel Lock, 1708 4in (10cm) long, 6oz.
$7,000-9,000

A biscuit box, with shaped sides, marked D M, S'Gravenhage, 1938, 5in (13cm).
$650-700

A biscuit box, with shaped sides, marked D M, S'Gravenhage, 1938, 6in (15cm).
$550-750

A William IV engraved cheroot case, with pull-off cover, by Henry Wilkinson & Co., stamped Wilkinson, Leeds, Sheffield 1832, 5½in (13cm) long, 10oz.
$6,500-8,000

The view on the case is of Harewood House.

A George IV snuff box, by John Bettridge, Birmingham 1823, 3in (8cm).
$450-550

A Victorian card case, chased in high relief with a view of Windsor Castle amongst strolling foliage, th reverse inscribed with monogram, by Nathaniel Mills, Birmingham 1843, 4in (10cm) long, 73gr.
$900-1,000

A box, with gadrooned edges, maker's mark G.G., 1860, 6in (15cm).
$650-700

A Dutch or German decorative box the hinged cover chased with a battle scene, the body with scroll and flower panels incorporating vacant cartouches, late 19thC, 6½i (17cm) wide, 9oz.
$900-1,000

A silver mounted tortoise vesta box, the body with realistically cast head and feet, with hinged tortoiseshell cover, restored, London 1901, 3½in (9cm). **$570-670**

A Spanish spice box, on 4 cast lion's paw feet and with central hinge, gadrooned hinged covers and central detachable grater with baluster finial, Valladolid, with the mark of Juan A. Sanz de Velasco, c1780, 4½in (11cm), 438gr.
$6,800-7,400

A German silver gilt double spice box, the interior with central divider, the hinged cover engraved with latticework and scrolls on a matted ground, by Johann Pepfenhauser, Augsburg, c1735, 2i (5cm), 80gr.
$3,600-5,600

A Victorian snuff box, the cover with presentation inscription 'To Donald Davidson Esq., Columbo by a few of his early friends, in Forres', and dated '1845', by Nathaniel Mills, Birmingham 1844, 4in (10cm), 7.5oz.
$3,300-4,500

Starting his career as a junior in a bank in Forres, Scotland, Donald Davidson helped finance and direct many businesses throughout the world, and was held in high esteem. Mount Davidson in Virginia was named after him.

A Victorian vinaigrette, the hinged cover cast depicting a view of Westminster Abbey, by Wheeler and Cronin, Birmingham 1842, 1½in (4cm).
$900-1,000

A Victorian novelty cigarette case, in the form of a letter, the name and address and franked postage stamp in enamel to the front, the reverse with a monogram, London 1883, 4in (10cm).
$500-650

An Edwardian silver embossed jewellery casket, with hinged cover gilded inside, with a silk lining, makers Goldsmiths and Silversmiths Co., London 1901, 17oz.
$1,400-1,500

A Victorian silver gilt five-light Corinthian column candelabrum, engraved with a crest, motto and Viscount's coronet, by Hawksworth, Eyre Ltd., Sheffield, 1899, 27½in (70cm), weight of branches 103oz.
$5,500-7,000

Candelabra

A four-light candelabrum and 5 candlesticks, by Shreve & Co., the candelabrum 13in (33cm) high.
$1,300-1,800

A George IV silver candelabrum centrepiece, the base with engraved coat-of-arms, crests and inscriptions: 'The Bequest of his Mother, 18th January 1833', on 3 foliate scroll feet, inscribed beneath 'Rundel Bridge & Rundell Aurifices Regis Londini', made by John Bridge for Rundell, Bridge & Rundell, fully hallmarked London 1824, 19in (48cm), 157oz.
$10,000-11,000

A pair of Austro-Hungarian four-light candelabra, with floral moulded knops and floral moulded central finials, the capitals with gadrooned edges, Vienna 1834, 20½in (52cm), 67oz.
$2,400-3,000

A pair of four-light candelabra, with 3 reeded scroll branches and central light each with similar socket, detachable nozzles and central flame finial, with foliage borders, by Matthew Boulton & Co., c1815, 25in (64cm).
$7,000-8,000

A pair of Continental seven-light candelabra, the stems terminating in foliate sprays and scroll branches, each applied with oak leaves and acorns, L. Janesich, 19thC, 23in (59cm), 3,779gr. **$6,500-10,000**

Refer to index for other candlesticks and candelabra in the lighting section

Candlesticks

A set of 4 George III Irish candlesticks, with 'cotton reel' nozzles and holders, made by John Walker, Dublin, c1775, 12in (30cm), 111.5oz. **$10,000-12,000**

A pair of George III candelabra, the bases stamped with rams' masks, paterae and husk festoons, engraved with a crest and motto, the two-light branches similarly decorated to the candlesticks, with detachable nozzles, the candlesticks by John Carter, overstriking Sheffield marks, the branches with the mark of John Carter and a lion passant only, 1775, 16in (41cm), weight of branches 70oz. **$10,000-14,500**

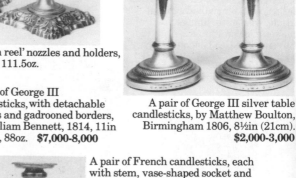

A pair of George III candlesticks, with detachable nozzles and gadrooned borders, by William Bennett, 1814, 11in (28cm), 88oz. **$7,000-8,000**

A pair of George III silver table candlesticks, by Matthew Boulton, Birmingham 1806, 8½in (21cm). **$2,000-3,000**

A pair of French candlesticks, each with stem, vase-shaped socket and detachable beaded nozzle, applied with husk swags, c1780, 11½in (30cm), 1,297gr. **$5,500-6,500**

A pair of late Victorian tapersticks in the mid-18thC taste, engraved with a crest and with a waisted socket and detachable nozzle, by Henry Eyre & Co., Sheffield 1897, 4½in (12cm). **$700-900**

A pair of Queen Anne table candlesticks, by John Elston, Exeter 1706, 8½in (21cm), 21.8oz. **$16,500-20,000**

Three George III Corinthian column candlesticks, by William Cafe, 1764, with a pair of two-light branches, with applied acanthus foliage and central vase finials, with square wax pans and vase shaped sockets, unmarked, 17½in (45cm), 104oz.
$9,000-10,000

A set of 4 George III cluster column table candlesticks, with detachable shaped circular nozzles, by John Carter, one nozzle unmarked, 1769, 13in (33cm).
$13,000-15,000

A York chamberstick, the angled handle with rectangular thumbpiece supporting detachable snuffer cone with gadrooned border, the central vase-form socket with detachable nozzle, crests engraved to base, nozzle and cone, by Robert Cattle and James Barber, fully hallmarked York 1812, 4½in (12cm), 15oz.
$1,200-1,800

A pair of George II style cast silver candlesticks, on shaped square bases with triple knopped stems, London assay, 7in (18cm), 40oz.
$2,000-2,800

A set of 4 Edwardian chamber candlesticks, each with scroll handle, vase-shaped socket, detachable nozzle and conical extinguisher with flame finial, with gadrooned borders, by Martin Hall & Co. Ltd., Sheffield 1901 and 1902, 6in (15cm), 34oz.   **$3,000-3,600**

Casters

A silver caster, maker's mark I.A, c1765, 6½in (16cm) high, 6oz.
$800-900

A silver octagonal pepper box, by Daniel Parker, Boston, c1740, 4in (10cm) high, 2½oz.
$2,200-2,500

A George II inverted pear-shaped sugar caster, the pierced domed cover with baluster finial, engraved with a crest and Earl's coronet, by Samuel Wood, 1756, 10in (25cm), 22oz.   **$4,000-4,800**

The crest and coronet are presumably those of Francis, Earl of Godolphin (d. 1766), whose second daughter and sole heiress, Mary, married Thomas, 4th Duke of Leeds in 1740.

A pair of pierced silver sugar casters, with blue glass liners, by Goldsmiths and Silversmiths Co., London 1924, 5in (13cm), 5oz.
$450-550

A caster by Samuel Edwards, Boston, marked, c1740, 3½in (9cm) high, 2¾oz.
$4,000-4,500

Centrepieces

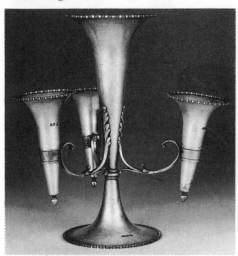

A George V centrepiece, Sheffield 1913, 906gr.
$1,000-1,200

A sugar sifter, the pierced and leaf engraved pull-off cover with baluster finial, monogram engraved to side, by Harrison & Howson, Sheffield 1931, 8in (20cm), 9oz.
$450-650

A Victorian centrepiece, the stem formed as 3 heroic female figures in Classical attire, with armorial and presentation inscription engraved to base, by Edward and John Barnard, London 1864, 108oz.
$10,000-12,000

A Continental two-handled centrepiece, import marks for 1897, 16in (41cm), 112oz.
$9,000-10,000

A Victorian candelabrum centrepiece, with 3 scroll branches each with wax pan and vase-shaped socket, with central foliage support for partly frosted glass bowl, engraved with a presentation inscription to Charles Manby Nainby, dated 16th April 1883, by Robert Hennell IV, 1873, 24in (61cm), 135oz.
$9,000-10,000

Accompanied by a leather-bound Testimonial.

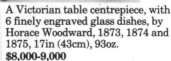

A Victorian table centrepiece, with 6 finely engraved glass dishes, by Horace Woodward, 1873, 1874 and 1875, 17in (43cm), 93oz.
$8,000-9,000

Cups

A Victorian two-handled parcel gilt cup and cover, the foot and body chased with foliage on a matted ground, the body with 2 panels chased with views within applied gilt surround, the handles formed as standing figures of fame, the cover with standing knight in armour finial, by Stephen Smith, 1871, 27½in (69cm), 170oz.
$6,500-10,000

A William IV table centrepiece, engraved with a contemporary coat-of-arms, later crest and presentation inscription, with an associated cut glass liner, by Paul Storr, also stamped Storr & Mortimer, 1833, 18½in (47cm), 110oz.
$7,000-8,000

The arms are those of Hall of Dunglass, Berwickshire, impaling Walker.

A set of 6 repoussé mint julep cups, by Schofield Co., Inc., Baltimore, c1904, 5½in (14cm) high, 38oz. **$3,600-4,000**

A Commonwealth wine cup, the bowl chased with flutes, the foot and bowl with matted oval-shaped panels, the base engraved and pricked with initials, maker's mark E.T. crescent below, 1650, 3½in (9cm), 2oz. **$16,500-18,000**

A German silver gilt cup and cover, with 8 flattened panels engraved with saints, 17thC, maker's mark only, I.C. a pellet below, for Johannes Clauss of Nuremberg, the standing figure finial and engraved cup rim added at a later date, 20in (51cm), 810gr. **$3,200-4,000**

A loving cup by Gorham, No. A237, 1898, 7in (18cm) high, 45oz. **$1,400-1,800**

Coffee Pots

Please see the Tea and Coffee Section

Cutlery

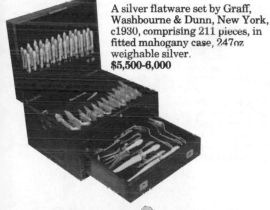

A silver flatware set by Graff, Washbourne & Dunn, New York, c1930, comprising 211 pieces, in fitted mahogany case, 247oz weighable silver. **$5,500-6,000**

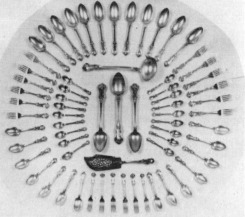

A Victorian Albert pattern silver single-struck table service, comprising 67 pieces, by John James Whiting, 1843, 152oz. **$4,500-5,500**

A silver flatware service by Tiffany & Co., New York, comprising 304 pieces, c1910, 367½oz weighable silver. **$22,000-25,000**

An Elizabethan spoon, with traces of gilding, the fig-shaped bowl with Exeter town mark, the stem with maker's mark I. Ions for John Jones, c1575, 29gr. **$2,700-3,600**

Dishes

A pair of George II meat dishes, later engraved with a coat-of-arms within a rococo cartouche, by David Willaume II, 1737, 18½in (47cm) long, 114oz.
$8,000-9,000

The arms are those of Forde impaling Knox for Matthew Forde of Seaford, M.P. for Downpatrick and Elizabeth Knox, daughter of Thomas Knox of Dungannon, whom he married in 1750.

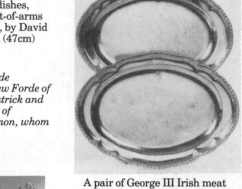

A pair of George III Irish meat dishes, each engraved with a coat-of-arms within a rococo cartouche, by John Lloyd, Dublin, c1760, 14in (36cm), 54oz.
$3,000-4,000

A silver venison platter, by Ball, Black & Co., New York, c1869, 29in (74cm) wide.
$3,500-4,000

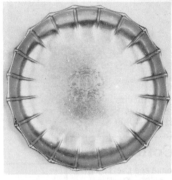

A George I strawberry dish, with lobed border, by John Hugh Le Sage, London 1720, 8½in (21cm), 14.5oz.
$10,000-11,000

A Charles II porringer, with beaded scroll handles, chased with a band of foliage and with a vacant cartouche, the base scratch engraved with initials, maker's mark indistinct, 1660, 3½in (9cm) wide, 7oz.
$4,500-5,500

A matched pair of George III entrée dishes and covers, engraved with armorials and crest, with gadroon edging, W. Burwash and R. Sibley, London 1807, one dish by another maker, London 1785, 10in (25cm) diam, 79oz.   **$2,000-2,700**

Twelve George III dinner plates, each with a gadrooned rim, engraved with the royal arms and crests, by Augustin le Sage, 1766, 9½in (24cm) diam, 196oz.
$28,000-36,000

Four George III soufflé dishes, each with foliage handles and gadrooned rim, engraved with a coat-of-arms, by Paul Storr, 1817, 10in (25cm) wide, 96oz.
$8,000-10,000

The arms are those of Osborne. The dishes were presumably made for George, 6th Duke of Leeds, but in the absence of a coronet they may possibly have been made for some other member of the family.

A Victorian butter dish, cover and stand, the sides, cover and border to the stand pierced and engraved with scrolling foliage, with vertical handles to the sides and flower finial to the slightly raised cover, by E. J. and W. Barnard, 1837, with frosted glass liner, 20oz.
$3,500-4,500

An Edward VII scallop shell shaped
dish, with chased and pierced
decoration on 3 shell feet, by Atkin
Brothers, Sheffield, 1907, 9in
(23cm) long, 10oz.   **$450-650**

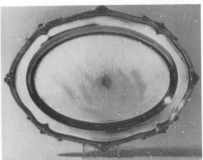

A George III meat dish,
with moulded shell and
foliage border, by Paul Storr,
1811, 22½in (57cm)
long, 85oz.
$4,500-5,500

A George III Irish dish ring, pierced
with laurel swags, slats, scrolls and
scalework and with oval medallions
enclosing portrait busts, engraved
with a crest, by William Hughes,
Dublin 1773, 8in (20cm) diam, 10oz.
$3,500-5,500

*The crest is probably that of the
Dukes of Abercorn.*

A set of 4 entréc dishes and
covers, each of the detachable
finials cast as a basket of flowers,
engraved with a coat-of-arms and
crest, by Paul Storr, London,
1801, 12in (31cm)
wide, 228oz, and 4 associated
Sheffield plate, two-handled
hotwater stands on stud feet.
$27,000-32,000

A William IV butter dish, formed as
a pail with a swing handle, the
tapering sides engraved to simulate
staves, engraved with cypher, crest
and Garter motto, by Robert
Garrard, 1834, 5in (13cm) diam,
11oz.
$4,500-5,500

*The arms are those of Gresley,
presumably for Sir Roger Gresley,
M.P. (1799-1837).*

Inkstands

An inkstandish on 4
scroll and stiff leaf
tab feet, by Mappin
& Webb, London
1925, 10in (25cm),
24oz.
$900-1,000

Jugs

A William IV inkstand, fitted with
3 silver mounted clear glass bottles,
the detachable covers chased with
scrolls, foliage and rocaille
ornament, 2 pierced with circular
apertures, by Edward Farrell, 1836,
13in (33cm) long, 59oz.
$6,500-10,000

A Victorian 2 bottle inkstand, with
2 pen depressions and 2 festoon
chased well holders, with
detachable flame finial covers, on
foliate paw corner panel supports,
fully marked, by Edward Barnard &
Sons, London, 1864, 11in (28cm)
wide, 36oz.
$3,500-5,500

*The inscription reads, 'Presented to
the Revd. Richard Joseph Farren
Lambert by the Parishioners of
Beckford with Ashton Underhill
annexed, on his leaving that parish,
as a mark of esteem for his Christian
piety & generosity especially to the
poor, during the 4 years he was
Curate, July 1865'.*

A silver gilt ewer by
Frank W. Smith Silver
Co., Gardner,
Massachusetts, c1898,
13in (33cm) high, 42oz.
$2,500-3,000

A pitcher by J. Conning, Mobile, Alabama, c1845, 10in (25cm) high, 23½oz.
$4,500-5,000

A water pitcher by Robert Keyworth, Washington, D.C., c1833, 12½in (32cm) high, 44oz.
$1,500-1,800

A Victorian silver mounted claret jug, with bracket handle, shell spout and hinged domed cover with baluster finial, chased with bands of foliage and engraved with a crest, by William Gough, Birmingham, 1869, 11in (28cm) high.
$2,000-3,000

A cream jug by George Washington Riggs, Washington, D.C., or Baltimore, marked on base, c1810, 5in (12cm) high, 6oz.
$3,500-4,500

A pitcher by Wood & Hughes, New York, c1850, 11in (28cm) high, 20½in.
$1,200-1,500

Mugs & Tankards

A silver mounted glass pitcher, by Gorham Mfg. Co., Providence, RI, 1886, 10½in (27cm) high.
$900-1,200

A Martini pitcher and mixing spoon by Gorham, the pitcher 12in (31cm) high, 29oz gross.
$1,000-1,200

A George II tankard, the body with applied rib and with scroll handle, hinged domed cover and scroll thumbpiece, engraved with a coat-of-arms, by John Langlands, Newcastle 1757, the cover unmarked, 7½in (19cm) high, 25oz.
$4,000-5,000

A cann by Samuel Casey, Rhode Island, marked on base, c1760, 4½in (12cm) high, 11½oz.
$4,200-4,500

A cann by Joseph and Nathaniel Richardson, Philadelphia, marked twice on base, c1780, 5½in (14cm) high, 12oz.
$2,200-2,500

A cann by Joseph and Nathaniel Richardson, Philadelphia, marked twice on base, c1780, 5in (12cm) high, 13oz.
$1,800-2,000

A George I tankard, the body with applied rib and scroll handle, hinged domed cover and corkscrew thumbpiece, the handle engraved with initials, by Henry Jay, 1718, 7in (18cm), 27oz.
$7,000-8,000

A George II tankard, the body with applied moulded band and with scroll handle, hinged domed cover and corkscrew thumbpiece, the handle engraved with initials SP, by John Payne, 1754, 7½in (19cm) high, 27oz.
$4,500-5,500

A cann by Nathaniel Hurd, Boston, c1765, 4½in (11cm) high, 12oz.
$13,500-14,000

A George III tankard, the body with applied rib and with scroll handle, hinged domed cover and corkscrew thumbpiece, engraved with initials, by Charles Wright, 1772, 8in (20cm), 24oz.
$4,000-5,000

A George II pint mug, engraved with a monogram, the underside scratch engraved with initials, maker's initials T.W. or J.W., London 1748, 5in (13cm), 14oz.
$1,000-1,200

A silver tankard by Bartholomew Le Roux, New York, c1730, 8in (20cm), 36oz.
$13,500-14,000

A pair of George II mugs, with leaf capped double scroll handles, Whipham & Wright, London 1759, 4in (10cm), 16oz.
$2,000-3,000

A silver cann by Edward Lownes, Philadelphia, c1820, 4in (10cm) high, 6½oz.
$1,700-2,000

A silver tankard by John Coddington, Newport, RI, c1715, 6½in (16cm) high, 25oz.
$3,600-4,000

A George III Newcastle tankard, with applied band to belly, scroll handle, the domed hinged cover with volute scroll thumbpiece, later chased with scrolls and flowers and leaves, by John Longlands, 1769, 7in (18cm) high, 20oz.
$3,000-3,600

A Victorian gilt lined baluster quart tankard, with double scroll handle, chased and embossed with rococo flowers, and with contemporary presentation inscription, Houles & Co., London 1868, 8in (20cm), 22oz.
$2,000-2,700

Salts

A pair of George III salts, each on 4 claw and ball feet, with blue glass liners, one damaged, by Robert Hennell, London 1786, 3in (8cm) long, 3oz.
$250-400

A pair of Victorian salts, in the form of an hour glass, each applied with a coat-of-arms and Royal monogram, the detachable tapering cover with beaded finial, by James Garrard, 1897, 5in (13cm) high, 12oz.
$6,500-7,000

The applied arms are those of the Salter's Company and the salts were made to commemorate Queen Victoria's Golden Jubilee.

A pair of salts and spoons, by Simon Chaudron, Philadelphia, c1810, 4in (10cm), 5oz.
$3,700-4,000

A pair of Victorian salt cellars in the form of sacks, engraved with initials, by John Charles Edington, London 1867, 2in (5cm), 7.3oz.
$1,500-1,700

A pair of George III salts, initialled, with blue glass liners, maker's mark W.A., London 1781, 3in (8cm) long, 2.6oz.
$350-450

A set of 4 Victorian salts modelled as figures, each on textured base, comprising gentleman and female companion in 18thC dress and a peasant boy and girl, by E & J Barnard, London 1863, 8in (20cm) high, 63oz.
$22,000-27,000

A pair of Victorian salts, with blue glass liners, open chased cast frames, with rococo scrolls and floral swags, by Elkington & Co., Birmingham 1852, 8oz.
$450-550

A set of 4 Victorian salts, with spoons and blue glass liners, in fitted case, London 1888, 2½in (6cm) diam, the spoons 1884/5, 6.6oz.
$550-650

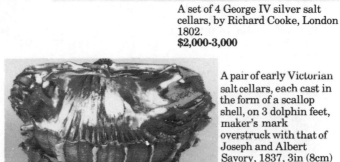

A set of 4 George IV silver salt cellars, by Richard Cooke, London 1802.
$2,000-3,000

A pair of Victorian salt cellars, each on cast simulated coral and seaweed base and with detachable shell shaped bowl, by John Mortimer and John S. Hunt, 1845, 4in (10cm) wide, 22oz.
$7,000-8,000

A pair of early Victorian salt cellars, each cast in the form of a scallop shell, on 3 dolphin feet, maker's mark overstruck with that of Joseph and Albert Savory, 1837, 3in (8cm) wide, 14oz.
$7,000-8,000

A matched set of 4 George III salts, on 4 claw-and-ball feet, with 4 blue glass liners, maker's mark indistinct, London 1774 and 1776, 3½in (9cm) long, 7oz.
$800-1,000

Salvers

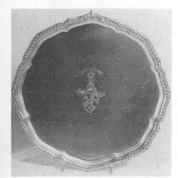

A salver, with shaped gadrooned border, on 3 volute scroll feet, crest and motto engraved to centre, by Edward Viner, Sheffield 1961, 12½in (31cm), 29oz.
$650-750

A George III salver, on 4 reeded scroll feet and with reeded border, by William Bennett, 1802, 19½in (49cm), 97oz.
$8,000-10,000

The arms are those of Gordon.

A Victorian silver Georgian style salver, with shaped Chippendale border, the centre with a coat-of-arms, with gentleman's helm, Turk's head crest and motto: 'Nemo me impune lacessit', on 4 scroll feet, makers W.C.J.L., made for Goldsmiths and Silversmiths Company, 112 Regent Street, London, 1895, 23in (59cm), 132oz.
$1,200-1,400

A Victorian salver, on 3 pierced acanthus supports, by E. J. J. & W. Barnard, London 1870, 9in (23cm), 15.2oz.
$650-750

A pair of George II sauceboats, each on 3 scroll and hoof feet, with shaped rims and foliage capped scroll handles, by Joseph Sanders, 1746, 16oz.
$8,000-10,000

A pair of sauceboats, possibly New England, 1816, 6½in (17cm) long, 20oz.
$1,600-2,000

A pair of George III salvers, engraved with armorials with an applied cast and pierced border of tied drapes and foliate oval medallions, with beaded edging, on 3 feet, by Robert Jones and John Scofield, London 1775, 9½in (24cm), 33.4oz.
$2,000-3,000

A pair of George III sauceboats, maker's mark indistinct, 1763, 9in (23cm) long, 30oz.
$6,500-8,000

An American sauceboat, on 4 scroll feet, complete with detachable liner, by Tiffany & Co., c1900, 8½in (21cm) wide, 25oz.
$2,000-3,000

Sauceboats

A pair of George III Irish sauceboats, each on cast spreading foot and with leaf capped scroll handle and gadrooned rim, engraved with a coat-of-arms, by Robert Calderwood, Dublin, c1760, 8in (20cm) long, 33oz.
$13,000-14,500

A pair of George III sauceboats, each on 3 shell feet and with quilted scroll handle and gadrooned rim, by William Cripps, 1763, 8in (20cm), 28oz.
$10,000-12,000

Services

A four-piece tea and coffee service
by Bigelow Bros. & Kennard,
Boston, c1845, the teapot and coffee
pot 12in (31cm), 76½in.
$4,000-4,500

A three-piece tea service, maker's
mark of Gorham, 1942, the teapot
7in (17cm) high, 23oz gross.
$780-840

A Mexican five-piece tea and coffee
service and two-handled tray, coffee
pot 10½in (27cm) high, 182½oz.
$3,500-4,000

A silver three-piece tea set, by
Baldwin Gardiner, New York,
c1825, teapot 9½in (24cm) high,
78oz.
$1,400-1,800

A Martele-style three-piece coffee
service and tray, by Reed & Barton,
c1905, coffee pot 10in (25cm) high,
53½oz.
$4,500-4,800

A five-piece tea and coffee service by Ball, Black & Co., New York,
c1865, coffee pot 10in (25cm) high, 105oz.   **$3,000-3,500**

A three-piece tea service in Georgian style, comprising
teapot, cream jug, sugar basin, London, 1915, 32oz gross.
$700-800

A silver five-piece tea and coffee set
and a butter dish, by S. Kirk & Son,
Baltimore, c1885, coffee pot 13in
(33cm) high, 191oz.
$7,000-8,000

A four-piece tea and coffee set of circular footed form, makers
Walker and Hall, Sheffield 1921, 61½oz.   **$1,400-1,500**

A silver three-piece tea set, by William Thompson, New York, c1815, 8in (20cm) high, 51oz. **$1,400-1,800**

A silver three-piece tea set by J. Sayre, New York, c1815, teapot 7½in (19cm) high, 44½oz. **$1,900-2,200**

A William IV three-piece tea service, of inverted baluster shape with everted rim, rose and scroll repoussé, on scalloped pedestal foot, London 1831, 48oz. **$1,200-1,400**

Trays

A square waiter by Peter David, Philadelphia, base marked PD, c1740, 6in (15cm), 9oz. **$19,000-21,000**

A Victorian tea tray, the border moulded with shells and scrolls, with presentation inscription dated 31st December 1906, by Mappin and Webb, Sheffield 1905, 121oz. **$3,200-4,200**

Tureens

A French two-handled soup tureen, cover and stand, the stand on 4 lion's paw feet, and with a foliage and beaded frieze, the cover with rosette cone finial on a palm leaf and ground, with narrow foliage borders and plain liner, by Jean-Nicolas Boulanger, Paris, c1800, 14in (36cm), 6,950gr. **$16,500-18,000**

A silver two-handled tray, by Gorham Mfg. Co., Providence, RI, 1901, 14in (36cm) diam, 31oz. **$2,200-2,500**

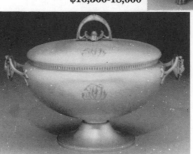

A silver soup tureen and cover, by Gorham Mfg. Co., Providence, RI, c1870, 14½in (37cm), 69½oz. **$3,000-3,300**

A pair of George IV entrée dishes and covers, with flower and foliage borders and similar detachable ring handles, by Marshall & Sons, Edinburgh 1829, 11½in (29cm) long, 112oz.
$7,000-9,000

A George III style soup tureen and cover of navette form, with looped handles and applied reeded rim, on oval spreading base, London 1902, 54oz.
$2,000-3,000

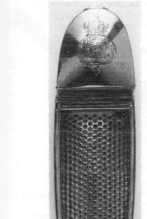

A George II quilted two-handled soup tureen and cover, with leaf capped gadrooned scroll handles, the domed cover with similar handle, by Peter Archambo and Peter Meure, 1756, 15½in (40cm) long, 100oz.
$16,500-20,000

A set of 4 George III sauce tureens and covers, with lion's mask and drop ring handles, each with gadrooned borders and engraved with a coat-of-arms and crest, by John Troby, 1806, 6½in (16cm) long, 93oz.
$10,000-11,000

The arms are those of Bell impaling another.

Miscellaneous

A pair of George III two-handled sauce tureens and covers, with beaded borders, loop handles and domed covers with urn finials, engraved with a crest, by Thomas Daniell, 1785, 44oz.
$6,500-7,500

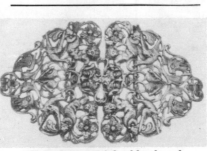

A Victorian nurse's buckle, chased and pierced, London 1898, 6in (15cm) long, 4.2oz.
$350-450

A Continental vase, chased and embossed on a matted ground, London imports for 1899, 10½in (27cm), 23oz.
$1,200-1,500

A George IV silver gilt nutmeg grater, with hinged rasp and container, engraved with Garter motto, crown and monogram GR, by Philip Rundell, 1823, 7in (18cm), 5oz.
$9,000-10,000

A miniature cow creamer, with hinged oval opening lid to the back of the animal, Chester 1907, 4in (10cm), 2oz.
$700-900

413

A pair of silver jardinières, by
S. Kirk & Son, Baltimore, with
wood bases and detachable metal
liners, late 19thC, 15in (38cm) long.
$6,000-8,000

A silver two-handled vase, by
Whiting Mfg. Co., Providence, RI,
c1890, 25in (64cm), 116oz.
$6,500-7,500

A measure, with moulded borders
and tapering cylindrical handle
with ring top, engraved with a
monogram and coat-of-arms, marks
not identified, a script B struck
twice and another mark also struck
twice, c1800, 4in (10cm) diam, 16oz.
$4,500-5,500

A George III ear trumpet,
with a reeded band to the
mid section, by Phipps &
Robinson, London 1796,
9½in (24cm).
$4,500-5,500

An octagonal serviette
ring, with engine
turned decoration,
Birmingham 1921.
$90-110

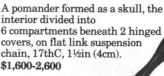

A silver plated stone set
kaleidoscope, signed Nitya, for
Nitya-prema, 1985, 13½in (35cm)
long.
$400-800

A pomander formed as a skull, the
interior divided into
6 compartments beneath 2 hinged
covers, on flat link suspension
chain, 17thC, 1½in (4cm).
$1,600-2,600

A George II baluster brandy
saucepan, with moulded rim and lip
and turned wood side handle,
engraved with initials, by Robert
Bailey, 1729, 6 oz gross.
$1,200-1,500

A two-handled replica of the
Warwick Vase, the body chased and
applied with masks, lions' pelts,
foliage and trailing vines, with vine
tendril handles and ovolo rim, by
Barnard Brothers, on silver-
mounted square ebonised wood
plinth, the plaques engraved with
coats-of-arms, inscription and dates,
1908, 10½in (27cm), 118oz.
$7,500-9,500

*One coat-of-arms is that of the
Turners' Company, the other that of
William Moore Shirreff, the recipient
of the vase.*

A South American picture
frame and a platter, the
picture frame 16in (41cm)
high, the platter 26in
(66cm) wide, 60½oz.
$1,200-1,800

An Edwardian silver-mounted pencil sharpener, fitted with a drawer to catch the shavings, A.B., London 1908, 4in (10cm).
$1,200-1,400

SILVER PLATE

Candlesticks

A pair of Victorian grape scissors.
$450-500

A pair of William IV cast naturalistic sugar nips, oak bough decorated, makers William Theobalds, London 1834.
$260-360

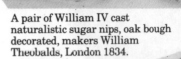

A pair of George III silver gilt grape scissors, with reeded and vineous handles and crowned Newcastle crest, makers Eley & Fearn, date letter missing, 3½oz.
$540-740

A pair of old Sheffield plate three-light candelabra, the central light with detachable flame finial, c1810, 20in (51cm).
$1,700-2,700

A set of 4 table candlesticks, the sockets with detachable nozzles, monograms engraved to stems, by S. C. Younge and Company, Sheffield 1821, 11in (28cm).
$4,500-6,500

A pair of five-light candelabra, each in Corinthian column form, 21in (53cm).
$1,500-1,700

A pair of early Victorian Sheffield plate bedroom candlesticks, with leaf scrolls to the borders, the spool shaped candleholders with detachable nozzles, the crested handles with detachable extinguishers, c1840.
$700-900

A Sheffield plate candelabrum centrepiece, the 4 detachable scroll branches each with vine border and vase-shaped sconce, lacking glass liner, c1830, 18½in (47cm).
$1,400-1,500

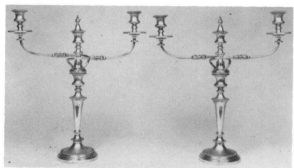

A pair of three-light candelabra, 20in (51cm).
$800-1,000

Miscellaneous

A Dutch silver gilt tobacco box, early 18thC.
$1,500-1,600

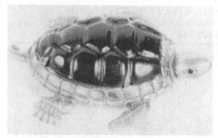

A novelty vesta in the form of a turtle, with embossed tortoiseshell back, the head and shoulders hinged, 2in (5cm).
$70-110

A Dixon's patent 24oz. spirit flask, in the form of a leather bound book, with EPNS leaves and quarters, the spine entitled 'A Pleasant Surprise'.
$450-650

An electroplate and cut glass centrepiece.
$3,500-4,500

A Victorian folding biscuit box, c1880, 10½in (27cm).
$850-1,000

Tureens

An Old Sheffield plate soup tureen and cover, with reeded loop handle, crest to cover and coat-of-arms to side, c1850, 17in (43cm) diam.
$1,800-2,800

A set of 6 Sheffield plate meat dish covers, with gadrooned rims, and detachable shell and foliage ring handles, by Matthew Boulton & Co., c1830.
$3,000-3,600

A soup tureen with 2 stags head handles, ladle with hoof handle and cover with fawn finial, beaded borders, 19thC, 13in (33cm).
$1,000-1,200

Make the Most of Miller's

Every care has been taken to ensure the accuracy of descriptions and estimated valuations. Price ranges in this book reflect what one should expect to pay for a similar example. When selling one can obviously expect a figure below. This will fluctuate according to a dealer's stock, saleability at a particular time, etc. It is always advisable to approach a reputable specialist dealer or an auction house which has specialist sales

DISCOVER THE WORLD OF ART DECO ORIGINALS

Good pieces of Clarice Cliff and other 30s pottery required for stock. Excellent prices paid.
Telephone Muir Hewitt (0422) 366657.
Evenings (0274) 882051.

MUIR HEWITT
HALIFAX ANTIQUES CENTRE

(NOT THE PIECE HALL!)
Queens Road Mills
Queens Road/Gibbet Street
Halifax, West Yorkshire HX1 4LR
Tel: Halifax (0422) 366657
Evenings: **Bradford (0274) 882051**

Open 5 Days Tuesday-Saturday 10am-5pm

A Clarice Cliff 'Age of Jazz'
figural group, modelled as
a two-dimensional pianist
and banjo player in
evening dress, 5in (12cm).
$7,000-8,000

A Linthorpe vase,
by C. Dresser.
$1,300-1,500

A Clarice Cliff
Bizarre pottery
chocolate pot,
in the form of a
chicken, with
lid, on circular
orange foot,
some damage,
6in (15cm)
high. **$210-270**

A Lorenzl Goldscheider
earthenware figure of an
odalisque, marked Lorenzl,
c1925, 18in (46.5cm).
$2,700-3,600

Two Clarice Cliff Fantasque pottery
comports: l. Hollyhock pattern. **$400-450**
r. Melon pattern. **$145-180**

A Goldscheider glazed earthenware
figure of a female dancer, marked,
c1930, 15½in (39.5cm).**$1,500-1,700**

A Gallé faience bulldog,
enamelled mark E Gallé à
Nancy, c1880, 12½in (31.5cm).
$9,500-10,000

A Coronaware vase, by
Hancock & Sons, designed by
Molly Hancock, 10in (25.5cm)
high. **$235-270**

A Clarice Cliff
Bizarre pottery
vase, 8in (20cm).
$540-650

A Lenci figure on a turtle,
c1930. **$3,600-4,700**

A New Hall plate, by Lucien
Bollumier, signed, c1925, 11½in
(29cm). **$320-400**

A bronze and
ivory figure,
marked Bruno
Zach, 15in
(38.5cm).
$4,500-6,000

A bronze figure,
c1930.
$3,000-4,500

A gold and enamel
buckle, now fitted with
a watch, stamped
Vever Paris, c1900,
3in (7.5cm).
$16,500-18,000

A parcel gilt cold
painted bronze figure,
23½in (60cm).
$11,000-13,000

A gilt and
enamelled bronze
figure of a snake
dancer, by Otto
Poertzel, c1930,
20½in (52cm).
$9,500-13,000

A bronze and ivory group, by Otto
Poertzel, 16½in (41.5cm).
$17,000-20,000

A bronze and ivory
figure, by Philippe,
14in (35cm).
$9,000-12,000

A parcel silvered bronze
and ivory figure of an
archer, by Pierre le
Faguays, early 20thC, 17in
(43cm). **$5,500-6,500**

An ivory figure of a
nude, Ecstasy, by
Ferdinand Preiss,
early 20thC, 17in
(43cm).
$9,000-10,000

A Chiparus bronze and ivory figure of a
dancer, 'Alméria', c1925, 25in (64cm).
$80,000-90,000

A cold painted bronze and ivory female
figure, by Ferdinand Preiss, early 20thC,
9in (23cm). **$9,000-10,000**

A bronze and
enamel clock,
with enamelled
dial, on marble
base, marked
Maple & Cie
Paris, c1920,
10½in (27cm).
$14,500-16,500

An Art Deco bronze and ivory figure, by
Demètre Chiparus, 21in (54cm).
$90,000-108,000

COLOUR REVIEW

Four Daum vases.
$4,500-8,000 each

A Daum internally decorated glass lamp, 17in (43cm).
$7,000-9,000

A Daum cameo glass and wheel carved vase, signed in intaglio, c1900, 7½in (18cm).
$2,700-3,500

A Daum enamelled vase, enamelled mark Daum Nancy, c1900, 13in (33cm).
$40,000-45,000

A Daum overlaid and etched glass lamp, 18in (45.5cm).
$22,000-27,000

Three Daum carved, and enamelled painted vases, painted signatures and cross of Lorraine. **$9,000-14,500 each**

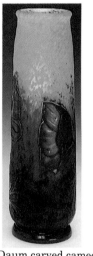

A Daum carved cameo and marqueterie sur verre glass vase, engraved mark Daum Nancy, c1900, 8in (20.5cm).
$18,000-21,000

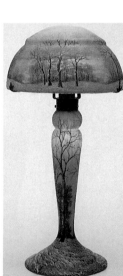

A Daum enamelled glass lamp, with mark Daum Nancy, c1900, 24½in (62cm).
$62,000-72,000

A Daum etched and enamelled cameo glass vase, signed, c1900, 7½in (18cm).
$6,000-7,000

An etched, enamelled and applied glass vase, Daum Nancy, 8in (20cm).
$63,000-72,000

Two Daum carved and acid etched lamps, carved signatures Daum Nancy.
$12,000-18,000 each

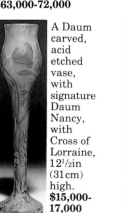

A Daum carved, acid etched vase, with signature Daum Nancy, with Cross of Lorraine, 12½in (31cm) high.
$15,000-17,000

A Daum carved and acid etched overlay vase, 9in (23cm).
$27,000-32,000

An Edgar Brandt wrought iron lamp, c1925. **$11,000-12,000**

A Daum vase, signed
Daum Nancy, 9¹/₂in
(24cm). **$4,700-5,700**

A Gallé double overlaid and
etched glass chandelier, the
domed shade with frosted
ground overlaid and etched to
depict blossoms, cameo
signature, 17¹/₂in (44cm).
$9,500-10,500

A Daum etched and
enamelled glass
vase, signature,
19¹/₂in (49cm).
$42,000-48,000

A Daum glass
vase, with Cross
of Lorraine,
7¹/₂in (19cm).
$2,700-3,600

A Gallé carved and acid etched double overlay
plafonnier, carved signature, 19in (49cm) diam.
$22,000-27,000

A Daum overlaid and
carved glass vase,
cameo signature,
16in (40cm).
$10,000-14,500

A Gallé overlaid and etched glass chandelier,
cameo signatures, 18in (46cm) diam. **$36,000-
40,000**

A Gallé overlaid, glass
lamp, 22in (56cm) high.
$22,000-27,000

A Gallé carved and acid etched
double overlay table lamp,
signed. **$63,000-80,000**

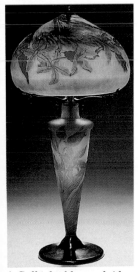

A Gallé double overlaid
etched glass lamp, 25in
(64cm). **$21,000-27,000**

A Gallé carved and acid
etched triple overlay
lamp. **$40,000-45,000**

A Gallé carved, acid
etched and fire
polished double overlay
table lamp, signed.
$38,000-45,000

A Gallé carved and acid
etched lamp, 15¹/₂in (39cm)
high. **$48,000-54,000**

COLOUR REVIEW

A Gallé intrecalaire, intaglio carved 'verrerie parlante' vase, signed, 4½in (11cm) high. **$54,000-63,000**

A Gallé glass vase, the frosted ground overlaid and etched to depict wisteria, cameo signature, 24½in (61cm). **$145,000-150,000**

A Gallé vase, signed in cameo, 12in (30.5cm) high. **$6,000-7,500**

A Gallé carved and acid etched double overlay landscape vase, carved Gallé signature, 33in (83cm). **$160,000-180,000**

A Gallé cameo glass vase, signed, c1900, 8½in (21cm). **$8,000-9,000**

A Gallé vase, carved signature, 6½in (16.5cm). **$12,000-14,500**

A Gallé triple overlaid and etched glass table lamp base, cameo signature, 15in (38cm), with metal mount. **$36,000-45,000**

A Gallé decorated martelé enamel vase, 12in (30.5cm) **$13,000-15,000**

A Gallé glass vase, c1900, 14in (35.5cm). **$18,000-21,000**

A Gallé cameo glass 'Iris' vase, cameo mark, c1900, 20½in (51.5cm). **$54,000-60,000**

A Gallé internally decorated carved cameo vase, c1900. **$63,000-72,000**

A Gallé double overlaid and etched vase, signature, 17in (43cm). **$28,000-32,000**

A Gallé carved and acid etched double overlay vase, cameo signature 17½in (43.5cm) high. **$72,000-80,000**

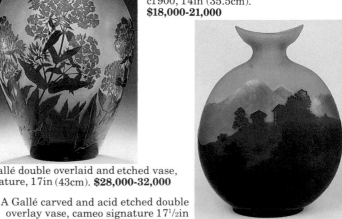

A frosted glass and bronze luminaire, the arched glass moulded with 3 peacocks and set in an electricfied bronze base, etched R Lalique France, 36in (91.5cm) wide. **$160,000-180,000**

A Lalique opalescent glass vase, 'Bacchantes', 9¹/₂in (24cm). **$22,000-28,000**

A Lalique glass vase, 'Languedoc', moulded in high relief with overlapping stylised leaves, engraved mark R Lalique France, 1929, 9in (22.5cm). **$12,000-14,500**

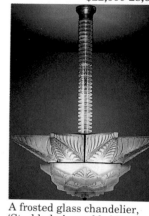

A frosted glass chandelier, 'Stockholm', moulded R. Lalique. **$9,000-10,000**

A Lalique opalescent figure, 'Suzanne', engraved R. Lalique France, 9in (23cm). **$18,000-21,000**

A pair of Lalique glass and nickel plated metal lamps, one shade with stencilled mark R Lalique, the other with wheel cut R Lalique France, c1928, 20in (50cm). **$16,500-18,000**

A Lalique table lamp, the base acid stamped, 10in (26cm). **$21,000-27,000**

A Lalique wall light, 18¹/₂in (47cm) diam. **$18,000-21,000**

'Le Jour et la Nuit' clock, stencilled mark R Lalique, 15in (38cm). **$145,000-160,000**

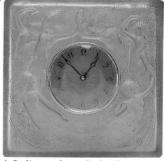

A Lalique glass clock, 'Sirènes', marked, c1928, 11in (28cm). **$9,500-11,000**

An Argy-Rousseau pâte-de-verre glass vase, marked, c1920, 4in (9,5cm). **$36,000-40,000**

A clear and frosted Alexandrite vase, 'Tortues', intaglio moulded R Lalique, 10½in (26cm). **$38,000-45,000**

A Muller Frères cameo glass vase, cameo mark, 12in (30.5cm). **$12,000-14,500**

A Lalique opalescent vase, 'Bacchantes', with engraved signature R Lalique, France, 9½in (24cm). **$34,000-38,000**

A leaded glass and earthernware table lamp, the shade by Tiffany, the base by Ruth Erikson. **$18,000-21,000**

A double overlaid and etched glass table lamp, cameo signature Muller Frères, Luneville, 21½in (54cm). **$14,000-18,000**

A blue and clear glass scent flaçon, 'Bouchon Mûres', chip to underside, moulded R Lalique, 4½in (11cm). **$63,000-72,000**

A Gabriel Argy-Rousseau pâte-de-verre table lamp, marked on both shade and base, 15½in (39.5cm). **$95,000-110,000**

A diamond, glass and yellow gold brooch, stamped Lalique, 3½in (9cm). **$80,000-90,000**

A French blue vase, 'Penthièvre', stencilled R Lalique, 10in (25.5cm). **$48,000-50,000**

A glass table, 'Cactus', by Lalique et Cie, engraved No 37 le 3/12/82, 60in (152cm) diam. **$24,000-27,000**

A Georges Dumoulin vase, with applied vertical grips, internally decorated with air bubbles, engraved G. Dumoulin, c1930. **$3,000-4,500**

An Argy-Rousseau enamelled glass vase, gilded mark, 1920s, 6in (15cm). **$5,500-7,000**

A Venini bottle vase, designed by Fulvio Bianconi, acid stamped mark, 9in (23cm). **$12,000-14,500**

A set of 6 Liberty & Co silver and turquoise enamel buttons, with an entrelac design of Celtic inspiration, stamped L&Co, cymric with Birmingham hallmark for 1907, original fitted case. **$900-1,000**

An Art Deco brooch, set with calibre cut black onyx and round diamonds, mounted in platinum, by Cartier. **$45,000-54,000**

A plique à jour pendant, German, Pforzheim, c1910, 2½in (6cm). **$1,500-2,000**

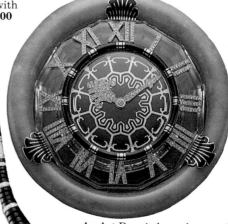

An Art Deco jade, rock crystal, diamond and enamel desk clock, signed Cartier, c1930, in fitted case. **$50,000-56,000**

Three Liberty & Co silver pendants. **$180-450 each**

Two Liberty pendants and one by Murrle Bennett & Co. **$180-360**

A Georg Jensen silver coloured metal necklace, monogrammed 'GJ', c1910, 9in (23cm) long. **$2,700-3,600**

An Art Deco carved emerald, diamond and enamel bracelet, by Cartier. **$80,000-90,000**

A Gabriel Argy-Rousseau pâte-de-verre vase, 'Loupes', moulded signature, 9½in (24cm) high. **$72,000-80,000**

A glass sculpture, by Clifford Rainey, 'Blue Figure', cast signature, 1989, 28in (71cm). **$6,000-8,000**

A copper and mica table lamp, the ginger jar vessel with 4 arms supporting a sweeping shade, stamped with windmill mark and Dirk Van Erp, c1911, 27in (69cm) high, with broken box. **$60,000-70,000**

A wrought iron and hammered copper five-light chandelier, by Gustav Stickley, c1905. **$8,000-9,500**

A leaded glass and copper table lamp, by the Roycrofters, stamped with the firm's orb mark, 18½in (47cm). **$9,000-10,000**

A glass sculpture, 'Cosmic Tides', by Ray Flavell, cut, polished and sand blasted, deeply engraved, engraved signature, 1990, 16½in (41cm). **$7,000-9,000**

A copper and mica table lamp, by Dirk Van Erp, stamped and windmill mark, c1919. **$9,000-10,000**

A copper and glass hanging ceiling light, by the Roycrofters. **$8,000-9,500**

A copper and mica table lamp, by Dirk Van Erp, stamp and windmill mark, c1912, 15½in (39cm). **$45,000-54,000**

An engraved glass globe, 'Walking the Earth', by Ronald Pennell, the hand blown glass body on cylindrical stem, wheel engraved with various animals, 1990, 10in (25cm). **$3,600-5,500**

A pair of Art Deco burr walnut bedside cabinets, by Mercier Frères, 23in (58cm) wide. **$6,000-7,000**

An oak sewing cabinet, by Gustav Stickley, firm's red decal, c1905, 20in (51cm) wide. **$4,500-5,500**

A walnut, maple and chrome display cabinet, by Gordon Russell workshops, c1930. **$6,000-8,000**

An oak smoker's cabinet, by Gustav Stickley, c1903, 17in (43cm) wide. **$5,500-7,000**

A carved mahogany, and marquetry cabinet, by Louis Majorelle, 25in (64cm). **$54,000-63,000**

An inlaid oak music cabinet, designed by Harvey Ellis for Gustav Stickley, c1903. **$7,000-8,000**

A carved mahogany and marquetry cabinet, by Louis Majorelle, 68in (173cm) high. **$36,000-45,000**

A mahogany and marquetry side cabinet, c1900, 55in (139cm) wide. **$5,500-7,000**

An oak hanging trophy case, by Gustav Stickley, c1904, 60½in (154cm) wide. **$8,000-9,500**

An Art Deco three-piece bedroom suite, comprising grand lit and 2 bedside tables, branded Leleu. **$10,000-12,000**

A carved mahogany and marquetry cabinet, by Louis Majorelle, boldly carved and inlaid, 75in (190.5cm) high. **$50,000-56,000**

An Art Deco ebony, macassar and vellum daybed, 86in (220cm) long. **$9,500-11,000**

A set of 8 Everaut pressed metal stacking chairs, c1930. **$7,000-9,000**

A pair of Apelli and Varesio side chairs, by Carlo Mollino, c1945. **$9,500-11,000**

A suite of leather furniture, comprising three-seater settee and 2 armchairs, c1930. **$3,600-5,500**

An Italian three-piece suite, comprising a chaise longue and 2 armchairs, c1950. **$2,000-3,600**

An aluminium chair, designed by Frank Lloyd Wright for the H. C. Price Company tower, c1954. **$16,500-18,000**

A 'Kota' chair, by Sue Golden, of fibreboard and steel construction, 1987. **$1,500-2,000**

An English Art Deco leather upholstered three-piece suite. **$7,000-9,000**

A Cassina chaise longue. **$2,000-2,700**

An inlaid oak side chair, designed by Harvey Ellis, produced by Gustav Stickley, red decal, model No.338, c1904 **$4,500-5,500**

An Irish pearwood Art Nouveau three-piece suite, by James Hayes, upholstered in brown leather, labelled Millar and Beatty Ltd, c1902. **$10,000-12,000**

A Carlo Bugatti painted vellum ebonised and inlaid side chair, seat restored, painted signature. **$7,000-9,000**

A pair of Liberty and Co., oak armchairs, with leather upholstery, manufacturers label. **$4,500-5,500**

A set of 6 dining chairs, designed by Harvey Ellis, produced by Gustav Stickley, model Nos 353 and 353A, c1910. **$4,500-6,000**

COLOUR REVIEW

An oak wardrobe, by
Peter Waals.
$4,500-6,000

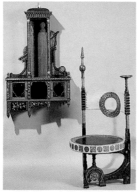

A Carlo Bugatti
inlaid chair and
hanging shelf.
**$7,000-9,000
each**

'Metropole', a Memphis
clock, designed by
George J. Sowden,
made in Italy, 1982.
$2,700-3,600

An oak dressing table mirror,
1906, 23in (58cm) wide.
$9,000-10,000

An oak blanket chest, by Gordon
Russell, dated 20.6.27, 65in
(166cm) wide. **$8,000-10,000**

An oak sideboard, by Gustav Stickley,
firm's branded mark, model No.804, 54in
(137cm) wide. **$14,500-18,000**

A Carlo Bugatti
ebonised and inlaid
pedestal, 51in (130cm).
$5,500-7,000

A Liberty and Co. oak
revolving bookcase,
c1900. **$10,000-12,000**

A black lacquered dining table, top
with curved corners, on U-shaped
base, c1930, 66in (168cm) long.
$3,600-5,500

'Three Thirds of a Table', by Ron Arad,
of mirror polished stainless steel, c1989,
98in (250cm) wide. **$21,000-27,000**

An oak serving table,
by Gustav Stickley,
firm's branded mark,
c1912. **$4,500-6,000**

A carved mahogany
and marquetry
cupboard, by Louis
Majorelle,
46in (117cm).
$10,000-12,000

A carved mahogany and marquetry
sideboard, by Louis Majorelle,
signed. **$15,000-18,000**

A spruce coffee table, designed by
Frank Lloyd Wright, c1950, 74in
(188cm). **$15,000-17,000**

A Shapland and Petter oak
sideboard, the central reserve
decorated with a copper relief
panel of stylised flowers, 90in
(228cm) wide. **$9,000-10,000**

A Fontana Arte glass topped bronze
coffee table, attributed to Gio Ponti,
stamped, 1950s. **$7,000-9,000**

A silver and rosewood powder box, bowl and circular box, made by Puiforcat, marked, 1927, 21½ oz gross. **$9,000-10,000**

An E. Bingham & Co electroplated table service, designed by Charles Rennie Mackintosh, comprising 42 pieces. **$14,500-18,000**

A silver two-handled tea tray, by Georg Jensen, 830 standard, inscribed and dated 1925, marked, 34in (86cm) wide. **$18,000-21,000**

A set of 12 silver plates, designed by Johan Rohde, 1930, made by Georg Jensen, post 1945, marked, 11in (28cm) diam. **$10,000-14,500**

A nickel plated metal smoker's companion, 1930s, 10½in (26cm) long. **$5,500-7,000**

A WMF electroplated metal photograph frame, marks, c1900, 14½in (36cm). **$2,700-3,600**

A Liberty and Co. silver and enamel ceremonial spoon, by Archibald Knox, Birmingham 1900. **$6,000-9,000**

A parcel gilt silver pitcher, by Georges Lecomte, Paris, marked, c1945, 18in (46cm), 133½oz. **$16,500-18,000**

A canteen of Georg Jensen cutlery, comprising 77 pieces, various Jensen marks. **$9,000-10,000**

A George Jensen muffin dish, cover and stand, various marks, c1920 and c1940. **$5,500-7,000**

A four-piece silver and glass tea and coffee service and tray, by Puiforcat, post 1973. **$21,000-23,000**

A silver and fluorite covered tureen, by Puiforcat, marked post 1973, 54oz gross. **$14,500-18,000**

A silver eight-piece tea and coffee service and tray, Georg Jensen, post 1945. **$54,000-63,000**

A Hukin & Heath electroplated tantalus, designed by Dr Christopher Dresser, stamped H&H, c1879, 11in (28cm) high. **$10,000-14,500**

A James Dixon & Son three-piece electroplated tea set, designed by Christopher Dresser, stamped, c1880. **$15,000-18,000**

A Hukin & Heath electroplated metal three-piece tea set, designed by Christopher Dresser, stamped H&H, c1878. **$9,000-12,000**

A silver ivory mounted vase, by Tétard Frères, Paris, marked, c1935, 15in (38cm), 170oz gross. **$14,500-18,000**

A silver vase, by Risler, Paris, marked, c1935, 22in (56cm) high, 164oz. **$14,500-18,000**

A silver covered soup tureen, by Tétard Frères, Paris, marked, c1935, 9½in (24cm) high, 101oz gross. **$12,000-14,500**

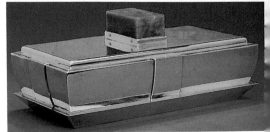

A silver and aventurine quartz covered serving dish, by Puiforcat, marked, c1935, 9in (23cm) long, 41oz gross. **$23,000-27,000**

A Flamand gilt bronze figural lamp, marked G. Flamand, c1900, 33in (84cm). **$6,000-7,500**

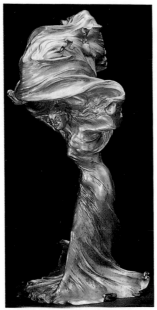

A gilt bronze two-light table lamp, 'Loie Fuller', by Raoul Larche, early 20thC. **$10,000-14,500**

A Gurschner bronze and nautilus shell lamp, marked, c1900, 21in (53cm). **$18,000-21,000**

A Cartier silver and lapis lazuli humidor, 1928, 9¹/₂in (24cm) long. **$12,000-14,000**

A pair of Bouval gilt bronze Art Nouveau lamps, marked M Bouval and with foundry mark 'Thiébaut Frères', c1900, 20in (50.5cm). **$18,000-21,000**

A WMF style electroplated metal tazza, c1900, 18in (45cm). **$3,600-5,500**

An Albert Cheuret alabaster and metal lamp, c1925. **$14,500-18,000**

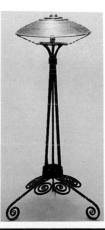

A wrought iron lamp, with Muller Frères etched glass shade, c1925, 41in (104cm). **$2,700-3,600**

A pair of Georg Jensen silver tureens and covers, 1928. **$12,000-14,500**

A pair of silver five-light candelabra, by Georg Jensen, marked, 1930, 10¹/₂in (26cm). 185¹/₂oz. **$42,000-48,000**

A napkin ring, by Henri Husson, c1905, 2¹/₂in (5cm). **$2,700-3,600**

433

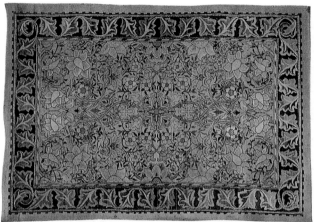

A William Morris 'Redcar' hand knotted carpet, probably woven at Merton Abbey, c1890, 135 by 98in (345 by 249cm). **$70,000-80,000**

A woollen tapestry, 'Moonlight', designed by Howard Hodgkin, woven at the West Dean Tapestry Studio by Dilys Stinson, dated 1983. **$8,000-9,000**

A pair of Liberty jardinières on pedestals, 31½in (80cm) high. **$3,600-5,500**

An Edgar Brandt wrought iron firescreen, marked, c1925, 36½in (93cm) high. **$18,000-21,000**

A spun silk wall hanging, by Sally Greaves-Lord, 1990, 75 by 35in (190 by 90cm). **$1,000-1,500**

A leaded glass window, c1913, 72in (183cm) high. **$7,000-9,000**

A Nigel Coates woollen carpet, 'L'Europea', signed, 1990, 110 by 63in (280 by 160cm). **$4,500-6,000**

A pair of Morris & Co woven compound twill Peacock and Dragon curtains, c1878. **$4,500-5,500**

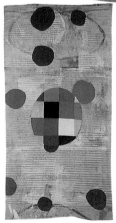

A cotton wall hanging, 'Core', by Ruston Aust, 1989. **$1,500-1,800**

A set of steel Dupré Lafon fireguards, with flat rectangular section and tubular crossbar, c1930, 40in (102cm) wide. **$4,500-6,000**

A gilt bronze and glass sconce, designed by Frank Lloyd Wright, c1902, 13½in (34cm). **$8,000-9,50**

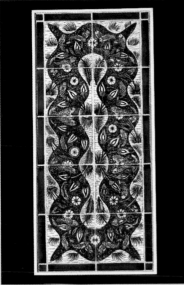

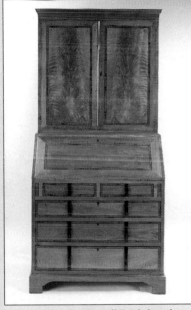

A stoneware sack form, by Hans Coper, with bronze disc top, seal, c1970, 7¹/₂in (19cm). **$13,000-15,000** *n*

An hour glass vase, by Hans Coper, c1963. **$17,000-18,000 -10,500** *Bon*

A cup form stoneware pot, by Hans Coper, impressed HC seal, c1970, 6in (15cm). **$10,000-14,500**

A Hans Coper vase, impressed HC seal, c1965, 7¹/₂in (19cm). **$18,000-21,000**

An early thistle form pot, by Hans Coper, impressed HC seal, c1958, 12in (31cm). **$11,000-13,000**

A Hans Coper spade vase, chip restored, impressed HC seal, c1970, 7in (17.5cm). **$9,500-11,000**

A hand painted and glazed vase, by Raoul Dufy, signed, marked, numbered 17, 12¹/₂in (32cm). **$80,000-90,000 50,000** *S*

An early stoneware bottle form, by Hans Coper, 11in (28cm(28cm). **$7,000-9,000**

A stoneware form, Hans Coper, impressed seal, c1970, 7in (18cm). **$12,000-14,500**

An early bottle form by Hans Coper, impressed seal, c1956, 13in (34cm). **$24,000-28,000** *Bon*

A spade form, by Hans Coper, impressed HC seal, c1965, 8in (20c(20cm). **$12,000-14,500**

A Hans Coper vase, impressed HC seal, c1965, 7in (18.5cm). **$16,500-18,000**

An enamelled terracotta plaque, 'Le Prophète', by Jean Arp, comprising 6 painted and partially glazed ceramic tiles, signed, inscribed XI on the reverse, 22in (56.5cm) high. **$14,500-16,500**

A cup and disc stoneware form, by Hans Coper, c1965. **$5,500-7,000**

A stoneware swollen sack form, by Elizabeth Fritsch, with brown glaze to rim and interior, 1983, 16in (41cm). **$10,000-14,500**

An Elizabeth Fritsch bowl, with bright blue interior, green exterior with wide rim border, 18in (45.5cm). **$8,000-9,500**

An Elizabeth Fritsch vase, decorated and incised with a geometric design, rim chip, 1975, 7½in (19cm). **$3,600-5,500**

A stoneware flask, by Elizabeth Fritsch, c1984, 16in (41cm). **$6,000-8,000**

A stoneware vase, by Elizabeth Fritsch, white with tinges of green, the rim with an ochre band, the interior in pale blue, 10in (26cm). **$5,500-6,500**

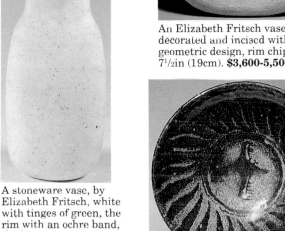

A stoneware charger, by Bernard Leach, impressed BL and St Ives Pottery seals, 13½in (34cm). **$6,000-7,500**

A stoneware container of 3 stacking compartments, by Kanjiro Kawai, c1950, 6½in (16.5cm). **$5,500-7,000**

An elliptical cup and saucer, by Elizabeth Fritsch, saucer 9in (23cm). **$9,000-10,000**

A stoneware vase, by Bernard Leach, glazed in tehmoku, impressed BL and St Ives seals, c1963. **$7,000-9,000**

A stoneware lidded bowl, by Bernard Leach, the rust brown body with sgraffito decoration, impressed BL and St Ives seals, c1967, 9in (23cm) diam. **$6,000-9,000**

An earthenware bowl, by George Ohr, stamped G.E. OHR Biloxi, Miss, 8in (20cm) diam. **$2,000-2,700**

A painted and partially glazed pitcher, by Pablo Picasso, inscribed, No 27/50, 14in (35.5cm). **$72,000-90,000**

A hand painted and glazed plate, by Pablo Picasso, signed and dated 7 juin 54, 18¹/₂in (22cm) wide. **$63,000-72,000**

A plate, by Pablo Picasso, inscribed 188/200, 1953, 9in (23cm). **$2,000-2,700**

A painted white earthenware vase, by Pablo Picasso, No. 12/25, 1951, 22in (55cm) high. **$72,000-80,000**

A hand painted and glazed plate, 'Oseau sur fond bleu', stamped, by Pablo Picasso, 1949, 14¹/₂in (37.5cm) long. **$90,000-108,000**

A hand painted and glazed vase, by Pablo Picasso, No.2/62, 22¹/₂in (57cm) high. **$72,000-80,000**

A hand painted and glazed plate, 'Oseau Mangeant un ver', by Pablo Picasso, 1949. **$95,000-108,000**

A painted white earthenware pitcher, 'Taureau', stamped Edition Picasso, Madoura plein feu, No. 17/100, 1955, 12in (30.5cm). **$80,000-90,000**

A painted and partially glazed plate by Pablo Picasso, 1956, 16¹/₂in (42cm). **$18,000-21,000**

A painted and partially glazed terracotta vase, by Pablo Picasso, dated 19.12.53, stamped and inscribed. **$19,000-21,000**

A hand painted and glazed plate, by Pablo Picasso, dated 25.3.48, stamped on reverse, 25¹/₂in (65cm) wide. **$108,000-125,000**

A painted and glazed pitcher, 'Visage aux yeux rieurs', by Pablo Picasso, stamped and inscribed. **$27,000-32,000**

A Lucie Rie stoneware compressed bowl, impressed LR seal, c1968, 11in (28cm) wide. **$7,000-9,000**

A Lucie Rie bowl, impressed LR seal, c1968, 9¹/₂in (24cm) diam. **$10,000-12,000**

A Lucie Rie stoneware bowl, impressed LR seal, c1972, 10¹/₂in (27cm) diam. **$7,000-9,000**

A Lucie Rie porcelain bowl, with impressed LR seal, c1960, 6in (15cm) high. **$7,000-9,000**

A Lucie Rie porcelain bowl, with feathered rim, impressed LR seal, c1968, 9in (23cm) **$6,000-7,000**

A Lucie Rie bowl, with yellow uranium glaze and running bronze rim, impressed LR seal, c1960, 5in (13cm) diam. **$4,500-5,500**

A Lucie Rie porcelain bowl, with bronze fluxed rim, impressed LR seal, c1965, 9in (23cm) diam. **$3,600-4,500**

A Lucie Rie porcelain bowl, with one inlaid circular line, LR seal, c1960, 7in (18cm) diam. **$6,000-8,000**

A Lucie Rie white porcelain bowl, with bronze running rim, impressed LR seal, c1975, 10in (26cm) diam. **$5,500-7,000**

A Lucie Rie stoneware inlaid sgraffito bowl, with brown vertical sgraffito, impressed LR seal, c1950, 14¹/₂in (37cm) diam. **$8,000-9,500**

A Lucie Rie stoneware 'knitted' bowl, with inlaid criss-cross lines, impressed LR seal, c1975, 7¹/₂in (19cm) diam. **$4,500-6,000**

A Lucie Rie porcelain bowl, impressed LR seal, c1978, 5in (12.5cm) diam. **$3,000-4,500**

A Lucie Rie porcelain bowl, impressed LR seal, c1968, 5in (12.5cm) diam. **$7,000-9,000**

A Lucie Rie bowl, with sgraffito decoration, c1965, 8in (21cm). **$9,000-9,500**

A Lucie Rie stoneware bowl, with feathered rim, LR seal, c1985, 9in (23cm) diam. **$5,500-7,000**

A Lucie Rie stoneware bowl, LR seal, c1982, 9in (23cm) **$5,500-7,000**

A Lucie Rie porcelain vase, with wide flaring rim, impressed LR seal, c1978, 9^1/$_2$in (24cm). **$20,000-21,000**

A Lucie Rie bronze porcelain vase, LR seal, c1972, 9^1/$_2$in (24cm). **$5,500-7,000**

A stoneware vase by Lucie Rie, impressed LR seal, c1965, 12in (31cm) high. **$4,500-6,000**

A Lucie Rie stoneware vase, LR seal, c1960, 11^1/$_2$in (29cm) high. **$11,000-13,000**

A Lucie Rie porcelain bowl, the terracotta foot and well with a ring of turquoise, impressed LR seal, c1986, 9in (23cm) diam. **$8,000-9,500**

A Lucie Rie stoneware bottle, impressed LR seal, c1960, 13^1/$_2$in (34.5cm) high. **$9,000-10,000**

A Lucie Rie stoneware pot, in a pitted 'volcanic' glaze, unglazed base, impressed LR seal, c1958, 6in (15.5cm) high. **$12,000-14,500**

A Lucie Rie bowl, impressed LR seal, c1975, 7in (43cm) diam. **$10,000-12,000**

A Lucie Rie stoneware bowl, with a pitted white and beige glaze, impressed LR seal, c1980, 9^1/$_2$in (24cm) wide. **$7,000-9,000**

A Lucie Rie tall vase, the shoulder and rim with sgraffito, impressed LR seal, c1965, 10in (25cm) high. **$10,000-12,000**

A Lucie Rie porcelain vase, with bronze rim, impressed LR seal, 11in (28in) high. **$2,700-3,600**

A Lucie Rie stoneware vase, with a heavily pitted glaze, impressed LR seal, c1960, 7in (19cm) high. **$3,600-5,500**

A Lucie Rie stoneware bowl, impressed LR seal, c1984, 8in (21cm) diam. **$5,700-6,200**

TEA & COFFEE

Ever since tea and coffee were introduced into Britain in the mid-17thC there has been, in addition to the actual tea and coffee pots, an array of equipage which was necessary in their making. Just as roasters and grinders were necessary for coffee, canisters, kettles, strainer spoons and sugar nips for example, were necessary for tea.

The early silversmiths were clearly aware of the commercial opportunities created by the need for tea and coffee accessories as also have all the pottery, porcelain and silver plate manufacturers ever since.

Unfortunately, it is such a big subject that we cannot hope to include all the equipage in this edition.

For coffee we have majored on silver coffee pots whilst for tea, the greater presentation is made on caddies and caddy spoons, tea kettles and urns, teapots and strainers.

It is only natural that as time passes certain items such as sugar nips, ratafia glasses, drip-catchers and even tea cosies can be forgotten, however fashionable they may have been in their day.

A good way for the new collector to understand more about tea and coffee equipment and accessories is to study the 'tea and coffee portrait' paintings which became a popular genre in the paintings of the 18th and 19thC. Such pictures as the poet John Gay and his sisters taking tea (V & A) or the 'Coffee Portrait' by Januarius Zick, Archiv fur Kunst und Geschichte Berlin, proved that tea and coffee had taken its place as an official element of European culture.

Caddy Spoons

These delightful spoons (alas no longer required with a teabag) originated from the strainer spoons which were considered such an essential part of early tea making equipage.

The early Chinese tea canisters with their high rounded turrets used pull off caps which doubled as measures, but since it is easier to measure tea out into a teapot by spoon – rather than shaking – the bowl of the strainer spoon (albeit pierced) would have been used.

This multi-purpose object would not only take tea out of the canister (no other spoon shape would fit into the narrow necks of early caddies) but also acted as a strainer as the tea was poured, and if that was not enough, you could dislodge with the pointed stem any tea leaves stuck in the spout.

The change to the shape associated with the caddy spoon came about around 1760 when the caddy openings became larger and they accepted the broad shell shaped caddy spoon more easily for use within the area of the caddy itself. It is reasonable to suggest that the British, preferring stronger tea to the Chinese, would wish to use more tea and it is significant that as the caddies became more open at the top the strainer spoons disappeared and the caddy spoon emerged triumphant.

A rare collection of English caddy spoons, dating from 1799-1809.
$70-900 each

A Victorian leaf bowl caddy spoon, with a hollow vine decorated handle, by George Unite, Birmingham 1869.
$260-360

A Victorian caddy spoon, by Hunt and Roskell, London 1867.
$550-650

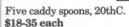

Five caddy spoons, 20thC.
$18-35 each

These inexpensive caddy spoons could prove to be an ideal start to a collection.

Make the Most of Miller's

In Miller's we do NOT just reprint saleroom estimates. We work from realised prices either from an auction room or a dealer. Our consultants then work out a realistic price range for a similar piece. This is to try to avoid repeating freak results – either low or high

Coffee Pots

When coffee first came to these shores from the Middle East in the early 17thC it was made by boiling after the Eastern tradition with either the Baghdad boiler, the Ethiopian Jabena, or the Turkish Ibrik.

In the coffee houses however, the coffee made in bulk over the fire grates was decanted into serving pots of ewer shape as depicted on coffee house tokens of the time. To the English silversmith it would have been easier to produce a tapering cylinder or beer tankard shape for coffee with a single seam and this became the mode for our first coffee pots.

Originally, to facilitate serving, the handle was at right angles to the spout, but gradually, as coffee began to be served in the home and people no doubt helped themselves at the table (servants served from a standing position) the handle was made opposite the spout. Ceramic coffee pots followed a similar course.

A George I coffee pot, engraved with armorials, with wood scroll handle, on a base with scratch weight 28:18 and initials I.S., maker's mark worn, Robert Timbrell and Joseph Bell, London 1714, 10½in (26cm) high, 29.1oz gross.
$10,000-14,500

Provenance: By descent in the Hoare family, traditionally known as part of the Kelsey plate. Charles Hoare, born 1767, purchased the estate of Luscombe, near Dawlish. He died in 1851 and bequeathed his property to his nephew, Peter Richard Hoare, of Kelsey Park, near Beckenham, Kent.

A George IV coffee pot, chased and embossed, engraved with a coat-of-arms, by Benjamin Smith, London 1825, the matched stand on 3 cast foliate feet, complete with burner, 13in (33cm) high, 63oz.
$7,000-7,500

The arms are those of Bogle. When such pots as this had a support inside for a linen bag to contain the coffee and were held on a spirit heater they were frequently called biggins.

A George II coffee pot, with leaf capped fluted curved spout, hinged domed cover and baluster finial, engraved with a coat-of-arms within a rococo cartouche, the base with initials, by John Swift, 1742, 9in (23cm) high, 23oz gross.
$5,500-7,000

A Staffordshire coffee pot, c1765, 7in (18cm) high.
$6,500-7,000

A Leeds coffee pot, painted with the Miss Pitt decoration, c1780, 9in (23cm).
$4,000-4,500

A Liverpool coffee pot and cover, painted in underglaze blue, iron red and gilding within trellis pattern rims, Philip Christian's factory, c1770, some damage, 9½in (24cm) high.
$650-750

A baluster coffee pot, with an ebonised wood scroll handle, in the French 18thC taste, S.W.S. & Co., London 1920, 7in (18cm), 25.25oz.
$700-800

A George III coffee pot, with Newcastle hallmark, c1755, 8½in (21cm) high, 19.5oz.
$650-800

A George III coffee pot, with a shell polished wood double scroll handle and gadrooned domed hinged cover with spiral twist finial, one side engraved with an armorial within a rococo foliate cartouche, the other side engraved with a crest, maker's initials I.K. with a pellet between, London 1770, 10½in (26cm) high, 29.75oz.
$5,500-7,000

A George III coffee jug on stand with burner, by Paul Storr, London 1803, 13in (34cm), 53.5oz.
$10,000-11,000

A George II coffee pot, with curved spout, waisted hinged cover and baluster finial, engraved with a coat-of-arms and flat chased with bands of scrolls, shells, strapwork and latticework, by John White, 1737, 8½in (21cm) high, 24oz.
$5,500-7,000

An early George III baluster pattern coffee pot with repoussé and chased decoration and blackwood scroll handle, 8in (20cm) high, 18oz.
$2,600-3,600

A Staffordshire saltglazed coffee pot, c1765, 8½in (21cm) high.
$4,500-5,500

A George II embossed and chased coffee pot, the spout with rocaille decoration, wood scroll handle, by Fuller White, London 1751, 10in (25cm) high, 26.5oz.
$3,500-4,500

Posters

A further way to study the history of tea and coffee is through its associated ephemera.

A Horniman's Almanac, 1887.
$200-250

An International Stores calendar advertising Ceylindo Tea, 1908.
$150-200

An advertisement for Indian tea depicting Queen Victoria offering tea to President McKinley of the United States, 1897.
$350-450

A Mazawattee Tea Calendar, 1927.
$150-200

A tea chest label, late 19thC.
$200-250

Labels on tea chests were necessary to identify the particular consignment of teas.

The front cover of a song sheet for Lewis's Beautiful Tea, early 20thC.
$200-250

Tea & Coffee Services

Towards the end of the 17thC tea and coffee services on trays became popular, with a servant carrying a tray into the drawing room, stating the social standing of the owners.

A Worcester boxed set of coffee cups and saucers, signed and painted by Harry Stinton, with gilt interiors and 6 silver gilt spoons, marked in puce, date code for 1931.
$5,000-6,500

A four-piece silver tea set and tray, Mappin and Webb, c1948.
$11,000-12,000

A New Hall topographical part tea and coffee service, each piece printed and painted in colours with country views or views of stately homes, some named, gilt line edges, comprising: 8 tea cups, 7 coffee cans, 8 saucers, milk jug, sucrier and cover, slop bowl, teapot stand, saucer dish, some faults, one saucer marked in brown with New Hall within rings, some pieces with puce pattern No. 984, the slop bowl with puce 'fern leaf' and pattern No. 984, 29 pieces.
$1,500-1,800

A Victorian tea and coffee service, retailed by Hunt & Roskell, late Storr, Mortimer & Hunt, London 1850, 64.5oz.
$3,000-3,500

A Sèvres monogrammed part tea service, printed with the gilt initials LP, the handles and rims enriched with gilding, comprising a teapot and cover, a milk jug, 2 sugar bowls and covers, 5 tea cups and 7 saucers, blue printed marks, some damage, various dates, iron red Château de Tuileries marks, incised marks, c1840.
$900-1,200

A four-piece silver tea set, by Georg Jensen, designed by Johan Rohde, c1950.
$11,000-12,000

An English porcelain part miniature tea service, painted in colours and signed Leighton, comprising a lobed hexagonal teapot and cover, a lobed milk jug, 6 cups and saucers, gilding slightly rubbed
$580-680

A Staffordshire part tea and coffee service, pattern No. 586, mid-19thC.
$2,000-3,000

A Meissen Hausmalerei part tea service, painted in underglaze blue in the Oriental style, enriched in overglaze enamels in the workshop of F. J. Ferner, the borders and underglaze blue decoration enriched with gilding, comprising: a teapot and cover, 4 tea bowls and saucers, with blue crossed sword marks, various painter's initials and numerals, various Dreher's marks and Pressnummern, some damage, the porcelain c1735, the decoration c1750.
$3,500-5,500

A Japanese export five-piece silver tea set and tray, c1880.
$32,000-36,000

A five-piece tea service, with cut card type trefoil terminals, Sheffield 1935, with a matching two-handled tray of oval form with piecrust border, London 1936, 3,599gr total.
$3,000-3,600

A Chinese export silver four-piece tea service with tongs, each engraved with initial, except tongs, in fitted wood box, late 19thC, teapot 5½in (14cm) high, 37.5oz.
$5,500-6,500

A George IV Irish three-piece tea service, by James Fray, each piece richly repoussé and engraved with an armorial crest, Dublin 1826, 1,543gr.
$2,000-3,000

A five-piece tea and coffee set, each piece of square baluster form with broad lobes, wooden handles and finials, the coffee pot Utrecht 1963, maker's mark VKB, the remainder Utrecht 1940/41, maker's mark VKG.
$1,200-1,800

An Edwardian Scottish composite eight-piece tea and coffee service, each piece engraved with a crest of a fly above the motto 'Non Sibi', comprising teapot, coffee pot, hot water jug and kettle, all with covers, ebony finials and handles, slop basin, two-handled sugar basin and milk jug and a large two-handled fitted tray, of rounded quatrefoil form, Glasgow 1903/4, by R. and W. Sorley, tea and coffee service, 2,904gr.
$4,000-4,500

A Coalport fluted part tea service, painted between bands in pink and gilding, comprising a teapot, cover and stand, a milk jug, a slop bowl, a sugar bowl and cover, a bread plate, 11 teacups, 4 coffee cans and 10 saucers, some damage.
$1,000-1,500

A set of 6 Meissen monogrammed tea cups and saucers, painted with garlands of flowers forming the initials VH beneath a gilt and iron red coronet, flanked by sprays of blue flowers, enriched with gilding, some damage, blue crossed swords and dot marks, blue Bs to cups, various Pressnummern to saucers and 18 to cups, c1770.
$2,600-3,600

FURTHER INFORMATION
For further information on the subject of Tea and Coffee Equipage, contact:-
The Bramah Tea Collection
3 Oakmount Road
Chandlers Ford
Hampshire SO5 2LG
Tel: (0703) 269443

Tea Caddies

It is not only because caddies take up such little space both to collect and display that we feature them so prominently in this section. They represent all the changes in style for the 18th and 19thC and the popularity and passing of different materials can be studied with total fascination. Tea canisters, tea chests and caddies represent so much of our history.

It was the tea canister from China that came first. Being made of china, silver, tin or pewter they combined the dual function of keeping the tea fresh and a means by which it could be measured out in their pull-off caps.

A fashion developed for placing two or three canisters together in what became known as a tea chest which frequently included sugar nips, a sugar strainer spoon and teaspoons.

The tea 'caddy', being simply a box for tea, came along later in the 18thC and the word is a corruption of 'catty' the Malayan Kati which is about 1⅓lb of tea, which is a convenient measure for packing.

Apart from the essential need to keep tea fresh, the tea chest and caddies coincided with the extremely high cost of tea and so the tea was kept under lock and key. Silver examples date mostly from the 18thC when silversmithing was at its best.

In addition to china and silver caddies, the materials used for either the total constitution or decoration included paper, papier mâché, tortoiseshell, ivory, glass, enamel and a whole host of woods for general marquetry and exotic veneers.

An English blue and white tea caddy, c1750, 4in (10cm) high.
$1,200-1,500

A pair of George II silver tea caddies and matching sugar bowl, the caddy covers now pierced and surmounted by cast rocaille finials, by Samuel Taylor, marked on bases, caddies London 1748, 6in (15cm) high, sugar bowl 1749, 5in (13cm) high, 29oz.
$3,500-4,500

A shagreen three-division tea caddy, with spoon compartments, the interior velvet lined, with brass handle and escutcheon plate, on paw feet, 11½in (29cm) wide.
$450-550

A George III silver sugar box and matching tea caddy, with a similar tea caddy, each marked on base and cover, by Pierre Gillois, London 1760 and 1765, each 5½in (14cm) high, 30oz.
$3,500-5,500

A Queen Anne silver tea caddy, by Samuel Thorne, London 1703, marked on side, cover and cap, 5in (13cm) high, 7oz.
$8,000-9,000

A George III silver tea caddy, marked on base and cover, by Pierre Gillois, London 1763, 5in (13cm) high, 8.5oz.
$1,500-2,500

A George II silver tea caddy, the hinged cover with a cast foliate finial, the sides and cover repoussé and chased with a wave pattern, marked on base and cover, by William Cripps, London 1756, 6in (15cm) high, 12.5oz.
$3,500-5,500

A commemorative tea caddy, depicting George III and Queen Charlotte, c1762, 6in (15cm) high.
$1,800-2,000

A Worcester porcelain tea canister and cover, 18thC.
$550-700

A Queen Anne tea caddy and detachable cover with shaped finial, the base engraved with initials, by Ebenezer Roe, 1711, 5in (13cm) high, 6oz.
$3,500-4,500

A pair of George III enamel tea caddies and a matching sugar box, the caddies inscribed 'Green' and 'Bohea', each enamelled green with 4 polychrome painted landscape scenes surrounded by gilt rocaille, South Staffordshire, c1760, caddies 4in (10cm) high and sugar box 3½in (9cm) high.
$12,000-14,500

Please refer to index for boxes elsewhere in this book

A Worcester tea jar, decorated in colours with the thunder and lightning pattern, c1770.
$250-450

A pair of George II tea caddies and a matching sugar box, the caddies each with sliding base and cover, the sugar box on 4 bracket feet, each engraved with a coat-of-arms within a rococo cartouche, maker's mark W.A., contained in a silver mounted shagreen case on 4 claw and ball feet, 1756, caddies 5in (13cm) high, 43oz.
$22,000-24,000

The arms are those of Medley quartering and impaling others.

A George III fruitwood tea caddy, in the form of an apple, 4in (10cm) high.
$1,500-1,800

A yew veneered and tulipwood banded tea caddy, the cut corners with boxwood inlay, the cover and front with conch shell paterae, late 18thC, 5in (13cm) wide.
$1,000-1,200

A set of 2 George II tea caddies and a sugar bowl and cover, the caddies with sliding bases and cap covers with shell finials, the sugar bowl on foliage foot, with domed cover and bud finial, engraved with a coat-of-arms and motto and a crest and motto, by Samuel Taylor, 1748, with 2 Hanoverian rat tailed teaspoons, 1887 and a pair of pierced sugar tongs, c1780, in a silver mounted fitted wood case, 41oz.
$14,500-16,500

The arms are those of Reid impaling Clayton for General Sir Thomas Reid G.C.B. who married in 1835 Elizabeth, daughter of John Clayton of Enfield Old Park, Middlesex, the crest and motto are those of Reid.

Two George II silver tea caddies, in a shagreen case, both with gadrooned rims, case with silver furniture and later velvet lining, one by Samuel Taylor, one unmarked, London, c1745, 6in (15cm) high, 25.5oz.
$5,500-7,000

A pair of George III silver tea caddies, each marked on base and cover, maker's mark WT, probably William Tuite, London 1773, 5in (13cm) high, 17.5oz.
$2,500-3,500

A set of 3 bombé tea caddies and sugar box, by Pierre Gillois, 1755, 33oz.
$10,000-11,000

A pair of George II silver tea caddies and a matching sugar box, in shagreen case with hinged cover opening to a velvet lined fitted interior with silver gadrooning, the exterior mounted with silver furniture, marked on bases and covers, by John Sidaway, caddies and sugar box marked WA, London 1759, each 5in (13cm) high, 31oz.
$4,500-5,500

A pair of black japanned and mother-of-pearl inlaid tole peinte tea canisters, with mother-of-pearl mosaic, gilt decoration to neck and lid, some damage, early 19thC, 19in (48cm).
$1,800-2,000

A George III silver tea caddy and a sugar basket, the caddy surmounted by a figure of a Chinese man, marked in interior, the sugar basket with a red glass liner, marked on the base, in a shagreen case with brass furniture and fitted with a velvet lined interior, c1771, caddy 5in (13cm) high, basket 5in (13cm) diam, 15.5oz.
$6,500-8,000

The maker's mark ED in script may be an unrecorded mark for Edward Darvill, a maker of tea caddies in this period.

A George III silver tea caddy, on 4 foliate scroll feet, marked on base and cover, by William Vincent, London 1768, 5½in (14cm) high, 11oz.
$2,000-3,000

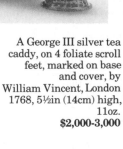

A George III tea caddy, the sides and cover finely engraved, with narrow feather edge borders, maker's mark I.L., 1772, 4½in (11cm) high, 6oz.
$3,500-4,500

An ivory veneered and tortoiseshell strung tea caddy of decagonal outline, with mother-of-pearl inlaid swag and silver mounts, later re-lined, late 18thC, 4in (10cm) wide.
$1,800-2,000

A George III tea caddy, the cover with urn finial and engraved crest over monogram, marked on base and cover, by William Vincent, London 1785, 5in (13cm) high, 13oz.
$2,600-3,600

A George III silver tea caddy, with an iron lock, marked on base and cover, by Henry Chawner, London 1793, 6in (14cm) high, 12oz.
$5,500-6,500

A wood and paper filigree caddy, early 19thC.
$1,000-1,200

A Victorian silver plated tea caddy, on a scrolled base, unmarked, after Paul de Lamerie, 19thC, 5½in (14cm) high.
$800-1,000

A Regency tortoiseshell tea caddy, the covers with turned ivory handles, the whole outlined and crossed with pewter stringing, upon 4 ball feet, 5in (13cm).
$1,000-1,200

A Georgian mahogany and satinwood shell inlaid tea caddy, with fitted interior and 2 glass containers with plated tops.
$1,200-1,600

A tortoiseshell and mother-of-pearl tea caddy, the hinged top enclosing 2 compartments, on bun feet, in need of restoration, 19thC, 7in (18cm) wide.
$700-800

A George III silver tea caddy, with inscription 'In remembrance/A mother's gift', and script initials centering a crest, marked on base and cover, by Thomas Holland, London 1806, 5in (12cm) high.
$2,000-3,000

A pair of George III tea caddies, in a fitted silver mounted and ivory case inlaid with flowers and foliage, by Robert Garrard, 1819, the silver mounts also 1819, 35oz.
$18,000-21,000

The design of these caddies follows that of a set by Thomas Heming of 1752 which is a variation of a model by Paul de Lamerie of 1751. It was later used by a number of goldsmiths including Frederick Vonham in 1763.

A quality veneered tea casket, mid-19thC.
$1,500-1,800

A pair of George II silver tea caddies, by Samuel Herbert & Co., London, marked on base, 1752, 5in (13cm) high, 14.5oz.
$3,000-4,500

The arms are those of Williams-Wynn impaling those of another.

A Georgian mahogany tea caddy, inlaid with stained and coloured woods, with classical columns and medallions containing stylised oak leaves, the hinged cover opening to reveal a zinc lined interior, slight damage, 5in (13cm) high.
$350-450

A Regency burr yew fitted tea caddy, the sides applied with brass lion's mask and ring handles, on 4 brass lion's paw feet, the interior with 2 covered compartments, c1815, 7in (18cm) wide.
$550-700

An early Victorian tortoiseshell tea caddy, the hinged top enclosing 2 compartments, on ivory bun feet, c1840, 7in (18cm) wide.
$1,000-1,500

A George III satinwood and mahogany fitted tea caddy with painted scenes, the compartment covers also painted with reserves labelled 'Bohea' and 'Green', within polychrome bouquets, c1790, 8in (19cm) wide.
$2,600-3,600

A George III silver tea caddy, with an iron lock, marked on base and cover, by Paul Storr, London 1793, 5in (13cm) high, 13.5oz.
$8,000-9,000

A George III fruitwood tea caddy, in the form of a pear, with associate turned ivory knop and steel escutcheon, 7½in (19cm) high.
$2,600-3,600

A George III tortoiseshell veneered tea caddy, 8in (20cm).
$1,000-1,200

A George III silver tea caddy, marked on base and cover, by Hester Bateman, London 1789, 5in (13cm) high, 13oz.
$3,500-5,500

A George III inlaid yew double tea caddy, the compartment with 2 later covers, the cover and front inlaid with green stained and shaded harewood oval panels, one with fox and grapes and one with heron, the edges with inlaid banding, c1800, 7in (18cm) wide.
$1,600-2,000

Two George II and George III engraved tea caddies, one by Edward Wakelin, c1755, maker's mark and lion passant only, the other by J. Langford and J. Sebille, 1764, 28oz.
$7,000-9,000

A Victorian silver tea caddy, engraved with armorials, marked on base, cover and finial, cover with French import control mark, by John Edward Terrey, London 1844, 7in (18cm) high, 35oz.
$2,600-3,600

A late Victorian tortoiseshell veneered tea caddy, the sides with foliate silver handles, the lid with foliate pierced mount, shield shaped escutcheon, raised on bun feet, the mounts with Chester assay office hallmark 1894, 5in (13cm) wide.
$2,600-3,600

A Victorian tortoiseshell veneered and pewter strung 2 division tea caddy, of pagoda shape, the interior with lidded compartments, 9in (23cm) wide.
$1,600-2,000

A pair of Regency silver tea caddies, marked on side and cover, by Samuel Hennell, London 1819, 5in (13cm) high, 20.5oz.
$3,500-5,500
The arms are those of Lees of Blackrock, Dublin, created baronets in 1804.

A promotional caddy, made by Maling for Ringtons Tea Company, early 20thC.
$200-300

A Regency tortoiseshell and pewter strung tea caddy, interior with 2 lidded compartments, raised on 4 ball feet, 6in (15cm) wide.
$1,000-1,500

453

A William IV 2 division tortoiseshell and pewter strung tea caddy, inlaid with foliate cut mother-of-pearl, pillars to the corners, on shaped base with ivory ball feet, 8in (20cm) wide.
$2,000-3,000

A Regency tortoiseshell veneered 2 division tea caddy, the bow front profusely inlaid with foliate cut brass scrolls, the cover with ball handle, 7in (18cm) wide.
$2,600-3,600

A Regency octagonal tortoiseshell and ivory outlined tea caddy, the lid with silvered loop handle and escutcheon plate, 5in (13cm) wide.
$1,500-2,000

A Continental silver tea canister, 19thC, 5in (12cm).
$550-650

A Russian silver tea caddy, marked on the base St. Petersburg, 1786, assaymaster Nikifor Moshchalkin, 5in (13cm) high, 9oz.
$1,800-2,800

A George III green stained tortoiseshell and ivory outlined tea caddy, the lid inset with a gold crest, the interior with 2 lidded compartments, 7in (18cm) wide.
$3,000-3,600

A pair of George III tea caddies and matching sugar box, finely cast and chased in the Chinese Chippendale manner, with hinged covers and lizard handles, by Peter Taylor, in original shark skin covered box, scroll handle and pierced escutcheon, London 1747, 4in (10cm) high, 53oz.
$32,000-36,000

An early Victorian tortoiseshell veneered, pewter strung serpentine fronted tea caddy, the cover and front inlaid with mother-of-pearl and haliotis shell designs of song birds amidst foliage, on bun feet, 9in (23cm) wide.
$1,600-1,800

A Regency boxwood, herringbone banded and paper scroll tea caddy, of navette shape, 8in (20cm) wide.
$1,000-1,200

A French glass tea caddy, late 19thC.
$650-800

A Meissen tea caddy and cover, brightly painted in underglaze blue, crossed swords in blue, minute chip, c1735, 4½in (11cm).
$5,500-6,500

A George IV silver double tea caddy, marked on side and covers, by Joseph Cradock and William K. Reid, London 1825, 7in (18cm) wide, 27oz.
$2,600-3,600

An Austro-Hungarian sugar box or tea caddy, with gilt interior, lock, and maker's mark AK, Vienna 1858, 6in (15cm), 12.25oz.
$650-750

A Regency Scottish silver tea caddy, fitted with an iron lock, marked on base, by William & Patrick Cunningham, Edinburgh 1818, 6½in (16cm) high, 26oz.
$1,800-2,800

An Austro-Hungarian caddy, the cover with a baluster finial, upper border embossed paterae and husk chains, foliate panel feet, with gilt interior, maker's mark R.O., 5in (13cm) wide, 9.25oz.
$450-550

A Meissen ormolu mounted tea caddy, painted, beneath a gilt line rim, blue crossed swords mark, the ormolu mount inscribed Escalier de Crystal Paris and the cover cast with foliage, gilding rubbed c1740, 5in (12cm) high.
$3,500-4,500

A Chinese black lacquer tea caddy inlaid with mother-of-pearl, the top enclosing a well with 2 silk-lined trays, the sides with carrying handles, on a later ebonised stand with square tapering legs, 19thC, 17in (43cm).
$1,500-1,800

A late Victorian tortoiseshell veneered tea canister.
$900-1,000

A Victorian burr elm tea caddy, with rosewood interior, fitted with 2 cut glass caddies and an open sugar bowl, mid-19thC, 14in (36cm) wide.
$650-800

A Russian silver mounted cut glass tea caddy, the silver cap chased with a foliate guilloche border and engraved with a monogram and coronet lifting above a silver rim and inner cover, the mounts marked with the Imperial warrant of Faberge, Moscow, 1899-1908, 6in (15cm) high.
$1,800-3,000

A Chinese silver and enamelled tea canister, made in Peking, c1880.
$3,000-4,000

A Meissen Kakiemon tea caddy, painted with sprays of peony and chrysanthemum and scattered insects, the sides each with a flying phoenix and the shoulders with iron red flower heads, Pressnummer 49, c1740, 4in (10cm) high.
$1,600-2,000

A Regency silver plated tea caddy, on 4 lion's paw feet, the front engraved with a coat-of-arms, the fitted interior with a pair of caddies and a cut glass sugar bowl, marked on base, c1815, 13½in (34cm) wide.
$2,600-3,600

A Russian silver tea caddy, marked Moscow, maker's mark Cyrillic G L, c1890, 5in (13cm) high, 13oz.
$1,600-2,600

A tortoiseshell veneered tea caddy, late Georgian, 8in (20cm) wide.
$1,200-1,400

Make the Most of Miller's

CONDITION is absolutely vital when assessing the value of an antique. Damaged pieces on the whole appreciate much less than perfect examples. However a rare, desirable piece may command a high price even when damaged

A Chinese export carved ivory tea caddy, the cover and sides relief-carved, on 4 claw and ball feet, the hinged cover opening to 2 compartments, 19thC, 9½in (24cm) long.
$1,400-1,800

An Indian Colonial silver tea caddy, with wood finial, the sides decorated with 4 reeded bands, the front with script monogram, fitted with iron lock, by William Henry Twentyman, marked on base, c1820, 5in (13cm), 18oz.
$3,500-4,500

Tea & Coffee Urns

In spite of their size, urns especially in silver, are outstandingly elegant. The boiling water – or made tea or coffee poured inside – could be kept hot by the red hot iron bar, dropped into a socket inside the urn, or by charcoals kept in the base from which hot air rose through a tub inside the urn, extending up to the lid.

A Scottish coffee urn, on leaf capped shell and paw cabriole supports, with serpent handles and plain spigot with ebony handle, by Hugh Gordon, other marks rubbed, Edinburgh, c1750, 11in (28cm), 53oz.
$3,000-3,600

A German japanned tea urn, mid-19thC.
$5,500-6,500

A German two-handled fluted pear-shaped coffee urn, the customary 3 taps have been removed, the cover has a later plated Walpole crest finial and the body is engraved 'Ye lucke of Walpole', by Johann Georg Kloss, Augsburg, 1747/1749, 12in (31cm).
$3,600-4,600

A George III silver chinoiserie tea urn, with 2 branch handles and a dolphin-form spigot with wood grip, the cover with a cast finial of a Chinaman, the front engraved with a coat-of-arms within rocaille cartouche, marked on body, base and cover, by Thomas Whipham and Charles Wright, London 1767, 20in (51cm), 97oz.
$18,000-22,000

The arms are those of Daubuz impaling those of Powderdon.

A George III vase shaped tea urn, with foliate scroll handles, shaped tap and detachable cover, engraved with a coat-of-arms within a foliate scroll cartouche, on later detachable wood base, by Daniel Smith and Robert Sharp, 1771, 20in (51cm), 107oz. excluding wood base.
$6,500-7,500

The arms are those of Stanmore, Middlesex, quartering Port, of Poole, Co. Dorset.

A Staffordshire tea urn, late 19thC.
$260-360

457

A George III tea urn, the cover with bud finial, with egg and dart and foliage borders and circular detachable lamp, engraved with a coat-of-arms, crest and motto, by Benjamin Smith, 1819, the spirit lamp by Paul Storr, 1812, 15½in (40cm), 181oz.
$7,000-9,000

The arms, crest and motto are those of Neeld, for Joseph Neeld, the great-nephew and principal beneficiary of Philip Rundell's will, from whom he inherited in 1827. He was M.P. for Chippenham from 1830 until his death in 1856, a governor of his old school, Harrow, from 1828 until 1836, and a member of many learned societies, including the Society of Arts, and the Royal Geographical Society.

A George III coffee urn, on 4 ball feet, with drop ring handles, detachable domed cover and spirally fluted finial, the interior with detachable sleeve, by Peter and Ann Bateman, 1799, 14in (36cm), 43oz.
$3,500-4,500

Tea Kettles

Since tea was made in the mid-18thC by the lady of the house the constant supply of hot water was catered for by the magnificent tea kettles which filled the delicate teapots. Through the years the tea kettle shape followed the teapot exactly, except for capacity. With the handle above and the tripod table and spirit heater and tray below they stood in total splendour. Towards the end of the 18thC however, the tea kettle was usurped by the tea urn, which with the convenience of a tap was more accurate in its use.

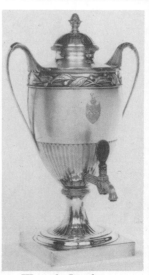

A George III partly fluted tea urn, engraved with a coat-of-arms, the cover with a crest, by John Wakelin and William Taylor, 1785, 18½in (47cm), 110oz.
$9,000-10,000

The arms are those of Robinson impaling Harris, for the Hon. Frederick Robinson, second son of the 1st Baron Grantham who married Catherine Harris.

A Queen Anne tea kettle, stand and lamp, with scrolling swing handle and detachable lamp, engraved with a coat-of-arms in Baroque cartouche, the kettle by John Jackson, 1708, the stand and lamp, c1710, maker's mark only, probably that of William Fawdery, 11in (28cm), 51oz.
$12,000-13,000

A Japanese silver tea kettle with Shakudo style decoration, c1880.
$6,500-7,000

A silver tea kettle, by Richard Gurney, London, 1756.
$5,500-6,500

A George III silver tea urn, with 2 beaded loop handles and a beaded spigot with stained bone grip, on 4 ball feet, the rim, shoulder and base applied with beaded borders, the front engraved with an oval cartouche enclosing a coat-of-arms in a shield, marked on base, body and cover, by Robert Hennell, London 1781, 13in (33cm), 95oz.
$4,500-65,00

TEA KETTLES
* ★ made from silver or other metals
* ★ a vessel intended for boiling water at the table
* ★ designed to sit over a spirit lamp

458

A Tetsubin tea kettle, mid-19thC.
$350-450

A George II inverted pear-shaped tea kettle, stand and lamp, the kettle with scalework and mask spout, partly wicker covered scroll swing handle and hinged domed cover with wrythen finial, the kettle and lamp engraved with a coat-of-arms, by John Jacobs, 1754, 15in (38cm), 76oz.
$6,500-7,500

A Victorian silver tea kettle, stand and burner, fully marked, by George John Richards, London 1851, 16½in (42cm), 75.5oz.
$3,000-3,500

A German ceramic tea kettle and cover, the body moulded in relief in the Chinese style, the body covered with a red-glazed imitation cinnabar lacquer, chipped, impressed marks, 12½in (32cm).
$180-220

A Tetsubin cast iron tea kettle, mid-19thC.
$550-700

Teapots

Teapots originated in China then went to Japan when a glazed stoneware became the accepted pottery of the Tea Ceremony. Holland was the first European country to see tea porcelains which arrived with the tea which served as the pattern for later productions in both china and silver wares made in Holland, Germany, France and England.

A George III silver teapot, with a hinged cover, an ebonised finial and carved wood handle, by Hester Bateman, marked on base and cover, 5½in (14cm), 12oz.
$2,000-3,000

A silver teapot with chinoiserie decoration, after Chinese export silver model, made by I. E. Terry, 1682 London hallmarks, 1816.
$10,000-11,000

A rare Worcester polychrome teapot and cover, painted with the spinning maiden pattern, with iron red saw-tooth borders, minor damage, c1760, 6in (15cm).
$2,000-3,000

A Chinese 'famille verte' porcelain teapot, with scroll spout and handle, Kang Hsi, 5in (12cm).
$3,200-4,000

An American silver tank teapot with similar milk and water tanks, early 1920s.
$21,000-27,000

Make the Most of Miller's

CONDITION is absolutely vital when assessing the value of an antique. Damaged pieces on the whole appreciate much less than perfect examples. However a rare, desirable piece may command a high price even when damaged

A late George III teapot, with melon fluted ivory finial, raised on 4 ball feet, by T. Robins, London 1811, 498gr.
$650-750

An early Victorian teapot with floral finial, on scroll cast feet, by Reiley & Storer, London 1843.
$800-900

A Meissen painted teapot and cover, with wishbone scroll handle picked out in gilt, minor chips to knop, crossed swords in underglaze blue, c1760, 3in (7cm).
$1,000-1,500

A Meissen teapot formed as a crowing cockerel, with black, grey and brown plumage, the exotic tail forming the handle and open beak the spout, with iron red wattle and comb beneath a feathered crest, tip of open beak missing, Pressnummer 4, c1740.
$5,500-6,500

A Japanese earthenware teapot, with cream coloured body, painted in enamels and gilt with wisteria, butterflies and garden flowers, partially rubbed seal mark in gilt, possibly of Meizan, 4in (10cm) high.
$650-900

A George III silver teapot, with carved wood handle and turned wood finial, by Paul Storr, London, 1793, marked on base and cover, 6in (15cm) high, 15oz.
$2,600-3,600

A Regency ogee teapot, chased in high relief, the cover with cast oak apple finial, scroll wood handle, on maiden head/paw feet, by Edward Cornelius Farrell, London 1817, 24oz.
$1,600-2,000

A George IV silver teapot of compressed circular form, maker's mark WH London 1823, 25.75oz.
$700-800

A George III silver teapot, part fluted, London 1812.
$550-650

A George III teapot, with elongated tapering spout and fruitwood scroll handle with spur thumbpiece, matching stand on claw and ball feet, maker's mark RG, Edinburgh, with incuse duty mark, 1784, 6in (15cm), 21oz.
$3,500-4,500

l. A Victorian silver teapot, London 1856.
$900-1,000
r. A Victorian silver teapot, by Charles Thomas Fox and George Fox, London 1841.
$450-550

An English creamware teapot and cover, painted in puce monochrome, with leaf handle terminals enriched in puce and green, restored, c1775, 5in (13cm).
$350-550

A teapot on stand after Paul Revere, by George C. Gebelein, Boston, c1930, 11in (28cm) wide, 28oz gross.
$2,200-2,800

A George III teapot with ebonised wood scroll handle, wood finial, bright cut with floral and foliate swags and later engraved with a monogram, by John Emes, London 1804, 5in (13cm), 16.5oz.
$1,000-1,200

A silver teapot by Ephraim Brasher, New York, c1790, 7in (17cm) high, 18oz gross.
$4,500-5,000

Tea Strainers

Three single cup tea strainers, complete with retaining chains, the forerunner of the teabag, 20thC.
$5-9 plated
$90+ each silver

A silver lemon strainer by Jacob Hurd, Boston, marked on each handle, c1750, 11in (28cm) long, 3½oz.
$3,500-4,000

A silver lemon strainer by William Burt, Boston, minor repairs, marked on each handle W. BURT, c1745, 10½in (27cm) long, 3½oz.
$5,000-5,500

A selection of tea strainers, 20thC.
$9-90 each

Two spring single cup tea makers, mid-20thC.
$9-18 each

Miscellany

An unusual pair of ceramic tea strainers, 19thC.
$180-230

A plated self-balancing tea strainer, ensuring that all drips are caught in the bottom basin, early 20thC.
$90-180

A silver strainer and stand, mid-20thC.
$140-200

A Victorian silk velvet and beadwork tea cosy, of typical form, the purple silk velvet ground applied with thistles and flowers on one side and Tudor roses and flowers on the other, the interior of quilted purple silk, with beaded carrying handle, 19thC, 15in (38cm) wide.
$450-550

Space prohibits us from showing more than one tea cosy in this section!

We wish to pose the question, where is all the miscellaneous tea and coffee equipment?

WINE ANTIQUES

A George III mahogany cellaret, the veneered and rosewood crossbanded top now enclosing a compartment tray, the sides applied with swing handles, on supports of square section with casters, c1790.
$2,000-3,000

A George III mahogany cellaret-on-stand, the hinged top enclosing compartments on a reduced stand with moulded supports, c1800.
$1,000-1,200

A rosewood liquor cabinet, containing 4 decanters and 12 glasses, the sides inlaid with beechwood lines, c1900, 11½in (29cm) wide.
$1,000-1,200

A late George III mahogany brass bound cellaret on stand, with crossbanded and fruitwood strung hinged lid, with later fitted interior between brass carrying handles, the stand possibly associated, 17½in (44cm) wide.
$2,600-3,600

A late George III mahogany and inlaid cellaret, the hinged lid enclosing a fitted interior, on a fluted banded base, adapted, 25½in (65cm) wide.
$2,600-3,600

A William IV mahogany cellaret, with stepped hinged lid, the interior with compartments, with panelled front on turned reeded legs headed by capitals, with brass caps, 27in (69cm) high.
$2,000-3,000

A Regency mahogany sarcophagus shaped wine cooler.
$3,000-4,500

A pair of mahogany brass bound wine coolers, zinc lined, 18thC, 14in (36cm) diam. **$6,500-7,000**

A George III brass bound mahogany wine cooler, the lead lined interior with zinc liner, the ends with brass carrying handles, on square tapering legs with brass caps, 26½in (68cm) wide.
$4,500-5,500

A George III brass bound mahogany wine cooler, the rim banded in fruitwood, with lead lined interior, the ends with brass carrying handles, 19in (48cm) wide.
$3,200-4,000

463

Five London delft bin labels named for Sherry and Champaign in manganese, and Cyder, Perry and Lisbon in underglaze blue, pierced for hanging, some restorations, c1780, 5½in (14cm) long.
$1,800-2,200

Four George III wine coasters, with trelliswork sides and gadrooned borders, the silver bases engraved with a coat-of-arms in plume mantling, by W. Burwash and R. Sibley, 1810.
$14,500-16,500

The arms are those of Henchman or Hinchman, Co. Northampton.

A Battersea enamel and gilt metal mounted wine funnel, the white ground painted in puce with sprays of flowers, 18thC, 3½in (9cm).
$650-750

A pair of Sheffield plate wine coasters, each with scalloped foliate pierced edges, scroll and bead embossed edge, and turned wood base, 6in (15cm).
$200-280

A George III Irish silver wine funnel and stand, by James le Bas, Dublin, 1822, 4.5oz.
$260-360

A pair of silver wine coasters, with turned fruitwood bases, Sheffield, 1925, 5in (13cm).
$1,000-1,100

A wine funnel with embossed decoration, by Charles Fox, London 1818.
$650-700

A brass barrelled King's Screw corkscrew with bone handle and steel side winding handle, applied with a Royal coat-of-arms plaque, the brush lacking.
$550-650

A nickel plated A1 double lever corkscrew, by James Heeley & Sons Ltd.
$260-360

A selection of turned wood handled corkscrews: top row, l. to r., c1840, **$110-130**; c1880, **$40-60**; c1870, **$55-70**; c1830, **$55-70**; c1870, **$95-115**; bottom row: c1840, **$60-75**; c1830 brass stem, **$125-145**

METALWARE

Gold

A Louis XVI gold mounted bonbonnière, the cover set with a miniature under glass, bordered by entwined gold wirework and seed pearls, 2 panels cracked, with the décharge of Henry Clavel, Paris, 1783-89, 2in (5cm) diam. **$3,500-4,500**

A gold mounted double ended hardstone desk seal, formed as an agate column with bloodstone matrices, one engraved with the crest, coronet and garter motto of the Prince of Wales, the base engraved 'to err is human, to forgive divine', the upper mount chased and engraved with foliate scrolls and a reeded band, the lower engraved with chevrons, c1820. **$2,600-3,600**

Pewter

A Scottish lidded pewter flagon, the interior bearing touch mark for J. Gardiner, Edinburgh, 19thC, and a similar unmarked flagon, each 10in (25cm) high. **$1,000-1,200**

Brass

A brass tavern tobacco box with central carrying handle, flanked by 2 lidded compartments, the right hand one having coin slot, retaining original mechanism, raised on bun feet, mid-19thC. **$350-550**

A cylindrical brass hand lantern with hinged door, the candle guard with pierced foliage, late 18thC, 4in (10cm) high. **$200-280**

A quart wine measure, West of England, c1850, 6½in (16.5cm). **$300-360**

An English or Dutch brass brazier, with pierced stand, on tripod scroll feet, with turned wood handle, 18thC, 12in (31cm) long, and 2 copper castellated jelly moulds. **$540-720**

A French copper and brass grape hod of tapering form, embossed with 2 figures carrying a vine branch, coat-of-arms and a cartouche inscribed within 'Armand Lesange, Longnoy, Anno 1749', with iron ring carrying handles, early 19thC, 36in (92cm) high. **$1,000-1,200**

A group of 4 English brass spice and pepper shakers, 18thC, 4-5in (10-12cm) high. **$90-180**

A brass shoe snuff box, c1795, 4½in (11cm). **$550-700**

A Victorian cast brass door stop, 24in (61cm) high. **$360-450**

A brass warming pan, the cover pierced and engraved with a deer shot by an arrow, within a foliate border and the inscription 'In God is all my trust', with iron handle, late 17thC.
$700-900

A brass warming pan, the cover incised with a leaping dog, surrounded by foliate motifs and pierced borders, with engraved steel handle, late 17thC.
$700-1,000

An English brass snuffer and stand, c1740, 6½in (17cm). **$650-800**

An Italian bronze bust of a young faun, on painted plaster socle, 19thC, 18in (46cm) high.
$5,500-7,000

Bronze

A Flemish bronze bust of Pomona, in the style of Gabriel Grupello, on gilt wood pedestal, late 17th/early 18thC, 5½in (14cm).
$2,600-3,600

A bronze bust of King George IV, wearing the Order of the Golden Fleece, after Pistrucci, 8in (20cm) high, on a white marble socle, 19thC.
$700-900

A pair of French bronze busts of Bacchantes, after Clodion, on marble socles and bronze bases, 19thC, 10½in (27cm).
$2,000-2,800

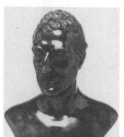

An English bronze bust of Wellington, early 19thC, 12in (31cm) high.
$1,400-1,800

The casting and quality of this bronze are similar to the work of Samuel Parker (fl. 1820-31), who made a series of small bronze busts, some of which are in the Scottish National Portrait Gallery and the Ashmolean Museum, Oxford.

An Italian bronze figure of Bacchus, after Jacopo Sansovino, from the workshop of Massimiliano Soldani-Benzi, some damage, 18thC, 12in (31cm) high.
$2,500-4,500

A bronze figure of a harvester by Charles Levy, signed Faneur Par Ch. Levy, Salon des Beaux-Arts and with foundry stamp, brown patination, c1880, 16½in (42cm).
$2,600-3,600

A French bronze model of a walking bear, cast from a model by Isidore Bonheur, signed I. Bonheur, 19thC, 5in (13cm).
$4,500-5,500

An Austrian cold painted bronze figure group of a quail and 3 chicks, 3in (8cm) high.
$1,200-1,400

A bronze group of 2 bloodhounds, signed A. Dubucard, traces of gilt patination now worn, c1870, 12in (31cm) long.
$2,600-3,600

A Viennese cold painted bronze of a rock dove, the underside of the tail stamped, 5in (13cm) high.
$1,500-1,600

A French bronze model of a bull, cast from a model by Isidore Bonheur, on naturalistic base, signed I Bonheur, numbered underneath in ink, golden brown patina, 19thC, 15in (38cm) high. **$8,000-9,000**

A French bronze figure of a Fribourg milking cow, cast from a model by Isidore Bonheur, the base signed I. Bonheur, the velvet base with title plaque inscribed 'Vache Laitiere Fribourgeoise, 1er Prix, Exposition Universelle 1889', late 19thC, 11in (28cm) high.
$2,000-3,000

A bronze group of 'Chasse à la Perdrix', cast after a model by Pierre-Jules Mêne (1810-79), signed P.J. Mêne, 9in (23cm) high.
$3,000-4,000

This is possibly one of Mêne's best known groups. It was first exhibited in wax at the Salon in 1848.

A French bronze group of 2 stallions, 'L'Accolade', cast from a model by Pierre-Jules Mêne, on naturalistic base signed P J Mêne, reddish gold patina, indistinct ink inscription under base, 19thC, 8in (20cm) high.
$4,500-6,500

A French bronze equestrian group of Louis XIV, cast from a model by Baron Francois-Joseph Bosio, signed Baron Bosio, mid-19thC, 18in (46cm) high.
$3,200-4,500

This sculpture is a reduction of the original commissioned in bronze by the King in 1819. It was cast in 1822 and erected in the Place des Victoires, Paris.

A French bronze group of 2 stalking hounds, cast from a model by Jules Moigniez, signed J. Moigniez, c1865, 8in (20cm) high.
$3,500-4,500

A pair of French bronze groups of Clorinda and Tancred, Clorinda in the process of clubbing her foe, Tancred drawing his sword, respectively inscribed Clorinde and Tancrede, mid-19thC, Clorinda 19in (48cm) and Tancred 18½in (47cm) high.
$2,000-3,500

The subject of Clorinda and Tancred derives from Torquato Tasso's epic of the first Crusade 'Jerusalem Delivered'. The Christian knight, Tancred, was in love with a maiden from his Saracen opposition, Clorinda. Unfortunately, he did not recognise her in her armour during the ensuing battle, and mortally wounded her.

A French bronze group of a mare and a dog, cast from a model by Pierre-Jules Mêne, signed P.J.Mêne, c1865, 10in (25cm) high.
$2,600-3,600

A French bronze model of a heron, with wings displayed and a fish in its beak, on naturalistic base cast with leaves and reeds, 19thC, 9in (23cm).
$800-1,000

Both Alfred Jacquemart and Jules Moigniez worked on similar models of herons.

A German bronze group of 2 rearing horses, on bronze base with stylised foliate trim, on marble pedestal base, 19thC, 13in (33cm) high.
$18,000-21,000

A pair of French bronzes of Henri IV and Charles I, above brass, tortoiseshell and ebonised 'boulle' plinths, dark brown patination, 19thC, 17½in (45cm).
$3,000-4,000

A French bronze group of 2 stallions, cast from a model by Jules Moigniez, the base signed J. Moigniez, with pale golden brown patina, on veined marble base, c1860, bronze 13in (33cm) high.
$6,500-7,000

A pair of Italian bronze figures of a horse and a bull, after Giambologna, probably cabinet figures, on marble bases, 17th or 18thC, 4½ and 4in (11 and 10cm) high.
$4,500-5,500

A pair of bronze lions, on moulded hexagonal bases edged with a band of ropetwist, mid-19thC, 14½in (37cm) high.
$3,000-4,000

A French bronze model of a walking lion, cast from a model by Antoine-Louis Barye, on naturalistic ground and stepped integrally cast base, signed Barye and with FB stamp for Barbedienne, 19thC, 9in (22cm) high.
$3,600-4,600

A bronze model of a standing rhinoceros, 4½in (11cm) high.
$1,600-2,000

A French bronze model of a stag, cast from a model by Pierre-Jules Mêne, signed P.J. Mêne, late 19thC, 23½in (60cm) high.
$5,000-6,000

A bronze model of a racehorse, saddled and bridled, on a shaped naturalistic base, signed Willis Good, 9in (23cm) high.
$2,000-3,000

A Russian bronze group of 3 cavalrymen on horseback, signed in Cyrillic E.A. Lanceray, and with the date 1880, Chopin foundry mark, 16in (41cm) high.
$18,000-21,000

A bronze figure of Albert Edward, Prince of Wales, after the painting by Franz Xaver Winterhalter, dressed in a sailor suit, English, mid-19thC, 21in (53cm) high.
$3,500-4,500

The celebrated painting of the Prince of Wales by Winterhalter is now in the Royal collection at Osborne House. Prince Albert commissioned the portrait in 1846, and included it amongst his 1846 Christmas presents to Queen Victoria.

A bronze figure of a nymph representing the river Thames, with the arms of the City of London on the ewer, English, mid-19thC, 11 by 17in (28 by 43cm).
$3,500-4,500

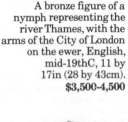

A bronze figure allegorical of Autumn, mid to dark brown patination, 15½in (39cm) high.
$700-1,000

A seated figure of a young girl by Ruth Milles, signed Ruth Milles on base, brown/green patination, c1910, 6½in (16cm) high.   **$1,500-2,000**

A French bronze group of The Rape of A Sabine, after Giambologna, bearing the signature Jean de Bologne, on rococo ormolu base numbered 51765 and with bronze label Houdebine Bronzier Paris, on a lacquered wood pedestal with pierced arches, 19thC, 38in (96cm) high.   **$6,500-10,000**

A pair of French bronze figures of Tragedy and Comedy, cast from models by Albert Carrier-Belleuse, both signed on the base A. Carrier, 19thC, 20½in (52cm) high.
$4,500-6,500

A bronze study of a crouching boy, cast from a model by Alfred Drury R.A., signed A. Drury, 1918, upon a marble plinth, dark green/black patination, 10in (25cm) high.
$3,500-4,500

A. Drury (1856-1944) first studied at the Oxford School of Art before going to South Kensington, where he studied under Jules Aimé Dalou, whom he accompanied to Paris in 1879. Although Drury became most famous for his portrait busts and large public commissions, such as his work for the Victoria Memorial 1901-24, he continued to produce small works in bronze, many of which, in the immediacy of their interpretation, reveal the lasting influence of Dalou.

A French bronze figure of a naked nymph, cast from a model by Henri Marius Ding, the base of the harp inscribed H. Ding, the circular base with founder's seal, on marble base with gilt bronze border, 19thC, 18in (46cm) high.
$2,600-3,600

A bronze figure of Henry Irving, shown as Mathias in 'The Bells', signed and dated E. Onslow Ford 1893 and inscribed Henry Irving as Mathias, presented by his comrades of the Lyceum Theatre on the 21st Anniversary of his first appearance Bells 25th Nov 1871 25th November 1892, c1892, 21½in (54cm) high.
$16,500-21,000
Sir Henry Irving (1838-1905), was renowned during his lifetime as the greatest actor in England. It was through his outstanding efforts that the Lyceum Theatre became nationally acclaimed for its dramatic acting and plays. The present bronze is not only a rare work of the contemporary 'New Sculpture' and of a contemporary subject, but also an interesting example of the rediscovered 'lost-wax' technique.

A French gilt bronze group of putti playing with a sedan chair, cast from a model by Louis Gossin, the 5 putti tumbling as the rococo chair is tilted, on naturalistic white marble base, signed L. Gossin, late 19th/early 20thC, 9½in (24cm) high.
$4,000-5,000

A bronze figure of Joan of Arc by Henri Chapu, the base signed H. Chapu and inscribed F. Barbedienne, fondeur, Paris and with A. Collas reduction stamp, pale brown patination, c1870, 18in (46cm) high.
$1,500-2,000

A pair of French bronze cupids, one holding a scroll entitled Contrat de Mariage, the other holding a heart pierced by an arrow, the bases signed Drouot upon moulded spreading Siena marble plinths, 14in (36cm) high.
$2,600-3,600

A pair of French bronze groups of Bacchantes, after Clodion, on shaped veined marble socles, late 19thC, 20in (51cm) high.
$5,000-6,000

A bronze group of a girl and her lover, on marble base, signed O. Hertel, late 19thC, 11in (28cm) high. **$1,000-1,600**

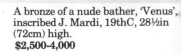

A French bronze figure of Cupid, after Charles Gabriel Lemire, the naked winged figure seated on a draped outcrop stringing a bow, pale brown patination, mid-19thC, 16in (41cm) high.
$1,800-2,000

A bronze group of 2 nymphs and a putto, after Claude Michel Clodion, clad in flowing dresses with vine leaves in their hair, on circular base signed Clodion, dark brown patination, mid-19thC, 21in (54cm).
$3,000-3,600

A bronze of a nude bather, 'Venus', inscribed J. Mardi, 19thC, 28½in (72cm) high.
$2,500-4,000

An Italian bronze group of Venus and Cupid, in the style of Pietro Tenerani, underside lined with resin, early 19thC, 25in (64cm) long.
$4,500-6,500

A bronze figure of a huntsman entitled 'Hallali' by Eugene Marioton and signed Eug. Marioton, brown patination, 40in (101cm).
$3,500-4,500

A French bronze figure of Father Time, standing scantily-clad, green/black patination, base missing, early 19thC, 11½in (30cm) high.
$700-800

A French bronze figure of a young naked woman, reclining on a bear skin rug, signed L. Pradier, 19thC, 9in (23cm) long.
$550-650

A bronze group of 2 children by Francois Hippolyte Moreau, signed Hte. Moreau and titled Un Secret par Hte. Moreau, Medaille au Salon, on veined marble base, patination rubbed, c1880, 17in (43cm) high.
$2,600-3,000

An Italian bronze figure of Apollo Sauroctonus, after the Antique, perhaps from the Zoffoli workshops, on Siena marble base, late 18thC, 11in (28cm) high.
$2,600-3,600

The Hellenistic Apollo Sauroctonus, formerly in the Borghese Collection, is now in the Musée du Louvre, Paris. During the 18thC, particularly thanks to Winckelmann's enthusiasm for the figure, the Apollo became popular. Bronze reductions were made at this time for the Grand Tourists. The present bronze example is probably one of these, and varies from the marble in some details, particularly in the position of Apollo.

A pair of French bronze figures of Hungarian warriors, by Emile Picault, clad in chainmail, armour and helmet, one holding a sword, the other an oil lamp, the base signed E. Picault, mid-brown patination, late 19thC, 18in (46cm).
$1,500-2,000

A pair of French bronze figures of semi-naked infants in the attitude of the dance, in the manner of Clodion, on marble stands, 19thC.
$1,200-1,400

A French gilt bronze and plated encrier, signed J. Moigniez, 19thC, 12in (31cm) wide.
$650-750

An Italian bronze figure of Marshal Ney, cast from a model by Giuseppe Grandi, inscribed Ney, late 19thC, 13in (33cm) high.
$10,000-11,000

A bronze on plaster figure of a classical male, numbered 122241, late 19thC, 50½in (129cm) high.
$2,600-3,600

A bronze figure of a fisherboy, signed Lavergne, pale brown patination, c1880, 12in (31cm).
$1,200-1,500

A bronze figure of an Italian shepherd boy, indistinctly signed, dark brown patination, c1870, 16½in (42cm).
$1,400-1,800

An Italian bronze figure of the seated Mars, after the Antique, green/brown patination, late 19thC, 19½in (49cm) high.
$1,200-1,400

An Italian bronze inkwell of a monkey playing with terrapins, cast from a model by Guido Righetti, one of the terrapins lifts to reveal an inkwell, on black marble base, signed G. Righetti, early 20thC, 7½in (19cm) long including base.
$2,600-3,600

Guido Righetti (1875-1958) was born in Milan. He was a pupil of Paul Troubetzkoy, but for most of his life worked in isolation at his estate in the Brianza region.

An Italian copper electrotype figure of a dancing faun, after the Antique, green/brown patination, late 19thC.
$1,000-1,500

A pair of French gilt bronze ornamental ewers, the handles modelled with putti, with satyr terminals, the bodies with raised bands of fruiting vines and amorini emblematic of the Arts, on stepped circular bases, 19thC, 22½in (57cm).
$650-800

An English bronze mortar, c1680, 5in (13cm) high.
$550-750

An Italian bronze hand bell, the sides cast in relief, the centre inscribed with the initials G di B F and dated 1560, the handle in the form of a female figure ringing a bell with an urn at her side, bell body cracked, c1560, 7in (18cm) high.
$2,600-3,600

A Northern Italian bronze vessel, the vessel cast in the shape of a mortar with the addition of 4 hollow lateral cylinders, the central vessel and cylinders with waisted decorative band, with feet in the form of seated lions, late 16th/early 17thC, 4in (10cm) high.
$1,500-2,000

An Italian bronze bell, surmounted with the Papal Tiara, the body with raised figure subjects, 19thC, 5½in (14cm) high.
$200-300

Did you know
MILLER'S Antiques Price Guide builds up year by year to form the most comprehensive photo-reference system available

Copper

A Limoges enamel and copper reliquary casket, in 12thC Mosan style, the lid and sides enamelled with biblical scenes and florets in blues, green, yellow and red, the reverse with a hinged opening, some damage, 6½ by 6in (16 by 15cm).
$8,000-10,000

This casket is inspired by 4 Mosan 12thC plaques in the Louvre, Paris, which entered their collection in 1820. They were until recently assumed to form part of a casket, but have now been associated with other similar plaques in various museums, and, in fact, form part of a large crucifix.

A North European copper lidded urn with brass banding, 28in (71cm) high.
$550-750

A moulded and painted copper and zinc sulky driver, with original paint, late 19thC, 13in (33cm) high.
$2,000-2,500

Firemarks

The Alliance British and Foreign Fire and Life Insurance Co., copper, c1830, 9in (23cm).
$90-140

The Salop Fire Office, copper, c1830, 8in (20cm).
$90-140

The Sun Fire Office, copper, c1850, 6in (15cm) diam.
$90-120

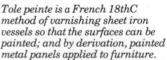

The District Fire Office, copper, c1860, 7½in (19cm).   **$90-110**

A tôleware bottle carrier, the 2 co-joined cylindrical canisters with a central carrying handle, the painted blue ground heightened in gilt with fruiting vine and painted with reserves of Italianate landscapes, 19thC, 13in (33cm).
$1,000-1,200

Tole peinte is a French 18thC method of varnishing sheet iron vessels so that the surfaces can be painted; and by derivation, painted metal panels applied to furniture.

Iron

An iron strong box of Armada type, the hinged lid opening to reveal a complex polished iron lock, the front with false cartouche key plate and a carrying handle to each side, late 17thC, 43in (109cm) wide.
$4,000-4,500

A cast iron fire back, c1685, 22in (56cm).
$700-900

A cast iron water font back, with a lion couchant in high relief, on moulded shelf with D-shaped back, 19thC, 33in (84cm) wide.
$900-1,000

ARTS & CRAFTS

A Bretby bowl, c1895, 8½in (21cm) diam.
$150-200

An unusual tea set, showing the influence of William Burgess, maker's mark A.L. unidentified, Chester, 1912.
$1,200-1,600

A Bretby earthenware 'bamboo' stick stand, with a seated monkey at the base, his arms wrapped around the stand, the monkey painted in naturalistic colours, the stand shading from yellow to amber and green, rim crack, impressed mark, 23in (59cm) high.
$650-800

A William de Morgan red lustre vase and cover, the white ground decorated in red, cover restored, the base impressed W. De Morgan, Sand Pottery, with Morris & Co. paper label, 13in (33cm) high.
$4,500-5,500

A pair of Bretby vases, c1885, 14in (36cm) high.
$900-1,000

A Minton's majolica teapot and cover in the form of a monkey, impressed marks and year code for 18?, 7in (17cm) high.
$2,000-3,000

A William De Morgan jar, decorated in the Persian style, in turquoise, blue, dark purple and grey with stylised floral arabesques, 16in (41cm) high.
$6,500-7,000

A pair of candle sconces, attributed to Edward Spencer and the Artificers Guild, in steel, 12in (31cm) high.
$3,500-4,500

A Minton pottery plaque, painted by W. S. Coleman, in pastel colours, printed Minton Art Pottery Studio, Kensington Gore, c1870, 18in (46cm) wide.
$5,800-6,800

A pair of Moser engraved glass vases, each deeply engraved with flowering daffodils, engraved mark 3, 13in (33cm) and 13½in (34cm) high.
$650-1,000

A Rookwood pottery vase, by Albert R. Valentien, decorated with yellow floral blooms with long curving tendrils against a dark brown ground, exhibiting in part a glimmering lustre, impressed 'Rookwood 1886', incised A.R.V. artist's monogram, 28½in (73cm) high.
$2,000-3,000

A Cotswold School dresser, in plain oak, 53½in (136cm) wide.
$1,500-2,000

An oak bedroom suite decorated with coloured glass panels, comprising a breakfront wardrobe, 83in (210cm) wide, a dressing table with swing-frame mirror, 48in (122cm) wide, a marble topped washstand with spindle turned superstructure, 50in (127cm) wide, and a pedestal bedside cupboard, 17in (43cm) wide.
$2,800-3,600

An oak cabinet designed by Ambrose Heal, the cupboard doors with elaborate locking mechanism, 44in (112cm) wide.
$1,500-2,000

An oak chair, probably by William Birch, with drop-in rush seat with stretchers below, on pad feet.
$900-1,000

An Edward Barnsley oak pedestal desk, with beaten metal handles, 53½in (136cm) wide.
$3,500-4,500

The records of the Barnsley Education Trust show that this desk was commissioned in 1923 – the year that Edward Barnsley established his workshop at Froxfield.

An inlaid oak desk, the top covered in red leather, with brass handles, one door enclosing 3 short drawers, the other a single shelf, the front, sides and back of the desk decorated with stylised foliate panels of marquetry, 59in (149cm) wide.
$3,000-4,000

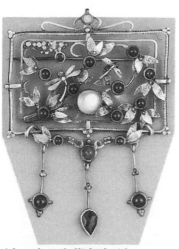

A brooch, embellished with wirework, garnet cabochons and a moonstone and opal cabochon, and dragonflies amid foliage, with garnet drops, 2in (5cm) wide.
$700-900

An important necklace by Edward Spencer of the Artificers' Guild, set with aquamarines, moonstones, rubies, emerald and opal, c1890, showing influences by Henry Wilson.
$4,000-5,000

A large rock crystal, crysophase and moonstone heart-shaped pendant, English, c1930, probably by Sybil Dunlop.
$1,500-2,000

A brooch in the form of a dragonfly, the body set with garnet cabochons and an amethyst, the eyes as moonstone cabochons, stamped GM maker's mark, 4½in (11cm) wide.
$800-1,000

Martin Bros.

A Martin Brothers stoneware bottle vase incised and painted with an insect, game birds and reeds, the neck with a geometric pattern in shades of blue and brown, 10in (25cm).
$500-700

Two Martin Brothers stoneware cache pots, l. the sides moulded with lizard-like creatures on a waved ground, coloured overall in shades of olive and brown, incised Martin Bros. London & Southall, 10-1900; r. the rim decorated with ovals, the sides moulded with various species of jellyfish on a hatched ground, coloured overall in shades of olive and brown, incised Martin Bros. London & Southall, 10-1900, 4½in (11cm) high.
$2,000-3,000 each

A Martin Brothers stoneware spill vase, incised and painted with birds on the branches of a fruit tree, in shades of blue on a light brown ground, inscribed R.W. Martin, Southall, 7½in (19cm).
$350-550

A Martin Brothers stoneware jug of compressed globular form, with narrow neck modelled and incised with peonies and foliage on a scaly ground, in shades of beige, brown and black, incised Martin Bros. London & Southall, 5in (12cm).
$800-1,000

MARTIN BROTHERS
★ Robert, Charles, Walter and Edwin founded the pottery in 1873, moved to Southall in 1877 and continued in production until 1914
★ Martinware is the Art Pottery made by the Martin brothers between 1873 and 1914, characterised by Grotesque human and animal figures in stoneware

ART NOUVEAU
Ceramics

A Brannam egg separator, c1910.
$110-125

A German tile, tube lined with a maiden in purple dress, contained within a wooden wall bracket embellished with gilt metal floral detail, 19in (49cm).
$1,000-1,500

A Poole blue and white geometric vase, 10in (25cm) high.
$900-1,000

A Goldscheider ceramic wall head, c1930.
$750-1,000

A Pilkingtons Royal Lancastrian highly decorated lustre bowl, by Mycock, c1900, 5in (13cm) diam.
$350-550

Make the Most of Miller's

Every care has been taken to ensure the accuracy of descriptions and estimated valuations. Price ranges in this book reflect what one should expect to pay for a similar example. When selling one can obviously expect a figure below. This will fluctuate according to a dealer's stock, saleability at a particular time, etc. It is always advisable to approach a reputable specialist dealer or an auction house which has specialist sales

---

An Ault vase, the design attributed to Christopher Dresser, 5½in (14cm) high.
$230-280

CHRISTOPHER DRESSER 1835-1905

★ an influential English pottery and glass designer who was inspired by Japanese art and worked for Tiffany as well as the pottery firms of Ault, Linthorpe and Pilkington

---

A Linthorpe jug, by Christopher Dresser, shape No. 346, 10in (25cm).
$1,800-2,800

A Linthorpe vase, designed by Dr. Christopher Dresser, decorated with 4 grotesque heads, each forming a handle, covered in a streaky green glaze, running and pooling, impressed facsimile signature Chr Dresser 254, 9in (23cm) high.
$1,000-1,200

A Royal Dux porcelain centrepiece, in tones of pink, green and mauve heightened with gilt, raised pink triangle to base, numbered 710, 16½in (42cm).
$1,200-1,800

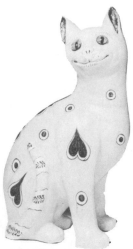

A Gallé faience model of a cat, with green glass eyes, glazed yellow and decorated with blue hearts and circles, unsigned, 13½in (35cm).
$1,000-1,500

A Minton Pottery Secessionist jardinière and stand, slip trailed and painted with a stylised design of candles and leaves, glazed in blood red and green enamels on a cream ground, printed mark, design No. 55, 41½in (105cm).
$1,400-1,800

A Gallé tin glazed earthenware flowerholder, covered in a white glaze, decorated with polychrome flowersprays and a pink ribbon, on an oval naturalistic base with a tree trunk vase, inset with red glass eyes, signed Gallé Nancy, 8in (20cm) high.
$4,000-5,000

A Rookwood ceramic vase, on 4 splayed feet, the white ground shaded into blue, with painted decoration of narcissi, with stamped monogram RP and numbered 597z, initialled R.F., 13½in (35cm).
$800-1,200

Clocks

A Tiffany Furnaces enamelled gilt bronze three-piece clock garniture, impressed LOUIS C. TIFFANY FURNACES INC./651 and 38, 1920s.
$2,000-3,000

A Gouda glazed earthenware clock case painted with colourful swirling flowers and plant forms, 16½in (42cm).   **$540-740**

A Tiffany and Co. clock, the face square with canted corners, set in a thin section of lapis lazuli, mounted in a gold coloured and enamelled bezel, the face signed Tiffany & Co. and etched to the base VAN 19539, 4½in (12cm).
$700-900

Did you know
MILLER'S Antiques Price Guide builds up year by year to form the most comprehensive photo-reference system available

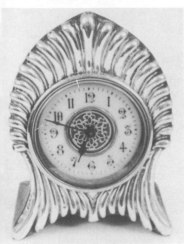

A clock, inscribed on the bezel St. Moritz 1900, with an interesting hallmark, c1891, 5in (12cm) high.
$700-800

A Liberty & Co. pewter and enamelled clock, embossed with a stylised leafy tree, the blue/green enamelled clock face with Roman numerals, the door on the reverse with a pierced tree, stamped marks, made in England, Tudric, c1900, 13in (33cm).
$4,500-5,500

A corner table with inlaid chrysanthemum design, 18½in (47cm) high.
$270-280

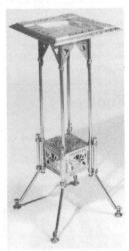

An Aesthetic Movement brass pedestal, the top with shallow well, on 4 angled tubular legs, with pierced and repoussé linear and foliate decoration, moulded marks PAT APL⁰ FOR, 32in (82cm) high.
$1,200-1,500

Furniture

A Liberty & Co. mahogany side table, the octagonal top with a lighter inlaid band, on square section legs, tapering to pad feet, with slotted stretchers between, with maker's label, 36in (92cm) diam.
$1,500-1,600

A pair of Morris & Co ebonised side chairs, each with toprails and cross splat, the rush seats on turned legs straight and curved bar stretchers.
$2,000-3,000

An Aesthetic Movement ebonised chest stool, decorated front and back with carved gilt emblematic roundels, supported on turned legs above a gallery, the seat upholstered in black horse hair 35½in (90cm) wide.
$4,500-5,500

A Liberty's style mahogany three-piece suite, comprising a two-seater settee and a pair of armchairs, with rosewood veneered backs with inlay, upholstered in Liberty's Peacock Feather linen, settee 54in (137cm) wide, armchairs 30in (76cm) wide.
$5,500-7,000

A chair designed by J. M. Olbrich, the back inlaid with stylised flowers in mother-of-pearl and fruitwoods, with upholstered seat and back, supported on tapering square section legs with pad feet.
$1,200-1,500

An inlaid display cabinet.
$700-1,000

An oak dining table, designed by M. H. Baillie-Scott, on 2 trestle supports, each composed of twin turned baluster columns and shaped transverse base, c1897, 72in (183cm) long.
$7,000-9,000

Figures

A German plated pewter lady holding a jewellery box, 13½in (35cm).
$720-1,000

An English Aesthetic Movement bedroom suite, comprising a wardrobe, dressing table and a bedside cabinet, each decorated with panels of fruitwood marquetry with hammered and pierced hinges and handles, the wardrobe 70in (177cm) high.
$4,000-5,000

A bronze figure by Eloe, signed.
$1,500-$2,000

A gilt bronze figure lamp by Agathon Léonard, the lamp concealed in the drape held above the female head, signed in the bronze, c1900.
$18,000-27,000

An Austrian bronze figure on marble base.
$700-1,000

A gilt bronze and ivory figure by Preiss, signed, c1930, 11in (28cm) high.
$2,700-4,500

Glass

Six enamelled glasses, each decorated in either blue, red or yellow with a painted flowerhead, each with gilt linear decoration, 6½in (16cm) high and smaller.
$3,000-4,000

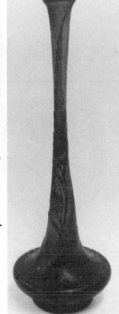

A Gallé cameo glass bottle vase, the compressed onion body and slender attenuated trumpet neck carved in relief with hollyhocks rising from dark to pale tint, signed, c1900, 15in (38cm) high.
$2,600-3,600

Emile Gallé (1846-1904) was the founder of a talented circle of designers based around Nancy. Simultaneously, in the 1880s, he designed delicate furniture embellished with marquetry and began experimenting with new glass techniques. In 1889 he developed cameo glass; in 1897 marquetry glass. After his death factories continued to produce his wares, signed Gallé but marked with a star, until the 1930s.

An orange and green satin glass vase, the undulating rim folded to form 3 handles, acid etched and carved to reveal green fronds, with gilt decorated border, monogrammed L.G. and indistinctly inscribed, chipped, 6in (15cm) high.
$550-650

Twelve Austrian enamelled glass goblets, the bowls decorated with a variety of stylised petals in shades of orange, blue, yellow, pink and green, with gilt highlights, most enamelled with letters or numerals, the largest 9in (23cm) high.
$3,000-4,000

A Morris & Co. stained glass panel, the pale yellow stained glass painted with red, yellow and white decoration in alternating designs of open and budding flowers, within charcoal border, 17½ by 18in (46 by 44cm).
$550-900

The decorative features of this panel can be seen in a pair of windows with minstrel figures which are in the Victoria and Albert Museum.

A Gallé cameo glass vase.
$6,500-7,000

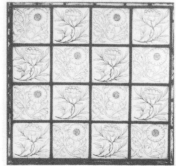

Fourteen wine glasses and 2 liqueur glasses, attributed to Heckart Petersdorfer Glashütte, on long green stems, with various gilt and polychrome enamelled stylised floral designs, 8½in (21cm) and 5½in (14cm) high.
$3,500-4,500

A Daum cameo class landscape lamp, in mottled orange/yellow glass, overlaid in green with trees on the bank of a lake, repeated on the wavy rimmed shade, cameo mark, Daum Nancy, Cross of Lorraine, c1900, 16½in (42cm).
$18,000-21,000

Jewellery

A Liberty & Co. silver belt buckle, in the style of Archibald Knox, with stylised spade-shaped flowers, supported on entwined entrelacs, the surface beaten, stamped marks, L & Co. Cymric, Birmingham 1901, 2in (5cm).
$260-360

A large 9ct gold pendant, by Murlle Bennett & Co., set with an opal flanked by 2 pale aquamarines and 2 citrines, c1900.
$1,200-1,600

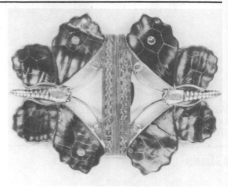

A silver buckle, each piece in the form of a butterfly with shaded mother-of-pearl wings, marked R.P. Birmingham 1910, 3½in (9cm) wide.
$180-300

A French 18ct gold brooch, the sculpture effect hand finished, c1900.
$1,000-1,500

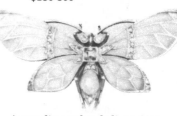

A rose diamond and plique à jour enamel butterfly brooch, with baroque pearl, untested, rose diamond and gem body.
$4,500-5,500

An unusual plique à jour and diamanté pendant, the ivory and mother-of-pearl bust mounted in a gilt white metal setting, the wings and fan tail with shades of green and turquoise plique à jour enamel, set with white and pink gems, in fitted leather case, 13in (33cm).
$5,800-6,800

A diamond and rose diamond cluster brooch, the pierced and chased floral scrollwork shoulders each set with 2 rose diamonds. **$650-750**

A Liberty & Co. silver and enamel belt buckle, attributed to Archibald Knox, enamelled in mottled blue and green, some enamel replaced, stamp marks L & Co. Cymric, Birmingham 1901, 3in (8cm).
$350-450

Lamps

A pair of Tiffany Favrile glass and bronze shield boudoir lamps, bases impressed TIFFANY STUDIOS/ NEW YORK, 1966 and 427 respectively, c1910, 15½in (40cm). **$4,000-5,000**

A Handel reverse painted glass and patinated metal lamp, shade impressed HANDEL PAT'D. NO./979284 and signed HANDEL 6004, base with woven label HANDEL, minor flecks to rim of shade, c1910, 21in (53cm) high. **$5,500-7,000**

A Tiffany Favrile glass and bronze acorn lamp, base impressed Tiffany Studios/New York/168 and S137, c1910, 22in (56cm). **$5,000-8,000**

l. A Tiffany Studios bronze lamp base, impressed TIFFANY STUDIOS/NEW YORK/2031, c1915, 24in (62cm). **$5,500-6,500**
r. A Tiffany Studios bronze counter-balance desk lamp base, impressed TIFFANY STUDIOS/ NEW YORK/417, c1915, 15½in (40cm). **$2,500-3,000**

A Tiffany Favrile cypriote glass vase, inscribed L.C. Tiffany Favrile and 6791K, c1916, 4in (10cm) high. **$6,000-10,000**

A Tiffany Favrile glass and gilt bronze counter-balance floor lamp, slight damage to shade, shade inscribed L.C.T. Favrile, base impressed TIFFANY STUDIOS/ NEW YORK/468, c1915, 53in (135cm). **$3,000-6,000**

A Tiffany Studios bronze bridge lamp, impressed TIFFANY STUDIOS/NEW YORK/423, c1915, 55in (140cm). **$3,000-6,000**

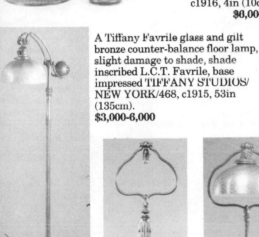

A Tiffany Studios bronze nautilus desk lamp, cracked shell, base impressed TIFFANY STUDIOS/ NEW YORK/403, c1910, 11½in (29cm). **$1,800-2,200**

A Tiffany Studios bronze floor lamp base, impressed TIFFANY STUDIOS/NEW YORK/386, c1910, 59in (150cm) high. **$5,500-8,000**

A Tiffany Favrile glass, bronze and wood standing smoker's lamp, with ashtray, wooden drink holder and magazine rack, shade inscribed L.C.T., base impressed TIFFANY STUDIOS/NEW YORK/582B, c1910, 54½in (138cm). **$5,000-6,000**

An iridescent glass and metal table lamp, with domed Palme Konig shade of pink tone with pale web-like stringing, 15in (38cm).
$2,600-3,600

A Tiffany Favrile glass and bronze acorn chandelier, some damage, shade impressed TIFFANY STUDIOS/NEW YORK, c1915, 25in (64cm).
$7,500-8,500

A copper and brass table lamp, by W. A. S. Benson.
$1,000-1,200

Metal

A silver flatware set by Tiffany & Co., New York, 196 pieces including 4 salt spoons by Mappin & Webb, c1900, 247oz excluding knives.
$6,500-7,000

A silver Art Nouveau water pitcher by Shreve & Co., San Francisco, c1900, 14in (36cm) high, 42oz. **$1,800-2,200**

A set of 4 silver table candlesticks, by Tiffany & Co., 20thC, 13½in (34cm) high. **$4,500-5,000**

A pair of silver gilt picture frames, maker's mark of Tiffany & Co., c1895, 9½in (24cm) long, 22½oz.
$3,500-4,000

A pitcher by Tiffany & Co., c1862, 9in (23cm) high, 35½oz.
$4,700-5,000

A silver and glass inkwell by Tiffany & Co., New York, c1895, 7½in (19cm) diam.
$2,600-3,000

A silver soup tureen and cover, by Tiffany & Co., New York, c1895, 15in (38cm) wide, 65oz.
$5,000-7,000

A silver standing bowl by Tiffany & Co., New York, c1885, 9in (22cm) high, 31½oz.
$2,500-3,000

A silver two-handled cup by Tiffany & Co., New York, c1895, 10in (25cm) high, 50oz.
$6,600-7,000

A pair of silver entrée dishes and covers, by Tiffany & Co., New York, the bases engraved with date February 23, 1899, 10in (25cm) long, 88oz.
$6,700-7,000

A pair of seven-light plated candelabra, maker's mark of Tiffany & Co., 22in (56cm) high.
$4,000-4,800

A vase by Tiffany & Co., New York, c1875, 7½in (19cm) high, 12½oz.
$3,500-4,000

A pair of silver vases by Tiffany & Co., New York, c1895, 14½in (37cm), 94oz.　$8,000-9,000

A three-light candelabrum centrepiece, maker's mark of Tiffany & Co., 9in (22cm) diam, 39½oz.　$2,700-3,000

A bridal basket vase by Tiffany & Co., with plated liner also by Tiffany, 1911, 11in (28cm) high, 6½oz weighable silver.
$1,200-1,500

A silver mounted bread board by Tiffany & Co., New York, c1890, 13in (33cm) diam.　$2,500-3,000

A silver flatware set by Tiffany & Co., New York, c1935, comprising 82 pieces, together with 2 Danish silver bottle openers, by Georg Jensen, modern, with a mahogany box.
$4,000-4,500

A centrepiece bowl by Tiffany & Co., New York, for the world's Columbian Exposition, Chicago, 1893, 19in (48cm) long, 61½oz.
$7,000-7,500

A silver soup tureen and cover by Tiffany & Co., New York, c1875, 14in (36cm), 52½oz.
$4,700-5,000

An electroplated bowl, designed by Christopher Dresser, with ebonised handle, with design registration lozenge for March 1878, 8½in (22cm) long.
$650-800

A Cymric Liberty & Co. bowl, designed by Oliver Baker, set with Connemara marble discs, Birmingham 1901, 8½in (21cm) diam.
$5,500-6,500

A pair of pewter figural candlesticks, marked B.G. imperial, 10½in (27cm).
$900-1,000

A Mappin and Webb vase, the handles with heart shaped terminals, the base with inverted hearts in relief, with inscription, maker's mark, London 1903, 5in (13cm).
$300-450

A C. R. Ashbee hammered silver goblet, the foot with a radiating repoussé pattern of stylised buds, stamped C R A with London hallmarks for 1899, 5in (12cm).
$1,000-1,200

A silver tea caddy by Tiffany & Co. New York, c1870, 6in (15cm) long, 18oz.
$2,000-2,300

A plated pewter pen and inkstand, 8½in (22cm) high.
$180-210

A W.M.F. silvered metal tea set, comprising a teapot, coffee pot, covered sugar and creamer, with two-handled lobed tray, all cast with curvilinear foliage, tray 24½in (62cm) diam.
$2,600-3,600

A Liberty & Co. silver pen tray, each end decorated with a cabochon turquoise, with owner's initials A.M.W., stamped marks L & Co. and Birmingham hallmarks for 1912, 7in (17cm) long, 60gr.
$450-550

W.M.F.
Short for the Austrian Württembergishe Metallwarenfabrik, one of the principal producers of Art Nouveau silver and silver plated objects, early 20thC.

Moorcroft

A Moorcroft Pottery vase, the body painted with the Anemone pattern on a red ground, 6½in (17cm).
$460-560

A Moorcroft MacIntyre pottery baluster vase with 2 loop handles, polychrome floral decoration on a white ground with gilt banding, 7½in (19cm).
$1,000-1,200

A rare Moorcroft flambé Eventide vase, tube-lined with trees in a hilly landscape and richly coloured in mauve, orange and red, minor chip restored on foot, impressed Moorcroft, Made in England and signed in blue W. Moorcroft, 8in (20cm).
$3,500-4,500

A Moorcroft pottery vase, painted with the Hibiscus design on a deep red ground, impressed marks and painted signature, 8½in (21cm).
$550-650

A Moorcroft pottery vase, painted with the Pomegranate and Grape design on a deep blue ground, impressed marks and painted signature, 6½in (17cm).
$300-400

A Moorcroft Eventide vase, decorated with green and brown trees and hills against a flame coloured sky, impressed mark, signature in green, 5½in (14cm).
$1,400-1,500

A Moorcroft Apple Blossom bowl, tube-lined with branches of flowers and berries in tones of green, hair crack, impressed Moorcroft Burslem 1914, signed in green W. Moorcroft and dated 1914, 10in (25cm).
$1,500-2,000

A Moorcroft Florian ware bottle vase with fluted rim, decorated in blue and green with the Poppy design on a white ground, pattern No. 401753, printed Florian ware mark and signed, 6in (15cm).
$700-800

A Moorcroft Florian ware vase, tube-lined with yellow and blue flowerheads and green foliage on a light and dark blue ground, printed Florian ware mark and signed in green W. Moorcroft, c1902, 11½in (30cm).
$2,600-3,600

DOULTON

A Doulton figure of a mandarin, wearing a yellow tunic with circular motifs over a plain blue full length skirt, his jacket with larger motifs on a black ground, small chip to hat, dated 7.24, HN 611, 10in (25cm). **$1,200-1,800**

A pair of Doulton Lambeth salt glazed stoneware bookends, one with a single monkey, the other with a monkey and child, on a foliate base under a green glaze, stamped factory mark, Doulton, Lambeth, England, c1890, 6in (15cm). **$550-700**

A 1930s style Doulton dinner service entitled 'Dubarry', comprising: 4 tureens and covers, 2 ladles, 5 graduated meat plates, 2 sauceboats, 22 plates and 2 petal edged plates, on a cream ground, with a geometric pattern of intersecting lines and semi-circles edged in green with a central motif of a stylised flower in orange, some plates worn. **$550-700**

A Doulton Lambeth stoneware vase, decorated by Edith Lupton, carved and glazed with flowers and grasses over a beige background with painted florets, dated 1887, 16in (41cm). **$800-1,000**

A Doulton figure, 'Contentment', decorated mainly in yellow, light green and pink, slight pitting to glaze, HN 395, 7½in (19cm). **$800-1,200**

A Doulton salt glazed stoneware vase, by Hannah B. Barlow, impressed factory marks and date, incised monogram, BHB and LAB for Lucy A. Barlow, c1884, 12in (31cm). **$1,200-1,400**

ROYAL DOULTON

A figure 'Coquette', HN 37, No. 258, cracked, 9½in (24cm) high. **$1,200-1,500**

A model of a bulldog, glazed in shades of brown, HN 1043, and a smaller model of a seated bulldog. **$450-550**

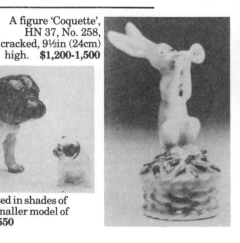

'A Yeoman of the Guard', HN 2122 6in (15cm) high. **$650-800**

A pair of Royal Doulton vases, c1900, 11in (28cm).
$270-320

A pair of salt glazed stoneware vases, by Hannah B. Barlow, in green and brown with tube lined Art Nouveau swirling motifs in a band above and below, large chip to rim of one, impressed factory marks, incised monogram, BHB and others of Assistants, c1885, 11in (28cm).
$1,500-2,000

A group, 'The Love Letter', HN 2149, withdrawn 1976.
$260-360

A brown and white model of a standing bulldog, HN 1045.
$650-720

A large loving cup, produced to commemorate the Silver Jubilee of King George V and Queen Mary, No. 980 of an edition limited to 1,000.
$450-700

A pair of flambé models of penguins, set on an alabaster ashtray with silver mounts, with assay mark for London 1919, 6½in (17cm).
$450-550

A coffee service, 'Reynard the Fox', with printed marks and pattern number H4927.
$550-700

'Simon the Cellarer', a white character jug, 3in (8cm).
$260-360

A salt glazed metal mounted stoneware biscuit barrel, by Hannah B. Barlow, highlighted in blue, with impressed factory mark and date, and incised monogram Hannah B Barlow, 1880, 7½in (19cm).
$800-1,000

A pottery vase, the body decorated with an extensive fox hunting scene between bands of flowers, 2 cracks, 22½in (57cm).
$350-550

A porcelain vase, dated 5.11, by Arthur Leslie, decorated with a maiden holding a white dove in a landscape, 9in (23cm). **$700-800**

'Collinette', HN 1999, withdrawn
$450-550

ART DECO
Lalique Glass

An opalescent bowl with beads graduating inside and forming a swirling pattern, with R. Lalique in upper case, 8in (20cm).
$550-720

A Lalique blue tinted opalescent glass bowl, moulded with fishes.
$1,200-1,500

A frosted desk clock, 'Roitelets', the glass face surrounded by a band of wrens in flight, with Omega timepiece, stencilled R. Lalique France, 8in (20cm).
$5,500-6,500

An opalescent table clock, 'Inseperables No. 765', minor damage, 4½in (11cm).
$1,500-1,800

An opalescent bowl, 'Perruches', moulded with a frieze of budgerigars perched on flowering branches, heightened with blue staining and etched R. Lalique France, 9½in (24cm).
$5,500-6,500

An opalescent glass bowl, entitled 'Lys' moulded with a frieze of 4 lilies, the stems tapering to form legs, stencil mark R. Lalique, France, c1925, 9½in (23cm).
$1,500-2,000

An opalescent bowl, 'Vase Coquilles', 9½in (24cm).
$650-800

A clear and green stained bowl, 'Coupe Filix', moulded on the underside with broad pinnated leaves, wheel cut mark R. Lalique France, 13in (33cm) diam.
$1,500-2,000

A clear and frosted glass clock, 'Naïdes', intaglio moulded with a band of mermaids with fanned and beaded hair, their limbs entwined, heightened with pale brown staining, etched R. Lalique France, 4in (11cm) diam.
$1,800-2,800

An opalescent and sienna stained dish, 'Anges', moulded in intaglio with facing pairs of kneeling angels, wheel cut R. Lalique France, 14½in (37cm) diam.
$6,500-7,000

An opalescent dish, decorated with birds, 8in (20cm). **$700-900**

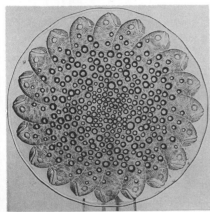

A clear blue stained dish, 'Roscoff', the underside moulded with radiating fish, the centre with a myriad of bubbles, engraved R. Lalique France, 14in (36cm).
$1,800-2,800

A glass pendant, in white metal frame, the foil backed and black stained glass with relief decoration of a nymph in a wooded landscape, the reverse with mirror, with engraved signature R. Lalique France, 3in (8cm) long. **$2,700-3,700**

A dark blue frosted dish, 'Phalènes', moulded to the underside with a stylised flower, the flat rim moulded in intaglio with moths, slight reduction to rim, wheel cut R. Lalique France, 15in (38cm).
$6,500-8,000

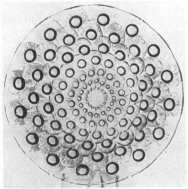

An opalescent dish, moulded on the underside with a peacock feather motif, engraved R. Lalique France, 12in (30cm).
$1,200-1,500

A glass pendant in white metal frame, the gold foil backed and black stained glass with relief decoration of a maiden's face framed with flowers, the reverse with mirror, the frame stamped Lalique, 3in (8cm) long.
$2,700-3,700

A green glass brooch, 'Sauterelles', signed LALIQUE, 3in (8cm) long
$5,500-7,000

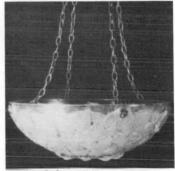

A frosted glass plaffonier of hemispherical form, 'Charmes', moulded in relief with overlapping beach leaves, with suspension chain and ceiling rose, moulded R. LALIQUE, 13½in (35cm) diam.
$1,200-1,500

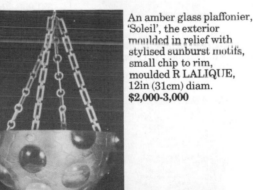

An amber glass plaffonier, 'Soleil', the exterior moulded in relief with stylised sunburst motifs, small chip to rim, moulded R LALIQUE, 12in (31cm) diam.
$2,000-3,000

A frosted glass plaffonier, 'Stalactites', moulded as pendant icicles, minor chips, wheel cut R. LALIQUE, 10½in (26cm).
$2,700-3,600

A black opaque pendant, moulded with 2 panels of wasps, heads facing inwards and with down-curved bodies, pierced at the top and base for suspension cord and tassel, engraved R. Lalique, 2in (5cm).
$2,600-3,600

A clear and frosted glass chandelier, 'Charmes', moulded twice R LALIQUE, 14in (36cm) diam.
$4,500-5,500

A hanging light, 'Boule de Gui', composed of 2 hemispherical and 8 rectangular glass panels, linked by metal rings to form a globe, moulded with mistletoe, with metal hanging ring and wired for electricity, 17½in (45cm) high.
$21,000-27,000

A frosted plafonnier, 'Deux Sirénes', moulded with 2 swimming water nymphs, their hair forming streams of bubbles, with matching ceiling rose, moulded R. Lalique, 15½in (39cm) diam.
$14,500-16,500

An opalescent glass and chromium plated metal table lamp, 'Coquilles', moulded with 4 clam shells, suspended from a C-shaped mount on stepped circular base, wheel cut R. Lalique France, 12in (31cm).
$3,500-4,500

A frosted glass vase, 'Druids', moulded with entwined sprigs of mistletoe with polished clusters of berries in relief, moulded to base R. Lalique, 7in (18cm) high.
$900-1,200

A rare, early frosted mirror, 'Anemones', moulded with flowerheads, with metal easel support, impressed Lalique, 15in (38cm) diam.
$21,000-27,000

A vase, 'Laurier', with raised leaves and berries in blue, etched near the base R. Lalique, 7in (17cm) high.
$550-720

A clear glass vase, 'Paquerettes', moulded in relief with stylised daisy-like blooms against a heavily textured ground heightened with black staining, etched R. Lalique France, 7½in (19cm) high.
$1,200-1,600

A clear and frosted vase, 'Annecy', moulded with alternating waved and serrated horizontal bands, stencilled R. Lalique France, 6in (15cm). **$1,000-1,200**

A turquoise stained vase, 'Oursin', the clear and satin finished glass moulded with protruding bubbles, with acid stamped signature R. Lalique France, 7½in (19cm) high. **$2,600-3,600**

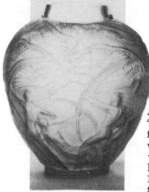

A grey stained vase, 'Archers', the satin finished glass moulded with archers and eagles, with engraved signature R Lalique France No 893, 10½in (26cm) high.
$7,000-9,000

An opalescent, clear and blue stained ashtray, 'Cendrier Statuette', in the centre a miniature 'Source de la Fontaine' figure, holding a lotus, etched R. Lalique, 4½in (12cm) high.
$1,200-1,600

Ceramics

A hand painted yellow and black vase, by Myott & Son, 8½in (22cm).
$90-150

A Beswick wall mask, with brown hair, wearing a green and yellow necklace, with blue and yellow petalled flowers behind, impressed Beswick, Made in England, 436, late 1930s, 12in (31cm).
$350-450

A Pilkington's Royal Lancastrian lapis-ware wall plate, decorated by W. S. Mycock, in grey on an orange ground, with impressed Pilkington mark and underglaze artist's monogram, 12½in (32cm) diam.
$180-280

A Charlotte Rhead Burslem ware jug, c1920, 9in (23cm).
$110-125

A Pilkington's Royal Lancastrian vase, by Mycock, 8½in (21cm).
$700-900

A Shelley Regent shape coffee service, transfer printed with a Lakeland scene, comprising coffee pot and cover, milk jug, sugar basin, 6 cups and 6 saucers, c1935, printed factory mark, Shelley, England, registration number 781613, painted number 12336.
$450-650

A Shelley porcelain tea service, each piece decorated with irises and stylised flowers on a pink and white ground, comprising: a teapot and cover, hot water jug, sugar basin, milk jug, 2 bread and butter plates, 12 tea plates and 12 teacups and saucers, slight damage to sugar basin.
$900-1,200

A Pilkington's Royal Lancastrian vase, by Mycock, 8½in (21cm).
$650-800

A Pilkington's Royal Lancastrian vase, by Cundall, 9in (23cm).
$700-900

A Shelley tea service, with abstract black pattern, some slight damage, 20 pieces, No. 756533.
$650-800

A Limoges
porcelain tea set,
glazed a lustrous
faux malachite
with silver trim,
with firm's
printed mark,
tray 15½in
(40cm) long.
$1,000-1,200

A cased Crown Devon coffee service,
decorated in yellow, purple and gilt,
with silver plastic beaded spoons,
chip to saucer, black printed factory
mark, Crown Devon, Fieldings,
England, painted number 2258,
c1930.
$550-900

A Pilkington's Royal Lancastrian
lapis-ware wall plate, decorated by
W. S. Mycock, in grey on an orange
ground, with impressed Pilkington
mark, underglaze artist's
monogram and date code for 1935,
12in (31cm).
$180-280

A Shelley fluted tea service with
cottage scene, in black, white and
yellow, 37 pieces, No. 11604131.
$650-800

Clarice Cliff

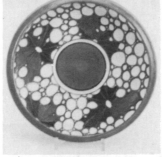

A Clarice Cliff Bizarre plate, from
the Circus Series designed by Dame
Laura Knight, all printed in pink
overpainted in green, black, yellow
and iron red heightened with gilt,
printed marks, impressed year
mark for 1934, 9in (23cm).
$1,000-1,400

A Clarice Cliff Fantasque Hiawatha
bowl, the interior decorated in the
Broth pattern in red, green, blue
and black, with multi-banded
exterior, minor wear to exterior,
rubber stamp mark, 9½in (24cm).
$550-900

A Clarice Cliff Fantasque Isis vase,
hand painted with repeating panels
in the Sunrise pattern of a sunburst
in green, orange, blue, yellow and
brown, factory marks and facsimile
signature to base, 10in (25cm).
$800-1,000

A Clarice Cliff Blue Firs flower
bowl, painted with tall black
stemmed trees, with various blue
foliage on treetops with a half
hidden cottage between the hills,
some surface scratching, black
printed factory mark, Hand
Painted, Bizarre, by Clarice Cliff,
Newport Pottery, England, c1930,
9in (23cm).
$450-550

A Clarice Cliff Bizarre
sandwich set, decorated in
the Idyll pattern, painted
in colours with black and
yellow banded borders,
lithograph marks, the
large plates 9in (23cm),
tea plates 6in (15cm).
$3,000-3,600

A Clarice Cliff Inspiration plate, painted with pink lilies, with black stems and black lily pads, on a green ground, black printed factory mark, Hand Painted, Bizarre, by Clarice Cliff, Wilkinson Ltd., England, 1931, 10in (25cm).
$550-700

A Clarice Cliff Persian Inspiration pottery vase, in vibrant azure blue with spiral and ogee motif in turquoise, lavender and amber, signed Persian and with printed Bizarre marks, 10in (25cm).
$1,500-1,800

A Clarice Cliff Melons plate, decorated with a band of fruits in yellow and orange with blue sections and green dots, minor damage to edge, printed mark, hand painted, Fantasque, by Clarice Cliff, Wilkinson Ltd., England, 10in (25cm).
$350-550

A pair of Clarice Cliff cottage bookends, decorated in red on a green ground with a blue sky, one cracked, the other chipped, black printed mark, Clarice Cliff, Wilkinson Pottery, retailer's mark, Lawleys, Regent Street, late 1930s, 5½in (14cm).
$500-600

A Clarice Cliff Bizarre Sliced Circle pattern single handled lotus jug, painted in bright colours, printed factory marks and facsimile signature, 10in (25cm).
$3,200-3,800

A Clarice Cliff pierced floral wall plaque, moulded in low relief with various flowers, printed factory mark, hand painted, Bizarre, Newport Pottery, England, painted The property of Threlfalls Brewery, signed on front Clarice Cliff, c1930, 13in (33cm).
$350-450

A Clarice Cliff Apples Isis vase, painted with apples and grapes, in pink, orange, black, yellow and green, fitted as lamp base, with electric fittings and shade, black printed factory mark, Fantasque, Hand Painted, Bizarre, by Clarice Cliff, Newport Pottery, England, c1932, 10in (25cm).
$1,600-2,000

A Clarice Cliff Isis vase, boldly painted with trees in Latona glazes, 10in (25cm).
$800-900

A Clarice Cliff Fantasque Summerhouse pattern vase, hand painted in colours around the 3 sides with a red roofed summerhouse and trees with pendant blooms, with orange banding top and bottom, facsimile signature and factory mark for Newport Pottery, 8in (20cm).
$700-900

Did you know
MILLER'S Antiques Price Guide builds up year by year to form the most comprehensive photo-reference system available

Ceramic Figures

A Goldscheider figure of a nude female, signed Lorenzl, No. 3802, 11in (28cm).
$900-1,000

A Cathaussen ceramic figure, 13in (33cm) long.
$550-1,000

Metal Figures

An Art Deco chrome lamp, 12in (31cm) high.
$175-200

A green patinated bronze figure of a dancing girl, on green onyx base, pitted and rubbed, marked Lorenzl and Argentor Wien, c1930, 14in (36cm).
$1,500-1,800

A cold painted silvered bronze figure of a nude girl, holding a bronze and ivory opened fan, on arched mottled marble base, Etling, Paris, 15½in (40cm).
$1,400-1,500

'O Mighty Woman', a bronze group cast from a model by J. J. Nielsons, on a naturalistic base, her distraught lover at her feet, signed in the bronze J.J. Nielsons, 14½in (37cm) high.
$1,000-1,500

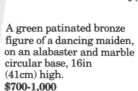

'Sword Dance' a bronze figure, cast from a model by F. Ouillon Carrere, on bronze base, on black marble plinth, signed in the bronze F. Ouillon Carrere 1919, 21in (54cm) high.
$2,000-3,000

A bronze figure, by Phillipe, on square marble base, signed P. Phillipe, R.U.M., 16in (41cm) high.
$1,600-2,000

A green patinated bronze figure of a dancing maiden, on an alabaster and marble circular base, 16in (41cm) high.
$700-1,000

Bronze & Ivory Figures

A pair of bronze and ivory figures, 6in (15cm) high.
$2,700-3,300

A bronze and ivory figure of a dancer by Lorenzl, 15in (38cm) high.
$3,300-4,600

A figure of a bronze and ivory dancer, on a large onyx dish, 8in (20cm) high.
$1,200-1,600

A Preiss carved ivory figure of a young girl with a skipping rope, on an onyx base, signed F. Preiss, 6in (15cm) high.
$1,000-1,500

A gilded bronze and ivory figure of a dancing girl, on a green onyx pedestal, signed in the bronze H. Fugiere, the base plate stamped Fabrication Francaise Paris – G.M., little finger of right hand missing, 19in (48cm) high.
$2,600-3,600

A bronze and ivory statue in the style of Preiss, the girl balancing an iridescent glass ball, minor damage to hands and feet, 12in (31cm).
$2,600-3,600

A bronze and ivory figure, by Claire J. Colinet, 12in (31cm).
$7,000-9,000

Furniture

An oak child's settle, model No. 215, and an oak child's rocker, model No. 341, red printed mark on each, c1910, settle 37½in (95cm) long.
$1,800-2,000

The Respectful Splits, a cold painted bronze and ivory figure, cast from a model by Paul Phillipe, on a green onyx base, signed P. Phillipe, 7in (18cm) high.
$4,500-5,500

A silvered bronze and ivory figure, by Lorenzl, modelled as a 1920s girl in short graduated party dress, on square marble base, signed Lorenzl, 7½in (19cm) high.
$550-700

An oak library table by Gustav Stickley, model No. 619, c1910, 30in (76cm) high.   **$5,000-5,500**

A Gustav Stickley oak single bed, model number 923, c1910, 82in (208cm) long. **$2,000-3,000**

An oak china cabinet, by Gustav Stickley, model number 815, c1904, 39½in (100cm). **$5,500-7,000**

Two oak smoker's cabinets, by Gustav Stickley, model number 89, c1910, 29in (74cm) high. **$7,500-8,000**

An oak spindle cube chair by Gustav Stickley, model No. 391, c1907. **$9,000-10,000**

An oak bent arm Morris chair, by Gustav Stickley, model No. 336, red printed mark, c1904. **$4,500-5,000**

Two oak spindle chests by Gustav Stickley, each retaining original label, c1907, 16in (41cm) high. **$7,000-7,500**

An oak dressing table by Gustav Stickley, model No. 907, printed red mark, 55in (140cm). **$3,000-3,500**

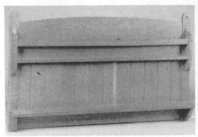

An oak plate rack by Gustav Stickley, model No. 801, c1910, 28in (71cm) high. **$4,500-4,800**

An oak music cabinet, by Gustav Stickley, model number 70, c1910, 20in (51cm). **$5,000-7,000**

An oak settle by Gustav Stickley, model No. 225, c1910, 68in (172cm). **$5,000-5,500**

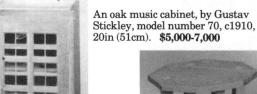

An oak octagonal taboret by L. and J. G. Stickley, model No. 558, c1910, 20in (51cm) high. **$1,200-1,500**

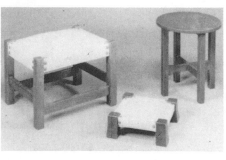

Two oak stools and a taboret by Gustav Stickley, c1910. **$1,700-$2,000**

Two oak benches by Gustav Stickley, c1910. **$2,500-4,000**

Glass

A pair of French frosted glass decanters, decorated with female forms.
$1,000-1,600

A black and clear glass decanter, 9in (23cm), and 6 glasses.   **$550-700**

Jewellery

A Georg Jensen brooch, with Danish maker's marks and numbered 70, 2in (6cm) diam.
$350-450

A black and clear glass decanter, c1930.
$180-360

A cameo vase by Le Verre Francais, 8½in (21cm) high.
$1,200-1,600

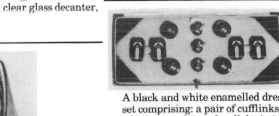

A black and white enamelled dress set comprising: a pair of cufflinks, 4 buttons and 3 studs, all depicting a gentleman in tuxedo, in original fitted case.
$800-1,000

A Georg Jensen silver ring, designed by Henning Koppel, of openwork almost heart-shape amoebic form, Danish marks, numbered 89 and bearing London import marks for 1967.
$140-180

A silver and enamel pendant watch, the reverse with green, black, yellow, blue and red enamel stripe design, the champagne dial with Arabic numerals, signed Fresard, Lucerne, the signed oval movement jewelled to the third with 3 adjustments, the hinged case with the maker's mark.
$450-650

A pearl bracelet, each section interspersed by 3 diamonds and with all diamond set white gold clasp, 2ct approx.
$2,000-3,000

A lady's Continental two-colour bracelet watch, the black dial signed Titus with square cut synthetic ruby twin line borders and diamond and synthetic ruby panel, scroll shoulders to the twin row Brazilian link bracelet.
$1,200-1,600

Make the most of Miller's

Unless otherwise stated, any description which refers to 'a set' or 'a pair' includes a valuation for the entire set or the pair, even though the illustration may show only a single item

A lady's Continental sprung bangle watch, with scrollwork terminals, the movement signed Periam Watch Co., with black dial.
$2,000-3,000

Metal

A Continental silver gilt and enamel cigarette box with cedar interior, in pale blue, pink and black design on a white ground, stamped import marks for London 1927, 4½in (11cm) wide.
$1,600-2,000

A sterling silver oblong cigarette case with sunburst cast decoration and gold coloured clasp set with a blue stone, 4½in (11cm) wide.
$550-650

A silver chalice by Charles Boyton, 1936, 7in (18cm).
$700-900

A pair of brass candlesticks, 11in (28cm) high.
$70-100

A James Dixon silver candelabra, c1920, 8in (20cm) high.
$700-1,000

A pair of Liberty pewter candlesticks, with separate sconces, maker's marks.
$550-650

A Georg Jensen hammer beaten beaker, marked Denmark Sterling, Georg Jensen, 296A, c1925, 4in (10cm).
$450-550

Georg Jensen (1886-1935) was a Danish designer of silverware and jewellery, whose workshop was established in 1904 in Copenhagen.

A silver dish, London, c1930, 11in (28cm) diam.
$650-800

A Georg Jensen silver butter dish and butter knife in the Blossom pattern, maker's marks and import marks for 1928 and 1930.
$700-900

A pair of bonbon dishes with applied ivory handles, by William Hutton & Sons, Sheffield 1935, 9in (23cm) wide   **$1,600-2,000**

A tea and coffee service, designed by Georg Jensen, comprising: teapot with ebonised wooden handle, terminating at the top in twin fruit cluster finial, London import marks for 1931, coffee pot, London import marks for 1929, 9½in (24cm) high, sugar bowl and milk jug, London import marks for 1931, and tea tray, marks for 1928, each with oval mark and crown, oval .925 mark, and Sterling Denmark, with GS import mark for George Stockwell, marked Dessin GI.
$7,000-9,000

A German electroplate cocktail shaker modelled as a Zeppelin, the interior containing flask, lemon squeezer, strainer, graduated cups, corkscrew box and cover, and spoon.
$2,000-2,700

A three-piece coffee set, by R. E. Stone, London, 1947.
$1,200-1,500

A Georg Jensen four-piece lightly hammered coffee service, with ebonised handles and finials, stamped with usual Georg Jensen marks and dated 1918, coffee pot 6in (15cm) high, 788gr.
$2,600-3,600

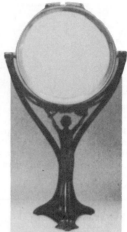

A pewter coffee set with tray, marked Liberty & Co.
$550-700

A W.M.F. electroplated pewter mirror, stamped factory marks, B, 1/O, OX, piece missing from top, c1900, 19in (48cm).
$1,000-1,200

A three-piece silver tea service of panelled rectangular design, comprising: teapot, sugar basin and cream jug, Birmingham 1932/3, 39oz gross.
$650-800

A four-piece tea service comprising: teapot, hot water jug, sugar and cream jug, of octagonal form, decorated with bands of chased scrollwork, Birmingham 1933, 58oz.
$1,000-1,200

Miscellaneous

A bronze and ivory figure and clock, by Ferdinand Preiss, 9in (23cm).
$3,500-4,500

A clock made in the Isle of Man, and featured on the front cover of Collectable Clocks, the rocking ship and changing background light are very effective, particularly at night, c1943, 13in (33cm) high.
$700-900

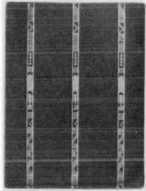

A Wiener Werkstätte embossed leather wallet, 'Gesiba', with popper fastener, with embossed gilt decoration of 3 bands each with a geometric pattern, stamped on the inside Gesiba Wiener Werkstätte, 6in (15cm) long.
$450-650

A Donegal tufted woollen carpet, the sage green field with central blue rose flowerhead within rose leaf and stem motifs in green and brown, 68½ by 37½in (173 by 96cm).
$1,000-1,200

An enamelled and chromed metal table lamp, on circular base, the curved part reeded column supporting swivel mounted reeded shade, 16½in (42cm) high.
$450-650

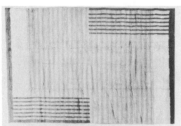

A Donegal tufted woollen carpet, the mushroom ground with patterns in shades of green, the reverse with printed number 1936, 159½ by 107½in (404 by 273cm).
$800-1,200

Post-War Design

Pipistrello, a table lamp designed by Gae Aulenti, for Martinelli Luce, marked Modello 620, Pipistrello, Martinello Luce design Gae Aulenti, Made in Italy, 35½in (91cm).
$1,800-2,800

Berthe Hill, 'Chippie', 1920s jazz singer, in fibreglass, by John Clinch, 34in (86cm).
$1,500-1,600

Jean Cocteau, a terracotta bust by Arno Breker, signed, numbered 5/50, on a rectangular dark grey stone base, 13½in (35cm) high.
$3,500-4,500

A Vistosi metal and glass stylised bird, the free-blown smoky grey glass internally decorated with a triple row of irregular blue and green rectangles, with applied millefiori eyes and mounted on folded metal legs with claw feet, 10½in (27cm).
$1,800-2,800

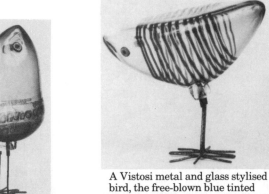

A Vistosi metal and glass stylised bird, the free-blown blue tinted glass internally decorated with a red spiral, with applied millefiori eyes and mounted on folded metal legs with claw feet, 7½in (19cm) high.
$1,800-2,800

A terracotta plate, designed by Jean Lurçat, with polychrome enamels, signed under the plate J. Lurçat Sant-Vicens, N.Z.C. III Dessin, 10in (25cm) diam.
$2,000-3,000

A Scandinavian blue tinted fruit bowl, signed and dated 1960, 15in (38cm) wide.
$110-150

A James Powell & Sons (Whitefriars) Ltd. vase, decorated with a spiral ribbon, in amethyst glass, 11in (28cm) high.
$260-360

A set of 8 Fornasetti plates, each with painted polychrome decoration of the sun in various shapes, with black printed signature 12 Mesi, 12 Soli, Fornasetti Milano, Made in Italy, 10½in (26cm) diam.
$5,500-7,000

IVORY

A Siculo-Arabic ivory casket, the lid and body with gilt copper mounts and lock plate, the lid with one side panel lacking, minor damage, 12th/13thC, 4½in (12cm) wide.
$5,800-9,800

A set of 6 Austrian carved ivory figures of musicians, on turned boxwood and ebonised barrel bases, 6in (15cm).
$4,500-6,500

A pair of South German ivory and wood figures of beggars, on naturalistically carved wooden bases, minor damage to one hat, early 18thC, 11in (28cm).
$8,000-9,000

These figures are stylistically very close to the style of Veit Grauppensberg (1698-1774).

l. An ivory goblet and cover, 14in (36cm) high.
$36,000-45,000
r. An ivory goblet and cover, 19in (48cm) high.
$63,000-72,000

An unusual Anglo Indian carved ivory miniature chiffonier, the upper section with mirror back and scroll supports, the base with 2 doors, enclosing a selection of bottles, goblets and jugs, slight damage, 19thC, 7in (18cm).
$900-1,000

A German or Austrian ivory and boxwood figure of a tonsured monk leaning on a wine barrel, dated 1895, 6in (15cm) overall.
$800-1,200

An ivory opera glass, three-draw with turned eyepiece and barrel, signed on the draw G. & C. Dixey, 3 New Bond Street, London.
$650-900

A German ivory figure of Venus with Cupid, on naturalistic base, on turned wooden socle, 19thC, 9in (23cm).
$3,500-4,500

A French ivory statuette of Parsifal, in period costume, on cylindrical turned socle, hand repaired, 19thC, 8in (20cm).
$1,800-2,800

A Dutch ivory handled knife and fork set, the handles carved in the round with a king and queen holding their sceptres, the steel knife blade with cutler's mark, the steel fork with 2 tines, in cuir bouilli case, some splits, late 17thC, the knife 8in (20cm) overall.
$1,800-2,800

A carved ivory portrait bust of a gentleman, raised on a black marble socle, 19thC, 3in (8cm). **$800-1,000**

An Italian sculpted white marble bust of the young Emperor Augustus, inscribed L. Clerici. Roma. 1879, 18in (46cm), on a socle. **$2,600-3,600**

An English white marble bust of a young girl, by Donald Campbell Haggart, inscribed and dated on the back D.G. Haggart. SCR.1902, on an ebonised wood pedestal base, early 20thC, 59½in (150cm) high. **$2,600-3,600**

Donald Campbell Haggart worked primarily in Glasgow during the late 19th and early 20thC. He exhibited at the Royal Academy in 1882.

MARBLE

A white marble bust of St. Theresa, in nun's habit, on square marble base, 19thC, 29½in (75cm).
$900-1,500

An Italian white marble bust of a faun, the smiling figure with tightly curling hair, set on a waisted socle, c1880, 22in (56cm).
$1,200-1,500

A white marble bust of a young woman, in Renaissance style, late 19thC, 21½in (54cm).
$6,500-7,000

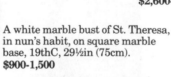

A reconstituted marble bust of a young clown, smiling and wearing a ruff, on a waisted socle, 20in (51cm).
$300-400

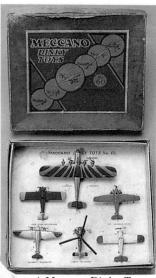

A C.I.J. tinplate clockwork P2 Alfa Romeo, some damage, 21½in (54cm) long, with original box and key. **$4,500-5,500**

A Bing spirit fired fire engine, re-painted, mechanism restored, hose missing, c1902, 10in (26cm) long. **$3,600-4,500**

A Merrythought Mickey Mouse doll, 14in (35.5cm). **$70-110**

A Meccano Dinky Toys boxed aeroplane gift set, No. 60, play worn, c1940. **$1,500-1,600**

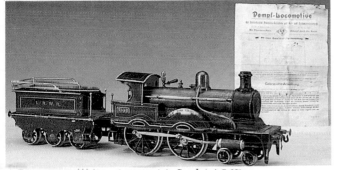

A Bing gauge III live steam spirit fired 4-4-0 King Edward Locomotive, damaged, c1902. **$10,000-12,000**

A German Baroque painted sledge, early 18thC, 109in (277cm) long. **$16,500-12,000**

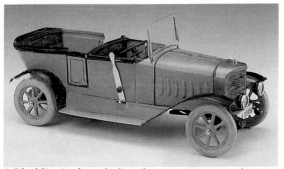

A Marklin tinplate clockwork open tourer, steering mechanism detached from front axle, c1927, 11in (28cm). **$7,000-9,000**

A musical automaton, French, c1870, 26in (66cm) high. **$10,000-12,000**

A Marklun tinplate 'Fidelitas' clown car train, hand painted, No. 8965, car lacking. **$26,000-28,000**

A carved flag horse, with American flag blanket, 54in (137cm) long. **$8,000-10,000**

A set of 2 carved wood rounding boards. **$2,300-2,800**

A carved double-sided chariot, depicting a woman riding a swan, 54in (137cm) long. **$3,000-3,500**

A carved wood 'Uncle Sam' chariot, with carved images. **$7,000-9,000**

A set of carved wood rounding boards, with carved nude angels. **$1,000-1,500**

A carved wood horse. **$2,000-2,700**

A carved prancing horse, with jewelled trappings, 53in (135cm) long. **$21,000-27,000**

A set of carved wood rounding boards. **$1,000-1,500**

A carved wood stork, carrying a baby, 67in (168cm) high. **$24,000-27,000**

A carved wood Zebra, 42in (107cm) long. **$9,000-10,000**

A carved wood cat, in leaping pose, 49in (125cm) long. **$20,000-21,000**

A carved wood carousel dog, with deeply carved fur and carved collar, chains and saddle, 53in (134.5cm) long. **$14,500-18,000**

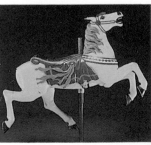

A carved wood cat, with expressive face, 51in (130cm) long. **$12,000-14,500**

A carved wood leaping frog, 41in (104cm) high. **$16,500-18,000**

A carved wood dog, with deep markings, carved buckle, collar and saddle, 43in (109cm) long. **$7,000-9,000**

A carved wood carousel horse, 47in (119cm) long. **$4,000-5,000**

A Kammer & Reinhardt bisque googlie eyed doll, c1914, 14¹/₂in (34cm). **$3,600-5,500**

A Lenci cloth doll of a Russian lady, c1930s, 41in (104cm). **$9,000-10,000**

A F. E. Winkler bisque doll, with Bahr and Proschild head, body by Adolf Wislizenus. **$5,500-9,000**

A French bisque doll, with ball jointed wood and composition body, impressed J1. **$5,500-7,000**

A Jumeau bisque doll. **$21,000-27,000**

A Steiff plush teddy bear, c1908, 29in (74cm). **$5,500-6,500**

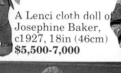

A Lenci cloth doll of Josephine Baker, c1927, 18in (46cm). **$5,500-7,000**

A J D Kestner bisque doll, c1914, 13¹/₂in (34cm). **$7,000-9,000**

A Jumeau bisque doll, some damage, impressed EJ ALO, c1875, 26in (66cm) high. **$36,000-45,000**

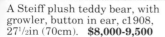

A Steiff plush teddy bear, with growler, button in ear, c1908, 27¹/₂in (70cm). **$8,000-9,500**

A Steiff golly, with button in ear, c1913, 17in (43cm). **$9,000-10,000**

A Steiff plush teddy bear, with button in ear, some wear, c1920, 30in (76cm). **$9,000-10,000**

An Etruscan bronze helmet, Vetulonia type, 480-460 BC, 8in (21cm). **$20,000-23,000**

An Apulian pottery pyxis and cover, associated with the Baltimore painter, 4thC BC. **$4,500-5,500**

A Hellenistic terracotta figure of a woman, 2nd-1st Century BC, 21¹/₂in (54cm). **$12,000-14,500**

An Egyptian limestone head of a goddess, 19th-21st Dynasty. **$8,000-9,000**

A Roman marble head, 1st Century AD, 9¹/₂in (24cm). **$16,500-20,000**

An Attic cup, 540 BC. **$12,000-14,500**

A Roman glass flask, restored, 1st Century BC, 31¹/₂in (9cm). **$45,000-50,000**

A Greek terracotta head of a Kouros, early 5th Century BC. **$16,500-21,000**

A Roman bronze figure of youth, 2nd Century AD, 5¹/₂in (14cm). **$16,500-18,000**

An Apulian pottery krater, late 4th Century BC. **$54,000-63,000**

An Egyptian limestone stele, c1075-30 BC, 11in (28cm) high. **$6,000-8,000**

An Attic krater, 540-530 BC, 11in (28cm) high. **$10,000-12,000**

An Egyptian bronze head of a cat, with a beryl scarab inset in the crown of its head, 712-730 BC, 3in (7.5cm). **$9,000-10,000**

COLOUR REVIEW

A celadon jade 'champion' vase and cover, Qianlong. **$30,000-36,000**

A Jadeite figure of a maiden, in flowing robe, 8¹/₂in (22cm) high, wood stand. **$4,500-6,000**

A bronze figure of Guanyin, losses, Song Dynasty, 9in (22cm). **$7,000-9,000**

A pottery cocoon jar, the oviform body with waisted neck, Han Dynasty, 18¹/₂in (47cm) wide. **$5,500-6,000**

An archaic bronze wine vessel and cover, Western Zhou Dynasty. **$54,000-72,000**

A Bronze group of Zhenwu, Ming Dynasty, 43in (110cm) high, with wood stand. **$16,500-20,000**

Two painted pottery Zodiac figures, one ear missing, six Dynasties, 9¹/₂in (24cm). **$7,000-9,000**

A celadon and russet jade boulder, carved with 2 deer on a river bank, 18thC, 7¹/₂in (19cm) long wood stand. **$7,000-9,000**

A Sancai pottery figure of a horse, 20in (50cm) high. **$20,000-23,000**

A Dingyao floral dish incised with a single lotus stem, rim chips, Song Dynasty, 5¹/₂in (14cm), with box. **$12,000-14,500**

A Yaozhou celadon bowl, the exterior incised with petal ribs, under a translucent celadon glaze suffused with bubbles, Song Dynasty, 8in (20cm) diam. **$18,000-21,000**

A recumbent jade bull, the mottled grey stone with scattered deep russet inclusions, small chip to nostril, Ming Dynasty, 51¹/₂in (13.5cm) long, wood box and stand. **$11,000-14,500**

A silver and shibuichi box and cover, decorated in gold wire and translucent enamels, signed, late 19thC, 5in (12.5cm) long. **$3,000-4,000**

A gilt bronze figure of Wei To, 17thC, 9in (23cm) high, wood stand. **$6,000-8,000**

A Ming style gilt copper seated figure of Buddha, with inscriptions, incised Qianlong Seven-character mark. 12½in (31cm). **$6,000-8,000**

A silver Kogo, decorated in takabori and gilt takazogan, signed Setsuho sei, late 19thC, 3in (7cm) diam. **$12,000-16,500**

A pair of archaic Ordos bronze openwork plaques, extensive malachite encrustation, Warring States, 5in (12cm) long. **$8,000-9,500**

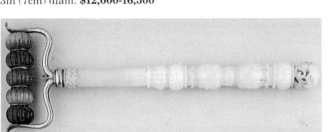

A celadon jade back massager, with revolving beads of lapis lazuli, coral and jade, mid-Qing Dynasty, 10½in (26cm) long. **$8,000-10,000**

A pair of inscribed beaten gold lotus cups, Tang Dynasty, 4in (9cm) diam. **$40,000-45,000**

A Shibuichi migaki-ji kogo and cover, signed Isshuhoru, late 19thC, 2½in (6cm) square. **$3,600-5,500**

An iron box, decorated in uchidashi, takabori and silver takazogan, late 19thC, 5in (12cm). **$1,600-2,000**

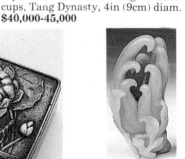

A jade carving of a finger citron, 18thC, 4in (10.5cm). **$2,000-2,700**

A celadon jade sceptre, 18thC, 14in (35cm). **$6,000-8,000**

An ivory netsuke, signed Shugetsu, 18thC, 6in (15cm) high. **$90,000-100,000**

An ivory netsuke of the God of Longevity, unsigned, 18thC, 3½in (8.5cm) high. **$32,000-36,000**

A rogin box and cover formed as Hotei's treasure bag, late 19thC, 4in (10cm) wide. **$14,500-16,500**

A bronze vase, signed in seal form Yuasa zo, late 19thC, 7in (18cm) high. **$6,000-7,500**

A silver box and cover, signed Yukiteru, late 19thC, 6½in (17cm) wide. **$8,000-9,500**

A silver lined shibuichi box and cover, base signed Kogyokusai, late 19thC, 5½in (13.5cm) wide. **$18,000-21,000**

A bronze moon flask, base signed Shoami Katsuyoshizo, c1880, 7in (18cm) high. **$14,500-16,000**

A Korean gilt bronze seal, inscription probably removed, Yi Dynasty, 15th/16thC. **$8,000-10,000**

An inlaid silver ox and ceremonial cart, with lapis lazuli, turquoise, mother-of-pearl and amber, late Qing Dynasty, 18½in (7cm) long. **$8,000-9,500**

A Shibuichi-ji natsume, unsigned, 19thC, 4in (10.5cm) high. **$3,000-3,600**

A Komai iron box and cover, shaped as a folding fan overlapping a gourd, signed Kyoto ju Komei sei, late 19thC, 7in (17.5cm) wide. **$3,600- 5,500**

An archaic gold and silver inlaid bronze axe head, some encrustations, Warring States, 5in (13cm) wide. **$14,500-16,500**

A suzuribako, decorated in fundame, silver heidatsu, aogai okibirame, the interior similarly decorated, damaged, unsigned, late 17thC, 8½in (21cm) high. **$2,700-3,600**

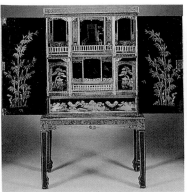

A Chinese Export gilt decorated black lacquer cabinet-on-stand, restoration to decoration, early 19thC, 35½in (90cm) wide. **$14,500-18,000**

A lacquer Momoyama period domed chest, latch replaced, c1600. **$6,000-7,000**

A Chinese six-leaf screen, 80in (203cm) high. **$145,000-160,000**

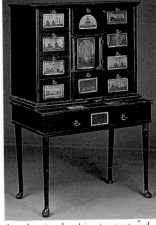

A Chinese painted four-leaf screen, the reverse painted with waterfront scenes and domestic utensils, 19thC, 74in (188cm) high. **$7,000-9,000**

An ebonised cabinet-on-stand, inset with pietra paesina panels, restorations, cabinet early 18thC, 35in (89cm) wide. **$9,000-10,000**

A Chinese six-leaf screen, 19thC, 81½in (206cm). **$27,000-32,000**

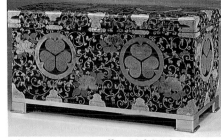

A lacquer storage coffer, 18th/19thC, 69in (175cm) long. **$215,000-230,000**

A Chinese Export black and gold lacquer coffer, mid-18thC. **$30,000-36,000**

An eight-leaf black lacquer hardwood screen, painted with a continuous scene, the reverse with landscape, 19thC, 72in (182cm) high. **$9,000-10,000**

A black lacquer tsuitate, 19thC, 51in (130cm) high. **$23,000-28,000**

A cloisonne enamel censer and cover, 19thC. **$5,500-7,000**

A Sino-Tibetan cloisonne enamel qilin, old enamel losses, Qianlong, 24in (62cm) high. **$13,000-15,000**

A carved marbled lacquer stand, chip to foot, 17th/18thC, 9in (23cm) wide. **$7,000-9,000**

A lacquer tray, some damage, late 19thC, 28½in (73cm) wide. **$45,000-50,000**

A cloisonne enamel bronze mounted vase, early 19thC, 33½in (85.5cm) high. **$7,000-9,000**

An enamelled silver koro and cover, minor damage, signed on a gilt tablet Hiratsuka, late 19thC, 5½in (13cm). **$8,000-10,000**

A lady's leather card case, with ivory spine and covers, leather torn, unsigned, Meiji period. **$4,500-6,000**

A carved marbled lacquer bowl, 15th/16thC, 7½in (19cm). **$9,500-11,000**

A lacquer dish, age cracks, mid-Ming Dynasty. **$14,500-16,500**

A leather laced armour, c1860. **$27,000-32,000**

A pair of wood sculptures, old wear and damage, Kamakura period, 19½in (50cm) high. **$100,000-108,000**

A Chinese mirror painting mid-18thC, in George III style giltwood carved frame. **$14,500-16,500**

A pair of Regency gilt bronze candelabra, c1820, 26in (66cm) high. **$12,000-14,500**

A pair of George III mahogany and brass candelabra, 20½in (52cm) high. **$9,500-10,500**

A pair of George III ormolu and giltwood candelabra, drilled for electricity, one base cracked, 27in (168cm) high. **$63,000-72,000**

A pair of Regency candlesticks, 13½in (34cm). **$2,700-3,600**

A pair of bronze and ormolu candelabra, early 19thC, 28in (71cm) high. **$72,000-80,000**

A pair of Irish George III giltwood and composition candelabra, restored, 44in (113cm). **$14,500-18,000**

A pair of Empire bronze and ormolu candelabra, supported on spreading triangular shafts, 7 later drip pans, 39½in (100cm) high. **$45,000-54,000**

A pair of Napoleon III bronze candelabra **$9,000-10,000**

A set of 4 gilt bronze candlesticks, French or English, c1775, 16½in (42cm) high. **$125,000-145,000**

A pair of Louis XVI ormolu and Meissen porcelain candelabra, some damage. **$9,000-10,000**

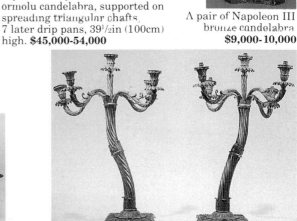

A pair of Regency ormolu candelabra, one drip pan lacking, one associated. **$13,000-15,000**

A pair of ormolu and bronze two-light candelabra, on marble plinths, 17½in (44cm) high. **$7,000-9,000**

A pair of Charles X bronze and ormolu candlesticks, 13in (33cm). **$4,500-6,000**

A pair of French bronze and ormolu twin-light candelabra, mid-19thC, 19in (48cm). **$32,000-36,000**

A pair of Restauration bronze candelabra, c1820, 32in (81cm). **$21,000-23,000**

A pair of George III paktong candlesticks, 11in (28cm). **$5,500-7,000**

A pair of Charles X ormolu candelabra, the central branches with flaming nozzles, 16½in (42cm) high. **$5,500-7,000**

A pair of Empire ormolu and polished steel candlesticks, each foliate nozzle on turned tapering applied with stars, with triple paw socle and stepped base with anthemia, 10in (25cm) high. **$2,500-2,800**

A pair of ormolu candlesticks in Louis XV style, after Meissonnier, 13in (33cm) high. **$45,000-54,000**

A pair of ormolu seven-light candelabra, 29in (74cm) high. **$3,600-5,500**

An ormolu and marble four-light candelabra, with beaded drip pans, drilled for electricity, 21in (53cm) high. **$3,600-5,500**

A brass six-light chandelier, surmounted by an eagle, late 17th/early 18thC, fitted for electricity, 26½in (67cm) high. **$4,000-4,800**

A pair of gilt bronze candlesticks, supported by seated male and female figures with cornucopia, 19thC, 13in (33cm) high. **$3,200-4,500**

A pair of Regency black painted plaster, gilt gesso and cut glass candelabra, 34in (86cm) high. **$8,000-9,500**

An ormolu and cut glass eight-light chandelier, mid-19thC. **$4,500-6,000**

A brass chandelier, the scroll arms with flat drip pans and ovoid nozzles, early 18thC, 39in (99cm) diam. **$15,000-18,000**

A cut glass chandelier, fitted for electricity, slight chips, 46in (117cm) high. **$7,000-9,000**

A Restauration gilt bronze and glass chandelier, c1820, 44in (112cm) high. **$16,500-18,000**

A German giltwood seven-light chandelier, 18thC, 41in (104m) high. **$14,500-16,500**

A brass twelve-light chandelier in 2 graduated tiers, 18thC, 25½in (65cm) diam. **$7,000-9,000**

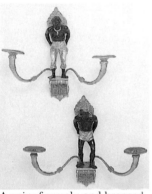

A pair of ormolu and bronzed twin-branch wall lights, later nozzles, fitted for electricity, 11in (28cm) high. **$6,000-9,000**

A pair of ormolu wall lights, bored for electricity, basically early 19thC, 9½in (24cm) wide. **$3,600-4,500**

A pair of ormolu four-branch wall lights, fitted for electricity, 12in (30cm) high. **$5,500-7,000**

A gilt metal, tôle and soft paste porcelain chandelier, fitted for electricity, 29in (74cm) high. **$4,500-6,000**

A William IV brass colza oil hanging light, lacking burners, 45in (114cm) high. **$6,000-8,000**

A pair of early Victorian painted and parcel gilt torchère lamps, 65in (165cm) high. **$4,500-5,500**

A Louis XV style ormolu eight-branch chandelier, lacking one branch, 53in (134.5cm) high. **$12,000-14,500**

A pair of French ormolu torchères, the bases with inset jasper limoges plaques, c1900, 72in (182cm). **$4,500-6,000**

A pair of Venetian parcel gilt polychrome and ebonised blackamoor torchères, lacking trays, mid-19thC, 66in (168cm) high. **$27,000-32,000**

A Second Empire torchère, 84¹/₂in (214cm) high. **$9,000-10,000**

A Regency gilt brass and glass colza light, c1815, with modern shades, 36in (91cm) high. **$24,000-27,000**

A pair of giltwood torchères, one as a merman and one as a mermaid, on simulated porphyry bases, one with damage to shell, redecorated, 18thC, 57¹/₂in (146cm) high. **$10,000-12,000**

A Regency ormolu colza oil hanging lamp, in Gothic style, later fitments and frosted glass shades, restorations, 51in (130cm) high. **$36,000-40,000**

A William IV glass chandelier, c1830, 64in (162cm) high. **$24,000-27,000**

An ormolu, cut and moulded glass chandelier, fitted for electricity, late 19thC. **$14,500-16,500**

A pair of Louis XVI style ormolu and cut glass electroliers, 48in (122cm) high. **$7,000-9,000**

An alabaster dish light, with crenellated top, painted with signs of the Zodiac, c1830, 11in (28cm) diam. **$8,000-9,500**

A pair of Louis XVI gilt bronze wall lights, c1785. **$21,000-24,000**

A pair of Regence style silvered wall lights, 29½in (75cm) high. **$9,500-11,000**

A pair of Viennese ormolu, tôle and enamel wall lights, mid-18thC. **$36,000-38,000**

A pair of Louis XV gilt bronze wall lights, mid-18thC, 22in (56cm) high. **$27,000-29,000**

A pair of Charles X ormolu lamps. **$20,000-21,000**

A gilt bronze and cut glass lamp. **$12,000-14,500**

A pair of Louis XV gilt bronze wall lights, mid-18thC. **$6,000-8,000**

A pair of Empire gilded and patinated bronze wall lights, each with a blackamoor mask. **$7,000-9,000**

A set of 6 ormolu and twin-branch wall lights, fitted for electricity, 24in (61cm). **$9,000-10,000**

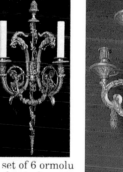

A pair of early Louis XVI gilt bronze wall lights, attributed to Pitoin, c1775. **$20,000-23,000**

A pair of Louis XVI ormolu lamps, fitted for electricity. **$18,000-21,000**

A pair of Empire ormolu and bronze wall lights, 9½in (24cm) wide. **$13,000-15,000**

A brass and engraved glass hanging light, fitted for electricity, 19thC, 25in (64cm). **$9,500-10,000**

A pair of Louis XV ormolu, tôle and Vincennes lights, 13in (33cm) high. **$27,000-29,000**

A pair of Louis XV gilt bronze wall lights, mid-18thC. **$5,500-7,000**

The Most Noble Order of the George, Lesser George sash badge, mid-18thC. **$74,000-78,000**

The Most Noble Order of the Garter. **$20,000-21,000**

Order of the Golden Fleece, Spain, Kingdom, late 18thC. **$10,000-14,500**

The Most Noble Order of the Garter, Lesser George sash badge, in fitted case. **$38,000-45,000**

The Most Noble Order of the Garter, Lesser George badge. **$18,000-21,000**

The Most Noble Order of the Garter, Lesser George. **$34,000-38,000**

The Most Noble Order of the Garter, Lesser George, c1650. **$50,000-54,000**

The Most Noble Order of the Garter, Lesser George, early 18thC. **$36,000-40,000**

The Most Noble Order of the Garter, breast star, gold, silver and enamel. **$6,000-8,000**

The Most Noble Order of the Garter, breast star, gold, silver and enamel, mid-19thC. **$5,500-7,000**

The Most Noble Order of the Garter, Lesser George, mid-17thC. **$82,000-90,000**

Order of the Osmanieh, Grand Cordon set of insignia, badge, Turkey. **$1,000-1,500**

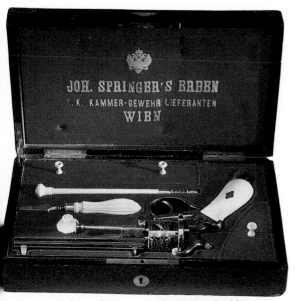

A composed set of 3 12-bore Churchill 'Premiere XXV' assisted-opening sidelock ejector gun, 25in (63cm). **$44,000-46,000**

A Continental cased 12mm six-shot pifire double-action revolver, No. 125656 and 641, c1875. **$13,000-15,000**

A 12-gauge Winchester model 101 Silver Anniversary Edition custom selective, single trigger over/under gun. **$3,000-4,500**

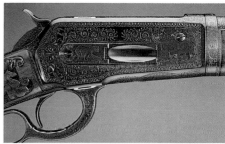

A factory engraved Winchester model 1886 Takedown rifle, by Angelo J Stokes, No. 145592, 24in (61cm) barrel. **$38,000-42,000**

A French model of an armourer's shop, signed Au Pere Masselin, Armurier du Roi, early 16thC. **$9,500-11,000**

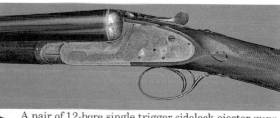

A pair of 12-bore single trigger sidelock ejector guns, No. 7083/4, standard easy-opening action, 29in (73.5cm) barrels. **$36,000-38,000**

A pair of 12-bore self-opening sidelock ejector guns, by J. Purdey, No. 27437/8, 28in (71cm) barrels. **$55,000-60,000**

A factory engraved and cased Winchester model 1892 lever-action carbine, No. 60909, 44-40 calibre, 20in (50.5cm) barrel, with brass and hickory cleaning rod. **$36,000-45,000**

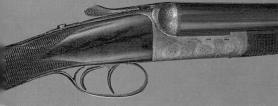

A pair of 12-bore round-action ejector guns, by J Dickson, No. 7067/8, 28in (71cm) barrels. **$28,000-32,000**

A pair of 12-bore sidelock ejector guns, by F. Beesley, No. 2221/2, 28in (71cm) barrels, with oak and leather case . **$34,000-36,000**

An Aubusson carpet, areas of repair, stained, backed. **$2,000-2,700**

A Heriz silk rug, with floral cartouche and vine border, 76 by 53in (193 by 134cm). **$30,000-36,000**

An Aubusson runner, the border with leafy cartouches, areas of wear and damage, backed, 168 by 46in (416 by 117cm). **$5,500-6,000**

An Aubusson carpet, slight-staining, backed, 203 by 159in (515 by 403cm). **$28,000-32,000**

An Agra carpet, the brickred field with herati patern, with flowering vine border, 144 by 120in (365 by 304cm). **$10,000-12,000**

An Aubusson carpet, with central moulded medallion and bouquet, slight damage, 256 by 124in (650 by 314cm). **$30,000-36,000**

An Aubusson carpet, areas of wear and repair, 122in (309cm) long. **$5,500-7,000**

An Aubusson carpet, with tracery flowering vine around a central medallion, areas of staining and repair, backed, 138 by 133in (350 by 337cm). **$8,000-9,500**

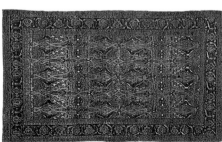

A bidjar carpet, 221 by 136in (560 by 245cm). **$12,000-14,000**

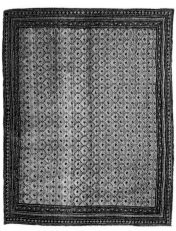

An Agra carpet, striped border, 131 by 100in (332 by 254cm). **$9,500-11,000**

A Melas prayer rug, a short kilim strip at each end, minor repairs, 71in (180cm) long. **$4,500-6,000**

A Kirman part silk pictorial rug, ends with minor damage, 93 by 63in (236 by 160cm). **$9,500-11,000**

A Senneh Hamadan rug, short kilim at each end, some damage, 81in (205cm) long. **$12,000-14,500**

A Kashan Mochtasham rug, with Royal Hawkers, in floral boarder with calligraphic cartouches, between calligraphic cartouche stripes, 91 by 55in (231 by 140cm). **$9,000-10,000**

A Kashan carpet, areas of extensive re-piling, 283 by 161in (718 by 408cm). **$20,000-21,000**

A Pontremoli carpet, the ivory field with a variety of loose open sprays, in a serrated minor border, signed JMP, 146 by 97in (370 by 246cm). **$34,000-38,000**

A Kashan Mochtasham rug, with pictorial scene of Bahram Gur, 82in long. **$7,000-9,000**

A Savonnerie carpet, with a central floral roundel with a moulded leaf frame, some damage and wear, 200in (762cm) long. **$45,000-54,000**

A Kashan carpet, with an angular lattice of
palmettes, flowerheads and floral lozenges
surrounding a central medallion, 200 by 121in
(508 by 307cm). **$20,000-21,000**

A Bakshaish carpet, with flowerheads and floral
motifs around a serrated and indented panel,
areas of slight wear, one end rewoven, 130 by
116in (330 by 294cm). **$18,000-21,000**

A Regency Axminster carpet, with large floral
bouquets, ribbons and bunches of leaves around
an octagonal panel, with leafy border, reduced,
130 by 120in (330 by 304cm). **$9,000-10,000**

A Kashan carpet, with palmettes and floral sprays
around a palmette medallion, 147 by 106in
(373 by 296 cm). **$21,000-23,000**

A Heriz carpet, with radiating floral
medallion, and flowering vine and
serrated leaf border, areas of wear,
some tinting, 228 by 179in (579 by
454cm). **$23,000-27,000**

A Kashan mochtacham carpet, with flowering vine
and perching bird striped border, 130 by 93in (330 by
236cm). **$28,000-32,000**

A Karabagh Kelleh , with flowering vine border,
222 by 66in (563 by 167cm). **$6,000-8,000**

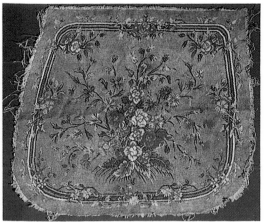

A set of needlework panels, for a bergère chair, worked in silks and wools, French, c1760.
$1,000-1,500

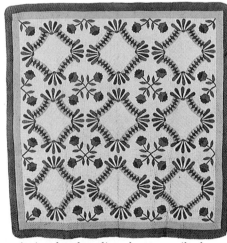

A pieced and appliqued cotton quilted coverlet, North Carolina, c1850, 88½in (224cm). **$1,600-2,000**

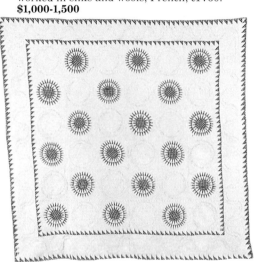

A pieced appliqued and trapunto quilted cotton coverlet American, 19thC, 90in (230cm) long.
$3,500-5,500

A Charles I stumpwork picture, probably depicting Charles I and Henrietta, mounted in black and gilt frame, c1645, 12in (30cm) wide.
$7,000-9,000

A Charles I embroidered picture, c1685, 17in (43cm) wide. **$13,000-15,000**

A velvet coat, stencilled in gold with thistles and roses, labelled Mariano Fortuny Venise, c1920. **$3,500-7,000**

A Charles II silver thread, needlework and stumpwork picture, c1660, in 18thC box, 13in (33cm) wide.
$14,000-16,000

A pair of lady's shoes, in spotted kid, with low heels, labelled Edwd. Hogg, St James's, London, c1795.
$1,200-1,800

A pair of lady's mules, embroidered in white thread wrapped in silver, with sunbursts with sequins, square toes, c1665.
$21,000-25,000

'Autumn', a tapestry depicting peasants at grape harvest, losses and restoration, 232$\frac{1}{2}$in (590cm). **$36,000-45,000**

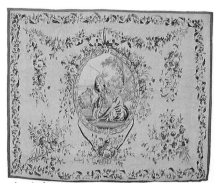

An Aubusson tapestry, late 18thC, 93in (236cm) wide. **$20,000-27,000**

A Brussels mythological tapestry, early 18thC, 99in (252cm) wide. **$28,000-32,000**

'Summer', a tapestry depicting harvest, losses and restorations, 248$\frac{1}{2}$in (631cm). **$36,000-45,000**

A Flemish biblical tapestry, probably depicting the continence of Scipio, within a floral and foliate border, 17thC, 166in (421cm). **$21,000-27,000**

A Bruges woven silk and wool tapestry, late 17thC, 99in (252cm) wide. **$63,000-72,000**

A suite of Spanish vestments early 18thC. **$7,000-9,000**

A Bruges woven tapestry, after an engraving by Lucas Vorsterman after the painting by Rubens, in silk and wool, mid-17thC, 81in (205cm) wide. **$63,000-72,000**

The detail of the embroidered borders of a velvet suit, altered, c1760. **$7,000-9,000**

A Flemish tapestry, c1600, 148in (375cm) wide. **$20,000-27,000**

A Besson echo cornet.
$1,000-1,400

A Bechstein vertical strung
iron framed piano, c1880.
$720-1,200

An overstrung iron framed
boudoir grand piano, by Ernest
Kaps, Dresden, No. 21849.
$1,700-2,700

A Victorian English vertical strung
piano, repolished burr walnut case.
$800-1,400

A violin, by Antonio
Stradivari, the two-
piece back of broad curl
descending from the
centre joint, c1720,
length of back
14in (35.5cm).
$1,600,000-1,800,000

An English overstrung under
damped piano, repolished
mahogany case, c1920.
$1,000-1,500

A Composite
Cremonese Violoncello,
with two-piece back,
c1670. **$30,000-32,000**

An Italian violin, by
Bernardo Calcagni,
with one-piece back,
c1751, 14in (35.5cm).
$54,000-72,000

A French Violoncello,
school of Bernadel,
with two-piece back,
29½in (75cm). **$32,000-
38,000**

A violin, by David
Tecchler, with two-
piece back, 18thC, 14in
(35.5cm).
$28,000-36,000

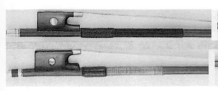

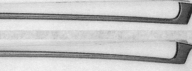

A silver mounted violin
bow, by Grand Adam.
$14,000-18,000

A silver mounted violin
bow, by Francois Tourte.
$36,000-54,000

Sangorski & Sutcliffe, binders, The Complete Angler, John Major, 1824. **$4,500-5,500**

Zaehnsdorf, binders, Burns Poetical works, Macmillan & Co., 1879. **$3,500-5,500**

Zaehnsdorf, binders, Posthumous Poems, J & H. L. Hunt, 1824. **$2,500-2,900**

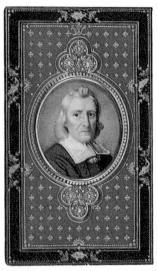

Zaehnsdorf, binders, The Parson's Horn-Book, by the Comet Literary and Patriotic Club, London, Effingham Wilson, 1832. **$450-550**

Stikeman & Co, binders, King of England, Vale Pres, London 1903. **$750-1,500**

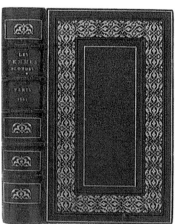

Masson-Debonelle, binders, Les Femmes Blondes, Paris, Aubry 1845. **$1,600-2,000**

Sangorksi & Sutcliffe, binders, a Complete View of the Dress and Habits of the People of London, H. G. Bohn, 1843. **$800-950**

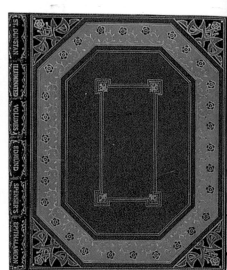

Trautz-Bauzonnet Bindery, Epithalamion, Edmund Spenser, George D. Sproul, 1902. **$540-900**

Webb of Liverpool, The Sketch Book of Geoffrey Crayon, John Murray, 1822. **$800-1,000**

Sangorski & Sutcliffe, Poems by Alfred Tennyson, Edward Moxon, 1842. **$1,000-1,500**

Zaehnsdorf, binders, Chastelard A Tragedy, by A. C. Swinburne, John Camden Hotten, 1866. **$550-720**

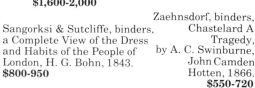

A Victorian white marble figure of a Classical style maiden, by John Randolph Rogers, signed Randolph Rogers, Rome, base detached, some chipping, 42in (107cm).
$3,500-5,500

John Randolph Rogers (1825-92). Born in New York, he studied both in Florence and Rome under Bartolini. Major commissions include many monuments to the American Civil War as well as a pair of doors for the Capitol. Smaller pieces include Biblical and Classical subjects such as Ruth and Nydia.

An Italian white marble bust of a pensive girl in a lace mantilla, by C. Lapini, signed and dated on the reverse C. Lapini Firenze 1888, associated green marble fluted column with rotating capital, the bust 20½in (52cm).
$4,500-6,500

A pair of Italian white marble busts, Venus and Adonis, after the Antique, on socles, with grey marble pedestals, 69in (175cm) high overall.
$5,500-6,500

A white marble armorial keystone, the face carved with a coat-of-arms flanked by foliate scrolls, 18thC, 5½in (14cm).
$550-700

An Italian white marble figure of a young boy, late 19thC, 22in (56cm).
$2,000-3,000

An Italian white marble portrait relief of a lady, in Florentine Renaissance style, within an oval giltwood frame with flowerheads at corners, 14½ by 11in (37 by 28cm).
$6,500-7,000

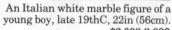

A white marble armorial plaque, the face with a coat-of-arms supported by a lion and a slave, inscribed Furth fortune and fill the letters, 18thC, 9in (23cm).
$900-1,000

The arms are those of Murray, Alexander Sutherland.

An Italian marble mortar, the sides richly carved in relief, and with the initials IN-B-G-M, 2 of the spouts carved for pouring, the other 2 plain, 17thC, 16in (41cm) wide.
$2,600-3,600

A Victorian white marble female figure, wearing a long skirt, monogrammed L.S., 25in (64cm).
$650-800

A pair of marble and gilt bronze urns, the mottled white and green marble forming the baluster body, stepped domed lids with pine cone finials, with gilt bronze feet decorated with stylised foliage, the body with gilt bronze satyr masks and swags of leaves and berries, the gilt bronze neck with guilloche design, 19thC, 6in (15cm). **$2,600-3,600**

An Italian white marble figure of Jesus of Nazareth, with a young boy at his side, some chips and weathering, late 19thC, 55in (140cm). **$1,700-2,700**

An Italian serpentine marble inkwell, the lid and sides decorated with plaster cameos after the Antique, enclosing a fitted interior with slightly ribbed body, mid-19thC, 5½in (14cm) diam. **$1,800-2,800**

An English white marble relief of Diana, probably from a chimneypiece, shown seated against a tree trunk, her quiver at her side and a boar's head and dead stag in the background, holding aloft a bird, at which her 2 hounds look, 18thC, 21 by 8in (53 by 20cm). **$3,000-4,000**

TERRACOTTA

Vertue records Rysbrack making the statuettes of Van Dyck, Rubens and Fiammingo (sic) in 1743, during the period that his popularity was briefly eclipsed by Scheemaker's successful Monument to Shakespeare of 1740 in Westminster Abbey. The 3 statuettes were, nevertheless, much admired at the time, and by 1744 the Daily Advertiser was carrying an advertisment for the casting in plaster of the 3 figures 'now in the Collection of Mr. Joseph van Hacken' for the price of seven and a half guineas the set, subscriptions to be taken by Mess. Claessens and Ven Hagen, at Mr. Rysbrack's in Vere Street. The production of these casts was continued after van Hacken's death in 1749 by John Cheere and Charles Harris. Although examples of the Rubens and van Dyck figures are relatively common, the figure of Duquesnoy, referred to in contemporary literature as Fiammingo, is very rare.

An English white terracotta figure of François Duquesnoy, cast from a model by Michael Rysbrack, leaning against the Belvedere Torso, which is partially draped with an embroidered coverlet, right and left foot missing, minor arm chips, late 18thC, 21½in (54cm). **$8,000-10,000**

A French painted terracotta bust of Marie Antoinette, with manufacturer's mark to the reverse, on an integral socle, 19thC, 30in (76cm). **$900-1,500**

WOODCARVINGS

A pair of polychrome and giltwood reliefs of the infant Christ and the infant St. John, Christ holding the globe, St. John embracing a lamb, minor damages and wear to polychrome, early 18thC, 6in (15cm) high. **$1,200-1,600**

530

A rare English carved oak figure of St. John, 16thC.
$6,500-7,000

A set of 5 Tyrolean wood figures of peasants, the wood stained to resemble marquetry, one figure lacking right arm, another lacking left hand, other minor losses, 18th/19thC, approximately 12½in (32cm) high.
$3,500-5,500

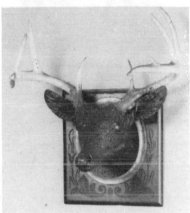

A pair of Anglo-Flemish wood figures of courtiers, one figure lacking right forearm, some damages, early 17thC, 24in (61cm).
$3,500-5,500

A German polychrome wood group of 3 winged putti, some repainting, later shaped wooden base, early 18thC, 21½in (55cm) high.
$9,000-10,000

A South German boxwood figure of St. John, formerly from a Crucifixion group, on wooden socle, tip of nose and base chipped, c1700, 7½in (19cm).
$2,600-3,600

The present boxwood figure with its delicate modelling is similar in style to a boxwood figure of approximately the same height in the Staatliche Museen zu Berlin.

A carved wood stag's head, signed H. Leach, c1870, 24in (61cm) high.
$1,500-2,000

A Hispano-Flemish polychrome and giltwood group of St. Martin, sword lacking, some worming and minor damages, later wooden base, early 16thC, 31½in (80cm). **$10,000-12,000**

A Franconian limewood relief of a bishop saint, traces of polychrome, staff and fingers lacking from right hand, early 16thC, 38in (97cm).
$4,500-6,500

A pair of Italian carved giltwood and gesso figures of amorini, on stepped square bases, late 18thC, 23in (59cm) high overall.
$1,800-2,000

A South German or Austrian wood appliqué, carved in high relief with a demi-figure of a bishop, later pierced wooden background with strapwork, 18thC, 11in (28cm) high.
$3,500-4,500

A Neapolitan polychrome wood figure of an ox, probably from a crib group, with glass eyes, on later wooden base, late 18th/early 19thC, 11½in (29cm) high.
$3,000-4,000

A German 16thC style oak panel, carved in high relief with Adam and Eve, after Albrecht Durer, head of serpent lacking, 26in (66cm) wide.
$2,600-3,600

A carved oak cartouche, the cresting with 2 putti interspersed with 'rays of light' above a panel of the Virgin Mary framed by leafy scrolls, c1750, 54 by 36in (137 by 92cm).
$1,200-1,800

Two wood carvings in the style of Grinling Gibbons, one depicting pine cones, fruit and peas in the pod, 23in (59cm) high, the other flowers and ears of wheat, 26in (66cm), 18thC.
$400-500

A pair of Italian giltwood and painted wall plaques, centred with scallop shells, within fruit and foliate surrounds, 28in (71cm).
$1,500-1,800

A pair of German pearwood reliefs, within ebonised wood mounts and giltwood frames, the oak reverse with old label, late 17th/early 18thC, 6in (15cm) high.
$7,000-9,000

The labels on the reverse of these reliefs read 'William of Orange landed at Torbay 1688. This carving was one of the panels round top of one of the ornamental vats which were brought over for his dining room so that he could always get at his favourite drink. When these vats were in possession of the L. Victuallers Co. were broken up, a parishioner on Epping Green secured the Panels for Rev. H. L. Neave'.

A South Tyrol polychrome and giltwood relief of God the Father and putti, mounted on metal bracket, minor repairs, 18thC, 19 by 17½in (48 by 45cm).
$9,000-10,000

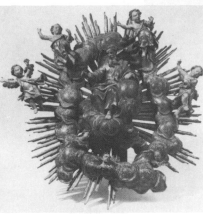

ANTIQUITIES
Marble

A Roman marble head of Caracalla, 2nd Century A.D., 11½in (29cm). **$32,000-40,000**

A Roman marble funerary relief, with inscription between the acroteria at either corner, reading 'Ioulianos, son of Menios, aged 35, farewell. Chrysea, wife of Ioulianos, (?age), farewell', the recessed niche below carved with 2 busts, Eastern Mediterranean, 3rd Century A.D., 23½in (60cm) high. **$11,000-12,000**

A Roman marble male figure, wearing a bulla decorated with a mask, his himation worn diagonally so as to leave his chest bare, the garment with notched edges, 1st Century A.D., 39½in (100cm). **$10,000-14,000**

A Roman marble cinerary urn, 3rd Century A.D., 27in (69cm) wide. **$14,500-18,000**

A Palmyran marble female bust, c150 A.D., 23in (59cm). **$2,600-3,600**

A Roman marble male torso, nude except for a fragment of drapery over the left shoulder, restored, 1st-2nd Century A.D., 31in (79cm). **$45,000-54,000**

A Roman marble head, from a togatus or palliatus figure, his himation drawn up over the back of his head, the face with furrowed brow and ageing features, 1st Century B.C. /1st Century A.D., 9½in (24cm). **$18,000-21,000**

Metalware

An Egyptian bronze figure of a cat, Late period, c600 B.C., 4½in (11cm). **$8,000-10,000**

A fragmentary Greek marble grave loutrophoros, carved in shallow relief, inscribed above the heads of the 2 principal figures, 'Polykrates and Polystratos', foot, handles and neck of loutrophoros broken away, 4th Century B.C., 44in (111cm). **$40,000-45,000**

Polykrates and Polystratos appear as son and father on a gravestone from Peiraeus (IG II 1771); on this loutrophoros the order of relationship seems reversed. It could perhaps be the same family, but neither are rare names in Athens.

An Egyptian bronze figure of a lion, reclining, with its left paw resting on its right paw, Late period, 712-30 B.C., 4½in (11cm). **$8,000-9,000**

An Egyptian bronze figure of Osiris, the God, of mummified form, standing holding the crook and flail, with plumed headdress and central uraeus, 26th Dynasty, c664-525 B.C., 8½in (21cm).
$6,000-7,000

A Roman bronze candelabrum, standing on 3 dolphin shaped feet with palmettes, 3 shell shaped dishes between, one foot restored, 1st-2nd Century A.D., 32½in (82cm).
$14,500-18,000

A Roman bronze lamp, with the inward curving handle terminating in a theatrical mask, a palmette under its chin, 3rd Century A.D., 6in (15cm).
$3,500-4,500

Pottery

An Italic bronze helmet, of the Pilos type, 2 appliques resembling wings to either side of the crown, mid-4th Century B.C., 10in (25cm).
$9,000-10,000

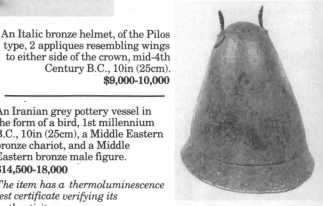

An Iranian grey pottery vessel in the form of a bird, 1st millennium B.C., 10in (25cm), a Middle Eastern bronze chariot, and a Middle Eastern bronze male figure.
$14,500-18,000
The item has a thermoluminescence test certificate verifying its authenticity.

A Corinthian pottery round bodied aryballos, decorated with the figure of a siren, standing with open wings between a panther and a goose, with added purple details, c600 B.C., 5in (13cm).
$2,600-3,600

Miscellaneous

A Palmyran limestone female bust, carved in relief, with an Aramaic inscription in the top left hand corner, nose restored, c150-200 A.D., 21in (53cm).
$9,000-10,000

A Roman limestone relief, with a male figure holding a scroll in his left hand, the head surmounted by a ?bird, 3rd Century A.D., 31in (79cm).   **$6,500-7,500**

A Greek terracotta female figure, 6th Century B.C., 8in (20cm).
$1,000-1,500

A Roman green glass single handled flask, a strap handle attached to the shoulder and neck, the base moulded with 3 concentric circles, with some weathering, 2nd-3rd Century A.D., 10in
$1,500-1,800

A Greek terracotta female figure, probably East Greek, early 5th Century B.C., 7in (18cm). **$1,000-1,500**

A boulle sewing box with original fittings, c1850, 9in (23cm) wide. **$3,000-3,600**

An Attic terracotta doll, in the form of a nude female figure, depicted only to the upper part of the legs, the arms not moulded, 5th Century B.C., 6in (15cm). **$3,000-3,600**

A Roman limestone draped female torso, 1st-2nd Century A.D., 49in (124cm). **$11,000-12,000**

SEWING

A collection of 51 lace bobbins, comprising 33 bearing names or messages, 6 pewter banded, 12 plain, 5 bobbins chipped, 19thC. **$1,000-1,200**

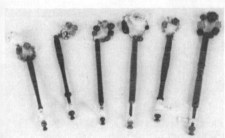

A selection of wooden lace bobbins, 4-6in (10-15cm). **$10-20 each**

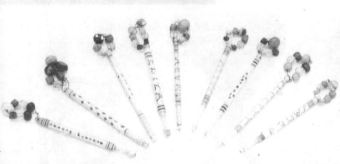

Nine variously named bone bobbins. **$250-300**

A silver mounted tortoiseshell novelty sewing case, in the form of an egg, mounted with the cast head of an emerging chick, its feet protruding from the base, containing a gilt thimble, silver gilt scissors, silver needle case and silver bodkin, London, 1901, 4in (10cm). **$1,000-1,200**

A selection of bone lace bobbins, 3½-4½in (9-12cm). **$25-70 each**

An ivory and brass inlaid sewing case, the cover and escutcheons inlaid with brass scrolls and stained mother-of-pearl, containing carved mother-of-pearl spools, 2 silver thimbles and various sewing items, including an ivory tape measure case. **$800-900**

A brass container for packets of needles, made by W. Avery, c1880.
$35-45

A Chelsea porcelain thimble, brightly painted within gold line bands, inscribed Souvenez vous de moy, hair crack, 1in (2cm).
$4,500-5,500

A Meissen style porcelain needlecase, with hinged cover, in the form of a baby, swathed in yellow and florally decorated clothes, 4½in (12cm). **$800-1,000**

A Meissen gilt metal mounted etui of cigar shape, painted with 4 scenes of gallants and ladies, in iron red, minute rim chips, c1770, 6½in (17cm).
$1,600-2,000

An enamel bodkin case, painted with urns and trophies in gilt cartouches on a turquoise ground, inscribed Amor and A Pledge of Love, and a group of 4 bodkins.
$450-550

A Meissen porcelain thimble, reserved on a powder-blue ground, the top with a flowerhead, with gilt interior, c1740.
$3,000-3,600

A Meissen porcelain thimble, the top painted with a gold flowerhead, c1740.
$4,500-5,500

A set of 6 buttons, each engraved with a dog, George Cray, London, c1780, 1in (2cm) diam, in fitted case. **$550-650**

A Ward's arm and platform machine, No. 15851, with gilt and coloured decoration. **$850-1,000**

A decoupage sewing box, French, c1850.
$1,600-2,000

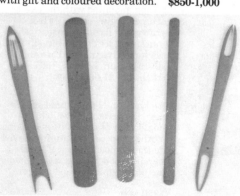

A selection of wooden netting tools – 2 needles and 3 gauges or meshes.
$9-18

A Grover & Baker No. 24 treadle sewing machine, No. 233295, with japanned arm, gilt decoration, patent dates to 1863, open treadle with drawer, instruction book, sales literature and original invoice; Bainbridge & Co., Newcastle, date June 11, 1870, for £8.8.0.
$2,600-3,600

TEXTILES
Costume

A set of viscount's and viscountess's ceremonial robes, by Ede and Ravenscroft, comprising a pair of coronets trimmed with ermine and silver balls, a scarlet velvet gown and matching cape trimmed with ermine, tasselled sash, an ermine trimmed waistcoat with matching cape, with deep ermine collar and trim, all in a wooden case, early 20thC. **$1,800-2,800**

A trained dress of white cotton, the sleeves, bodice and hem with deep muslin insertions embroidered in white silk with laurel wreaths and key pattern borders, the bodice also worked with monogram C.M., c1800. **$3,500-7,000**

A trained dress of white muslin, the sleeves and borders embroidered with garlands of white flowers outlined in black, c1800. **$9,000-10,000**

A dress of yellow cotton printed with vignettes of palm trees and shells, in red, with gigot sleeves, and a miniature version of the same dress for a little girl, both c1828. **$3,500-4,500**

A printed cotton gown, in black, gold and rust, c1810. **$1,200-1,600**

A dress of grey silk, embroidered in emerald green, yellow and white silk, trimmed with green velvet and black lace, with sleeved and sleeveless bodice, one bodice altered, French, c1865. **$1,600-2,000**

A Schiaparelli evening gown and cape, the gauze striped with bands of orange and gold, the skirt with asymmetrical fishtail, complete with silk underslip, labelled Schiaparelli, Paris, numbered 41677, c1935. **$4,500-5,500**

A trained wedding dress of ivory silk and cream silk, with a spray of artificial orange blossom at the neck, the Vandyked hem trimmed with a blue bow and a spray of heather, c1878. **$550-650**

A sleeveless evening dress of crushed raspberry pink velvet, the off the shoulder bodice trimmed with a large velvet flourish, labelled Chanel, 1930s. **$3,500-7,000**

Napoleon Bonaparte's black silk socks, contained in purpose made leather presentation book shaped case, together with letter of provenance from Mr. Dixon dated 1916, early 19thC. **$7,000-8,000**

Provenance: these socks were allegedly presented by Madame Bertrand to W. Dixon Esq., Surgeon on H.M. Camel at St. Helena. In a letter dated 1916 a descendant of his, H. Dixon, donates the socks to raise money for the war effort.

A wedding dress of ivory silk, with high waist and slight train, with matching bolero and cloak, some alterations, unlabelled, probably by Balenciaga, c1968.
$1,200-1,600

A pair of brocaded satin ankle boots, the soles stamped Hird, the gold and white striped satin woven with yellow, pink and pale blue flowers, and fastened with 9 gold buttons, 2in (5cm) heels, c1885. **$1,200-1,300**

A straw hat, c1920. **$40-70**

A brocaded silk shoe and clog, woven in pale blue and ivory, the clog of pale blue satin, c1760.
$1,000-1,200

Five Bes Ben hats, American, some damage, c1950. **$550-900**

A woven Kashmir shawl, with central quatrefoil ground densely bordered by green, pink, scarlet and blue intertwined botehs, c1840. **$700-900**

A Bes Ben crystal water lily toque, American, of black felt applied with huge blooms and enamelled leaves, with veil, c1950.
$270-360

A pair of lady's court shoes of navy blue satin figured with gilt thread arabesques and printed with bold floral designs, with long pointed tongue, stamped Made Expressly for Mme Neal Ltd, Bradford, c1910.
$350-550

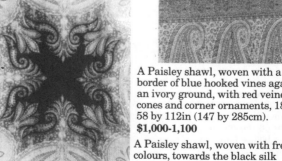

A topi. **$50-100**

A Paisley shawl, woven with a border of blue hooked vines against an ivory ground, with red veined cones and corner ornaments, 1840, 58 by 112in (147 by 285cm).
$1,000-1,100

A Paisley shawl, woven with fresh colours, towards the black silk central medallion, c1860, 72in (183cm) square. **$900-1,000**

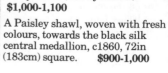

A gentleman's sleeved waistcoat of linen, the borders worked with exotic leaves in corded and knotted work, with small ball-shaped self-embroidered buttons to the hem, the buttonholes finish at pocket height, c1690. $4,500-5,500

A red facecloth suit, comprising wide trousers, with gilt thread embroidered front, fastening with gilt covered buttons, and outer jacket with open embroidered sleeves, 19thC.
$350-550

A gentleman's pale grey-green grosgrain coat embroidered in colours with floral garlands and bows, and with embroidered buttons, c1775.
$1,000-1,200

A jacket of red cotton woven with a quilted effect and printed with sprays of berries, with pouched hem and wrap over, three-quarter length sleeves, with large ceramic buttons, labelled Schiaparelli, 12 Place Vendome, Paris, inscribed on the reverse 82542, 1940s.
$1,600-2,000

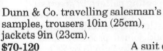

Dunn & Co. travelling salesman's samples, trousers 10in (25cm), jackets 9in (23cm).
$70-120

A suit of pink and apple green checked bouclé wool, the jacket weighted with a chain at the hem, with matching pale pink sleeveless blouse, the jacket labelled Chanel, 1960s. $450-800

A lady's waistcoat of linen embroidered in brightly coloured red, blue and green silks, against a yellow herringbone motif, bound with yellow silk braid, enlarged down the sides, English, early 18thC. $9,000-14,000

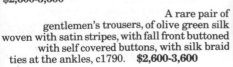

An apron of ivory silk embroidered in gold thread in various stitches, the scalloped border edged with gold lace, English, c1735.
$2,600-3,600

A rare pair of gentlemen's trousers, of olive green silk woven with satin stripes, with fall front buttoned with self covered buttons, with silk braid ties at the ankles, c1790. $2,600-3,600

An Italian miniature linen robe for an effigy, embroidered in pink silk, the central medallion with the IHS symbol and the 2 side ones with hearts and the initials S.A.N. and M.R.A., 17thC. $900-1,200

A Queen Victoria souvenir beadwork purse, the gilt clasp marked 'Victoria June 28th 1938', together with another Victorian beadwork purse, a beadwork bracelet, a muff purse and a beadwork cuff.
$140-200

Such combined lots are quite common at auction, and can prove very good value.

A Swiss linen handkerchief, embroidered in red silk, the centre with clasped hands, the symbol of fidelity, and the initials H.S. and K.P., the border with a zigzag pattern of leaves and acorns, trimmed with lace, probably commemorating an engagement, 17thC, 18in (46cm) square.
$3,000-4,000

A reticule of ivory silk, embroidered in coloured silks, the edges trimmed with green braid and blue and pink flowers, lined with ivory silk, c1820, 7in (18cm) long.
$900-1,000

A miniature corset, possibly for a doll but probably an apprentice's masterpiece of linen, the front woven in silk damask with a pattern of berries and trimmed with lacing, boned and laced at the back, c1770, 6in (15cm) high.
$2,600-3,600

Embroidery

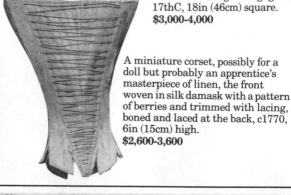

An English needlework picture, embroidered in coloured silks, on an ivory satin ground, c1660, 9 by 11in (23 by 28cm), framed and glazed.
$4,500-5,500

A linen border, woven with a repeating pattern in green silk, depicting pairs of dragons between castles and fountains, trimmed with braid, joined, probably Italian, 16thC, 3 by 96in (8 by 243cm).
$1,600-2,000

A Swiss linen cushion cover, embroidered in scarlet coloured silk, trimmed with lace, c1650, 15 by 13in (38 by 33cm).
$3,600-4,500

A pair of needlework panels, embroidered in coloured silks, mounted on a stretcher, late 16thC, 23in (59cm) square.
$3,000-3,600

A needlework pelmet, worked in coloured silks, with large bizarre type flowerheads among smaller blossoms and petals, against a dark brown ground, with scalloped edge, c1680, 14 by 168in (36 by 426cm).
$2,600-3,600

A silkwork picture on silk ground, depicting a woman watching a boy feeding 2 pigs, church and cottages to background, in gilt gesso frame, early 19thC, 16½ by 20in (42 by 51cm).
$900-1,500

A needlework picture, worked in coloured silks, against an ivory satin ground, unfinished, with drawing visible, framed and glazed, English, mid-17thC, 9 by 8in (23 by 20cm).
$8,000-9,000

A needlework mirror, embroidered in coloured silks and gilt threads, with the initials MD at the top, dated 1652, 24 by 20in (61 by 51cm), in a black and gold painted chinoiserie 19thC frame.
$4,500-5,500

Lace

A pair of needlework pictures, worked in coloured silks, one depicting a shepherdess, the other with a shepherd, early 18thC, 8 by 11in (20 by 28cm), framed and glazed.
$3,500-4,500

A linen point de Saxe cover, worked within an elaborate strapwork frame, the details worked with white silk embroidery and drawn thread work, Dresden, c1730, 68 by 64in (172 by 162cm).
$9,000-10,000

A pair of Brussels bobbin lace lappets with oval cartouches containing asymmetric floral sprays, c1745.
$650-700

A border of Italian needlelace, composed of framed vignettes of birds and mythical beasts and devices from the arms of the Colona family, 16th/17thC, 3 by 30in (8 by 76cm). **$900-1,000**

A panel of Spanish needlelace, worked with 2 rows of framed vignettes, including ships, birds and horse riders, 16th/17thC, 6 by 33in (15 by 84cm).
$3,600-4,500

A panel of fine Italian filet, worked with leafy scrolls with 2 mermaids bearing a cup, 17thC, 7 by 28in (18 by 71cm).
$1,200-1,500

A length of Flemish bobbin lace, Vandyked border, worked with flowers and bows, 17thC, 3 by 82in (8 by 208cm). **$1,600-1,800**

Two borders of bobbin lace worked with stylised figures and trees, possibly Italian, 17thC, 18 and 44 by 2in (46 and 111 by 5cm). **$180-280**

A length of Italian bobbin lace with a Vandyked edge with pendant florets and perching birds, 16th/17thC, 3 by 17in (8 by 43cm). **$650-700**

A flounce of point de France large scale lace, worked with bold designs, c1710, 25 by 108in (64 by 274cm). **$5,500-9,000**

A border of needlelace, worked with a top edge of scrolling carnations, with a Vandyked edge of pendant carnations, with crown like motifs above, Italian, 17thC, 30 by 5in (76 by 13cm). **$1,200-1,500**

A border of Punto Tagliato, worked with alternating blocks of figures, geometric cutwork and reticella patterns, 17thC, 2½ by 18½in (6 by 47cm). **$450-550**

Quilts

A red, white and navy blue pieced cotton crib quilt, probably Pennsylvania, mid-19thC, approx. 48 by 47in (122 by 119cm). **$1,400-1,800**

A pieced and embroidered red, white and blue cotton 'Daughters of America' quilt, dated September 23, 1924, approx. 84 by 92in (213 by 234cm). **$2,000-2,500**

A pieced red and white cotton quilt, initialled LBS, Amsterdam, New York, some discolouration and stain, some minor fraying, dated 1915, approx. 71 by 78in (180 by 198cm). **$1,200-1,800**

A pieced and appliquéd calico quilt, probably Pennsylvania, 19thC, approx. 92in (234cm) square. **$3,600-4,000**

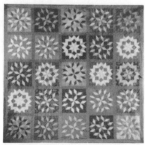

A pieced calico quilt, some breaks in the fabric, 19thC, 86½ by 85in (220 by 216cm). **$1,700-2,000**

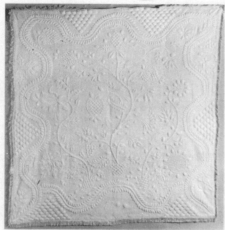

An all-white stuff-work quilt, probably New England, some repairs to fringe, breaks and weakness, dated 1796, approx. 88 by 92in (224 by 234cm).
$14,000-18,000

A pieced blue and white calico crib quilt, probably New England, early 19thC, approx. 45 by 33in (114 by 84cm).
$1,800-2,200

A red and white cotton quilt, probably East Central Indiana, c1920, approx. 76in (193cm) square.
$1,200-1,800

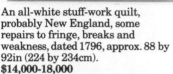

An Amish 'Bar' quilt, probably Pennsylvania, some imperfections, early 20thC, 72in (183cm) square.
$850-1,000

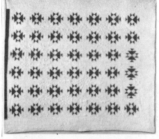

A pieced and stuff-work cotton quilt, initialled C.A.C. and W.F.L., probably Virginia, some stain and fading, dated 1888, approx. 72 by 84in (183 by 213cm).
$3,000-4,000

An all white stuff-work quilt, attributed to Sarah Cook, Litchfield, Connecticut, c1810, approx. 100in (254cm) square.
$5,500-6,000

A pieced and appliquéd blue and white calico quilt, New York or New England, c1880, approx. 77 by 85in (196 by 216cm).
$1,500-1,800

A rare pieced blue and white cotton 'Carpenter's Square' quilt, probably Dover, Ohio, c1890, approx. 79in (201cm) square.
$7,500-8,000

A blue resist printed bed cover, Eastern Seaboard, some discolouration, c1775, 87½ by 93in (222 by 236cm).
$5,300-5,800

A pieced and trapunto blue and white cotton quilt, probably Ohio, c1870, approx. 76½ by 79in (194 by 201cm).
$2,000-2,500

A pieced and appliquéd cotton quilted coverlet, Hawaii, slight discolouration, 20thC, 90 by 80in (229 by 203cm).
$1,200-1,800

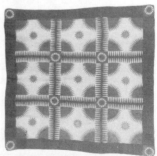

A pieced cotton quilted coverlet, some soiling, late 19thC, 88in (224cm) square.
$1,500-2,000

Samplers

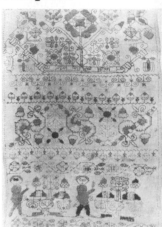

An English sampler, worked in shades of blue, green and cream silk, with bands of patterns, including rows of flowers and vines, and an alphabet, mid-17thC, 39in (99cm) long.
$2,600-3,600

An early Victorian needlework sampler, 1845.
$650-800

A darning sampler, worked in coloured silks, framed and glazed, late 18th/early 19thC, 17 by 13in (43 by 33cm).
$1,500-1,700

A William IV needlework sampler by Elizabeth Lammiman, aged 10, depicting Holwood House, Kent, the seat of the Rt. Hon. William Pitt, November 25th 1832, 17 by 13in (43 by 33cm).
$1,000-1,200

A needlework sampler, by Polly Shores, Warren, Rhode Island, some darkening of the linen ground, dated April 6, 1792, 22 by 17in (56 by 43cm).
$5,300-5,800

A needlework sampler by Hannah Carter, worked in cross stitch with verse above Adam and Eve and the Tree of Life, dated 1832, 17½ by 16in (45 by 41cm).
$800-900

Tapestries

A silkwork sampler, Louisa Benford Aged 9 years, 1818, in plain gilt frame, 16 by 12½in (41 by 32cm).
$1,800-2,000

A pair of miniature needlework samplers, initialled M.M., Philadelphia, some minor stain, early 19thC, 8 by 7in (20 by 18cm) framed.
$1,700-2,000

An Aubusson tapestry portière, woven in many colours, trimmed with fringing, French, late 19thC, 63 by 80in (160 by 203cm).
$2,000-3,000

A tapestry lunette, worked in many colours, depicting the Annunciation to the Virgin after Filippo Lippi, from the workshop of Morris and Company, in gesso frame, damaged, c1912, 80 by 34in (203 by 86cm).
$30,000-40,000

This tapestry was woven by the weavers John Martin and Gordon Berry for St Mary's Convent, Chiswick.

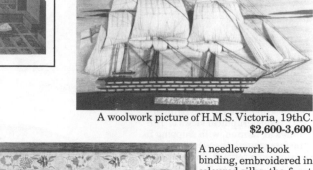

A woolwork picture of H.M.S. Victoria, 19thC.
$2,600-3,600

A needlework book binding, embroidered in coloured silks, the front and back depicting Adam and Eve and the Tree of Knowledge, unfinished, with the pattern drawn on the ground, English, mid-17thC, framed and glazed, 12 by 19in (31 by 48cm).
$5,500-9,000

A gros point wool picture, Summer, by Edna Oddy, 1810, in moulded frame, 34 by 24in (86 by 61cm).
$4,500-5,500

Miscellaneous

A Charles II beadworked picture, the satin ground densely covered with glass beads and pearls, in softwood frame, c1660, 9 by 11½in (23 by 29cm).
$2,000-3,500

A Dutch fan, the guards pierced with chinoiseries, the sticks with Chinese figures carrying umbrellas, c1760.
$700-900

A patchwork cover top, with original templates intact, one dated 1853, 82in (208cm) square.
$360-450

The autograph fan of Miss Katherine Grant, 'White Lady' of Sir Hubert Herkomer R.A., with wooden stick, one guardstick inlaid with mother-of-pearl chrysanthemum, in green kid box tooled in gold with sprays of flowers by Johanna Birkenroth, London, lined with grey and pink figured silk, with a tall booklet listing many of the autographs bound in the same silk, c1880, 13in (33cm).
$3,500-4,500

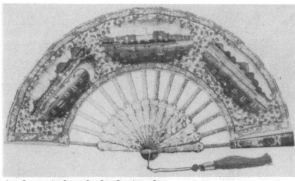

A telescopic fan, the leaf painted with 3 topographical views of The Hongs at Canton, with shipping in the foreground, the verso with figures on a terrace, their faces of ivory, their clothes of silk, with lacquer sticks, verso rubbed, 10in (25cm) extended, in lacquer box for a non-telescopic fan.
$1,200-1,800

An Italian fan, the leaf centred by a painted panel of 2 bound slaves being assessed by a lady and attendants flanked by medallions and vignettes, plain ivory sticks and guards.
$700-900

A fan, the leaf painted with a country dance, the figures dressed in pink, blue and mauve, the ivory sticks carved and pierced with figures, c1720, 10in (25cm), in 19thC fan box.
$2,600-3,600

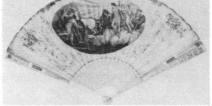

A fan, the leaf printed with an oval hand coloured stipple engraving of Apollo, by Thomas Kirk, the ivory sticks carved and pierced with flowers, in contemporary red morocco fan box, c1800, 9in (23cm).
$550-700

A Royal Marriage fan, commemorating the marriage of King George III and Queen Charlotte, with silver paper decoupe leaf, the ivory sticks carved and pierced and painted with chinoiserie and crowns, with a gold tassel, probably 1761, 11in (28cm).
$3,000-4,000

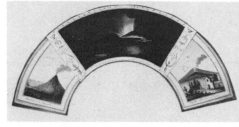

Five Neapolitan School fan designs, gouache on kid skin, 19thC, overall 21in (53cm) wide.
$3,000-3,600

An English fan, the ivory sticks carved and pierced and painted with chinoiserie and cloute with mother-of-pearl and decorated with glitter, c1740, 12in (31cm).
$700-1,400

The fan appears to have been designed for larger sticks and to have been cut down slightly at the sides.

A fan, the leaf painted with Chinese ladies in a garden, the wooden sticks painted with figures in European dress, the guardstick painted with a musician, Chinese, for the European market, late 17th/early 18thC, in glazed fan case inscribed: One of the Court fans for the Wedding of William the 3rd and Mary of England Nov. 4.1677, leaf damaged.
$450-800

Did you know

MILLER'S Antiques Price Guide builds up year by year to form the most comprehensive photo-reference system available

An English fan, the sticks and guards pierced and painted with chinoiserie panels, and 2 painted ivory fans, c1760.
$3,500-4,500

A Cantonese mandarin fan, the leaf painted with a multitude of ivory faced figures, the gilt filigree guards and sticks pierced with figures of tortoiseshell, stained ivory and mother-of-pearl, in a lacquer case, c1880.
$650-1,000

A French fan, the leaf painted with 3 vignettes in 18thC style, against a pink ground painted with putti en grisaille, the verso with monogram J.E.L., c1840, in fan box, 11in (28cm).
$1,000-1,200

Les Riches du Jour, a printed fan, the leaf a stipple engraving printed in blue with 3 scenes, c1790, 9in (23cm).
$700-1,000

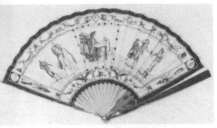

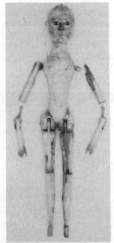

Souvenir de l'Exposition Universelle de 1867, Paris, a printed fan, designed by Guilletat, 48 rue de Belleville and engraved by Tuillot, with wooden sticks, 10in (25cm).
$700-900

DOLLS

Wooden Dolls

A Japanese ivory brisé fan, lacquered in gold with peacocks, the eyes on their tails cloute with mother-of-pearl, the guardsticks decorated with shibayama work fruit and insects, late 19thC, 3 stones missing from guardsticks, 11in (28cm), in bamboo box.
$5,500-7,000

A carved and painted wooden doll, with dark inset stitched eyes, rouged cheeks, carved ears, the cream painted body and limbs jointed at shoulders, elbows, hips and knees, damaged, English, 18thC, 16in (41cm) high.
$1,200-1,600

It is likely that there was one maker who constructed dolls in this manner, with fine joints, all-over painted flesh tones and well shaped body and limbs.

A late Georgian painted wooden doll, with painted rouged cheeks, red mouth and nostrils, inserted black pupil-less eyes, blonde mohair wig, the body with high pigeon chest, wooden peg-jointed hips and knees with hoof feet, wound linen upper arms nailed to the shoulders, the kid lower arms each having 3 stitched fingers, unmarked, 15in (38cm) high.
$1,500-1,800

A wooden pedlar doll, with painted hair and features, wearing red cape and printed dress, carrying basket of wares including lace and buttons, 11½in (29cm) high, under glass dome, on ebonised wood plinth base.
$550-650

A pair of wooden head and shoulder
character dolls, each with a carved
and painted wig, features, wooden
lower limbs and stuffed fabric body,
wearing national costume, 20thC,
14in (35cm) high.
$450-650

A wax over papier mâché headed
doll, with pink kid arms and
separated fingers in original pink
silk spencer with matching quilted
bonnet, white piqué dress,
pantaloons, lace edged cap, petticoat
and pink figured cotton laced boots
and extra clothes, English, c1812,
18in (46cm) high.
$2,000-3,000

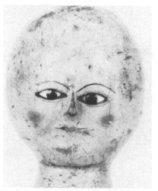

A painted wooden doll's torso, with
inset enamel eyes, rouged cheeks
and remains of kid arm, wearing
printed cotton frock and petticoat,
English, early 19thC, 9in (23cm)
high.
$1,200-1,500

An English poured shoulder-wax
doll, with fixed blue glass eyes,
inserted blonde hair and cloth body
with poured wax lower limbs, in
original lace panelled and
pintucked white dress, one leg
bandaged, head and shoulder colour
faded, late 19thC, 25in (64cm).
$900-1,200

A wax over composition pumpkin
headed doll, with dark inset eyes,
and moulded blonde hair, the
stuffed body with squeaker, papier
mâché lower section and wooden
limbs, dressed in contemporary blue
and white cotton print frock, c1860,
12in (31cm) high.
$450-650

Wax

A wax over composition headed doll,
with fixed blue eyes, wearing
original underclothes and faded
pink silk frock trimmed with lace
and ribbons, c1865, 16in (41cm)
high.
$900-1,000

A waxed shoulder composition bride
doll, with fixed spiralled blue glass
eyes, painted mouth, applied
ringletted blonde real hair, kid
leather body, with separately
stitched fingers, earrings, wax and
fabric floral headdress, wearing
underclothes, ivory brocaded satin
lace trimmed wedding gown with
train and heeled light brown shoes,
some lace frail, German, c1890,
14½in (37cm).
$1,000-1,500

A pair of wax over composition dolls,
one with blue eyes the other with
black weighted eyes, painted
mouths, fabric bodies with leather
lower arms, dressed in matching
maroon silk lace trimmed gowns,
bead necklaces, and pearlised brown
shoes with silk trim, minor cracking
to faces, one shoe to each doll with
hole in sole, German, c1890, 15in
(38cm).
$1,800-2,800

A poured wax baby doll, with fixed blue eyes, inset short blonde wig and stuffed body, with wax limbs attached through metal eyelets, wearing a petticoat, with Lucy Peck square stamp on the body reading "FROM Mrs Peck THE DOLL'S HOME 131 REGENT STREET W", 20in (51cm) high.
$700-900

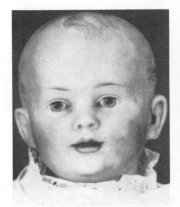

A bisque headed character baby doll, with brown painted eyes with red line above, open/closed mouth, dressed in white, impressed 131 2, 11½in (29cm) high.
$800-1,000

A bisque doll's shoulder head, with painted features, pierced ears, moulded and painted hair, marked 18, 5in (13cm) high.
$260-360

Bisque & Papier Mâché

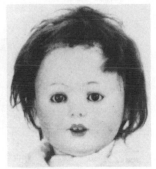

A bisque headed character baby doll, with blue sleeping eyes, feathered brows, brown mohair wig and bent limbed composition body, marked Jutta 1914 12½. by Cuno & Otto Dressel, one finger damaged, 23in (59cm) high.
$650-800

A brown bisque headed child doll, with brown sleeping eyes, pierced ears and jointed body, 29in (74cm) high.
$1,600-2,000

A bisque headed child doll, with fixed blue eyes, pierced ears and jointed body dressed in cream silk gauze over satin, underclothes, shoes and socks, impressed DEP 12, and on the body 12, 28in (71cm) high.
$1,500-2,000

A bisque headed character doll, with blue lashed sleeping eyes, feathered brows, brown mohair wig and bent limbed composition body dressed in cotton print romper and velvet cap, marked 201 S & Q 12, 21in (53cm) high.
$550-700

A bisque flange necked fashionable doll, with unusual construction allowing the head to turn only 90° on a bisque protrusion, remains of skin wig and gussetted kid body wearing black kid slippers, Swiss straw hat, tortoiseshell comb, and later dress, c1870, 14½in (37cm) high.
$1,200-1,600

A bisque headed doll, with fixed spiralled blue glass eyes, Belton head, closed painted mouth, metal torso and skirt with clockwork mechanism within, in red satin skirt, black velvet bodice peasant costume and matching hat, impressed N/9, costume frail, German, c1885, 11in (28cm).
$650-900

A bisque swivel head fashion doll, with fixed blue glass eyes, fair mohair wig over cork pate and gussetted kid body with separately stitched fingers, unclothed except for leather boots with silk rosettes, impressed 1, French, c1875, 15in (38cm).
$1,600-2,000

A Kohl Wengenroth bisque character doll, with weighted brown glass eyes, open mouth, 5 piece curved limb composition body, replaced brown human hair, redressed in underclothes, white gauze dress, knitted pants and vest, brown shoes, impressed KW in an oval /12, German, c1910, 21in (53cm).
$1,000-1,200

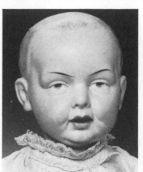

An 'Einco' Kaiser-baby type bisque character doll, with intaglio blue eyes, open/closed mouth, brushstroked hair, curved limb 5 piece composition body, in white shift, hands rubbed, impressed Einco Germany 3, c1910, 15in (38cm).
$700-900

A bisque headed bébé, with blue yeux fibres, feathered brows, pierced ears, dark brown wig, the jointed wood and composition body dressed in navy and green striped woollen frock, underwear and brown leather shoes, small chip to neck, marked 10 1, 24in (61cm).
$3,500-4,500

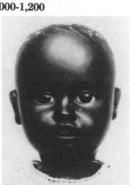

A brown bisque headed character doll, with brown sleeping eyes and rigid limb body, impressed 34 – 26, by Gebruder Kuhnlenz, 16½in (42cm).
$1,500-1,700

A bisque swivel headed Parisienne, with blue eyes, feathered brows and blonde mohair wig, the gussetted kid body with replaced composition arms dressed in white cotton gown, body marked with faint Simonne stamp, Passage Delorme, Paris circa 1860, 17½in (45cm).
$2,000-2,700

Bru

A rare early bisque shoulder headed Parisienne, with short blonde mohair curls, cork pate, fixed bright blue eyes, unpierced ears and kid over wood jointed body, the bisque arms with pink tinting at elbow and back of hand, possibly by Bru, c1870, 10½in (27cm) high.
$2,600-3,600

Gebruder Heubach

A bisque headed character doll, with blue sleeping eyes, and rigid limb child body with moulded shoes and socks, in original 18thC style fancy dress and powdered wig, impressed Gebruder Heubach 5½ O G. 5/0½ H, 11½in (29cm).
$450-650

A pair of Laurel and Hardy bisque head and shoulder dolls, the stuffed bodies with bisque lower limbs dressed in felt costumes, 18 and 21in (46 and 53cm).
$110-180

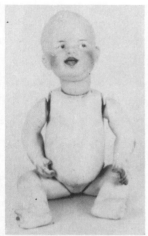

A rare bisque headed character doll, moulded hair and composition baby's body, impressed Gebruder Heubach square mark and 8191 27 5, 11½in (29cm).
$1,500-1,800

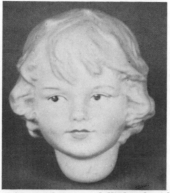

A bisque character doll's head, with open/closed mouth, light blue intaglio eyes and moulded blonde hair, impressed Heubach square mark 79, late production, 3½in (9cm).
$1,200-1,600

A bisque headed bébé, with pale blue eyes, fixed wrist papier mâché body dressed in blue, impressed DEPOSE E 8 J, and with painter's mark, the body stamped Jumeau Medaille d'Or Paris, the shoes marked EJ Depose, 19in (48cm).
$10,000-11,000

Jumeau

A bisque character doll, with weighted brown glass eyes, brown mohair wig and ball jointed wood and composition body in orange and white dress, impressed 8192 5, c1912, 20in (51cm).
$1,200-1,600

A bisque doll, with jointed wood and composition body, dressed in white cotton dress edged with lace, stringing loose, paint worn on body, stamped in red DÉPOSÉ TÊTE JUMEAU Bte. S.G.D.G. 7 and with red check mark, c1880, 17in (43cm).
$4,500-6,500

An English poured shoulder wax doll, with fixed blue glass eyes, one inside head, blonde mohair and cloth body with poured wax lower limbs, in original dress and cream cape, quilted cream satin bonnet, 22in (56cm), together with extra clothes including a pair of Jumeau ice blue satin shoes stamped on sole in gold BÉBÉ JUMEAU MED'OR PARIS DÉPOSÉ.
$1,600-2,000

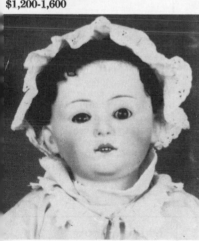

A bisque headed child doll, with blue sleeping eyes and jointed composition body, impressed with the Gebruder Heubach square mark and 10532 13, 31in (79cm).
$1,200-1,600

A Mulatto bisque doll, with black real hair wig and jointed wood and composition body, in pink ribbed dress with lacy top, slight damage and repair, embossed with a J, c1885, 17in (43cm).
$900-1,200

An early pressed bisque headed bébé, with closed mouth, blue almond shaped eyes, light brows, pierced ears, skin wig and fixed wrist jointed body, dressed in red with original cream satin and lace hat, impressed 3 over 0 and stamped on the body JUMEAU MEDAILLE d'OR, c1880, 13½in (34cm).
$10,000-11,000

A swivel head bisque fashion doll, wearing yellow metal thread brocaded top, pink figured silk bloomers and pink and yellow striped silk shawl and headscarf, marked with red check marks and incised 4, with stamp on back JUMEAU MEDAILLE d'OR PARIS, c1880, 14in (36cm).
$1,800-2,800

An 'Oriental Jumeau' bisque doll, with fixed brown glass eyes, lined in black, with stiffened shaped black wig on wooden pate, pierced ears, wood and composition straight limbed body with fixed wrists, in attractive original Chinese style robe and leggings, and matching raised slippers, hands rubbed, impressed 6, late 19thC, 19in (48cm), complete with silk covered wooden stand.
$2,000-3,000

A bisque doll, with 8 ball jointed wood and composition body, very slight wig pull on left side of face and raised firing line at left of mouth, blue stamp on bottom JUMEAU MEDAILLE D'OR PARIS, in later blue and white dress, brown kid shoes with cut silk rosettes incised 8 E. JUMEAU MÉD d'OR 1878 PARIS, c1875, 23in (58cm).
$5,500-7,000

A bisque walking/talking doll, with brown glass eyes, blonde real hair wig and jointed wood and composition body with straight walking legs causing the head to turn and the voice box to scream, firing line from left ear to centre of cheek, one wrist joint loose, hand paint scuffed, impressed 1907 10, 22½in (57cm), c1907, together with an extra white bonnet.
$1,800-2,800

An unusual 'crying' bisque doll, with open/closed mouth, fixed brown glass eyes, pierced applied ears, black wig over cork pate and wood and composition jointed body containing pull string 'Mama' voice box, in brown and white spotted silk dress, some chips and cracks, impressed 8 on head, c1880, 17in (43cm).
$2,500-4,500

A bisque doll, with fixed blue eyes, auburn real hair wig and jointed wood and composition body, crack from wig socket to right eyebrow, one finger missing and body paint scuffed, impressed 8 and 0 and indistinctly stamped TÊTE, c1905, 19in (49cm), together with a bodice and a blue and white striped extra bonnet.
$1,500-1,800

A bisque headed bébé, dressed in pale blue with shoes and socks, impressed 7, and stamped in red TETE JUMEAU, and on the body BÉBÉ JUMEAU Diplome d'Honneur, 18in (46cm).
$3,500-4,500

A bisque doll with blue glass eyes, blonde mohair wig over plaster pate, jointed wood and composition body in original pink dress and bonnet, impressed 1924, c1910, 14in (35cm), and her trunk covered in cream linen and metal studs, containing clothing and trinkets.
$2,600-3,600

A bisque headed character baby doll, with painted hair, brown sleeping eyes and composition body dressed in silk robe, bib and bonnet, impressed J D K 20, 24in (61cm).
$1,000-1,200

A bisque doll, French head on German body, with auburn wig, jointed wood and composition body, in cream lacy dress with maroon tartan overdress, hairline crack from wig socket to edge of right eye, impressed 6, c1880, 17in (43cm).
$700-1,000

Lenci

J. D. Kestner

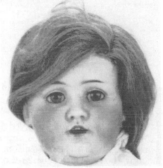

A bisque headed child doll, with blue lashed sleeping eyes, feathered brows, fair wig and jointed wood and composition body, dressed in white, 5 fingers broken, marked 13 J.D.K. 249, 24in (61cm).
$800-1,000

A cloth soldier doll, with felt face, painted lips and brown eyes, auburn hair and stitched ears, the body jointed at shoulders and hips and with joined middle fingers, in original sludge green serge uniform and hat, brown leather boots with metal studs and backpack, Italian, c1930, 17in (43cm).
$1,500-2,000

A large Kaiser baby type bisque character doll, with weighted brown glass eyes, open/closed mouth, brown mohair wig, 5 piece curved limb composition body, in long infant gown, napkin, knitted socks and bib, probably Kestner, impressed 50 at neck, c1910, 18½in (47cm).
$1,500-2,000

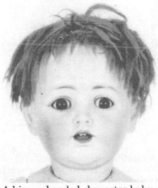

A bisque headed character baby doll, with quivering tongue, brown sleeping flirting eyes, short fair wig and baby's body, impressed J.D.K. 257 51, 19in (48cm).
$650-1,000

An all bisque googlie eyed doll, with blue eyes, water melon mouth, brown wig and painted blue socks and black shoes, probably a wigged swivel necked version of the Campbell Kid, chip to back of neck, impressed on legs 179 0, by Kestner, c1930, 6½in (16cm).
$800-1,000

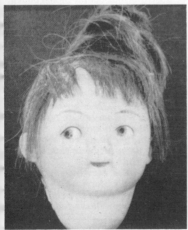

A pair of cloth dolls of Laurel and Hardy, featuring felt, hand finished faces, wearing 18thC costumes including tri-cornered hats, 10in (25cm) each.
$2,600-3,600

A cupid cloth doll, with felt face, painted blue eyes, knotted red felt hair, swivel neck, butterfly wings in red, orange and yellow discs, blue felt top and brown shorts embroidered with red hearts, yellow felt socks in brown sandals with red straps, red felt gloves holding a blue tipped bow in one hand, an arrow in the other, a blue and yellow painted wooden sheath holding 4 red shafted arrows round his neck, c1930, 7½in (19cm).
$3,000-3,600

Armand Marseille

A bisque socket head girl doll, 390 ASM, 22½in (57cm).
$550-750

A bisque socket head doll, with mohair wig, painted features, blue eyes, composition body and bent limbs, wearing a lemon petticoat under a cream lace dress with rosebuds and matching bonnet tied with pink ribbon, head and neck impressed Armand Marseille, Germany 990,A5/0M, 11in (28cm).
$350-550

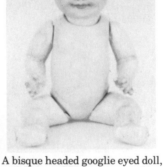

A bisque headed googlie eyed doll, with brown sleeping eyes, smiling closed mouth and composition baby's body, impressed 323 A 5/0 M, 8½in (22cm).
$900-1,000

A bisque shoulder headed doll, with brown eyes, blonde wig and stuffed body, with chamois leather breeches, leather gaiters and boots, impressed 370 AM 2½ DEP, 23in (59cm).
$700-900

A bisque headed googlie eyed doll, with blue eyes and rigid limb composition body, dressed in combinations, impressed 323 A 3/0 M, 11½in (30cm).
$1,600-2,000

S.F.B.J.

A French bisque character boy doll, with open/closed mouth, fixed blue glass eyes, domed brush stroked head and jointed wood and composition body, in blue sailor outfit, impressed 226, c1910, 16in (41cm).
$1,200-1,800

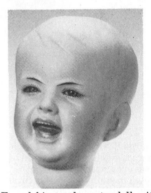

A French bisque character doll, with open/closed mouth showing tongue and teeth, fixed blue glass eyes, moulded hair and curved limb composition body, unclothed and unstrung, body paint flaked on legs and hands, impressed 233 4, c1910, 13in (33cm).
$2,000-3,000

Make the Most of Miller's

CONDITION is absolutely vital when assessing the value of an antique. Damaged pieces on the whole appreciate much less than perfect examples. However a rare, desirable piece may command a high price even when damaged

---

554

Simon & Halbig/ Kammer & Reinhardt

A French bisque doll, with brown glass eyes, pierced ears, red-blonde real hair wig and wood and composition jointed body, in cream fine lawn dress, cream calf fur shoes with pom-poms, lacy bonnet with lace flowers and green silk and satin ribbons, 3 fingers cracked, impressed 13, c1900, 28in (71cm).
$2,000-2,700

A Simon and Halbig bisque headed doll, with blue sleeping eyes, pierced ears and composition ball jointed body, in cream embroidered net dress, impressed Simon and Halbig DEP 1079 Germany 12, 25½in (65cm).
$900-1,000

A Kammer & Reinhardt/Simon & Halbig bisque headed doll, with sleeping blue eyes, auburn wig, composition ball jointed body, in blue velvet dress with straw bonnet, impressed K star R Simon and Halbig 117n, 32in (81cm).
$1,600-2,000

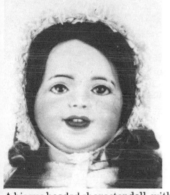

A bisque headed character doll, with open/closed mouth, blue sleeping eyes, brown wig, and baby's body wearing embroidered dress with lace insertions, impressed S.F.B.J. 236 Paris 11, 25in (64cm).
$1,500-2,000

A Kammer & Reinhardt bisque character doll, with blue eyes, blonde mohair plaited wig and jointed wood and composition body in blue-grey striped dress and white pinafore, impressed 114 23, c1909, 9in (23cm).
$1,800-2,800

A Simon & Halbig swivel head bisque doll, with fixed blue eyes, real hair over cork pate and canvas covered French wooden body with joints at shoulders, elbows, hips, knees and ankles, with bisque forearms, in rose pink cotton dress embroidered with blue flowers, black and blue bonnet with linen flowers, one little finger chipped, unmarked, c1880, 17in (43cm), together with broken glass dome.
$2,000-3,000

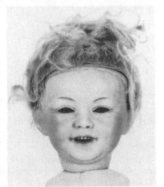

A rare bisque headed character boy doll, with fixed blue laughing eyes, blonde wig and jointed body, impressed S.F.B.J. 229 Paris 6, 16in (41cm).
$2,800-5,500

A bisque swivel headed doll, with kid neck lining, closed mouth, blue fixed eyes and blonde mohair wig, on a stuffed body with composition limbs, impressed S 14 H 949, 26½in (68cm).
$2,600-3,600

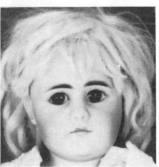

A bisque shoulder headed doll, with pierced ears and brown eyes, the cloth and kid body with bisque arms, dressed in white, impressed S 1 1 H 950, 20in (51cm).
$1,800-2,200

A Martin swimming doll, the French body with German head, with open mouth and upper teeth, fixed blue glass eyes, pierced ears, auburn wig and the pink jointed wooden body with metal hands, with keywind swimming mechanism, in original eau-de-nil swimming suit, impressed 1079 S & H 2½, c1895, 16in (41cm).
$1,800-2,800

A Simon & Halbig Oriental bisque doll, with brown eyes, black mohair wig, jointed wood and composition body, in mustard silk short robe, pale blue and white striped trousers, stringing loose, small firing fault under left eye, c1910, 13in (33cm).
$1,500-1,800

A Kammer & Reinhardt/Simon & Halbig flirty eyed bisque character doll, with five-piece curved limb composition body, in knitted pink dress and cotton underslip, stringing loose, hands and feet rubbed, replaced wig, impressed K star R Simon & Halbig 126/46, c1920, 18½in (47cm).
$700-1,000

A bisque headed character doll, with grey painted eyes and jointed composition body, wig pulls at back, body washed, impressed K star R 114 43, 15½in (40cm).
$3,000-4,000

A Simon & Halbig bisque doll, with weighted blue glass eyes, original brown mohair wig, pierced ears, wood and composition body, in original cream costume, lacking shoes and socks, impressed 1078/14½, c1895, 30in (76cm).
$1,800-2,800

Jules Steiner

A Simon & Halbig Gibson Girl bisque character doll, with fixed blue eyes, pierced ears, original wig, jointed wood and composition body, in original costume, lacking one earring, impressed 1159 Simon & Halbig DEP 6, c1894, 18½in (47cm).
$1,200-1,800

A French bisque doll, with moving blue eyes, pierced ears, dark real hair wig and jointed papier mâché body, in blue and white checked dress, straw bonnet and with small white teddy bear, some damage, impressed J. Steiner Bte. S.G.D.G. Paris FIre. A.11, c1895, 17in (43cm).
$1,800-2,000

A French bisque doll, with blue eyes, pierced ears, dark mohair wig and jointed papier mâché body, in white dress with blue sash, some damage, impressed J. Steiner Bte. S.G.D.G. Paris Fre., A 17, c1880, 24in (61cm).
$1,000-1,500

Dolls Houses

A dolls house designed as a double fronted Georgian residence with front gable pilaster and gallery, with hinged front gable and interior with furniture, 19thC, 29in (74cm) high.
$450-650

A painted and furnished wooden dolls house, with slate roof, opening at the front to reveal 3 rooms with staircase, the base with shaped apron, 41in (104cm) high.
$1,000-1,200

A dolls house chair made of yellow beads, 7in (18cm) high.
$30-40

A George III three-storey painted wooden baby house, opening at the front to reveal 6 rooms, hall, staircase, landings, interior doors and chimney breasts, 50in (127cm) high.
$4,500-7,000

A set of dolls bedroom furniture, comprising: bed, wardrobe, night cupboard and dressing table, with ebonised tops and brass handles, the dressing table 15½in (40cm) high.
$350-450

A German miniature kitchen, early 20thC, 20in (51cm) high.
$1,800-2,800

Six pieces of silver dolls house furniture, hallmarked variously 1896-1907, some restorations, the tallest 2in (5cm) high.
$650-1,000

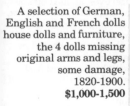

A selection of German, English and French dolls house dolls and furniture, the 4 dolls missing original arms and legs, some damage, 1820-1900.
$1,000-1,500

A collection of dolls house miniatures and furniture, of approximately 150 pieces, the majority in good condition, c1920.
$1,500-1,800

Two Hepplewhite shield style chairs, one of mahogany decorated with Prince of Wales feathers, and both with front tapering square legs with splayed feet, made and signed by A.C. Lowe Esq., 1935-1985, 7in (18cm) and 7½in (19cm) high.
$700-900

A group of 'cherry wood' dolls house furniture, with embossed Art Nouveau decoration, one armchair upholstered in plum velvet, and an elaborate bronze painted soft metal fireplace, with shop label from The Bon Marché Liverpool.
$450-700

The Bon Marché was founded by David Lewis in 1879, and is mentioned in the Liverpool Directory in 1880 as 'millinery, haberdashery and fancy repository 10-18, Basnett Street'. The shop is now a part of the John Lewis Partnership.

A quantity of dolls house furnishings and chattels, including 4 Waltershausen pieces, a helmet coal scuttle and shovel, a gilt metal vase with lamp shade and a china headed dolls house doll, with cloth body with china limbs, the doll c1865.
$1,200-1,400

A quantity of dolls house furniture and chattels, including a Waltershausen bureau and 4 chairs, a fender and fire irons.
$800-1,000

A pair of German fabric dolls, by Käthe Kruse, Cristabel with painted hazel eyes, applied blonde hair, in blue and white striped dress, with red handbag; Friedebald with painted brown eyes, applied blonde hair, in khaki shorts; each doll in original green cardboard box complete with head support and descriptive leaflet, c1950, each 19in (48cm).
$2,400-3,200

A selection of dolls house furniture, c1900.
$1,800-2,000

Miscellaneous

A talking doll with movable limbs, dressed in modern fabric, c1945, 19in (48cm).
$90-110

Two early English paper dolls, one in ivory silk dress with hand painted rose border to hem, dress frail, 10in (25cm); the other in gauze dress with applied paper leaf and flower decoration, inscribed to the back of head 'E G Ludlow, The Gift of the Bishop of Northumberland, 1809', 13in (33cm); together with a cut-out figure of a man in a frock coat, 10½in (27cm), and a watercolour portrait of a woman with 6 overlay transformation images, each labelled with inscription to reverse, and cut-out images of Prince Albert and Sir Walter Scott, c1810.
$650-800

A Russian doll in peasant costume, 9in (23cm).
$110-150

A German shoulder parian doll, with painted blue eyes, bald head with black yarn wig, fabric body with kid leather arms, in original peasant costume, c1860, 19in (48cm).
$1,000-1,500

A composition headed clockwork walking doll, mounted on a green painted three-wheeled platform, with movable front wheel and head movement, wearing original straw padded bonnet and later blue wool frock and cotton pinafore, some damage and repainting, probably by Theroude, c1860, 11in (28cm).
$1,800-2,800

A set of Punch and Judy hand puppets, the painted wooden heads on original felt and cotton outfits and wooden legs, some damaged, mid-19thC, Punch head 5½in (14cm).
$1,800-2,800

> **Did you know**
>
> *MILLER'S Antiques Price Guide builds up year by year to form the most comprehensive photo-reference system available*

Two miniature French prams, the larger of cream painted metal wire with cream cotton interior and folding canopy, on 4 spoked flat metal wheels, with curved handle, some paint loss, 7in (18cm) long; the other similar and smaller, with pink cotton lining and canopy, paint loss, 5in (12cm), both early 20thC.
$450-650

TOYS
Automata

A Roullet et Decamps musical rabbit in cabbage automaton, the moving mouth chewing a cabbage leaf, pricking up his ears and turning his head, with keywind stop/start musical movement, slighty soiled, nose rubbed, French, c1890, 10½in (27cm).
$1,600-2,000

A maracca playing Roullet et Decamps fur covered rabbit automaton, with amber and black glass eyes, tall pricked up ears, clockwork mechanism, with integral keywind causing him to dance and play his celluloid maraccas, French, early 20thC, 15in (38cm).
$1,400-1,500

A Hoyt smiling negro automaton picture, the clockwork mechanism causing the negro's face to change from a sleeping to a smiling expression, German, back cover missing, late 19thC, 27 by 22in (69 by 56cm) framed.
$5,500-6,500

A Roullet automaton of a drumming bear, the brown fur covered and muzzled beast with black and white glass eyes, with wooden hands holding metal drumsticks playing a metal drum, with keywind clockwork mechanism inoperative, French, c1900, 12in (31cm).
$700-900

A Decamps walking pig automaton, the kid covered animal with glass eyes, raised on 4 wheels, mechanism causing him to walk haltingly and emit grunting noise, with key, leather faded, some soiling, c1900, 12in (31cm) long.
$1,200-1,400

A rare Hoyt smiling lady automaton picture, the clockwork mechanism causing her eyes, mouth and head to move from sleeping to smiling expression, back cover and key missing, spring broken, German, late 19thC, 27 by 22in (69 by 56cm) framed.
$4,500-5,500

Teddy Bears

A Decamps walking cat automaton, the white rabbit fur covered animal with green and black glass eyes, pink painted nose, opening mouth, long tail, on 4 black painted wooden wheels, mechanism overwound, whiskers missing, c1900, 10in (25cm).
$700-1,000

A French singing bird automaton, the cage with feathered bird on perch, gessoed gilded base containing musical movement, carrying ring to top, some wear, early 20thC, 17in (43cm).
$1,800-2,800

A Steiff cinnamon plush teddy bear, with button in ear and white label 5328, swivel joints and excelsior stuffed, inoperative growler, some small holes, c1905, 16in (41cm).
$1,600-2,000

A long blond plush teddy bear, with brown stitched nose and mouth, cotton pads, brown stitched claws, swivel limbs, straw and fibre filled, snout worn, amber and black glass eyes replaced, possibly American, c1920, 26in (66cm).
$800-1,200

A Steiff dark golden plush covered roly poly bear, with boot button eyes, pronounced snout and wide apart ears, missing half an arm, small patches of wear, c1909, 5½in (14cm).
$800-1,000

A Steiff blond plush teddy bear, excelsior filled, with black boot button eyes, black stitched snout, humped back, long arms and pale felt paws, button to ear, growl box inoperative, early 20thC, 18in (46cm).
$5,500-6,500

A Steiff blond plush covered teddy bear, with boot button eyes, elongated limbs, slight hump, pronounced cut muzzle and felt feet pads, dressed as a sailor in blue trousers, white jersey and blue beret, worn, 8½in (21cm).
$550-700

A Steiff gold plush teddy bear, with button in ear, wide apart pricked ears, hump back, swivel joints, excelsior stuffed, some plush sparse, stuffing shifted, snout stitching sparse, c1908, 24in (61cm).
$2,600-3,600

A golden plush covered teddy bear, with elongated limbs, cut muzzle, glass eyes, wide apart ears, cloth pads, stitched nose with 2 outer edges extended, hump and growler, 21in (53cm).
$1,400-1,800

A Steiff blond teddy bear, with button in ear, brown and black glass eyes, brown stitched snout, hump back, swivel joints, excelsior stuffed, small holes to pads, c1930, 13½in (35cm).
$1,500-2,000

A Steiff blond plush teddy bear, with button in ear, swivel joints, some stitching worn, stuffing shifted at joints, one foot detached, c1908, 25in (64cm).
$1,000-1,500

A Steiff gold plush teddy bear, with button in ear, amber and black glass eyes, black stitched nose and mouth, straw filled, swivel limbs, ball growler, stuffing slipped, left ear torn and partially detached, early 20thC, 19in (48cm).
$1,200-1,400

A Steiff gold plush polar bear, with button in ear, swivel head with brown glass eyes, black stitched nose on white snout, tail key moving head from side to side, large hole on one paw, minor holes to 2 others, ears torn, c1930, 9in (23cm).
$3,000-3,600

A Steiff gold plush teddy bear, with button in ear, black stitched snout, black glass eyes, hump back, swivel joints, excelsior stuffed, inoperative growler, c1930, 18in (46cm).
$1,200-1,400

A straw gold plush covered teddy bear, with pronounced snout, glass eyes, felt pads, hump, growler, stitched nose and Steiff button in ear, probably c1909, 24in (61cm).
$3,500-4,500

A set of 12 miniature painted lead foxhunting figures and hounds.
$180-280

An early Steiff Burlap bear on wheels, with black stitched snout, black boot button eyes and swivel neck, hole in one paw, c1896, 20in (51cm) long.
$900-1,200

Lead Soldiers & Figures

A collection of 19 Britains painted lead anthropomorphic animals.
$260-360

A set of 5 Britains painted lead bandsmen.
$180-280

A collection of 20 rare Lucotte Napoleonic figures, exceptionally well hand painted, French, paint chipped and lifting on some figures.
$2,400-3,400

A Tipp & Co. 'Führerwagen' Mercedes tinplate clockwork staff car, with one composition figure in SS uniform, and key, in original box, together with 4 Lineol and 16 Elastolin figures, including Hitler with moving arm, in Jungfolk (Hitler Youth) uniform, Hess Goebbels, Jungfolk standard and flag bearers, Labour Corps flagbearer and worker, SS Motorcycle Corps with flagbearer, SS guard with flagbearer and others, some figures with fatigue, c1936.
$5,500-6,500

A set of 5 Britains painted lead Salvation Army figures.
$260-360

Money Banks

A cast iron savings bank featuring Andy and Bim Gump standing at each side, with a cast iron money bag at the slot area, 6in (15cm), together with a tinplate lithographed Andy Gump thrift bank, 4in (10cm).
$800-900

A John Harper & Co. Kiltie cast iron money bank, a coin placed in the figure's hand is placed into his shirt pocket, some damage and paint loss, English, c1935, 7in (18cm).
$1,000-1,200

Tinplate

A Shepherd Hardware Co. Uncle Sam cast iron money bank, coin trap with patent date June 8 1886, with key, paint loss and chipping, operating lever missing, American, c1890, 11½in (30cm).
$900-1,200

A Fischer clockwork lithographed tinplate six-light limousine, with chauffeur, finished in buff, red and ochre lining, in original box, 1920s, 13in (33cm) long.
$3,000-3,600

A Shepherd Hardware Co. Humpty Dumpty cast iron mechanical bank, hand depositing coin in clown's mouth, causing him to roll his eyes, with orange hat, blue and orange costume, American, paint loss and lacking coin trap, c1885, 7½in (19cm).
$540-740

A German lithographed tinplate money box, with lever action eyes and extending tongue, c1925, 7½in (19cm).
$650-800

A Bing tinplate sedan, lithographed in pale blue with dark blue lining, some repairs and repainting, wheels and edges rubbed, c1920, 12in (31cm).
$900-1,000

A Japanese Trademark tinplate open topped vintage car, with spring driven motor, patent No. 27579, 5½in (14cm) long.
$180-280

A large scale Lesney Massey Harris farm tractor, 8in (20cm) long.
$180-280

A Spanish tinplate wind-up Charlie Chaplin on a tricycle, a highly lithographed, smiling Charlie pedals the three-wheeled cycle while looking over his shoulder, c1920, 3½in (9cm).
$1,800-2,000

A German tinplate clockwork 4 seat open tourer, finished in off-white with orange lining, yellow spoked wheels, and scarlet seats, damage to paint, tyres distressed or missing, maker unknown, c1912, 10½in (27cm) long.
$3,500-4,500

A Karl Bub keywind sedan, c1929, 20in (51cm) long, in original heavy wooden box.
$6,500-7,000

A Karl Bub lithographed limousine, c1919, 13½in (35cm).
$1,400-1,800

A Linemar tinplate Bubble Blowing Popeye figure, battery operated, a highly lithographed Popeye, using his pipe, blows soap bubbles when operated, boxed, 8½in (21cm).
$2,000-3,000

A George Brown keywind 'Monitor' sidewheeler river boat, some paint distress, c1800, 14in (36cm) long.
$4,000-4,500

A Louis Marx tinplate Popeye Express, a wind-up toy featuring Popeye carrying a trunk in a wheelbarrow, on which sits a squawking stationary parrot, in original box, 8in (20cm).
$1,000-1,200

An Ives tinplate and wood 'Old Uncle Tom, the Fiddler', c1885, in original wood box, 9in (23cm) high.
$15,000-16,000

A Moxie flat lithographed horse and rider in an early car, c1924, 8½in (21cm) long.
$1,000-1,500

A Linemar tinplate Smoking Popeye, battery operated, featuring Popeye with pipe in hand, seated on a can of spinach and waving, with original box, 8½in (21cm).
$4,500-5,500

A Tippco keywind monoplane bomber, c1936, 5in (13cm) high.
$900-1,100

Cast Iron Toys

A Stevens and Brown painted mechanical hoop with lady and flag, flag partially repainted, c1870.
$13,000-15,000

A Harris painted goat cart with driver, c1903, 9½in (24cm).
$1,500-1,800

A Hubley motorcycle crash car, 11½in (29cm).
$3,300-3,800

A Hubley Indian motorcycle and sidecar with 2 uniformed policemen, paint worn, 9in (23cm) long.
$1,100-1,400

A Hubley painted motorcycle and driver, c1933, 9in (23cm) long.
$4,000-4,500

A Wilkins 3 horse-drawn water tower, missing counter-balance and hose, c1900, 43in (109cm) long.
$2,000-2,400

A Dent 3 horse-drawn hook and ladder wagon, c1910, 33in (84cm) long.
$2,300-2,800

A rare Hubley motorcycle with sidecar and 2 policemen, c1934, 8½in (21cm) long.
$1,400-1,800

A Wilkins horse-drawn two-wheel road cart, c1895, 11in (28cm) long.
$550-750

A Hubley J & B Express truck with driver, driver not original, tailgate missing, c1915, 15in (38cm).
$600-900

Miscellaneous

An Ives 'Bull Dog' savings mechanical bank, c1878, 8in (20cm).   **$5,300-5,800**

A Shepard 'trick pony' mechanical bank, c1885, 8in (20cm) long.
$800-900

A J. & E. Stevens 'I always did 'spise a mule' mechanical bank, c1880, 10½in (27cm).
$700-900

A painted wooden Noah's ark, with sliding side and approximately 140 painted animals and 7 turned wooden figures, by Sonneburg, mid-19thC, 15in (38cm) long.
$1,500-1,600

A Flowerpot Man glove puppet by Palitoy, together with a quantity of other toys including The Tricky Tractor, Penguin Clyde Cruiser, Roll Over Cat, etc., some boxed.
$280-380

A pair of chalkware figures of Mutt and Jeff, in appropriate clothes and individual top hats, some repairs to Mutt, Mutt 21in (53cm).
$450-550

A Steiff cloth Humpty Dumpty figure.
$2,000-3,000

A carved and painted pine child's horse and buggy, dated 1909, 28in (71cm) long.
$3,000-3,500

A French flock covered carton Boston terrier, with chain pull growl, moving lower jaw and glass eyes, 21in (53cm) long.
$650-1,000

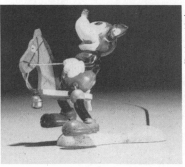

A Celluloid Mickey Mouse riding a wooden hobby horse, featuring Mickey in full colour, with large red shoes, riding on hand painted hobby horse, c1935, 4½in (11cm).
$2,600-3,600

A 6in gauge engineered model of an 0–4–0 coal fired Jubilee locomotive, of largely brass construction, with matching six-wheeled tender, bearing brass plaque reading T Hall, 1897, in GWR livery, lined in red and white, some paint loss and rubbing, 1897, 40in (101cm) long.
$6,000-7,000

This model was made for Lord Derby, on the occasion of Queen Victoria's Jubilee, and ran upon an elevated track in his garden.

MODELS

A Bing for Bassett-Lowke electric gauge 1 express locomotive, 4–6–0, Sir Sam Fay, No. 423, German, finished in Great Central Railways livery with matching six-wheeled tender, slight wear and rubbing to paint and transfers, headlamps missing, with quantity of three-rail track, original Bassett-Lowke pro-forma invoice, 1926, and sales catalogues, c1922.
$2,700-3,600

A Märklin bo-bo 'Gothard'-type 110 volt AC locomotive, Catalogue Ref. 1302, c1923.
$5,500-6,000

A Hornby 0 gauge tinplate snow plough, with original working drive belt, pre-war.
$360-450

A Bing gauge 3 live steam spirit fired 4–4–0 locomotive, Clyde, No. 1932, with brass boiler dome, finished in black with red and white lining, lacking chimney stack, spirit burner, rusted and dusty condition, lacking tender, with Bing gauge 3 L & N W R fitted First Class carriage and fitted guards/goods van, both with hinged lids lifting to reveal interiors, both chipped, crazed and rusted in places, 1904.
$3,600-4,500

A rare Märklin gauge 1 4–6–2 Swiss electric locomotive, catalogue No. HS 65/13021, finished in green with white roof livery with brown lining, red wheels and buffer plates, slight chips and crazing to paint, with quantity of Märklin gauge 1 track, c1932.
$6,000-7,000

A 2½in gauge model locomotive, probably American, mounted on a green painted chassis, boiler and firebox door detached, with a caged tender, lettered De Witt Clinton, carrying 2 barrels and spare wood, one wheel missing, and a yellow and gold painted stage coach, mounted on a 2½in gauge railway chassis, all pieces dusty and with minor damage, c1890.
$2,400-3,600

A model of the brig Marie Sophie, by L. D. Taylor, painted in blue and white, with 2 lifeboats, 2 life belts, 2 anchors and cabins, on a wooden stand, 32in (81cm) high.
$1,600-2,000

A model boat, c1900, 48in (122cm) long.
$1,600-2,000

GAMES
Chess Sets

A Cantonese carved ivory chess set, one side stained red, natural side as European royalty, rooks as knights as horsemen, complete, some damage, mid-19thC, white king 4in (10cm) high.
$900-1,000

A large Cantonese ivory chess set, red and natural, each carved piece with concentric pedestal bases, some old repairs and damage, kings 6½in (17cm) high, with lacquered chess/backgammon board with mother-of-pearl white squares, late 19thC, with velum transit case.
$1,000-1,400

A Spanish pulpit form bone chess set, each piece within an acanthus gallery, one side stained brown/black, one side natural, rooks as castellated towers, knights with horses heads, 7 pieces detached from bases, 5 pieces with losses, white queen lacking crown finial, late 18thC, the kings 5½in (14cm) high.
$14,500-16,000

A natural and red stained carved ivory chess set, kings 4in (10cm) high.
$550-900

Miscellaneous

A boxed games compendium, the burr thuya veneered box with ivory and ebony decorative edging with fitted interior, some replacements and damage, c1880, box 18½in (47cm) wide.
$8,000-9,500

A Victorian burr walnut games compendium, the interior with ivory retailer's label, W. Thornhill & Co., 144 New Bond Street, with a compartmented tray containing counters, shells, dominoes, chessman and other pieces, fitted below with 2 drawers containing a miniature croquet set, cards and other counters, 16in (41cm) wide.
$2,000-2,700

An oak cased penny operated Worlborl game, c1920, 26½in (67cm) high.
$360-450

Did you know

MILLER'S Antiques Price Guide builds up year by year to form the most comprehensive photo-reference system available

An oak cased playball machine, all win with 9 winning chutes, c1920.
$270-360

An oak cased old penny operated skill machine, c1920, 18in (46cm) high.
$270-360

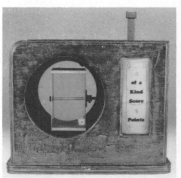

A coin operated Throw a Dice game, early 20thC, 14½in (37cm) wide.
$180-270

A carved wood and cast iron cribbage board, 19thC, 11in (28cm) long.
$180-270

An Embriachi horn and ivory games board, the sides decorated with intarsia pattern 'alla certosina', minor losses, restored, 15thC, 12in (30cm).
$5,500-6,000

MUSICAL
Musical Instruments

A single action pedal harp by J. Erat, of Wardour Street, Soho, London, the body and scroll arm veneered with maple, painted in black and gilt, the base carved with recumbent lions and on paw feet, with 43 strings, 8 pedals and 5 louvre boards, the brass machine head inscribed with maker's name and numbered 488, slight damage, some strings missing, early 20thC, 69in (175cm) high. **$1,500-1,800**

An Astor & Company chamber barrel organ, the 27cm cylinder playing 10 tunes on 6 rack and wood and metal pipes, contained in mahogany Gothic revival case with winding handle, set of simulated organ pipes and 6 organ stops at the front, tune changing knife at the side, English, early 19thC, 80in (203cm) high. **$3,200-3,800**

A grand pianoforte by John Broadwood & Sons, in a mahogany case with simple inlaid lines and a rosewood interior, the legs and pedal board enriched with ebony, with music desk, c1817, 97in (246cm) long. **$11,000-14,500**

An English violoncello by Arthur Richardson, labelled Made By/Arthur Richardson/Crediton Devon 1921, the varnish of a golden orange colour, length of back 30in (76cm), in case. **$9,000-10,000**

A violin, the two-piece back with medium to narrow near horizontal curl, the ribs and head of a similar wood, the table with narrow grain, the varnish of a mid-brown colour, with short neck, ebonised finger board and rosewood turners, together with a violin bow, the silver plated button and ebony frog inlaid with mother-of-pearl, late 19thC, length of back 14½in (37cm). **$700-800**

An English violin by John Byrom, labelled John Byrom ..... Liverpool 1902, with red-brown colour varnish over a golden ground, in case with silver mounted bow branded G.A. Chanot, length of back 14in (36cm). **$4,500-5,500**

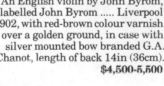

A six-keyed glass flute by Claude Laurent, engraved C. Laurent à Paris 1819/Brevete, with silvered keys and end cap, set with coloured glass, silver mounts, sounding length 21in (53cm), in fitted case. **$10,000-12,000**

An I. Willis & Co. chamber barrel organ, the 18 key movement playing on 4 racks of wooden and metal pipes, with 6 pinned wooden barrels each playing 10 popular airs and hymns, contained in mahogany case with winding handle on the front, together with panel of simulated organ pipes and 4 stops, the base housing spare cylinders, mid-19thC, 70in (178cm) high. **$5,500-7,000**

A German rosewood cased boudoir grand pianoforte by Blüthner, on bold turned and fluted tapering legs ending in brass cappings and casters, c1887, 78in (198cm) long. **$2,600-3,600**

Gramophones

An 11⅞in Symphonion rococo disc musical box, German, Style 25C, the 'sublime harmonie' arrangement of 2 combs together with 12 metal discs, 18½in (47cm) wide.
$5,500-6,500

An early His Master's Voice gramophone.
$700-900

An E. M. Ginn Expert Senior hand made gramophone with Expert 4 spring sound box, electric motor, counter-balanced goose neck tone arm and papier mâché horn, 28in (71cm) diam.
$3,500-4,500

A rare hand-cranked Berliner gramophone, German, with cast iron base, mounted with 5in turntable, flywheel and handcrank, original sound box and papier mâché horn, distressed, c1899, 10in (25cm) long, together with one damaged disc. **$6,500-7,000**

A rare HMV Model 251 console cabinet gramophone, with No. 4 sound box and folded internal horn enclosed by louvres and doors flanked by record compartments, finished in Chinese lacquer on black ground, c1925.
$1,600-2,000

The last of the Gramophones Company's derivatives of the 'Humpbacked Victrola', and the only one to appear with the new acoustic system of October 1925. The lacquer finish does not figure in HMV catalogues, and was probably applied for Harrods, whose label is in the machine.

BOXES

An early Victorian ebony, red tortoiseshell and boulle artist's box, inlaid in brass and pewter, the lid enclosing trays on 2 levels with paint holders, mixing tray and brush holders and green leather portfolio folder, lock stamped Turners Patent Hampton, 16½in (41cm) wide.
$1,400-1,800

A pair of Regency amboyna boxes, each hinged top inset with a boulle, red tortoiseshell, mother-of-pearl, copper and brass panel, one with a satyr and snakes, the other with putti, birds and snakes, enclosing a red velvet interior with pen tray, 10in (25.5cm) square.
$2,000-2,700

A Victorian biscuit box on stand, with hinged action opening to reveal pierced liners with cast handles and ornate cast legs terminating in hoof feet, 7½in (19cm) wide.
$650-720

A mahogany, chequer strung and painted knife box, the interior converted for stationery, 19thC, 18½in (47cm) high.
$3,000-4,000

A Britannia metal biscuit box,
c1890, 8½in (21cm) high.
$450-500

A Japanese export black and gilt
lacquer bow fronted decanter box,
the top enclosing a fitted green
velvet lined interior, with a set of
6 cut glass decanters with stoppers
and 2 smaller glass bottles, the sides
with carrying handles, on later bun
feet, late 18thC, 11in (28cm) wide.
$3,000-4,000

A French ivory counter box, the
cover with games marker, painted
and engraved with figures and
foliage, with a collection of counters,
18thC, 3in (7.5cm) wide.
$540-720

A George III mahogany and chequer
banded serpentine fronted knife
box, with later fitted interior, 13½in
(34cm) high. **$800-900**

A calamander dressing box, the
hinged top with an initialled brass
plaque, enclosing a fitted interior
with cut glass fittings with silver
mounts, above a sprung drawer,
19thC, 7½in (19cm) high.
$1,500-1,700

A snakewood and ebony decanter
box, with quarter veneered top
enclosing a cut glass decanter
with stopper, 6in (15cm) wide.
$1,800-2,000

A George III burr elm and
marquetry knife box, crossbanded
overall with fruitwood and inlaid
with boxwood and ebonised
stringing, enclosing a green baize
lined interior, the front with an oval
inlaid with an urn, possibly Dutch,
15½in (39cm) high. **$1,200-1,600**

A George IV rosewood and brass
bound dressing case,
countersunk handles and an
engraved plaque, the velvet lined
interior with a concealed mirror
above trays and compartments
including engraved silver
mounted cut glass containers,
hallmarked London 1822, 14½in
(37cm). **$2,000-2,700**

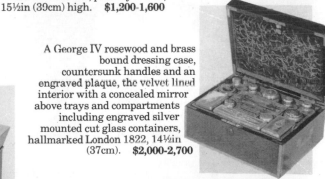

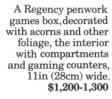

A Regency rosewood jewellery box.
$720-900

A Regency penwork
games box, decorated
with acorns and other
foliage, the interior
with compartments
and gaming counters,
11in (28cm) wide.
$1,200-1,300

A Victorian rosewood and boulle jewellery casket, inlaid overall à premiere partie with brass and pewter, the hinged lid enclosing an interior with tray containing a glass fronted silver gilt red leather display box, the reverse embossed in gilt, Honble. Elizabeth Ingram, Mrs. Hugo Meynell, enclosing an ormolu saucer, on a moulded base, 13in (33cm) wide.
$720-1,000

A George II red stained shagreen veneered knife box, the cover with brass handle and escutcheon plate, the interior fitted and lined with silk and velvet and braid, 8in (20cm) high. **$360-450**

A Sheraton period mahogany knife box, crossbanded in satinwood, with original interior and silver plated mounts.
$800-900

A pair of George III mahogany stationery boxes, inlaid overall with chevron banding, the top banded with rosewood and inlaid with later compass medallions with waved front, enclosing a later fitted interior, 13in (33cm) high.
$2,700-3,600

A George III mahogany cutlery urn, inlaid with chevron stringing, the domed top with later turned finial, the chamfered stem on a later hexagonal base, 25in (64cm) high.
$1,200-1,400

A French gold mounted portrait box, with reeded mounts, the box of green lacquer with plain mounts and tortoiseshell lining, c1790.
$800-1,000

A pair of George III urn-shaped mahogany knife boxes, the lids and bodies with boxwood and ebony stringing, the pedestal bases with tulipwood banding, on ogee bracket feet, interiors missing, 27in (68cm) high. **$3,600-4,500**

A French enamel powder box, painted with young lovers strolling through countryside, 8cm.
$800-900

A Victorian pierced gilt brass scent casket, with carrying handle, the interior velvet lined and with 3 clear and blue flashed glass scent bottles, decorated in gilt, 5in (12.5cm) wide.
$800-1,000

A Regency Anglo-Indian ivory sewing box, in the form of a house, 6in (15cm) wide.
$2,700-4,500

A gold snuff box, the cover engraved with a scene of a Roman ruin, the borders chased and carved with leafy scrolls, engine turned base and sides, 19thC, 8cm.
$2,700-3,600

A gilt lined snuff box with reeded sides, the lid engraved with a two-masted sailing ship in a floret border and, on the inside, 'The passenger on The Falcon, Capt. John Adams to accept this small token in admiration of his Seamanship on the passage to Port Sydney, 21st Day of May 1829', the base stamped Dick, 4 pseudo-hallmarks, and N.S.W.
$36,000-45,000

An English gold mounted ivory snuff box, the cover engraved, the base piqué and engraved, with plain reeded mount, c1720, 3½in (8cm) wide.
$2,700-3,600

An English gold mounted tortoiseshell snuff box, with reeded mounts and hinge, the cover set with a gold plaque engraved with a coat-of-arms, c1725, 3in (8cm) wide.
$3,600-4,500

The similarity of the engraving of the cartouche to a number of coats-of-arms on silver by Paul de Lamerie may suggest that it is the work of Ellis Gamble.

A South Staffordshire enamel snuff box, the cover painted on a raised white scroll cartouche, the sides and base with similar cartouches enclosing flowersprays, against a green ground with raised white trelliswork, restored, c1765, 3in (7.5cm) wide.
$1,200-1,400

A Viennese enamel and silver mounted snuff box, painted all over with figures in landscapes and buildings in riverscapes, 19thC, 3in (7.5cm) wide.
$800-900

A French enamel snuff box, the red ground with raised white scrolls, painted with panels of flowers, 3in (7.5cm) wide.
$270-360

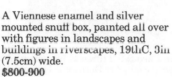

A French enamel snuff box, the blue ground with raised scrolls, painted with reserves of flowers, 19thC, 3in (7.5cm) wide.
$270-360

A gold and enamel mounted toothpick case, applied with a turquoise enamel panel and bordered with ivory beads, mirrored interior, c1800, 3½in (9cm).
$650-900

A pair of Dutch mahogany and fruitwood hanging tobacco jars, banded with ebonised mouldings with pierced roundel above a hinged lid, one with pottery jar, 19thC, 11½in (29cm) high.
$2,700-3,600

ELECTRICAL

A Gecophone 'Victor 3' three-valve receiver, in crinkle finish metal case with hinged lid, and an Orphean horn speaker.
$350-450

A Pilot Model U-650 six-valve receiver, in upright walnut veneered case with circular tuning dial with 'Magic Eye', 19½in (49cm) high.
$550-650

A Pye Model 350 four-valve receiver, in horizontal walnut case with sloping control panel above fret, 17in (43cm) wide, and a Celestion Model 79 speaker in case
$450-550

An Ekco Model 313 AC mains receiver, in horizontal brown Bakelite case, c1930, 17in (43cm) wide, and a Celestion speaker in mahogany case.
$350-450

An Ekco R.S.2 three-valve mains receiver, in Art Deco style brown Bakelite case, with triple speaker grille, 16in (41cm) high.
$260-360

A Magneto telephone, by Ericsson Telephones Ltd., in an oak case.
$450-550

Miscellaneous

A red telephone No. 232, with bell set 26, c1955.
$700-800

A Sterling intercommunication telephone, c1910.
$90-180

A 328 G.P.O. telephone, with bell on/off facility, c1955.
$130-140

A Siemens
neophone, c1938.
$180-200

A red Federal telephone, used on the
Government system, c1948.
$450-550

An ivory telephone
No. 232, with
bell set 26, c1955.
$650-700

A Post Office neophone, black
Bakelite with cast iron base, c1929.
$550-1,000

A Salter Improved No. 5 typewriter,
No. 2694, with gilt lining and
decoration, mahogany baseboard
and japanned and gilt lined steel
cover, by Geo. Salter & Co., West
Bromwich.
$5,500-6,500

A 52in (132cm)
Ordinary bicycle,
the backbone with
mounting step,
stamped Humber
& Co., Makers,
c1885.
$4,000-4,800

TRANSPORT

Vehicles

A Dursley Pederson bicycle, size 3,
with chain guard and tool box,
c1910.
$1,700-2,000

A 50in (127cm) Ordinary
bicycle, with sprung leather
saddle, mounting step,
and turned wood handles
mounted on shaped bar,
c1885.
$3,500-4,500

A Dursley Pederson bicycle, with
string saddle, tubular cross frame,
gears and bell, painted green,
size 5,
c1910.
$1,800-2,000

Car Mascots

'Epsom', a frosted modelled head of a racehorse, relief moulded mark R. Lalique, 7in (18cm) high, on chromed radiator mount, base with shallow rim chip.
$15,500-17,500

'Archer', a clear and frosted car mascot, the disc intaglio moulded with a kneeling male archer, moulded R. Lalique, wheel cut France, 5in (13cm).
$1,700-3,000

A red Ashay car mascot, c1930, 9in (23cm) long.
$1,800-2,200

'Tête de Bélier', a clear glass car mascot with amethyst tinge, in the form of a ram's head, the face exhibiting a waxy translucence, 4in (9cm) high, complete with Breves Galleries metal mount on illuminated square wooden stand, signed R. Lalique France and Breves Galleries Knightsbridge SW3, stand 8½in (21cm) high.
$9,000-10,000

'Barbillon', a frosted and clear car mascot, moulded as a fish with upright fin, on rectangular block base, stencilled R. Lalique, 3in (8cm).
$650-700

LEATHER & LUGGAGE
Leather & Luggage

A bound domed top canvas covered trunk, late 19thC, 32in (81cm) wide.
$90-120

Top. A photographic equipment trunk, covered in zinc and brass bound, with leather carrying handles, the interior fitted with polished wood and labelled Louis Vuitton Paris, London P1073, lock No. 0376752, 24in (61cm) wide.
$4,800-5,500

Bottom. A cabin trunk, vermin proof for use in the tropics, covered in zinc and brass bound, with carrying handles, on casters, interior finished in white cotton and labelled Louis Vuitton London, Paris No. N32043, lock No. 0215, lacking tray, 33½in (85cm) wide.
$4,500-5,000

A shoe secrétaire, covered in LV material, on casters bound in leather and brass, fitted with 29 shoe boxes with lids, one drawer and tray, all lined in white felt, labelled inside twice Louis Vuitton, Paris, Nice, Cannes, Vichy, London, number indistinct, lock No. 078463, 44½in (112cm) high.
$8,000-9,000

A gentleman's tan pigskin dressing case, with ivory fittings, monogrammed C.E.F., 15in (38cm) wide.
$450-550

A Fortnum and Mason travelling drinks set, comprising 3 shaped flasks and centre container with cups and lemon squeezer, in brown leather case, 8in (20cm) high.
$180-280

A Regency leather covered and gilt metal mounted lady's dressing table compendium, the chamfered, reeded top with gilt metal plaque inscribed Eliza B. Swayne, March 5th 1817, revealing a secret sprung jewellery compartment, the tan leather interior with 2 short and 3 long drawers, fitted with a paint box, a sewing box with thimbles, thread, ivory measuring tape and other items, the lower drawer with a pull-out writing slope containing 2 compartments and twin bottles, raised on claw feet, 12in (31cm) wide.
$1,600-1,700

On opening the writing slope a watermark can be detected which reads Ansell 1807.

A German trunk with leather, brass and wood trim, fitted interior, with drawers, some lined with silk, by Madler Koffer, 46in (116cm).
$270-280

A gentleman's tan leather fitted dressing case, the interior finished in polished hide lined leather, fitted with real ebony hair, hat and clothes brushes, silver topped glass bottles initialled G.P.R., and other accessories, nickel plated locks, Harrods, 26in (66cm) wide.
$550-650

A leather trunk banded in wood with brass fittings, with interior tray.
$350-400

A William and Mary leather and iron mounted travelling trunk, the hinged cover with Royal coronet and initials M.R., with iron carrying handles and key, standing on later twin rectangular oak stands with turned feet, the interior now unlined, c1690, 45½in (115cm) wide.
$8,000-9,000

This trunk reputedly was the property of Queen Mary, wife of William, Prince of Orange.

A crocodile skin travelling dressing case, the interior lined in maroon watered silk and fitted with silver mounted bottles, brushes, manicure set and curling tongs, further fitted with writing folder with ivory paper knife, pen and pencil, various maroon leather wallets, instrument case, French clock etc., makers Samuel Summers Drew and Earnest Drew, and CD, London, c1905, 18½in (47cm) wide.
$1,000-1,400

A car trunk with 3 matching trunks inside, all with white cotton interiors and straps, all labelled Louis Vuitton, Paris, Nice, Lille, London, Nos. 190383 to 190386, with monogram locks.
$7,000-8,000

SPORT
Cricket

J. Wisden's Cricketers' Almanack for 1879, original soft covers, spine distressed.
$450-500

J. Wisden's Cricketers' Almanack for 1881, original soft covers, spine distressed.
$300-360

J. Wisden's Cricketers' Almanack for 1880, original soft covers, spine distressed, covers loose.
$430-490

J. Wisden's Cricketers' Almanack for 1882, original soft covers.
$300-360

A Parian bust of W. G. Grace, by Robinson and Leadbetter, 6½in (17cm).
$700-1,000

England Australia Official Cricket Souvenir, Season 1911-12, souvenir programme issued by Authority of the Board of Control, with half tone portraits of the England Eleven and individual team members, original pictorial wrappers.
$350-550

A rare tour programme not listed by Padwick.

A metal admission ticket, obverse die-stamped with a central 'W' and name 'Darnall Cricket Ground', reverse with scene of a cricket field with inscription 'Grand Match Admission Ticket' on surround, 1in (3cm) diam.
£350-400   CSK

Fishing

A 3in Ogden Smith of London Improved Zefer reel, 1930s.
$55-70

A 3in Allcock of Redditch 'the Ousel' reel, made by Walter Dingley, c1930.
$35-40

A 2½in Farlow brass reel, crank wind handle made specially for the top to be bent down for protection while travelling, pre-1880.
$90-120

A 3³⁄₁₆in LRH Lightweight, with 3 screw latch, and duplicated Mk. II check, post-war model but the first type made.
$90-110

A 4in Allcock of Redditch the Marvel salmon reel, probably wartime.
$55-70

A small spinning reel by Allan of Glasgow, the Spinet, c1912.
$70-90

A Spanish knife, with tortoiseshell and ivory handle, and brass picture of a mounted spearing soldier, probably pre-war, 13½in (35cm).
$25-35

A carved painted wood half model of a salmon, 48in (122cm).
$3,200-3,800

A 2⅝in Moscrop brass reel, many unusual mechanisms, only designed by Moscrop, who died 1903.
$70-90

A 4in spinning reel, made by Young's of Redditch, named the Windex, post-war but collectable.
$35-55

A mahogany fishing rod cabinet and contents, 19thC, 25in (64cm) wide.
$6,500-7,000

A 2½in brass reel with embossed fisherman on back and front, rare, but poor condition.
$55-70

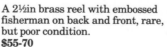

A 2⅝in Uniqua, a wartime model when there was a shortage of the blacklead finish, so lacquered over the aluminium, now known as the Spitfire model, c1945.
$110-125

A 4½in Westley Richards of Birmingham, by Walter Dingley, with elaborate ball bearings.
$70-90

A Hardy Test Montague black japanned fly box, with special compartment outside lid, very good condition, pre-1940.
$35-45

Football

A Staffordshire pottery mug, transfer printed in blue, depicting a football match on a pale brown ground, the interior rim with a garland of flowers, mid-19thC, 4in (10cm) high.
$770-850

Welsh Football Union Winners 1901-02 Triple Crown, 17 oval head and shoulders portrait photographs of the team, all mounted in one frame with central caption.
$350-450

A bronze statue of a footballer about to throw a ball into play, on wooden base, early 20thC, 13in (33cm).
$300-400

An Art Deco style clock, surmounted by a spelter statue of a footballer in action, 11in (28cm).
$450-550

Miscellaneous

Four early badminton rackets, contained in a wood box with other relics of a lawn tennis and badminton set.
$540-720

Golfing

A William Park Transitional and scared and head brassie, with lead insert and horn sole, restored.
$400-470

A Standard Golf Co. Mills Patent aluminium head putter, SS model Medium Lie, 10oz.
$70-110

Did you know

MILLER'S Antiques Price Guide builds up year by year to form the most comprehensive photo-reference system available

---

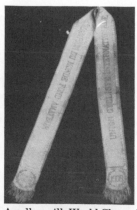

A half size mahogany billiard table, by Thurston & Co., with 6 turned and fluted tulip legs, c1880.
$3,500-5,500

A billiard/pool wall scoring board in mahogany, with centre slate marker, roller numbering, lower ball storage and coin sections, c1875.
$2,000-3,000

A yellow silk World Champion Cycling sash, embroidered with white metal thread with inscription 'Union Cycliste Internationale Champion Du Monde Fond Amateur 1908'.
$350-550

A Victorian style billiard table, with turned legs, c1900.
$4,500-6,500

An Olympic torch in steel with outline of the route taken by the runners from Olympia to Berlin, inscribed at the top 'Organisations-Komitee für die XI. Olympiade Berlin 1936, Als Dank Dem Trager', and on the underside 'Stiftung der Fried. Krupp A.G., Essen, Krupp Nirosta V2A Stahl', 11in (28cm).
$10,000-11,000

A full size mahogany billiard table, by Orme & Sons, c1900.
$15,000-21,000

A full size light oak billiard table, by Burroughes & Watts, with matching lights and other accessories and adjustable legs for levelling, c1890.
$32,000-40,000

A full size mahogany billiard table by Burroughes & Watts, c1870.
$14,500-18,000

A circular mahogany carousel cue stand, to hold 12 cues, c1900.
$700-900

A half size mahogany billiard/dining table, by Burroughes & Watts, shown with dining leaves removed and raised ready for play, c1890.
$6,500-7,500

> ## Use the Index!
>
> *Because certain items might fit easily into any of a number of categories, the quickest and surest method of locating any entry is by reference to the index at the back of the book.*
> *This has been fully cross-referenced for absolute simplicity*

LIGHTING

A miniature chamber candlestick, the feather moulded base painted with flowers within a gold rim, by J. Rose & Co., Coalport, 4in (9cm). **$650-700**

A Worcester, Flight, Barr & Barr pink ground and gilt chamber candlestick, impressed and script marks, c1820, 4in (10cm) wide. **$2,000-2,700**

A pair of bronze and gilt bronze candlesticks after the antique, of tripod form with paw feet, concave sided platforms, circular bases, applied gilt bronze florettes and gilt bronze sconces, 19thC, 11in (28cm). **$1,200-1,500**

A pair of brass candlesticks, the tall shafts with ejectors, on domed bases, early 19thC, 20in (51cm) high. **$800-1,200**

A pair of Dutch brass candlesticks, each with knopped stem on a slightly dished base, c1700. **$1,500-1,700**

A pair of stained beech candlesticks, the turned knopped columns with wide drip pans, on spreading conforming bases, late 19thC, 53in (134cm). **$1,400-1,500**

A pair of bronze and gilt bronze candlesticks, on bronze bronze stepped bases, engine turned and moulded key patterns, 19thC, 6in (15cm). **$450-650**

A pair of Northern bronze pricket candlesticks, raised on 3 stylised lion's feet, the knopped faceted stems with spirally twisted prickets, one pricket broken, bases with splits, 14th/15thC, 10in (25cm) high. **$6,000-6,500**

A pair of late 18thC style wrought iron floor standing pricket candlesticks, with knopped columns on trefoil bases, 49½in (126cm) high. **$700-1,000**

A bronzed metal three-light candelabrum, in the form of a street lamp, modelled with a figure of a swaggering young man, the base formed to simulate cobblestones and with a cartouche shaped plaque inscribed SIFFLEUR, early 20thC, 36in (92cm) high. **$700-1,000**

A large pair of six-light bronze patinated brass candelabra, in the form of male and female partially clad figures each supporting the 6 scrolling foliate branches, on open rococo bases, 19thC, 27in (69cm) high.
$1,200-1,500

A pair of George III cut glass two-branch candelabra, 23in (59cm) high. $1,400-1,500

A pair of ormolu ornate three-branch candelabra, 19thC, 20in (51cm) high.
$700-900

A pair of gilt metal five-branch, six-light candelabra with cut glass drops, 26in (66cm) high.
$900-1,000

A pair of bronze and ormolu five-light candelabra, on a stepped alabaster plinth and toupie feet, fitted for electricity, one plinth restored, 18in (46cm) high.
$5,500-6,500

A pair of French ormolu table candelabra, raised on 3 acanthus leaf sheathed knurl feet, 30½in (77cm) high.
$1,500-1,800

A George II gilt metal hall lantern, with 4 double arched panels, one forming the door with arched ribs, door panel missing, c1750, 17½in (44cm) diam.
$2,600-3,600

A pair of French ormolu and black painted seven-light candelabra, the concave bases with variegated marble plinths and acanthus decoration, late 19thC, 31in (79cm) high.
$2,000-3,000

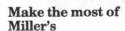

A Georgian glass and bronze hall lantern, the tapering cylindrical glass body with guilloche decorated metal rim with 3 hooks for chains, the base with a screw-on candle nozzle with urn pendant finial, c1810, 16½in (42cm).
$2,600-3,600

> ## Make the most of Miller's
>
> *Unless otherwise stated, any description which refers to 'a set' or 'a pair' includes a valuation for the entire set or the pair, even though the illustration may show only a single item*

A French style pentagonal hall lantern, with an open scroll corona, late 18thC, 41in (104cm) high.
$5,500-6,500

A pair of George III style gilt bronze framed four-light hall lanterns, of pentagonal outline, with curved glass panels and scroll corona, 32in (81cm) high.
$6,500-8,000

A French brass framed eight-light hall lantern of square section with canted corners, the frame with applied stylised caryatid figures, with open scrollwork corona, 48in (122cm) high.
$3,500-4,500

A George III style hexagonal brass hall lantern, the glazing bars surmounted by anthemion leaves, below an open scrollwork corona, 30in (76cm) high.
$900-1,000

A green painted wrought iron hexagonal hall lantern, with stylised foliate and open scrollwork corona and terminal, 36in (92cm) high.
$650-700

A Royal Worcester female Bringaree Indian lamp base, her clothes coloured rust-brown and green, a cream coloured staff held in her right hand, after a model by James Hadley, puce printed crowned circle, shape number 2028 and Rd. No., impressed mark, c1898, 26in (66cm).
$4,500-5,500

A tôleware adjustable twin-light table lamp, the pierced shades heightened in gilt, 19thC, 19½in (49cm) high.
$650-700

A black painted wrought iron hexagonal hall lantern in the form of a castle, with a central spire flanked by 2 smaller turrets, the base with stylised foliate mounts, 30in (76cm) high.
$800-1,000

An ormolu three-light electrolier, the scrolling foliate chased branches emanating from a circular lobed corona, late 19th/early 20thC, 21in (53cm) high.
$1,200-1,300

A George IV gilt brass and glass four-light Colza hanging oil lamp, hung with chains from a foliate corona, the burners with later frosted glass shades, 20in (51cm) diam. **$10,000-12,000**

A pair of Empire style ormolu eight-light chandeliers, with pineapple terminal and suspension chains below a stellar corona, 58in (147cm) high. **$5,500-9,000**

A set of 5 French twin-light wall appliqués, late 19thC, 17½in (45cm) high. **$2,000-3,000**

A set of 4 gilt bronze twin-light wall appliqués, of Empire design, the fluted branches emanating from narrow backplates, centred by a laurel wreath and hung with ribbon tie surmount, 17½in (44cm) high. **$2,600-3,500**

A pair of Victorian silver plated on copper Adam style oil lamps/candlesticks, with removable cranberry glass reservoirs. **$450-650**

A large brass chandelier, eight-branch electric candle fitments with eagle mount to top. **$1,000-1,200**

A pair of French ormolu five-branch wall lights of Louis XVI design, 12in (31cm). **$1,200-1,800**

A collection of 4 gilt metal Louis XVI style wall lights, the foliate candle arms with cast acanthus leaves and berries attached to quiver backplates, the central arms above putti blowing twin trumpets, with frosted glass torch shades, one wall bracket slightly damaged, 24½in (62cm) high. **$1,000-1,200**

A set of 6 French gilt bronze wall lanterns, the glazing bars with foliate mounts, crown surmount and pineapple terminal, late 19thC, 18½in (47cm) high. **$3,500-4,500**

A six-light snooker table electric light fitting with highly decorative wrought oxidised metal frame. **$1,500-1,800**

TRIBAL ART

A Tami Island bowl, carved in relief with a stylised mask to one end with zigzags about the eyes, the carved teeth heightened with lime, a frigate bird to each side below the rim, a serrated band in high relief to each side joining the tail, dark glossy patina, tail broken, 23in (58cm) long.
$700-1,000

A Hawaiian bowl, of flaring form tapering in from the shoulder, a hooked projection emerging from one side, shiny smooth yellow brown turning to dark brown patina, 7in (18cm) diam.
$7,000-9,000

A Yoruba horseman, wearing a turban and holding a flywhisk, his jacket with incised chevrons the horse wearing striped collar, painted in red, blue, black and white, crack to base, left arm and reins repaired, from Ota, 19thC, 10in (25cm) high.
$1,200-1,600

This fine small carving shows all the characteristics of the work of the carving house in Ota which produced the carvers Labitan and Olaniyan at the beginning of this century.

Two Borneo figures, male and female, the male with conical hat and concave face, the female with hands curving about the swollen abdomen, wood bases, 28 and 24½in (71 and 63cm) high.
$1,600-1,800

A Nias large female figure, the hands holding an object against the chest, wood stand, 26in (66cm) high.
$1,200-1,400

A Senufo female figure, the median crest terminating in two knobs at nape of neck, thick crusty patina, 15in (38cm) high.
$6,500-7,000

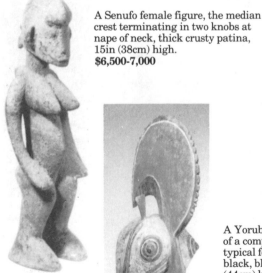

A Yoruba female figure, the blued coiffure with 2 tufts at the top, the eyes with metal stud pupils, carved wearing several bracelets and band about the waist, wearing 3 necklaces of coloured beads, from Ilobu, 16in (41cm) high.
$1,000-1,500

A Yoruba helmet mask, in the form of a compressed oval head with typical features, remains of white, black, blue and red pigment, 17½in (44cm) high.
$3,500-5,500

Two West African animal face masks, painted in red, white and black, one with incised details in white, 31 and 18in (79 and 46cm) high.
$2,700-5,500

A Maprik river ancestral figure, Abelam people, of openwork form, with a stylised lizard supporting a large standing male figure, decorated with dotted and geometric details in yellow, white, black and dark red, 74½in (189cm) high.
$2,000-3,000

A Middle Sepik river ancestral board, with details painted in dotted outline white against a faded red, yellow and black field, together with a Southern New Britain war shield, decorated with opposed stylised figures, flanking a broad rectangular projection emerging to bracket handles, bound at the centre and either end with red dyed raffia, 47 and 52in (119 and 132cm) high.
$2,700-3,600

A Yaka initiation mask, surmounted by a double tiered canvas headdress supporting an embracing couple, painted in bright blue, red, yellow and white, 24in (61cm) high.
$2,700-5,500

A Hawaiian Islands ivory pendant, of hooked form, strung on bundled thinly plaited human hair strands, bound at the top and attached to an olana fibre cord, 14in (36cm) long.
$7,000-9,000

A Mossi helmet mask, in the shape of a bird's head, the hemispherical lower part with a long narrow pointed beak surmounted by a backward turning jagged crest, the whole covered by a rich brown patina with traces of white, black and red painted designs on the sides of the helmet and the crest, 11in (28cm) high.
$3,000-4,500

The Wagadugu style masks are small, wooden zoomorphic masks. They are coloured with patterns in dark earth red, black and white, and represent animals commonly found in Mossi country. The type of animal represented can usually be recognised by certain stylised features of the animal. Thus, the hawk and other birds of prey are recognised by their short powerful beak and tri-lobed head crest feathers.

A Marquesan Islands stilt step, dark brown patina, 12in (31cm) high.
$4,500-5,500

A Lower Sepik river mask, 21½in (54cm) high.
$900-1,200

A Makonde ceremonial staff with zig-zag and diamond scarification on the face, smooth black patina, 19in (48cm) high.
$3,500-5,500

A Western Australian Aborigine shield, decorated with angular and grooved parallel lines on the front, striated lines on the back and arched handle, remains of red, white and black pigment, 31in (79cm)
$3,500-4,500

A Maori adze, with hooked cylindrical handle surmounted on the curved top by a seated figure covered with typical scrolling motifs, the pommel bound with twisted fibre, a rectangular jade blade emerging from the mouth of a stylised animal's head, pierced through the base for attachment of a wrist cord, reddish brown patina on the shaft, turning to darker brown, mottled green jade, 14in (36cm) long.
$4,500-5,500

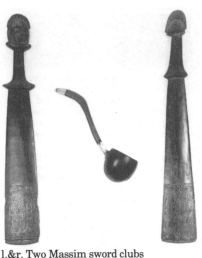

An Australian Aborigine bull roarer, of oval form, incised on each side with 5 spirals and crescents, dark glossy patina, 13in (33cm) long.
$3,500-4,500

A Kongo staff, the finial carved as a kneeling female, the cloth revealing three rows of ornaments at the back, incised swag headgear with topknot, a band of cowrie shell ornament at base, dark glossy patina, inagaki wood stand, 12½in (32cm) high.
$1,800-3,600

l.&r. Two Massim sword clubs incised on both sides with scroll designs, 26½in (67cm).
$300-360 each
c. An Oceanic ladle with stained coconut bowl, ivory and wood shaped handle, 13½in (34cm).
$150-200

A Solomon Islands model boat, in the form of a narrow dug-out canoe, inset with serrated mother-of-pearl geometric elements into the pitched surface, a long row of seashells attached to a ladder shaped device bound in red cloth on one end, broken off and reattached with native repair, an arched tapering element bound in similar cloth on the other end, 73½in (187cm) long.
$1,000-1,200

A Kongo flywhisk, the grip decorated with typical geometric design and surmounted by a human torso, eyes inset with metal discs, and coiffure in the form of a long braid hanging on the nape, animal's hair inset into the whisk with a wooden peg, brown patina with metal inlays, some missing, 16½in (42cm) high.
$550-650

A pair of Benin brass armlets, each with repoussé bands of heads of Portuguese, alternating with quatrefoils, a border of interlaced geometric ornament, each applied with 12 Maltese crosses in darker metal, minor damage, 19thC, 5½in (14cm) high.
$450-650

Cloisonné & Enamel

A pair of Japanese cloisonné vases, worked in silver wire with birds among flowering trees on green grounds, signed Ota Kichishaburo, 6in (15cm) high.
$1,000-1,600

Two Marquesan Island objects, a stone pounder with curved base, tapering sides and cylindrical shaft, surmounted by a Janus head with broad upturned mouth and scrolling ears, and a wood bowl with cylindrical base and rounded sides, decorated with traditional scrolling geometric elements and stylised human faces, pounder 9½in (24cm) high, bowl 12in (31cm) diam.
$3,600-4,500

A Japanese cloisonné vase, worked in silver wire with a writhing dragon on a dark blue ground, minor scratches, 9½in (24cm) high.
$1,200-1,500

A Chinese cloisonné baluster vase of diamond cross section with mask ring handles, decorated on a turquoise ground, 19in (48cm) high.
$700-1,000

A Japanese cloisonné vase, decorated with chyrsanthemum sprays, on a dark blue ground, signed Tamura, 7½in (19cm) high.
$350-550

A Chinese cloisonné bottle decorated on a turquoise ground, Qianlong, 5½in (14cm) high.
$650-800

Costume

A Chinese robe of bronze coloured silk, embroidered in coloured silks and gilt threads against a gilt thread lattice ground, with a sea-wave border at the base, with inscription in lining, fastened by ribbons, 19thC.
$1,200-1,800

The inscription translates: In the peach month (the third lunar month) of the sixth year of the Guangxu period (ie 1880) written under auspicious circumstances.

A Japanese 'furisode' of midnight blue silk, embroidered in gilt threads and coloured silks, lined with red silk crepe, with padded hem, mid/late 19thC.
$1,000-1,500

A Chinese image robe of green silk, embroidered in coloured silks and couched gilt threads, the lining with inscription, early 18thC.
$4,500-7,000

The inscription translates: This robe was offered on the 2nd day of the 2nd month, the sixth year of Qianlong (ie 1741 AD), followed by a list of the officers then the signature of the person who prepared the offering note.

A Chinese dragon robe, of brown kossu silk, woven in many coloured silks and gilt threads, with horseshoe cuffs, trimmed with fur, late 19thC.
$2,700-3,600

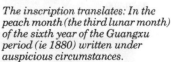

A ceremonial cover of three natural linen panels, each end embroidered with a band of pink florets, boteh outlined with blue hearts, and metal thread flowersprays, late 18thC, 108 by 54in (274 by 137cm).
$1,000-1,800

It is thought that these covers were placed on the marriage bed.

A Chinese formal robe, of blue kossu silk, woven in coloured silks and gilt threads, mid/late 19thC.
$2,000-3,000

A Chinese dragon robe of blue silk, embroidered with coloured silks and gilt threads, lined with blue silk, early/mid 19thC.
$1,600-2,000

A Chinese lady's informal jacket of midnight blue silk, embroidered in coloured silks, the sleeve bands of sea green embroidered silk, lined with red silk damask, with jade buttons, 19thC.
$800-1,200

A 'kosode' of pale blue cotton, printed with a bold overall design in yellow, white, brown and black, also with large hats and tassels, lined with red, padded, early 19thC.
$700-900

A Chinese lady's informal jacket of red silk, embroidered in coloured silks and gilt threads, the sleeve bands and trimmings of yellow silk embroidered with blossom and butterflies, lined with red silk, padded, mid/late 19thC.
$550-900

A Chinese lady's informal robe, of red silk, embroidered in coloured silks, trimmed with black embroidered braid, the sleeve bands of ivory embroidered silk, lined with blue silk, mid-19thC.
$1,800-2,800

Furniture

A Chinese wood six-leaf screen, the leaves set with a total of 92 'famille rose' porcelain plaques variously depicting Immortals in landscapes or scrolling foliage, each leaf 40½ by 12½in (103 by 32cm).
$3,000-3,600

A Japanese gold and black lacquered wood two-leaf screen with cloisonné panels, the exterior with panels of gold lacquer on wood, some damage, 67in (170cm) high.
$4,500-4,800

A Chinese export black and gilt lacquered tripod table, with tilt-top, mid-19thC, 36in (92cm) wide.
$4,500-5,500

A pair of Oriental hardwood jardinière stands, the marble tops above prunus carved friezes, on cabriole supports headed by masks and ending in claw-and-ball feet, 18in (46cm) diam.
$1,200-1,800

A Chinese lacquered sewing table, the hinged top enclosing a fitted interior, on lyre shaped end supports with floral carved scrolled feet tied by a turned stretcher, 19thC.
$450-650

A Chinese hardwood corner table, the serpentine top inset with marble, above a profusely carved and pierced frieze, on three massive carved cabriole supports and claw-and-ball feet, tied by a roundel and curved stretcher, 19thC, 41½in (105cm) wide.
$1,000-1,600

Glass

A Chinese black and gold japanned tray-on-stand, with hoof feet, early/mid-18thC, 32in (81cm) wide.
$3,000-3,600

A Chinese huanghualiwood stool, with rimmed top above beaded edge with pierced frieze and bowed supports joined by a shaped stretcher, 16½in (42cm) wide.
$700-1,000

A Peking yellow glass bottle shaped vase, with tapering neck decorated in relief with birds among prunus branches, 7in (18cm) high.
$1,800-2,000

A Chinese hardwood side cabinet, with raised sides to the cleated top, 3 frieze drawers, 2 doors to the panelled front, flanked by pierced and carved side sections and on square supports, 85in (216cm) wide.
$900-1,200

A Japanese padouk wood netsuke cabinet, 38in (96cm) wide.
$4,500-5,500

A Chinese hardwood window seat, carved with bamboo throughout, the solid seat enclosing a compartment and flanked by raised side sections, pierced underframe below, on cabriole legs, some restoration, 40in (101cm) wide.
$550-700

A Peking aquamarine green glass pear-shaped vase, 20in (51cm) high.
$1,800-2,000

Ivory

A Japanese ivory figure group, depicting three warriors in a circle wielding swords and weapons, some damage, signed sword blades and some digits, 5in (13cm) high.
$1,200-1,400

An ivory okimono of Kanyu and Chohi, 3in (8cm) high.
$900-1,000

A Japanese sectional ivory carving of a farmer with a wood frame of bundles of sticks on his back, a bird in a bird's nest in his left hand, a hare at his feet and an eagle perched on the frame watching the bird, the details in black, signed Gyokushi, 16½in (42cm) high.
$5,500-7,000

A Japanese ivory group of a farmer supporting a wood frame of bundles of wheat and a small child, a further child at his left with a basket of fruit and a rake, minor damage, signed on a red lacquer tablet, 9in (23cm) high.
$2,600-3,600

An ivory okimono of a lady peering into the ear of a grimacing man, his elbow resting on his cabinet, a pipe in his left hand, a case in his right, pipe bowl broken off, signed Munehiro, 2in (5cm) long.
$1,200-1,500

An ivory okimono of Kakkio and his family, 3in (8cm) high.
$900-1,000

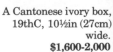

A Japanese ivory carving of a man, standing wearing a loosley fitting jacket with a large straw hat slung over his back, holding a tobacco pipe in his left hand and a pouch in his right, the details in black, signed on a red lacquer tablet, Hideyuki wood stand, 13in (33cm) high.
$4,500-5,500

A Japanese ivory carving of a girl dressed in a girl guides' uniform, holding a bunch of peony, 8in (20cm) high.
$650-700

A Cantonese ivory box, 19thC, 10½in (27cm) wide.
$1,600-2,000

A Japenese marine ivory carving of Shoki, 2 onis and 3 skeletons, the reverse with a lady pouring sake for a further skeleton, 4½in (12cm) high.
$550-700

Jade

A Japanese ivory carving of a figure, holding a bird of prey on his right arm, a basket slung at his waist, damaged, signed on a red lacquer tablet, 6in (15cm) high.
$180-360

An ivory netsuke style okimono of Daikoku holding his sack on which he plays with a drum and two mice, signed, 1½in (4cm) high.
$580-900

A Japanese ivory group of two farmers, the details in black, signed on a red lacquer tablet, Sekizan wood stand, 11½in (30cm) high.
$4,500-5,500

A jade and white metal mounted mirror, attached by an incised white metal frame to a pale celadon jade belt hook handle carved with an openwork chilong, Qing Dynasty, 10½in (26cm) long, with box.
$2,600-3,600

A pair of Chinese mottled green and brown jadeite carvings of ladies seated on deer, each holding a ruyi spray, the animals heads turned left and right, one broken at the ankles, 10in (25cm) high, on pierced wood stands.
$1,800-2,000

A Chinese apple green jadeite saddle ring, with slight russet inclusions, 1in (3cm) wide.
$900-1,500

A Chinese decorative jade carving on stand, early 19thC, 5in (13cm) long.
$550-700

A Chinese pale celadon jade figure group, 12½in (32cm) high.
$2,000-2,700

A Chinese dark green nephrite jade bowl of shallow form, the everted rim rising from a short foot, 8in (20cm) diam., with box.
$1,500-1,600

Metal

A pair of Japanese silvered bronze Manchurian cranes, on wood stand, some damage, signed Hidehisa, 9½ and 14½in (24 by 37cm) high.
$1,200-1,600

A pair of bronze mythical beasts, the bushy upright tails resembling flames, traces of gilt and red lacquer remaining, some wear, 17thC, 21in (54cm) high.
$12,350-13,350

A Chinese bronze figure of Buddha, with tightly curled hair and pendulous earlobes, the cloak falling over both shoulders, some degrading, late Ming Dynasty, 12½in (32cm) high.
$2,600-3,600

A Japanese bronze jardinière, cast in relief with several monkeys playing, some holding persimmon, signed Genryusai (Seiya Zo), 14in (36cm) diam.
$7,350-9,000

An archaic Ordos bronze dagger, the tapered blade of thin lozenge section, deeply patinated with some malachite encrustation, small losses to blade edges, 4th Century B.C., 13in (35cm) long.
$4,500-6,500

A Chinese bronze gilt and white metal inlaid twin headed duck, each head in opposite direction, late Ming Dynasty, 3½in (9cm) long.
$1,000-1,200

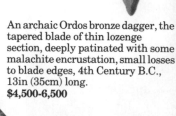

An Oriental silver coloured incense burner, with dragon handles supported by 3 elephant heads, on carved hardwood stand, 16in (41cm) high.
$650-800

A set of 12 Japanese bronze lanterns, with pagoda type tops and pierced doors and panels with foliage and cherry blossom, on shaped bases, 13in (33cm) high.
$4,500-5,500

A silver inlaid bronze figure of Guanyin, inlaid in silver with scrolling lotus, one finger missing, 17thC, 11in (28cm) high, on wood stand.
$2,600-3,600

Netsuke

An ivory netsuke of a recumbent karashishi scratching its back with a hind leg, the eyes inlaid, signed, 2in (5cm) long.
$550-650

A boxwood mask netsuke of Bugatu, signed Hozan and inscribed Shichi ju issai, aged 71.
$550-650

An ivory netsuke of a man standing clasping a bear, the animal's head turned, the details stained black, minor chips, signed, 2in (5cm) high.
$180-270

An ivory netsuke of an ox carrying wheat, with a girl by its side holding a pipe, signed, 2in (5cm) wide.
$550-750

A large ivory manju netsuke, carved in deep relief with 2 tennin wearing flowing robes and celestial scarves, one holding a lotus and necklace the other beating a drum with 2 sticks, the reverse with a pine tree, signed Insai, 3in (8cm) diam
$1,500-1,700

An ivory netsuke of a blind man straining to lift a large stone, the details in red, signed on a rectangular reserve Ryoun.
$900-1,000

> **Use the Index!**
> *Because certain items might fit easily into any of a number of categories, the quickest and surest method of locating any entry is by reference to the index at the back of the book.*
> *This has been fully cross-referenced for absolute simplicity*

Snuff Bottles

An agate snuff bottle, the darker skin in relief with a horseman holding a banner, 3in (7cm) high.
$700-1,000

An amber snuff bottle carved as a gourd, with leaves and tendrils in relief, 2in (5cm) high.
$800-900

Miscellaneous

An amber snuff bottle and stopper modelled as a lingzhi fungus, 2½in (7cm) high.
$450-550

Two Oriental brass inlaid hardwood jewel boxes, with trays, 9 by 8in (23 by 20cm).
$120-180

ISLAMIC ART

A Tibetan gilt bronze figure of a monk, seated in dhyanasana on a waisted throne, a vajra in relief in front of him, his hands in bhumisparsa and dhyana mudra, wearing a patchwork sanghati, with closely cropped black hair, the face with painted features, re-sealed, 17th/18thC, 9in (23cm).
$3,500-4,500

A Qajar pottery dish, decorated in dull blue and purple, with a Persian poem at the rim in 8 cartouches separated by rosettes, at the centre a hunter with his bow has just shot a lion, a tree between, the hunter wears pantaloons and boots with curled tips, a pointed helmet with chain mail and a shield on his back, beside his head are the Arabic numbers 82, 9in (23cm) diam.
$900-1,000

An Islamic inlaid table, the top inlaid with mother-of-pearl and various woods decorated with a geometric pattern and a central inscription against arabesques within a cube band border, the sides with inscribed panels above pairs of lobed arches supporting 8 legs, early 20thC, 24in (61cm) high.
$2,000-2,700

A large Qajar pottery tile, with a moulded design, decorated in cobalt blue, yellow, turquoise, purple and light brown with dark brown outlines, and a raised border with a grapevine, 19thC, 20 by 16in (51 by 41cm).
$3,500-4,500

A pair of Channakale pottery horses, of reddish ware with mottled greenish glaze and opaque red splashes, and with a filler hole on their hindquarters, decorated with a moulded rosette on their chests and a bridle lying curled on their saddles, the tubular legs with a ridge at the centre, 19thC, 9in (23cm) high.   **$4,500-6,000**

A panel of 10 Syrian pottery tiles, decorated in underglaze greyish blue, apple green, olive green, turquoise and purple with black outlines, with an elaborate design based on a tall flower filled vase decorated with cintimani holding a bouquet of flowers, other flowers and floral borders on either side, the stems of the central bouquet clasped together, mid/late 16thC, tiles 9in (23cm) square.   **$2,300-2,700**

An Ottoman inlaid wooden table, the octagonal recessed top inlaid with mother-of-pearl and coloured woods in a geometric design with the tughra of Abdülhamid II at the centre, the sides with pointed arches and inlaid geometric panels above, late 19th/early 20thC, 21in (54cm) high.
$700-1,000

A Safavid tinned copper bowl, with squat bulbous sides and waisted neck, the decoration consisting of 3 continuous inscribed bands round the neck, shoulder and body, a cable band on the shoulder and a festoon frieze below the inscriptions, 8in (20cm) diam.
$1,000-1,500

A Safavid tinned copper bowl, with squat bulbous sides, waisted neck and everted rim, incised on the rim with a large band containing 2 lines of inscription framed by 2 friezes of quadrilobes, the body with an overall intricate design of overlapping palmette and arabesque patterns within a scrolling foliate frieze and a strapwork border, late 17thC, 8in (20cm) diam. **$1,800-2,000**

A Sino-Tibetan brass figure of Vajrabhairava, standing in pratyalidhasana on birds, animals and Hindu deities, on a lotus throne, clasping his sakti in yab-yum, with 34 arms and numerous heads, the central one that of a ferocious bull, wearing typical garments and jewellery, traces of colour, c1800, 7in (18cm).
$2,000-2,300

A south Indian bronze figure of Buddha, standing on a waisted throne on a square base, his hands in abhaya and varada mudra, wearing a long diaphanous sanghati, the hair with flamiform finial, the separately cast aureole with columnar supports and scroll edged arch flanked by openwork floral medallions, the base inscribed, c17thC, 17in (43cm). **$4,500-5,500**

Three Qajar pottery tiles, each of moulded design with floral borders at the top, painted in underglaze polychrome colours with an equestrian figure holding a hawk in a floral landscape, 2 of them with buildings in the background, 19thC, largest 8 by 5in (20 by 13cm).
$2,000-2,300

A Qajar pottery tile, of moulded design, decorated in underglaze polychrome colours with a crowned figure in profile holding a sword in her left hand and seated on a throne between floral sprays against a blue ground, framed by a frieze of flowers, 19thC, 13 by 11in (33 by 28cm). **$1,200-1,500**

A Qajar pottery tile, with moulded frame and central design, decorated in underglaze blue, green, yellow, purple, grey and brown with black outlines, 19thC, 11in (28cm) square.
$1,800-2,800

An Egyptian carved and inlaid wooden corner cupboard, the central shelf with 2 lobed arches surmounted by a mashrabiyyah panel, the 2 other shelves with a central arch surrounded by 4 smaller, decorated with carved arabesques and inlaid mother-of-pearl rosettes, with trefoil cresting, late 19thC, 69½in (176cm) high. **$2,600-3,600**

An Indo-Persian tinned copper pedestal bowl, the inscription of calling God's blessing on the Twelve Innocents, owner's mark in a pointed medallion, 18th/19thC, **$1,000-1,600**

A Qajar pottery tile, decorated in shades of grey, blue, purple and turquoise with black outlines, framed, 19thC, 11½ by 10in (29 by 25cm). **$1,800-3,300**

A Qajar pottery tile, decorated in cobalt blue, turquoise, pale yellow, brown and purple with black outline, 19thC, 10in (25cm) square.
$1,800-2,700

An Armenian silver gilt plaque of the Virgin and Child, decorated in repoussé with engraved details, the Virgin holding the Child in the crook of her left arm, both gesturing with their right hands towards a cross hanging from the Virgin's neck, the Virgin with a triple pointed crown and a cross at the centre, with a pleated and scalloped robe, the lower half of the plaque with a rectangular chevron frame, 16thC, 5½in (14cm) high.
$2,500-2,800

A pair of Channakale pottery jugs, of green glazed earthenware with traces of unfired gold decoration, 19thC, 20in (51cm) high.
$3,500-4,500

An Indo-Persian steel axe, the watered blade with gold damescening on edges and hammer, the lacquered shaft with a floral trellis on the upper and lower halves and spiral floral sprays in the middle section, 18thC, 26in (66cm) long.
$900-1,200

An Ottoman silver bowl, with a raised boss at the centre, and decorated in repoussé in high relief, 19thC, 7in (17cm) diam.
$3,300-4,000

A Turkish bronze stirrup, the sides and top with chiselled floral motifs within a double lined frame, with openwork scrolls on top corners, 18thC, 5in (13cm) wide.
$900-1,200

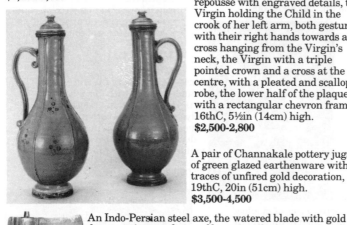

A carved black basalt Islamic tombstone, each face with a panel containing a lengthy inscription on a stippled ground including the name of the deceased, an arched panel above with pendant mosque lamp, slight damage and staining, Arabia 12th-14thC, 18in (46cm) high.
$2,600-3,600

A Persian silver bowl with flat base, rounded sides and thick rim, the rim extruded at one side into a cusped lobed panel, areas of slight corrosion, c14thC, 5in (13cm) diam.
$2,600-3,600

An Ottoman mail shirt, composed of interlocking riveted rings, a rectangular inscribed button on the front left side near the edge, 16thC, 38in (96cm) long.
$1,500-3,300

An Indo-Persian tinned copper bowl, with inscribed band interrupted by a roundel and framed by 2 scrolling foliate friezes, below a band of interlacing floral scrollwork and a row of trilobed escutcheons, the inscription calling God's blessing on the Fourteen Innocents, 18th/19thC, 11in (28cm) diam.
$1,000-1,600

EPHEMERA

Pop Ephemera

An album, Beatles For Sale, Parlophone Records, 1964, signed on the cover by each member of the group.
$2,600-3,600

A set of 4 glasses, each transfer printed with a portrait of a Beatle and his name, c1964, 4in (10cm) high.
$350-550

A souvenir table lamp, with yellow metal base and paper shade printed with the Beatles portraits and their facsimile signatures, 12in (31cm) high.
$450-800

A presentation Gold disc 'Reel Music', by the Beatles, the album mounted above a 'Gold' cassette, a reduction of the album cover and a plaque bearing the R.I.A.A. Certified Sales Award and inscribed Presented to Gary Benson to commemorate the sale of more than 500,000 copies of the Capitol Records Inc. album and cassette 'Reel Music', framed, 21 by 17in (53 by 43cm).
$1,800-2,700

A single sided acetate, I am The Walrus, by the Beatles, on white Emidisc label, inscribed with artists and song details and dated 2-10-67, with unpublished variations from the final release.
$2,000-2,700

A piece of paper signed by the 4 Beatles and inscribed Love to Barbara from Paul McCartney, framed, 7 by 5in (18 by 13cm).
$900-1,000

A set of 4 plastic dolls with movable heads, each labelled with a printed facsimile signature, and a set of 4 rubber character dolls, each 4in (10cm) high, another plastic Beatle doll dressed in a grey suit, 7in (18cm) high, and a John Lennon puzzle poster in box, 16 by 11½in (41 by 29cm).
$300-450

A presentation Gold disc, Dancing Machine, inscribed Presented to The Jackson Five to commemorate the sale of more than 500,000 copies of the Motown Records album, cassette and C.D. 'Dancing Machine', 21 by 17in (53 by 43cm).
$900-1,500

A Kalamazoo Oriole acoustic guitar, Serial No. 971 F27, in maple with solid spruce top, rosewood fingerboard, simulated tortoiseshell scratchplate and trim, the body signed Jon Bon Jovi in black felt pen, in case, 41in (104cm) long.
$900-1,800

Peter Sander's TV cartoon series, The Performing Beatles, gouache on celluloid, window mounted and framed, 1964, 8½ by 13½in (22 by 35cm).
$1,000-1,200

This image was used on the cover of a Beatles Tour programme, 1965.

A tooled leather guitar strap decorated with artist's name Bill Haley, and a floral pattern, 49in (124cm) long, used by Haley in the late 1970s, accompanied by a printed itinerary for Bill Haley and The Comets British Tour, March-April 1979, featuring a machine print photograph of Haley playing guitar and wearing this strap, signed and inscribed To Jerry – a pleasure working with you pal, Bill Haley.
$2,700-4,500

An illustrated souvenir concert programme, New Victoria Theatre, London, 24th August, 1976, signed on the cover Luck, Fats Domino, accompanied by a piece of paper, signed and inscribed Luck and Love to Jerry from your Boy, Fats Domino.
$550-700

Four Beatles Christmas flexi-discs in original sleeves, 1966, two 1967 and 1968, 2 demonstration singles, Lady Madonna and All You Need is Love, Parlophone Records, green labels with white 'A' motif, 45 r.p.m., 1967 and 1968 respectively, and 4 other Parlophone Records factory sample singles.
$1,000-1,200

An original photomontage artwork for Fashion, 12in and 7in single covers, 1980, signed and inscribed by artist Edward Bell on mount, framed, 10½ by 10½in (26 by 26cm).
$1,500-2,000

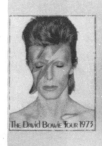

An ivory crepe shirt and a rust coloured cotton cap, the peak decorated with silver painted letters G.C., both garments worn by David Bowie in the 1969 film Love You Till Tuesday, accompanied by a letter of authenticity.
$1,000-2,000

The initials G.C. stand for Ground Control.

A typescript letter, signed by David Bowie, to a fan thanking him for his card, on headed paper, in common mount with 2 machine print photographs, framed, 19 by 32in (48 by 81cm).
$900-1,000

An original photomontage artwork for Scary Monsters album cover, signed by artist Edward Bell, dated 1980 and inscribed in artist's hand giving various instructions including one for Bowie's hair colour Dye red, window mounted and framed, 10½ by 13in (27 by 33cm).
$4,000-4,500

Four pages from an autograph book bearing the signatures of The Sex Pistols, in common mount with 2 publicity photographs of the band, overall measurement 16 by 29in (41 by 74cm).
$2,000-3,300

A mask of black net trimmed with black and gold lace, worn by Prince in the 1984 Warner Bros film Purple Rain accompanied by a copy of a letter from co-star Apollonia Kotero.
$1,000-1,500

A pair of ornate 17thC style gauntlets of black and silver lace also worn by Prince in the film Purple Rain.
$1,500-1,800

A pair of high heeled ankle boots brocaded in a purple and gold Paisley pattern, hand made by Franco Puccetti and worn by Prince in the film Purple Rain.
$6,500-8,000

All the above items accompanied by a letter of authenticity from co-star Apollonia.

A large collection The Sex Pistols and others punk clothing, including approximately 40 punk T-shirts, all decorated with various slogans, logos and band names.
$550-700

A rare handwritten playlist for a Beatles concert 1964, with 10 abbreviated song titles, signed and inscribed on the reverse To Wendy love from John Lenon xx, 4 by 2½in (10 by 6cm).
$3,500-4,500

The song titles included in the playlist suggest that it was written some time between January and April 1964.

A wide brimmed black felt hat allegedly owned by John Lennon and worn by him in the photograph on the cover of A Spaniard In The Works, 1965, accompanied by an affidavit confirming the provenance and John Lennon, A Spaniard In The Works, Jonathan Cape, 1965, illustrations, original boards.
$1,600-2,000

A polished bronze of John Lennon by John Somerville entitled Imagine, number 4 from a limited edition of 20, with certificate signed by sculptor, 1983, 25in (64cm) high including marble base.
$3,200-4,000

The Great Rock N Roll Swindle, 1979, Sid Vicious, 5 gouache on celluloid, window mounted, 9 by 12in (23 by 31cm).
$2,800-3,600

A bronze of Mick Jagger, numbered 2 from an edition limited to 20 by John Somerville, with a certificate of authenticity, signed by the sculptor, 25in (64cm) high, including marble base.
$2,000-4,000

A sheriff's badge inscribed Captain-Deputy Sheriff Shelby County, State of Tennessee, 2½ by 2½in (6 by 6cm), and corresponding identification card No. 499 with a head and shoulders photograph of Vernon Presley on the obverse, accompanied by a certificate of authenticity from The Elvis Presley Museum.
$3,000-4,000

The bicycle allegedly used in the 'Heaven' sequence of The Rocky Horror stage show, 1960s, the frame applied with gilded press-metal leaves, foliate scrolls and flowerheads.
$2,000-3,300

Film & Theatre

Twelve polychrome film posters, the majority featuring Humphrey Bogart and Errol Flynn, various titles include The Left Hand Of God, The Harder They Fall, Too Much Too Soon, African Queen, Sabrina Fair and In A Lonely Place, 2 framed, majority 40 by 30in (101 by 76cm).
$260-360

A black trilby of pure wool, stamped Cacharel in gilt lettering on inside leather band and silk lining, and letter of authenticity from Apollonia, Prince's co-star in the film Purple Rain, stating that she…received this black felt hat from Prince while we were working on the film…
$540-900

A concert bill for Jerry Lee Lewis's cancelled tour, advertising a concert at the Gaumont Theatre, Doncaster, 1958, with a Rank Organisation printed announcement slip fixed to the front withdrawing Lewis's name … The Rank Organisation feel they are carrying out the wishes of the majority in withdrawing this name from the bill…, 15 by 10in (38 by 25cm).
$700-1,000

Jerry Lee Lewis's fortunes plummeted in 1958 when news of his marriage to his 13-year-old second cousin Myra broke whilst he was on a concert tour of England. The condemnation was so great that concerts were cancelled.

A signed and inscribed photograph of Ingrid Bergman, obtained in person at 14 Hill Street, London, where she was staying whilst she starred in 'The Constant Wife', 1970, 10 by 8in (25 by 20cm).
$145-180

A shirt of cream silk woven with purple stripes and trimmed with purple and cream braid, worn by Rudolph Valentino as Ahmed, The Sheik in the early scenes of his last film The Son of the Sheik, United Artists, 1926, and 2 stills of subject wearing the shirt in the film, in common frame, overall measurement 36 by 27in (92 by 69cm).
$8,000-11,000

A portrait still of Marlene Dietrich in the 1941 film Manpower, signed in blue ink, 9½ by 7½in (24 by 19cm).
$450-550

A silver foil, cane and leather theatrical mask shaped as a life size horse's head, 30in (76cm) long, and a corresponding pair of leather and painted metal shoes resembling hooves, the soles shaped as horseshoes, 10in (25cm) high, worn in Peter Schaeffer's Equus, produced by the National Theatre at the Old Vic, July 26th 1973. **$900-1,500**

A collection of assorted tricks, props and novelties, and a letter of authenticity from Mrs Gwen Cooper confirming that these tricks and props were taken by Tommy Cooper for his final performance at Her Majesty's Theatre, April 1984. **$2,000-3,300**

A collection of correspondence from Stan Laurel to Mr and Mrs Wray, fans from Tyneside, and one corresponding envelope. **$800-1,200**

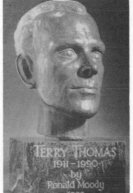

A Ronald Moody bronze portrait head of Terry Thomas, inscribed with gilt lettering, on marble base, 13in (33cm) high. **$350-550**

A theatre programme with Gracie Fields on the bill, c1930. **$15-18**

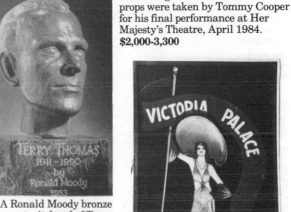

APOLLO THEATRE
SHAFTESBURY AVENUE, W.1

H. M. TENNENT LTD. and L. O. P. LTD.

DUEL OF ANGELS

By JEAN GIRAUDOUX

Translated by CHRISTOPHER FRY

First Performance at this Theatre: Thursday, 24th April, 1958

PROGRAMME SIXPENCE

A theatre programme signed on front cover by Vivien Leigh, Duel of Angels, at the Apollo Theatre, London, 24th April 1958, obtained in person. **$145-180**

A publicity photograph of Vivien Leigh as Scarlet O'Hara in the Twelve Oaks barbeque sequence signed by subject, 4 by 5in (10 by 13cm) window mounted and framed, and an illustrated Atlanta premiere programme for Gone With The Wind, 1939, in common frame, overall measurements 16½ by 24in (42 by 61cm). **$800-1,200**

A Ketubbah/Jewish marriage contract, inscribed with the bride and groom's names Arthur Miller and Marilyn Monroe and further details including the city Lewisboro, Weschester, the secular date July 1, 1956 and Hebrew date 22nd of Tammuz 5716, Rabbi Robert E. Goldburg, window mounted and framed, 20½ by 13½in (52 by 34cm). **$12,000-16,500**

The marriage between Arthur Miller, one of America's greatest intellectuals, and Marilyn Monroe, one of America's most famous film stars, caused an orgy of publicity. Marilyn was instructed in the Jewish faith by Rabbi Robert Goldburg, and a double-ring ceremony took place in Katonah at the home of Kay Brown, Arthur Miller's literary agent. Lee Strasberg gave Marilyn away and also signed the contract as one of the 2 witnesses, the other being Miller's brother Kermit. The Millers flew to England for their honeymoon to work on The Prince and the Showgirl, the couple and their 27 pieces of luggage were met at the airport by Laurence Olivier and Vivien Leigh, and a thirty-car caravan took them to a large rented estate at Egham in the grounds of Windsor Park.

Posters

A Marcella Cigars poster, comedy of old man at bookstall, framed, 2 screw holes to frame, some foxing, 14 by 10in (36 by 25cm).
$160-200

A Hignett's Virginia Honey Crop poster, framed and glazed with 2 screw holes to frame, some creasing and tears to edges, 19½ by 14½in (49 by 37cm). **$145-160**

An Ogden's Special Mixture poster, framed and glazed, with 2 screw holes to frame, some cracking and surface damage, 19 by 14in (48 by 35.5cm).
$110-160

A Pacific Line brochure, 1930s.
$18-25

A felt newspaper advertisement, 1930s.
$30-40

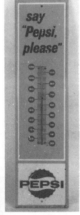

A Pepsi thermometer, American, c1950, 28in (71cm) high.
$90-125

A Hignett's True Bird's Eye poster, showing a yokel smoking a pipe, framed and glazed, with 2 screw holes to frame, 14½ by 11½in (37 by 29cm).
$180-200

A Hignett's Cavalier Brand poster, showing Cavalier with horse, on canvas, framed and glazed with 2 screw holes to frame, cracking and scuffing to canvas, 23 by 16in (59 by 41cm).
$90-145

A Hignett's Honey-Crop Brand poster, showing plantation workers tending tobacco plants, framed and glazed, with 4 screw holes to frame, creases, 11½ by 16½in (29 by 42cm).
$300-360

CRAFTS

An earthenware cider flagon, by Henry Hammond, in dark brown with trailed ochre slip decoration, impressed HH seal, 14½in (37cm).
$450-650

A Bernard Leach vase, covered with a grey and orange peel glaze, incised with a band of stylised flying birds, impressed BL and St. Ives, c1965, 7in (18cm).
$3,500-4,000

A stoneware bottle vase, by William Marshall, covered in an iron brown glaze beneath mottled dark caramel, with incised floral decoration, impressed WM and St. Ives seals, 11½in (29cm).
$540-720

A stoneware bottle vase, by Ewen Henderson, covered in textured mottled green glazes, 12½in (31.5cm).
$900-1,200

A Bernard Leach slab bottle, grey oatmeal and dark brown quartered and decorated with red tree motifs, impressed BL and St. Ives seals, c1955, 8in (20cm).
$7,000-8,000

A Bernard Leach incense box and cover, decorated with a rich brown and 'tenmoku' glaze, the domed cover incised with a quartered design, impressed BL and St. Ives seals, c1950, 4in (10cm).
$1,500-1,800

A stoneware bowl, by Hans Coper, the interior covered in a matt manganese glaze, the underside with a bluish matt glaze burnished to reveal matt manganese beneath, rim restored, impressed seal HC, 11in (28cm) diam.
$5,500-9,000

A stoneware flared bowl, by Lucie Rie, the slate grey body covered in a pitted thick white glaze, the exterior running and pooling, slight restoration by artist, seal, c1980, 12in (30cm).
$1,000-1,500

A deep porcelain bowl, by Mary Rich, covered in a mottled lavender blue and pink glaze with gilt bands of zig-zag and cross-hatched cell motif and purple band with gilt rim, impressed M seal, 10½in (26.5cm) diam.
$720-800

PAPIER MÂCHÉ

A papier mâché bread basket, decorated in colours and gilt against a black ground, the base impressed Clay, King St., Covt. Garden, c1820, 13½in (34cm) wide.
$720-900

Henry Clay, working 1772-1822, achieved wealth and fame after patenting in 1772 his 'new improved paper ware'. In 1792 he claimed the title 'Japanner to His Majesty', he died in 1812, the business continuing until 1822 at the King St. address.

A lacquered papier mâché blotter, heightened with tinted inlaid mother-of-pearl leaves and petals, within a gilt penwork and mother-of-pearl border, c1835, 12 by 9in (30.5 by 23cm).
$180-270

A Victorian papier mâché and parcel gilt lady's chair, the back inlaid with mother-of-pearl and painted with a flowerspray, above a caned seat, on cabriole legs.
$360-540

A pair of early Victorian black lacquered papier mâché pole screens, with adjustable panels, mother-of-pearl inlaid and gilt patterned with differing designs of exotic birds, flowers and scrolls, on triple splay supports.
$2,000-3,000

A Victorian papier mâché tray, inlaid with mother-of-pearl, the border decorated in gilt and with a hatched border, 31in (79cm) wide.
$650-800

JEWELLERY

A Victorian Golden Jubilee ring, 1887.
$180-270

A Victorian Tara brooch, set with malachite, the reverse with applied registration plaque and raised maker's name, West & Son, College Green, Dublin, Reg.
$360-540

A Victorian silver Aesthetic locket pendant, with applied two-colour owl, bird and linear decoration against an engraved background, suspended from a silver shield link collar.
$720-800

A Victorian gold locket, enamelled with the monogram G.L. above date 1864, enclosing a portrait of a gentleman with a lock of hair.
$450-650

A Victorian gold and banded onyx locket back brooch, the solitaire centre with banded onyx and half pearl floral border. **$540-650**

PINE FURNITURE
Beds

A pine cot/cradle, c1850, 34in (86cm) long. **$540-650**

A pine cot, with porcelain handles, 41in (104cm) long.
$250-320

A pine single bed head and foot from an Austrian sleigh bed, 75in (190cm).
$540-720

A pine sleigh bed, c1880.
$210-280

Bookcases

An open bookcase, early 19thC, 46in (116cm) high. **$1,200-1,500**

A glazed bookcase, with broken pediment, 50in (127cm). **$1,600-2,000**

A Victorian grey painted pine bookcase, in the Gothic taste, the upper section with a moulded cornice, the base with Gothic panelled cupboard doors, on a plinth, slightly reduced in length, late 19thC. **$54,000-63,000**

Chairs

A primitive small chair, c1840.
$180-210

A Scottish primitive chair, new rush seat, c1840.
$180-210

An armchair, with new rush seat, c1870.
$360-500

Chests

A painted and decorated pine blanket chest, signed Jacob Seltzer, dated 1797, feet reduced, some restoration to paint, 52in (132cm).
$5,000-6,000

A painted and decorated poplar seaman's chest, New England, restoration to paint, c1850, 39½in (100cm). **$3,500-4,500**

607

A pine box, with candle box, c1840, 41in (104cm). **$300-360**

A painted and decorated pine blanket chest, dated 1850, restoration to paint and top, 48½in (123cm). **$1,500-2,000**

Clocks

A Danish pine eight-day grandfather clock, with original paint, by J. M. Kofoed, 73in (185cm) high. **$1,700-2,000**

A Danish pine eight-day grandfather clock, with later paint, c1860, 73in (186cm) high. **$1,700-2,000**

A Danish eight-day grandfather clock, with painted dial, c1862, 76in (192cm) high. **$1,700-2,000**

Commodes

A mid-Victorian commode, 17in (43cm) square. **$125-180**

A commode, with initials TD on lid and date 1890. **$180-270**

A painted pine bowfronted corner cupboard, with panelled doors, original paint, 19thC, 46in (118cm). **$1,500-1,700**

A glazed cupboard with arched top, 36in (91.5cm). **$450-540**

Cupboards

An English corner cupboard, 80in (203cm) high. **$800-900**

A Scandinavian pine bowfront corner cupboard, with panelled doors enclosing 2 shelves, c1845, 48in (122cm). **$1,400-1,500**

A Swedish pot cupboard, c1910, 24½in (62cm). **$250-320**

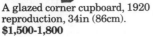

A glazed corner cupboard, 1920 reproduction, 34in (86cm). **$1,500-1,800**

A hanging corner cupboard, 19thC, 28in (71cm). **$650-720**

An Austrian hanging corner cupboard, with 3 coloured glass panels in the single door, 31½in (80cm) high. **$280-320**

A warming cupboard, c1830, 43in (109cm). **$550-650**

Dressers

A dresser base, c1840, 39in (99cm).
$1,000-1,200

A painted arched top dresser, 19thC,
98in (249cm).   **$3,600-4,500**

A Shetland Islands
dresser, with iron
handles, c1880, 51in
(130cm).
$1,000-1,200

A Yorkshire serpentine front
dresser, 54in (137cm).
$2,700-3,600

A George III dresser, with moulded
cornice above plate rack, the lower
section with 3 frieze drawers above
a pair of fielded arched panel
cupboard doors, on square section
feet, 54in (137cm).   **$3,000-6,000**

A Scottish dresser,
51in (129.5cm).
$1,000-1,200

A miniature
dresser, 26in
(66cm).
$450-540

A Bavarian
pine kitchen
dresser,
replacement
handles, 49in
(124.5cm).
$1,000-1,200

Hazel pine is a more
correct name for the
timber that has
previously been
described as satinwood
or satin walnut. Hazel
pine is an accepted
alternative, and more
commercially
attractive name for
American red
gum – Liquidambar
Styraciflua.

Stools

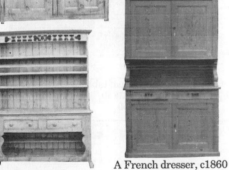

An Irish country
dresser, 54in
(137cm). **$1,200-1,400**

A French dresser, c1860
$800-900

An Austrian dresser, 40in
(101.5cm).   **$1,200-1,400**

A pine stool, (25cm) diam.   **$18-25**

Dressing Tables

A hazel pine dressing chest,
c1890, 42in (106.5cm).
$900-1,000

A hazel pine dressing
chest, c1890, 36in
(92cm).   **$900-1,000**

A pitch pine dressing
chest, c1870, 42in
(106.5cm).   **$800-900**

A stool or small table, c1860, 15in
(38cm) diam.   **$60-80**

Tables

A sycamore and pine cricket table, mid-18thC, 30in (76cm) diam. **$650-720**

A pine drop leaf table, with a drawer under, 59½in (150cm) long. **$540-720**

A pine work bench, c1840, 46in (117cm). **$270-360**

A cricket table, c1840, 26in (66cm) diam. **$360-450**

A French side table, c1890. **$170-210**

A Regency bowfronted side table, 36in (92cm). **$270-360**

A picnic table and 4 folding chairs, c1930. **$540-650**

A cricket table, c1840, 28in (71cm). **$360-450**

A drop leaf table, with drawer under, c1840, 60in (152cm). **$360-450**

Wardrobes

A pine wardrobe/armoire, 19thC, 78in (198cm) high. **$1,000-1,200**

A Dutch carved linen press, 93in (236cm) high. **$2,500-2,700**

An Austrian painted armoire, c1807, 73in (185cm) high. **$10,000-12,000**

A Danish single door wardrobe, 72in (182cm) high. **$600-720**

A Danish wardrobe, 76in (193cm) high. **$1,400-1,500**

A Hungarian wardrobe, c1885. **$800-1,000**

A hazel pine wardrobe, c1890, 54in (137cm). **$800-1,000**

A pine double wardrobe, c1870, 66in (167cm) wide. **$1,100-1,200**

A hazel pine combination wardrobe, with feature panels in East Indian satinwood, dated 1891, 72in (182.5cm). **$2,600-3,600**

Washstands

A single pine washstand, c1860, 24in (61cm) wide. **$400-540**

A hazel pine, marble top, washstand, c1890, 42in (106cm) wide. **$450-540**

A pine cupboard washstand, with marble top, c1910, 42½in (107cm) high. **$250-350**

Miscellaneous

A pine luggage rack, c1880, 25in (64cm) wide. **$145-160**

A pine plant stand, tin lined, c1880, 46in (116cm) wide. **$180-360**

An Austrian grape barrel, 28in (71cm) high. **$180-200**

A primitive plant stand, c1840, 25in (64cm) high. **$110-125**

A counter with panelled back, English, 76in (193cm) wide. **$1,200-1,400**

A pine over mantel, c1860, 44in wide. **$145-180**

Liberty pine shelves, 31in (79cm) high. **$110-120**

KITCHENALIA

A selection of horn beakers, 2½ to 4in (6 to 11cm) high.
$18-35 each

A wooden lemon squeezer, 6in (15cm) long.
$25-35

An apple corer, 6in (15cm) long.
$20-25

A bone apple corer, 4in (10cm) long.
$45-55

A wooden bowl scoop, 8in (20cm) diam.
$25-35

A Scottish oatmeal bowl, 19thC, 7in (18cm) diam.
$55-60

A German painted pine bread board, c1833, 23in (59cm) diam.
$70-90

A German painted pine bread board, dated 1890, 24in (61cm) diam.
$125-145

A 19thC shaving soap bowl, 4in (10cm) diam.
$18-25

A wooden butter pat, 9½in (24cm) long.
$55-60

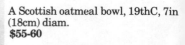

A selection of butter stamps, 19thC.
$45-90 each

Wooden butter moulds, 5½ by 3½in (14 by 9cm).
$65-70

A 19thC butter whisk, 7½in (19cm) long.
$25-35

A coffee grinder, 7½in (19cm) high.
$50-55

A 19thC butter churn, 17in (43cm) high.
$145-155

A thatcher's mallet, 12½in (32cm) long.
$15-18

A butter stamp and bowl with acorn pattern, bowl 4½in (11cm) diam.
$135-145

A wooden paper knife, 6in (15cm) large.
$15-25

A 19thC wooden grain measure, 7½in (19cm) diam.
$60-70

A Victorian pastry brush, 8in (20cm) long.
$25-30

An oak, metal banded measure, 7in (18cm) high.
$100-110

A Victorian beech ½ pint measure, lathe turned, 4in (10cm) high.
$100-110

A selection of brass pastry tools, 4½ to 6½in (11 to 16cm) long.
$40-55 each

A lemon squeezer, 9½in (24cm) long.
$60-70

A pastry press, 5in (13cm) long.
$55-60

A set of Mintons Art Deco storage jars, early 20thC.
$125-180

A French wooden spoon, 8in (20cm) long.   **$25-35**

A Devonshire tedding chopper, 12in (31cm) long.   **$15-25**

A pine spoon rack, 13in (33cm) high, with spoons.   **$90-100**

A wooden spoon rest, 5½in (14cm) long.
$9-18

A carved wooden spoon, 10in (25cm) long.   **$30-35**

A cheese press with lid and liner, 19thC, 8in (20cm) diam.
$80-90

A chrome sieve, 6in (15cm) high.
$30-35

A wool comb, 6in (15cm) wide.
$45-55

A cheese thermometer and holder, 10in (25cm) long.   **$45-55**

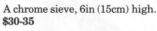

Crocodile nut crackers, 8in (20cm) long. **$35-45**

A spice tin, 7in (18cm) diam, with brass handle. **$80-90**

A French wire egg basket, 19thC. **$55-60**

Treen

Three darners, 5 to 6½in (13 to 17cm). **$9-12 each**

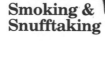

A pair of travelling olivewood candlesticks, each with a shallow cylindrical socket, on a detachable dished circular base, the 2 bases screwing together to form a cushioned circular box, together with a conical extinguisher, 4in (10cm) diam. **$270-360**

A brass and copper Aladdin's lamp, 18in (46cm) high. **$55-60**

A washboard with glass panel, early 20thC, 28in (71cm) high. **$35-45**

A wooden lemon squeezer, the semi-ovoid shaped body with finial shaped nozzle to the base and screw-off cover fitted with threaded plunger and T shaped handle, 19thC, 7in (18cm) high. **$350-450**

Tools

Smoking & Snufftaking

A leather marker, 6½in (17cm). **$15-18**

A meerschaum pipe, the bowl modelled as an open flowerhead, and carved with a running deer, amber stemmed, the bowl 3in (8cm) high, in a case. **$260-360**

Two rug making tools, 6½in (16cm). **$10-15** 11½in (29cm). **$30-40**

A Victorian Scandinavian pipe, 12in (31cm) long. **$60-90**

A massive meerschaum pipe bowl, carved with figures and hounds hunting bears, 7½in (19cm) long. **$380-480**

A pig scraper, 9in (23cm). **$70-75**

WALKING STICKS & CANES

A horn and bone banded walking cane, carved with a terminal in the form of a hoof, the whole stick made up of long sections of horn alternating with 2 short sections of bone, brass tip, c1840, 34½in (88cm).
$450-650

A sword stick in bamboo scabbard, the horn handle carved with a gun dog, game bird, oak leaves and an acorn, 19thC.
$350-450

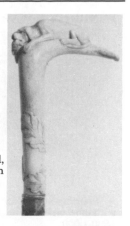

A pair of walking canes, the carved nut grips modelled with grimacing and smiling infants, 19thC.
$350-450

A gentleman's malacca cane, the ivory grip with piqué inlay, with initials and date, I.I. 90.
$1,800-2,500

A bamboo walking stick, the handle carved with the head of a gun dog, with overlaid silvered metal and inset glass eyes.
$700-900

A bamboo walking cane, the carved nut grip modelled in the form of a bulldog's head, the white metal collar stamped BRIGG, 19thC.
$450-650

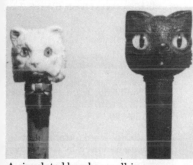

A malacca cane, with gilt metal collar, the ivory knop carved with the head of a child emerging from the beak of a chick, and a bamboo walking cane, the carved ivory grip modelled with an Arab's head.
$350-450

A German malacca cane, the silver and gilt hinged pommel inset with an automaton of an insect with cut and coloured glass wings and body, 19thC.
$2,300-3,300

A simulated bamboo walking cane, the ivory grip carved in the form of a cat's head, with inset glass eyes and yellow metal collar, and another with the wooden handle carved in the form of a cat's head.
$1,600-1,800

A Continental rose quartz, seed pearl, enamel and silver coloured metal parasol handle, decorated with engine turned bands and encircled by a husk garland, rose quartz terminal, part of original wooden shaft, in original Dreyfou tooled leather case, terminal 3in (7cm).
$350-450

A simulated rosewood cane, the plated silver top formed as a vesta, incorporating a sovereign case and with 2 pencils, a malacca cane, the silver top with glass scent phial, and an ebonised cane with silver metal match case handle.
$550-700

TUNBRIDGE WARE

A Tunbridge ware box by R. Russell, with label on base, 7in (18cm) wide.
$900-1,000

A Tunbridge ware money box, 4in (10cm).
$210-270

A Tunbridge ware dressing box with floral band to sides of pin cushion, jewellery tray under scent bottles on either side, on 4 stickware feet, 9in (23cm) wide.
$720-750

A Tunbridge ware postal card box, 5½in (14cm) wide.
$300-340

A triangular Tunbridge ware cribbage board, with a central motif of rose, shamrock and thistle, 7½in (19cm).
$400-450

A Tunbridge ware desk box, with fitted interior and geometric pattern on lid, 7in (18cm) wide.
$450-550

A Tunbridge ware pin cushion, in the form of a stickware kettle, 2in (5cm) diam.
$270-320

A Tunbridge ware sewing clamp, 2in (5cm) wide.
$320-360

A Tunbridge ware watch stand, with decorated base, 6½in (17cm) high.
$400-450

A Tunbridge ware glove darner, 5½in (14cm) long.
$150-180

A Tunbridge ware pins and needles box, 3 by 2in (8 by 5cm).
$125-145

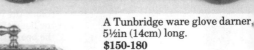

A Tunbridge ware letter rack with stickware handle, 8 by 5in (20 by 13cm).
$580-650

Stickware is when wood is fashioned long ways, not cut in cube design.

A Tunbridge ware inkwell with lid, 5in (13cm) diam.
$650-700

A Tunbridge ware tray with cube pattern, 4 by 3in (10 by 8cm).
$170-180

A Tunbridge ware standish desk set, with Vandyke pattern, c1840, 13in (33cm) wide.
$1,000-1,200

A Tunbridge ware sewing box, original interior fitted with various compartments and 2 inlaid lids, top with view of Penshurst Place, 8in (20cm) wide.
$1,100-1,200

A Tunbridge ware needle booklet, 2½ by 2in (6 by 5cm).
$130-145

A Tunbridge ware puzzle, 2in (5cm) square.
$170-210

A Tunbridge ware paper knife, 9½in (24cm) long.
$70-90

A Tunbridge ware lady's toilet box, decorated with an intricate floral motif mainly in bird's-eye maple, with key and 3 perfume/toilet water bottles, 6in (15cm) wide.
$1,100-1,200

Bilbouquet, a very expensive toy, 8in (20cm) long.
$900-1,000

A Tunbridge ware napkin ring, 2in (5cm) diam.
$55-70

Three Tunbridge ware items, a scent bottle, taperstick and box with glass lining, 1 to 1½in (3 to 4cm) high.
$170-270 each

Tunbridge ware book ends showing Herstmonceux and Hever castles, base in rosewood, 13in (33cm) long.
$800-900

A Tunbridge ware folding lectern, with original pegs, 16½in (42cm) high.
$900-1,000

A Tunbridge ware brooch, 3in (8cm) long.
$70-90

A Tunbridge ware clothes brush, 6in (15cm) long.
$35-55

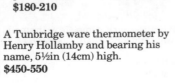

A Tunbridge ware sewing item with pin wheel to base, tape measure and pin cushion.
$180-210

A Tunbridge ware seam weight, 2in (5cm).
$250-280

A Tunbridge ware thermometer by Henry Hollamby and bearing his name, 5½in (14cm) high.
$450-550

ARMS & ARMOUR
Armour

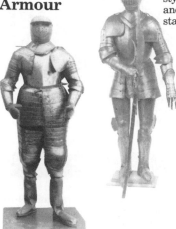

A complete suit of armour, in 16thC style, all etched with floral sprays and trophies of arms, mounted on stand. **$2,000-3,000**

A reproduction suit of 16thC armour. **$2,600-3,600**

A Continental breast and back plate, etched overall with religious scenes, c1680. **$1,800-2,700**

A suit of armour, the visor with rising peak above fretted eye pieces and fretted front, the breast plate with period indented test mark, articulated thigh and knee cover, on a stand covered in blue velvet and with later leather boots, on a dwarf panelled oak pedestal, early 17thC, 70in (177cm) high. **$10,000-11,000**

Helmets

l. A north Italian 'Spanish' morion, with skull rising to a stalk, slightly cracked, late 16thC, 11½in (29cm) high.
$10,000-11,000
r. A pikeman's pot, of russet iron, pierced and shaped iron plume-pipe, and retaining some original gilding throughout, c1630, probably Flemish, 12in (31cm) high.
$10,000-12,000

A Saxon electoral guard comb morion, with roped comb and brim, the base of the skull encircled by 16 gilt brass lion masks capping the lining rivets, laminated ear pieces, one replaced, the brim struck with the Nuremberg mark, c1580, 12in (31cm) high. **$22,800-27,000**

A Milanese Spanish morion, the base of the skull and brim with strapwork and guilloche borders, and remains of original red silk lining, late 16thC, 9in (23cm) high.
$14,500-18,000

A composite German, 'Maximilian' close helmet, shaped at the bottom to form a neck plate, the lower edges recessed, painted black throughout, minor repairs, the skull early 16thC, 12in (31cm) high.
$7,000-9,000

Daggers

An Arab silver mounted jambiya dagger.
$650-800

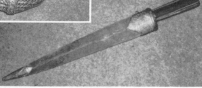

An Indian pesh-kabz dagger, with stone hilt, 19thC. **$900-1,200**

A British midshipman's dirk, c1800.
$260-360

A Scottish dirk, complete with small knife and fork, c1870. **$550-800**

Three Russian nielloed kinjals, 19thC. **$700-1,200 each**

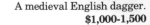

A medieval English dagger.
$1,000-1,500

Knives

An American hunting knife, c1800.
$650-800

An American bowie knife, with engraved blade and American eagle in centre panel of hilt.
$3,500-5,500

Swords

A Spanish Bilbao rapier, c1720.
$550-650

A basket hilt sword, Scandinavian or North German, c1650.
$1,200-1,500

A French officer's sword, by Le Page, c1810.
$7,000-9,000

A two-handled processional sword in 16thC style, etched and gilt throughout with bands and panels of scrollwork against a gilt ground, and bottle shaped leather covered wooden grip, with coloured fringe at the top, some worming to wooden grip, 46in (116cm) blade.
$5,500-7,000

Swords – Eastern

A bronze sword from Luristan.
$650-800

A sword from Tibet, with gilt brass sheath, 19thC.
$350-550

Blunderbuss

A brass barrelled flintlock blunderbuss, by Coner, Dublin, 18thC.
$2,000-3,000

Pistols

A pair of English percussion pocket pistols, c1840.
$450-650

A pair of flintlock duelling pistols, by H. Nock, cased, c1780.
$7,000-9,000

A pair of silver mounted flintlock pistols, c1770.
$4,500-6,500

A French military percussion pistol.
$270-450

An English all brass tap flintlock action pistol, c1790.   **$540-720**

A silver mounted Turkish flintlock pistol, c1800.   **$650-800**

A flintlock box-lock pocket pistol, 19thC, 5in (13cm).
$1,200-1,400

Uniforms & Bits

A Danish military shako.
$200-280

A pair of double barrelled flintlock box-lock pistols, with brass turn-off cannon barrels numbered from 1 to 4, brass actions engraved with rococo ornament, signed within a ribbon on the right side and with sliding cut-off on the left, engraved steel trigger-guard safety catches, rounded walnut butts finely inlaid with silver wire scrolls and flowers, some restoration, vacant silver escutcheons, and silver grotesque mask caps, by Joseph Bunney, London, Birmingham silver hallmarks, maker's mark of Charles Freeth, c1780, 8in (20cm).
$3,500-4,500

A 'Greener' Light Model martini action harpoon gun, by W. W. Greener, No. 79, nickel-plated finish, worn in places, manual lever-safe, cocking-indicator, stock with butt-plate, the forestock with brass mounting for a line-release frame, 20in (51cm) barrel, nitro proof, for 10oz harpoon, in its wooden case with instruction label, 5 stainless-steel barbed-harpoons, approx. 11oz, 2 line-release frames, a spare line and miscellaneous cleaning accessories.
$1,500-1,800

The harpoon fits over the barrel and the gun must not be used with any other projectile.

A selection of 19thC tipstaffs.
$180-650

Sporting

A .450 express martini-action sporting rifle by G. E. Lewis, No. 8632/42380, with some original blued finish, well-figured stock with iron butt-plate, horn-capped fore-end, sling-eyes, the barrel with matt top-flat and open-sights, 29in (74cm) barrel, black powder proof.
$1,200-1,500

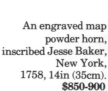

A cow's horn powder flask, all over decorated with scrimshaw work with hinged brass cover, 19thC, 9in (22cm) long.
$350-550

Miscellaneous

A German sporting crossbow, with robust steel bow struck with a mark and retained by its original cords, original string of twisted cord, together with a cranequin, probably original, curved crank handle with swelling wooden grip, and later belt hook, some wear, early 17thC, 26 and 13in (66 and 33cm).
$10,000-14,500

A hand painted leather ceremonial parade fire bucket, Asa C Dix, Enterprise Fire Club, dated 1810, rope handle broken, 13in (33cm) high.
$3,000-4,000

A pair of bronze cannon, each with tapering barrel with prominent muzzle ring, a blank shield with ermine lined mantling, date 1668, on 19thC wheeled pierced bronze carriages, probably French, 24½in
$10,500-12,000

An engraved map powder horn, inscribed Jesse Baker, New York, 1758, 14in (35cm).
$850-900

DIRECTORY OF INTERNATIONAL AUCTIONEERS

This directory is by no means complete. Any auctioneer who holds frequent sales should contact us for inclusion in the 1992 Edition. Entries must be received by April 1991. There is, of course, no charge for this listing. Entries will be repeated in subsequent editions unless we are requested otherwise.

America

Acorn Farm Antiques,
15466 Oak Road, Carmel,
IN 46032
Tel: (317) 846-2383

ALA Moanastampt Cain (David H Martin),
1236 Ala Moana Boulevard,
Honolulu, HI 96814

Alabama Auction Room Inc,
2112 Fifth Avenue North,
Birmingham, AL 35203
Tel: (205) 252-4073

B Altman & Co,
34th & Fifth Avenue, New York,
NY 10016
Tel: (212) OR 9 7800 ext 550 & 322

Ames Art Galleries,
8729 Wilshire Boulevard, Beverly
Hills, CA 9021
Tel: (213) 655-5611/652-3820

Arnette's Auction Galleries Inc,
310 West Castle Street,
Murfreesboro, TN 37130
Tel: (615) 893-3725

Associated Appraisers Inc,
915 Industrial Bank Building,
Providence, RI 02906
Tel: (401) 331-9391

Atlanta's ABCD Auction Gallery
(Clark, Bate and Depew),
1 North Clarendon Avenue,
Antioch, IL 30002
Tel: (312) 294-8264

Bakers Auction,
14100 Paramount Boulevard,
Paramount, CA 00723
Tel: (213) 531-1524

Barridoff Galleries,
242 Middle Street, Portland,
ME 04 101
Tel: (207) 772-5011

C T Bevensee Auction Service,
PO Box 141/A, Botsford, CT 06404
Tel: (203) 426-6698

Frank H. Boos Gallery, Inc.,
420 Enterprise Ct., Bloomfield
Hills, MI 48013

Richard A Bourne Co Inc,
Corporation Street, PO Box 141/A,
Hyannis Port, MA 02647
Tel: (617) 775-0797

Bridges Antiques and Auctions,
Highway 46, PO Box 52A,
Sanford, FL 32771
Tel: (305) 323-2801/322-0095

George C Brilant & Co,
191 King Street, Charleston,
SC 29401

R W Bronstein Corp,
3666 Main Street, Buffalo,
NY 14226
Tel: (716) 835-7666/7408

Brookline Auction Gallery,
Proctor Hill Road, Route 130,
Brookline, NII 03033
Tel: (603) 673-4474/4153

Brzostek's Auction Service,
2052 Lamson Road, Phoenix,
NY 13135
Tel: (315) 678-2542

Buckingham Galleries Ltd,
4350 Dawson Street, San Diego,
CA 92115
Tel: (714) 283-7286

Bushell's Auction,
2006 2nd Avenue, Seattle,
WA 98121
Tel: (206) 622-5833

L Butterfield,
605 W Midland, Bay City,
MI 48706
Tel: (517) 684-3229

Butterfield,
808 N La, Cienega Boulevard, Los
Angeles, CA 90069

Butterfield & Butterfield,
1244 Sutter Street, San Francisco,
CA 94109
Tel: (415) 673-1362

California Book Auction Galleries,
358 Golden Gate Avenue, San
Francisco, CA 94102
Tel: (415) 775-0424

C B Charles Galleries Inc,
825 Woodward Avenue, Pontiac,
MI 48053
Tel: (313) 338-9023

Chatsworth Auction Rooms,
151 Mamaroneck Avenue,
Mamaroneck, NY 10543

Christie, Manson & Wood
International Inc,
502 Park Avenue, New York
Tel: (212) 826-2388 Telex: 620721

Christie's East,
219 East 67th Street, New York,
NY 10021
Tel: (212) 570-4141

Representative Offices:
California:
9350 Wilshire Boulevard, Beverly
Hills, CA 902 12
Tel: (213) 275-5534

Florida:
225 Fern Street, West Palm Beach,
FL 33401
Tel: (305) 833-6592

Mid-Atlantic:
638 Morris Avenue, Bryn Mawr,
PA 19010
Tel: (215) 525-5493

Washington:
1422 27th Street NW, Washington,
DC 20007
Tel: (202) 965-2066

Midwest:
46 East Elm Street, Chicago,
IL 60611
Tel: (312) 787-2765

Fred Clark Auctioneer Inc,
PO Box 124, Route 14, Scotland,
CT 06264
Tel: (203) 423-3939/0594

Cockrum Auctions,
2701 North Highway 94,
St Charles, MO 63301
Tel: (314) 723-9511

George Cole, Auctioneers and
Appraisers,
14 Green Street, Kingston,
NY 12401
Tel: (914) 338-2367

Coleman Auction Galleries,
525 East 72nd Street, New York,
NY 10021
Tel: (212) 879-1415

Conestoga Auction Company Inc,
PO Box 1, Manheim, PA 17545
Tel: (717) 898-7284

Cook's Auction Gallery,
Route 58, Halifax, MA 02338
Tel: (617) 293-3445/866-3243

Coquina Auction Barn
40 S Atlantic Avenue, Ormond
Beach, FL 32074

Danny's Antique Auction Service
(Pat Lusardi),
Route 46, Belvidere, NH 07823
Tel: (201) 757-7278

Douglas Galleries,
Route 5, South Deerfield,
MA 01373
Tel: (413) 665-2877

William Doyle,
175 East 87th Street, New York,
NY 10128
Tel: (212) 427-2730

DuMochelle Art Galleries,
409 East Jefferson, Detroit,
MI 48226
Tel: (313) 963-6255

John C Edelmann Galleries Inc,
123 East 77th Street, New York,
NY 10021
Tel: (212) 628-1700/1735

Robert C Eldred Co Inc,
Box 796, East Dennis, MA 02641
Tel: (617) 385-3116/3377

The Fine Arts Company of
Philadelphia Inc,
2317 Chestnut Street,
Philadelphia, PA 19103
Tel: (215) 564-3644

Fordem Galleries Inc,
3829 Lorain Avenue, Cleveland,
OH 44113
Tel: (216) 281-3563

George S Foster III,
Route 28, Epsom, NH 03234
Tel: (603) 736 9240

Jack Francis Auctions,
200 Market Street, Suite 107,
Lowell, MA 01852
Tel: (508) 441-9708

S T Freeman & Co,
1808 Chestnut Street,
Philadelphia, PA 19103
Tel: (215) 563-9275

Col K R French and Co Inc,
166 Bedford Road, Armonk,
NY 10504
Tel: (914) 273-3674

Garth's Auctions Inc,
2690 Stratford Road, Delaware,
OH 43015
Tel: (614) 362-4771/369-5085

Gilbert Auctions,
River Road, Garrison, NY 10524
Tel: (914) 424-3657

Morten M Goldberg,
215 N Rampart Street, New
Orleans, LA 70112
Tel: (504) 522-8364

Gramercy Auction Galleries,
52 East 13th Street, New York,
NY 10003
Tel: (212) 477-5656

Grandma's House,
4712 Dudley, Wheatridge,
CO 80033
Tel: (303) 423-3640/534-2847

The William Haber Art Collection
Inc,
139-11 Queens Boulevard,
Jamaica, NY 11435
Tel: (212) 739-1000

Charlton Hall Galleries Inc,
930 Gervais Street, Columbia,
SC 29201
Tel: (803) 252-7927/779-5678

Hampton Auction Gallery,
201 Harwick Street, Belvidere,
NH 07823
Tel: (201) 475-2928

Hanzel,
1120 S Michigan Avenue, Chicago,
IL 60605
Tel: (312) 922-6234

Harbor Auction Gallery,
238 Bank Street, New London,
CT 06355
Tel: (203) 443-0868

Harmer's of San Francisco Inc,
49 Geary Street, San Francisco,
CA 94102
Tel: (415) 391-8244

Harris Auction Galleries,
873-875 North Howard Street,
Baltimore, MD 21201
Tel: (301) 728-7040

Hart,
2311 Westheimer, Houston,
TX 77098
Tel: (713) 524-2979/523-7389

Hauswedell & Nolte,
225 West Central Park, New York,
NY 10024
Tel: (212) 787-7245

G Ray Hawkins,
7224 Melrose Avenue, Los
Angeles, CA 90046
Tel: (213) 550-1504

Elwood Heller & Son Auctioneer,
151 Main Street, Lebanon,
NJ 08833
Tel: (201) 23 62 195

William F Hill Auction Sales,
Route 16, East Hardwick,
VT 05834
Tel: (802) 472-6308

Leslie Hindman,
215 West Ohio Street, Chicago,
IL 60610
Tel: (312) 670-0010

The House Clinic,
PO Box 13013A, Orlando, Fl 32859
Tel: (305) 859-1770/851-2979

Co Raymond W Huber,
211 North Monroe, Montpelier,
OH 43543

F B Hubley Et Co,
364 Broadway, Cambridge,
MA 02100
Tel: (617) 876-2030

Iroquois Auctions,
Box 66, Broad Street, Port Henry,
NY 12974
Tel: (518) 942-3355

It's About Time,
375 Park Avenue, Glencoe,
IL 60022
Tel: (312) 835-2012

Louis Joseph Auction Gallery
(Richard L Ryan),
575 Washington Street, Brookline,
MA 02146
Tel: (617) 277-0740

Joy Luke,
The Gallery, 300 East Grove
Street, Bloomington, IL 61701

Julia's Auction Service,
Route 201, Skowhegan Road,
Fairfield, ME 04937
Tel: (207) 453-9725

Sibylle Kaldewey,
225 West Central Park, New York,
NY 10024
Tel: (212) 787-7245

Kelley's Auction Service,
PO Box 125, Woburn, MA 01801
Tel: (617) 272-9167

Kennedy Antique Auction
Galleries Inc,
1088 Huff Road, Atlanta,
GA 30318
Tel: (404) 351-4464

Kinzie Galleries Auction Service,
1002 3rd Avenue, Duncansville,
PA 16835
Tel: (814) 695-3479

La Salle,
2083 Union Street, San Francisco,
CA 94123
Tel: (415) 931-9200

L A Landry (Robert Landry),
94 Main Street, Essex, MA 01929
Tel: (603) 744-5811

Jo Anna Larson,
POB 0, Antioch, IL 60002
Tel: (312) 395-0963

Levins Auction Exchange,
414 Camp Street, New Orleans,
LA 70130

Lipton,
1108 Fort Street, Honolulu,
HI 96813
Tel: (808) 533-4320

F S Long & Sons,
3126 East 3rd Street, Dayton,
OH 45403

R L Loveless Associates Inc,
4223 Clover Street, Honeoye Falls,
NY 14472
Tel: (716) 624-1648/1556

Lubin Galleries,
30 West 26th Street, New York,
NY 10010
Tel: (212) 924-3777

Main Auction Galleries,
137 West 4th Street, Cincinnati,
OH 45202
Tel: (513) 621-1280

Maison Auction Co Inc,
128 East Street, Wallingford,
CT 06492
Tel: (203) 269-8007

Joel L Malter & Co Inc,
Suite 518, 16661 Ventura
Boulevard, Encino, CA 91316
Tel: (213) 784-7772/2181

Manhattan Galleries,
1415 Third Avenue, New York,
NY 10028
Tel: (212) 744-2844

Mapes,
1600 West Vestal Parkway,
Vestal, NY 13850
Tel: (607) 754-9193

David W Mapes Inc,
82 Front Street, Binghamton,
NY 13905
Tel: (607) 724-6741/862-9365

Marvin H Newman,
426 South Robertson Boulevard,
Los Angeles, CA 90048
Tel: (213) 273-4840/378-2095

Mechanical Music Center Inc,
25 Kings Highway North, Darien,
CT 06820
Tel: (203) 655-9510

Milwaukee Auction Galleries,
4747 West Bradley Road,
Milwaukee, WI 53223
Tel; (414) 355-5054

Wayne Mock Inc,
Box 37, Tamworth, NH 03886
Tel: (603) 323-8057

William F Moon & Co,
12 Lewis Road, RFD 1, North
Attleboro, MA 02760
Tel: (617) 761-8003

New England Rare Coin Auctions,
89 Devonshire Street, Boston,
MA 02109
Tel: (617) 227-8800

Kurt Niven,
1444 Oak Lawn, Suite 525, Dallas,
TX 75207
Tel: (214) 741-4252

Northgate Gallery,
5520 Highway 153, Chattanooga,
TN 37443
Tel: (615) 842-4177

O'Gallerie Inc,
537 SE Ash Street, Portland,
OR 97214
Tel: (503) 238-0202

Th J Owen & Sons,
1111 East Street NW, Washington,
DC 20004

Palmer Auction Service,
Lucas, KS 67648

Park City Auction Service,
925 Wood Street, Bridgeport,
CT 06604
Tel: (203) 333-5251

Pennypacker Auction Centre,
1540 New Holland Road,
Kenhorst, Reading, PA 19607
Tel: (215) 777-5890/6121

Peyton Place Antiques,
819 Lovett Boulevard, Houston,
TX 77006
Tel: (713) 523-4841

Phillips,
867 Madison Avenue, New York,
NY 10021
Tel: (212) 570-4830

525 East 72nd Street, New York,
NY10021
Tel: (212) 570-4852

Representative Office:
6 Faneuil Hall, Marketplace,
Boston, MA 02109
Tel: (617) 227-6145

Pollack,
2780 NE 183 Street, Miami,
FL 33160
Tel: (305) 931-4476

Quickie Auction House,
Route 3, Osseo, MN 55369
Tel: (612) 428-4378

R & S Estate Liquidations,
Box 205, Newton Center,
MA 02159
Tel: (617) 244-6616

C Gilbert Richards,
Garrison, NY 10524
Tel: (914) 424-3657

Bill Rinaldi Auctions,
Bedell Road, Poughkeepsie,
NY 12601
Tel: (914) 454-9613

Roan Inc,
Box 118, RD 3, Logan Station,
PA 17728
Tel: (717) 494-0170

Rockland Auction Services Inc,
72 Pomona Road, Suffern,
NY 10901
Tel: (914) 354-3914/2723

Rome Auction Gallery (Sandra A
Louis Caropreso),
Route 2, Highway 53, Rome,
GA 30161

Rose Galleries Inc,
1123 West County Road B,
Roseville, MN 55113
Tel: (612) 484-1415

Rosvall Auction Company,
1238 & 1248 South Broadway,
Denver, CO 80210
Tel: (303) 777-2032/722-4028

Sigmund Rothschild,
27 West 67th Street, New York,
NY 10023
Tel: (212) 873-5522

Vince Runowich Auctions,
2312 4th Street North, St
Petersburg, FL 33704
Tel: (813) 895-3548

Safran's Antique Galleries Ltd,
930 Gervais Street, Columbia,
SC 29201
Tel: (803) 252-7927

Sage Auction Gallery,
Route 9A, Chester, CT 06412
Tel: (203) 526-3036

San Antonio Auction Gallery,
5096 Bianco, San Antonio,
TX 78216
Tel: (512) 342-3800

Emory Sanders,
New London, NH 03257
Tel: (603) 526-6326

Sandwich Auction House,
15 Tupper Road, Sandwich,
MA 02563
Tel: (617) 888-1926/5675

San Francisco Auction Gallery,
1217 Sutter Street, San Francisco,
CA 94109
Tel: (415) 441-3800

Schafer Auction Gallery,
82 Bradley Road, Madison,
CT 06443
Tel: (203) 245-4173

Schmidt's Antiques,
5138 West Michigan Avenue,
Ypsilanti, MI 48 197
Tel: (313) 434-2660

K C Self,
53 Victory Lane, Los Angeles,
CA 95030
Tel: (213) 354-4238

B J Selkirk & Sons,
4166 Olive Street, St Louis,
MO 63108
Tel: (314) 533-1700

Shore Galleries Inc,
3318 West Devon, Lincolnwood,
IL 60659
Tel: (312) 676-2900

Shute's Auction Gallery,
70 Accord Park Drive, Norwell,
MA 02061
Tel: (617) 871-3414/238-0586

Ronald Siefert,
RFD, Buskirk, NY 12028
Tel: (518) 686-9375

Robert A Siegel Auction Galleries
Inc,
120 East 56th Street, New York,
NY 10022
Tel: (212) 753-6421/2/3

Robert W Skinner Inc,
Main Street, Bolton, MA 01740
Tel: (617) 779-5528

585 Boylston Street,
Boston, MA 02116
Tel: (617) 236-1700

C G Sloan & Co,
715 13th Street NW, Washington,
DC 20005
Tel: (202) 628-1468

Branch Office:
403 North Charles Street,
Baltimore, MD 21201
Tel: (301) 547-1177

Sotheby,
101 Newbury Street, Boston,
MA 02116
Tel: (617) 247-2851

Sotheby Park Bernet Inc,
980 Madison Avenue, New York,
NY 10021
Tel: (212) 472-3400

1334 York Avenue, New York,
NY 10021

171 East 84th Street, New York,
NY 10028

Mid-Atlantic:
1630 Locust Street, Philadelphia,
PA 19103
Tel: (215) 735-7886

Washington:
2903 M Street NW, Washington,
DC 20007
Tel: (202) 298-8400

Southeast:
155 Worth Avenue, Palm Beach,
FL 33480
Tel: (305) 658-3555

Classic Auction Gallery
(formerly Sterling Auctions),
62 No. 2nd Avenue, Raritan,
NJ 08869
Tel: (201) 526-6024

Midwest:
700 North Michigan Avenue,
Chicago, IL 60611
Tel: (312) 280-0185

Southwest:
Galleria Post Oak,
5015 Westheimer Road, Houston,
TX 77056
Tel: (713) 623-0010

Northwest:
210 Post Street, San Francisco,
CA 94108
Tel: (415) 986-4982

Pacific Area:
Suite 117, 850 West Hind Drive,
Honolulu, Hawaii 96821
Tel: (808) 373-9166

Stack's Rare Coin Auctions,
123 West 57th Street, New York,
NY 10019
Tel: (212) 583-2580

Stremmel Auctions Inc,
2152 Prater Way, Sparks,
NV 89431
Tel: (702) 331-1035

Summit Auction Rooms,
47-49 Summit Avenue, Summit,
NJ 07901

Superior Stamp & Coin Co Inc,
9301 Wiltshire Boulevard,
Beverly Hills, CA 90210
Tel: (213) 272-0851/278-9740

Swann Galleries Inc,
104 East 26th Street, New York,
NY 10021
Tel: (212) 254-4710

Philip Swedler & Son,
850 Grand Avenue, New Haven,
CT 06511
Tel: (203) 624-2202/562-5065

Tait Auction Studio,
1209 Howard Avenue,
Burlingame, CA 94010
Tel: (415) 343-4793

Tepper Galleries,
110 East 25th Street, New York,
NY 10010
Tel: (212) 677-5300/1/2

Louis Trailman Auction Co,
1519 Spruce Street, Philadelphia,
PA 19102
Tel: (215) K1 5 4500

Trend Galleries Inc,
2784 Merrick Road, Bellmore,
NY 11710
Tel: (516) 221-5588

Trosby Auction Galleries,
81 Peachtree Park Drive, Atlanta,
GA 30326
Tel: (404) 351-4400

Valle-McLeod Gallery,
3303 Kirby Drive, Houston,
TX 77098
Tel: (713) 523-8309/8310

The Watnot Auction,
Box 78, Mellenville, NY 12544
Tel: (518) 672-7576

Adam A Wechsler & Son,
905-9 East Street NW,
Washington, DC 20004
Tel: (202) 628-1281

White Plains Auction Rooms,
572 North Broadway, White
Plains, NY 10603
Tel: (914) 428-2255

Henry Willis,
22 Main Street, Marshfield,
MA 02050
Tel: (617) 834 7774

The Wilson Galleries,
PO Box 102, Ford Defiance,
VA 24437
Tel: (703) 885-4292

Helen Winter Associates,
355 Farmington Avenue,
Plainville, CT 06062
Tel: (203) 747-0714/677-0848

Richard Withington Inc,
Hillsboro, NH 03244
Tel: (603) 464-3232

Wolf,
13015 Larchmere Boulevard,
Shaker Heights, OH 44120
Tel: (216) 231-3888

Richard Wolffers Inc,
127 Kearney Street, San
Francisco, CA 94 108
Tel: (415) 781-5127

Young,
56 Market Street, Portsmouth,
NH 03801
Tel: (603) 436-8773

Samuel Yudkin & Associates,
1125 King Street, Alexandria,
VA 22314
Tel: (703) 549-9330

Australia

ASA Stamps Co Pty Ltd,
138-140 Rundle Mall, National
Bank Building, Adelaide, South
Australia 5001
Tel: 223-2951

Associated Auctioneers Pty Ltd,
800-810 Parramatta Road,
Lewisham, New South Wales 2049
Tel: 560-5899

G J Brain Auctioneers Pty Ltd,
122 Harrington Street, Sydney,
New South Wales 2000
Tel: 271701

Bright Slater Pty Ltd,
Box 205 GPO, Lower Ground
Floor, Brisbane Club Building,
Isles Lane, Brisbane, Queensland
4000
Tel: 312415

Christie, Manson & Woods
(Australia) Ltd,
298 New South Head Road, Double
Bay, Sydney, New South Wales
2028
Tel: 326-1422

William S Ellenden Pty Ltd,
67-73 Wentworth Avenue,
Sydney, New South Wales 2000
Tel: 211-4035/211-4477

Bruce Granger Auctions,
10 Hopetoun Street, Huristone
Park, New South Wales 2193
Tel: 559-4767

Johnson Bros Auctioneers & Real
Estate Agents,
328 Main Road, Glenorchy,
Tasmania 7011
Tel: 725166 492909

James A Johnson & Co,
92 Boronia Road, Vermont,
Victoria 3133
Tel: 877-2754/874-3632

Jolly Barry Pty Ltd,
212 Glenmore Road, Paddington,
New South Wales 2021
Tel: 357-4494

James R Lawson Pty Ltd,
236 Castlereagh Street, Sydney,
New South Wales
Tel: 266408

Mason Greene & Associates,
91-101 Leveson Street, North
Melbourne, Victoria 3051
Tel: 329-9911

Mercantile Art Auctions,
317 Pacific Highway, North Sydey,
New South Wales 2060
Tel: 922-3610/922-3608

James R Newall Auctions Pty Ltd,
164 Military Road, Neutral Bay,
New South Wales 2089
Tel: 903023/902587 (Sydney ex)

P L Pickles & Co Pty Ltd
655 Pacific Highway, Killara, New
South Wales 2071
Tel: 498-8069/498-2775

Sotheby Parke Bernet Group Ltd,
115 Collins Street, Melbourne,
Victoria 3000
Tel: (03) 63 39 00

H E Wells & Sons,
326 Rokeby Road, Subiaco, West
Australia
Tel: 3819448/3819040

Young Family Estates Pty Ltd,
229 Camberwell Road, East
Hawthorn, Melbourne 2123
Tel: 821433

New Zealand

Devereaux & Culley Ltd,
200 Dominion Road, Mt Eden,
Auckland
Tel: 687429/687112

Alex Harris Ltd,
PO Box 510, 377 Princes Street,
Dunedin
Tel: 773955/740703

Roger Moat Ltd,
College Hill and Beaumont Street,
Auckland
Tel: 37 1588/37 1686/37 1595

New Zealand Stamp Auctions,
PO Box 3496, Queen and
Wyndham Streets, Auckland
Tel: 375490/375498

Alistair Robb Coin Auctions,
La Aitken Street, Box 3705,
Wellington
Tel: 727-141

Dunbar Sloane Ltd,
32 Waring Taylor Street,
Wellington
Tel: 721-367

Thornton Auctions Ltd,
89 Albert Street, Auckland 1
Tel: 30888 (3 lines)

Daniel J Visser,
109 and 90 Worchester Street,
Christchurch
Tel: 68853/67297

Austria

Christie's,
Ziehrerplatz 4/22, A-1030 Vienna
Tel: (0222) 73 26 44

Belgium

Christie, Manson & Woods
(Belgium) Ltd,
33 Boulevard de Waterloo, B-1000
Brussels
Tel: (02) 512-8765/512-8830

Sotheby Parke Bernet Belgium,
Rue de l'Abbaye 32, 1050 Brussels
Tel: 343 50 07

Canada

A-1 Auctioneer Evaluation
Services Ltd,
PO Box 926, Saint John,
NB E2L 4C3
Tel: (508) 762-0559

Appleton Auctioneers Ltd,
1238 Seymour Street, Vancouver,
BC V6B 3N9
Tel: (604) 685-1715

Ashton Auction Service,
PO Box 500, Ashton, Ontario,
KOA 180
Tel: (613) 257-1575

Canada Book Auctions,
35 Front Street East, Toronto,
Ontario M5E 1B3
Tel: (416) 368-4326

Christie's International Ltd,
Suite 2002, 1055 West Georgia
Street, Vancouver, BC V6E 3P3
Tel: (604) 685-2126

Miller & Johnson Auctioneers Ltd,
2882 Gottingen Street, Halifax,
Nova Scotia B3K 3E2
Tel: (902) 425-3366/425-3606

Phillips Ward-Price Ltd,
76 Davenport Road, Toronto,
Ontario M5R 1H3
Tel: (416) 923-9876

Sotheby Parke Bernet (Canada)
Inc,
156 Front Street, Toronto, Ontario
M5J 2L6
Tel: (416) 596-0300
Representative:
David Brown,
2321 Granville Street, Vancouver,
BC V6H 3G4
Tel: (604) 736-6363

Denmark

Kunsthallens,
Kunstauktioner A/S,
Købmagergade 11 DK 1150
Copenhagen
Tel: (01) 13 85 69

Nellemann & Thomsen,
Neilgade 45, DK-8000 Aarhus
Tel: (06) 12 06 66/12 00 02

France

Ader, Picard, Tajan,
12 rue Favart, 75002 Paris
Tel: 261.80.07

Artus,
15 rue de la Grange-Batelière,
75009 Paris
Tel: 523.12.03

Audap,
32 rue Drouot, 75009 Paris
Tel: 742.78.01

Bondu,
17 rue Drouot, 75009 Paris
Tel: 770.36.16

Boscher, Gossart,
3 rue d'Amboise, 75009 Paris
Tel: 260.87.87

Briest,
15 rue Drouot, 75009 Paris
Tel: 770.66.29

de Cagny,
4 rue Drouot, 75009 Paris
Tel: 246.00.07

Charbonneaux,
134 rue du Faubourg Saint-
Honoré, 75008 Paris
Tel: 359.66.57

Chayette,
10 rue Rossini, 75009 Paris
Tel: 770.38.89

Delaporte, Rieunier,
159 rue Montmartre, 75002 Paris
Tel: 508.41.83

Delorme,
3 rue Penthièvre, 75008 Paris
Tel: 265.57.63

Godeau,
32 rue Drouot, 75009 Paris
Tel: 770.67.68

Gros,
22 rue Drouot, 75009 Paris
Tel: 770.83.04

Langlade,
12 rue Descombes, 75017 Paris
Tel: 227.00.91

Loudmer, Poulain,
73 rue de Faubourg Saint-Honoré,
75008 Paris
Tel: 266.90.01

Maignan,
6 rue de la Michodière, 75002 Paris
Tel: 742.71.52

Maringe,
16 rue de Provence, 75009 Paris
Tel: 770.61.15

Marlio,
7 rue Ernest-Renan, 75015 Paris
Tel: 734.81.13

Paul Martin & Jacques Martin,
3 impasse des Chevau-Legers,
78000 Versailles
Tel: 950.58.08

Bonhams, Baron Foran,
Duc de Saint-Bar, 2 rue Bellanger,
92200 Neuilly sur Seine
Tel: (1) 637-1329

Christie's, Princess Jeanne-Marie
de Broglie,
17 rue de Lille, 75007 Paris
Tel: (331) 261-1247

Sotheby's, Rear Admiral J A
Templeton-Cotill, CB,
3 rue de Miromesnil, 75008 Paris
Tel: (1) 266-4060

Monaco

Sotheby Parke Bernet Group,
PO Box 45, Sporting d'Hiver, Place
du Casino, Monte Carlo
Tel: (93) 30 88 80

Hong Kong

Sotheby Parke Bernet (Hong
Kong) Ltd,
PO Box 83, 705 Lane Crawford
House, 64-70 Queen's Road
Central, Hong Kong
Tel: 22-5454

Italy

Christie's (International) SA,
Palazzo Massimo Lancellotti,
Piazza Navona 114, 00186 Rome
Tel: 6541217

Christie's (Italy) SR1,
9 Via Borgogna, 20144 Milan
Tel: 794712

Finarte SPA,
Piazzetta Bossi 4, 20121 Milan
Tel: 877041

Finarte SPA,
Via delle Quattro, Fontane 20,
Rome
Tel: 463564

Palazzo International delle Aste ed
Esposizioni SPA,
Palazzo Corsini, Il Prato 56,
Florence
Tel: 293000

Sotheby Parke Bernet Italia,
26 Via Gino Capponi, 50121
Florence
Tel: 571410

Sotheby Parke Bernet Italia,
Via Montenapoleone 3, 20121
Milan
Tel: 783907

Sotheby Parke Bernet Italia,
Palazzo Taverna, Via di Monte
Giordano 36, 00186 Rome
Tel: 656 1670/6547400

The Netherlands

Christie, Manson & Woods Ltd,
Rokin 91, 1012 KL Amsterdam
Tel: (020) 23 15 05

Sotheby Mak Van Waay BV,
102 Rokin 1012, KZ Amsterdam
Tel: 24 62 15

Van Dieten Stamp Auctions BV,
2 Tournooiveld, 2511 CX The
Hague
Tel: 70-464312/70-648658

Singapore & Malaysia
Victor & Morris Pte Ltd,
39 Talok Ayer Street, Republic of
Singapore
Tel: 94844

South Africa
Ashbey's Galleries,
43-47 Church Street, Cape Town
8001
Tel: 22-7527

Claremart Auction Centre,
47 Main Road, Claremont, Cape
Town 7700
Tel: 66-8826/66-8804

Ford & Van Niekerk Pty Ltd
156 Main Road, PO Box 8,
Plumstead, Cape Town
Tel: 71-3384

Sotheby Parke Bernet South
Africa Pty Ltd,
Total House, Smit and Rissik
Streets, PO Box 310010,
Braamfontein 2017
Tel: 39-3726

Spain
Juan R Cayon,
41 Fuencarral, Madrid 14
Tel: 221 08 32/221 43 72/222 95 98

Christie's International Ltd,
Casado del Alisal 5, Madrid
Tel: (01) 228-9300

Sotheby Parke Bernet & Co,
Scursal de Espana, Calle del
Prado 18, Madrid 14
Tel: 232-6488/232-6572

Switzerland
Daniel Beney,
Avenue des Mousquines 2,
CH-1005 Lausanne
Tel: (021) 22 28 64

Blanc,
Arcade Hotel Beau-Rivage, Box
84, CH-1001 Lausanne
Tel: (021) 27 32 55/26 86 20

Christie's (International) SA,
8 Place de la Taconnerie, CH-1204
Geneva
Tel: (022) 28 25 44

Steinwiesplatz,
CH-8032 Zurich
Tel: (01) 69 05 05

Auktionshaus Doblaschofsky AG,
Monbijoustrasse 28/30, CH-3001
Berne
Tel: (031) 25 23 72/73/74

Galerie Fischer,
Haldenstrasse 19, CH-6006
Lucerne
Tel: (041) 22 57 72/73

Germann Auktionshaus,
Zeitweg 67, CH-8032 Zurich
Tel: (01) 32 83 58/32 01 12

Haus der Bücher AG,
Baumleingasse 18, CH-4051 Basel
Tel: (061) 23 30 88

Adolph Hess AG,
Haldenstrasse 5, CH-6006 Lucerne
Tel: (041) 22 43 92/22 45 35

Auktionshaus Peter Ineichen,
CF Meyerstrasse 14, CH-8002
Zurich
Tel: (01) 201-3017

Galerie Koller AG,
Ramistrasse 8, CH-8001 Zurich
Tel: (01) 47 50 40

Koller St Gallen,
St Gallen
Tel: (071) 23 42 40

Kornfeld & Co,
Laupenstrasse 49, CH-3008 Berne
Tel: (031) 25 46 73

Phillips Son & Neale SA,
6 Rue de la Cité, CH-1204 Geneva
Tel: (022) 28 68 28

Christian Rosset,
Salle des Ventes, 29 Rue du Rhone,
CH-1204 Geneva
Tel: (022) 28 96 33/34

Schweizerische Gesellschaft der
Freunde von Kunstauktionen,
11 Werdmühlestrasse, CH-8001
Zurich
Tel: (01) 211-4789

Sotheby Parke Bernet AG,
20 Bleicherweg, CH-8022 Zurich
Tel: (01) 202-0011

24 Rue de la Cité, CH-1024 Geneva
Tel: (022) 21 33 77

Dr Erich Steinfels, Auktionen,
Rämistrasse 6, CH-8001 Zurich
Tel: (01) 252-1233 (wine) &
(01) 34 1233 (fine art)

Frank Sternberg,
Bahnhofstrasse 84, CH-8001
Zurich
Tel: (01) 211-7980

Jürg Stucker Gallery Ltd,
Alter Aargauerstalden 30,
CH-3006 Berne
Tel: (031) 44 00 44

Uto Auktions AG,
Lavaterstrasse 11, CH-8027
Zurich
Tel: (01) 202-9444

West Germany
Galerie Gerda Bassenge,
Erdener Strasses 5a, D-1000 West
Berlin 33
Tel: (030) 892 19 32/891 29 09

Kunstauktionen Waltraud Boltz,
Bahnhof Strasse 25-27, D-8580
Bayreuth
Tel: (0921) 206 16

Brandes,
Wolfenbütteler Strasse 12, D-3300
Braunschweig 1
Tel: (0531) 737 32

Gernot Dorau,
Johann-Georg Strasse 2, D-1000
Berlin 31
Tel: (030) 892 61 98

F Dörling,
Neuer Wall 40-41, D-2000
Hamburg 36
Tel: (040) 36 46 70/36 52 82

Roland A Exner,
Kunsthandel-Auktionen,
Am Ihmeufer, D-3000
Hannover 91
Tel: (0511) 44 44 84

Hartung & Karl,
Karolinenplatz 5a, D-8000
Munich 2
Tel: (089) 28 40 34

Hauswedell & Nolte,
Pöseldorfer Weg 1, D-2000
Hamburg 13
Tel: (040) 44 83 66

Karl & Faber,
Amiraplatz 3 (Luitpoldblock),
D-8000 Munich 2
Tel: (089) 22 18 65/66

Graf Klenau Ohg Nachf,
Maximilian Strasse 32, D-8000
Munich 1
Tel: (089) 22 22 81/82

Numismatik Lanz München,
Promenadeplatz 9, D-8000
Munich 2
Tel: (089) 29 90 70

Kunsthaus Lempertz,
Neumarkt 3, D-5000 Cologne 1
Tel: (0221) 21 02 51/52

Stuttgarter Kunstauktionshaus,
Dr Fritz Nagel,
Mörikestrasse 17-19, D-7000
Stuttgart 1
Tel: (0711) 61 33 87/77

Neumeister Münchener
Kunstauktionshaus KG,
Barer Strasse 37, D-8000
Munich 40
Tel: (089) 28 30 11

Petzold KG- Photographica,
Maximilian Strasse 36, D-8900
Augsburg 11
Tel: (0821) 3 37 25

Reiss & Auvermann,
Zum Talblick 2, D-6246
Glashütten im Taunus 1
Tel: (06174) 69 47/48

Gus Schiele Auktions-Galerie,
Ottostrasse 7 (Neuer Kunstblock),
D-8000 Munich 2
Tel: (089) 59 41 92

Galerie,
Paulinen Strasse 47, D-7000
Stuttgart 1
Tel: (0711) 61 63 77

J A Stargardt,
Universitäts Strasse 27, D-3550
Marburg
Tel: (06421) 234 52

Auktionshaus Tietjen & Co,
Spitaler Strasse 30, D-2000
Hamburg 1
Tel: (040) 33 03 68/69

Aachener Auktionshaus, Crott &
Schmelzer,
Pont Strasse 21, Aachen
Tel: (0241) 369 00

Kunstauktionen Rainer
Baumann,
Obere Woerthstrasse 7-11,
Nuremburg
Tel: (0911) 20 48 47

August Bödiger oHG,
Oxford Strasse 4, Bonn
Tel: (0228) 63 69 40

Bolland & Marotz,
Feldören 19, Bremen
Tel: (0421) 32 18 11

Bongartz Gelgen Auktionen,
Münsterplatz 27, Aachen
Tel: (0241) 206 19

Christie's International Ltd,
Düsseldorf:
Alt Pempelfort 11a, D-4000
Düsseldorf
Tel: (0211) 35 05 77

Hamburg:
Wenzelstrasse 21, D-2000
Hamburg 60
Tel: (4940) 279-0866

Munich:
Maximilianstrasse 20, D-8000
Munich 22
Tel: (089) 22 95 39

Württenberg:
Schloss Langenburg, D-7183
Langenburg

Sotheby Parke Bernet GmbH,
Munich:
Odeonsplatz 16, D-8000 Munich 22
Tel: (089) 22 23 75/6

Kunstauktion Jürgen Fischer,
Alexander Strasse 11, Heilbronn
Tel: (07 131) 785 23

Galerie Göbig,
Ritterhaus Strasse 5 (am
Thermalbad ad Nauheim)
Tel: (Frankfurt) (611) 77 40 80

Knut Günther,
Auf der Körnerwiese 19-21,
Frankfurt
Tel: (611) 55 32 92/55 70 22

Antiquitaeten Lothar Heubel,
Odenthaler Strasse 371, Cologne
Tel: (0221) 60 18 25

Hildener Auktionshaus und
Kunstgalerie,
Klusenhof 12, Hilden
Tel: (02103) 602 00

INDEX